SolidWorks 2009 for Designers

CADCIM Technologies

525 St. Andrews Drive
Schererville, IN 46375
USA
(www.cadcim.com)

Contributing Authors

Sham Tickoo

Professor
Department of Mechanical Engineering Technology
Purdue University Calumet
Hammond, Indiana
USA

Sandeep D

CAD Engineer
CADCIM Technologies
USA

CADCIM Technologies

SolidWorks 2009 for Designers
Sham Tickoo

ISBN 978-1-932709-65-0

CADCIM Technologies Staff:

Business Managers Meenu Bhat	**Technical Editor** D. Saravanan	**Sr. Copy Editor** Anju Jethwani
Marketing Managers Santosh Tickoo Shafali Pandita	**Art/Cover Designers** Vikas Saini Richa Garg	**Copy Editors** Sudam C. Mishra Rajendra Badola

www.cadcim.com

DEDICATION

*To teachers, who make it possible to disseminate knowledge
to enlighten the young and curious minds
of our future generations*

*To students, who are dedicated to learning new technologies
and making the world a better place to live in*

THANKS

*To the faculty and students of the MET department of
Purdue University Calumet for their cooperation*

To engineers of CADCIM Technologies for their valuable help

Online Training Program Offered by CADCIM Technologies

CADCIM Technologies provides effective and affordable virtual online training on various software packages including Computer Aided Design and Manufacturing (CAD/CAM), computer programming languages, animation, architecture, and GIS. The training is delivered 'live' via Internet at any time, any place, and at any pace to individuals, students of colleges, universities, and CAD/CAM training centers. The main features of this program are:

Training for Students and Companies in a Class Room Setting

Highly experienced instructors and qualified Engineers at CADCIM Technologies conduct the classes under the guidance of Prof. Sham Tickoo of Purdue University Calumet, USA. This team has authored several textbooks that are rated "one of the best" in their categories and are used in various colleges, universities, and training centers in North America, Europe, and in other parts of the world.

Training for Individuals

The cost effective and time saving initiative of CADCIM Technologies strives to deliver the training in the comfort of your home or work place, thereby relieving you from the hassles of traveling to training centers.

Training Offered on Software Packages

We provide basic and advanced training on the following software packages:

CAD/CAM/CAE: CATIA, Pro/ENGINEER Wildfire, SolidWorks, Autodesk Inventor, Solid Edge, NX, AutoCAD, AutoCAD LT, Customizing AutoCAD, EdgeCAM, ANSYS, and Mastercam

Computer Programming Languages: C++, VB.NET, Excel, Dreamweaver, Oracle, Ajax, and Java

Animation and Styling: Autodesk 3ds Max, Maya, and AliasStudio

Architecture and GIS: Autodesk Revit Building, Autodesk Civil 3D, and Autodesk Map 3D

For more information, please visit the following link:
http://www.cadcim.com

Note

The free teaching and learning resources, mentioned in the cover page of this textbook, are available only for the students who buy the textbook from our web site www.cadcim.com or the university/college bookstores. We need proof of purchase when you request the technical support from us.

Table of Contents

Chapter 3: Editing and Modifying Sketches

Chapter 4: Adding Relations and Dimensions to Sketches

Chapter 5: Advanced Dimensioning Techniques and Base Feature Options

Chapter 6: Creating Reference Geometries

Chapter 7: Advanced Modeling Tools-I

Chapter 8: Advanced Modeling Tools-II

Chapter 9: Editing Features

Chapter 10: Advanced Modeling Tools-III

Chapter 11: Advanced Modeling Tools-IV

Chapter 12: Assembly Modeling-I

Chapter 13: Assembly Modeling-II

Chapter 14: Working with Drawing Views-I

Chapter 15: Working with Drawing Views-II

Chapter 16: Sheet Metal Design

Chapter 17: Equations, Configurations, and Library Features

Chapter 18: Working with Blocks

Chapter 19: Surface Modeling

Preface

SolidWorks 2009

SolidWorks, developed by SolidWorks Corporation, is one of the world's fastest growing solid modeling software. It is a parametric feature-based solid modeling tool that not only unites the three-dimensional (3D) parametric features with two-dimensional (2D) tools, but also addresses every design-through-manufacturing process. The latest in the family of SolidWorks, SolidWorks 2009, includes a number of customer requested enhancements, substantiating that it is completely tailored to the customer's needs. Based mainly on the user feedback, this solid modeling tool is remarkably user-friendly and it allows you to be productive from day one.

In SolidWorks, the 2D drawing views of the components are easily generated in the **Drawing** mode. The drawing views that can be generated include detailed, orthographic, isometric, auxiliary, section, and so on. You can use any predefined standard drawing document to generate the drawing views. Besides displaying the model dimensions in the drawing views or adding reference dimensions and other annotations, you can also add the parametric Bill of Materials (BOM) and balloons in the drawing view. If a component in the assembly is replaced, removed, or a new component is assembled, the modification will be automatically reflected in the BOM placed in the drawing document. The bidirectional associative nature of this software ensures that any modification made in the model is automatically reflected in the drawing views and any modification made in the dimensions in the drawing views automatically updates the model.

SolidWorks 2009 for Designers is a textbook written with an intent of helping the users who are interested in learning 3D design. This textbook is written with the tutorial point of view and the learn-by-doing theme. Real-world mechanical engineering industry examples and tutorials have been used to ensure that the user can relate the knowledge of this text book with the actual mechanical industry designs. In this latest edition, two new chapters have been added on Surfacing and Blocks to enhance the knowledge of the readers. The main features of the book are as follows:

- **Tutorial Approach**
  The author has adopted the tutorial point-of-view and the learn-by-doing theme

throughout the textbook. This approach guides the users through the process of creating the models in the tutorials.

- **Real-world Mechanical Engineering Projects as Tutorials**

  The author has used the real-world mechanical engineering projects as tutorials in this textbook so that the reader can correlate the tutorials with the real-time models in the mechanical engineering industry.

- **Coverage of Major SolidWorks Modes**

  All major modes of SolidWorks are covered in this textbook. These include the **Part** mode, the **Assembly** mode, and the **Drawing** mode.

- **Tips and Notes**

  Additional information related to various topics is provided to the users in the form of tips and notes.

- **Learning Objectives**

  The first page of every chapter summarizes the topics that are covered in the chapter.

- **Self-Evaluation Test, Review Questions, and Exercises**

  Each chapter ends with a Self-Evaluation test that enables the users to assess their knowledge of the chapter. The answers to the Self-Evaluation test are given at the end of the chapter. Also, the Review Questions and Exercises are given at the end of each chapter, which can be used by the Instructors as test questions and exercises.

- **Heavily Illustrated Text**

  The text in this textbook is heavily illustrated with the help of around 800 line diagrams and 900 screen captures that support the tool sections and tutorials.

Chapter 1

Introduction to SolidWorks 2009

Learning Objectives

After completing this chapter, you will be able to:

- *Understand how to start SolidWorks.*
- *Learn about the system requirements to run SolidWorks.*
- *Learn about various modes of SolidWorks.*
- *Learn about various CommandManagers of SolidWorks.*
- *Understand various important terms and definitions of SolidWorks.*
- *Save files automatically in SolidWorks.*
- *Change the color scheme of SolidWorks.*

INTRODUCTION TO SolidWorks 2009

Welcome to the world of Computer Aided Designing (CAD) with SolidWorks. If you are a new user of this software package, you will be joining hands with thousands of users of this parametric, feature-based, and one of the most user-friendly software packages. If you are familiar with the previous releases of this software, you will be able to upgrade your designing skills with the tremendous improvement in this latest release.

SolidWorks, developed by the SolidWorks Corporation, USA, is a feature-based, parametric solid-modeling mechanical design and automation software. SolidWorks is the first CAD package to use the Microsoft Windows graphic user interface. The use of the drag-drop (DD) functionality of Windows makes this CAD package extremely easy to learn. The Windows graphic user interface makes it possible for the mechanical design engineers to innovate their ideas and implement them in the form of virtual prototypes or solid models, large assemblies, subassemblies, and detailing and drafting.

SolidWorks is one of the products of SolidWorks Corporation, which is a part of Dassault Systemes. SolidWorks also works as the platform software for a number of software. This implies that you can also use other compatible software within the SolidWorks window. There are a number of software provided by the SolidWorks Corporation, which can be used as Add-Ins with SolidWorks. Some of the software that can be used on SolidWorks's work platform are listed below:

1. SolidWorks Animator
2. PhotoWorks
3. FeatureWorks
4. COSMOS/Works
5. COSMOS/Motion
6. COSMOS/Flow
7. eDrawings
8. SolidWorks Piping
9. CAMWorks
10. Toolbox
11. Mold Base

As mentioned earlier, SolidWorks is a parametric, feature-based, and easy to use mechanical design automation software. It enables you to convert the basic 2D sketch into a solid model using simple, but highly effective modeling tools. SolidWorks does not restrict you to 3D solid output, but it extends to the bidirectional associative generative drafting. It also enables you to create the virtual prototype of a sheet metal component and its flat pattern, which help you in the complete process planning for designing and creating a press tool. SolidWorks helps you to extract the core and the cavity of a model that has to be molded or casted. With SolidWorks, you can also create complex parametric shapes in the form of surfaces. Some of the important modes of SolidWorks are discussed next.

Part Mode

The **Part** mode of SolidWorks is a feature-based parametric environment in which you can create solid models. You are provided with three default planes named as the **Front Plane**, **Top Plane**, and the **Right Plane**. First, you need to select the sketching plane to create the sketch for the base feature. On selecting the sketching plane, you enter the sketching environment. The sketches for the model are drawn in the sketching environment using easy to use tools. After drawing the sketches, you can dimension them and apply the required relations in the same sketching environment. The design intent is captured easily by adding relations and equations and using the design table in the design. You are provided with the standard hole library known as the **Hole Wizard** in the **Part** mode. You can create simple holes, tapped holes, counterbore holes, countersink holes, and so on using this wizard. The holes can be of any standard such as ISO, ANSI, JIS, and so on. You can also create complicated surfaces using the surface modeling available within the **Part** mode. Annotations such as weld symbols, geometric tolerance, datum references, and surface finish symbols can be added to the model within the **Part** mode. The standard features that are used frequently can be saved as library features and retrieved when needed. The palette feature library is also provided in SolidWorks, which contains a number of standard mechanical parts and features. You can also create the sheet metal components in the **Part** mode of SolidWorks using the related tools. Besides this, you can also analyze the part model for various stresses applied to the model in the real physical conditions. SimulationXpress is an easy and user-friendly tool for doing stress analysis in SolidWorks. It helps you to reduce the cost and time in testing your design in real physical testing conditions (destructive tests). You can analyze the component during modeling in the SolidWorks windows. In addition, you can work with the weld modeling within the **Part** mode of SolidWorks by creating steel structures and adding weld beads. All standard weld types and welding conditions are available for your reference. You can extract the core and the cavity in the **Part** mode by using the mould design tools.

Assembly Mode

In the **Assembly** mode, you can assemble components of the assembly with the help of the required tools. There are two methods of assembling the components:

1. Bottom-up assembly
2. Top-down assembly

In the bottom-up assembly method, the assembly is created by assembling the previously created components and maintaining their design intent. In the top-down method, the components are created in the assembly mode. You may begin with some ready-made parts and then create other components in the context of the assembly. You can refer to the features of some components of the assembly to drive the dimensions of other components. You can assemble all components of an assembly by using a single tool, the **Mate** tool. While assembling the components of an assembly, you can also animate the assembly by dragging. Besides this, you can also check the working of your assembly. Collision detection is one of the major features of the SolidWorks assembly. You can rotate and move the components and detect the interference and collision between the components that you have assembled using this feature. You can see the realistic motion of the assembly by using physical dynamics. Physical simulation is used to simulate the assembly with the effects of motors, springs, and gravity on the assemblies.

Drawing Mode

The **Drawing** mode is used for the documentation of the parts or the assemblies created earlier, in the form of drawing views and the details in the drawing views. There are two types of drafting done in SolidWorks:

1. Generative drafting
2. Interactive drafting

Generative drafting is a process of generating drawing views of a part or an assembly created earlier. The parametric dimensions and the annotations added to the component in the **Part** mode can be generated in the drawing views. Generative drafting is bidirectionally associative in nature. Automatic BOMs and balloons can be added while generating the drawing views of an assembly.

In interactive drafting, you have to create the drawing views by sketching them using the normal sketching tools, after which you have to add dimensions to them.

SYSTEM REQUIREMENTS

The system requirements to ensure the smooth functioning of SolidWorks on your system are as follows:

- Microsoft Windows XP Professional or Windows Vista.
- Intel Pentium, Xeon, or AMD Athlon-based computer.
- 512 MB RAM minimum (1 GB or higher recommended).
- Graphic card OpenGL (recommended).
- Mouse or any other compatible pointing device.
- Internet Explorer version 5.5 or higher recommended.

GETTING STARTED WITH SolidWorks

Install SolidWorks on your system and then start it by choosing the **Start** button available on the lower left corner of the screen. Choose **Programs** to display the **Program** menu. Choose **SolidWorks 2009 SP0.0** to display the cascading menu and then choose **SolidWorks 2009 SP0.0**, as shown in Figure 1-1.

Tip. *You can also start **SolidWorks 2009** by double-clicking on the **SolidWorks 2009 SP0.0** shortcut icon available on the desktop of your computer. You need to create the shortcut icon of **SolidWorks 2009** if it is not created by default. The shortcut icon of **SolidWorks 2009** is created by choosing the **Start** button available on the lower left corner of the screen. Choose **Programs** to display the **Program** menu and choose **SolidWorks 2009 SP0.0** to display the cascading menu. Move the cursor on **SolidWorks 2009 SP0.0** and right-click to display the shortcut menu. Move the cursor to the **Send To** option; a cascading menu will be displayed. Choose the **Desktop (create shortcut)** option from the cascading menu; the **SolidWorks 2009** shortcut icon will be placed on the desktop of your computer.*

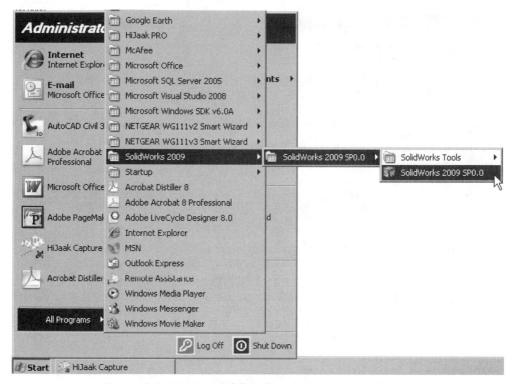

Figure 1-1 Starting SolidWorks using the taskbar shortcut

The system will now prepare to start SolidWorks. The SolidWorks window will be displayed on the screen. On opening SolidWorks for the first time, the **SolidWorks License Agreement** dialog box will be displayed, as shown in Figure 1-2; choose the **Accept** button from this dialog box.

The SolidWorks 2009 window is opened and the **SolidWorks Resources** task pane is displayed on the right, as shown in Figure 1-3. This window can be used to open a new file or an existing file. From this release of SolidWorks, the interface has been modified in such a way that the user can use the maximum space.

If the **SolidWorks Resources** task pane is not displayed by default, choose the **SolidWorks Resources** button to display the **SolidWorks Resources** task pane. This window can be used to open online tutorials and also to visit the website of the SolidWorks partners. Choose the **New Document** button from the **Getting Started** group in the **SolidWorks Resources** task pane to open a new file. Alternatively, you can also choose the **New** button from the Menu Bar. The **New SolidWorks Document** dialog box will be displayed, as shown in Figure 1-4.

Tip. *In SolidWorks, the tip of the day will be displayed at the bottom of the task pane. You can choose **Next Tip** to view additional tips. These tips help you to use SolidWorks efficiently. It is recommended to view at least 2 or 3 tips every time you start a new session of SolidWorks 2009.*

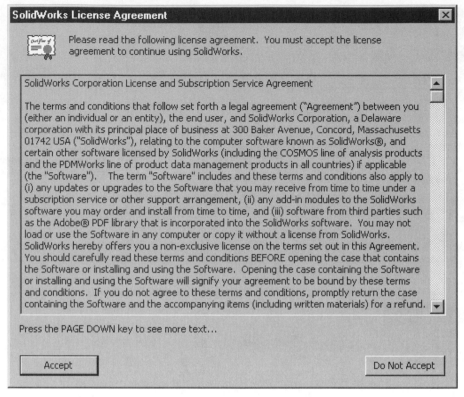

Figure 1-2 *The **SolidWorks License Agreement** dialog box*

Choose the **Part** button to create a part model and then choose **OK** from the **New SolidWorks Document** dialog box to enter the **Part** mode of SolidWorks. Move the cursor to the SolidWorks logo at the top of the screen; the SolidWorks menus will be displayed. Note that the task pane is automatically closed if you start a new file and click in the drawing area. The initial screen display when you start a new part file of SolidWorks using the **New** button in the Menu Bar is shown in Figure 1-5.

It is evident from the screen that SolidWorks is a very user-friendly solid modeling tool. Apart from the default **CommandManager** shown in Figure 1-5, you can also invoke other **CommandManagers**. To do so, move the cursor on a **CommandManager** tab and right-click; the shortcut menu will be displayed. Select the required **CommandManager** from the shortcut menu; the selected **CommandManager** will be added. Besides the existing **CommandManager**, you can also create a new **CommandManager**.

MENU BAR AND SolidWorks MENUS

In SolidWorks, the display area of the screen has been increased by grouping the tools that have similar functions or purposes. The tools that are in the **Standard** toolbar are now available in the Menu Bar, as shown in Figure 1-6. This toolbar is available above the drawing area. When you move the cursor on the SolidWorks logo on the top left corner of the display area, the SolidWorks menus will be displayed as cascading menu, as shown in Figure 1-7. You can also fix them by choosing the push-pin button.

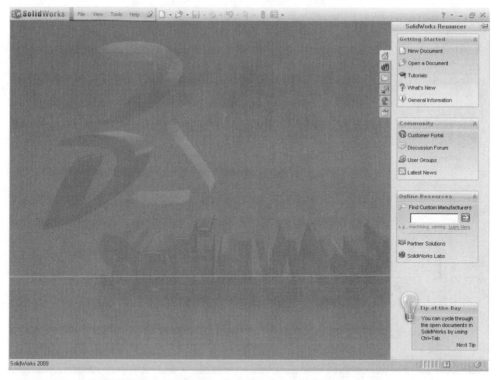

Figure 1-3 SolidWorks 2009 window and the **SolidWorks Resources** task pane

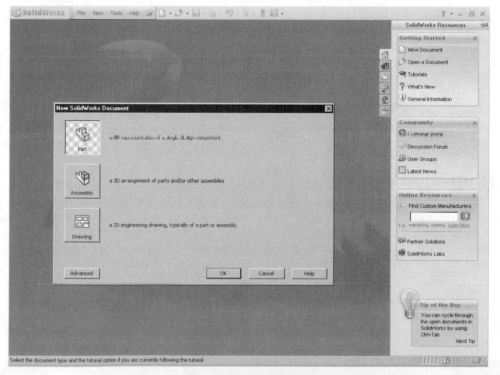

Figure 1-4 The **New SolidWorks Document** dialog box

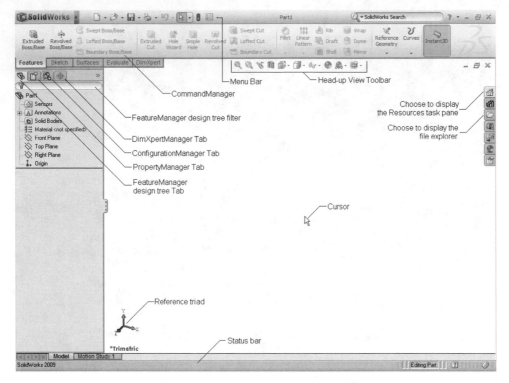

Figure 1-5 *The Components of a new part document*

Figure 1-6 *The Menu Bar*

Figure 1-7 *The SolidWorks menus*

CommandManager

There are four methods to invoke a tool in SolidWorks, the **CommandManager**, the SolidWorks menus on the top of the screen, the toolbar, and the shortcut menu. The **CommandManagers** are docked above the drawing area. While working with **CommandManager**, you will realize that this is the most convenient method to invoke a tool. Different types of **CommandManagers** are used for different design environments. These **CommandManagers** are discussed next.

Part Mode CommandManagers

A number of **CommandManagers** can be invoked in the **Part** mode. The **CommandManagers** that are extensively used during the designing process in this environment are described next.

Sketch CommandManager

This **CommandManager** is used to enter and exit the 2D and the 3D sketching environment. The tools available in the **CommandManager** are used to draw sketches for the features. This **CommandManager** is also used to add relations and smart dimensions to the sketched entities. The **Sketch CommandManager** is shown in Figure 1-8.

Figure 1-8 The Sketch CommandManager

Features CommandManager

This is one of the most important **CommandManagers** provided in the **Part** mode. Once the sketch is completed, you need to convert the sketch into a feature using the modeling tools. This **CommandManager** provides all the modeling tools that are to be used for feature-based solid modeling. The **Features CommandManager** is shown in Figure 1-9.

Figure 1-9 The Features CommandManager

DimXpert CommandManager

This **CommandManager** is used to add dimensions and tolerances to the features of a part. The **DimXpert CommandManager** is shown in Figure 1-10.

Figure 1-10 The DimXpert CommandManager

SheetMetal CommandManager

This **CommandManager** provides you the tools that are used to create the sheet metal parts. In SolidWorks, you can also create sheet metal parts while working in the **Part** mode. This is done with the help of the **SheetMetal CommandManager** shown in Figure 1-11.

Figure 1-11 The SheetMetal CommandManager

Mold Tools CommandManager

The options in this **CommandManager** are used to design the mold and extract its core and cavity. The **Mold Tools CommandManager** is shown in Figure 1-12.

Figure 1-12 The Mold Tools CommandManager

Evaluate CommandManager

This **CommandManager** is used to measure the distance between two entities, add the equations in the design, calculate the mass properties of a solid model, and so on. The **Evaluate CommandManager** is shown in Figure 1-13.

Figure 1-13 The Evaluate CommandManager

Surface CommandManager

The options available in this **CommandManager** are used to create complicated surface features. These surface features are also converted into the solid features. The **Surface CommandManager** is shown in Figure 1-14.

Figure 1-14 The Surface CommandManager

Assembly Mode CommandManagers

The **CommandManagers** in the **Assembly** mode are used to assemble the components, create an explode line sketch, and simulate the assembly. The **CommandManagers** in the **Assembly** mode are discussed next.

Assemble CommandManager

This **CommandManager** is used to insert a component and apply various types of mates to the assembly. Mates are the constraints that can be applied to the components to restrict their degree of freedom. You can also move and rotate the component in the assembly, change the hidden and the suppression state of the assembly and individual components, edit the component of an assembly, and so on. The **Assemble CommandManager** is shown in Figure 1-15.

Figure 1-15 The Assemble CommandManager

Drawing Mode CommandManagers

A number of **CommandManagers** can be invoked in the **Drawing** mode. The **CommandManagers** that are extensively used during the designing process in this mode are discussed next.

View Layout CommandManager

This **CommandManager** is used to generate the drawing views from an existing model or an assembly. The views that can be generated using this **CommandManager** are model view, three standard views, projected view, section view, aligned section view, detail view, crop view, relative view, auxiliary view, and so on. The **View Layout CommandManager** is shown in Figure 1-16.

Figure 1-16 The View Layout CommandManager

Annotate CommandManager

The **Annotate CommandManager** is used to generate the model items and to add the notes, balloons, geometric tolerance, surface finish symbols, and so on to the drawing views. The **Annotate CommandManager** is shown in Figure 1-17.

Figure 1-17 The Annotate CommandManager

Tip. *You can also create 2D drawings and drawing views using the normal sketching tools available in the **Sketch Tools** toolbar. The **Sketch Tools** toolbar is also available in the **Drawing** mode.*

Customized CommandManager

If you work on a particular set of tools often, you can create a customized **CommandManager** to cater your needs. To do so, choose a **CommandManager** tab and right-click; the shortcut menu will be displayed. Choose the **Customize CommandManager** option from the shortcut menu; the **Customize** dialog box will be displayed. Also, a new tab will be added along with the existing **CommandMangers** tab. Choose the new tab and rename it. Next, choose the **Commands** tab from the **Customize** dialog box. Select a command from the **Categories** list box; the tools of the corresponding command will be displayed in the **Buttons** area. Select a tool, press and hold the left mouse button, and drag the tool to the customized **CommandManager**; the tool will be added to the customized **CommandManager**. Choose **OK** from the **Customize** dialog box.

To delete a customized **CommandManager**, invoke the **Customize** dialog box as discussed earlier. Next, choose the **CommandManager** tab to be deleted and right-click; the shortcut menu will be displayed. Choose the **Delete** option from the shortcut menu; the **CommandManager** will be deleted.

Note
You cannot delete the default CommandManagers.

TOOLBAR

In SolidWorks, you can choose most of the tools from the **CommandManager** or from the SolidWorks menus. However, if you hide the **CommandManager** to increase the drawing area, you can use the toolbars to invoke a tool. To display a toolbar, right-click on a **CommandManager**; the list of toolbars available in SolidWorks will be displayed. Select the required toolbar.

Pop-up Toolbar

This toolbar was introduced in SolidWorks 2008. If you select a feature or an entity and do not move the mouse; a pop-up toolbar will be displayed. Figure 1-18 shows a pop-up toolbar that is displayed on selecting a feature. Remember that this toolbar will disappear, if you move the cursor away from the selected feature or entity.

Figure 1-18 *The pop-up toolbar*

You can switch off the display of the pop-up toolbar. To do so, invoke the **Customize** dialog box. In this dialog box, the **Show on Selection** check box is selected by default in the **Context toolbar Settings** area. It means that the display of the pop-up toolbar is on, by default. To turn off the display of the pop-up toolbar, clear this check box and choose the **OK** button.

Heads-up View Toolbar

In SolidWorks, some of the display tools are grouped together and displayed in the drawing area, as shown in Figure 1-19. This toolbar is known as **Heads-up View** toolbar.

Figure 1-19 *The **Heads-up View** toolbar*

Customizing the CommandManagers and Toolbars

In SolidWorks, all buttons are not displayed by default in toolbars or **CommandManagers**. You need to customize and add buttons to them according to your need and specifications. Follow the procedure given below to customize the **CommandManagers** and toolbars.

1. Choose **Tools > Customize** from the SolidWorks menus to display the **Customize** dialog box. You can also right-click on a **CommandManager** and choose the **Customize** option which is at the end of the toolbars list.
2. Choose the **Commands** tab from the **Customize** dialog box.
3. Select a name of the toolbar from the **Categories** area of the **Customize** dialog box; the tools available in the toolbars will be displayed.
4. Left-click on a button in the **Buttons** area; the description of the selected button will be displayed in the **Description** area.
5. Press and hold the left mouse button on a button from the **Buttons** area of the **Customize** dialog box.
6. Drag the mouse to a **CommandManager** or a toolbar and release the left mouse button to place the button on that **CommandManager** or toolbar.
7. Choose **OK** from the **Customize** dialog box.

To remove a tool from the **CommandManager** or toolbar, invoke the **Customize** dialog box and drag the tool that you need to remove from the **CommandManager** to the graphics area.

Note
*You cannot customize the **Heads-up View** toolbar. However, you can add or remove the tools that will be displayed when you right-click on a tool in the **Heads-up View** toolbar. To add a tool, right-click on a tool in the **Heads-up View** toolbar; a list of tools will be displayed. Select the check box of the corresponding tool and clear the check box to remove a tool.*

Shortcut Bar

In SolidWorks, when you press the S key on the keyboard, some of the tools that can be used in the current mode will be displayed near the cursor. To customize the tools in the shortcut bar, right-click on it and choose the **Customize** option. Then, follow the procedure discussed above.

Tip. *You can display some of the tools by pressing a key on the keyboard. To assign a shortcut key to a tool, invoke the **Customize** toolbar and choose the **Keyboard** tab. Enter the key in the **Shortcut** column for the corresponding tool and choose **OK**.*

DIMENSIONING STANDARD AND UNITS

While installing SolidWorks on your system, you can specify the units and the dimensioning standard for dimensioning the model. You are provided with many dimensioning standards such as ANSI, ISO, DIN, JIS, BSI, and GOST. You are also provided with various units such as millimeters, centimeters, inches, and so on. This book follows millimeters as the units and ISO as the dimensioning standard. Therefore, it is recommended that you install SolidWorks with ISO as the dimensioning standard and millimeters as units.

IMPORTANT TERMS AND THEIR DEFINITIONS

Before you proceed further in SolidWorks, it is very important to understand the following terms as they have been widely used in this book.

Feature-based Modeling

A feature is defined as the smallest building block that can be modified individually. In SolidWorks, the solid models are created by integrating a number of these building blocks. A model created in SolidWorks is a combination of a number of individual features with each feature related to the other, directly or indirectly. These features understand their fits and functions properly, and therefore can be modified at any time during the design process. If proper design intent is maintained while creating the model, these features automatically adjust their values to any change in their surrounding. This provides greater flexibility to the design.

Parametric Modeling

The parametric nature of a software package is defined as its ability to use the standard properties or parameters in defining the shape and size of a geometry. The main function of this property is to derive the selected geometry to a new size or shape without considering its original dimensions. You can change or modify the shape and size of any feature at any stage of the design process. This property makes the designing process very easy.

For example, consider the design of the body of a pipe housing shown in Figure 1-20. In order to change the design by modifying the diameter of the holes and the number of holes on the front, top, and the bottom face, you need to select the feature and change the diameter and the number of instances in the pattern. The modified design is shown in Figure 1-21.

Figure 1-20 *Body of pipe housing*

Figure 1-21 *Design after modifications*

Bidirectional Associativity

As mentioned earlier, SolidWorks has different modes such as the **Part** mode, **Assembly** mode, and **Drawing** mode. There exists a bidirectional associativity between all these modes, which ensures that any modification made in the model in any one of the modes of SolidWorks is automatically reflected in the other mode immediately. For example, if you modify the dimension of a part in the **Part** mode, the change will be reflected in the **Assembly** and the **Drawing** modes. Similarly if you modify the dimensions of a part in the drawing views generated in the **Drawing** mode, the changes will be reflected in the **Part** and **Assembly** modes. Consider the drawing views shown in Figure 1-22. These are the drawing views of the body of the pipe housing shown in Figure 1-20. Now, when you modify the model of the body of pipe housing in the **Part** mode, the changes will be reflected in the **Drawing** mode automatically. Figure 1-23 shows the drawing views of the pipe housing after increasing the diameter and the number of holes.

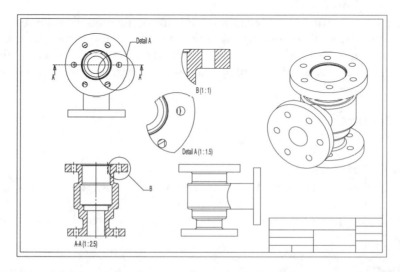

Figure 1-22 *Drawing views of the body part before making the modifications*

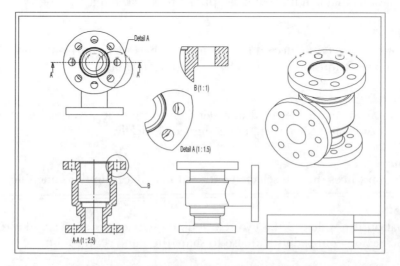

Figure 1-23 *Drawing views after modifications*

Windows Functionality

SolidWorks is the first Windows-based 3D CAD package. It uses the graphical user interface of Windows, also its drag and drop, and the copy paste functionality. For example, consider a case, where you had created a hole feature on the front planar surface of a model. Now, to create another hole feature on the top planar surface of the same model, select the hole feature and press CTRL+C (copy) on the keyboard. Next, select the top planar surface of the base feature and press CTRL+V (paste). You can also drag and drop the standard features from the feature pallet library on the face of the model on which the feature has to be added. Therefore, SolidWorks is the easiest 3D CAD package to learn.

Geometric Relations

Geometric relations are the logical operations that are performed to add a relationship (like tangent or perpendicular) between the sketched entities, planes, axes, edges, or vertices. When adding the relations, one entity can be a sketched entity and the other can be a sketched entity, or an edge, face, vertex, origin, plane, and so on. There are two methods to create the geometric relations:

1. Automatic Relations
2. Add Relations

Automatic Relations

The sketching environment of SolidWorks has been provided with the facility of autorelations. This facility ensures that the geometric relations are applied to the sketch automatically while creating it. Automatic relations are also provided in the **Drawing** mode while working with interactive drafting.

Add Relations

Add relations is used to add geometric relations manually to the sketch. The sixteen types of geometric relations that can be manually applied to the sketch are as follows:

Horizontal

This relation forces the selected line segment to become a horizontal line. You can also select two points and force them to be aligned horizontally.

Vertical

This relation forces the selected line segment to become a vertical line. You can also select two points and force them to be aligned vertically.

Collinear

This relation forces the two selected entities to be placed in the same line.

Coradial

This relation is applied to the two selected arcs, circles, or an arc and a circle to force them to become equi-radius and also to share the same centerpoint.

Perpendicular

This relation is used to make the selected line segment perpendicular to another selected segment.

Parallel

This relation is used to make the selected line segment parallel to another selected segment.

Tangent

This relation is used to make the selected line segment, arc, spline, circle, or ellipse tangent to another arc, circle, spline, or ellipse.

 Note

In case of splines, the relations are applied to their control points.

Concentric

This relation forces two selected arcs, circles, a point and an arc, a point and a circle, or an arc and a circle to share the same centerpoint.

Midpoint

This relation forces a selected point to be placed on the midpoint of a line.

Intersection

This relation forces a selected point to be placed at the intersection of two selected entities.

Coincident

This relation is used to make two points, a point and a line, or a point and an arc coincident.

Equal

The equal relation forces the two selected lines to become equal in length. This relation is also used to force two arcs, or two circles, or an arc and a circle to have equal radii.

Symmetric

The symmetric relation is used to force the selected entities to become symmetrical about a selected centerline, so that they remain equidistant from the centerline.

Fix

This relation is used to fix the selected entity to a particular location with respect to the coordinate system of the current sketch. The endpoints of the fixed line, arc, spline, or an elliptical segment are free to move along the line.

Pierce

This relation forces the sketched point to be coincident to the selected axis, edge, or curve where it pierces the sketch plane. The sketched point in this relation can be the endpoint of the sketched entity.

Merge

This relation is used to merge two sketched points or endpoints.

Blocks

A block is a set of entities grouped together as a single entity. The blocks are used to create complex mechanisms as sketches and check their functioning before developing them into complex 3D models.

Library Feature

Generally, in a mechanical design, some features arc used frequently. In most of the other solid modeling tools, you need to create these features whenever you need them. However, SolidWorks allows you to save these features in a library so that you can retrieve them whenever you want. This saves a lot of designing time and effort of a designer.

Design Table

Design tables are used to create a multi-instance parametric component. For example, some components in your organization have the same geometry but different dimensions. Instead of creating each component of the same geometry with a different size, you can create one component and then using the design table, create different instances by changing the dimension as per your requirement. You can access all these components in a single part file.

Equations

Equations are the analytical and numerical formulae applied to the dimensions during the sketching of the feature sketch or after sketching the feature sketch. The equations can also be applied to the placed features.

Collision Detection

Collision detection is used to detect the interference and collision between the parts of an assembly when the assembly is in motion. While creating the assembly in SolidWorks, you can detect the collision between the parts by moving and rotating them.

What's Wrong Functionality

While creating a feature of the model or after editing a feature created earlier, if the geometry of the feature is not compatible and the system is not able to construct that feature, then the **What's Wrong** functionality is used to detect the possible error that may occur while creating the feature.

2D Command Line Emulator

The 2D command emulator is an **Add-In** of SolidWorks. You can activate this by choosing **Tools** > **Add-Ins** from the SolidWorks menus. On choosing this option, the **Add-Ins** dialog box will be displayed. Select the **SolidWorks 2D Emulator** check box and choose **OK** from the **Add-Ins** dialog box. A command section will be displayed at the bottom of the graphics area. This 2D Command line emulator is useful for invoking the commands by typing them. You can type the commands in the 2D Command line emulator.

SimulationXpress

In SolidWorks, you are provided with SimulationXpress, which is an analysis tool to execute the static or stress analysis. In SimulationXpress you can only execute the linear static analysis. Using the linear static analysis, you can calculate the displacement, strain, and stresses applied on a component with the effect of material, various loading conditions, and restraint conditions applied on a model. A component fails when the stress applied to it reaches a certain permissible limit. The Static Nodal stress plot of the crane hook designed in SolidWorks and analyzed using SimulationXpress is shown in Figure 1-24.

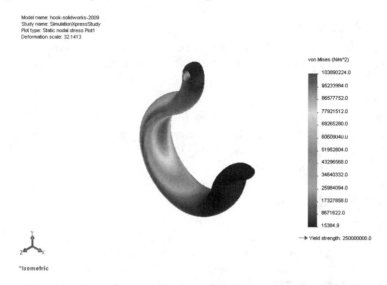

Figure 1-24 *The crane hook analyzed using SimulationXpress*

Physical Dynamics

The Physical Dynamics is used to observe the motion of the assembly. With this option selected, the component dragged in the assembly applies a force to the component that it touches. As a result, the other component is moved or rotated within its allowable degrees of freedom.

Physical Simulation

The Physical Simulation is used to simulate the assemblies created in the assembly environment of SolidWorks. You can assign and simulate the effect of different simulation elements such as linear, rotary motors, and gravity to the assemblies. After creating a simulating assembly, you can record and replay simulation.

Seed Feature

The original feature that is used as the parent feature to create any type of pattern or mirror feature is known as the seed feature. You can edit or modify only a seed feature. You cannot edit the instances of the pattern feature.

FeatureManager design tree

The **FeatureManager design tree** is one the most important components of SolidWorks screen. It contains the information about the default planes, material, lights, and all the features that are added to the model. When you add features to the model using various modeling tools, the same are also displayed in the **FeatureManager design tree**. You can easily select and edit the features using the **FeatureManager design tree**. When you invoke any tool to create a feature, the **FeatureManager design tree** is replaced by the respective **PropertyManager**. At this stage, the **FeatureManager design tree** is displayed in the drawing area.

Absorbed Features

Features that are directly involved in creating other features are known as absorbed features. For example, the sketch of an extruded feature is an absorbed feature of the extruded feature.

Child Features

The features that are dependent on their parent and whose existence is not possible without their parent features are known as child features. For example, consider a cube with the filleted edges. If you delete the cube, the fillet feature will also be deleted because its existence is not possible without its parent feature.

Dependent Features

Dependent features are those that depend on their parent feature but can still exist without the parent feature with some minor modifications. If the parent feature is deleted, then by specifying other references and modifying the feature, you can retain the dependent features.

AUTO-BACKUP OPTION

SolidWorks also allows you to set the option to save the SolidWorks document automatically after a regular interval of time. While working on a design project, if the system crashes, you may loose the unsaved design data. If the auto-backup option is turned on, your data is saved automatically after regular intervals. To turn this option on, choose **Tools** > **Options** from the SolidWorks menus; the **System Options - General** dialog box is displayed. Select the **Backup/Recover** option from the display area provided on the left of this dialog box. Now, choose the **Save auto recover info every** check box. The spinner and the drop-down list provided on the right of the check box are enabled. Use this spinner and drop-down list, you can set the number of changes or minutes after which the document will be saved automatically. By default, the backup files are saved in *X:\Documents and Settings\Administrator <name of your machine>\Local Settings\TempSWBackupDirectory\swxauto* location (where *X* is the drive in which you have installed SolidWorks 2009 and the *Local Settings* folder is a hidden folder). You can also change the path of this location. To change this path, choose the button provided on the right of the edit box; the **Browse For Folder** dialog box is displayed. You can specify the location of the folder to save the backup files using this dialog box. If you need to save the backup files in the current folder, select the **Number of backup copies per document** check box and then select the **Save backup files in the same location as the original** radio button. You can set the number of backup files that you need to save using the **Number of backup copies per document** spinner. After setting all the options, choose the **OK** button from the **System Options - Backup/Recover** dialog box.

SELECTING HIDDEN ENTITIES

Sometimes, while working on a model, you need to select an entity that is either hidden behind another entity or is not displayed in the current orientation of the view. SolidWorks allows you to select these entities using the **Select Other** option. For example, consider a case where you need to select the back face of a model, which is not displayed in the current orientation. In such cases, you need to move the cursor over the visible face such that the cursor is also in line with the back face of the model. Now, right-click and choose **Select Other** from the shortcut menu; the cursor changes to the select other cursor and the **Select Other** list box is displayed. This list box displays all entities that can be selected. The item on which you move the cursor in the list box is highlighted in the drawing area. You can select the hidden face using this box.

COLOR SCHEME

SolidWorks allows you to use various color schemes as the background color of the screen, color and display style of **FeatureManager design tree**, and for displaying the entities on the screen. Note that the color scheme used in this book is neither the default color scheme nor the predefined color scheme. To set this color scheme, choose **Tools > Options** from the SolidWorks menus; the **System Options - General** dialog box is displayed. Select the **Colors** option from the left of this dialog box; the option related to the color scheme is displayed in the dialog box and the name of the dialog box is changed to **System Options - Colors** dialog box. In the list box available in the **Color scheme settings** area, the **Viewport Background** option is available. Select this option and choose the **Edit** button from the preview area on the right. Select white color from the **Color** dialog box and choose the **OK** button. After setting the color scheme, you need to save it so that next time if you need to set this color scheme, you do not need to configure all the settings. You just need to select the name of the saved color scheme from the **Current Color Scheme** drop-down list. Choose the **Save As Scheme** button; the **Color Scheme Name** dialog box is displayed. Enter the name of the color scheme as **SolidWorks 2009** in the edit box in the **Color Scheme Name** dialog box and choose the **OK** button. Now, choose the **OK** button from the **System Options - Colors** dialog box.

Note

The colors of the entities that are mentioned in the description or tutorials in this book are those that are displayed if the operating system is Windows XP. However, if you use Windows 2000, the colors of the entities that you get on the screen may be different from those mentioned in this book.

SELF-EVALUATION TEST

Answer the following questions and then compare them to those given at the end of this chapter:

1. The **Part** mode of SolidWorks is a feature-based parametric environment in which you can create solid models. (T/F)

2. Generative drafting is the process of generating drawing views of the part or assembly created earlier. (T/F)

3. The tip of the day will be displayed at the bottom of the task pane. (T/F)

4. In SolidWorks, the solid models are created by integrating a number of building blocks, called features. (T/F)

5. The _____ property ensures that any modification made in the model in any of the modes of SolidWorks is reflected in the other modes immediately.

6. The _____ relation forces two selected arcs, circles, a point and an arc, a point and a circle, or an arc and a circle to share the same centerpoint.

7. The _____ relation is used to make two points, a point and a line, or a point and an arc coincident.

8. The _____ relation forces the two selected lines to become equal in length.

9. The _____ is used to detect the interference and collision between the parts of an assembly when the assembly is in motion.

10. _____ are the analytical and numerical formulae applied to the dimensions during the sketching of the feature sketch or after sketching the feature sketch.

Answers to Self-Evaluation Test
1. T, **2.** T, **3.** T, **4.** T, **5.** bidirectional associativity, **6.** concentric, **7.** coincident, **8. Equal**, **9.** collision detection, **10.** Equations

Chapter 2

Drawing Sketches for Solid Models

Learning Objectives

After completing this chapter, you will be able to:

* *Understand the requirement of the sketching environment.*
* *Open a new part document.*
* *Understand various terms used in the sketching environment.*
* *Work with various sketching tools.*
* *Use the drawing display tools.*
* *Delete the sketched entities.*

THE SKETCHING ENVIRONMENT

Most of the products designed by using SolidWorks are a combination of sketched, placed, and derived features. The placed and derived features are created without drawing a sketch, but the sketched features require a sketch to be drawn first. Generally, the base feature of any design is a sketched feature and is created using a sketch. Therefore, while creating any design, the first and foremost point is to draw a sketch for the base feature. Once you have drawn the sketch, you can convert it into the base feature and then add the other sketched, placed, and derived features to complete the design. In this chapter, you will learn to create the sketch for the base feature using various sketching tools.

In general terms, a sketch is defined as the basic contour for the feature. For example, consider the solid model of a Spanner shown in Figure 2-1.

Figure 2-1 Solid model of a Spanner

This Spanner consists of a base feature, cut feature, mirror feature (cut on the back face), fillets, and an extruded text feature. The base feature of this spanner is shown in Figure 2-2. It is created using a single sketch drawn on the **Front Plane**, as shown in Figure 2-3. This sketch is drawn in the sketching environment using various sketching tools. Therefore, to draw the sketch of the base feature, you first need to invoke the sketching environment where you will draw the sketch.

Note
Once you are familiar with various options of SolidWorks, you can also use a derived feature or a derived part as the base feature.

The sketching environment of SolidWorks can be invoked at any time in the **Part** mode or the **Assembly** mode. You just have to specify that you want to draw the sketch of a feature and then select the plane on which you want to draw the sketch.

Note
You will learn how to invoke the sketching environment in SolidWorks 2009 later in this chapter.

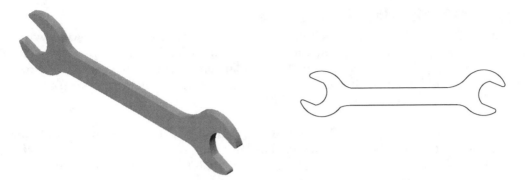

Figure 2-2 *Base feature of the Spanner*   **Figure 2-3** *Sketch for the base feature of the Spanner*

STARTING A NEW SESSION OF SolidWorks 2009

To start a new session of SolidWorks 2009, choose **Start** > **All Programs** > **SolidWorks 2009 SP0.0** > **SolidWorks 2009 SP0.0** from the **Start** menu or double-click on the **SolidWorks 2009 SP0.0** icon on the desktop of your computer; the SolidWorks 2009 window will be displayed. If you are starting SolidWorks application for the first time after installing it, the **SolidWorks License Agreement** dialog box will be displayed. Choose **Accept** from this dialog box; the **Welcome to SolidWorks** dialog box will be displayed, as shown in Figure 2-4. This dialog box welcomes you to SolidWorks and helps you customize SolidWorks installation. The options in this dialog box are discussed next.

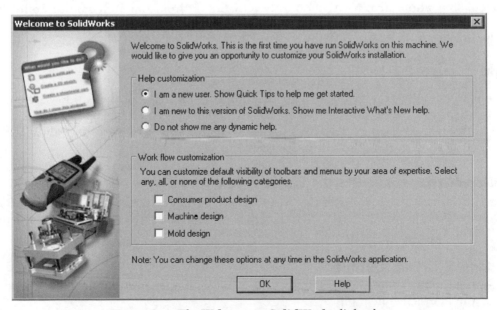

Figure 2-4 *The **Welcome to SolidWorks** dialog box*

Help customization Area

The options in this area are used to define the type of help you need to invoke while working with SolidWorks. By default, the **I am a new user. Show Quick Tips to help me get started** radio button is selected from this area. With this radio button selected, you are provided with quick tips that will guide you through the process of starting as a new user. Keep this radio button selected if you are a new user of SolidWorks.

If you are an existing user of SolidWorks, select the **I am new to this version of SolidWorks. Show me Interactive What's New help.** radio button. This ensures that the **Interactive What's New** help is displayed while you are working with the tools that are enhanced or introduced in this release of SolidWorks.

If you do not want to invoke any dynamic help topic, select the **Do not show me any dynamic help.** radio button.

Work flow customization Area

The options in the **Work flow customization** area of this dialog box are used to customize the visibility of toolbars and menu bars. The toolbars and the menu bars are customized on the basis of the area of your work such as product design, machine design, and mold design. Select the check box corresponding to the area of your work.

This textbook follows a beginner's point of view. Therefore, you need to keep the default radio button selected in the **Help customization** area and clear all check boxes in the **Work flow customization** area. Next, choose the **OK** button from the **Welcome to SolidWorks** dialog box; the **Welcome to SolidWorks** dialog will disappear and the SolidWorks 2009 window will be displayed, as shown in Figure 2-5.

TASK PANES

In SolidWorks 2009, the task panes are displayed on the right of the window. These task panes are provided with various options that are used to start a new file, open an existing file, browse the related links of SolidWorks, and so on. Various task panes in SolidWorks are discussed next.

SolidWorks Resources Task Pane

 By default, the **SolidWorks Resources** task pane is displayed when you start the SolidWorks session. Different rollouts available in this task pane are discussed next.

Getting Started Rollout

The options in this rollout are used to start a new document, open an existing document, and invoke the interactive help topics.

Community Rollout

The options in this rollout are used to invoke various SolidWorks communities such as subscription services, discussion forum, user groups, and so on.

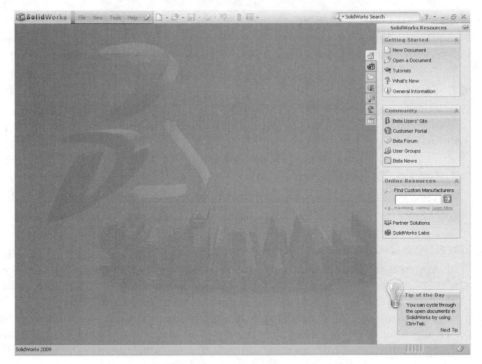

Figure 2-5 *The SolidWorks window*

Online Resources Rollout

The options in this rollout are used to invoke the discussion forum of SolidWorks, subscription services, partner solutions, manufacturing network, and print 3D websites. In SolidWorks, a search engine is provided in the **Online Resources** task pane. To find information about a particular topic, you need to enter the related term and then choose the **Start searching** button; you will be redirected to the website of customer search engine.

Tip of the Day Message Box

The **Tip of the Day** message box provides you with a useful tip that will help you make the full utilization of tools available in SolidWorks. Click on the **Next Tip** text provided at the lower right corner of the **Tip of the Day** message box to view the next tip.

Design Library Task Pane

The **Design Library** task pane is invoked by choosing the **Design Library** tab from the task pane. This task pane is used to browse the default **Design Library** available in SolidWorks or the toolbox components, and also to access the **3D ContentCentral** website. To access the toolbox components, **Toolbox Add-ins** needs to be installed in your computer. To add toolbox, choose **Tools > Add-ins** from the SolidWorks menus; the **Add-Ins** dialog box will be displayed. Select the **SolidWorks Toolbox Browser** check box and choose **OK**. To access the **3D ContentCentral** website, your computer needs to be connected to the Internet.

File Explorer Task Pane

 The **File Explorer** task pane is used to explore the files and folders that are saved in the hard disk of your computer.

Search Task Pane

 You can notice the **Search** task Pane at the upper right corner of the window. If you use this search option to search any SolidWorks file, document, and so on, the results will be displayed in the **Search** task pane.

View Palette Task Pane

 The **View Palette task pane** is used to drag and drop the drawing views into a drawing sheet.

Appearance/Scenes Task Pane

 The **Appearance/Scenes** task pane is used to change the appearance of the model or the display area. On choosing the **Appearance/Scenes** tab from the task pane, you will notice two nodes, **Appearance** and **Scenes** in the **Appearance/Scenes** task pane. The **Appearances** node is used to change the appearance of the model and the **Scenes** node is used to change the background of the drawing area. To change the appearance of the model, expand the **Appearances** node and select a category; the preview of the different materials available for that category will be displayed. Drag and drop the material in the drawing area; the appearance of the model will be changed. If you drag and drop the material by pressing and holding the ALT key, the **Appearances PropertyManager** will be displayed. You can change the properties of the material added using this **PropertyManager** about which you will learn in the later chapters.

If you need to change the background of the drawing area, expand the **Scenes** node from the **Appearance/Scenes** task pane and select a category; the preview of the different backgrounds available for that category will be displayed. Drag and drop the background in the drawing area; the background of the drawing area will be changed. You can also choose the **Scenes** button in the **Heads-up View** toolbar which will be discussed in the later chapters.

Custom Properties Task Pane

The **Custom Properties** task pane is invoked by choosing the **Custom Properties** tab from the task pane. This task pane is used to view the properties of the files. If you do not have a property template for the files, then you can create it by choosing the **Create now** button from the **Custom Properties** task pane. On choosing this button, the **Property Tab Builder** window will be displayed. Set the properties in this window and save it. After saving, you can view these properties in the **Custom Properties** task pane. To do so, choose **Tools > Options** from the SolidWorks menus; the **System Options** dialog box will be displayed. Choose the **File Location** option from this dialog box. The options related to the **File Location** option will be displayed on the right of the dialog box. Select the **Custom Property Files** option from the **Show folders for** drop-down list. Next, browse the property template in the **Folders** area by choosing the **Add** button. Choose the **OK** button from the dialog box to exit from it. Now, you can view these properties in the **Custom Properties** task pane.

Note

In assemblies, you can assign properties to multiple parts at the same time.

STARTING A NEW DOCUMENT IN SolidWorks 2009

To start a new document in SolidWorks 2009, select the **New Document** option from the **Getting Started** rollout of the **SolidWorks Resources** task pane; the **New SolidWorks Document** dialog box will be displayed, as shown in Figure 2-6. You can also invoke this dialog box by choosing the **New** button from the Menu Bar. The options in this dialog box are discussed next.

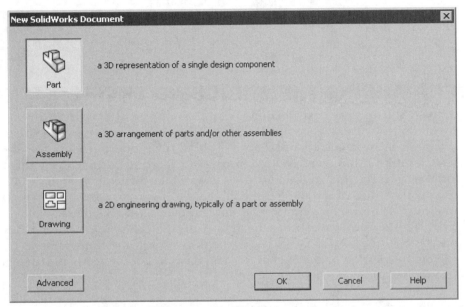

Figure 2-6 The New SolidWorks Document dialog box

Part

The **Part** button is chosen by default in the **New SolidWorks Document** dialog box. Choose the **OK** button to start a new part document to create solid models or sheet metal components. When you start a new part document, you will enter the **Part** mode.

Assembly

Choose the **Assembly** button and then the **OK** button from the **New SolidWorks Document** dialog box to start a new assembly document. In the assembly document, you can assemble the components created in the part documents. You can also create components in the assembly document.

Drawing

Choose the **Drawing** button and then the **OK** button from the **New SolidWorks Document** dialog box to start a new drawing document. In a drawing document, you can generate or create the drawing views of the parts created in the part documents or the assemblies created in the assembly documents.

Note
*When you start a new file in SolidWorks, the **What would you like to do?** window is displayed, which assists you in working with SolidWorks. To close this window, choose the **?** button available at the lower right corner of the **SolidWorks** window. You can choose this button to again display the **What would you like to do?** window.*

Tip. *If you invoke the **New SolidWorks Document** dialog box using the task pane and start a new document, the task pane will remain expanded even when the new document is started. If you invoke the **New SolidWorks Document** dialog box using the SolidWorks menus or the Menu Bar, the task pane will be collapsed and remain collapsed after starting the new document.*

UNDERSTANDING THE SKETCHING ENVIRONMENT

Whenever you start a new part document, by default, you are in the part modeling environment. But you need to start the design by first creating the sketch of the base feature in the sketching environment. To invoke the sketching environment, choose the **Sketch** tab from the **CommandManager**. Next, choose the **Sketch** button from the **Sketch CommandManager**. For your convenience, you can add the **Sketch** button to the Menu Bar and invoke the sketching environment using this button. To do so, right-click on any toolbar and choose the **Customize** option from the shortcut menu; the **Customize** dialog box will be displayed. Choose the **Commands** tab and select the **Sketch** option from the **Categories** list box; all tools in the sketch categories will be displayed in the **Buttons** area. Press and hold the left mouse button on the **Sketch** tool and then drag it to the Menu Bar. Figure 2-7 shows the **Sketch** button added to the Menu Bar.

When you choose the **Sketch** button from the Menu Bar or invoke any tool from the **Sketch CommandManager**; the **Edit Sketch PropertyManager** will be displayed on the left of the drawing area and you are prompted to select the plane on which the sketch will be created. Also, the three default planes available in SolidWorks 2009 (**Front Plane**, **Right Plane**, and **Top Plane**) are temporarily displayed on the screen, as shown in Figure 2-8.

You can select any plane to draw the sketch of the base feature depending on the requirement of the design. The selected plane will automatically be oriented normal to the view, so that you can easily create the sketch. Also, the **CommandManager** now displays various sketching tools to draw the sketch.

The default screen appearance of a SolidWorks part document in the sketching environment is shown in Figure 2-9.

Tip. *To expand the task pane at any stage of the design cycle, choose any one of the tabs provided on the task pane. Choose the **Auto Show** button to pin the task pane. To collapse the task pane, click anywhere in the drawing area when the **Auto Show** button is not chosen.*

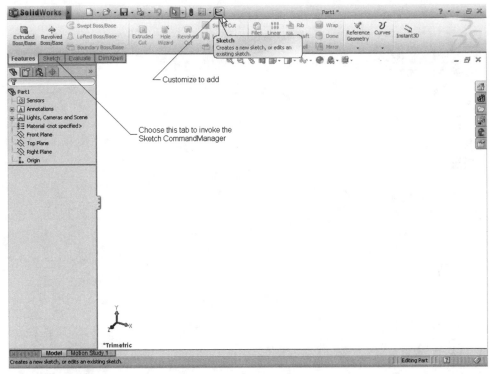

Figure 2-7 *Different methods of invoking the sketching environment in SolidWorks 2009*

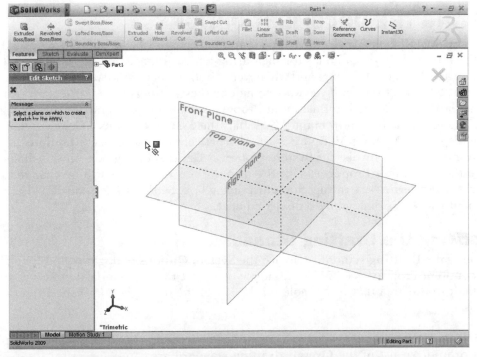

Figure 2-8 *The three default planes displayed on the screen*

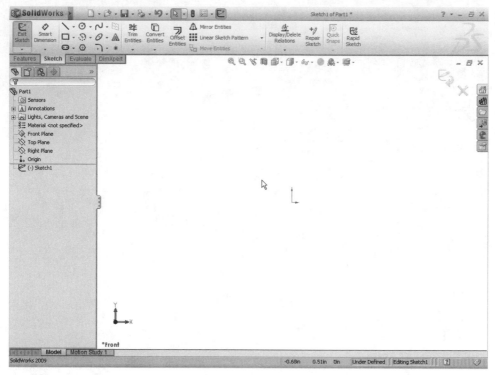

Figure 2-9 *Default screen display of a part document in the sketching environment*

SETTING THE DOCUMENT OPTIONS

When you install SolidWorks on your computer, you will be prompted to specify the dimensioning standards and units for measuring linear distances. The settings specified at that time are the default settings and whenever you start a new SolidWorks document, it will use these settings. However, if you want to modify these settings for a particular document, you can easily do it using the **Document Properties** dialog box. To invoke this dialog box, choose the **Options** button from the Menu Bar; the **System Options - General** dialog box will be displayed, as shown in Figure 2-10. Alternatively, choose **Tools > Options** from the SolidWorks menus to invoke the **System Options - General** dialog box. In this dialog box, choose the **Document Properties** tab; the name of this dialog box will be changed to the **Document Properties - Drafting Standard** dialog box. Setting the options for the current document using this dialog box is discussed next.

Modifying the Drafting Standards

To modify the **Drafting** standards, invoke the **System Options** dialog box and then choose the **Document Properties** tab. You will notice that the **Drafting Standard** option is selected by default in the area that is available on the left of the dialog box to display the drafting options.

The default drafting standard that was selected while installing SolidWorks will be displayed in the drop-down list in the **Overall drafting standard** area. You can select the required

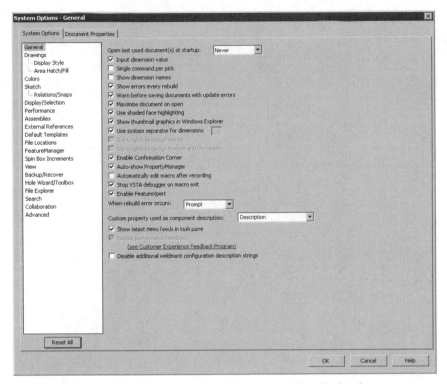

Figure 2-10 The **System Options - General** *dialog box*

drafting standard from this drop-down list. The standards that are available in this drop-down list are ANSI, ISO, DIN, JIS, BSI, GOST, and GB. You can select any one of these drafting standards for the current document.

Modifying the Linear and Angular Units

To modify the linear and angular units, invoke the **System Options** dialog box and then choose the **Document Properties** tab. In this tab, select the **Units** option from the area that is available on the left of the dialog box to display the options related to linear and angular units, as shown in Figure 2-11. The default option that was selected for measuring the linear distances while installing SolidWorks will be available in the **Length** field and the **Unit** column. You can set the units to be used for the current document from the options in the **Unit system** area. To specify the units other than the standard unit system in this area, select the **Custom** radio button; the options in the tabulation will be enabled. Select the cell corresponding to **Length** and **Unit**; a drop-down list will be displayed. Set the units from the drop-down list. The units that can be selected for **Length** are angstroms, nanometers, microns, millimeters, centimeters, meters, microinches, mils, inches, feet, and feet & inches. To change the units for angular dimensions, select the cell corresponding to **Angle** and **Unit**; a drop-down list will be displayed. The angular units that can be selected from this drop-down list are degrees, deg/min, deg/min/sec, and radians. Set the number of decimal places in the corresponding field under the **Decimals** column.

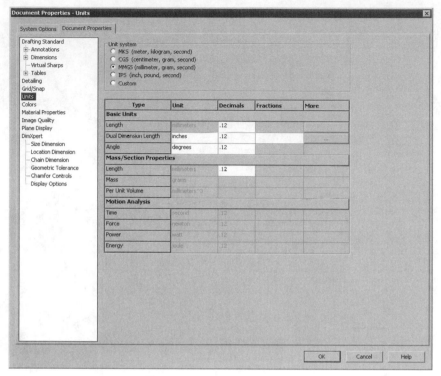

Figure 2-11 *Setting the dimensioning standards*

Modifying the Snap and Grid Settings

In the sketching environment of SolidWorks, you can make the cursor jump through a specified distance while creating the sketch. Therefore, if you draw a sketched entity, its length will change in the specified increment. For example, while drawing a line, if you make the cursor jump through a distance of 10 mm, the length of the line will be incremented by a distance of 10 mm. To do so, choose **Options** button from the Menu Bar to display the **System Options** dialog box. To ensure that the cursor jumps through the specified distance, you need to invoke the snap option. Select the **Relations/Snaps** branch of the **Sketch** option to display the related options. From the options available on the right, select the **Grid** check box. Next, clear the **Snap only when grid is displayed** check box, if it is selected. If this check box is selected, then the cursor will snap the sketched entities only when the grid is displayed.

Now, choose the **Go To Document Grid Settings** button to invoke the **Document Properties - Grid/Snap** dialog box, as shown in Figure 2-12. The distance through which the cursor jumps is dependent on the ratio between the values in the **Major grid spacing** and **Minor-lines per major** spinners available in the **Grid** area. For example, if you want the coordinates should be incremented by 10 mm, you will have to make the ratio of the major and minor lines to 10. This can be done by setting the value of the **Major grid spacing** spinner to **100** and that of the **Minor-lines per major** spinner to **10**. Similarly, to make the cursor jump through a distance of 5 mm, set the value of the **Major grid spacing** spinner to **50** and that of the **Minor-lines per major** spinner to **10**.

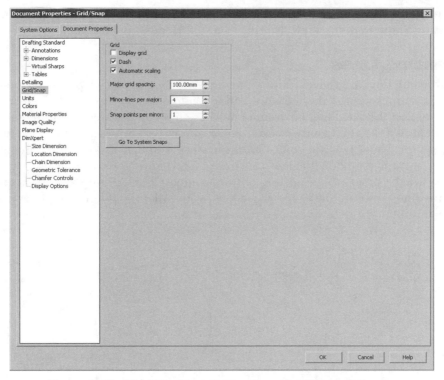

*Figure 2-12 The **Document Properties - Grid/Snap** dialog box*

Note

Remember that these settings will be only for the current documents. When you open a new document, it will have the settings that were defined while installing SolidWorks.

Tip. *If you want to display the grid in the sketching environment, select the **Display grid** check box from the **Grid** area of the **Document Properties - Grid/Snap** dialog box. Alternatively, choose **Hide/Show Items > View Grid** from the **Heads-up View** toolbar.*

While drawing a sketched entity by snapping through grips, the grips symbol will be displayed below the cursor on the right.

LEARNING SKETCHER TERMS

Before you learn about various sketching tools, it is important to understand some terms that are used in the sketching environment. These tools and terms are discussed next.

Origin

The origin is represented by a red colored point displayed at the center of the sketching environment screen. By default, there are two arrows at the origin displaying the X and Y axes directions of the current sketching plane. The point of intersection of these two axes is the origin point and the coordinates of this point are 0,0. To display or hide the origin, choose **Hide/Show Items** > **View Origins** from the **Heads-up View** toolbar.

Inferencing Lines

The inferencing lines are the temporary lines that are used to track a particular point on the screen. These lines are the dashed lines and are automatically displayed when you select a sketching tool in the sketching environment. These lines are created from the endpoints or the midpoint of a sketched entity or from the origin. For example, if you want to draw a line from the point where two imaginary lines intersect, you can use the inferencing lines to locate the point and then draw the line from that point. Figure 2-13 shows the use of inferencing lines to locate the point of intersection of two imaginary lines. Figure 2-14 shows the use of inferencing lines to locate the center of a circle. Notice that the inferencing lines are created from the endpoint of the line and also from the origin.

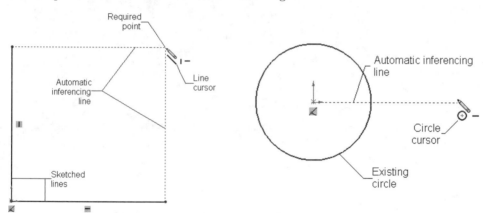

Figure 2-13 *Using inferencing lines to locate a point*

Figure 2-14 *Using inferencing lines to locate the center of a circle*

Note
The inferencing lines that are displayed on the screen will be either blue or yellow. The blue inferencing lines suggest that the relations are not added to the sketched entity and the yellow inferencing lines suggest that the relations are added to the sketched entity. You will learn about various relations in the later chapters.

Inferencing lines will be displayed only when a sketching tool is active.

Tip. *You can disable the inferencing line temporarily by pressing the CTRL key.*

Select Tool

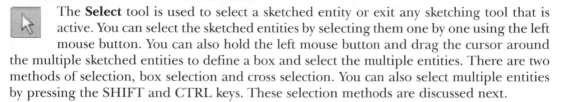

SolidWorks menus: Tools > Select

The **Select** tool is used to select a sketched entity or exit any sketching tool that is active. You can select the sketched entities by selecting them one by one using the left mouse button. You can also hold the left mouse button and drag the cursor around the multiple sketched entities to define a box and select the multiple entities. There are two methods of selection, box selection and cross selection. You can also select multiple entities by pressing the SHIFT and CTRL keys. These selection methods are discussed next.

Note

*When a sketching tool is active, you can invoke the **Select** tool or press the ESC key to exit the sketching tool. You can also right-click and choose the **Select** option from the shortcut menu to exit the tool.*

Selecting Entities Using the Box Selection

A box is a window that is created by pressing the left mouse button and dragging the cursor from left to right in the drawing area. The selection box will be displayed by continuous lines. When you create a box, the entities that lie completely inside it will be selected. The selected entities will be displayed in light blue and a pop-up toolbar will be displayed near the cursor.

Selecting Entities Using the Cross Selection

When you press the left mouse button and drag the cursor from right to left in the drawing area, a box of dashed lines is drawn. The entities that lie completely or partially inside this box or the entities that touch the dashed lines of the box will be selected. The selected entities will be displayed in light blue and a pop-up toolbar will be displayed near the cursor. This method of selection is known as cross selection.

Selecting Entities Using the SHIFT and CTRL Keys

You can also use the SHIFT and CTRL keys to manage the selection procedure. To select multiple entities, press and hold the SHIFT key and select the entities. After selecting some entities, if you need to select more entities using the windows or cross selection, press and hold the SHIFT key. Now, create a window or a cross selection; all the entities that touch the crossing or are inside the window will be selected.

If you need to remove a particular entity from a group of selected entities, press the CTRL key and select the entity. You can also invert the current selection using the CTRL key. To do so, select the entities that you do not want to be included in the selection set. Next, press the CTRL key and create a window or a cross selection.

Note

In SolidWorks 2009, when you select an entity, a pop-up tool bar will be displayed with options to edit the sketch. You will learn about these options in the later chapters.

Invert Selection Tool

SolidWorks menus:	Tools > Invert Selection

This tool will be active only when an entity is selected and is used to invert the selection set. This tool is used to remove the entities from the current selection set and select all the other entities that are not in the current selection set. To invert the selection, select the entities that you do not want to be included in the final selection set and then choose **Tools > Invert Selection** from the SolidWorks menus. You can also invoke the **Invert Selection** tool from the shortcut menu. All entities that were not selected earlier are now selected and the entities that were in the selection set earlier are now removed from the selection set.

Now, you are familiar with the important sketching terms. Next, you will learn about the sketching tools available in SolidWorks.

DRAWING LINES

CommandManager:	Sketch > Line
SolidWorks menus:	Tools > Sketch Entities > Line
Toolbar:	Sketch > Line

Lines are one of the basic sketching entities available in SolidWorks. In general terms, a line is defined as the shortest distance between two points. As mentioned earlier, SolidWorks is a parametric solid modeling tool. This property allows you to draw a line of any length and at any angle so that it can be forced to the desired length and angle. To draw a line in the sketching environment of SolidWorks, invoke the **Line** tool from the **Sketch CommandManager**; the **Insert Line PropertyManager** will be displayed, as shown in Figure 2-15. You will notice that the cursor, which was an arrow, is replaced by the line cursor. The line cursor is actually a pencil-like cursor with a small inclined line below the pencil. You can also invoke the **Line** tool by pressing the L key.

Figure 2-15 The Insert Line PropertyManager

The **Message** rollout of the **Insert Line PropertyManager** informs you to edit the settings of the next line or sketch a new line. The options in this **PropertyManager** can be used to set the orientation and other sketching options to draw a line. All these options are discussed next.

Orientation Rollout

The **Orientation** rollout is used to define the orientation of the line to be drawn. By default, the **As sketched** radio button is selected, so you can draw the line in any orientation. If you need to draw only horizontal lines, select the **Horizontal** radio button. On selecting this radio button, the **Parameters** rollout will be displayed and you can specify the length of the line in the **Length** spinner provided in this rollout. You will learn more about dimensioning in the later chapters. After specifying the parameters, choose the start point and the endpoints in succession to create the horizontal line. Choose **OK** twice to exit the **Line** tool.

Similarly, to draw a vertical line, select the **Vertical** radio button, specify the parameters in the **Parameters** rollout, and then choose the start point and the endpoints in succession.

 Note
*If the value 0 is set in the **Length** spinner of the **Parameters** rollout, you can draw horizontal/ vertical line of any length. Make sure that the corresponding radio button is chosen in the **Orientation** rollout of the **Insert Line PropertyManager**.*

The **Angle** radio button is selected to draw lines at a specified angle. When you select this radio button, the **Parameters** rollout will be displayed, where you can set the values of the length of the line and the angle or the orientation.

Options Rollout

The **For construction** check box available in this rollout is used to draw a construction line. You will learn more about the construction lines later in this chapter. The **Infinite length** check box is used to draw a line of infinite length.

On selecting the **As sketched** radio button in the **Orientation** rollout, you can draw lines by using two methods. The first method is to draw continuous lines and the second method is to draw individual lines. Both these methods are discussed next.

Drawing a Chain of Continuous Lines

This is the default method of drawing lines. In this method, you have to specify the start point and the endpoint of the line using the left mouse button. As soon as you specify the start point of the line, the **Line Properties PropertyManager** will be displayed. The options in the **Line Properties PropertyManager** will not be available at this stage.

After specifying the start point, move the cursor away from it and specify the endpoint of the line using the left mouse button. A line will be drawn between the two points. You will also notice that the line has filled rectangles at the two ends. The line will be displayed in light blue color because it is still selected.

Move the cursor away from the endpoint of the line and you will notice that another line is attached to the cursor. The start point of this line is the endpoint of the last line and the length of this line can be increased or decreased by moving the cursor. This line is called a rubber-band line as this line stretches like a rubber-band when you move the cursor. The point that you specify next on the screen will be taken as the endpoint of the new line and a line will be drawn such that the endpoint of the first line is taken as the start point of the new line and the point you specify is taken as the endpoint of the new line. Now, a new rubber-band line is displayed starting from the endpoint of the last line. This is a continuous process and you can draw a chain of as many continuous lines as needed by specifying the points on the screen using the left mouse button.

You can exit the continuous line drawing process by pressing the ESC key, by double-clicking on the screen, or by invoking the **Select** tool from the Menu Bar. You can also right-click to display the shortcut menu and choose the **End chain** or **Select** option to exit the **Line** tool.

Figure 2-16 shows a sketch drawn using the continuous lines. This sketch is started from the lower left corner and the horizontal line is drawn first. Draw the other lines and to close the loop, move the cursor attached to the last line close to the start point of the first line; you will notice that a orange colored circle will be displayed at the start point. If you specify the endpoint of the line at this stage, the loop will be closed and no rubber-band line will be displayed now. This is because the loop is already closed and you may not need another continuous line now. However, the **Line** tool is still active and you can draw other lines.

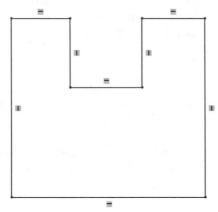

Figure 2-16 Sketch drawn using the continuous lines

Note
When you terminate the line drawing process by double-clicking on the screen or by choosing
End chain *from the shortcut menu, the current chain is ended but the **Line** tool is still active.*
*So, you can draw other lines. However, you can exit the **Line** tool by choosing **Select** from the*
shortcut menu.

Drawing Individual Lines

This is the second method of drawing lines. This method is used to draw individual lines and the start point of the new line will not necessarily be the endpoint of the previous line. To draw individual lines, you need to press and hold the left mouse button to specify the start point, drag the cursor without releasing the mouse button. Once you have dragged the cursor to the endpoint, release the left mouse button; a line will be drawn between the two points.

To make the sketching process easy in SolidWorks, you are provided with the **PropertyManager**. The **PropertyManager** is a table that will be displayed on the left of the screen as soon as you select the first point of any sketched entity. The **PropertyManager** has all parameters related to the sketched entity such as the start point, endpoint, angle, length, and so on. You will notice that as you start dragging the mouse, the **Line Properties PropertyManager** is displayed on the left of the drawing area. All options in the **Line Properties PropertyManager** will be available when you release the left mouse button. Figure 2-17 shows a partial view of the **Line Properties PropertyManager**.

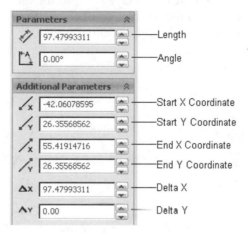

*Figure 2-17 Partial view of the **Line Properties PropertyManager***

Note

*The **Line Properties PropertyManager** will also display additional options about relations. You will learn more about relations in the later chapters.*

After you have drawn the line, modify the parameters in the **Line Properties PropertyManager** to make the line to the desired length and angle. You can also modify the line dynamically by holding its endpoints and dragging them.

Line Cursor Parameters

When you draw lines in the sketching environment of SolidWorks, you will notice that a numeric value is displayed above the line cursor, see Figure 2-18. This numeric value indicates the length of the line you draw. This value is the same as that in the **Length** spinner of the **Line Properties PropertyManager**. The only difference is that in the **Line Properties PropertyManager**, the value will be displayed with more precision.

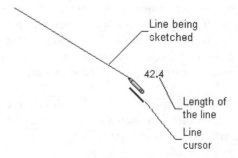

Figure 2-18 The length of the line displayed on the screen while drawing the line

The other thing that you will notice while sketching is that a ▬ or ▮ symbol is displayed below the line cursor, when you are drawing horizontal or vertical lines. These are the symbols of the **Vertical** and **Horizontal** relations. SolidWorks applies these relations automatically to the lines. These relations ensure that the lines you draw are vertical or horizontal and not inclined. Figure 2-19 shows the symbol of the **Vertical** relation on a line and Figure 2-20 shows the symbol of the **Horizontal** relation on a line.

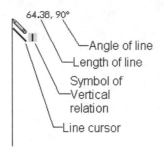

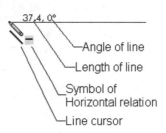

Figure 2-19 *Symbol of the **Vertical** relation*   ***Figure 2-20*** *Symbol of the **Horizontal** relation*

Note

*In addition to the **Horizontal** and **Vertical** relations, you can apply a number of other relations such as **Tangent**, **Concentric**, **Perpendicular**, **Parallel**, and so on. You will learn about all these relations and other options in the **Line Properties PropertyManager** in the later chapters.*

Drawing Tangent or Normal Arcs Using the Line Tool

SolidWorks allows you to draw tangent or normal arcs originating from the endpoint of the line while drawing continuous lines. Note that these arcs can be drawn only if you have drawn at least one line, arc, or spline. To draw such arcs, draw a line by specifying the start point and the endpoint. Move the cursor away from the endpoint of the last line to display the rubber-band line. Now, when you move the cursor back to the endpoint of the last line, the arc mode will be invoked. The angle and the radius of the arc will be displayed above the arc cursor. You can also invoke the arc mode by right-clicking and choosing **Switch to arc** from the shortcut menu or pressing the A key on the keyboard.

To draw a tangent arc, invoke the arc mode by moving the cursor back to the endpoint of the last line. Now, move the cursor through a small distance along the tangent direction of the line; a dotted line will be drawn. Next, move the cursor in the direction in which the arc should be drawn. You will notice that a tangent arc is drawn. Specify the endpoint of the tangent arc using the left mouse button. Figure 2-21 shows an arc tangent to an existing line.

To draw a normal arc, invoke the arc mode. Now, move the cursor through a small distance in the direction normal to the line and then move it in the direction of the endpoint of the arc; the normal arc will be drawn, as shown in Figure 2-22.

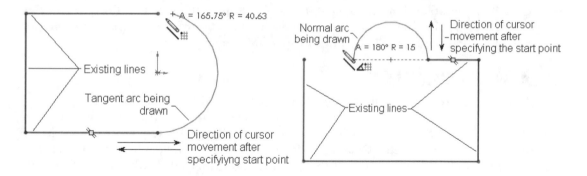

Figure 2-21 *Drawing a tangent arc using the* **Line** *tool*

Figure 2-22 *Drawing a normal arc using the* **Line** *tool*

As soon as the endpoint of the tangent or the normal arc is defined, the line mode will be invoked again. You can continue drawing lines using the line mode or move the cursor back to the endpoint of the arc to invoke the arc mode.

Note
If the arc mode is invoked by mistake while drawing lines, you can cancel the arc mode and invoke the line mode again by pressing the A key. Alternatively, you can right-click and choose **Switch to Line** *from the shortcut menu or move the cursor back to the endpoint and press the left mouse button to invoke the line mode.*

Drawing Construction Lines or Centerlines

CommandManager:	Sketch > Line > Centerline
SolidWorks menus:	Tools > Sketch Entities > Centerline
Toolbar:	Sketch > Line > Centerline

The construction lines or the centerlines are ones that are drawn only for the aid of sketching. These lines are not considered while converting the sketches into features.

You can draw a construction line similar to the sketched line by using the **Centerline** tool. You will notice that when you draw a construction line, the **For construction** check box in the **Options** rollout of the **Line Properties PropertyManager** is selected. You can also draw a construction line using the **Line** tool. To do so, invoke the **Insert Line PropertyManager**, select the **For construction** check box in the **Options** rollout, and draw the line.

Drawing the Lines of Infinite Length

SolidWorks allows you to draw lines of infinite length. Note that these lines can be drawn only if the **Line** or **Centerline** tool is invoked. To draw lines of infinite length, invoke the **Insert Line PropertyManager** and then select the **Infinite length** check box available in the **Options** rollout of this **PropertyManager**. Next, specify two points in the drawing area. A line of infinite length will be drawn.

To convert the solid infinite length line to a construction infinite length line, you need to select the **For construction** check box in the **Options** rollout of the **Line Properties PropertyManager**. You can also set the angle value for infinite lines in the **Angle** spinner available in the **Parameters** rollout of this **PropertyManager**.

DRAWING CIRCLES

In SolidWorks, there are two methods of drawing circles. The first method is by specifying the center point of a circle and then defining its radius. The second method is drawing a circle by defining three points that lie on its periphery. The tools for drawing a circle are grouped together in the **Sketch CommandManager**. To draw a circle, select the down arrow on the **Circle** tool; a flyout with both the tools will be displayed. Invoke a tool from this flyout; the **Circle PropertyManager** will be displayed, as shown in Figure 2-23. Alternatively, right-click and choose the **Circle** option from the shortcut menu to display the **Circle PropertyManager**.

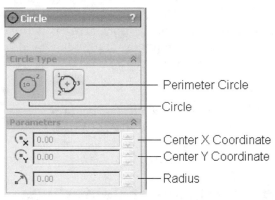

Figure 2-23 The Circle PropertyManager

Select the appropriate method from the **Circle Type** rollout to draw the circle. Both the methods to draw the circles are discussed next.

Drawing Circles by Defining Their Center Points

CommandManager:	Sketch > Circle
SolidWorks menus:	Tools > Sketch Entities > Circle
Toolbar:	Sketch > Circle

When you invoke the **Circle PropertyManager**, the **Circle** button is chosen by default in the **Circle Type** rollout. This button is chosen to draw a circle by specifying its center. You will notice that the arrow cursor is replaced by the circle cursor. The circle cursor consists of a pencil and a circle below the pencil. Specify the center point of the circle and then move the cursor to define its radius. The current radius of the circle will be displayed above the circle cursor. This radius will change as you move the cursor. Click on a point to define the radius. This radius can be modified by using the **Circle PropertyManager**. Also, the coordinates of the center point of the circle can be modified. Figure 2-24 shows a circle being drawn using the **Circle** tool by specifying the center point and dragging the cursor.

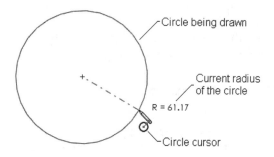

Figure 2-24 *Drawing a circle by specifying the centerpoint*

Drawing Circles by Defining Three Points

CommandManager:	Sketch > Circle > Perimeter Circle
SolidWorks menus:	Tools > Sketch Entities > Perimeter Circle
Toolbar:	Sketch > Circle > Perimeter Circle

The **Perimeter Circle** tool is used to draw a circle by defining three points that lies on the periphery of a circle. To draw a circle using this tool, click on the down arrow on the right of the **Circle** button; a flyout will be displayed. Choose the **Perimeter Circle** tool. Alternatively, invoke the **Circle PropertyManager** and choose the **Perimeter Circle** button from the **Circle Type** rollout; the select cursor will be replaced by a three-point circle cursor. Specify the first point of the circle in the drawing area. Now, specify the other two points of the circle. The resulting circle will be highlighted in light blue and you can modify the circle by setting its parameters in the **Circle PropertyManager**.

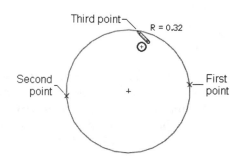

Figure 2-25 *Drawing a circle by specifying three points*

Figure 2-25 shows a circle being drawn by specifying three points.

Drawing Construction Circles

If you want to sketch a construction circle, draw a circle using the **Circle** tool and then select the **For construction** check box in the **Options** rollout of the **Circle PropertyManager**.

Tip. *To convert a construction entity back to the sketched entity, invoke the **Select** tool and then select the construction entity; the **PropertyManager** will be displayed. Clear the **For construction** check box; the construction entity will be changed into a sketched entity and it will be displayed with a continuous line.*

DRAWING ARCS

In SolidWorks, you can draw arcs using three tools: **Centerpoint Arc**, **Tangent Arc**, and **3 Point Arc**. All these tools are grouped together and they can be invoked separately from the flyout displayed by choosing the down arrow on the right of the **Centerpoint Arc** tool from the **Sketch CommandManager**. These methods are discussed next.

Drawing Tangent/Normal Arcs

CommandManager:	Sketch > Centerpoint Arc > Tangent Arc
SolidWorks menus:	Tools > Sketch Entities > Tangent Arc
Toolbar:	Sketch > Centerpoint Arc > Tangent Arc

 The tangent arcs are the ones that are drawn tangent to an existing sketched entity. The existing sketched entities include the sketched and construction lines, arcs, and splines. The normal arcs are the ones that are drawn normal to an existing entity. You can draw tangent and normal arcs using the **Tangent Arc** tool.

To draw a tangent arc, invoke the **Tangent Arc** tool; the arrow cursor will be replaced by the tangent arc cursor. Move the arc cursor close to the endpoint of the entity that you want to select as the tangent entity. You will notice that an orange colored dot is displayed at the endpoint. Also, a yellow symbol displaying two concentric circles appears below the pencil. Now, press the left mouse button once and move the cursor along the tangent direction through a small distance and then move the cursor to size the arc. The arc will start from the endpoint of the tangent entity and its size will change as you move the cursor. Note that the angle and the radius of the tangent arc are displayed above the cursor, see Figure 2-26.

To draw a normal arc, invoke the **Tangent Arc** tool. Move the cursor close to the endpoint of the entity that you want to select as the normal entity; an orange colored dot will be displayed at the endpoint. Also, a yellow symbol displaying two concentric circles appear below the pencil. Now, press the left mouse button once and move the cursor along the normal direction through a small distance and then move the cursor to size the arc, refer to Figure 2-27.

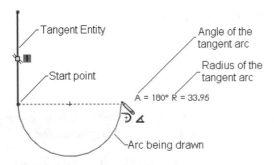

Figure 2-26 Drawing a tangent arc

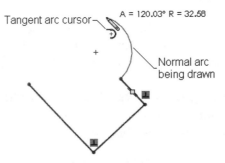

Figure 2-27 Drawing a normal arc

On invoking the **Tangent Arc** tool, the **Arc PropertyManager** will be displayed. However, the options in the **Arc PropertyManager** will not be enabled at this stage. These options will be enabled only after you have completed drawing the tangent or the normal arc.

You can draw an arbitrary arc and then modify its value using the **Arc PropertyManager**. Figure 2-28 shows the partial view of the **Arc PropertyManager**.

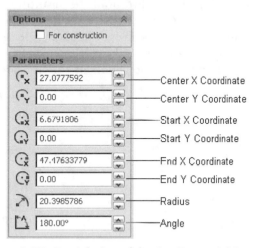

Figure 2-28 *Partial view of the **Arc PropertyManager***

Note

*When you select a tangent entity to draw a tangent arc, the **Tangent** relation is applied between the start point of the arc and the tangent entity. Therefore, if you change the coordinates of the start point of the arc, the tangent entity will also be modified accordingly.*

Drawing Centerpoint Arcs

CommandManager:	Sketch > Centerpoint Arc
SolidWorks menus:	Tools > Sketch Entity > Centerpoint Arc
Toolbar:	Sketch > Centerpoint Arc

The centerpoint arcs are the ones that are drawn by defining the centerpoint, start point, and endpoint of the arc. When you invoke this tool, the arrow cursor is replaced by the arc cursor. An arc cursor consists of a pencil and a centerpoint arc below the pencil.

To draw a centerpoint arc, invoke the **Centerpoint Arc** tool and then move the arc cursor to the point that you want to specify as the centerpoint of the arc. Press the left mouse button once at the location of the centerpoint and then move the cursor to the point from where you want to start the arc. You will notice that a dotted circle is displayed on the screen. The size of this circle will modify as you move the mouse. This circle is drawn for your reference and the centerpoint of this circle lies at the point that you specified as the center of the arc. Press the left mouse button once at the point that you want to select as the start point of the arc. Next, move the cursor to specify the endpoint of the arc. You will notice that the reference circle is no longer displayed and an arc is being drawn with the start point as the point that you specified after specifying the centerpoint. Also, the **Arc PropertyManager**, similar to the one that is shown in the tangent arc, is displayed on the left of the drawing area. Note that the options in the **Arc PropertyManager** will not be available at this stage.

If you move the cursor in the clockwise direction, the resulting arc will be drawn in the clockwise direction. However, if you move the cursor in the counterclockwise direction, the resulting arc will be drawn in the counterclockwise direction. Specify the endpoint of the arc using the left mouse button. Figure 2-29 shows the reference circle displayed when you move the mouse button after specifying the centerpoint of the arc and Figure 2-30 shows the resulting centerpoint arc.

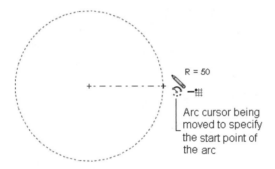

Figure 2-29 Specifying the centerpoint and the start point of the centerpoint arc

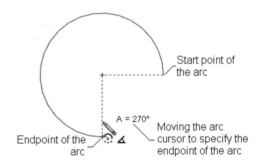

Figure 2-30 Moving the cursor to specify the start point and the endpoint of the arc

Drawing 3 Point Arcs

CommandManager:	Sketch > Centerpoint Arc > 3 Point Arc
SolidWorks menus:	Tools > Sketch Entities > 3 Point Arc
Toolbar:	Sketch > Centerpoint Arc > 3 Point Arc

 The three point arcs are the ones that are drawn by defining the start point and the endpoint of the arc, and a point on the circumference or the periphery of the arc. When you invoke this tool, the arrow cursor is replaced by the three-point arc cursor.

To draw a 3 point arc, invoke the **3 Point Arc** tool and then move the three-point arc cursor to the point that you want to specify as the start point of the arc. Press the left mouse button once at the location of the start point and then move the cursor to the point that you want to specify as the endpoint of the arc. As soon as you invoke the **3 Point Arc** tool, the **Arc PropertyManager** will be displayed. Note that when you start moving the cursor after specifying the start point, a reference arc will be displayed. However, the options in the **Arc PropertyManager** will not be available at this stage.

Specify the endpoint of the arc using the left mouse button. You will notice that the reference arc is no longer displayed. Instead, a solid arc is displayed and the cursor is attached to it. As you move the cursor, the arc will also be modified dynamically. Using the left mouse button, specify a point on the screen to create the arc. The last point that you specify will determine the direction of the arc. The options in the **Arc PropertyManager** will be displayed once you draw the arc. You can modify the properties of the arc using the **Arc PropertyManager**. Figure 2-31 shows the reference arc that is drawn by specifying the start point and the endpoint of the arc and Figure 2-32 shows specifying the third point for drawing the arc.

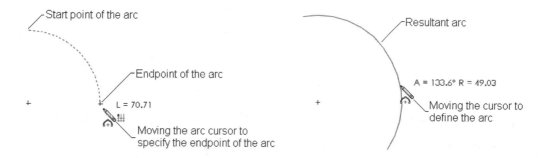

Figure 2-31 Specifying the start point and the endpoint of the arc

Figure 2-32 Specifying the third point for drawing the arc

DRAWING RECTANGLES

In SolidWorks 2009, the tools that are used to draw rectangles are grouped together. On invoking the **Rectangle** tool from the **Sketch CommandManager**, the **Rectangle PropertyManager** will be displayed. Select an appropriate method to draw a rectangle from the **Rectangle Type** rollout. Alternatively, right-click and choose the **Corner Rectangle** option from the shortcut menu to display the **Rectangle PropertyManager**. The various methods to create a rectangle are discussed next.

Drawing Rectangles by Specifying Their Corners

CommandManager:	Sketch > Corner Rectangle
SolidWorks menus:	Tools > Sketch Entities > Rectangle
Toolbar:	Sketch > Corner Rectangle

To draw a rectangle by specifying the two diagonally opposite corners, choose the **Corner Rectangle** button from the **Rectangle Type** rollout in the **Rectangle PropertyManager**, if it is not chosen by default. Next, move the cursor to the point that you want to specify as the first corner of the rectangle. Press the left mouse button once at the first corner and then move the cursor and specify the other corner of the rectangle using the left mouse button. You will notice that the length and width of the rectangle are displayed above the rectangle cursor. The length is measured along the X-axis and the width is measured along the Y-axis. Figure 2-33 shows a rectangle being drawn by specifying two diagonally opposite corners.

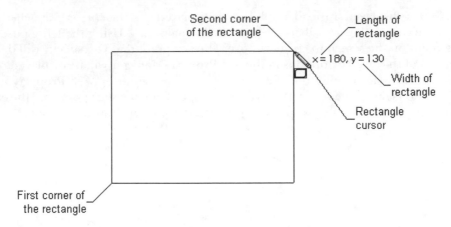

Figure 2-33 *Drawing a rectangle by specifying two diagonally opposite corners*

Drawing Rectangles by Specifying the Center and a Corner

CommandManager:	Sketch > Corner Rectangle > Center Rectangle
SolidWorks menus:	Tools > Sketch Entities > Center Rectangle
Toolbar:	Sketch > Corner Rectangle > Center Rectangle

To draw a rectangle by specifying the center and one of the corners, choose the **Center Rectangle** button from the **Rectangle Type** rollout in the **Rectangle PropertyManager**. Next, move the cursor to the point that you want to specify as the center of the rectangle and press the left mouse button. Then, move the cursor and specify one of the corner of the rectangle using the left mouse button. You will notice that the length and width of the rectangle are displayed above the rectangle cursor. The length is measured along the X-axis and the width is measured along the Y-axis. Figure 2-34 shows a rectangle being drawn by specifying its center and one of the corners.

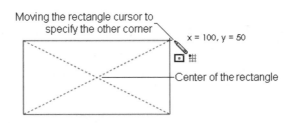

Figure 2-34 *Drawing a rectangle by specifying*
the center and one of the corners

Drawing Rectangles at an Angle

CommandManager:	Sketch > Corner Rectangle > 3 Point Corner Rectangle
SolidWorks menus:	Tools > Sketch Entities > 3 Point Corner Rectangle
Toolbar:	Sketch > Rectangle > 3 Point Corner Rectangle

To draw a rectangle at an angle, choose the **3 Point Corner Rectangle** button from the **Rectangle Type** rollout in the **Rectangle PropertyManager**. Move the cursor to the point that you want to specify as the start point of one of the edges of the rectangle. Press the left mouse button at this point and move the cursor to size the edge. You will notice that a reference line is being drawn. Depending on the current position of the cursor, the reference line will be horizontal, vertical, or inclined. The current length of the edge and its angle will be displayed above the rectangle cursor. Specify the second point as the endpoint of the edge such that the reference line is at an angle.

Next, move the cursor to specify the width of the rectangle. You will notice that a reference rectangle is drawn at an angle. Also, irrespective of the current position of the cursor, the width will be specified normal to the first edge, either above or below. Specify the third point using the left mouse button to define the width of the rectangle, as shown in Figure 2-35; the reference rectangle will be converted into a sketched rectangle.

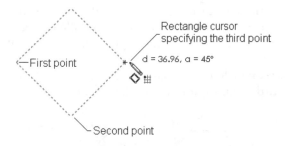

Figure 2-35 Drawing a rectangle at an angle

Drawing Centerpoint Rectangles at an Angle

CommandManager:	Sketch > Corner Rectangle > 3 Point Center Rectangle
SolidWorks menus:	Tools > Sketch Entities > 3 Point Center Rectangle
Toolbar:	Sketch > Corner Rectangle > 3 Point Center Rectangle

To draw a centerpoint rectangle at an angle, choose the **3 Point Center Rectangle** button from the **Rectangle Type** rollout in the **Rectangle PropertyManager**. Next, move the cursor to the point that you want to specify as the centerpoint of the rectangle. Press the left mouse button once at this point and move the cursor to a distance that is equal to half the length of the rectangle to be drawn. You will notice that a reference line is being drawn. Depending on the current position of the cursor, the reference line can be horizontal, vertical, or inclined. The current length of the edge and its angle will be displayed above the rectangle cursor. Specify the second point using the left mouse button. Next, specify the third point to define the width of the rectangle, as shown in Figure 2-36.

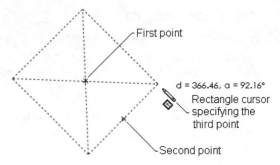

Figure 2-36 *Drawing a centerpoint rectangle at an angle*

Drawing Parallelograms

CommandManager:	Sketch > Corner Rectangle > Parallelogram
SolidWorks menus:	Tools > Sketch Entities > Parallelogram
Toolbar:	Sketch > Corner Rectangle > Parallelogram

To draw a parallelogram, choose the **Parallelogram** button from the **Rectangle Type** rollout of the **Rectangle PropertyManager**. Specify two points on the screen to define one edge in the parallelogram. Next, move the mouse to define the width of the parallelogram. As you move the mouse, a reference parallelogram will be drawn. The size and shape of the reference parallelogram will depend on the current location of the cursor.

Specify a point on the screen to define the parallelogram. Figure 2-37 shows the parallelogram cursor specifying the third point to draw a parallelogram.

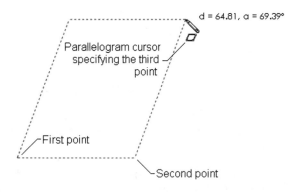

Figure 2-37 *Drawing a parallelogram*

Tip. *In SolidWorks 2009, when you are in the sketching environment, press the S key to invoke the shortcut bar that contains the tools for sketching.*

Note

*Though the **Rectangle PropertyManager** is displayed while creating a rectangle, a rectangle is considered as the combination of four individual lines. Therefore, after drawing the rectangle, if you select one of the lines of the rectangle, the **Line Properties PropertyManager** will be displayed. You can modify the parameters of the selected line using the **Line Properties PropertyManager**.*

*Remember that because the relations are applied to all four corners of the rectangle, if you modify the parameters of one of the lines using the **Line Properties PropertyManager**, the other three lines will also be modified accordingly.*

*You can convert a rectangle into a construction rectangle by selecting all lines together using a window and then selecting the **For construction** check box from the **PropertyManager**.*

Tip. *You can invoke the list of recently used tools by right-clicking in the drawing area. Choose the **Recent Command** option from the shortcut menu; a cascading menu will be displayed with the eight most recently used tools.*

DRAWING POLYGONS

CommandManager:	Sketch > Polygon
SolidWorks menus:	Tools > Sketch Entities > Polygon
Toolbar:	Sketch > Polygon

A regular polygon is defined as a multisided geometric figure in which the length of all sides and the angle between them are the same. In SolidWorks, you can draw a regular polygon with the number of sides ranging from 3 to 40. The dimensions of a polygon are controlled using the diameter of a construction circle that is inscribed inside the polygon or circumscribed outside the polygon. If the construction circle is inscribed inside the polygon, the diameter of the construction circle will be taken from the edges of the polygon. If the construction circle is circumscribed about the polygon, the diameter of the construction circle will be taken from the vertices of the polygon.

To draw a polygon, invoke the **Polygon** tool; the **Polygon PropertyManager** will be displayed, as shown in Figure 2-38.

Set the parameters such as the number of sides, inscribed or circumscribed circle, and so on, in the **Polygon PropertyManager**. You can also modify these parameters after drawing the polygon. When you invoke this tool, the arrow cursor will be replaced by the polygon cursor. Press the left mouse button at the point that you want to specify as the centerpoint of the polygon and then move the cursor to size the polygon. The length of each side and the rotation angle of the polygon will be displayed above the polygon cursor as you drag it. Using the left mouse button, specify a point on the screen after you get the desired length and rotation angle of the polygon. You will notice that based on whether you selected the **Inscribed circle** or the **Circumscribed circle** radio button in the **Polygon PropertyManager**, a construction circle will be drawn inside or outside the polygon. After you have drawn the polygon, you can modify the parameters such as the centerpoint of the polygon, the diameter of the construction circle, the angle of rotation, and so on using the **Polygon PropertyManager**.

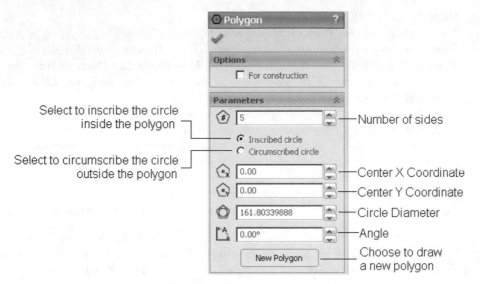

Figure 2-38 *The Polygon PropertyManager*

If you want to draw another polygon, choose the **New Polygon** button provided below the **Angle** spinner in the **Polygon PropertyManager**.

Figure 2-39 shows a six-sided polygon with the construction circle inscribed inside the polygon and Figure 2-40 shows a five-sided polygon with the construction circle circumscribed about the polygon. Note that the reference circle is retained with the polygon. Remember that this circle will not be considered while converting the polygon into a feature.

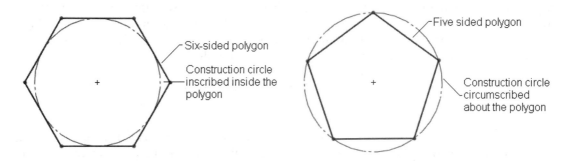

Figure 2-39 *Six-sided polygon with the construction circle inscribed inside it*

Figure 2-40 *Five-sided polygon with the construction circle circumscribed about it*

Tip. *You can also invoke the tools to draw lines, arcs, circles, or rectangles using the shortcut menu that is displayed when you right-click in the drawing area.*

DRAWING SPLINES

CommandManager:	Sketch > Spline
SolidWorks menus:	Tools > Sketch Entities > Spline
Toolbar:	Sketch > Spline

 In SolidWorks, you can draw a spline using the left mouse button by continuously specifying the points through which the spline will pass. This method of drawing splines is similar to that of drawing continuous lines. After specifying all points of the spline, right-click to invoke the shortcut menu. If you need to exit the current spline and draw another spline, choose the **End Spline** option. Now, you can draw a new spline. If you need to exit the **Spline** tool, choose the **Select** option. Figure 2-41 shows a spline drawn with its start point at the origin.

Note

*When you select a spline using the **Select** tool, handles are displayed on the points. These handles are used to edit a spline. You will learn more about these handles in the later chapters while editing splines.*

Similar to individual line, you can also create individual spline segments by specifying the start point and then dragging the mouse to specify the endpoint.

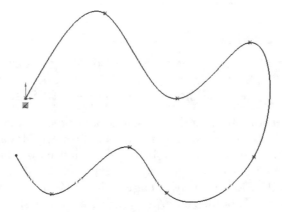

Figure 2-41 Sketched spline with its start point at the origin

 Tip. *After creating the spline, when you select it using the **Select** tool, the **Spline PropertyManager** will be displayed. The current control point will be displayed with a green filled square and its number and the corresponding X and Y coordinates will be displayed in the **Spline PropertyManager**. You can modify these coordinates to modify the position of the selected control point. A double-sided arrow will also be displayed along with the handle. You will learn more about this in the later chapters.*

DRAWING SLOTS

In SolidWorks 2009, the tools that are used to draw slots are grouped together. To draw a slot, invoke the **Slot PropertyManager** by choosing the **Straight Slot** button from the **Sketch CommandManager** and select the appropriate method to draw a slot from the **Slot Type** rollout. Alternatively, right-click and choose the appropriate option from the shortcut menu to draw a slot. Various methods to create a slot are discussed next.

Creating a Straight Slot

CommandManager:	Sketch > Straight Slot
SolidWorks menus:	Tools > Sketch Entities > Straight Slot
Toolbar:	Sketch > Straight Slot

To create a straight slot, choose the **Straight Slot** button from the **Sketch CommandManager**; the **Slot PropertyManager** will be displayed. Next, move the cursor where you want to specify the first end point of the straight slot. Press the left mouse button once at the first end point, then move the cursor and specify the second end point of the straight slot; a preview of the slot will be attached to the cursor. The options in the **Slot PropertyManager** will not be enabled at this stage. Move the cursor and specify the width of the straight slot, as shown in Figure 2-42. The options in the **Slot PropertyManager** will be enabled once you draw the straight slot. You can modify the properties of the straight slot using the options available in the **Slot PropertyManager**.

Creating a Centerpoint Straight Slot

CommandManager:	Sketch > Straight Slot > Centerpoint Straight Slot
SolidWorks menus:	Tools > Sketch Entities > Centerpoint Straight Slot
Toolbar:	Sketch > Straight Slot > Centerpoint Straight Slot

To draw a centerpoint straight slot, choose **Straight Slot > Centerpoint Straight Slot** from the **Sketch CommandManager**; the **Slot PropertyManager** will be displayed. Specify the center point of the slot by using the left mouse button. Next, move the cursor and specify the end point of the slot; a preview of the slot will be attached to the cursor. The options in the **Slot PropertyManager** will not be enabled at this stage. Move the cursor and specify the width of the centerpoint straight slot, as shown in Figure 2-43. The options in the **Slot PropertyManager** will be enabled once you draw the centerpoint straight slot. You can modify the properties of the centerpoint straight slot using the options available in the **Slot PropertyManager**.

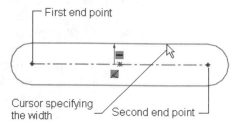

Figure 2-42 *Specifying points to create a straight slot*

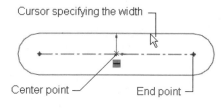

Figure 2-43 *Specifying points to create a centerpoint straight slot*

Creating a 3 Point Arc Slot

CommandManager:	Sketch > Straight Slot > 3 Point Arc Slot	
SolidWorks menus:	Tools > Sketch Entities > 3 Point Arc Slot	
Toolbar:	Sketch > Straight Slot > 3 Point Arc Slot	

To create a 3 point arc slot, choose **Straight Slot > 3 Point Arc Slot** from the **Sketch CommandManager**; the **Slot PropertyManager** will be displayed. You need to specify three points in the drawing area to create a 3 point arc slot. Move the cursor to the point where you want to specify the start point of the slot and then specify the start point of the slot by using the left mouse button. Note that as soon as you specify the start point, a reference arc will be attached to the cursor. Move the cursor to the location where you want to specify the second point of the slot and then specify the second point of the slot. Next, specify the third point of the slot; a preview of the 3 point arc slot will be attached to the cursor. The options in the **Slot PropertyManager** will not be enabled at this stage. Move the cursor and specify the width of the 3 point arc slot, as shown in Figure 2-44. The options in the **Slot PropertyManager** will be enabled once you draw the 3 point arc slot. You can modify the properties of the 3 point arc slot using the options available in the **Slot PropertyManager**.

Creating a Centerpoint Arc Slot

CommandManager:	Sketch > Straight Slot > Centerpoint Arc Slot	
SolidWorks menus:	Tools > Sketch Entities > Centerpoint Arc Slot	
Toolbar:	Sketch > Straight Slot > Centerpoint Arc Slot	

To create a centerpoint arc slot, choose **Straight Slot > Centerpoint Arc Slot** from the **Sketch CommandManager**; the **Slot PropertyManager** will be displayed. Specify the center point of the slot; a reference circle will be attached to the cursor. Move the cursor and specify the start point of the slot. Next, specify the end point of the slot using the left mouse button; a preview of the centerpoint arc slot will be attached to the cursor. Move the cursor and specify the point to create the centerpoint arc slot, as shown in Figure 2-45.

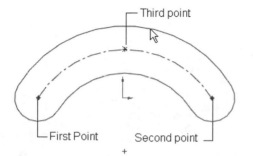

Figure 2-44 *Specifying points to create a 3 point arc slot*

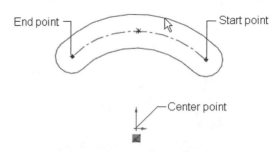

Figure 2-45 *Specifying points to create a centerpoint arc slot*

PLACING SKETCHED POINTS

CommandManager:	Sketch > Point
SolidWorks menus:	Tools > Sketch Entities > Point
Toolbar:	Sketch > Point

To place a sketched point, choose the **Point** button from the **Sketch CommandManager** and then specify the point on the screen where you want to place it; the **Point PropertyManager** will be displayed with the X and Y coordinates of the current point. You can change/shift the location of the point by modifying its X and Y coordinates in the **Point PropertyManager**.

DRAWING ELLIPSES

CommandManager:	Sketch > Ellipse > Ellipse
SolidWorks menus:	Tools > Sketch Entities > Ellipse
Toolbar:	Sketch > Ellipse > Ellipse

In SolidWorks, an ellipse is drawn by specifying its centerpoint and then specifying the two ellipse axes by moving the mouse. To draw an ellipse, invoke the **Ellipse** tool from the **Sketch CommandManager**; the arrow cursor will be replaced by the ellipse cursor. Move the cursor to the point that you want to specify as the centerpoint of the ellipse. Press the left mouse button once at that point and then move the cursor to specify one of the ellipse axes. You will notice that a reference circle is drawn and two values are displayed above the ellipse cursor, see Figure 2-46. The first value that shows R = * is the radius of the first axis that you are defining and the second value that shows r = * is the radius of the other axis. While defining the first axis, the second axis is taken equal to the first axis. This is the reason why a reference circle is drawn and not a reference ellipse.

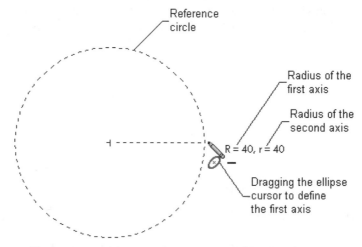

Figure 2-46 Dragging the cursor to define the ellipse axis

Specify a point on the screen to define the first axis. Next, move the cursor to size the other ellipse axis. As you move the cursor, the second value above the ellipse cursor that shows r = *

and the value in the **Radius 2** spinner in the **Ellipse PropertyManager** will change dynamically. Specify a point in the drawing area to defines the second axis of the ellipse, refer to Figure 2-47.

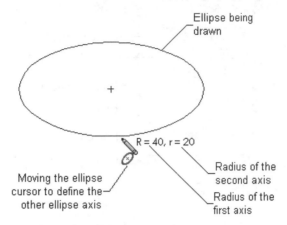

Figure 2-47 *Defining the second axis of the ellipse*

DRAWING ELLIPTICAL ARCS

CommandManager:	Sketch > Ellipse > Partial Ellipse
SolidWorks menus:	Tools > Sketch Entities > Partial Ellipse
Toolbar:	Sketch > Ellipse > Partial Ellipse

In SolidWorks, the process of drawing an elliptical arc is similar to that of drawing an ellipse. You will follow the same process of defining the ellipse first. The point that you specify on the screen to define the second axis of the ellipse is taken as the start point of the elliptical arc. You can define the endpoint of the elliptical arc by specifying a point on the screen, as shown in Figure 2-48.

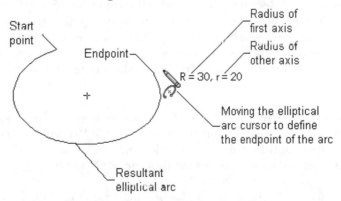

Figure 2-48 *Drawing an elliptical arc*

After drawing the elliptical arc, you can also modify its parameters in the **Ellipse PropertyManager**, as shown in Figure 2-49.

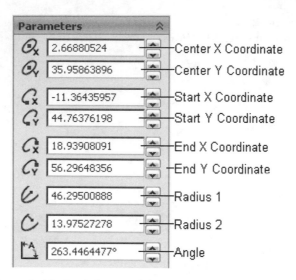

Figure 2-49 *Partial view of the **Ellipse PropertyManager***

DRAWING PARABOLIC CURVES

CommandManager:	Sketch > Ellipse > Parabola
SolidWorks menus:	Tools > Sketch Entities > Parabola
Toolbar:	Sketch > Ellipse > Parabola

In SolidWorks, you can draw a parabolic curve by specifying the focus point, apex point, and then two endpoints of the parabolic curve. To draw a parabolic curve, choose **Ellipse > Parabola** from the **Sketch CommandManager**; the cursor will be replaced by the parabola cursor. Move the cursor to the point that you want to specify as the focal point of the parabola. Press the left mouse button once at that point. You will notice that a reference parabolic arc is displayed. Then move the cursor to define the apex point and to size the parabola. As you move the cursor away from the focal point, the parabola will be flattened. After you get the basic shape of the parabolic curve, specify a point using the left mouse button. This point is taken as the apex of the parabolic curve. Next, specify two points with respect to the reference parabola to define the guide of the parabolic curve, see Figure 2-50.

As you move the mouse after specifying the focal point of the parabola, the **Parabola PropertyManager** will be displayed. But the options in the **Parabola PropertyManager** will not be available. These options will be available only after you have drawn the parabola. Figure 2-51 shows a partial view of the **Parabola PropertyManager**.

Tip. *To dislodge the task pane, choose the **Auto Show** button and double-click on the gray bar at the top where its name is displayed. Now, you can move it at the desired location. To place it back on its original position, again double-click on the gray bar or choose the **Dock Task Pane** button provided on the top right corner of the task pane.*

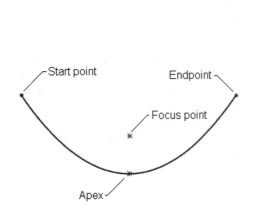

Figure 2-50 *Parabola and its parameters*

Options	☆
☐ For construction	

Parameters	☆

↻x	4.03660046	Start X Coordinate
↻y	72.67962164	Start Y Coordinate
↻x	6.04350065	End X Coordinate
↻y	28.88636949	End Y Coordinate
↻x	-23.50940171	Center X Coordinate
↻y	47.8202603	Center Y Coordinate
↻x	8.81602564	Apex X Coordinate
↻y	47.8202603	Apex Y Coordinate

Figure 2-51 *Partial view of the **Parabola** PropertyManager*

DRAWING DISPLAY TOOLS

The drawing display tools are one of the most important tools provided in any of the solid modeling software. These tools allow you to modify the display of a drawing by zooming or panning it. In SolidWorks 2009, some of these tools are displayed in the drawing area in the **Heads-up View** toolbar. Some of the drawing display tools available in SolidWorks are discussed in this chapter. The remaining tools will be discussed in the later chapters.

Zoom to Fit

Heads-up View: View > Modify > Zoom to Fit

You can find this tool in the drawing area. Choose the **Zoom to Fit** button to increase or decrease the drawing display area so that all sketched entities or dimensions are fitted inside the current view. You can also press the F key to invoke this tool. Alternatively, you can double-click on the middle mouse button in the drawing area to invoke this tool.

Zoom to Area

Heads-up View: View > Modify > Zoom to Area

You can find this tool in the drawing area. The **Zoom to Area** button is used to magnify a specified area so that the part of the drawing inside the magnified area can be viewed in the current window. The area is defined inside a window that is created by dragging the cursor. When you choose this button, the cursor is replaced by a magnifying glass cursor. Press and hold the left mouse button and drag the cursor to specify the opposite corners of the window. The area enclosed inside the window will be magnified.

Zoom In/Out

SolidWorks menus: View > Modify > Zoom In/Out

 The **Zoom In/Out** tool is used to dynamically zoom in or out of the drawing. When you invoke this tool, the cursor will be replaced by the zoom cursor. To zoom out of a drawing, press and hold the left mouse button and drag the cursor in the downward direction. Similarly, to zoom in a drawing, press and hold the left mouse button and drag the cursor in the upward direction. As you drag the cursor, the drawing display will be modified dynamically. After you get the desired view, exit this tool by choosing the **Select** tool from the **Sketch** toolbar. You can also exit this tool by right-clicking and choosing **Select** from the shortcut menu or by pressing the ESC key. If you have a mouse with scroll wheel, then scroll the wheel to zoom in/out. You can also press the Z key to zoom out of a drawing and press the SHIFT+Z keys to zoom in the drawing .

Zoom to Selection

SolidWorks menus: View > Modify > Zoom to Selection

 The **Zoom to Selection** tool is used to modify the drawing display area such that the selected entity is fitted inside the current display. After selecting the entity, choose the **Zoom to Selection** button. The drawing display area will be modified such that the selected entity fits inside the current view. Press and hold the CTRL key while selecting multiple entities. In SolidWorks 2009, if you select an entity a pop-up toolbar will be displayed and you can invoke the **Zoom to Selection** tool from it.

Pan

SolidWorks menus: View > Modify > Pan

The **Pan** tool is used to drag the view in the current display. You can also press the CTRL key and the middle mouse button and then drag the cursor to move the entities.

 Tip. *You can also invoke the **Pan** tool using the CTRL key and the arrow keys on the keyboard. For example, to pan toward the right, press the CTRL key and then press the right arrow key. Similarly, to pan upward, press the CTRL key and then press the up arrow key.*

Previous View

SolidWorks menus: View > Previous View

This tool is used to display the last view of the model and can be useful if you have zoomed the model at many levels. You can view the last ten views using this tool. You can invoke this tool from the drawing area or press the CTRL+Z keys.

Tip. *You can also invoke some of the drawing display tools from the shortcut menu. To do so, right-click and choose **Zoom/Pan/Rotate**; a flyout will be displayed with the display tools.*

Redraw

SolidWorks menus:	View > Redraw

The **Redraw** tool is used to refresh the screen. Sometimes when you draw a sketched entity, some unwanted elements remain on the screen. To remove these unwanted elements from the screen, use this tool. The screen will be refreshed and all the unwanted elements will be removed. You can invoke this tool by pressing the CTRL+R keys.

DELETING SKETCHED ENTITIES

You can delete the sketched entities by selecting them using the **Select** tool and then pressing the DELETE key on the keyboard. You can select the entities individually or select more than one entity by defining a window or crossing around the entities. When you select the entities, they turn light blue. When they turn light blue, press the DELETE key. You can also delete the sketched entities by selecting them and choosing the **Delete** option from the shortcut menu that is displayed on right-clicking.

TUTORIALS

Tutorial 1

In this tutorial, you will draw the basic sketch of the revolved solid model shown in Figure 2-52. The sketch of the revolved solid model is shown in Figure 2-53. Do not dimension the sketch. The solid model and dimensions are given only for your reference.

(Expected time: 30 min)

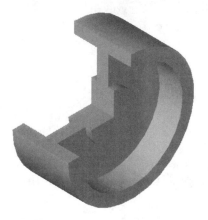
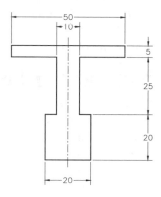

Figure 2-52 *Revolved solid model for Tutorial 1* ***Figure 2-53*** *Sketch for the revolved solid model*

The following steps are required to complete this tutorial:

a. Start a new part document.
b. Switch to the sketching environment.
c. Modify the settings of the snap and grid so that the cursor jumps through a distance of 5 mm instead of 10 mm.
d. Draw the sketch of the model using the **Line** tool.
e. Save the sketch and then close the document.

Starting SolidWorks and Starting a New Part Document

1. Start SolidWorks by choosing **Start > All Programs > SolidWorks 2009 > SolidWorks 2009** or by double-clicking on the shortcut icon of SolidWorks 2009 available on the desktop of your computer; the **SolidWorks 2009** window is displayed along with the **SolidWorks Resources** task pane on its right. The **Getting Started Community**, **Online Resources**, and **Tip of the Day** are displayed in this task pane.

> **Tip**. *If the shortcut icon of SolidWorks is not created automatically on the desktop of your computer when you install SolidWorks, you can create it manually. To do so, choose **Start > All Programs > SolidWorks 2009** to display the SolidWorks cascading menu. Right-click on **SolidWorks 2009** in the cascading menu and then choose **Send To > Desktop (create shortcut)** from the shortcut menu.*

You can get many valuable tips from the **Tip of the Day** message box. These tips are helpful in making the full utilization of this CAD package.

2. Choose the **New Document** option from the **Getting Started** rollout of the **SolidWorks Resources** task pane; the **New SolidWorks Document** dialog box is displayed, as shown in Figure 2-54.

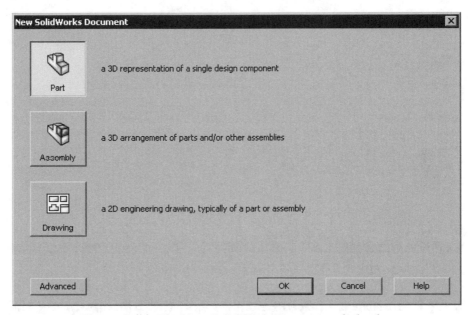

Figure 2-54 The New SolidWorks Document dialog box

3. The **Part** button is chosen by default. Choose the **OK** button from the **New SolidWorks Document** dialog box; a new SolidWorks part document is started. Also, the part modeling environment is active by default.

You need to invoke the sketching environment to draw the sketch.

4. Choose the **Sketch** tab from the **CommandManager** and then choose the **Sketch** button in the **Sketch CommandManager**; the **Edit Sketch PropertyManager** is displayed and you are prompted to select a plane on which you want to draw the sketch.

5. Select **Front Plane** from the drawing area; the sketching environment is invoked and the plane is oriented normal to the view. You will notice that a red colored arrow is displayed at the center of the screen indicating that you are in the sketching environment. Also, the confirmation corner is displayed with the **Exit Sketch** and **Delete Sketch** options on the upper right corner in the drawing area. The screen display in the sketching environment of SolidWorks is shown in Figure 2-55.

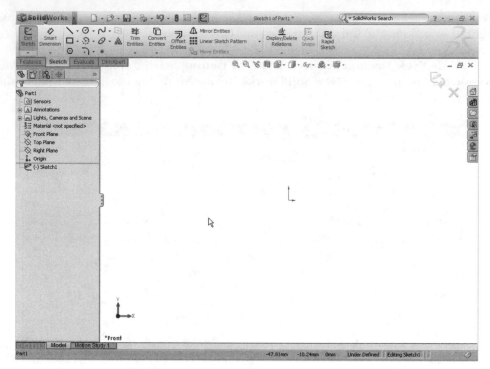

Figure 2-55 Screen display in the sketching environment

Modifying the Snap and Grid Settings and the Dimensioning Units

It is assumed that while installing SolidWorks, you have selected the **MMGS (millimeters, gram, second)** option for measuring the length. So, the length of an entity will be measured in millimeters in the current file. But if you have selected some other unit while installation, you need to make some initial settings to change the linear and angular units before drawing the sketch. For this tutorial, you need to modify the grid and snap settings so that the cursor jumps through a distance of 5 mm.

Note
If you had selected millimeters as the unit while installing SolidWorks, skip the first four points in this section.

1. Choose the **Options** button from the Menu Bar; **System Options - General** dialog box is displayed.

2. Choose the **Document Properties** tab; the name of the dialog box is changed to **Document Properties - Drafting Standard**.

3. Select the **Units** option from the area on the left to display the options related to the linear and angular units.

4. Select the **MMGS (millimeter, gram, second)** radio button in the **Unit system** area. Also, select the **degrees** option from the **Angle** area in the **Units** column.

As evident in Figure 2-53, the dimensions in the sketch are multiples of 5. Therefore, you need to modify the grid and snap settings so that the cursor jumps through a distance of 5 mm instead of 10 mm.

5. Select the **Grid/Snap** option from the area on the left to display the options related to grids. Set the value in the **Major grid spacing** spinner to **50**. Set the value in the **Minor-lines per major** spinner to **10**.

6. Select the **Display grid** check box, if it is cleared. Now, choose the **Go To System Snaps** button; the system options related to relations and snaps are displayed.

7. Select the **Grid** check box from the **Sketch snaps** area and clear the **Snap only when grid is displayed** check box. Choose **OK** to exit the dialog box.

    Note that in the sketching environment, the lower right corner of the drawing area displays information about, editing sketch, status of the sketch, and location of the cursor in the X, Y, and Z coordinates. You will use the coordinates display to draw the sketch of the model. These coordinates will be modified as you move the cursor around the drawing area. When you move the cursor after the initial settings, the coordinates will show an increment of 5 mm instead of the default increment of 10 mm.

Drawing the Sketch

As evident from Figure 2-53, the sketch will be drawn using the **Line** tool. You will start drawing the sketch from the lower left corner of the sketch.

1. Choose the **Line** button from the **Sketch CommandManager**; the arrow cursor is replaced by the line cursor.

2. Move the line cursor to a location whose coordinates are 40 mm, 0 mm, 0 mm.

3. Press the left mouse button at this point and move the cursor horizontally toward the right. You will notice that the symbol of the **Horizontal** relation is displayed below the line cursor and the length and angle of the line is displayed above the line cursor.

4. Press the left mouse button again when the length of the line above the line cursor shows the value 20.

    The first horizontal line is drawn. As you are drawing continuous lines, the endpoint of the line drawn is automatically selected as the start point of the next line.

5. Move the line cursor vertically upward. The symbol of the **Vertical** relation is displayed on the left of the line cursor and the length of the line is displayed above the line cursor. Press the left mouse button when the length of the line on the line cursor displays the value 20.

6. Move the cursor horizontally toward the left and press the left mouse button when the length of the line on the line cursor displays the value 5.

7. Move the line cursor vertically upward and press the left mouse button when the length of the line on the line cursor displays the value 25.

8. Move the line cursor horizontally toward the right and press the left mouse button when the length of the line on the line cursor displays the value 20.

9. Move the line cursor vertically upward and press the left mouse button when the length of the line on the line cursor displays the value 5.

10. Press F from the keyboard to fit the sketch on the screen.

11. Move the line cursor horizontally toward the left and press the left mouse button when the length of the line on the line cursor displays the value 50.

12. Move the line cursor vertically downward and press the left mouse button when the length of the line on the line cursor displays the value 5.

13. Move the line cursor horizontally toward the right and press the left mouse button when the length of the line on the line cursor displays the value 20.

14. Move the line cursor vertically downward and press the left mouse button when the length of the line on the line cursor displays the value 25.

15. Move the line cursor horizontally toward the left and press the left mouse button when the length of the line on the line cursor displays the value 5.

16. Move the line cursor vertically downward to the start point of the first line. Press the left mouse button when the red circle is displayed. The final sketch for Tutorial 1 is created, as shown in Figure 2-56. In this figure, the display of the grid is turned off for clarity.

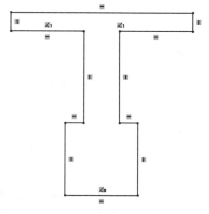

Figure 2-56 *Final sketch for Tutorial 1*

17. Right-click and choose **Select** from the shortcut menu to exit the **Line** tool.

Tip. *To turn off the grid display, right-click in the drawing area to display the shortcut menu. The **Display grid** option has a check mark on it's left, indicating that this option is chosen. Choose the option again.*

Saving the Sketch

It is recommended that you create a separate folder for saving the tutorial files of this book. When you invoke the option to save a document, the default folder *My Documents* will be displayed. You will create a folder with the name *SolidWorks* in the *My Documents* folder and then create the folder of each chapter inside the *SolidWorks* folder. As a result, you can save the tutorials of a chapter in the folder of that chapter.

1. Choose the **Save** button from the Menu Bar to invoke the **Save As** dialog box. Create the *SolidWorks* folder inside the *My Documents* folder and then create the *c02* folder inside the *SolidWorks* folder.

2. Enter the name of the document as *c02tut1* in the **File name** edit box and choose the **Save** button. The document will be saved in the *My Documents\SolidWorks\c02* folder.

3. Close the document by choosing **File > Close** from the SolidWorks menus.

Tutorial 2

In this tutorial, you will draw the sketch of the solid model shown in Figure 2-57. The sketch of the model is shown in Figure 2-58. Do not dimension the sketch. The dimensions and the solid model are given for your reference only. **(Expected time: 30 min)**

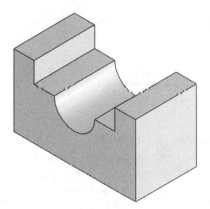

Figure 2-57 Solid model for Tutorial 2

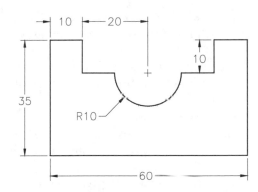

Figure 2-58 Sketch for Tutorial 2

The following steps are required to complete this tutorial:

a. Start SolidWorks and then start a new part document.
b. Invoke the sketching environment.
c. Modify the settings of the snap and grid so that the cursor jumps through a distance of 5 mm instead of 10 mm.

d. Draw the sketch using the **Line** tool, refer to Figure 2-59.

e. Save the sketch and then close the file.

Opening a New File

1. Choose the **New** button from the Menu Bar to invoke the **New SolidWorks Document** dialog box.

2. The **Part** button is chosen by default in the **New SolidWorks Document** dialog box. Now, choose the **OK** button.

    Invoke the sketching environment, as you need to draw the sketch of the model first.

3. Choose the **Sketch** button from the **Sketch CommandManager** and select the **Front Plane** to invoke the sketching environment.

Modifying the Snap and Grid Settings and Dimensioning Units

As evident in Figure 2-58, the dimensions in the sketch are multiples of 5. Therefore, you need to modify the grid and snap settings so that the cursor jumps through a distance of 5 mm instead of 10 mm.

1. Choose **Options** from the Menu Bar to invoke the **System Options - General** dialog box. Choose the **Document Properties** tab.

2. Select the **Grid/Snap** option from the area on the left to display the options related to linear and angular units. Set the value in the **Major grid spacing** spinner to **50** and value in the **Minor-lines per major** spinner to **10**.

3. Make sure the **Grid** check box is selected in the **System Options - Relations/Snaps** dialog box. Choose **OK** to close the dialog box.

    When you move the cursor, the coordinates displayed close to the lower right corner of the drawing area show an increment of 5 mm.

Drawing the Sketch

The sketch will be drawn using the **Line** tool. The arc in the sketch will also be drawn using the same tool. You will start drawing from the lower left corner of the sketch.

1. Invoke the **Line** tool by pressing the L key; the arrow cursor is replaced by the line cursor.

2. Move the line cursor to a point whose coordinates are 30 mm, 0 mm, 0 mm.

3. Press the left mouse button at this point and move the cursor horizontally toward the right. Press the left mouse button again when the length of the line above the line cursor shows the value 60; the bottom horizontal line of 60 mm length is drawn.

4. Move the line cursor vertically upward and press the left mouse button when the length of the line displayed above the line cursor shows the value 35.

5. Choose the **Zoom to Fit** button from the **Heads-up View** toolbar to fit the sketch on the screen.

    As mentioned earlier, you can also invoke the drawing display tools while some other tool is active. After modifying the drawing display, the tool that was active before invoking the drawing display tool will be restored and you can continue using that tool. Therefore, after the drawing display area is modified, the **Line** tool will be restored and you can continue drawing lines.

6. Move the line cursor horizontally toward the left and press the left mouse button when the length of the line above the line cursor shows the value 10.

7. Move the line cursor vertically downward and press the left mouse button when the length of the line above the line cursor shows the value 10.

8. Move the line cursor horizontally toward the left and press the left mouse button when the length of the line above the line cursor shows a value of 10.

    Next, you need to draw the arc that is normal to the last line. As mentioned earlier, you can draw an arc using the **Line** tool also. Drawing arcs using the **Line** tool is a recommended method when you need to draw a sketch that is a combination of lines and arcs. This increases the productivity by reducing the time taken in invoking the tools for drawing an arc and then invoking the **Line** tool to draw lines.

9. Move the line cursor away from the endpoint of the last line and then move it back close to the endpoint; the arc mode is invoked.

10. Move the arc cursor vertically downward up to the next grid point.

11. Move the arc cursor toward the left.

    You will notice that a normal arc is being drawn and the angle and radius of the arc is displayed above the line cursor.

12. Move the cursor to left and press the left mouse button when the angle value on the arc cursor is 180 and the radius value is 10. An arc normal to the last line is drawn and the line mode is activated.

13. Move the line cursor horizontally toward the left and press the left mouse button when the length of the line on the line cursor shows a value of 10.

14. Move the line cursor vertically upward and press the left mouse button when the length of the line on the line cursor shows a value of 10.

15. Move the line cursor horizontally toward the left and press the left mouse button when the length of the line on the line cursor shows the value 10.

16. Move the line cursor to the start point of the first line and press the left mouse button when the orange circle is displayed.

17. Press the ESC key to exit the **Line** tool.

This completes the sketch. However, you need to modify the drawing display area such that the sketch fits the screen.

18. Press the F key to modify the drawing display area. The final sketch for Tutorial 2, without the grid display, is shown in Figure 2-59.

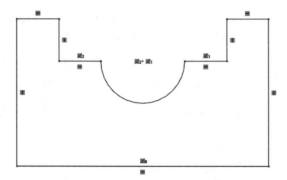

Figure 2-59 *Final sketch for Tutorial 2*

Saving the Sketch

1. Choose the **Save** button from the Menu Bar to invoke the **Save As** dialog box.

2. Enter the name of the document as *c02tut2* in the **File name** edit box and choose the **Save** button.

3. Close the document by choosing **File > Close** from the SolidWorks menus.

Tutorial 3

In this tutorial, you will draw the basic sketch of the model shown in Figure 2-60. The sketch to be drawn is shown in Figure 2-61. Do not dimension the sketch; the solid model and dimensions are given for your reference only.   **(Expected time: 30 min)**

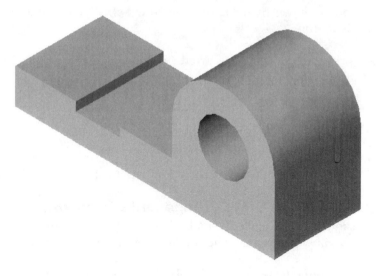

Figure 2-60 *Solid model for Tutorial 3*

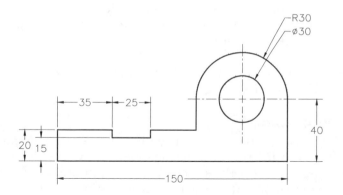

Figure 2-61 *Sketch for Tutorial 3*

The following steps are required to complete this tutorial:

a. Start SolidWorks and then start a new part file.
b. Switch to the sketching environment.
c. Modify the settings of the snap and grid so that the cursor jumps through a distance of 5 mm instead of 10 mm.
d. Draw the outer loop of the sketch using the **Line** tool.
e. Draw the inner circle using the **Circle** tool, refer to Figure 2-63.
f. Save the sketch and then close the file.

Starting a New File

1. Choose the **New** button from the Menu Bar to invoke the **New SolidWorks Document** dialog box.

2. The **Part** button is chosen by default in the **New SolidWorks Document** dialog box. Choose the **OK** button.

A new SolidWorks part document is started. To draw the sketch of the model, you need to invoke the sketching environment.

3. Choose the **Sketch** button from the **Sketch CommandManager**; the **Edit Sketch PropertyManager** is displayed. Select **Front Plane** from the drawing area.

The sketching environment is displayed with the confirmation corner with the **Exit Sketch** and **Delete Sketch** options on the upper right corner of the drawing area.

Modifying the Snap and Grid Settings and Dimensioning Units

As the dimensions in the sketch are multiples of 5, you need to modify the grid and snap settings so that you can make the cursor jump through a distance of 5 mm.

1. Choose **Options** from the Menu Bar to invoke the **System Options - General** dialog box. Choose the **Document Properties** tab.

2. Select the **Grid/Snap** option from the area on the left to display the options related to linear and angular units. Set the value of the **Major grid spacing** spinner to **50** and set the value of the **Minor-lines per major** spinner is **10**.

3. Make sure the **Grid** check box is selected in the **System Options - Relations/Snaps** dialog box. Choose **OK** to close the dialog box.

Drawing the Outer Loop

As evident from Figure 2-61, the sketch consists of an outer loop and an inner circle. Therefore, this sketch will be drawn using the **Line** and **Circle** tools. You will start drawing from the lower left corner of the sketch. As the length of the lower horizontal line is 150 mm, you need to modify the drawing display area such that the drawing area in the first quadrant is increased. This can be done using the **Pan** tool.

1. Press the CTRL key and the middle mouse button and drag the cursor toward the bottom left corner of the screen.

You will notice that the origin also moves toward the bottom left corner of the screen, thus increasing the drawing area in the first quadrant.

2. After dragging the origin close to the lower left corner, release the left mouse button.

3. Choose the **Line** button from the **Sketch CommandManager**.

4. Move the line cursor to a location whose coordinates arc 40 mm, 0 mm, 0 mm.

5. Press the left mouse button at this point and move the cursor horizontally toward the right. Press the left mouse button again when the length of the line above the line cursor shows a value of 150.

6. Move the line cursor vertically upward and press the left mouse button when the length of the line on the line cursor displays the value 40.

   The next entity that has to be drawn is a tangent arc. This arc will be drawn by invoking the **Arc** tool from the **Line** tool

7. Move the line cursor away from the endpoint of the last line and then move it back to the endpoint.

   The arc mode is invoked and the line cursor is replaced by the arc cursor.

8. Move the arc cursor vertically upward to a small distance.

9. When the dotted line is displayed, move the cursor toward the left.

   You will notice that a tangent arc is being drawn. The angle of the tangent arc and its radius are displayed above the arc cursor.

10. Press the left mouse button when the angle value above the arc cursor shows 180 and the radius shows a value of 30 to complete the arc.

    The required tangent arc is drawn. As mentioned earlier, the line mode is automatically invoked after you have drawn the arc using the **Line** tool.

11. Move the line cursor vertically downward and press the left mouse button when the length of the line on the line cursor displays the value 20.

12. Move the line cursor horizontally toward the left and press the left mouse button when the length of the line on the line cursor displays the value 30.

13. Move the line cursor vertically downward and press the left mouse button when the length of the line on the line cursor displays the value 5.

14. Move the line cursor horizontally toward the left and press the left mouse button when the length of the line on the line cursor displays the value 25.

15. Move the line cursor vertically upward and press the left mouse button when the length of the line on the line cursor displays the value 5.

Tip. *While drawing the lines, if the arc mode is invoked by mistake, press the A key; the line mode will be invoked again.*

16. Move the line cursor horizontally toward the left and press the left mouse button when the length of the line on the line cursor displays the value 35.

17. Move the line cursor to the start point of the first line. Press the left mouse button when the orange circle is displayed.

    The length of the line at this point will be 20 mm.

18. Right-click and choose **Select** from the shortcut menu to exit the **Line** tool.

19. Choose the **Zoom to Fit** button to fit the sketch on the screen. This completes the outer loop of the sketch. The sketch, after drawing the outer loop, is shown in Figure 2-62.

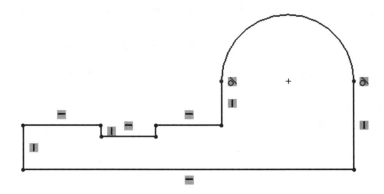

Figure 2-62 Sketch after drawing the outer loop

Drawing the Circle

The circle in the sketch will be drawn using the **Circle** tool. The centerpoint of the circle will be the centerpoint of the arc, which will be displayed by a plus sign. This plus sign is automatically drawn when you draw the arc. You can select this centerpoint to draw the circle.

1. Choose the **Circle** button from the **Sketch CommandManager** to invoke the **Circle PropertyManager**. Choose the **Circle** button from the **Circle Type** rollout, if it is not chosen already.

2. Move the circle cursor close to the centerpoint of the arc and press the left mouse button when the orange circle is displayed.

3. Move the cursor toward the left and when the radius of the circle above the circle cursor shows a value of 15, press the left mouse button. A circle of 15 mm radius is drawn.

 Tip. *You will notice that the bottom horizontal line in the sketch is black and the remaining lines are blue. In the next chapter, you will learn about the reason why some entities in the sketch have a different color.*

4. This completes the sketch for Tutorial 3. Right-click and choose the **Select** option from the shortcut menu to exit the **Circle** tool.

The final sketch for Tutorial 3 is shown in Figure 2-63.

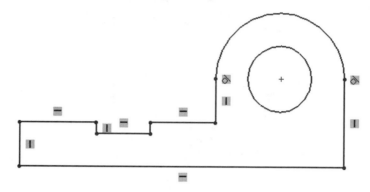

Figure 2-63 *Final sketch for Tutorial 3*

Saving the Sketch

1. Choose the **Save** button from the Menu Bar to invoke the **Save As** dialog box.

2. Enter the name of the document as *c02tut3* in the **File name** edit box and choose the **Save** button.

3. Close the document by choosing **File > Close** from the SolidWorks menus.

Tutorial 4

In this tutorial, you will draw the sketch of the model shown in Figure 2-64. The sketch of the model is shown in Figure 2-65. You will not dimension the sketch. The solid model and the dimensions are given for your reference only. **(Expected time: 30 min)**

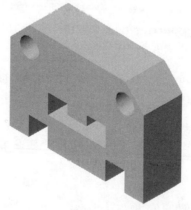

Figure 2-64 *Solid model for Tutorial 4*

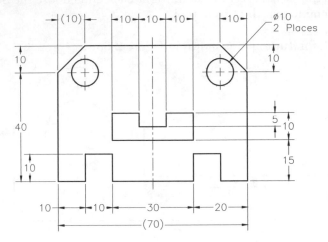

Figure 2-65 *Sketch of the model for tutorial 4*

The following steps are required to complete this tutorial:

a. Start SolidWorks and then start a new part document.
b. Switch to the sketching environment.
c. Draw the sketch of the model using the **Line** and **Circle** tools, refer to Figures 2-66 through 2-70.
d. Save the sketch and then close the document.

Modifying Unit and Grid Settings

You need to make some initial settings to change the linear and angular units before drawing the sketch.

1. Choose the **Options** button from the Menu Bar to invoke the **System Options - General** dialog box.

2. Choose the **Document Properties** tab; the name of the dialog box is changed to **Document Properties - Drafting Standard**.

3. Select the **Units** option from the area on the left to display the options related to the linear and angular units.

4. Select the **MMGS (millimeter, gram, second)** radio button from the **Unit system** area, if it is not selected by default. Also, select the **degrees** option from the **Angle** area, if it is not selected by default.

Note
*If you had selected **Millimeters** as the unit while installing SolidWorks, skip the points discussed earlier in this section.*

5. Select **Grid/Snap** from the area on the left and select the **Display Grid** check box, if it is cleared.

6. Set the value of the **Major grid spacing** spinner to **100** and the value of the **Minor-lines per major** spinner to **20**. Now, choose the **Go To System Snaps** button; the system options related to relations and snap are displayed.

7. Select the **Grid** check box from the **Sketch snaps** area, if it is cleared. Make sure that you clear the **Snap only when grid is displayed** check box, if it is selected. Choose **OK** to exit the dialog box.

> **Tip**. *If the grid is displayed on the screen when you invoke the sketching environment for the first time, then you can set the option to turn off the grid display. Right-click in the drawing area to display the shortcut menu. The **Display Grid** option has a check mark on its left, indicating that this option is chosen. Select this option again to turn the grids off.*

Drawing the Outer Loop of the Sketch

The sketch of the model consists of an outer loop, which has two circles and a cavity inside it. You will first draw the outer loop and then the inner entities. Therefore, the sketch will be drawn using the **Line** and **Circle** tools.

The outer loop will be drawn using the continuous lines. You will start drawing the sketch from the lower left corner of the sketch.

1. Choose the **Line** button from the **Sketch CommandManager** to invoke the **Line** tool; the arrow cursor is replaced by the line cursor.

2. Move the cursor in the first quadrant close to the origin; the coordinates of the point are displayed close to the lower left corner of the screen.

3. Press the left mouse button at the point whose coordinates are 10 mm, 10 mm, 0 mm and then move the cursor horizontally toward the right.

4. Press the left mouse button when the length of the line displayed above the line cursor shows a value of 10. Horizontal line is created. Refer to Line 1 in Figure 2-66.

5. Move the line cursor vertically upward. The symbol of the **Vertical** relation is displayed below the line cursor and the length of the line is displayed above the line cursor.

6. Press the left mouse button when the length of the line displayed above the line cursor shows a value of 10. Vertical line is created. Refer to Line 2 in Figure 2-66.

7. Move the line cursor horizontally toward the right. Press the left mouse button when the length of the line above the line cursor shows a value of 10; the next horizontal line of 10 mm length is drawn. Refer to Line 3 in Figure 2-66.

8. Move the line cursor vertically downward and press the left mouse button when the length of the line on the line cursor shows the value 10. Refer to Line 4 in Figure 2-66.

9. Move the line cursor horizontally toward the right and press the left mouse button when the length of the line on the line cursor shows the value 30. Refer to Line 5 in Figure 2-66.

10. Move the line cursor vertically upward and press the left mouse button when the length of the line on the line cursor shows the value 10. Refer to Line 6 in Figure 2-66.

11. Move the line cursor horizontally toward the right and press the left mouse button when the length of the line on the line cursor shows the value 10. Refer to Line 7 in Figure 2-66.

12. Move the line cursor vertically downward and press the left mouse button when the length of the line on the line cursor shows the value 10. Refer to Line 8 in Figure 2-66.

13. Move the line cursor horizontally toward the right and press the left mouse button when the length of the line on the line cursor shows the value 10. Refer to Line 9 in Figure 2-66.

14. Move the line cursor vertically upward and press the left mouse button when the length of the line on the line cursor displays the value 40. Refer to Line 10 in Figure 2-66.

The next line that you need to draw is an inclined line that makes an angle of 135-degree. To draw this line, you need to move the cursor in a direction that makes an angle of 135-degree.

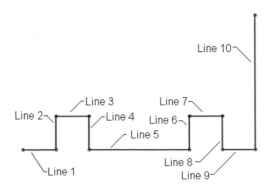

Figure 2-66 *Partial outer loop of the sketch*

15. Move the line cursor such that the line is drawn at an angle of 135-degree and the length of the line displays the value 14.14 above the cursor. The angle can be checked from the **Angle** spinner in the **Parameters** rollout of the **Line PropertyManager**.

16. Press the left mouse button at this location to specify the endpoint of the inclined line.

17. Move the line cursor horizontally toward the left and press the left mouse button when the length of the line on the line cursor displays the value 50.

    You will notice that some yellow inferencing lines are displayed when you move the cursor.

18. Move the line cursor in the direction diagonally downward where the value of the angle displays a value of 135-degree and the length of the lines displays the value 14.14.

19. Press the left mouse button at this location.

20. Move the cursor vertically downward to the start point of the first line.

    You will notice that when you move the cursor close to the start point of the first line, a red circle is displayed. Symbols of the **Vertical** and **Coincident** relations are displayed on the right of the cursor. The length of the line shows the value 40.

21. Press the left mouse button when the red circle is displayed. Right-click to display the shortcut menu and choose the **Select** option to exit the **Line** tool.

    This completes the sketch of the outer loop. Note that the display of the sketch is small. Therefore, you need to modify the drawing display area such that the sketch fits the screen. This is done using the **Zoom to Fit** tool.

22. Choose the **Zoom to Fit** button from the **Heads-up View** toolbar to fit the current sketch on the screen. The outer loop of the sketch is completed and is shown in Figure 2-67. Note that in this figure, the display of the grid is temporarily turned off for a better visibility. This can be done by right-clicking in the drawing area and choosing the **Display grid** option from the shortcut menu.

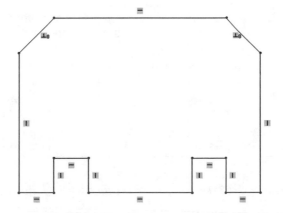

Figure 2-67 Outer loop of the sketch

Drawing Circles

The circles will be drawn using the **Circle** tool. You will use the inferencing lines originating from the start points and endpoints of the inclined lines to specify the centerpoint of the circles. At a given time, you can snap to grid or use inferencing lines to draw the sketches. Therefore, you need to turn off the snapping to grid.

1. Right-click in the drawing area and choose the **Relations/Snaps Options** option from the shortcut menu; the **System Options - Relations/Snaps** dialog box is displayed with the **Relations/Snaps** option selected. Clear the **Grid** check box and choose the **OK** button from this dialog box.

2. Choose the **Circle** button from the **Sketch CommandManager** to invoke the **Circle PropertyManager**. Choose the **Circle** button from the **Circle Type** rollout, if it is not chosen already.

    When you invoke the **Circle** tool, the arrow cursor will be replaced by the circle cursor.

3. Move the circle cursor close to the lower endpoint of the right inclined line and then move it toward the left. Remember that you will not press the left mouse button at this moment. An inferencing line is displayed originating from the lower endpoint of the right inclined line. On moving the cursor toward the left, you will notice that at the point where the cursor is vertically in line with the upper endpoint of the right inclined line, another inferencing line originates from the upper endpoint of the right inclined line. This inferencing line will intersect the inferencing line generated from the lower endpoint of the inclined line, as shown in Figure 2-68.

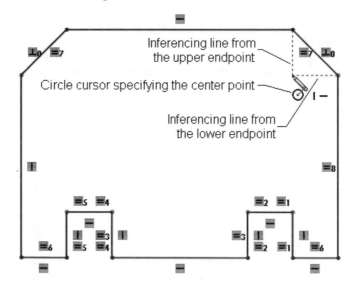

Figure 2-68 *Drawing a circle with the help of inferencing lines*

4. Press the left mouse button at the point where the inferencing lines from both the endpoints of the inclined lines intersect. Now, move the circle cursor toward the left to define a circle.

5. Press the left mouse button when the radius of the circle displayed above the circle cursor shows a value close to 5.

6. Now, the options in the **Circle PropertyManager** are activated. Set the value in the **Radius** spinner to **5** in the **Parameters** rollout of the **PropertyManager** and press **ENTER**.

7. Similarly, draw the circle on the left using the inferencing lines generating from the endpoints of the left inclined line. The sketch, after drawing the two circles inside the outer loop, is shown in Figure 2-69.

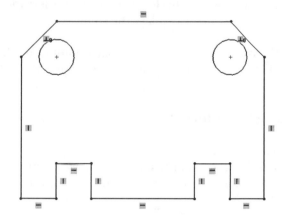

Figure 2-69 *Sketch after drawing the two inner circles*

8. Right-click in the drawing area and choose **Select** to exit the **Circle** tool.

Drawing the Sketch of the Inner Cavity

Next, you will draw the sketch of the inner cavity. You will start drawing with the lower horizontal line. Before proceeding further, you need to invoke the snap to grid option.

1. Select the **Grid** check box in the **System Options - Relations/Snaps** dialog box. Now, invoke the **Line** tool by pressing the L key; the arrow cursor is replaced by the line cursor.

2. Move the line cursor to a location whose coordinates are 30 mm, 25 mm, 0 mm.

3. Press the left mouse button at this point and move the cursor horizontally toward the right. Press the left mouse button when the length of the line above the line cursor displaying the value of 30.

4. Move the line cursor vertically upward and press the left mouse button when the length of the line on the line cursor displays the value 10.

5. Move the line cursor horizontally toward the left and press the left mouse button when the length of the line on the line cursor displays the value 10.

6. Move the line cursor vertically downward and press the left mouse button when the length of the line on the line cursor displays the value 5.

7. Move the line cursor horizontally toward the left and press the left mouse button when the length of the line on the line cursor displays the value 10.

8. Move the line cursor vertically upward and press the left mouse button when the length of the line on the line cursor displays the value 5.

9. Move the line horizontally toward the left and press the left mouse button when the length of the line on the line cursor displays the value 10.

10. Move the line cursor vertically downward to the start point of the first line. Press the left mouse button when the red circle is displayed. The length of the line at this point will show the value 10.

11. Right-click and choose **Select** from the shortcut menu. This completes the sketch for Tutorial 4.

12. Choose the **Zoom to Fit** button from the **Heads-up View** toolbar to fit the display of the sketch on the screen. The final sketch for Tutorial 4 is shown in Figure 2-70.

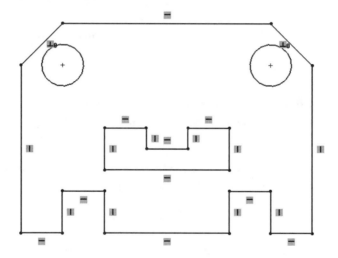

Figure 2-70 Final sketch for Tutorial 4

Saving the Sketch

It is recommended that you create a separate folder for saving the tutorial files of this book. When you invoke the option to save a document, the default folder *My Documents* will be displayed. You will create a folder with the name *SolidWorks* in the *My Documents* folder and then create the folder of each chapter inside the *SolidWorks* folder. As a result, you can save the tutorials of a chapter in the folder of that chapter.

1. Choose the **Save** button from the Menu Bar to invoke the **Save As** dialog box.

2. Enter the name of the document as *c02tut4* in the **File name** edit box and choose the **Save** button. The document will be saved in the *My Documents\SolidWorks\c02* folder.

3. Close the document by choosing **File** > **Close** from the SolidWorks menus.

SELF-EVALUATION TEST

Answer the following questions and then compare them to those given at the end of this chapter:

1. The base feature of any design is a sketched feature and is created by drawing the sketch. (T/F)

2. You can also invoke the **3Point Arc** tool using the **Line** tool. (T/F)

3. By default, the cursor jumps through a distance of 5 mm. (T/F)

4. If you save a file in the sketching environment, it is opened in the part modeling environment when you open it the next time. (T/F)

5. You can convert a sketched entity into a construction entity by selecting the _____ check box provided in the **PropertyManager**.

6. To draw a rectangle at an angle, you need to use the _____ tool.

7. The _____ are the temporary lines that are used to track a particular point on the screen.

8. You can also invoke the _____ tool or press the ESC key to exit the sketching tool.

9. When you select a tangent entity to draw a tangent arc, the _____ relation is applied between the start point of the arc and the tangent entity.

10. In SolidWorks, a rectangle is considered as a combination of individual _____

REVIEW QUESTIONS

Answer the following questions:

1. The three point arcs are drawn by defining the start and endpoints of the arc and a point on the arc. (T/F)

2. You can also delete the sketched entities by selecting them and choosing the **Delete** option from the shortcut menu, which is displayed on right-clicking. (T/F)

3. The origin is a blue icon that is displayed in the middle of the sketcher screen. (T/F)

4. In SolidWorks, circles are drawn by specifying the centerpoint of the circle and then entering the radius of the circle in the dialog box that is displayed. (T/F)

5. When you open a new SolidWorks document, it is not maximized in the SolidWorks window. (T/F)

6. In SolidWorks, a polygon is considered as a combination of which of the following entities?

    (a) Lines   (b) Arcs
    (c) Splines   (d) None

7. Which one of the following options is not displayed in the **New SolidWorks Document** dialog box?

    (a) **Part**   (b) **Assembly**
    (c) **Drawing**   (d) **Sketch**

8. Which one of the following entities is not considered while converting a sketch into a feature?

    (a) Sketched circles   (b) Sketched lines
    (c) Construction lines   (d) None

9. When you select a line of the rectangle, which of the following **PropertyManagers** will be displayed?

    (a) **Line Properties PropertyManager**   (b) **Line/Rectangle PropertyManager**
    (c) **Rectangle PropertyManager**   (d) None

10. While drawing an elliptical arc, which of the following **PropertyManagers** will be displayed?

    (a) **Arc PropertyManager**   (b) **Ellipse PropertyManager**
    (c) **Elliptical Arc PropertyManager** (d) None

EXERCISES

Exercise 1

Draw the sketch of the model shown in Figure 2-71. The sketch to be drawn is shown in Figure 2-72. Do not dimension the sketch. The solid model and dimensions are given for your reference only.   **(Expected time: 30 min)**

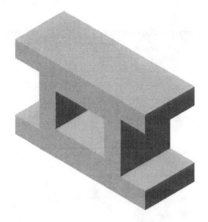

Figure 2-71 Solid model for Exercise 1

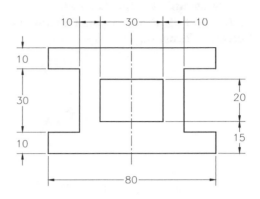

Figure 2-72 Sketch for Exercise 1

Exercise 2

Draw the sketch of the model shown in Figure 2-73. The sketch to be drawn is shown in Figure 2-74. Do not dimension the sketch. The solid model and dimensions are given for your reference only. **(Expected time: 30 min)**

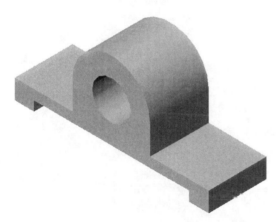

Figure 2-73 Solid model for Exercise 2

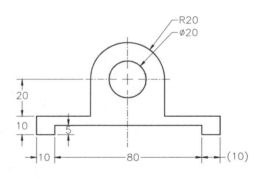

Figure 2-74 Sketch for Exercise 2

Answers to Self-Evaluation Test

1. T, **2.** F, **3.** F, **4.** F, **5. For construction**, **6. 3 Point Corner Rectangle**, **7.** inferencing lines, **8. Select**, **9. Tangent**, **10.** lines

Chapter 3

Editing and Modifying Sketches

Learning Objectives

After completing this chapter, you will be able to:
- *Edit sketches using various editing tools.*
- *Create rectangular patterns of sketched entities.*
- *Create circular patterns of sketched entities.*
- *Write text in the sketching environment.*
- *Modify sketched entities.*
- *Modify sketches by dynamically dragging sketched entities.*

EDITING SKETCHED ENTITIES

SolidWorks provides you with a number of tools that can be used to edit the sketched entities. Using these tools, you can trim, extend, offset, or mirror the sketched entities. You can also perform various other editing operations. The tools to perform these operations are discussed next.

Trimming Sketched Entities

CommandManager:	Sketch > Trim Entities
SolidWorks menus:	Tools > Sketch Tools > Trim
Toolbar:	Sketch > Trim Entities

The **Trim Entities** tool is used to trim the unwanted entities in a sketch. You can use this tool to trim a line, arc, ellipse, parabola, circle, spline, or centerline that is intersecting another line, arc, ellipse, parabola, circle, spline, or centerline. You can also extend the entities using the **Trim** tool. To use the trim option, choose the **Trim Entities** button from the **Sketch CommandManager**; the **Trim PropertyManager** will be displayed, as shown in Figure 3-1.

The options available in the **PropertyManager** to trim the sketched entities are discussed next.

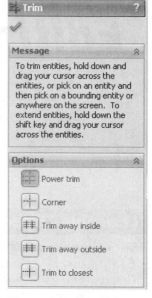

*Figure 3-1 The **Trim** PropertyManager*

Message Rollout

The **Message** rollout in this **PropertyManager** will inform you about the procedure of trimming and extending the sketched elements, depending upon the option that is selected in the **Options** rollout of the **Trim PropertyManager**.

Options Rollout

The **Options** rollout displays all the options available in the **Trim PropertyManager** to trim the sketched entities. These options are discussed next.

Power trim

When the **Power trim** button is chosen in the **Options** rollout, the **Message** rollout in this **PropertyManager** will inform you about the procedure of trimming and extending the sketched elements using this option. To trim the unwanted portion of the sketch using this option, press and hold the left mouse button and drag the cursor. You will notice that a gray-colored drag trace line is displayed along the path of the cursor. When you drag the cursor across the unwanted sketched entity, it will be trimmed and a small red-colored box will be displayed in its place. You can continue trimming the entities by dragging the cursor across them. After trimming all unwanted entities, release the left mouse button.

To extend the sketched entities using this tool, press and hold the SHIFT key and the left mouse button. Now, drag the cursor over the entity that needs to be extended. As the cursor reaches the entity, it will extend to the nearest entity to intersect. If there is no entity to intersect, the entity will not be extended. You can continue extending the entities by dragging the cursor on them. After extending the entities, release the SHIFT key and the left mouse button.

Note
To trim or extend an entity dynamically using this tool, click once on the entity and then move the cursor; the entity will trim or extend dynamically. Move the cursor upto the level to which the entity has to be trimmed or extended. Press the left mouse button to complete the operation.

Corner

The **Corner** button in the **Options** rollout is used to trim or extend the sketched entities in such a way that the resulting entities form a corner. To trim the unwanted elements using this option, choose the **Corner** button from the **Options** rollout; you will be prompted to select an entity. Select the entity from the geometry area; you will be prompted to select another entity. When you move the cursor over the second entity, the preview of the resulting entity will be displayed in different color. Select the portion of the second entity that has to be retained, as shown in Figure 3-2. The portion of the entity from where the selection was made will be retained and the resulting entities form a corner, as shown in Figure 3-3.

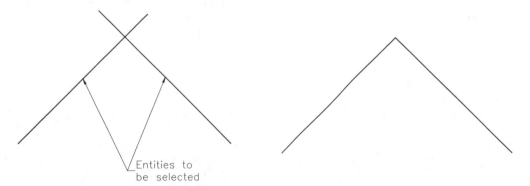

Figure 3-2 Entities to be selected for trimming   *Figure 3-3 Trimmed entities*

You can also extend the entities using this tool. To do so, choose the **Corner** button from the **Options** rollout. Select the entities to be extended; the selected entities will be extended to their apparent intersection, refer to Figures 3-4 and 3-5.

Trim away inside

The **Trim away inside** button in the **Options** rollout is used to trim the portion of the selected entity that lies inside two bounding entities. To trim the entities using this tool, invoke the **Trim PropertyManager** and choose the **Trim away inside** button from the **Options** rollout; the **Message** rollout will inform you to select two bounding entities, and then to select the entities to be trimmed. Select the bounding entities from the drawing area, refer to Figure 3-6. Now, select the entities to be trimmed from the drawing area. As you select an entity to be trimmed, the portion of the entity inside the bounding entities will be removed and the portion outside the bounding entities will be retained, refer to Figure 3-6.

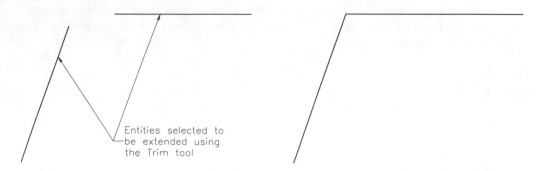

Figure 3-4 Entities selected to extend   *Figure 3-5 Sketch after extension*

Trim away outside

The **Trim away outside** button in the **Options** rollout is used to trim the portion of the entity that is outside the bounding entities. To trim the entities using this tool, invoke the **Trim PropertyManager** and choose the **Trim away outside** button from the **Options** rollout; the **Message** rollout will inform you to select the two bounding entities, and then to select the entities to be trimmed. Select the bounding entities from the drawing area, refer to Figure 3-7. Now, select the entities to be trimmed from the drawing area. As soon as you select an entity to be trimmed, the portion of the entity outside the bounding entities will be removed and the portion inside will be retained, refer to Figure 3-7.

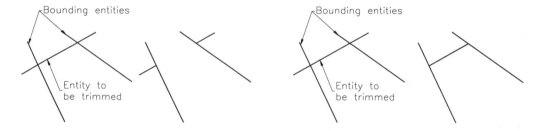

*Figure 3-6 Entity trimmed using the **Trim away inside** option*

*Figure 3-7 Entity trimmed using the **Trim away outside** option*

Trim to closest

The **Trim to closest** button is used to trim the selected entity to its closest intersection. To trim the entities using this tool, invoke the **Trim PropertyManager** and choose the **Trim to closest** button from the **Options** rollout; the cursor will be replaced by the trim cursor. Move the trim cursor near the portion of the sketched entity to be removed. The entity or the portion of the entity to be removed will be highlighted in orange. Press the left mouse button to remove the highlighted entity. Figure 3-8 shows the entities to be trimmed and Figure 3-9 shows the sketch after trimming the entities.

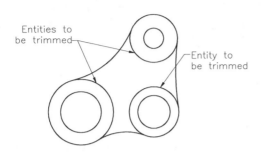

Figure 3-8 *Entities to be trimmed*

Figure 3-9 *Sketch after trimming the entities*

You can also use this option to extend the sketched entities. To do so, move the trim cursor to the entity to be extended. When the sketched entity turns orange, press the left mouse button and drag the cursor to the entity up to which it has to be extended. You will notice the preview of the extended entity. Release the left mouse button when the preview of the extended entity appears; the entity will be extended.

 Tip. *You can toggle between the **Trim Entities** and **Extend Entities** tools using the shortcut menu that will be displayed on right-clicking when one of these tools is active.*

Extending Sketched Entities

CommandManager:	Sketch > Trim Entities > Extend Entities
SolidWorks menus:	Tools > Sketch Tools > Extend
Toolbar:	Sketch > Trim Entities > Extend Entities

The **Extend Entities** tool is used to extend the sketched entity to intersect the next available entity. The tool is used to extend a line, arc, ellipse, parabola, circle, spline, or centerline to intersect another line, arc, ellipse, parabola, circle, spline, or centerline. The sketched entity is extended up to its intersection with another sketched entity or a model edge. Choose the **Extend Entities** button from the **Sketch CommandManager** and move the extend cursor close to the portion of the sketched entity that is to be extended. The entity to be extended will be highlighted and the preview of the extended entity will also be displayed. Press the left mouse button to complete the extend operation. Figure 3-10 shows the sketched entities to be extended and Figure 3-11 shows the sketched entities after extending.

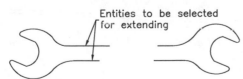

Figure 3-10 *Sketched entities before extending*

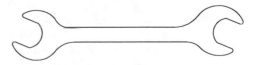

Figure 3-11 *Sketched entities after extending*

Tip. *If the preview of the sketched entity to be extended is shown in the wrong direction, move the extend cursor to a position on the other half of the entity and observe the new preview.*

Filleting Sketched Entities

CommandManager:	Sketch > Sketch Fillet
SolidWorks menus:	Tools > Sketch Tools > Fillet
Toolbar:	Sketch > Sketch Fillet

A fillet creates a tangent arc at the intersection of two sketched entities. It trims or extends the entities to be filleted, depending on the geometry of the sketched entity. You can apply a fillet to two nonparallel lines, two arcs, two splines, an arc and a line, a spline and a line, or a spline and an arc. The fillet between the two arcs, or between an arc and a line depends on the compatibility of the geometry to be extended or filleted along the given radius. You can invoke the **Sketch Fillet** tool first and then select the entities to be filleted or select the vertex formed at the intersection of the two entities to be filleted. You can also hold the CTRL key, select the two entities to be filleted and then invoke this tool. When you invoke this tool, the **Sketch Fillet PropertyManager** will be displayed, as shown in Figure 3-12.

Figure 3-12 The Sketch Fillet PropertyManager

Set the value of the **Radius** spinner and press ENTER or choose the **OK** button from the **Sketch Fillet PropertyManager** to create the fillet. If the **Keep constrained corners** check box is selected, the dimension and geometric relations applied to the sketch will not be deleted. If you clear the **Keep constrained corners** check box, you will be prompted to delete the relations applied to the corners of the sketched entities to be filleted. The **Undo** button will be displayed in the **Sketch Fillet PropertyManager** only when you create at least one sketch fillet. Figure 3-13 shows the intersecting entities before and after applying the fillet. You can also select the nonintersecting entities for creating a fillet. In this case, the selected entities will be extended to form a fillet, as shown in Figure 3-14.

Note
The consecutive fillets with the same radius are not dimensioned individually. An automatic equal radii relation is applied to all fillets.

The fillet creation between two splines, a spline and a line, and a spline and an arc depends on the compatibility of the spline to be trimmed or extended.

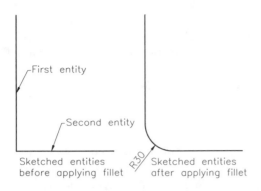

Figure 3-13 Intersecting entities before and after applying a fillet

Figure 3-14 Nonintersecting entities before and after applying a fillet

Tip. *You can also create a fillet by selecting the two entities by drawing a window around them after invoking the* **Sketch Fillet** *tool. To fillet the entities using this method, invoke the* **Sketch Fillet** *tool. Set the* **Radius** *spinner to the required value. Now, drag the cursor to create a window around the two entities to be filleted such that they are enclosed inside the window. As soon as you release the left mouse button, the fillet will be created.*

Chamfering Sketched Entities

CommandManager:	Sketch > Sketch Fillet > Sketch Chamfer
SolidWorks menus:	Tools > Sketch Tools > Chamfer
Toolbar:	Sketch > Sketch Fillet > Sketch Chamfer

The **Sketch Chamfer** tool is used to apply a chamfer to the adjacent sketch entities at the point of intersection. The chamfer can be specified by two lengths or angle and length from the point of intersection. You can apply a chamfer between two nonparallel lines that may be intersecting or nonintersecting. The creation of a chamfer between two nonintersecting lines depends on the length of the lines and the chamfer distance. To create a chamfer, choose the down arrow on the **Sketch Fillet** tool in the **Sketch CommandManager** and choose the **Sketch Chamfer** button from the flyout; the **Sketch Chamfer PropertyManager** will be displayed, as shown in

Figure 3-15 The Sketch Chamfer PropertyManager

Figure 3-15. Next, select the two entities to be chamfered. You can also select the two entities before invoking the **Chamfer** tool. The options in the **Sketch Chamfer PropertyManager** are discussed next.

Angle-distance

The **Angle-distance** radio button is selected to create the chamfer by specifying the angle and the distance. When you select this radio button, the **Direction 1 Angle** spinner will be displayed below the **Distance 1** spinner. Specify the distance and angle values in the **Distance 1** and **Direction 1 Angle** spinners, respectively. Next, select the two entities to which the chamfer needs to be applied; the chamfer will be created, as shown in Figure 3-16(a). Note that the angle will be measured from the first entity you have selected.

Distance-distance

When you invoke the **Sketch Chamfer PropertyManager**, the **Distance-distance** radio button and the **Equal distance** check box are selected by default. Clear this check box to specify two different distances for creating the chamfer, refer to Figure 3-16(b). When you clear this check box, the **Distance 2** spinner will be displayed below the **Distance 1** spinner to set the value of the distance in the second direction. Specify the distance value in both the spinners. Next, select the two entities which need to be chamfered; the chamfer will be created, as shown in Figure 3-16(b). Note that the distance 1 value will be measured along the first entity that you have selected and the distance 2 value will be measured along the second entity.

Equal distance

When you invoke the **Sketch Chamfer PropertyManager**, the **Distance-distance** radio button and the **Equal distance** check box is selected by default. Therefore, you can create an equal distance chamfer between the selected entities. Specify the distance value in the **Distance 1** spinner and select the entities; the chamfer will be created, as shown in Figure 3-16(c).

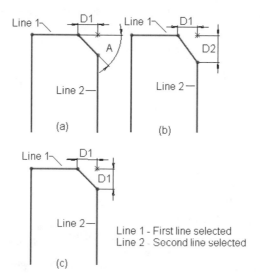

Figure 3-16 *Chamfer and its parameters*

You can also invoke the shortcut menu to select the options discussed to create a chamfer. Choose the **OK** button from the **PropertyManager** to exit the tool.

Note

*If you apply a sketch chamfer to the entities that are constrained using some relations or dimensions, the **SolidWorks** message box will be displayed. It will show the message: **At least one sketch constraint is about to be lost, Chamfer anyway?** Choose the **Yes** button from this message box. You will learn more about the relations and dimensions that constrain the sketch in the later chapters.*

Tip. *While performing any kind of editing operation, if you want to clear the current selection set, right-click in the drawing area and choose **Clear Selections** from the shortcut menu.*

Offsetting Sketched Entities

CommandManager:	Sketch > Offset Entities
SolidWorks menus:	Tools > Sketch Tools > Offset Entities
Toolbar:	Sketch > Offset Entities

Offset is one of the easiest methods to draw parallel lines or concentric arcs and circles. You can select the entire chain of entities as a single entity or select an individual entity to be offset. You can offset the selected sketched entities, edges, loops, and curves. You can also select the parabolic curves, ellipses, and elliptical arcs to be offset. When you choose the **Offset Entities** button from the **Sketch** toolbar, the **Offset Entities PropertyManager** will be displayed, as shown in Figure 3-17. The options in the **Offset Entities PropertyManager** are discussed next.

Figure 3-17 The Offset Entities PropertyManager

Offset Distance

The **Offset Distance** spinner is used to set the distance through which the selected entity needs to be offset. You can set the value of the offset distance in this spinner or by dragging the offset entity in the drawing area.

Add dimensions

The **Add dimensions** check box is selected by default in the **Parameters** rollout. When selected, this check box will add a dimension representing the offset distance between the parent entity and the resulting offset entity.

Reverse

The **Reverse** check box is selected to change the direction of the offset. Note that while offsetting the entities by dragging, you do not need this check box. This is because you can change the direction of the offset by dragging the entities in the required direction.

Select chain

The **Select chain** check box is selected to select the entire chain of continuous sketched entities that are in contact with the selected entity. When you invoke the **Offset** tool, the

Select chain check box will be selected by default. If you clear this check box, only the selected sketched entity will be offset.

Bi-directional

The **Bi-directional** radio button is selected to create the offset of the selected entity in both the directions of the selected entity. If the **Bi-directional** check box is selected, the **Reverse** check box will not be available in the **Parameters** rollout.

Make base construction

The **Make base construction** check box is selected to convert the parent entity into a construction entity.

Cap ends

The **Cap ends** check box is available only if the **Bi-directional** check box is selected. On selecting this check box, the ends of the bidirectionally offset entities will be closed. You can select the **Arcs** or the **Lines** radio button to specify the type of cap to close the ends. If you are offsetting a closed entity on both the directions, this option will not be available.

Figure 3-18 shows a new chain of entities created by offsetting the chain of entities and Figure 3-19 shows offsetting of a single entity.

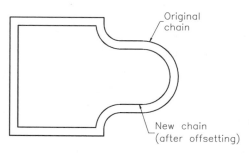

Figure 3-18 *Offsetting a chain of entities*

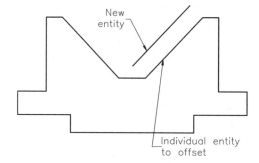

Figure 3-19 *Offsetting a single entity*

Mirroring Sketched Entities

CommandManager:	Sketch > Mirror Entities
SolidWorks menus:	Tools > Sketch Tools > Mirror
Toolbar:	Sketch > Mirror Entities

The **Mirror Entities** tool is used to create the mirror image of the selected entities. The entities are mirrored about a centerline. When you create the mirrored entity, SolidWorks applies the symmetric relation between the sketched entities. If you change the entity, its mirror image will also change. To mirror the existing entities, choose the **Mirror Entities** button from the **Sketch CommandManager**; the **Mirror PropertyManager** will be displayed, as shown in Figure 3-20.

You are prompted to select the entities to be mirrored. Select the entities from the drawing area. The name of the selected entities will be displayed in the **Entities to mirror** selection box. After selecting all entities to be mirrored, click once in the **Mirror about** selection box. Alternatively, if you pause the mouse after selecting an entity, the **Select** symbol will be displayed below the cursor. Right-click when this symbol is displayed; the **Mirror about** selection box will be activated automatically and you will be prompted to select a line or a linear model edge to mirror about. Select a line or a centerline from the drawing area that will be used as the mirror line; the preview of the mirrored entities will be displayed. You need to make sure that the **Copy** check box is selected in the **Mirror PropertyManager**. If you clear this check box, the parent selected entities will be removed and only the mirror image will be retained when you mirror the sketched entities. Choose the **OK** button from the **Mirror PropertyManager**.

Figure 3-20 The Mirror PropertyManager

Figure 3-21 shows the sketched entities with the centerline and Figure 3-22 shows the resulting mirror image of the sketched entities.

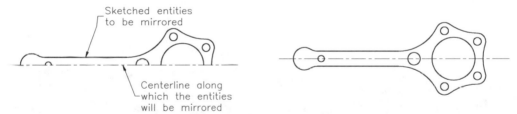

Figure 3-21 Selecting the sketched entities and the centerline

Figure 3-22 Sketch after mirroring the geometry

Mirroring While Sketching (Dynamic Mirror Entities)

CommandManager:	Sketch > Dynamic Mirror Entities	*(Customize to add)*
SolidWorks menus:	Tools > Sketch Tools > Dynamic Mirror	
Toolbar:	Sketch > Dynamic Mirror Entities	*(Customize to add)*

The **Dynamic Mirror Entities** tool is used to mirror the entities dynamically about a symmetry line while sketching. This tool is recommended when you are drawing the symmetric sketches. To use this tool, choose the **Dynamic Mirror Entities** button from the **Sketch CommandManager**; the **Mirror PropertyManager** will be displayed, as shown in Figure 3-23.

The **Message** rollout of the **Mirror PropertyManager** informs that you need to select a sketch line or a linear model edge to mirror about. Select a line or a centerline from the drawing that will be used as symmetry line. The symmetry symbols appear at both ends of the centerline to indicate that automatic mirroring is activated, as shown in Figure 3-24. Now, start drawing

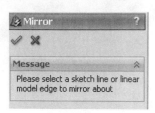

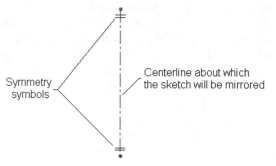

Symmetry
symbols

Centerline about which
the sketch will be mirrored

Figure 3-23 The **Mirror PropertyManager**

Figure 3-24 *The centerline and the symmetry symbols*

the sketch. The entity that you draw on one side of the centerline will automatically be created on the other side of the mirror line (centerline). As evident in Figure 3-25, the entities are mirrored automatically while sketching. Figure 3-26 shows the complete sketch with automatic mirroring. After completing the sketch using the automatic mirroring option, you need to choose the **Dynamic Mirror Entities** tool again to exit the tool.

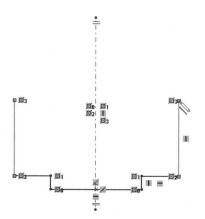

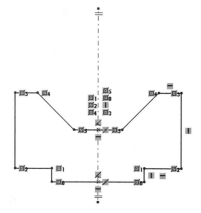

Figure 3-25 *Sketching using the **Dynamic Mirror Entities** tool*

Figure 3-26 *Sketch drawn using the **Dynamic Mirror Entities** tool*

Moving Sketched Entities

CommandManager:	Sketch > Move Entities
SolidWorks menus:	Tools > Sketch Tools > Move
Toolbar:	Sketch > Move Entities

The **Move Entities** tool is used to move the selected entities from one location to a desired location. To do so, invoke the **Move Entities** tool by choosing the **Move Entities** button from the **Sketch CommandManager** or right-click to display the shortcut menu and choose the **Move Entities** option from it to invoke this tool. Remember that this tool will be available only when at least one sketched entity is drawn. When you invoke this tool, the **Move PropertyManager** will be displayed, as shown in Figure 3-27, and you will be prompted to select the sketched items or the annotations to be moved. The options in this **PropertyManager** are discussed next.

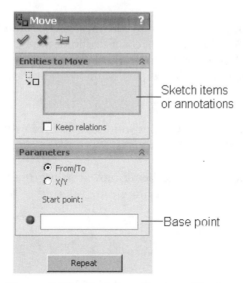

Figure 3-27 The Move PropertyManager

Entities to Move Rollout

The options in this rollout are used to select the entities to be moved. You will notice that the **Sketch items or annotations** selection box is active in this rollout. The names of the entities selected to be moved will be displayed in this selection box. To remove an entity from the selection set, select it again from the drawing area. Alternatively, you can select its name from the **Sketch items or annotations** selection box and right-click to display the shortcut menu. Choose the **Delete** option from the shortcut menu. If you choose the **Clear Selections** option from the shortcut menu, all the entities in the selection set will be removed.

You will notice that by default, the **Keep relations** check box is cleared. If you move the sketched entities with this check box cleared, the relations applied to the entities to be moved will be removed. If you select this check box and then move the entities, then the relations applied to the sketched entities are retained even if you move the entities. You will learn more about relations later in this chapter.

Parameters Rollout

The **Parameters** rollout is used to specify the origin and destination positions of the entities selected to move. The options available in this rollout are discussed next.

From/To

The **From/To** radio button is selected by default. So, you can move the selected entities from one point to another. To move the selected entities using this option, click once in the **Base point** selection box; you are prompted to define the base point. Click anywhere in the drawing area to specify the base point; a yellow circle is displayed where the start point is specified and you are prompted to define the destination point. Select a point anywhere in the drawing area to place the selected entities.

X/Y

The **X/Y** radio button is selected to move the selected entities by specifying the relative coordinates of X and Y. When you select this radio button, the **Delta X** and the **Delta Y** spinners will be displayed below this radio button. Set the value of the destination coordinates in these spinners with respect to the current location.

Repeat

If the **Repeat** button is chosen, the entities will move further with the incremental distance specified in the **Delta X** and **Delta Y** spinners.

Figure 3-28 shows the selected entities being moved using the **Move Entities** tool. In this figure, the upper and right edges of a rectangle are selected to be moved.

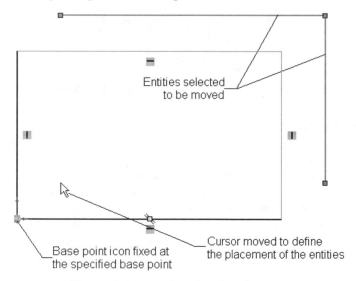

Figure 3-28 Moving the selected entities

Rotating Sketched Entities

CommandManager:	Sketch > Move Entities > Rotate Entities
SolidWorks menus:	Tools > Sketch Tools > Rotate
Toolbar:	Sketch > Move Entities > Rotate Entities

To rotate the sketched entities, choose the down arrow on the right of the **Move Entities** tool in the **Sketch CommandManager**; a flyout will be displayed. Choose the **Rotate Entities** option from the flyout. You can also select the entities and right-click to display the shortcut menu. Choose **Rotate Entities** from the shortcut menu; the **Rotate PropertyManager** will be displayed, as shown in Figure 3-29, and you will be prompted to select the sketched items or annotations.

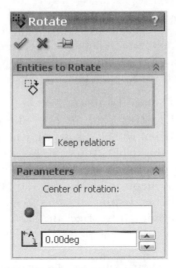

*Figure 3-29 The **Rotate PropertyManager***

Select the entities to be rotated; their names will be displayed in the **Sketch items or annotations** selection box of the **Entities to Rotate** rollout. Next, click in the **Base point** selection box in the **Parameters** rollout; you will be prompted to specify the center point of rotation.

As soon as you specify the center point, the **Angle** spinner in the **Parameters** rollout will be highlighted. You can specify the angle of rotation using this spinner. You can also drag the mouse on the screen to define the angle of rotation.

Figure 3-30 shows a rectangle being rotated by dragging the cursor to define the angle of rotation. The lower right vertex of the rectangle is taken as the center point of rotation.

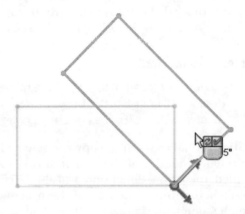

Figure 3-30 Dragging the cursor to rotate the rectangle

Scaling Sketched Entities

CommandManager:	Sketch > Move Entities > Scale Entities
SolidWorks menus:	Tools > Sketch Tools > Scale
Toolbar:	Sketch > Move Entities > Scale Entities

To resize the entities, choose the down arrow on the right of the **Move Entities** tool in the **Sketch CommandManager**; a flyout will be displayed. Choose the **Scale Entities** option from the flyout. You can also select the entities and right-click to display the shortcut menu. Choose **Scale Entities** from the shortcut menu to invoke this tool; the **Scale PropertyManager** will be displayed, as shown in Figure 3-31, and you will be prompted to select the sketched items or annotations.

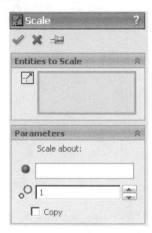

Select the entities to be resized; their names will be displayed in the **Sketch items or annotations** selection box of the **Entities to Scale** rollout. After selecting the entities to be scaled, right-click; you will be prompted to specify the base point about which to scale. Select the base point in the drawing area by clicking the left mouse button.

Figure 3-31 The Scale PropertyManager

After specifying the base point, specify the magnification factor in the **Scale Factor** spinner of the **Parameters** rollout. The entities will be resized based on the value set in this spinner.

If you need to create copies of the selected entities, select the **Copy** check box. Else, choose the **OK** button from the **Scale PropetyManager**; the selected entities will be resized. On selecting the **Copy** check box, the **Number of Copies** spinner will be displayed. Set the number of instances in this spinner and choose the **OK** button from the **Scale PropertyManager**; the entities will be resized and their copies will be created with an incremental scale factor with respect to the original entity selected.

Copying Sketched Entities

CommandManager:	Sketch > Move Entities > Copy Entities
SolidWorks menus:	Tools > Sketch Tools > Copy
Toolbar:	Sketch > Move Entities > Copy Entities

The **Copy Entities** tool allows you to copy the selected sketched entities from one location to the other. Note that if the dimensions are also selected along with the entities to be copied, then those dimensions will also be copied along with the sketched entities. To copy the sketched entities, choose the down arrow on the right of the **Move Entities** tool in the **Sketch CommandManager**; a flyout will be displayed. Choose the **Copy Entities** option from the flyout; the **Copy PropertyManager** will be displayed, as shown in Figure 3-32.

Select the entities that you want to copy and then select the **From/To** radio button, if it is not selected

Figure 3-32 The Copy PropertyManager

by default. Next, click once in the **Base point** selection box and then specify the base point. Now, move the cursor; you will notice that the preview of the entities to be copied will be attached to the cursor. Click at a location in the drawing area to place the copied entities. If you need to create multiple copies, left-click at different locations. Else, right-click to invoke the shortcut menu and choose the **OK** option from it to exit the tool. On selecting the **X/Y** radio button in the **Parameters** rollout of the **Copy PropertyManager,** you need to specify the X and Y coordinates of the new entities with respect to their current location and choose the **OK** button. Note that on selecting the **X/Y** radio button, you cannot create multiple copies of the selected entities.

CREATING PATTERNS

Sometimes you may need to place the sketched entities in a particular arrangement such as along linear edges or around a circle while creating the base feature. For example, refer to Figures 3-33 and 3-34, which show the base features with slots. These slots are created with the help of linear and circular patterns of the sketched entities. The tools that are used to create the linear and circular patterns of sketched entities are discussed next.

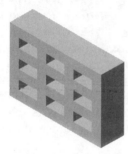

Figure 3-33 Base feature with slots created along the linear edges

Figure 3-34 Base feature with slots created around a circle

Creating Linear Sketch Patterns

CommandManager:	Sketch > Linear Sketch Pattern
SolidWorks menus:	Tools > Sketch Tools > Linear Pattern
Toolbar:	Sketch > Linear Sketch Pattern

In SolidWorks, the linear pattern of the sketched entities is created using the **Linear Sketch Pattern** tool. To create the linear pattern, select the sketched entities from the drawing area. Then, choose the **Linear Sketch Pattern** button from the **Sketch CommandManager**; the **Linear Pattern PropertyManager** will be displayed, as shown in Figure 3-35 and the preview of the linear pattern will be displayed. Also, the arrow cursor will be replaced by the linear pattern cursor. Note that if you have not selected the sketched entities to be patterned before invoking this tool, you will have to select them one by one using the linear pattern cursor. You cannot select more than one entity by drawing a window using the linear pattern cursor. The name of the selected instances are displayed in the **Entities to Pattern** rollout.

Figure 3-35 *The **Linear Pattern PropertyManager***

The options available in this **PropertyManager** are discussed next.

Direction 1 Rollout

The options in the **Direction 1** rollout are used to define the first direction, distance between the instances, number of instances, and the angle of pattern direction.

When the **Linear Pattern PropertyManager** is invoked, you will notice that only the options in the **Direction 1** rollout are active. Also a callout is attached to the direction arrow. The edit boxes in this callout are used to define the number of instances and the distance between the instances to be created. Alternatively, you can define these values in the **Spacing** and the **Number** spinners in the **Direction 1** rollout. You can also define the distance between the instances by dragging the select point provided on the tip of the direction arrow. By default, direction 1 is parallel to the X-axis. If you need to select any existing line or a model edge to define direction 1, click in the selection box in the **Direction 1** rollout and select a line or an edge of the existing feature. Click on the direction arrow or choose the **Reverse direction** button from this rollout to reverse the pattern direction, if required. The **Angle** spinner is used to define the angle of the direction of the pattern. By default, the direction of pattern is set to 0-degree. If the **Add dimension** check box is selected, the dimension will be attached between the parent instance and the first instance of the pattern.

Figure 3-36 shows the preview of the entities being patterned along the first direction. Figure 3-37 shows a linear pattern at an angle of 30-degree.

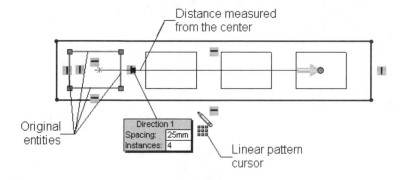

Figure 3-36 Preview of the linear pattern with three instances along direction 1 and one instance along direction 2

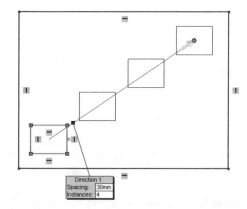

Figure 3-37 Preview of the linear pattern at an angle of 30-degree along direction 1

Direction 2 Rollout

You will notice that the preview is not displayed in the second direction. This is because the value of the number of instances is set to 1 in the **Number** spinner. This means that by default, only one instance will be created in the second direction and that is the parent instance. If you set the value of the number of instances to more than 1, then the options in this rollout will be enabled. All options in this rollout are the same, except the **Add angle dimension between axes** check box. Select this check box to apply an angular dimension to the reference direction lines of both the directions. Figure 3-38 shows a linear pattern created by specifying instances in both the directions.

Tip. *You can also specify the spacing and angle values dynamically in the preview of the linear pattern. To do so, press the left mouse button on the control points displayed at the end of the arrow in the pattern preview and drag the cursor. After placing the arrow at the desired location, release the left mouse button; the new spacing and angle values will be displayed in their respective spinners.*

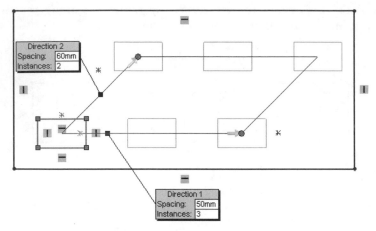

Figure 3-38 *Preview of the linear pattern at an angle of 0-degree along direction 1 and 45-degree along direction 2*

Instances to Skip Rollout

The **Instances to Skip** rollout is used to remove some of the instances from the pattern temporarily. By default, this rollout is not invoked. To invoke it, click on the down arrow on the right side of the rollout. As soon as you activate the selection box in this rollout, pink dots are displayed at the center of each pattern instance. To remove an instance from a pattern temporarily, move the cursor on the pink dot; a hand symbol will be displayed and its location will be displayed in the tooltip below the hand symbol in the matrix format. Click at the pink dot to remove the particular instance; the display of the instance will be turned off and its location will be displayed in the selection box. Also, the pink dot will change to an orange dot. Similarly, remove as many instances that you do not want to include in the pattern.

To restore the temporarily removed instances, select the orange dot displayed after hiding the instances. Alternatively, you can select the name of the instance from the **Instances to Skip** rollout and then press the DELETE key.

Tip. *You can also add entities from the current selection set by selecting them using the linear pattern cursor. To remove an entity from the selection set, select the entity, right-click, and choose **Delete** from the shortcut menu. As you add or remove the instances, the effect can be seen dynamically in the preview of the pattern.*

Creating Circular Sketch Patterns

CommandManager:	Sketch > Linear Sketch Pattern > Circular Sketch Pattern
SolidWorks menus:	Tools > Sketch Tools > Circular Pattern
Toolbar:	Sketch > Linear Sketch Pattern > Circular Sketch Pattern

In SolidWorks, the circular pattern of the sketched entities is created using the **Circular Sketch Pattern** tool. To create circular pattern of an entity, select it, choose the down arrow on the right of the **Linear Sketch Pattern** tool in the **Sketch CommandManager**; the flyout will be displayed. Choose the **Circular Sketch Pattern** option from the flyout; the

Circular Pattern PropertyManager will be displayed, as shown in Figure 3-39, and the preview of the circular pattern will be displayed. Also, the arrow cursor will be replaced by the circular pattern cursor. The names of the selected entities will be displayed in the **Entities to Pattern** rollout.

The options provided in the **Circular Pattern PropertyManager** are discussed next.

Parameters Rollout

The options in the **Parameters** rollout are used to define the centerpoint of the circular pattern, coordinates of the centerpoint of the reference circle, number of instances, angle between the instance or the total angle of pattern, radius of the reference circle, and so on. Figure 3-40 shows the parameters associated with the circular pattern. The options to define all these parameters are discussed next.

The **Reverse direction** button is used to reverse the default direction of the circular pattern. The selection box on the right of this button is used to select the center point of the circular pattern. By default, the origin is selected as the center of the circular pattern. You can modify this location using the **Center X** and **Center Y** spinners. Alternatively, click once in the selection box and select the point that you want to be the new centerpoint.

Figure 3-39 The Circular Pattern PropertyManager

You can set the value of the number of instances using the **Number of Instances** spinner.

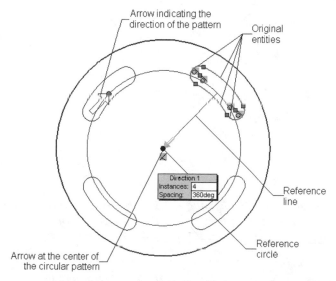

Figure 3-40 Parameters associated with the circular pattern

By default, the **Equal spacing** check box is selected and the value of angle in the **Angle** spinner is set to 360-degree. When this check box is selected the specified number of instances are equi-spaced radially. If you modify the default value in the **Angle** spinner, the angle between the instances will be adjusted accordingly. However, if the **Equal Spacing** check box is cleared, then you need to specify the incremental angle between the instances using the **Angle** spinner.

The **Radius** spinner is used to modify the radius of the reference circle around which the circular pattern will be created. The **Arc Angle** spinner provided in this rollout is used to modify the angle between the centerpoint of the original pattern instance and the center of the reference circle.

The **Add dimensions** check box is used to display the dimensions of the circular pattern.

Note

If you know the location of the centerpoint of the circular pattern, then it is recommended to drag the arrow to the center of the reference circle for defining the center of the circular pattern.

Instances to Skip Rollout

The **Instances to Skip** rollout is used to remove the instances temporarily from the pattern. The procedure to skip the instances is the same as discussed while creating the linear pattern.

Figure 3-41 shows the preview of the circular pattern with a 70-degree incremental angle between two successive instances. Figure 3-42 shows a circular pattern with the angle and radius dimension values displayed in the pattern.

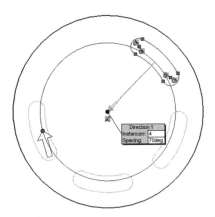

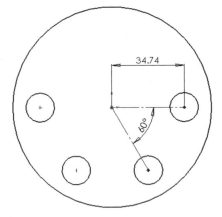

Figure 3-41 *Creating circular pattern by defining incremental angle between individual instances*

Figure 3-42 *Radius and angle values placed in the circular pattern*

Tip. *You can modify the total angle between the instances by pressing the left mouse button on the tip of the direction arrow and dragging the cursor.*

EDITING PATTERNS

You can edit the patterns of the sketched entities by using the shortcut menu that will be displayed when you right-click on any instance of the pattern. Depending on whether you right-click on the instance of the linear or the circular pattern, the **Edit Linear Pattern** or the **Edit Circular Pattern** option will be available in the shortcut menu. Figure 3-43 shows the partial view of the shortcut menu that will be displayed when you right-click on one of the instances of a circular pattern.

Depending on whether you choose the option to edit a linear pattern or a circular pattern, the **Linear Pattern Property Manager** or the **Circular Pattern PropertyManager** will be displayed. Note that only the parameters that can be edited will be available in these **PropertyManagers**.

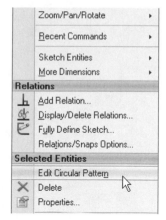

Figure 3-43 The shortcut menu displayed on right-clicking on the instance of a circular pattern

WRITING TEXT IN THE SKETCHING ENVIRONMENT

CommandManager:	Sketch > Text
SolidWorks menus:	Tools > Sketch Entities > Text
Toolbar:	Sketch > Text

You can also create text in the sketching environment of SolidWorks that can be later used to create join or cut features. To write the text, choose the **Text** button from the **Sketch CommandManager**; the **Sketch Text PropertyManager** will be displayed, as shown in Figure 3-44. Enter the text in the box in the **Text** rollout; the text will start from the sketch origin. To place the text at a specified location, exit the **Sketch Text PropertyManager** after writing the text. You will notice a dot at the start of the text. Drag the text and place it at the required location. You can also change the format, font, justification, and so on using the options in the **Text** rollout. Figure 3-45 shows the text created using the **Text** tool.

You can also create the text along a curve. To do so, you first need to create a curve. The curve can be an arc, a spline, a line, or a combination of a line, arc, and spline. Next, choose the **Text** button to invoke the **Sketch Text PropertyManager**. Select the curve or curves along which you need to create the text. Now, enter the text in the **Text** edit box; you will observe that the text is created along the arc. You can use the **Flip Horizontal** and **Flip Vertical** buttons to modify the position of the text. Figure 3-46 shows the text created along an arc.

Tip. *If the text that you write appears reversed, you can draw a line from left to right and then use it as an element to align the text.*

Figure 3-44 The **Sketch Text PropertyManager**

Figure 3-45 Sketch created using the **Text** tool

Figure 3-46 Text created along an arc

MODIFYING SKETCHED ENTITIES

Most of the sketches require modification at some stages of design. Therefore, it is important for a designer to understand the process of modification in SolidWorks. Modification of various sketched entities is discussed next.

Modifying a Sketched Line

You can modify a sketched line by using the **Line Properties PropertyManager**, which is displayed when you select the line using the **Select** tool. Note that if the selected line is a part of a rectangle, polygon, or a parallelogram, the entire object will be modified as you modify the line. This is because relations are applied to all lines of a rectangle, polygon, and a parallelogram.

Similarly, you can also modify a centerline using the **Line Properties PropertyManager**, which will be displayed when you select the centerline.

Modifying a Sketched Circle

To modify a sketched circle, select it using the **Select** tool; the **Circle PropertyManager** will be displayed with the coordinate values of the centerpoint of the circle and the value of the radius in the **Parameters** rollout. You can modify the values in the respective edit boxes.

Tip. *The status of the sketched entity that you select for modification is displayed in the **Existing Relations** rollout of the **PropertyManager** that is displayed on selecting an entity. For example, if the selected entity is fully defined, it will be displayed in the **PropertyManager** and if the entity is underdefined, the **PropertyManager** will display a message that the entity is underdefined.*

Modifying a Sketched Arc

To modify a sketched arc, select it using the **Select** tool; the **Arc PropertyManager** will be displayed with the coordinate values of the centerpoint, start point, and endpoint. The values of the radius and the included angle will also be displayed. You can modify the values in the respective edit boxes.

Modifying a Sketched Polygon

To modify a sketched polygon, right-click on any one edge of the polygon to display the shortcut menu. Choose the **Edit polygon** option from the shortcut menu to display the **Polygon PropertyManager**. You can modify the selected polygon using the options in the **Polygon PropertyManager** or draw a new polygon.

Note

*If you right-click on the reference circle that is automatically drawn when you draw a polygon, the **Edit polygon** option will not be available in the shortcut menu.*

Modifying a Spline

You can perform four types of modifications on a spline. The first is the modification of the coordinates of the selected control point. The second modification is by using the Spline

Handles. The third type of modification is by using the Control polygons. The fourth is the addition of a curvature control symbol. These modifications are discussed in detail next.

Modifying a Spline Using the Control Points

To modify the location of the control points of a spline, select the spline; the **Spline PropertyManager** will be displayed. The control points of the spline will be displayed with a square and the current control point will also be highlighted with a filled circle. The number of current control point and its coordinates will also be displayed in the **Parameters** rollout of the **Spline PropertyManager**, as shown in Figure 3-47. When you set the value in the **Spline Point Number** spinner, the corresponding control point will be selected in the spline. Now, you can modify its coordinates using the **X Coordinate** and **Y Coordinate** spinners. Alternatively, you can select and drag a control point, to place it on the desired location.

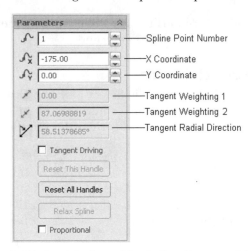

*Figure 3-47 Partial view of the **Spline PropertyManager***

You can also add more control points to a spline. To do so, choose **Tools > Spline Tools > Insert Spline Point** from the SolidWorks menus. Alternatively, select the spline and right-click to invoke the shortcut menu. In this menu, choose the **Insert Spline Point** option. Now, specify the location on the spline where you need to add the control point; a point and a spline handle will be displayed at the point specified on the spline. Spline handles are discussed in the next section. Similarly, you can add as many control points as needed. After adding the required number of control points, invoke the **Select** tool and selcct the spline again. You will notice that the boxes of control points are displayed on all points including the newly added points.

Modifying a Spline Using the Spline Handles

The spline handle is a line with diamond handle, arrow, and circular handle on both its endpoints. The spline handles will be displayed when you select a spline using the **Select** tool. The default spline handles will be displayed in gray, which implies that they are not selected. When you move the cursor over a spline handle, it will be highlighted in orange. Additionally, a rotate symbol will be displayed if you move the cursor near the diamond handle. A red colored arrow symbol will be displayed, if you move the cursor near the arrow. If you move the cursor near the circular handle, both the symbols will be displayed, as shown in Figure 3-48.

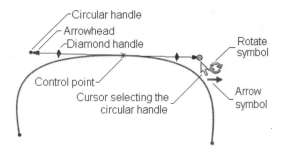

Figure 3-48 *The spline and the spline handle*

Move the cursor near the diamond handle, arrows, or the circular handle; it will be highlighted. On selecting any of these entities, the number of respective control points and their coordinates will be displayed in the **Parameters** rollout. Select and drag the diamond handle to dynamically modify the direction of the tangent. As you drag the diamond handle, the value in the **Tangent Radial Direction** spinner will change dynamically. The **Tangent Driving** check box is also selected automatically when you drag the cursor. After modifying the shape of the spline, click anywhere in the drawing area to exit the current selection set. You will notice that the currently modified spline handle is displayed in blue, which implies that the default setting of this spline handle is modified. Select and drag the arrowhead to modify the tangent weighting. As you drag the arrowhead, the value in the **Tangent Weighting** spinner will change dynamically. If you press the ALT key while dragging the arrowhead, the spline will get deformed symmetrically. Similarly, you can edit the spline using the circular handle. In this case, both the symbols will be displayed. So, the values in the **Tangent Radial Direction** and **Tangent Weighting** spinners will change dynamically.

Choose the **Reset This Handle** button to reset the current handle to the original position. Choose the **Reset All Handles** button to reset all handles to the default position. To create a smooth curvature after editing the handles, choose the **Relax Spline** button.

To add more spline handles, select the spline and right-click to invoke the shortcut menu. Choose the **Add Tangency Control** option from the shortcut menu; a spline handle will be attached to the selected spline. Move the cursor to the location where you want to place the spline handle and click on that location. A spline control point will also be added along with the spline handle. You can also apply relations to the spline handles. You will learn more about relations in the later chapters. You can also delete the spline handles by selecting the control point and pressing the DELETE key.

You can also apply dimensions to the spline handles to accurately shape the spline. You will learn more about dimensioning in the later chapters.

Modifying a Spline Using the Control Polygon
To display the control polygon, select a spline and right-click; a shortcut menu will be displayed. Choose the **Display Control Polygon** option; the control polygons are displayed, as shown in Figure 3-49. When you select a control polygon, the **Spline Polygon PropertyManager** will

be displayed. You can also set the location of the control points by using the **X Coordinate** and **Y Coordinate** spinners in the **Spline Polygon PropertyManager**. You can modify the location of the control point by dragging it. To turn off the display of the control polygon, select a spline, invoke the shortcut menu, and choose **Display Control Polygon** again.

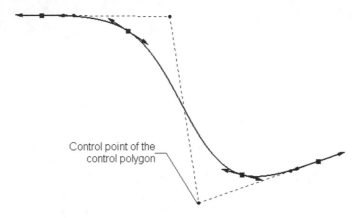

Figure 3-49   Control point of the control polygon

Adding the Curvature Control

You can also add a curvature control symbol which is used to modify the curvature of the spline. To add a curvature control, select the spline and invoke the shortcut menu. Choose the **Add Curvature Control** option from it; the curvature control symbol will be attached to the selected spline. Move the cursor to the location where you want to place the curvature control symbol. A spline handle will also be placed tangent to the spline at the location where the curvature control symbol is attached. Now, select and drag the dot symbol at the bottom of this symbol. You will notice that the curvature of the spline is modified dynamically as you drag the cursor. After modifying the shape of the spline, release the left mouse button. You can also delete the curvature control symbol by selecting it and pressing the DELETE key.

Modifying the Coordinates of a Point

To modify the location of a point, select it using the **Select** tool; the **Point PropertyManager** will be displayed. You can modify the coordinates of the sketched point using this **PropertyManager**.

Modifying an Ellipse or an Elliptical Arc

To modify an ellipse or an elliptical arc, select it using the **Select** tool; the **Ellipse PropertyManager** will be displayed. You can modify the parameters using the options in this **PropertyManager**.

Modifying a Parabola

To modify a parabola, select the parabola using the **Select** tool; the **Parabola PropertyManager** will be displayed. Modify the parameters of the parabola from this **PropertyManager**.

Dynamically Modifying and Copying Sketched Entities

In the sketching environment of SolidWorks, you can relocate the sketched entities by dynamically dragging them using the left mouse button. For example, consider a case where you create a sketch of a rectangle and you want to increase the size of the rectangle. You simply have to select any of the lines of the rectangle or any of its vertices and hold the left mouse button to drag the cursor. Drag the sketch according to your requirement and then release the left mouse button. Alternatively, if you choose **Tools** > **Sketch Settings** > **Detach Segment on Drag** from the SolidWorks menus and select a line of a rectangle to drag, the line segment will be detached from the rectangle. As this option is not activated by default, the segments of the selected entities are not detached on dragging.

You can also copy the sketched entities dynamically. Select the sketched entity or entities to be copied. Press and hold the CTRL key and then drag the selected entity or entities; the preview of the copied entities will be displayed. Release the left mouse button at the location where you want to place the new entities. You can make multiple copies of the selected entities by repeating this procedure.

Splitting Sketched Entities

CommandManager:	Sketch > Split Entities	(Customize to add)
SolidWorks menus:	Tools > Sketch Tools > Split Entities	
Toolbar:	Sketch > Split Entities	(Customize to add)

The **Split Entities** tool is used to split a sketched entity into two or more entities. To split an entity, choose the **Split Entities** tool from the **Sketch CommandManager**; the current cursor will be replaced by the split entities cursor. Move the cursor to an appropriate location where you want to split the sketched entity. When the cursor snaps to the entity, press the left mouse button to add a split point. Now, right-click to display the shortcut menu and choose the **Select** option from the shortcut menu. Select the sketched entity using the select cursor. You will notice that the sketched entity is divided in two entities and a split point is added between the two sketched entities. You can add as many split points as you need. Remember that to split a circle, a full ellipse, or a closed spline, you need to split them at least at two points.

You can also delete the split points to convert the split entity into a single entity. To delete the split point, select the split point and press the DELETE key. You can also right-click on the split point to display the shortcut menu and choose the **Delete** option from the shortcut menu.

TUTORIALS

Tutorial 1

In this tutorial, you will create the base sketch of the model shown in Figure 3-50. The sketch of the model is shown in Figure 3-51. You will create the sketch with a mirror line and mirror tool. After creating the sketch, you will modify it by dragging the sketched entities.

(Expected time: 30 min)

Figure 3-50 *Solid model for Tutorial 1*   *Figure 3-51* *Sketch for Tutorial 1*

The following steps are required to complete this tutorial:

a. Start SolidWorks and then start a new part document.
b. Invoke the sketching environment.
c. Create the centerlines and convert one of the centerlines to mirror line using the **Dynamic Mirror Entities** tool.
d. Create the sketch in the third quadrant; the sketch will automatically be mirrored on the other side of the mirror line, refer to Figure 3-52.
e. Mirror the entire sketch along the second mirror line, refer to Figure 3-53.
f. Modify the sketch by dragging the sketched entities, refer to Figure 3-54.

Starting SolidWorks and a New SolidWorks Document

1. Start SolidWorks by choosing **Start > Programs > SolidWorks 2009 SP0.0 > SolidWorks 2009 SP0.0** or by double-clicking on the shortcut icon of **SolidWorks 2009 SP0.0** on the desktop of your computer.

    The **SolidWorks Resources** task pane is displayed on the right of this window.

2. Select the **New Document** option in the **Getting Started** rollout of the **SolidWorks Resources** task pane; the **New SolidWorks Document** dialog box is displayed.

3. The **Part** button is chosen by default. Choose the **OK** button from this dialog box.

Next, you need to invoke the sketching environment.

4. Choose the **Sketch** tab from the **CommandManager**. Next, choose the **Sketch** button from the **Sketch CommandManager**; the **Edit Sketch PropertyManager** is invoked and you are prompted to select the plane to create the sketch.

5. Select the **Front Plane**; the sketching environment is invoked and the plane is oriented normal to the view.

Modifying the Snap and Grid Settings and the Dimensioning Units

Before drawing the sketch, you need to modify the grid and snap settings to make the cursor jump through a distance of 10 mm.

1. Choose the **Options** button from Menu Bar; the **System Option - General** dialog box is displayed.

2. Choose the **Document Properties** tab and select the **Grid/Snap** option from the area on the left. Set the values **100** and **10** in the **Major grid spacing** and the **Minor-lines per major** spinners, respectively.

3. If the grid is displayed by default, when you invoke the sketching environment, you can turn off its display by clearing the **Display grid** check box in the **Grid** area.

4. Choose the **Go To System Snaps** button and select the **Grid** check box. Next, clear the **Snap only when grid is displayed** check box, if it is already selected.

    If you had selected a unit other than the millimeter to measure the length while installing SolidWorks, you need to select the units for the current drawing.

5. Choose the **Document Properties** tab and select the **Units** option from the area on the left of the **Document Properties - Grid/Snap** dialog box.

6. Select the **MMGS (millimeter, gram, second)** radio button in the **Unit system** area. Next, select **degrees** from the drop-down list in the cell corresponding to the **Angle** row and **Unit** colomn.

7. After making the necessary settings, choose the **OK** button.

    The coordinates displayed close to the lower right corner of the SolidWorks window will show an increment of 10 mm when you move the cursor in the drawing area after exiting the dialog box.

Drawing the Centerlines and Converting Them into a Mirror Line

It is recommended to draw the sketches that are symmetrical along any axis using the mirroring tool. In this tutorial, you will draw the sketch using the **Dynamic Mirror** and **Mirror Entities** tools. However, you can also complete this tutorial by using the **Line** and **Dynamic Mirror** tools.

1. Choose **Line > Centerline** from the **Sketch CommandManager**.

2. Move the line cursor to a location where the value of the coordinates are 0 mm, 100 mm, 0 mm. You may have to zoom the drawing to reach that point.

3. Specify the start point of the centerline at this point and move the cursor vertically downward and draw a line of 200 mm length. You may have to zoom and pan the drawing to draw a line of this length.

4. Now, double-click anywhere on the screen to end the current chain. You can also press the right mouse button anywhere in the drawing area to invoke the shortcut menu and choose the **End chain** option from it.

5. Move the line cursor to a location where the coordinates are -100 mm, 0 mm, 0 mm.

6. Specify the start point of the centerline and move the cursor horizontally toward the right to draw a line of 200 mm length. Pan the drawing, if required.

7. Press F to fit the drawing in the screen. Right-click and choose the **Select** option from the shortcut menu; the line cursor will be replaced by the select cursor.

8. Select the vertical centerline.

9. Choose **Tools > Sketch Tools > Dynamic Mirror Entities** from the SolidWorks menus; the vertical centerline is converted to mirror line and the dynamic mirror option is activated.

    You can confirm the creation of the mirror line and the activation of the dynamic mirror option by observing the symmetrical symbol applied to both ends of the centerline.

Drawing the Sketch

Next, you need to draw the sketch of the base feature. You will draw the sketch in the third quadrant and the same sketch will be created automatically on the other side of the mirror line. The symmetrical relation is applied between the parent entity and the mirrored entity.

1. Press the L key on the keyboard; the **Line** tool is invoked.

2. Move the line cursor to a location where coordinates are 0 mm, -100 mm, 0 mm.

3. Specify the start point of the line at this location and move the cursor horizontally toward the left.

4. Specify the endpoint of the line when the length of the line above the line cursor shows the value 90.

    You will notice that as soon as you specify the endpoint of the line, a mirror image is automatically created on the other side of the mirror line. The line drawn as the mirrored entity is merged with the line drawn on the left. Therefore, the entire line becomes a single entity. Remember that the lines will merge only if one of the endpoints of the line you draw is coincident with the mirror line.

5. Move the cursor vertically upward and specify the endpoint of the line when the length of the line above the line cursor shows the value 30.

    You will notice that as soon as you specify the endpoint of a line, a mirror image is automatically created on the other side of the mirror line.

6. Move the line cursor toward the right and specify the endpoint of the line when the length of the line above the line cursor shows the value 30; a mirror image is automatically created on the other side of the mirror line.

7. Move the line cursor vertically upward and specify the endpoint of the line when the line cursor snaps to the horizontal centerline. Exit the **Line** tool. The sketch after drawing the lines is shown in Figure 3-52.

Mirroring the Entire Sketch

After creating one half of the sketch, you need to mirror the entire sketch about the horizontal centerline. But first, you need to disable the automatic mirroring.

1. Right-click and choose **Recent Commands > Dynamic Mirror Entities** from the shortcut menu to disable dynamic mirroring.

2. Use the box selection method to select all the lines sketched earlier and also the horizontal centerline. Make sure you do not select the vertical centerline.

3. Choose the **Mirror Entities** button from the **Sketch CommandManager**; the entire sketch is mirrored about the horizontal centerline. The sketch after mirroring is shown in Figure 3-53.

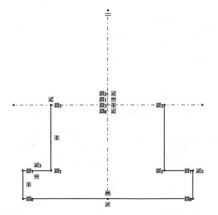

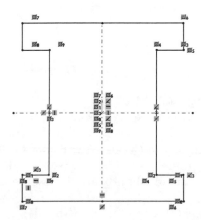

Figure 3-52 *Sketch after drawing the lines*   *Figure 3-53* *Sketch after mirroring the sketched entities*

Modifying the Sketch by Dragging

Next, you need to modify the sketch by dragging. While dragging the entities, you will observe that the corresponding mirrored entity will also be modified.

1. Select the lower right vertical line; the **Line PropertyManager** will be displayed on the left of the drawing area. You will notice that the value of the length in the **Length** spinner is **30**.

2. Set the value in the **Length** spinner to **20** in the **Parameters** rollout, as the required length of this line is 20. You will observe that all dependent lines are also modified. This is because they are created as mirror images.

3. Choose the **OK** button or click once in the drawing area.

4. Select the midpoint of the right vertical line that passes through the horizontal centerline; the **Point PropertyManager** is displayed. You will notice the coordinates are 60, 0.

5. Press and hold the left mouse button and drag the point toward the origin; the value in the **X Coordinate** spinner of the **Parameters** rollout will change dynamically.

6. Release the left mouse button when the **X Coordinate** spinner shows the value 10. The final sketch after modifying the sketched entities by dragging is shown in Figure 3-54.

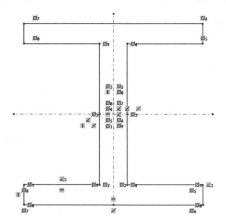

Figure 3-54 *Final sketch for Tutorial 1*

Saving the Sketch

1. Choose the **Save** button from the Menu Bar to invoke the **Save As** dialog box.

2. Choose the **Create New Folder** button from the **Save As** dialog box. Enter the name of the folder as *c03* and press ENTER. Enter the name of the document as *c03tut1* in the **File name** edit box and choose the **Save** button.

3. Press CTRL+W to close the file.

Tutorial 2

In this tutorial, you will create the sketch of the model shown in Figure 3-55. The sketch is shown in Figure 3-56. Do not dimension the sketch; the solid model and the dimensions are given only for your reference.   (**Expected time: 30 min**)

Figure 3-55 *Solid model for Tutorial 2*   *Figure 3-56* *Sketch for Tutorial 2*

The following steps are required to complete this tutorial:

a.   Start a new part document.
b.   Invoke the sketching environment.
c.   Create a centerline.
d.   Draw and edit the sketch using the **Mirror Entities** and **Trim Entities** tools, refer to Figure 3-57.
e.   Offset the entire sketch, refer to Figure 3-58.
f.   Complete the final editing of the sketch using the **Extend Entities** and **Trim Entities** tools, refer to Figures 3-59 and 3-60.

Starting a New Document

1.   Choose the **New** button from the Menu Bar to invoke the **New SolidWorks Document** dialog box.

2.   The **Part** button is chosen by default in the **New SolidWorks Document** dialog box. Choose the **OK** button .

3.   Choose the **Sketch** button from the **Sketch CommandManager** and select **Front Plane** to invoke the sketching environment.

4.   Invoke the **Document Properties - Grid/Snap** dialog box. Now, set the value in the **Major grid spacing** spinner to **100** and value in the **Minor-lines per major** spinner to **10**.

Drawing the Centerline

Before drawing the sketch, you need to draw a centerline that will act as a reference for the other sketch entities. This centerline will also be used for mirroring.

1. Choose **Line > Centerline** from the **Sketch CommandManager**.

2. Move the cursor to a location where the value of the coordinates is -70 mm, 0 mm, 0 mm.

3. Specify the start point at this location and move the cursor horizontally toward the right.

4. Specify the endpoint of the centerline when the value of the length of the centerline above the line cursor shows the value 140.

5. Double-click anywhere in the drawing area to end the line creation.

Drawing the Outer Loop of the Sketch

Next, you need to draw the outer loop of the sketch using the sketch tools. As evident from Figure 3-56, the sketch is drawn using the **Circle** and **Line** tools.

1. Choose the **Circle** button from the **Sketch CommandManager**; the line cursor will be replaced by the circle cursor.

2. Choose the **Circle** button from the **Circle Type** rollout, if it is not selected by default. Move the circle cursor to the origin, when the orange circle is displayed, press the left mouse button to specify the center point of the circle.

3. Move the cursor horizontally toward the right and draw a circle of 50 mm radius.

4. Choose the **Zoom to Fit** button from the **Heads-up View** toolbar to increase the display of the sketch.

5. Choose the **Line** button from the **Sketch CommandManager** and move the cursor to a location where the coordinates are -60 mm, 10 mm, 0 mm. Specify the start point of the line at this location.

6. Move the cursor horizontally toward the right and press the left mouse button to specify the endpoint of the line when the line cursor snaps the circle. Exit the **Line** tool.

7. Press and hold the SHIFT key and using the left mouse button, select the horizontal line created in the last step and the centerline.

8. Choose the **Mirror Entities** button from the **Sketch CommandManager**; the mirror image of the horizontal line is created on the other side of the centerline.

9. Choose the **Line** button from the **Sketch CommandManager** and move the cursor to the left endpoint of the upper horizontal line. Specify the start point of the line when the orange circle is displayed.

10. Move the cursor vertically downward. Specify the endpoint of the line when the cursor snaps to the left endpoint of the lower horizontal line.

11. Choose the **Trim Entities** button from the **Sketch CommandManager**; the **Trim PropertyManager** is displayed.

12. Choose the **Power trim** button. Press and hold the left mouse button and drag the cursor over the portion to be removed. Choose the **OK** button. The sketch after removing the unwanted portion is shown in Figure 3-57.

 Tip. *If you have trimmed the centerline, invoke the shortcut menu and choose the* ***Extend Entities*** *option. Then, move the cursor over one end of the centerline and press the left mouse button to extend the line. Alternatively, perform the undo operation.*

Offsetting the Entities

After drawing the outer loop of the sketch, you need to draw the inner loop. The first step in drawing the inner loop of the sketch is offsetting the entire sketch inwards.

1. Choose the **Offset Entities** button from the **Sketch CommandManager**; the **Offset Entities PropertyManager** is displayed on the left of the drawing area.

2. Set the value of the **Offset Distance** spinner to **4**. Select the **Add dimensions** and **Select chain** check boxes. Select any one entity of the sketch; the entire sketch is selected.

   When you select the sketch, the preview of the offset sketch is displayed in the drawing area. But the direction of the offset is outside the sketch. The required direction of offset should be inside the sketch. Therefore, you need to flip the direction.

3. Move the cursor inside the sketch and press the left mouse button to offset the sketch inside the original sketch; a dimension with the value 4 is displayed with the sketch.

   The sketch after offsetting the outer loop is shown in Figure 3-58.

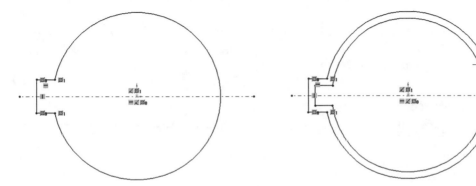

Figure 3-57 *The sketch after removing the unwanted portion*   ***Figure 3-58*** *Sketch after offsetting the outer loop*

Extending and Trimming the Entities

1. Choose **Trim Entities** > **Extend Entities** from the **Sketch CommandManager**.
   The select cursor is replaced by the extend cursor.

2. Move the cursor close to the left end of the lower horizontal line of the inner loop. You
   can preview the extended line in orange.

   You need to move the cursor a little toward the left if the preview of the extended line
   appears on the right.

3. Press the left mouse button to extend the line.

4. Similarly, extend the upper horizontal line of the inner sketch. The sketch after extending
   the lines is shown in Figure 3-59.

5. Right-click and choose the **Trim Entities** option from the shortcut menu; the extend
   cursor is replaced by the select cursor.

6. Trim the unwanted entities as discussed earlier. The final sketch is shown in Figure 3-60.

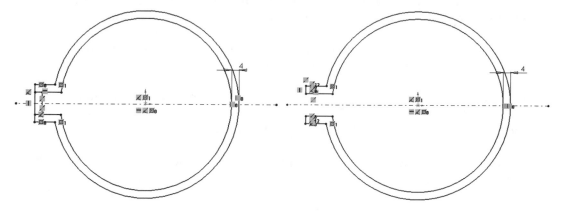

Figure 3-59 *Sketch after extending the lines*   *Figure 3-60* *Final sketch for Tutorial 2*

 Tip. *You can turn on/off the display of the relation symbols on the sketched entities,
by choosing **Hide/Show Items** > **View Sketch Relations** button from the
Heads-up View toolbar.*

Saving the Sketch

1. Choose the **Save** button from the Menu Bar to invoke the **Save As** dialog box.

2. Enter the name of the document as *c03tut2* in the **File name** edit box and choose the
   Save button.

3. Close the file by choosing **File** > **Close** from the SolidWorks menus.

Tutorial 3

In this tutorial, you will create the base sketch of the model shown in Figure 3-61. The sketch of the model is shown in Figure 3-62. You will create the sketch of the base feature using the sketch tools. Also, modify and edit the sketch using various modifying options. Do not create the center marks and centerlines, as they are for your reference only.

(Expected time: 30 min)

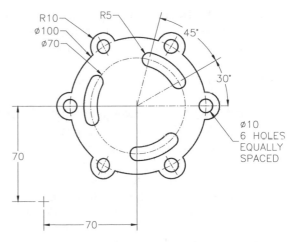

Figure 3-61 *Solid Model for Tutorial 3*   ***Figure 3-62*** *Sketch for Tutorial 3*

The following steps are required to complete this tutorial:

a. Start a new part document.
b. Invoke the sketching environment.
c. Draw the outer loop of the sketch of the given model, refer to Figures 3-63 and 3-64.
d. Create the inner cavity using the **Centerpoint Arc Slot** tool, refer to Figures 3-65 through 3-67
e. Use the **Circular Sketch Pattern** tool to create a circular pattern of the inner cavity, refer to Figure 3-68.
f. Complete the sketch by creating the circles that define the hole in the outer loop.
g. Use the **Circular Sketch Pattern** tool to create a circular pattern of holes in the outer loop, refer to Figure 3-69.

Starting a New Document

1. Choose the **New** button from the Menu Bar to invoke the **New SolidWorks Document** dialog box.

2. The **Part** button is chosen by default. Choose the **OK** button from the **New SolidWorks Document** dialog box.

Next, you need to invoke the sketching environment.

3. Choose the **Sketch** button from the **Sketch CommandManager**; the **Edit Sketch PropertyManager** is invoked and you are prompted to select the plane to create the sketch.

4. Select the **Front Plane**; the sketching environment is invoked and the plane is oriented normal to the view.

5. Choose **Options** button from Menu Bar; the **System Option - General** dialog box is displayed.

6. Choose the **Document Properties** tab and select the **Grid/Snap** option from the area on the left. Set the value of the **Minor-lines per major** spinner to **20** and the **Major grid spacing** spinner to **100**. In addition to this, set the units to millimeters.

7. Choose the **OK** button after making the necessary settings.

Drawing the Outer Loop of the Sketch

As evident from Figure 3-62, the sketch consists of the outer loop and inner cavities. It is recommended to create the outer loop of the sketch first and then the inner cavities.

The origin of the sketching environment is placed in the middle of the drawing area and you have to create the sketch in the first quadrant. Therefore, it is recommended that you modify the drawing area by relocating the origin.

1. Press the CTRL key and the middle mouse button and drag the cursor in such a way that the sketch origin is moved near the lower left corner of the drawing area.

2. Choose the **Circle** button from the **Sketch CommandManager**; the **Circle PropertyManager** is displayed.

3. Choose the **Circle** button in the **Circle Type** rollout of the **Circle PropertyManager**, if it is not already chosen.

4. Move the cursor to a location where the coordinates are 70 mm, 70 mm, 0 mm.

5. Specify the center point of the circle at this location and move the cursor horizontally toward the right. When the radius above the circle cursor shows a value 50, press the left mouse button and exit the tool.

6. Choose the **Zoom to Area** button from the **Heads-up View** toolbar. Press and hold the left mouse button and drag the cursor to define a window such that the sketched circle and the origin are placed in the window.

7. Release the left mouse button; the display area of the sketch is increased.

8. Choose the **Circle** button from the **Sketch CommandManager** and move the cursor to the right quadrant of the circle. All quadrants of the circle are displayed, and the right quadrant on which you have placed the cursor is displayed in orange. The symbol of coincident constraint is displayed below the cursor.

9. Specify the center point of the circle at this location and move the cursor horizontally toward the right. When the value of the radius above the circle cursor shows a value 10, press the left mouse button.

10. Choose the **Trim Entities** button from the **Sketch CommandManager** and choose the **Trim to closest** button from the **Trim PropertyManager**.

11. Trim a part of the sketch such that the sketch looks similar to that shown in Figure 3-63.

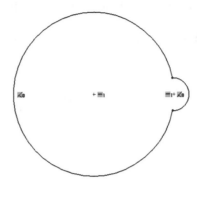

Figure 3-63 *Sketch after trimming the unwanted entities*

12. Choose the **Linear Sketch Pattern > Circular Sketch Pattern** button from the **Sketch CommandManager**; the **Circular Pattern PropertyManager** is displayed and the cursor is replaced by the circular pattern cursor.

13. Select the trimmed circle of radius 10 mm using the circular pattern cursor; the preview of the circular pattern with the default setting is displayed in the drawing area.

You will notice that the center of the circular pattern is placed at the origin and an arrow is displayed. As the origin is not the center of the circular pattern, you need to modify it. This can be done by entering the coordinates of the point in the **Center X** and the **Center Y** spinners in the **Parameters** rollout of this **PropertyManager**. But it is recommended to drag the arrow displayed at the center of the pattern to the required location.

14. Move the circular pattern cursor to the control point that is available at the end of the arrow.

15. Press and hold the left mouse button at the control point and drag it to the center of the 100 mm diameter circle. Release the left mouse button when an orange circle is displayed at the center point of the circle.

You will notice that both the **Center X** and the **Center Y** spinners display the value 70 mm. This is because the center of the 100 mm diameter circle is located at a distance of 70 mm along the X and Y axis directions.

16. Set the value of the **Number** spinner to **6**. Accept all other default values and choose the **OK** button to create the pattern.

17. Trim the unwanted portion of the 100 mm diameter circle using the **Trim Entities** tool. You need to use the **Trim to closest** button for this trimming.

18. Choose **OK** after trimming. The outer loop of the sketch is created, as shown in Figure 3-64.

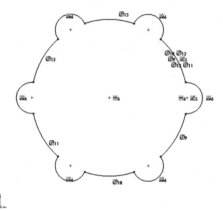

Figure 3-64 *Outer loop of the sketch*

Drawing the Sketch of the Inner Cavity

Next, you will draw the sketch of one of the cavities and create a circular pattern.

1. Choose the **Centerpoint Arc Slot** button from the **Sketch CommandManager**; the **Slot PropertyManager** is displayed and the cursor is replaced by the slot cursor.

2. Move the slot cursor to the center of the 100 mm diameter circle. When the cursor snaps to the center of the circle, specify the center point of the slot.

3. Move the slot cursor toward the right and above the horizontal axis. Now, specify the start point of the slot at a location, where the radius of the slot above the slot cursor shows a value close to 35-degree, as shown in Figure 3-65.

4. Move the slot cursor in the counterclockwise direction and specify the end point of the slot, when the angle of the slot above the slot cursor shows a value close to 45-degree; a reference slot is attached to the slot cursor.

5. Specify a point in the drawing area, when the width of the slot shows a value close to 10 mm in the **Parameters** rollout of the **Slot PropertyManager**. As soon as you specify the point, the options in the **Parameters** rollout are enabled. Enter the value 35 mm, 45 deg,

and 10 mm in the **Radius of Arc**, **Angle of Arc**, and **Slot Width** spinners of the **Parameters** rollout, respectively and then exit the tool. The resultant profile is shown in Figure 3-66.

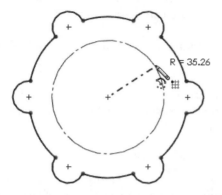

Figure 3-65 *The slot cursor selecting the start point of the slot*

Figure 3-66 *The profile after creating the slot*

6. Choose the **Smart Dimension** button from the **Sketch CommandManager**. Next, select the points from the drawing area to apply the radial dimension, as shown in Figure 3-67 and enter the value **30** in the **Modify** dialog box.

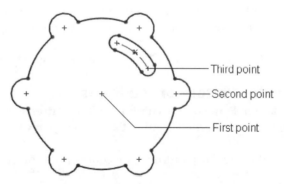

Figure 3-67 *The points to be selected for applying the radial dimension*

Creating a Pattern of the Inner Cavity

Next, you need to create a pattern of the inner cavity using the **Circular Sketch Pattern** tool. The pattern of the inner cavity consists of three instances. The center point of the pattern lies at the center point of the 100 mm diameter circle.

1. Select the arc profile of the inner cavity.

2. Choose **Linear Sketch Pattern > Circular Sketch Pattern** from the **Sketch CommandManager**; the **Circular Pattern PropertyManager** will be displayed and the preview of the circular pattern is displayed with an arrow in the center.

3. Move the circular pattern cursor to the control point that is available at the end of the arrow indicating the center point of the pattern. Press and hold the left mouse button at the control point and drag it to the center of the 100 mm diameter circle. Release the left mouse button when an orange circle is displayed at the center point of the circle.

The default value of the number of items in the pattern is 4. You need to modify this value because you need three items in the pattern.

4. Set the value in the **Number** spinner of the **Parameters** rollout to **3**. Accept all other default values and choose the **OK** button to create the pattern. The sketch, after creating the pattern of the inner cavity, is shown in Figure 3-68.

Sketching the Holes

Next, you need to draw the sketch of the holes. As evident from Figure 3-62, you need to create six circles. After drawing the first circle, you need to create the other five circles by creating a circular pattern of the parent circle.

1. Choose the **Circle** button from the **Sketch CommandManager**.

2. Select the center point of the 10 mm radius arc at the left quadrant of the larger circle as the center point of the new circle.

3. Press and hold the CTRL key and draw a circle of radius close to 5. Make sure you press the CTRL key so that the cursor does not snap to the points or grid.

4. Set the value in the **Radius** spinner to **5** in the **Circle PropertyManager**.

Creating the Circular Pattern of the Holes

1. Choose **Linear Sketch Pattern** > **Circular Sketch Pattern** from the **Sketch CommandManager** to invoke the **Circular Pattern PropertyManager**.

2. Move the center of the circular pattern to the center point of the larger trimmed circle.

3. Set the value **6** in the **Number** spinner. Accept all other default values and choose **OK** in this **PropertyManager**. Convert the sketch to a fully define sketch. The final sketch for Tutorial 3 is shown in Figure 3-69.

Saving the Sketch

1. Choose the **Save** button from the **Standard** toolbar to invoke the **Save As** dialog box.

2. Enter the name of the document as *c03tut3* in the **File name** edit box and choose the **Save** button.

The document will be saved in the */My Documents/SolidWorks/c03* folder.

3. Close the file by choosing **File** > **Close** from the SolidWorks menus.

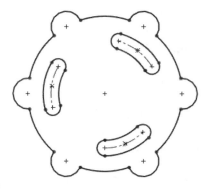

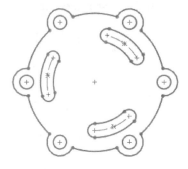

Figure 3-68 *Sketch after creating the pattern of the inner cavity*

Figure 3-69 *Final sketch for Tutorial 3*

SELF-EVALUATION TEST

Answer the following questions and then compare them to those given at the end of this chapter:

1. The **Trim** option is also used to extend the sketched entities. (T/F)

2. In the sketching environment, you can apply fillets to two parallel lines. (T/F)

3. You can apply a fillet to two nonparallel and nonintersecting entities. (T/F)

4. You cannot offset a single entity using the **Offset Entities** tool. (T/F)

5. You can choose **Insert > Customize** from the SolidWorks menus to display the **Customize** dialog box. (T/F)

6. The design intent is not captured in the sketch created using the mirror line. (T/F)

7. The _____ tool is used to create a linear pattern in the sketching environment of SolidWorks.

8. The _____ tool is used to create a circular pattern in the sketching environment of SolidWorks.

9. To modify a sketched circle, select it using the _____ tool to display the _____ **PropertyManager**.

10. The _____ tool is used to invoke the dynamic mirroring.

REVIEW QUESTIONS

Answer the following questions:

1. You cannot extend the sketched entity using the **Trim** tool. (T/F)

2. The preview of the entity to be extended is displayed in red. (T/F)

3. There are 4 types of slot tools available in SolidWorks 2009. (T/F)

4. The sketched entities can be mirrored without using a centerline. (T/F)

5. The **Add angle dimension between axes** check box in the **Linear Pattern PropertyManager** is selected to display the angular dimension between the two directions of the pattern. (T/F)

6. Which **PropertyManager** is displayed when you choose the **Sketch Fillet** button from the **Sketch CommandManager**?

        (a) **Sketch Fillet**   (b) **Fillet**
        (c) **Surface Fillet**   (d) **Sketching Fillet**

7. Which **PropertyManager** is displayed on the left of the drawing area when you choose **Tools > Sketch Tools > Chamfer** from the SolidWorks menus?

        (a) **Sketch Chamfer**   (b) **Sketcher Chamfer**
        (c) **Sketching Chamfer**   (d) **Chamfer**

8. Which tool is used to create an automatic mirror line?

        (a) **Dynamic Mirror Entities**   (b) **Mirror**
        (c) **Automatic Mirror**   (d) None

9. Which tool is used to break a sketched entity into two or more entities?

        (a) **Split Entities**   (b) **Trim Sketch**
        (c) **Break Curve**   (d) **Trim Curve**

10. Which tool is used to create a circular pattern in SolidWorks?

        (a) **Pattern**   (b) **Circular Sketch Pattern**
        (c) **Array**   (d) None

EXERCISES

Exercise 1

Create the sketch of the model shown in Figure 3-70. The sketch of the model is shown in Figure 3-71. The solid model and dimensions are given only for reference.

(Expected time: 30 min)

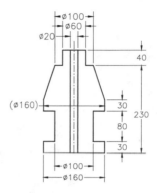

Figure 3-70 Solid model for Exercise 1

Figure 3-71 Sketch for Exercise 1

Exercise 2

Create the sketch of the model shown in Figure 3-72. The sketch of the model is shown in Figure 3-73. This model is created using a revolved feature. Therefore, you will create the sketch on one side of the centerline. The solid model and dimensions are given only for reference.

(Expected time: 30 min)

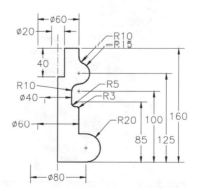

Figure 3-72 Solid model for Exercise 2

Figure 3-73 Sketch for Exercise 2

Exercise 3

Create the sketch of the model shown in Figure 3-74. The sketch of the model is shown in Figure 3-75. The solid model and dimensions are given only for reference. Create the sketch on one side and then mirror it on the other side. Make sure you do not use the **Dynamic Mirror** tool to draw this sketch. This is because if you draw the sketch using this tool, some relations are applied to the sketch. These relations interfere while creating fillets.

(Expected time: 30 min)

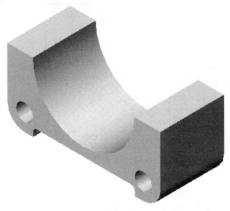

Figure 3-74 Solid model for Exercise 3

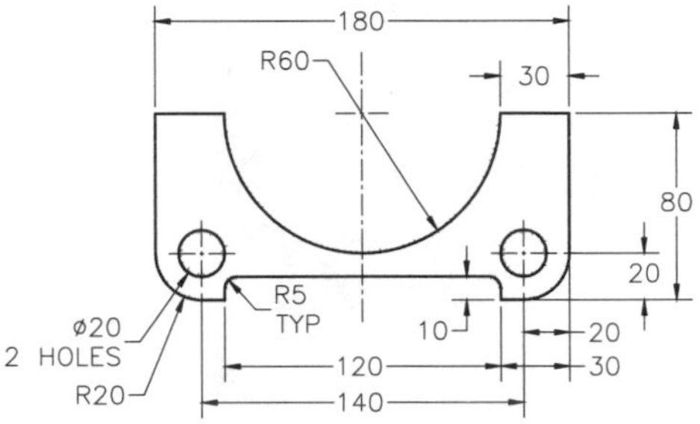

Figure 3-75 Sketch for Exercise 3

Exercise 4

Create the sketch of the model shown in Figure 3-76. The sketch of the model is shown in Figure 3-77. The solid model and dimensions are given only for reference. Create the sketch using the sketching tools and then edit the sketch using the **Circular Pattern** tool and the **Trim** tool.

(Expected time: 30 min)

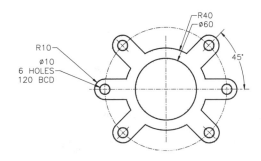

Figure 3-76 Solid model for Exercise 4

Figure 3-77 Sketch for Exercise 4

Answers to Self-Evaluation Test
1. T, **2.** F, **3.** T, **4.** F, **5.** F, **6.** F, **7. Linear Sketch Pattern**, **8. Circular Sketch Pattern**, **9. Select, Circle**, **10. Dynamic Mirror Entities**

Chapter 4

Adding Relations and Dimensions to Sketches

Learning Objectives

After completing this chapter, you will be able to:
- *Add geometric relations to sketches.*
- *Dimension sketches.*
- *Modify the dimensions of sketches.*
- *Understand the concept of fully defined sketches.*
- *View and examine the relations applied to sketches.*
- *Open an existing file.*

APPLYING GEOMETRIC RELATIONS TO SKETCHES

Geometric relations are the logical operations that are performed to add relationships (such as tangent or perpendicular) between the sketched entities, planes, axes, edges, or vertices. The relations applied to the sketched entities are used to capture the design intent. Geometric relations constrain the degree of freedom of the sketched entities. There are two methods of applying relations to the sketch:

1. Add Relations PropertyManager
2. Automatic Relations

Applying Relations Using the Add Relations PropertyManager

CommandManager:	Sketch > Display/Delete Relations > Add Relation
SolidWorks menus:	Tools > Relations > Add
Toolbar:	Sketch > Display/Delete Relations > Add Relation

The **Add Relations PropertyManager** is widely used to apply relations to the sketch in the sketching environment of SolidWorks. It is invoked by choosing **Display/Delete Relations > Add Relation** from the **Sketch CommandManager**. Alternatively, select an entity and right-click in the drawing area. Next, choose the **Add Relation** option from the shortcut menu; the **Add Relations PropertyManager** will be displayed, as shown in Figure 4-1. Also, when you invoke this **PropertyManager**, the confirmation corner is displayed at the top right corner of the drawing area. The different rollouts in the **Add Relations PropertyManager** are discussed next.

Figure 4-1 *The* ***Add Relations*** *PropertyManager*

Selected Entities Rollout

The **Selected Entities** rollout displays the name of the entities that are selected to apply the relations. The entities that you select are displayed in light blue and are added in the area below the **Selected Entities** rollout. You can remove the selected entity from the selection set by selecting the same entity again in the drawing area.

Existing Relations Rollout

The **Existing Relations** rollout displays the relations that are already applied to the selected sketch entities. It also shows the status of the sketch entities. You can delete the already existing relation from this rollout. To do so, select the existing relation from the selection box and right-click to display the shortcut menu. Choose the **Delete** option from this shortcut menu to delete the selected relation. If you choose the **Delete All** option, all relations displayed in the selection box of the **Existing Relations** rollout will be deleted.

Tip. *You can also remove the selected entity from the selection set by selecting that entity in the **Selected Entities** rollout and invoking the shortcut menu. Choose the **Delete** option from the shortcut menu to remove the selected entity from the selection set. If you choose the **Clear Selections** option from the shortcut menu, all entities will be removed from the selection set.*

Add Relations Rollout

The **Add Relations** rollout is used to apply the relations to the selected entity. The list of relations that can be applied to the selected entity or entities is shown in the **Add Relations** rollout. The most appropriate relation for the selected entities appears in bold letters.

Tip. *You can apply a relation to a single entity or between two or more entities. To apply a relation between two or more entities, at least one entity should be a sketched entity. The other entity or entities can be sketched entities, edges, faces, vertices, origins, plane, or axes. The sketch curves from other sketches that form lines or arcs, when projected on the sketch plane, can also be included in the relation.*

The relations that can be applied to the sketches using the **Add Relations** rollout are discussed next.

Horizontal

The **Horizontal** relation forces one or more selected lines or centerlines to become horizontal. You can also select an external entity such as an edge, plane, axis, or sketch curve on an external sketch that will act as a line to apply this relation. You can also force two or more points to become horizontal using the **Horizontal** relation. A point can be a sketch point, a center point, an endpoint, a control point of a spline, or an external entity such as origin, vertex, axis, or point in an external sketch. To use this relation, invoke the **Add Relations PropertyManager**. Select the entity or entities to apply the **Horizontal** relation. Choose the **Horizontal** button from the **Add Relations** rollout in the **Add Relations PropertyManager**. You will notice that the name of the horizontal relation will be displayed in the **Existing Relations** rollout.

Vertical

The **Vertical** relation forces one or more selected lines or centerlines to become vertical. You can force two or more points to become vertical using the **Vertical** relation. To use this relation, invoke the **Add Relations PropertyManager** and select the entity or entities to apply the **Vertical** relation. Choose the **Vertical** button from the **Add Relations** rollout. You will notice that the name of the vertical relation is displayed in the **Existing Relations** rollout.

Collinear

The **Collinear** relation forces the selected lines to lie on the same infinite line. To use this relation, select the lines to apply the **Collinear** relation. Choose the **Collinear** button from the **Add Relations** rollout.

Coradial

  The **Coradial** relation forces the selected arcs or circles to share the same radius and the same center point. You can also select an external entity that projects as an arc or a circle in the sketch to apply this relation. To use this relation, invoke the **Add Relations PropertyManager**. Select two arcs or circles, or an arc and a circle to apply the **Coradial** relation. Choose the **Coradial** button from the **Add Relations** rollout.

Perpendicular

The **Perpendicular** relation forces the selected lines to become perpendicular to each other. To use this relation, invoke the **Add Relations PropertyManager**. Select two lines and choose the **Perpendicular** button from the **Add Relations** rollout. Figure 4-2 shows two lines before and after applying the **Perpendicular** relation.

Parallel

The **Parallel** relation forces the selected lines to become parallel to each other. To use this relation, invoke the **Add Relations PropertyManager**. Select two lines and choose the **Parallel** button from the **Add Relations** rollout. Figure 4-3 shows two lines before and after applying this relation.

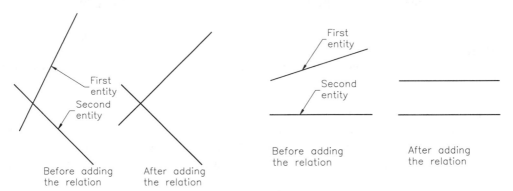

Figure 4-2 *Entities before and after applying the Perpendicular relation*

Figure 4-3 *Entities before and after applying the Parallel relation*

ParallelYZ

The **ParallelYZ** relation forces a line in the three-dimensional (3D) sketch to become parallel to the YZ plane with respect to the selected plane. To use this relation, invoke the **Add Relations PropertyManager**. Select the line in the 3D sketch and then select a plane. Next, choose the **ParallelYZ** button from the **Add Relations** rollout.

Note
You will learn more about the 3D curves in the later chapters.

ParallelZX

The **ParallelZX** relation forces a line in the 3D sketch to become parallel to the ZX plane with respect to the selected plane. To use this relation, invoke the **Add Relations PropertyManager**. Select the line in the 3D sketch and then select a plane. Next, choose the **ParallelZX** button from the **Add Relations** rollout.

AlongZ

AlongZ The **AlongZ** relation forces a line in the 3D sketch to become normal to the selected plane. To use this relation, invoke the **Add Relations PropertyManager**. Select the line in the 3D sketch and then select a plane. Next, choose the **AlongZ** button from the **Add Relations** rollout.

Tangent

Tangent The **Tangent** relation forces the selected arc, circle, spline, or ellipse to become tangent to the other arc, circle, spline, ellipse, line, or edge. To use this relation, invoke the **Add Relations PropertyManager**. Select two entities and choose the **Tangent** button from the **Add Relations** rollout. Figures 4-4 shows a line and circle before and after applying the **Tangent** relation. Figure 4-5 shows two arcs after applying the **Tangent** relation.

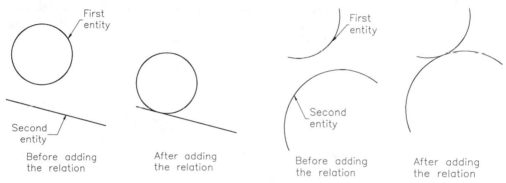

Figure 4-4 Applying the **Tangent** relation to a line and a circle

Figure 4-5 Applying the **Tangent** relation to two arcs

Concentric

Concentric The **Concentric** relation forces the selected arc or circle to share the same center point with the other arc, circle, point, vertex, or circular edge. To use this relation, invoke the **Add Relations PropertyManager**. Select the required entity to apply the **Concentric** relation and then choose the **Concentric** button from the **Add Relations** rollout.

Equal

Equal The **Equal** relation forces the selected lines to have equal length and the selected arcs, circles, or arc and circle to have equal radii. To use this relation, invoke the **Add Relations PropertyManager**. Select the required entity to apply the **Equal** relation and choose the **Equal** button.

Intersection

Intersection The **Intersection** relation forces the selected point to move at the intersection of two selected lines. To use this relation, invoke the **Add Relations PropertyManager**. Select the required entity to apply the **Intersection** relation. Choose the **Intersection** button from the **Add Relations** rollout.

Coincident

The **Coincident** relation forces the selected point to be coincident with the selected line, arc, circle, or ellipse. To use this relation, invoke the **Add Relations PropertyManager**. Select the required entity to apply the **Coincident** relation. Choose the **Coincident** button from the **Add Relations** rollout.

Midpoint

The **Midpoint** relation forces the selected point to move to the midpoint of a selected line. To use this relation, invoke the **Add Relations PropertyManager**. Select the point and the line to which the midpoint relation has to be applied. Choose the **Midpoint** button from the **Add Relations** rollout.

Symmetric

The **Symmetric** relation forces two selected lines, arcs, points, and ellipses to remain equidistant from a centerline. This relation also forces the entities to have the same size and orientation. To use this relation, invoke the **Add Relations PropertyManager**. Select the required entity to apply the **Symmetric** relation and select a centerline. Choose the **Symmetric** button from the **Add Relations** rollout.

Fix

The **Fix** relation forces the selected entity to be fixed at the specified position. If you apply this relation to a line or an arc, its location will be fixed but you can change its size by dragging the endpoints. To use this relation, invoke the **Add Relations PropertyManager**. Select the required entity and choose the **Fix** button.

Merge Points

The **Merge Points** relation forces two sketch points or endpoints to merge in a single point. To use this relation, invoke the **Add Relations PropertyManager**. Select the required entities to apply the **Merge Points** relation and choose the **Merge Points** button from the **Add Relations** rollout.

Pierce

The **Pierce** relation forces a sketch point or an endpoint of an entity to be coincident with an entity of another sketch. To use this relation, invoke the **Add Relations PropertyManager**. Select the required entities to apply the **Pierce** relation and choose the **Pierce** button from the **Add Relations** rollout.

Tip. *You can also apply the relations using the **Properties PropertyManager**. This **PropertyManager** is automatically invoked if you select more than one entity from the drawing area. The possible relations for the selected geometry will be displayed in the **Add Relations** rollout. Choose the relation you need to apply to the selected geometry.*

Alternatively, select the entity or entities to which you need to apply the relation and do not move the mouse for a while; a pop-up toolbar will be displayed with few relations. Select the relations from the pop-up toolbar. You can also select the entity or entities and invoke the shortcut menu to display these relations.

Automatic Relations

Automatic relations are applied automatically to the sketch while drawing. For example, you will notice that when you specify the start point of a line and move the cursor horizontally toward the right or left, the horizontal line symbol is displayed below the line cursor. This is the symbol of the **Horizontal** relation that is applied to the line while drawing. If you move the cursor vertically downward or upward, the vertical line symbol for the **Vertical** relation will be displayed below the line cursor. If you move the cursor to the intersection of two or more sketched entities, the intersection symbol will appear below the cursor. Similarly, other relations are also automatically applied to the sketch when you draw it.

You can activate the automatic relations option if it is not activated. To do so, choose the **Options** button from the Menu Bar; the **System Options - General** dialog box will be displayed. Select the **Relations/Snaps** option from the area on the left, then select the **Automatic relations** check box from this dialog box and finally choose the **OK** button. The relations that can be applied automatically are listed below:

1. Horizontal
2. Vertical
3. Coincident
4. Midpoint
5. Intersection
6. Tangent
7. Perpendicular

Tip. *You will observe that while sketching, two types of inferencing lines are displayed, one is in blue and the other in yellow. The yellow inferencing line indicates that the relation is applied automatically to the sketch, whereas, the blue inferencing line indicates that no automatic relation is applied.*

DIMENSIONING THE SKETCH

After drawing the sketches and adding the relations, dimensioning is the most important step in creating a design. As mentioned earlier, SolidWorks is a parametric software. This property of SolidWorks ensures that irrespective of the original size, the selected entity is driven by the dimension value that you specify. Therefore, when you apply and modify the dimension of an entity, it is forced to change its size in accordance with the specified dimension value.

In SolidWorks, you can use the **Smart Dimension** tool in the **Sketch CommandManager** to dimension any kind of entity. If you use the **Smart Dimension** tool, the type of dimension that will be applied will depend on the type of entity selected. For example, if you select a line, then a horizontal, vertical, or aligned dimension will be applied. If you select a circle, a diametric dimension will be applied. Similarly, if you select an arc, a radius dimension will be applied. However, if you want to apply a particular type of dimension, click on the down arrow in **Smart Dimension** button and select the required tool from the flyout that is displayed. You can also invoke these the **Dimensions/Relations** toolbar for applying various dimensions. As soon as you place the dimension, the **Modify** dialog box will be displayed, as shown in

Figure 4-6. You can modify the default dimension value using the spinner or by entering a new value in the edit box available in the **Modify** dialog box. In SolidWorks, a thumbwheel is also provided below the spinner. You can drag this thumbwheel to the right to increase and to the left to decrease the value.

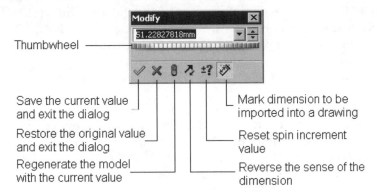

*Figure 4-6 The **Modify** dialog box*

> **Tip**. *If the **Modify** dialog box is not displayed when you place the dimension, you need to set its preference manually. To do this, invoke the **System Options - General** dialog box and select the **Input dimension value** check box.*

The buttons available in the **Modify** dialog box are discussed next.

The **Save the current value and exit the dialog** button is used to accept the current value and exit the dialog box. The **Restore the original value and exit the dialog** button is used to restore the last dimensional value applied to the sketch and exit the dialog box. The **Regenerate the model with the current value** button is used to preview the geometry of the sketch with the modified dimensional value. The **Reverse the sense of the dimension** button is used to flip the dimension value of an entity. This button will be available in the **Modify** dialog box when the selected dimension is a linear dimension. The **Reset spin increment value** button is used to modify the increment value in the spinner. If you choose this button, the **Increment** dialog box will be displayed. Enter a value and press ENTER. This new value will be added to or subtracted from the current value when you click on the spinner arrow. The **Mark dimensions to be imported into a drawing** button is chosen to make sure that the selected dimension is generated as a model annotation in the drawing views. If this button is not chosen, the dimensions will not be generated in the drafting environment. You can drive the dimension by an equation and also link the dimension to other dimensions using the **Add equation** and **Link value** options available in the drop-down list of the **Modify** dialog box. You will learn more about these options in the later chapters.

> **Tip**. *You can also enter the arithmetic symbols directly into the edit box of the **Modify** toolbar to calculate the dimension. For example, if you have a dimension as a complex arithmetic function such as (220*12.5)-3+150, which is equal to 1247, you do not need to calculate this function using the calculator. Just enter the statement in the edit box and press ENTER; SolidWorks will automatically solve the mathematical expression to get the value of the dimension.*

In SolidWorks 2009, you can also specify numeric input while creating lines, rectangles, circles, and arcs. To do so, choose the **Options** button from the Menu Bar; the **System Options - General** dialog box will be displayed. Select the **Sketch** option from the left area of the dialog box; the options related to the sketch are displayed on the right of the dialog box. Select the **Enable on the screen numeric input on entity creation** check box and then choose the **OK** button to apply the changes and close the dialog box. Now, you can specify the numeric input while creating the lines, rectangles, circles, and arcs. For example, choose the **Corner Rectangle** button from the **Sketch CommandManager** and specify the first corner of the rectangle in the drawing area. Next, move the cursor away from the first corner. Note that the vertical and horizontal dimensions will be attached to the reference rectangle, as shown in Figure 4-7. Now, you can specify the required dimensions of the rectangle in the drawing area.

Figure 4-7 *Linear dimensioning of lines*

The types of dimensions that can be applied to the sketches in the sketching environment of SolidWorks 2009 are discussed next.

Horizontal/Vertical Dimensioning

CommandManager:	Sketch > Smart Dimension > Horizontal/Vertical Dimension
SolidWorks menus:	Tools > Dimensions > Horizontal/Vertical
Toolbar:	Dimensions/Relations > Horizontal/Vertical Dimension

These dimensions are used to define the horizontal or vertical dimensions of a selected line or between two points. The points can be the endpoints of lines or arcs, or the center points of circles, arcs, ellipses, or parabolas. You can dimension a vertical or a horizontal line by directly selecting it. To invoke these tools, choose the **Smart Dimension > Horizontal Dimension/Vertical Dimension** from the **Sketch CommandManager**. You can also right-click in the drawing area and choose **More Dimensions > Horizontal/Vertical** from the shortcut menu. When you move the cursor on the line, the line will be highlighted and turn orange. As soon as you select the line, it will turn light blue, and the dimension will be attached to the cursor. Move the cursor and place the dimension at an appropriate place using the left mouse button. The **Modify** dialog box will be displayed with the default value in it. Enter the new value of the dimension in the **Modify** dialog box and press ENTER. Figure 4-8 shows the horizontal and vertical dimensioning linear of lines.

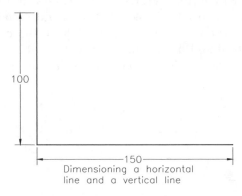

Figure 4-8 Linear dimensioning of lines

If the dimension is selected from the drawing area, the **Dimension PropertyManager** will be displayed, as shown in Figure 4-9. The different rollouts in the **Value** tab of the **Dimension PropertyManager** are discussed next.

Style Rollout

The **Style** rollout, as shown in Figure 4-10, is used to create, save, delete, and retrieve the dimension style in the current document. You can also retrieve the dimension styles saved in other documents using this rollout. The options available in this rollout are discussed next.

Apply the default attributes to selected dimensions

The **Apply the default attributes to selected dimensions** button is used to apply the default attributes to the selected dimension or dimensions. The attributes include the tolerance, precision, arrow style, dimension text, and so on. This option is generally used when you modify the settings applied to a dimension and then you want to restore the default settings on that dimension.

Add or Update a Style

The **Add or Update a Style** button is used to add a dimension style to the current document for a selected dimension. After invoking the **Dimension PropertyManager**, set the attributes using various options provided in this **PropertyManager**. Now, choose the **Add or Update a Style** button; the **Add or Update a Style** dialog box will be displayed, as shown in Figure 4-11. Enter the name of the dimension style in the edit box and press ENTER; the dimension style will be added to the current document.

Figure 4-9 The **Dimension PropertyManager**

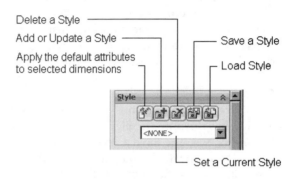

Figure 4-10 The **Style** rollout

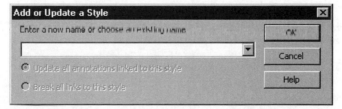

Figure 4-11 The **Add or Update a Style** dialog box

You can apply the new dimension style to the selected dimension by selecting the dimension style from the **Set a current Style** drop-down list in the **Style** rollout. You can also update the dimension style. To do so, select the dimension and set the options of the dimension style according to your need. Next, choose the **Add or Update a Style** button to invoke the **Add or Update a Style** dialog box. Select the dimension style to update from the drop-down list provided in the dialog box; the two radio buttons in this dialog box are enabled. Select the **Update all annotations linked to this Style** radio button and choose the **OK** button to update all the dimensions linked with the selected **Style**. If you select the **Break all links to this Style** radio button and choose the **OK** button, then the link between the other dimensions that have the same **Style** and the selected **Style** will be broken.

Delete a Style

The **Delete a Style** button is used to delete a dimension style. Select a dimension style from the **Set a current Style** drop-down list and choose the **Delete a Style** button. Note that even after you delete the dimension style, the properties of the dimensions will be the same as those with the deleted style. You can set the properties of a dimension to the default settings using the **Apply the default attributes to selected dimension** button.

Save a Style

The **Save a Style** button is used to save a dimension style so that it can be retrieved in some other document. Select the dimension style from the **Set a current Style** drop-down list and choose the **Save a Style** button; the **Save As** dialog box will be displayed. Browse to the folder in which you want to save the style and enter its name in the **File name** edit box. Choose the **Save** button from the **Save As** dialog box. The style file will be saved with the extension *.sldstl*.

Load Style

The **Load Style** button is used to open a saved Style in the current document. The properties of that favorite will be applied to the selected dimension. To load a Style, choose the **Load Style** button to invoke the **Open** dialog box. Browse the folder in which the Style is saved. Now, select the file with the extension *.sldstl* and choose the **Open** button; the **Add or Update a Style** dialog box will be displayed. Choose the **OK** button from this dialog box.

Tip. *You can load more than one style by pressing the SHIFT key and selecting the style from the **Open** dialog box. All style will be displayed in the **Set a current Style** drop-down list.*

Tolerance/Precision Rollout

The **Tolerance/Precision** rollout, as shown in Figure 4-12, is used to specify the tolerance and precision in the dimensions. The options in this rollout are discussed next.

*Figure 4-12 The **Tolerance/Precision** rollout*

Tolerance Type

The **Tolerance Type** drop-down list is used to apply the tolerance to the dimension. By default, the **None** option is selected. Therefore, no tolerance is applied to the dimensions. The other tolerance types available in this drop-down list are discussed next.

Basic

The basic dimension is the one that is enclosed in a rectangle. To display the basic dimension, select the dimension that you want to display as a basic dimension and then select the **Basic** option from the **Tolerance Type** drop-down list. You will notice that the dimension is enclosed in a rectangle, indicating that it is a basic dimension, see Figure 4-13.

Bilateral

The bilateral tolerance provides the maximum and minimum variation in the value of the dimension that is acceptable in the design. To apply the bilateral tolerance, select the dimension and then the **Bilateral** option from the **Tolerance Type** drop-down list; the **Maximum Variation** and **Minimum Variation** edit boxes will be enabled, where you can enter the maximum and minimum variation for a dimension. The **Show parentheses** check box will also be displayed. If you select this check box, the bilateral tolerance will be displayed with parentheses. The dimension with a bilateral tolerance is shown in Figure 4-14.

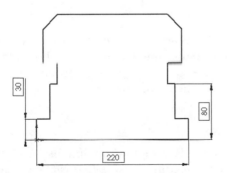

Figure 4-13 Basic dimension

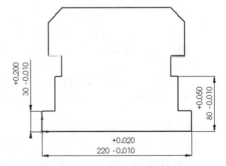

Figure 4-14 Bilateral tolerance

Note
The ISO standard has been used as the dimension standard for the sketches in this book.

Limit

The maximum and minimum permissible dimensional values of an entity are displayed on selecting the **Limit** option. To apply this tolerance type, select the dimension to be displayed as limit dimension and select the **Limit** option; the **Maximum Variation** and **Minimum Variation** edit boxes will be enabled. Enter the value of the maximum and minimum variation. The dimension along with the limit tolerance is shown in Figure 4-15.

Symmetric

The symmetric tolerance is displayed with plus and minus signs. To use this tolerance, first select the dimension and then select the **Symmetric** option; the **Maximum Variation** edit box will be displayed. You can enter the value of the tolerance in this edit box. Also, you can select the **Show parentheses** check box to show the tolerance in parentheses. The dimension along with the symmetric tolerance is shown in Figure 4-16.

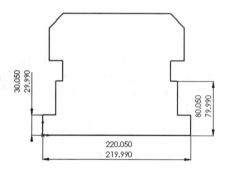

Figure 4-15 *Limit tolerance*   **Figure 4-16** *Symmetric tolerance*

MIN

In this dimensional tolerance, the **min.** symbol is added to the dimension as a suffix. This implies that the dimensional value is the minimum value that is allowed in the design. To display this dimensional tolerance, select the dimension and the **MIN** option from the **Tolerance Type** drop-down list. The dimension, along with the minimum tolerance, is shown in Figure 4-17.

MAX

In this dimensional tolerance, the **max.** symbol is added to the dimension as suffix. This implies that the dimensional value is the maximum value that is allowed in the design. To display this dimensional tolerance, select the dimension and the **MAX** option from the **Tolerance Type** drop-down list. The dimension, along with the maximum tolerance, is shown in Figure 4-18.

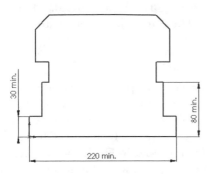

Figure 4-17 *Minimum tolerance*

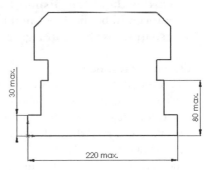

Figure 4-18 *Maximum tolerance*

Fit

The **Fit** option is used to apply the fit according to the Hole Fit and Shaft Fit systems. The **Tolerance/Precision** rollout with the **Fit** option selected in the **Tolerance Type** drop-down list is shown in Figure 4-19. Select the type of fit from the **Classification**

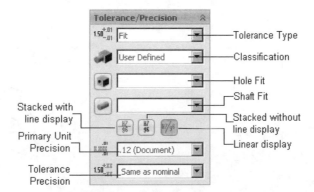

Figure 4-19 *The **Tolerance/Precision** rollout with the **Fit** option selected from the **Tolerance Type** drop-down list*

drop-down list. The **Classification** drop-down list is used to define the **User Defined** fit, **Clearance** fit, **Transitional** fit, or **Press** fit. To apply the fit using the Hole Fit system or the Shaft Fit system, select the dimension and the **Fit** option from the **Tolerance Type** drop-down list. The **Classification**, **Hole Fit**, and **Shaft Fit** edit drop-down lists will be displayed below the **Tolerance Type** drop-down list. Select the required fit from the **Classification** drop-down list and select the fit standard from the **Hole Fit** drop-down list or the **Shaft Fit** drop-down list. If you select the **Clearance**, **Transitional**, or **Press** option from the **Classification** drop-down list and the fit standard from the **Hole Fit** drop-down list, then only the standards that match the selected hole fit will be displayed in the **Shaft Fit** drop-down list and vice versa. However, if you select the **User Defined** option from the **Classification** drop-down list, you can select any standard from the **Hole Fit** and **Shaft Fit** drop-down lists. The **Stacked with line display** button is chosen to display the stacked tolerance with a line. You can also display the tolerance as stacked without a line using the

Stacked without line display button. If you choose the **Linear display** button, the tolerance will be displayed in the linear form. The dimension, along with the hole fit and shaft fit, is shown in Figure 4-20.

Fit with tolerance

The **Fit with tolerance** option in the **Tolerance Type** drop-down list is used to display the tolerance along with the hole fit and shaft fit in a dimension. To apply the fit with the tolerance, select the dimension and the **Fit with tolerance** option from the **Tolerance Type** drop-down list. Select the type of fit from the **Classification** drop-down list. Now, select the fit standard from the **Hole Fit** drop-down list or the **Shaft Fit** drop-down list. The tolerance will be displayed with the fit standard only if you select a fit system from the **Hole Fit** or **Shaft Fit** drop-down list. The tolerance will be displayed along with the fit standard in the drawing area. In SolidWorks, the tolerance is calculated automatically, depending on the type and standard of the selected fit. The **Show parentheses** check box can be selected to show the tolerance in parentheses. The dimension along with the fit and tolerance is shown in Figure 4-21.

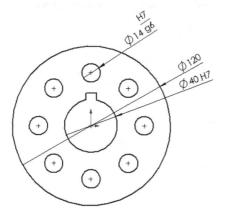

Figure 4-20 Hole fit and shaft fit

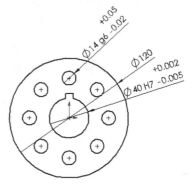

Figure 4-21 Dimensioning along with the fit and tolerance

Fit (tolerance only)

The **Fit (tolerance only)** option in the **Tolerance Type** drop-down list is used to display the tolerance in a dimension based on the hole fit or shaft fit.

None

The **None** option in the **Tolerance Type** drop-down list is used to display the dimensional value without any tolerance.

Primary Unit Precision

The **Primary Unit Precision** drop-down list is used to specify the precision of the number of places after the decimal for dimensions. By default, the selected precision is two places after the decimal.

Tolerance Precision

The **Tolerance Precision** drop-down list is used to specify the precision of the number of places after the decimal for tolerance. By default, the selected precision is two places after the decimal. This drop-down list will not be available if the **None** option is selected in the **Tolerance Type** drop-down list.

Dimension Text Rollout

The **Dimension Text** rollout, as shown in Figure 4-22, is used to add the text and symbols to the dimension. The text box provided in this rollout is used to add the text to the dimension. The **<DIM>** text displayed in the text box symbolizes the dimensional value. You can add the text before or after the dimension value. In SolidWorks, four new buttons have been added above the text box. Choose the **Add Parentheses** button to enclose the dimension text in parentheses. Choose the **Center Dimension** button to place the dimension at the center of the dimension line. Choose the **Inspection Dimension** button to enclose the dimension text in an obround shaped and this dimension will be checked during the inspection. If you need to place the text at a distance from the dimension line, choose the **Offset Text** button and drag the dimension to the required location. Note that you can also choose all four buttons simultaneously for a specified dimension.

This rollout also provides buttons to modify the text justification and add symbols such as **Diameter**, **Degree**, **Plus/Minus**, **Centerline**, and so on to the dimension text. You can add more symbols by choosing the **More Symbols** button from the **Dimension Text** rollout. When you choose this button, the **Symbols** dialog box will be displayed, as shown in Figure 4-23.

*Figure 4-22 The **Dimension Text** rollout*

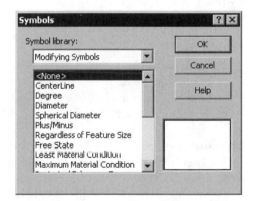

*Figure 4-23 The **Symbols** dialog box*

Dual Dimension Rollout

You need to select the check box in the **Dual Dimension** rollout to enable the options in this rollout. The options in this rollout are used to display the dimension value in alternate units. Also, the dual dimension value will be displayed in square brackets, as shown in Figure 4-24. The options in this rollout are similar to those discussed in the earlier sections. Note that the alternate unit is set in the **Dual Dimension Length** cell in the **Document Property - Units** dialog box. To invoke this dialog box, choose **Tools > Options** from the SolidWorks menus; the **System Options** dialog box will be displayed. Choose the **Document Properties** tab; the name of this dialog box will be changed to the **Document**

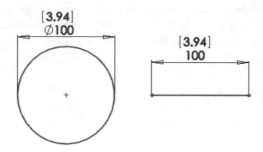

Figure 4-24 Circle and line with dual dimension

Property - Drafting Standard dialog box. In this dialog box, select the **Units** option from the area on the left to display the options for setting units. Note that, on selecting the **Unit** option, the name of this dialog box will be changed to **Document Property - Units** dialog box. Sometimes, you may need to change the type of arrowheads or place the dimension at a distance from the entity because of space constraint. In SolidWorks 2009, these actions can be performed by choosing the **Leaders** tab in the **Dimension PropertyManager**. The rollouts in this tab are discussed next.

Witness/Leader Display Rollout

The **Witness/Leader Display** rollout is used to specify the arrowhead style in the dimensions, as shown in Figure 4-25. The options in this rollout are discussed next.

Outside
The **Outside** button is used to display the arrows outside the extension line. To do so, select a dimension from the drawing area and choose the **Outside** button from the **Witness/Leader Display** rollout.

Inside
The **Inside** button is used to display the arrows inside the extension line. To do so, select a dimension from the drawing area and choose the **Inside** button. You can also click on the control point displayed on the arrowhead to reverse its direction.

Smart
The **Smart** button is chosen by default and the arrows are displayed inside or outside the extension line, depending on the space available between the extension lines.

*Figure 4-25 The rollouts in the **Leaders** tab*

Style

The **Style** drop-down list is used to select the style of the arrowhead. The unfilled triangular arrow is selected by default. You can select any arrowhead style for a particular dimension or dimension style. To change the arrowhead style, select a dimension from the drawing area and then the arrowhead style from the **Style** drop-down list. Figure 4-26 shows dimensions with different styles of arrowheads.

Use document bend length

To change the length of the leader line after the bend, clear this check box and specify the length in the edit box given below the check box. By default, the value specified in the **Document Properties - Detailing - Dimensions** dialog box will be displayed in the edit box given below this check box. Figure 4-27 shows the dimensions with leader lines.

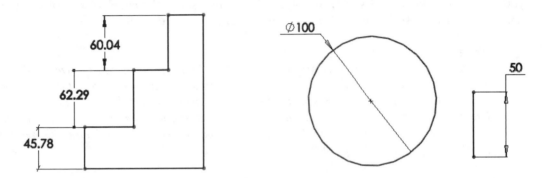

Figure 4-26 *Dimensions with different arrowheads* *Figure 4-27* *Dimensions with leader lines*

Leader Style Rollout

To enable the options in the **Leader Style** rollout, you need to clear the **Use document display** check box in it. After clearing this check box, the **Leader Style** and **Leader Thickness** drop-down lists will be enabled. The **Leader Style** drop-down list is used to specify the leader style and the **Leader Thickness** drop-down list is used to specify the thickness of the leader. You can also select the **Custom size** option from the **Leader Thickness** drop-down list. On selecting this option, you can specify the thickness value of the leader in the spinner available below this drop-down list as per your requirement.

Custom Text Position Rollout

The options in this rollout are used to specify the position of the text on the dimension line. Select the check box in the **Custom Text Position** rollout to enable the options in this rollout. The options in this rollout are discussed next.

Solid Leader, Aligned Text

If you choose this button, the leader line will be placed parallel to the dimension line along with the text.

Broken Leader, Horizontal Text

On choosing this button, leader line will be placed parallel to the horizontal axis along with the text.

Broken Leader, Aligned Text

Choose this button to place the dimension line to the center of the text. In this case, the text and the leader line will be placed parallel to the dimension line.

In SolidWorks, you can change the units and the font of the dimension text by choosing the **Other** tab. The rollouts in this tab are discussed next.

Override Units Rollout

If you need to change the existing units of the dimension, select the check box in this rollout to expand it and select the units from the **Length Units** drop-down list.

Note

*On selecting the units such as **Microinches**, **Mils**, **Inches**, and so on, the **Decimal** and **Fractions** radio buttons will be displayed in the **Override Units** rollout. Select the **Decimal** radio button to display the dimensional value in the decimal format. Select the **Fractions** radio button to display the dimensional value in the fractional format. On selecting the **Fractions** radio button, you need to specify the denominator value and select the **Round to nearest fraction** check box to display the value as fractions.*

Text Fonts Rollout

The font style set in the **Document Property - Detailing - Annotations Font** dialog box will be the default font style. To change the font style, clear the **Use document's font** check box and change the font style by choosing the **Font** button in the **Text Fonts** rollout.

Options Rollout

If you select the **Read only** check box in this rollout, the dimensional value cannot be changed. If you select the **Driven** check box, the value will be the driven value.

Horizontal/Vertical Dimensioning Between Points

As mentioned earlier, you can add a horizontal or a vertical dimension between two points. To do so, choose the required button from the **Dimensions/Relations** toolbar. Select the first point, and then the second point. Specify a point to place the dimension; the **Modify** dialog box will be displayed. Enter a new dimension value in this dialog box and press ENTER. Figure 4-28 shows the horizontal and vertical dimensions between two points. Figure 4-29 shows horizontal and vertical dimensions of an inclined lines.

You can also apply horizontal or vertical (linear) dimensioning to a circle. However, note that these types of dimensions can only be applied to a circle only by using the **Smart Dimension** tool. To apply this type of dimension to a circle, choose the **Smart Dimension** button from the **Sketch CommandManager** and select the circle; the dimension will be attached to the cursor. If you want to apply the vertical dimension, move the cursor to the right or left of the sketch. If you want to apply the horizontal dimension, move the cursor to the top or bottom

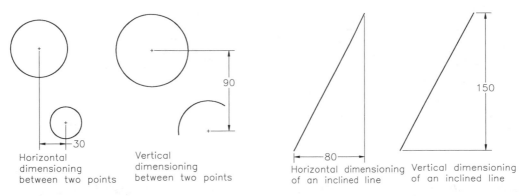

Figure 4-28 *Applying horizontal and vertical dimensions between two points*

Figure 4-29 *Applying horizontal and vertical dimensions of an inclined lines*

of the sketch. Use the left mouse button to place the dimension and enter a new value in the **Modify** dialog box. The linear dimensioning of a circle is shown in Figure 4-30.

Aligned Dimensioning

CommandManager:	Sketch > Smart Dimension
SolidWorks menus:	Tools > Dimensions > Smart
Toolbar:	Sketch > Smart Dimension

 Aligned dimensions are used to dimension lines that are at an angle with respect to the X-axis and the Y-axis. These types of dimensions measure the actual length of the inclined lines. You can directly select an inclined line or two points to apply this dimension. The points that can be used to apply aligned dimensions include the endpoints of a line, arc, parabolic arc, or spline and the center points of arcs, circles, ellipse, or parabolic arc. To apply an aligned dimension to an inclined line, choose the **Smart Dimension** button from the **Sketch CommandManager** and select the line. Move the cursor at an angle such that the dimension line is parallel to the inclined line. Place the dimension at an appropriate place and enter a new value in the **Modify** dialog box

To apply an aligned dimension between two points, choose the **Smart Dimension** button, select the first point, and then the second point to apply the dimension; the dimension will be attached to the cursor. Move the cursor such that the dimension line is parallel to the imaginary line that joins the two points. Now, place the dimension at an appropriate location. Enter a new value in the **Modify** dialog box and press ENTER. Figure 4-31 shows aligned dimensioning of an inclined line between two points.

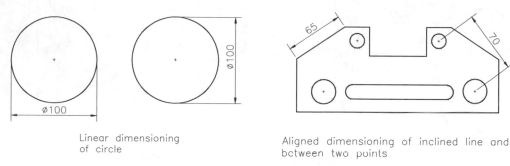

Linear dimensioning
of circle

Figure 4-30 *Linear dimensioning of a circle*

Aligned dimensioning of inclined line and
between two points

Figure 4-31 *Aligned dimensioning*

Angular Dimensioning

Angular dimensions are used to dimension angles. You can apply angular dimensions between two line segments or between three points of an arc. All these options of angular dimensioning are discussed next.

Angular Dimensioning Between Two Line Segments

CommandManager:	Sketch > Smart Dimension
SolidWorks menus:	Tools > Dimensions > Smart
Toolbar:	Sketch > Smart Dimension

To apply angular dimensions between two lines, choose the **Smart Dimension** button from the **Sketch CommandManager** and select the first line segment; a dimension will be attached to the cursor. Now, select the second line segment; an angular dimension will be attached to the cursor. Place the angular dimension and enter the new value of angular dimension in the **Modify** dialog box. Depending on the location of the dimension placement, the interior angle, exterior angle, major angle, or minor angle will be displayed. Therefore, you need to be very careful while placing the angular dimension. Figures 4-32 through 4-35 illustrate various angular dimensions, depending on the placement of the dimension.

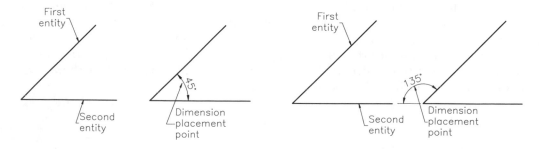

Figure 4-32 *Angular dimension displayed according to the dimension placement point*

Figure 4-33 *Angular dimension displayed according to the dimension placement point*

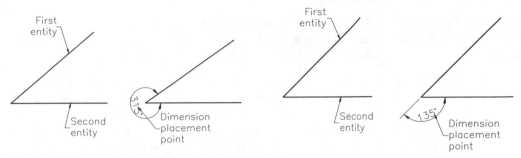

Figure 4-34 *Angular dimension displayed according to the dimension placement point*

Figure 4-35 *Angular dimension displayed according to the dimension placement point*

Angular Dimensioning Between Three Points

To add angular dimensions between three points, you need to be extremely careful while selecting the points. To apply angular dimensions between three points, choose the **Smart Dimension** button from the **Sketch CommandManager**. Select the first point using the left mouse button. This is the angle vertex point. Select the second point; a linear dimension will be attached to the cursor. Next, select the third point; an angular dimension will be attached to the cursor. Place the angular dimension at an appropriate location and enter a new value of angular dimension in the **Modify** dialog box, if you need to change the value. Figure 4-36 shows the angular dimensioning between three points.

Angular Dimensioning of an Arc

You can use angular dimensions to dimension an arc. To do so, select the two endpoints and the center point of the arc. Figure 4-37 shows the angular dimensioning of an arc.

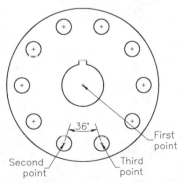

Figure 4-36 *Angular dimension specified between three points*

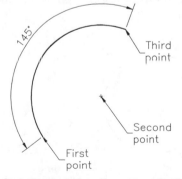

Figure 4-37 *Angular dimension displayed on an arc*

Diameter Dimensioning

CommandManager:	Sketch > Smart Dimension
SolidWorks menus:	Tools > Dimensions > Smart
Toolbar:	Sketch > Smart Dimension

Diameter dimensions are applied to dimension a circle or an arc in terms of its diameter. To apply the diameter dimension, choose the **Smart Dimension** button from the **Sketch CommandManager**. Select a circle or an arc and place the dimension. In SolidWorks, when you select a circle to dimension, the diameter dimension is applied to it by default. However, when you select an arc, the radius dimension is applied to it. To apply the diameter dimension to an arc, select the dimensional value; the **Dimension PropertyManager** will be displayed. Choose the **Diameter** button in the **Witness/Leader Display** rollout of the **Leaders** tab and choose **OK**. Alternatively, select the dimension, invoke the shortcut menu, and choose **Display Options > Display As Diameter** from the shortcut menu. Figure 4-38 shows a circle and an arc with the diameter dimension.

Radius Dimensioning

CommandManager:	Sketch > Smart Dimension
SolidWorks menus:	Tools > Dimensions > Smart
Toolbar:	Sketch > Smart Dimension

Radius dimensions are applied to dimension a circle or an arc in terms of its radius. As mentioned earlier, by default, the dimension applied to a circle is in the diameter form and the dimension applied to an arc is a radius dimension. To apply a radius dimension to circle, select the dimensional value; the **Dimension PropertyManager** will be displayed. Choose the **Radius** button in the **Witness/Leader Display** rollout of the **Leaders** tab and choose **OK**. Alternatively, select the dimension, invoke the shortcut menu and choose **Display Options > Display As Radius** from the shortcut menu. Figure 4-39 displays the radius dimensioning of a circle and an arc.

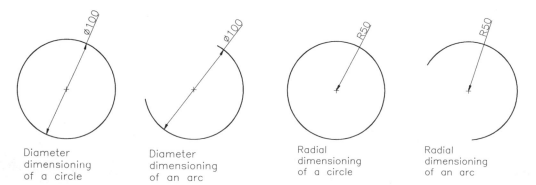

Diameter dimensioning of a circle   Diameter dimensioning of an arc   Radial dimensioning of a circle   Radial dimensioning of an arc

Figure 4-38 *Diameter dimensioning of a circle and an arc*

Figure 4-39 *Radial dimensioning of a circle and an arc*

Linear Diameter Dimensioning

CommandManager:	Sketch > Smart Dimension
SolidWorks menus:	Tools > Dimensions > Smart
Toolbar:	Sketch > Smart Dimension

Linear diameter dimensioning is used to dimension the sketch of a revolved component. An example of a revolved component is shown in Figure 4-40. The sketch for the revolved component is drawn using the sketching tools, as shown in Figure 4-41. If you dimension the sketch of the base feature of the given model using the linear dimensioning method, the same dimensions will be generated in the drawing views. This may be confusing because in the shop floor drawing, you need the diameter dimension of a revolved model. To overcome this problem, it is recommended that you create a linear diameter dimension, as shown in Figure 4-41. To create a linear diameter dimension, choose the **Smart Dimension** button from the **Sketch CommandManager**. Select the entity to be dimensioned and then select the centerline around which the sketch will be revolved. Move the cursor to the other side of the centerline; a linear diameter dimension will be displayed. Place the dimension and enter a new value in the **Modify** dialog box.

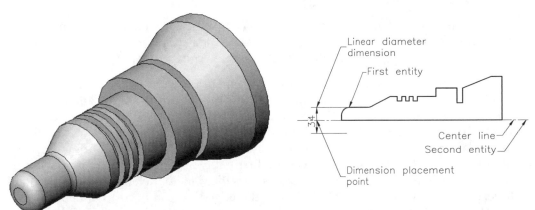

Figure 4-40 *A revolved component*

Figure 4-41 *Sketch for the revolved feature and linear diameter dimensioning*

Ordinate Dimensioning

The ordinate dimensions are used to dimension the sketch with respect to a specified datum. Depending on the requirement of the design, the datum can be an entity in the sketch or the origin. The ordinate dimensions are of two types, horizontal and vertical. The methods of creating these types of ordinate dimensions are discussed next.

Horizontal Ordinate Dimensioning

CommandManager:	Sketch > Smart Dimension > Horizontal Ordinate Dimension
SolidWorks menus:	Tools > Dimensions > Horizontal Ordinate
Toolbar:	Dimensions/Relations > Horizontal Ordinate Dimension

Horizontal ordinate dimensions are used to dimension the horizontal distances of the selected entities from the specified datum, see Figure 4-42. Note that when you apply the ordinate dimensions, the **Modify** dialog box will not be displayed to modify the dimension values. After placing all ordinate dimensions, you need to exit the tool and then double-click on the dimensions to modify their values.

To apply a horizontal ordinate dimension, choose **Smart Dimension > Horizontal Ordinate Dimension** from the **Sketch CommandManager**; you will be prompted to select an edge or a vertex. Note that the first entity selected is taken as the datum entity from where the remaining entities will be measured. Select the first entity and place the dimension above or below it. You will notice that the dimension shows the value 0; refer to the dimension of the left vertical line in Figure 4-42.

After placing the first dimension, you will again be prompted to select an edge or a vertex. Select the edge that you need to dimension with respect to the first selected edge as the datum. As soon as you select the edge, a horizontal dimension between the datum and this entity will be placed. Similarly, place the other dimensions to apply multiple horizontal ordinate dimensions, refer to Figure 4-42.

Vertical Ordinate Dimensioning

CommandManager:	Sketch > Smart Dimension > Vertical Ordinate Dimension
SolidWorks menus:	Tools > Dimensions > Vertical Ordinate
Toolbar:	Dimensions/Relations > Vertical Ordinate Dimension

Vertical ordinate dimensions are used to dimension the vertical distances of the selected entities from the specified datum, see Figure 4-43. To add a vertical ordinate dimension, choose **Smart Dimension > Vertical Ordinate Dimension** from the **Sketch CommandManager**; you will be prompted to select an edge or a vertex. As mentioned earlier, the first entity that you select is taken as the datum entity from where the remaining entities will be measured. Select the first entity and place the dimension on its right or left. You will notice that the dimension shows the value 0. Refer to the dimension of the left vertical line in Figure 4-43. Next, select the edge that you need to dimension with respect to the first selected edge as datum. As soon as you select the edge, a vertical dimension will be placed between the datum and this entity. Similarly, place the other dimensions to create multiple vertical ordinate dimensions, refer to Figure 4-43.

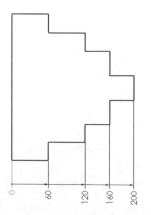

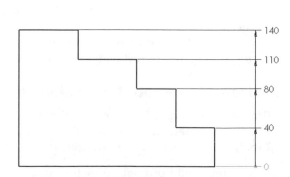

Figure 4-42 *Horizontal ordinate dimensions*   ***Figure 4-43*** *Vertical ordinate dimensions*

CONCEPT OF A FULLY DEFINED SKETCH

It is important for you to understand the concept of fully defined sketches. While creating a model, you first need to draw the sketch of the base feature and then proceed further for creating other features. After creating the sketches, you have to add the required relations and dimensions to constrain the sketch with respect to the surrounding environment. After adding the required relations and dimensions, the sketch may exist in any of the six states discussed below:

1. Fully Defined
2. Overdefined
3. Underdefined
4. Dangling
5. No Solution Found
6. Invalid Solution Found

Fully Defined

A fully defined sketch is the one in which all entities of the sketch and their positions are fully defined by the relations or dimensions, or both. In a fully defined sketch, all degrees of freedom of a sketch are constrained. Therefore, the sketched entities cannot move or change their size and location unexpectedly. If the sketch is not fully defined, it can change its size or position at any time during the design because all degrees of freedom are not constrained. All entities in a fully defined sketch are displayed in black.

Overdefined

An overdefined sketch is the one in which some of the dimensions, relations, or both are conflicting or the dimensions or relations have exceeded the required number. The overdefined sketch is displayed in red. It is recommended not to proceed further for creating the feature with an overdefined sketch. When a sketch is overdefined, you need to delete the extra and conflicting relations or dimensions. An overdefined sketch can be changed to fully defined or underdefined sketch by deleting the conflicting relations or dimensions. You will learn more about deleting the overdefining relations or dimensions later in this chapter.

Tip. *In SolidWorks, it is not necessary to fully dimension or define the sketches before you use them to create the features of the model. However, it is recommended that you fully define the sketches before you proceed further for creating the feature.*

*If you always want to use fully defined sketches before proceeding further, you can do so by choosing **Tools > Options** from the SolidWorks menus to display the **System Options - General** dialog box. Select the **Sketch** option from the area on the left. Select the **Use fully defined sketches** check box and choose **OK** from this dialog box.*

Underdefined

An underdefined sketch is the one in which some of the dimensions or relations are not defined and the degree of freedom of the sketch is not fully constrained. In these types of sketches, the entities may move or change their size unexpectedly. As a result, the sketched entities of the underdefined sketch are displayed in blue. When you add relations and dimensions, the color of the entities in the sketch changes to black, suggesting that the sketch is fully defined. If the entire sketch is displayed in black and only some of the entities are displayed in blue, it means that the entities in blue require some more dimensions or relations.

Note
From this chapter onward, you will work with fully defined sketches. Therefore, follow the above mentioned procedure to use the fully defined sketches in future.

Dangling

In a dangling sketch, the dimensions or relations applied to an entity lose their reference because of deletion of the entity from which they were referenced. These entities are displayed in brown. You need to delete the dangling entities, dimensions, or relations that conflict.

No Solution Found

In the no solution found state, the sketch is not solved with the current constraints. Therefore, you need to delete the conflicting dimensions or relations and add other dimensions or relations. In such cases, the sketched entity, dimension, or relation will be displayed in pink.

Invalid Solution Found

In the invalid solution found state, the sketch is solved but it will result in invalid geometry such as a zero length line, zero radius arc, or self-intersecting spline. The sketch entities in this state are displayed in yellow.

Sketch Dimension or Relation Status

In SolidWorks, while applying the dimensions and relations to the sketches, sometimes you apply the ones that are not compatible with the geometry of the sketched entities or they make the dimensioned entity overdefined. In addition to the fully defined state, the sketch dimensions or relations may have any of the following states:

1. Dangling
2. Satisfied
3. Overdefining
4. Not Solved
5. Driven

Dangling

A dangling dimension or relation is the one that cannot be resolved because the entity to which it was referenced is deleted. The dangling dimension appears in brown.

Satisfied

A satisfied dimension is the one that is completely defined and is displayed in black.

Overdefining

An overdefining dimension or relation overdefines one or more entities in the sketch. An overdefining dimension appears in red.

Not Solved

The not solved dimension or relation cannot determine the position of the sketched entities. The not solved dimension appears in pink.

Driven

In a sketch, the driven dimension's value is driven by other dimensions that solve the sketch. The driven dimension appears in gray.

 Tip. *While working in the sketching environment, the status bar of the SolidWorks window is divided into four areas. The **Sketch Definition** area of the status bar always displays the status of the sketch, dimension, and relation. If the sketch is underdefined, the status area will display **Under Defined**; if the sketch is overdefined, the message displayed in the status area will be **Over Defined**; if the sketch is fully defined, the message displayed in the status area will be **Fully Defined**.*

DELETING OVERDEFINING DIMENSIONS

In SolidWorks, when you add a dimension that overdefines a sketch, the sketch and dimension turn different color and the **Make Dimension Driven?** dialog box is displayed, as shown in Figure 4-44.

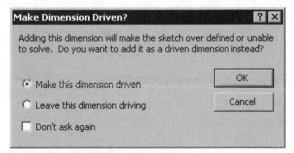

*Figure 4-44 The **Make Dimension Driven?** dialog box*

The **Make Dimension Driven?** dialog box informs you that adding this dimension will overdefine the sketch or the sketch will not be solved. You are also prompted to specify whether you want to add the dimension as driven dimension. If you select the **Make this dimension driven** radio button and choose **OK**, then the selected dimension will become a driven dimension. The driven dimension is displayed in gray and it cannot be modified. Its value depends on the value of the driver dimension. If you change the value of the driver dimension, the value of the driven dimension will be automatically changed.

If you select the **Leave this dimension driving** radio button and choose **OK**, then some of the entities and dimensions in the sketch will be displayed in red. Next, you need to delete the relation or dimension which is overdefining the sketch. In SolidWorks, the **Over Defined** button is provided in the status bar, as shown in Figure 4-45.

*Figure 4-45 The **Over Defined** button in the status bar*

To resolve the overdefining relations or dimensions, click on the **Over Defined** button displayed in the status bar; the **SketchXpert PropertyManager** will be displayed, as shown in Figure 4-46. You can choose the **Diagnose** button in the **Message** rollout to automatically resolve the possible errors or choose the **Manual Repair** button to resolve the errors manually. On choosing the **Diagnose** button, the relations or dimensions that need to be deleted will be displayed in the **Results** rollout. Also, in the **More Information/Options** rollout, the conflicting relations will be listed. Choose the arrows in the **Results** rollout to view various solutions. In SolidWorks, on choosing the arrows, the additional relation or the dimension to be deleted will be displayed with a strike mark. Figure 4-47 shows the sketch that is overdefined because of the additional vertical dimension 100. Figure 4-48 shows the striked out additional vertical relation. To remove a particular relation or dimension, choose the **Accept** button

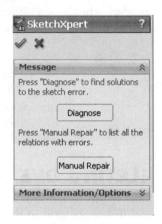

*Figure 4-46 The **SketchXpert** PropertyManager*

in the **Results** rollout; the striked out relation or dimension will be removed and the sketch will be fully defined. Also, a message informing you that the sketch is now fully defined will be displayed in the **SketchXpert PropertyManager**. Choose the **OK** button.

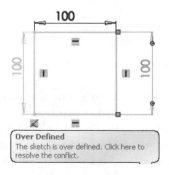

Figure 4-47 The overdefined sketch

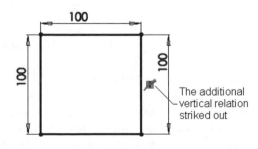

Figure 4-48 The additional vertical relation striked out

Choose the **Manual Repair** button from the **Message** rollout; the relations or dimensions that are responsible for over defining the sketch are displayed in the **Conflicting Relations/Dimensions** rollout, as shown in Figure 4-49. Select any of the relation or dimension that is responsible for over defining the sketch and choose the **Delete** button. If the over defining status of the sketch is removed, then the **Message** rollout displays a message in green that the sketch can now find a valid solution. If the dimensions or relations deleted are not sufficient to find a valid solution, the **Conflicting Relations/Dimensions** rollout is still displayed. Therefore, you need to delete few more dimensions or relations to remove the overdefining status from the sketch.

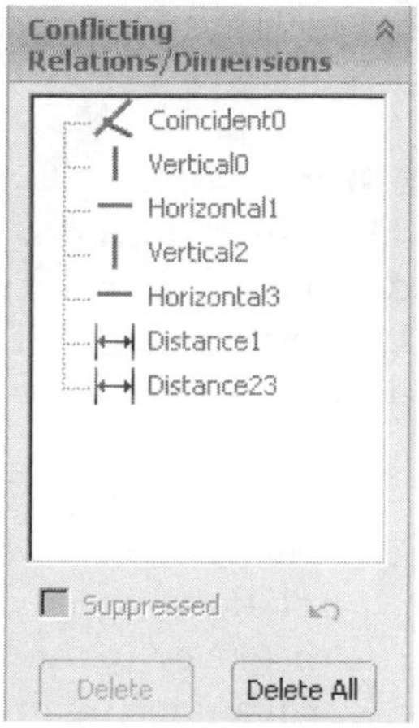

Figure 4-49 The Conflicting Relations/Dimensions rollout

You need to delete the relation or dimension displayed in red to make sure that the sketch is no longer overdefined. When the sketch is not overdefined any more, the **Message** rollout in the **SketchXpert PropertyManager** will inform you that the sketch is no longer overdefined. Choose **OK** from the **SketchXpert PropertyManager**; the sketch will be displayed in black or blue, depending on the current state of the sketch. Note that if you select the **Always open this dialog box when sketch error occurs** check box in the **More Informations/Options** rollout of the **SketchXpert PropertyManager**, the **SketchXpert PropertyManager** will be displayed automatically when a sketch is overdefined.

You can also prevent the sketch from being overdefined by choosing the **Cancel** button from the **Make Dimension Driven?** dialog box. If you choose **Cancel** from the **Make Dimension Driven?** dialog box, the **SolidWorks** information dialog box will be displayed with a message that the sketch is no longer overdefined.

Displaying and Deleting Relations

CommandManager:	Sketch > Display/Delete Relations
SolidWorks menus:	Tools > Relations > Display/Delete
Toolbar:	Sketch > Display/Delete Relations

If the sketch is overdefined after adding the dimensions and relations, you need to delete some of the overdefining, dangling, or not solved relations or dimensions. You can view and delete the relations applied to the sketch using the **Display/Delete Relations PropertyManager**. To invoke this **PropertyManager**, choose the **Display/Delete Relations** button from the **Sketch CommandManager**. You can also right-click in the drawing area to display the shortcut menu and choose the **Display/Delete Relations** option; the **Display/Delete Relations PropertyManager** will be displayed as shown in Figure 4-50. The rollouts in this **PropertyManager** are discussed next.

Relations Rollout

The **Relations** rollout is used to check, delete, and suppress the unwanted and conflicting relations. The status of the sketch or the selected entity is displayed below the **Relations** list

in this rollout. The options in the **Relations** rollout are
discussed next.

Filter

The **Filter** drop-down list is used to select the filter to
display the relations in the **Sketch Relation
PropertyManager**. The options in the **Filter** drop-down
list are discussed next.

All in this sketch

The **All in this sketch** option is used to display all
relations applied to the sketch. The first relation
displayed in the list will be selected by default and it
will appear against a blue background. The status of
the selected relations is displayed below the list box
in the **Relations** rollout. The overdefined relations
are highlighted in yellowish green. If you select a
relation highlighted in yellowish green in the
Relations rollout, the status of the selected relation
will be displayed as **Over Defining**. The dangling
relation is highlighted in brownish green. When you
select the dangling relation, the status of the relation

*Figure 4-50 The **Display/Delete
Relations PropertyManager***

will be displayed as **Dangling** below the **Relations** list. Similarly, the not solved relation
will be highlighted in yellow and the driven relation in gray.

Dangling

This option is used to display only the dangling relations applied to the sketch.

Overdefining/Not Solved

The **Overdefining/Not Solved** option is used to display only the overdefining and
not solved relations. The dangling relations are also not solved relations. Therefore,
they will also be displayed in the list box.

External

The **External** option is used to display the relations that have a reference with an
entity outside the sketch. This entity can be an edge, vertex, or origin within the
same model or it can be an edge, vertex, or origin of different models within an
assembly.

Defined In Context

The **Defined In Context** option is used to display only the relations that are in the
context of a design. They are the relations between the sketched entity in one part
and an entity in another part. These relations are defined while working with the
top-down assemblies.

Locked

The **Locked** option is used to display only the locked relations.

Broken
The **Broken** option is used to display only the broken relations.

Note
*The **Locked** and **Broken** relations are applied while creating a part within the assembly environment. You will learn more about creating parts within an assembly in the later chapters.*

Selected Entities
The **Selected Entities** option is used to display the relations of only the selected set of entities. When you select this option from the **Filter** drop-down list, the **Selected Entities** selection box will be displayed in the **Relations** rollout. When you select an entity to display the relations, the name of the selected entity will be displayed in the **Selected Entities** selection box and the relations applied to this entity will be displayed in the **Relations** rollout. To remove the selected entity from the selection set, select it and then right-click to display the shortcut menu. Choose the **Delete** option from the shortcut menu. If you choose the **Clear Selections** option, all entities will be removed from the selection set.

Suppressed
The **Suppressed** check box is selected to suppress the selected relation. When you suppress a relation, it will be displayed in gray in the list box. The status of the suppress relation will be displayed as **Satisfied** or **Driven** in the information area. If you suppress the overdefining dimensions, the **SolidWorks** information dialog box will be displayed with a message that **The sketch is no longer over defined**. Choose the **OK** button from this dialog box.

Delete
The **Delete** button is used to delete the relation selected in the **Relations** rollout.

Delete All
The **Delete All** button is used to delete all relations that are displayed in the **Relations** rollout.

Undo last relation change
The **Undo last relation change** button is used to undo the action performed by using the **Delete**, **Replace**, or the **Suppressed** options earlier. The **Replace** option is discussed later in this chapter.

Entities Rollout
The **Entities** rollout is used to display the entities that are referred to in the selected relation. This rollout is also used to display the status of the selected relation and the external reference, if any. By default, the **Entities** rollout is collapsed. You can expand this rollout by clicking on the down arrow displayed on the right of this rollout, refer to Figure 4-51. The options in this rollout are discussed next.

Entities used in the selected relation
The **Entities used in the selected relation** area is used to display the information about the entities used in the selected relation. This area provides you the information about

the name of the entity, the status of the entity, and the place where the entity is defined. This area is divided into three columns, which are discussed next.

Entity

The **Entity** column is used to display the entity or entities to which the selected relation is applied.

Status

The **Status** column is used to display the status of the selected relation. The status can be **Fully Defined**, **Dangling**, **Over Defined**, or **Not Solved**.

Figure 4-51 *The Entities rollout*

Defined In

The **Defined In** column is used to display the placement of the entity. The entity can be placed in any of the following places:

Current Sketch

The **Current Sketch** option is displayed in the **Defined In** column when the entity is placed in the same sketch.

Same Model

The **Same Model** option is displayed in the **Defined In** column when the entity to be defined is placed in the same model. This means that the entity is placed in the same model, but outside the sketch. This entity can be an edge, vertex, or origin of the same model.

Tip. *By default, the **Override Dims on Drag/Move** option is not chosen from **Tools > Sketch Settings** menu in the SolidWorks menus. As a result, if you drag a dimensioned sketched entity, the entity will not be modified automatically. If the sketch is not fully defined, the entities that are not properly dimensioned or constrained will move. You can use this option to change a dimensioned sketched entity by dragging it.*

*By default, the **Automatic Solve** option is selected from the **Tools > Sketch Settings** menu in the SolidWorks menus. This option helps you solve the relations and dimensions automatically when you drag or modify a sketched entity. If you clear this option, a message will be displayed that will inform you that the sketch cannot be dragged because **Auto Solve** mode is off. It will further inform you to drag the sketch, please turn the **Auto Solve** mode on. If you modify the dimension value using the **Modify** dialog box, the dimension will not be updated automatically, and you have to update the new dimension manually. To update and solve the dimension, you need to choose the **Rebuild** button from the Menu Bar or press CTRL+B on the keyboard.*

External Model

The **External Model** option is displayed in the **Defined In** column when the entity is placed in some other model but within the same assembly. This entity can be an edge, vertex, or origin of a different model, but in the same assembly.

Entity

The **Entity** display box is used to display the name of the entity and the name of the part in which the selected entity is placed. This entity is selected in the **Entity** column of the **Entities used in the selected relation** area. The selected entity is also highlighted in the drawing area.

Owner

The **Owner** display box is used to display the name of the model in which the entity is placed when the **External Model** option is displayed in the **Defined In** column.

Assembly

The **Assembly** display box is used to display the path of the assembly in which the entity is placed when the **External Model** option is displayed in the **Defined In** column.

Replace

The **Replace** button is used to replace the selected entity from the **Entity** column with some other entity from the drawing area. When you select the entity from the drawing area, the entity will be displayed in the **Entity to replace the one selected above** display box available right of the **Replace** button. Choose the **Replace** button to replace the entity. If the sketch is overdefined, you will be given a warning message. Sometimes after replacing the entity, the status of the entity is changed to not solved or overdefining. In such cases, you need to undo the last operation.

Options Rollout

The check box available in this rollout is selected to display the **Display/Delete PropertyManager** when the sketch becomes overdefined or cannot be solved.

Tip. *By default, the relations applied to the sketched entities are displayed when you draw them or apply a relation to them. Therefore, sometimes the sketch looks untidy as all relations concerned with the sketch are displayed. To turn off the display of these relations, choose* **View > Sketch Relations** *from the SolidWorks menus. To turn on the display of these relations, again, choose* **View > Sketch Relations** *from the SolidWorks menus.*

OPENING AN EXISTING FILE

Toolbar:	Menu Bar > Open
SolidWorks menus:	File > Open

 The **Open** dialog box is used to open an existing SolidWorks part, assembly, or drawing document. You can also use this dialog box to import files from other applications saved in some standard file formats. Choose the **Open** button from the Menu Bar, or press the CTRL+O keys to invoke the **Open** dialog box, as shown in Figure 4-52. The options in this dialog box are discussed next.

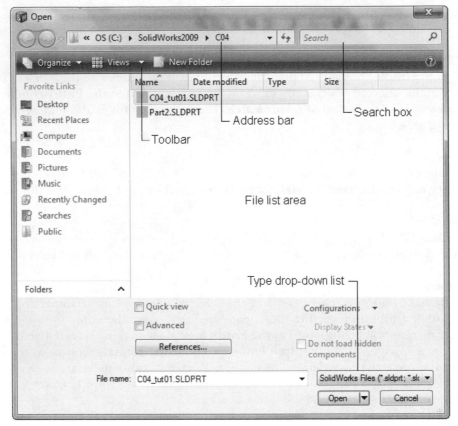

*Figure 4-52 The **Open** dialog box (displayed in Windows Vista)*

Address Bar

The **Address bar** drop-down list is used to specify the drive or directory in which the file is saved. The location of the file and the folder that you browse is displayed in this drop-down list.

File name

The name of the selected file is shown in the **File name** edit box. You can also enter the name of the file to open in this edit box.

Type Drop-down List

The **Type** drop-down list is used to specify the type of file to open. You can use this drop-down list to select a particular type of file such as the part file, assembly file, drawing file, all SolidWorks files, and so on. You can also define the standard file format in this drop-down list to import the files saved in those file formats.

Open as Read-Only

The **Open as Read-Only** option is selected to open the document as a read-only file. This option is available in the flyout that will be displayed on choosing the down arrow on the right of the **Open** button. If you modify the design in a read-only file, the changes will be saved in a new file, and the original file will not be modified. This option also allows other users to access the document while it is open on your computer.

Quick view

The **Quick view** check box is selected to open a SolidWorks document in the view-only format. When you open a view-only file, only the tools related to viewing the models are enabled. The rest of the tools will not be available. Therefore, you cannot make any modifications in the view-only document. You can use only the zoom, pan, or dynamically rotate tools. However, if you want to edit the design, right-click in the drawing area and choose the **Edit** option from the shortcut menu; all tools will be available to edit the design.

References

The **References** button is used to check the references of an assembly or a drawing.

Configurations

The configurations available in the selected file are displayed in this drop-down list. Select the required configuration from this drop-down list.

Display States Area

The options in this area will be available if the selected file is an assembly file. Select the required display state from the drop-down list in this area. If you select the **Do not load hidden components** check box, the components that are in the hidden state will not be displayed.

TUTORIALS

Tutorial 1

In this tutorial, you will draw the sketch of the model shown in Figure 4-53. This is the same sketch that was drawn in Tutorial 4 of Chapter 2. You will draw the sketch using the mirror line and then add the required relations and dimensions to it. The sketch is shown in Figure 4-54. The solid model is given only for reference.   **(Expected time: 30 min)**

The following steps are required to complete this tutorial:

a. Start SolidWorks and then start a new part document.
b. Create a mirror line using the **Centerline** and **Dynamic Mirror** tool.
c. Draw the sketch of the model on one side of the mirror line so that it is automatically drawn on the other side, refer to Figures 4-55 through 4-60.
d. Add the required relations to the sketch, refer to Figures 4-61 and 4-62.
e. Add the required dimensions to the sketch and fully define the sketch, refer to Figure 4-63.
f. Save the sketch and then close the document.

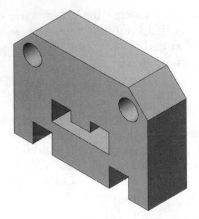

Figure 4-53 *Solid Model for Tutorial 1*   *Figure 4-54* *Sketch of the model*

Starting SolidWorks and Starting a New Part Document

1. Start SolidWorks by double-clicking on the shortcut icon of SolidWorks 2009 available on the desktop of your computer.

    The SolidWorks 2009 window is displayed and the **SolidWorks Resources** task pane is displayed on the right of the SolidWorks window.

2. Choose the **New** button from the Menu Bar; the **New SolidWorks Document** dialog box is displayed.

3. The **Part** button is chosen by default. Choose the **OK** button from the **New SolidWorks Document** dialog box; a new SolidWorks part document is started.

4. Choose the **Sketch** button from the **Sketch CommandManager** and then select the **Front Plane** to invoke the sketching environment.

    In the previous chapters, you used the grid and snap settings to create the sketches. From this chapter onward, it is recommended that not to use those settings. This way you can get familiar with drawing sketches at arbitrary locations and then using dimensions and relations to move them to their actual locations.

5. If the grid is displayed, invoke the **System Options - Relations/Snaps** dialog box and then clear the **Grid** check box from the **Sketch snaps** area to hide the grid.

6. Set the units for measuring linear dimensions to millimeters and the units for angular dimensions to degree using the **Document Properties - Units** dialog box. However, if you selected millimeters as units while installing SolidWorks, you can skip this point.

Drawing the Mirror Line

In this tutorial, you will draw the sketch of the given model with the help of the **Dynamic Mirror** tool. So, when you draw an entity on one side of the centerline, the same entity is drawn automatically on the other side of it. Also, the symmetrical relation is applied to the entities on both sides of the centerline. Therefore, if you modify an entity on one side of the centerline, the same modification is reflected in the mirrored entity and vice versa. However, to follow these steps, you first need to draw a centerline to proceed to the next steps.

The origin of the sketching environment is placed at the center of the drawing area and you need to create the sketch in the first quadrant. Therefore, it is recommended that you modify the drawing area such that the area in the first quadrant is increased. This can be done using the **Pan** tool.

1. Press CTRL and the middle mouse button and drag the cursor toward the bottom left corner of the drawing area.

2. Choose **Line > Centerline** from the **Sketch CommandManager**; the **Insert Line PropertyManager** is displayed.

3. Move the line cursor to a location whose coordinates are close to 45 mm, 70 mm, 0 mm. You do not need to move the cursor exactly to this location. You can move it to a point close to this location.

4. Specify the start point of the centerline and move the line cursor vertically downward to draw a line of length close to 80 mm.

   As soon as you specify the endpoint of the centerline, a rubber-band line is attached to the line cursor. Right-click to display the shortcut menu and choose the **Select** option from the shortcut menu to exit the **Line** tool.

5. Press F key; the sketch is zoomed and it fits on the screen.

6. Select the centerline and choose **Tools > Sketch Tools > Dynamic Mirror** from the SolidWorks menus to convert the centerline into a mirror line.

Drawing the Sketch

You will draw the sketch on the right of the mirror line and the same sketch will automatically be drawn on the other side of the mirror line.

1. Choose the **Line** button from the **Sketch CommandManager**; the arrow cursor is replaced by the line cursor.

2. Move the line cursor close to the centerline; the cursor snaps to the mirror line and a coincident symbol is displayed below the cursor.

3. Specify the start point of the line at this point and move the cursor horizontally toward the right. Specify the endpoint of the line when its length above the line cursor shows a value close to 15. As soon as you press the left mouse button to specify the endpoint of the line, a line of the same length is drawn automatically on the other side of the mirror

line. Figure 4-55 shows the mirrored entity created automatically on the other side of the mirror line. The display of relations in this figure can be turned off by choosing **Hide/Show Items > View Sketch Relations** from the **Heads-up View** toolbar.

Note that the mirrored entity that is automatically created on the left of the mirror line is merged with the line drawn on the right. Therefore, the entire line becomes a single entity. The mirror image of the line will merge with the line you draw only if one of the endpoints of the line is coincident with the mirror line.

4. Move the cursor vertically upward. Specify the endpoint of the line when the length of the line on the line cursor displays a value close to 10. Figure 4-56 shows the sketch after drawing the vertical lines.

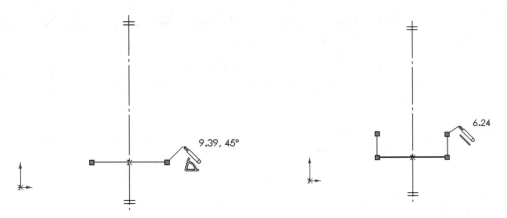

Figure 4-55 *Sketching using automatic mirroring*   ***Figure 4-56*** *Left line drawn by mirroring*

5. Move the line cursor horizontally toward the right. Specify the endpoint of the line when the length of the line on the line cursor displays a value close to 10.

6. Move the line cursor vertically downward. Specify the endpoint when the length of the line on the line cursor displays a value close to 10.

7. Move the line cursor horizontally toward the right. Specify the endpoint when the length of the line on the line cursor displays a value close to 10.

8. Move the line cursor vertically upward. Specify the endpoint when the length of the line on the line cursor displays a value close to 40.

9. Move the line cursor at an angle close to 45-degree and specify the endpoint of the line. Figure 4-57 shows the sketch after drawing this inclined line.

10. Move the line cursor horizontally toward the left. Specify the endpoint when the cursor snaps to the mirror line and the mirror line is highlighted. Double-click anywhere in the drawing area to exit the line tool. The sketch after completing the outer profile is shown in Figure 4-58.

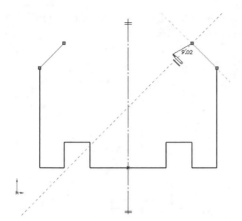

Figure 4-57 Sketch after drawing the inclined line

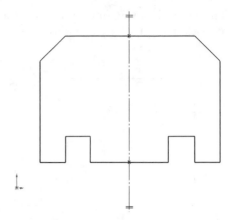

Figure 4-58 Sketch after completing the outer profile of the sketch

Next, you will draw the sketch of the inner cavity. To draw the sketch of the inner cavity, you will start with the lower horizontal line.

11. Specify the start point of the line in the mirror line and move the cursor horizontally toward the right. Specify the endpoint when the length of the line above the line cursor shows a value close to 15.

12. Move the line cursor vertically upward. Specify the endpoint when the length of the line on the line cursor displays a value close to 10.

13. Move the line cursor horizontally toward the left. Specify the endpoint when the length of the line on the line cursor displays a value close to 10.

14. Move the line cursor vertically downward. Specify the endpoint when the length of the line on the line cursor displays a value close to 5.

15. Move the line cursor horizontally toward the left. Specify the endpoint when the line cursor snaps to the mirror line.

16. Double-click anywhere in the drawing area to end the line creation. The sketch, after completing the inner cavity, is shown in Figure 4-59.

17. Choose the **Circle** button from the **Sketch CommandManager** to invoke the **Circle** tool.

18. Move the circle cursor to the point where the inferencing line originating from the endpoints of the inclined line intersect.

19. Specify the center of the circle at this point and move the circle cursor toward the left to define the radius of the circle. Press the left mouse button when the radius of the circle above the circle cursor shows a value close to 5.

The circle is automatically mirrored on the other side of the mirror line. The sketch, after drawing the circle, is shown in Figure 4-60.

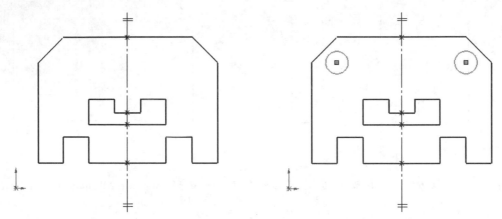

Figure 4-59 *Sketch after drawing the inner cavity*   **Figure 4-60** *Sketch after drawing the circle*

20. Exit the **Dynamic Mirror** tool by choosing **Tools > Sketch Tools > Dynamic Mirror** from the SolidWorks menus.

Adding the Required Relations

After drawing the sketch, you need to add relations using the **Add Relations PropertyManager**. The relations are applied to a sketch to constrain its degree of freedom, to reduce the number of dimensions in the sketch, and also to capture the design intent of the sketch.

1. Press the ESC key to remove the circles created previously from the selection set.

2. Choose **Display/Delete Relations > Add Relation** from the **Sketch CommandManager**; the **Add Relations PropertyManager** is displayed. Also, the confirmation corner is displayed at the upper right corner of the drawing area.

3. Select the center point of the circle on the right and then select the lower endpoint of the right inclined line. The names of the selected entities are displayed in the **Selected Entities** rollout of the **Add Relations PropertyManager**.

The relations that can be applied to the two selected entities are displayed in the **Add Relations** rollout of the **Add Relations PropertyManager**, as shown in Figure 4-61. The **Horizontal** option is highlighted, suggesting that the horizontal relation is the most appropriate relation for the selected entities.

 Tip. *If you have generated the drawing views of the current model, as soon as you suppress any feature in the model, it will not be displayed in the drawing views. Similarly, as soon as you unsuppress the feature, it will be displayed in the views.*

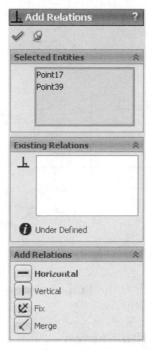

*Figure 4-61 The **Add Relations** PropertyManager*

Note
*The names of the entities displayed in the **Selected Entities** rollout of the **Add Relations** PropertyManager may be different from those displayed on your computer screen.*

4. Choose the **Horizontal** button from the **Add Relations** rollout to apply the **Horizontal** relation to the selected entities.

5. Move the cursor to the drawing area and right-click to display the shortcut menu. Choose the **Clear Selections** option to remove the selected entities from the selection set.

6. Select the center point of the circle on the right and the upper endpoint of the right inclined line.

    The relations that can be applied to the selected entities are displayed and the **Vertical** button is highlighted in the **Add Relations** rollout.

7. Choose the **Vertical** button from the **Add Relations** PropertyManager. Right-click in the drawing area and choose the **Clear Selections** option.

8. Select the entities, as shown in Figure 4-62. Choose the **Equal** button in the **Add Relations** rollout in the **Add Relations** PropertyManager.

9. Choose the **OK** button from the **Add Relations** PropertyManager or choose **OK** from

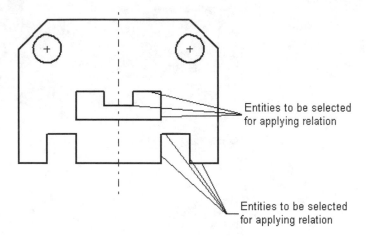

Entities to be selected
for applying relation

Entities to be selected
for applying relation

Figure 4-62 *Entities to be selected to apply the **Equal** relation*

the confirmation corner to close the **PropertyManager**. Click anywhere in the drawing area to clear the selected entities.

Applying Dimensions to the Sketch

Next, you will apply the dimensions and fully define the sketch. As mentioned earlier, the sketched entities are shown in blue, suggesting that the sketch is underdefined. It will be changed to black after you apply the required dimensions to the sketch. This indicates that the sketch is fully defined.

1. Choose **Options** from the Menu Bar; the **System Options - General** dialog box is displayed. Select the **Input dimension value** check box, if it is cleared, and choose **OK** from the **System Options - General** dialog box. This check box is selected to invoke the **Modify** dialog box to enter a new dimension value and modify the sketch as you place the dimension.

2. Choose the **Smart Dimension** button from the **Sketch CommandManager**. You can also right-click in the drawing area and choose the **Smart Dimension** option.

   The cursor is replaced by the dimension cursor.

3. Move the dimension cursor to the lower right horizontal line; the line is highlighted.

4. Select the line; a linear dimension is attached to the cursor.

5. Move the cursor downward and click to place the dimension below the line, refer to Figure 4-63. As you place the dimension, the **Modify** dialog box is displayed.

6. Enter the dimension value **10** in this dialog box and press ENTER, the dimension is placed and the length of line is also modified to **10**.

7. Move the dimension cursor to the lower-middle horizontal line, refer to Figure 4-63. Select the line when the line is highlighted; a dimension is attached to the cursor.

8. Move the cursor downward and click to place the dimension. Enter the value **30** in the **Modify** dialog box and press ENTER.

9. Move the cursor to the outer left vertical line and when the color of the line is highlighted, select the line; a dimension is attached to the cursor.

10. Move the cursor to the left and then click to place the dimension. Enter the value **40** in the **Modify** dialog box and press ENTER.

11. Select the right inclined line; a dimension is attached to the cursor. Move the cursor vertically upward to apply the horizontal dimension to the selected line. Click to place the dimension at an appropriate place, see Figure 4-63.

12. Enter the value **10** in the **Modify** dialog box and press ENTER.

13. Again, select the right aligned line; a dimension is attached to the cursor. Move the cursor horizontally toward the right to apply the vertical dimension for the selected line. Click to place the dimension at an appropriate place, see Figure 4-63.

14. Enter a value of **10** in the **Modify** dialog box and press ENTER.

15. Move the cursor to the left circle and when the circle is highlighted, select it. A diameter dimension is attached to the cursor. Move the cursor outside the sketch.

16. Place the diameter dimension. Enter the value **10** in the **Modify** dialog box and press ENTER.

17. Select the lower horizontal line of the inner cavity; a linear dimension is attached to the cursor. Select the lower right horizontal line of the outer loop.

    A vertical dimension between the lower horizontal line of the inner cavity and the lower right horizontal line of the outer sketch is attached to the cursor.

18. Move the cursor horizontally toward the right and place the dimension. Enter the value **15** in the **Modify** dialog box and press ENTER.

19. Select the inner right vertical line of the cavity and place the dimension outside the sketch. Enter the value **5** in the **Modify** dialog box and press ENTER.

20. Select the lower left horizontal line of the outer sketch and the origin.

21. Move the cursor horizontally toward the left and place the dimension. Enter a value of **10** in the **Modify** dialog box.

Notice that some of the entities are displayed in black. This indicates that these entities are now fully defined. But you have to fully define the entire sketch. So you need to add some more dimensions.

22. Select the left vertical line of the outer sketch and the origin. Move the cursor vertically downward and place the dimension. Enter the value **10** in the **Modify** dialog box.

Notice that now all entities are displayed in black. This indicates that the sketch is fully defined. If the sketch is not fully defined, then you have to add a dimension between the outer right vertical line and the outer left vertical line. The value of the dimension should be maintained to 70. The fully defined sketch after applying all required relations and dimensions is shown in Figure 4-63.

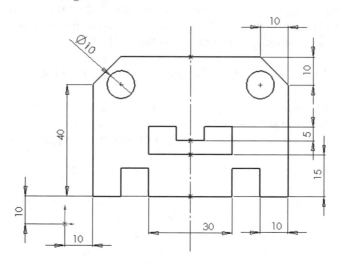

Figure 4-63 Fully defined sketch after applying all the required relations and dimensions

Saving the Sketch

1. Choose the **Save** button from the Menu Bar to invoke the **Save As** dialog box. Browse to the \My Documents\SolidWorks folder. Choose the **Create New Folder** button from the **Save As** dialog box. Enter the name of the folder as c04 and press ENTER.

2. Enter the name of the document as c04tut1 in the **File name** edit box and choose the **Save** button. The document will be saved in the \My Documents\SolidWorks\c04 folder.

3. Close the document by choosing **File > Close** from the SolidWorks menus.

Tutorial 2

In this tutorial, you will draw the sketch of the revolved model shown in Figure 4-64. The sketch of the feature is shown in Figure 4-65. The solid model is given only for your reference.

(Expected time: 30 min)

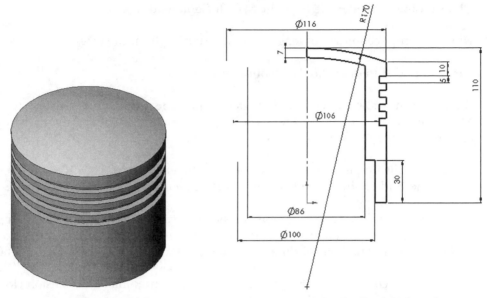

Figure 4-64 *Solid model of the piston*   **Figure 4-65** *The sketch of the base feature*

The following steps are required to complete this tutorial:

a. Start a new part document and then invoke the sketching environment.
b. Draw a centerline that will be used to add the linear diameter dimensions to the sketch of the piston.
c. Create the sketch using various sketching tools, refer to Figures 4-66 and 4-67.
d. Use the **Offset Entities** tool to offset the required lines, refer to Figure 4-68.
e. Draw the arcs and trim the unwanted entities, refer to Figure 4-70.
f. Add the required relations.
g. Add the required dimensions and fully define the sketch, refer to Figure 4-72.

Starting a New Part Document

1. Choose the **New** button from the Menu Bar; the **New SolidWorks Document** dialog box is invoked.

2. The **Part** button is chosen by default. Choose the **OK** button; a new SolidWorks part document is started.

3. Choose the **Sketch** button from the **Sketch CommandManager** and select the **Front Plane** to invoke the sketching environment.

4. Invoke the **System Options - General** dialog box and set the units and grids for this tutorial.

Drawing the Sketch

To draw the sketch of the revolved model, you need to draw the centerline around which the sketch of the base feature will be revolved.

1. Choose **Line > Centerline** from the **Sketch CommandManager**.

2. Draw a vertical centerline of length 120 mm starting from the origin.

   Next, you need to draw the sketch of the piston.

3. Right-click in the drawing area and choose the **Line** option from the shortcut menu. Move the cursor to a location whose coordinates are close to 58 mm, 0 mm, 0 mm. Click at this point to specify the start point of the line.

4. Move vertically upward and left-click when the dimension is close to 100. Right-click and choose the **End chain** option from the shortcut menu, refer to Line 1 in Figure 4-66.

5. Move the cursor to the lower endpoint of the line drawn earlier. Specify the start point of the line when the end point is highlighted. Move the cursor horizontally toward the left and draw a horizontal line of dimension close to 8, refer to Line 2 in Figure 4-66.

6. Move the line cursor vertically upward and draw a vertical line of dimension close to 30, refer to Line 3 in Figure 4-66.

7. Move the cursor horizontally toward the left and draw a horizontal line of dimension close to 7. Sketch after drawing the horizontal line is shown in Figure 4-66.

8. Move the line cursor vertically upward and draw a vertical line of dimension close to 70.

9. Right-click and choose the **3 Point Arc** option from the shortcut menu. Move the cursor near the upper endpoint of the right vertical line.

10. Specify the first point of the arc when the endpoint is highlighted. Move the cursor horizontally toward the left; the reference arc is attached to the cursor. Specify the second point of the arc when the value of the length is close to 116, refer to Figure 4-67.

11. Move the cursor toward the right. Specify the third point of the arc when the value of the radius is close to 170, refer to Figure 4-67.

12. Invoke the **Line** tool. Move the line cursor near the outer vertical line on the right-side and specify the start point of the line on this line such that the start point is on the vertical line and its Y and Z coordinates are close to 90, 0.

13. Move the cursor horizontally toward the left to draw a line of a dimension close to 5. Double-click anywhere in the drawing area to end the line creation. The sketch after drawing the horizontal line is shown in Figure 4-67.

14. Choose **Zoom To Fit** from the **Heads-up View** toolbar to fit the sketch in the drawing area.

Offsetting the Lines

You need to offset the entities created earlier using the **Offset Entities** tool.

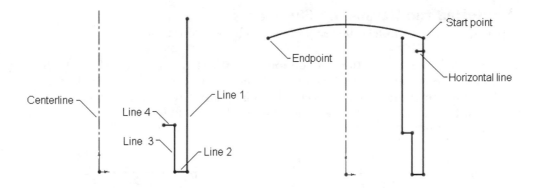

*Figure 4-66 Sketch drawn using the **Line** tool*   *Figure 4-67 Sketch after drawing the arc and line*

1. Invoke the **Select** tool to select the line of 5 mm length created earlier.

2. Choose the **Offset Entities** button from the **Sketch CommandManager** to invoke the **Offset Entities PropertyManager**. The confirmation corner is also displayed at the upper right corner of the drawing area.

3. Choose the **Keep Visible** button from the **Offset Entities PropertyManager** to pin the **PropertyManager**.

4. Set the value in the **Offset Distance** spinner to **5**. Now, select the **Reverse** check box to offset the entity in the reverse direction. The preview of the entity to be offset is modified in the drawing area.

5. Choose the **OK** button from the **Offset Entities PropertyManager**.

    You will notice that an entity is created at an offset distance of 5 mm from the original entity. Also, a dimension is applied between the newly created entity and the original entity with a value of **5**. This dimension is the offset distance between the two entities.

6. Select the newly created entity. Move the cursor vertically downward; the preview of the entity and the direction of the offset creation are also displayed. Press the left mouse button to offset the selected line.

    Repeat this procedure of offsetting the entities until you get eight entities, including the original entity.

7. Set the value in the **Offset Distance** spinner to **7** and clear the **Select chain** check box. Now, select the upper arc. The preview of the offset arc is displayed in the drawing area.

8. Choose the **OK** button twice from the **Offset Entities PropertyManager**. The sketch after creating the offset entities is as shown in Figure 4-68.

Completing the Remaining Sketch

Next, you will complete the remaining sketch using the **Line** tool.

1. Right-click and choose the **Line** option from the shortcut menu. Move the line cursor close to the left endpoint of the original line that was used to create offset lines. When the endpoint is highlighted, specify the start point. Specify the endpoint of the line at the end point of the last offset line. The sketch after drawing the vertical line is shown in Figure 4-69.

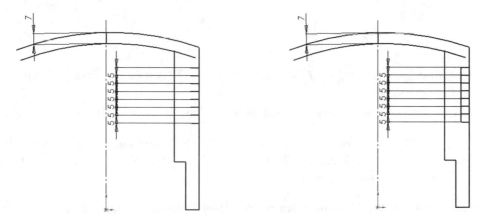

Figure 4-68 Sketch after offsetting the entities   *Figure 4-69 Sketch after drawing the vertical line*

2. Move the cursor to the intersection point of the upper arc and the centerline. When the cursor snaps to the intersection, draw a vertical line that snaps to the intersection point of the lower arc and the centerline.

Trimming the Unwanted Entities

Next, you will trim the unwanted entities using the **Trim Entities** tool.

1. Choose the **Trim Entities** button from the **Sketch CommandManager**.

2. Choose the **Trim to closest** button from the **Trim PropertyManager** and trim the unwanted entities using the left mouse button. When you trim the arc, a message stating that the trimming will delete the relations will be displayed. Choose **OK**. The sketch after trimming the unwanted entities is shown in Figure 4-70.

Adding the Required Relations

Now, you will add the required relations to the sketched entities.

1. Right-click and choose the **Select** option from the shortcut menu. Press and hold the CTRL key and select one of the endpoints of the lower horizontal line and then select the origin. Release the CTRL key after the selection; the pop-up toolbar will be displayed. Choose the **Make Horizontal** option from the pop-up toolbar to add the horizontal relation to the selected entities. Click anywhere in the drawing area to clear the selection set.

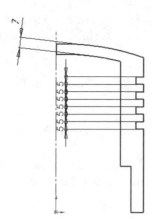

Figure 4-70 *Sketch after trimming the unwanted entities*

2. Press and hold the CTRL key and then select the horizontal lines created by offsetting. Release the CTRL key after making the selection; a pop-up toolbar will be displayed. Choose the **Make Equal** option to apply the **Equal** relation.

3. Zoom out using the **Zoom In/Out** tool and apply the Vertical relation between the center point of the upper arc and the centerline.

Adding Dimensions to the Sketch

After drawing, editing, and applying the relations to the sketch, you need to add the required dimensions to fully define the sketch.

1. Select the dimension with the value **7**, which is placed between the upper arcs and press the DELETE key to delete this dimension.

    This dimension needs to be deleted because during the design and manufacturing practices, the dimension between the tangents should be avoided.

2. Right-click and choose the **Smart Dimension** option from the shortcut menu to invoke the **Dimension** tool.

3. Now, select the inner vertical line and then select the centerline, refer to Figure 4-71. Move the cursor to the other side of the centerline and click to place the dimension below the sketch.

4. Enter the value **86** in the **Modify** dialog box and press ENTER.

5. Now, select the middle vertical line and then select the centerline, refer to Figure 4-71. Move the cursor to the other side of the centerline and click to place the dimension below the sketch.

6. Enter the value **100** in the **Modify** dialog box and press ENTER.

7. Select the outer vertical line, refer to Figure 4-71. Now, select the centerline and move the cursor to the other side of the centerline. You will notice that the diameter dimension is displayed along the cursor.

8. Click to place the dimension above the sketch and enter the value **116** in the **Modify** dialog box and press ENTER.

9. Add the remaining dimensions to fully define the sketch.

10. Select one of the dimensions that are created after offsetting the entities, use the left mouse button and drag the cursor toward the right and left-click to place the dimension at an appropriate place.

11. Arrange all dimensions using the above method. The fully defined sketch is shown in Figure 4-72. In this figure, the display of relations is turned off.

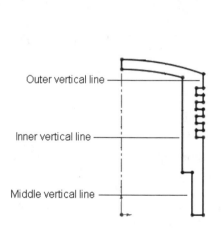

Figure 4-71 *Reference to create the dimension*

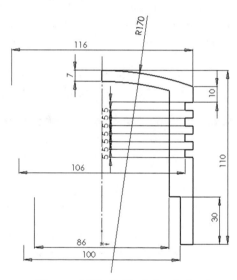

Figure 4-72 *Fully defined sketch*

Saving the Sketch

1. Choose the **Save** button from the Menu Bar and save the sketch with the name and location as *My Documents\SolidWorks\c04\c04tut2.sldprt*.

2. Choose **File > Close** from the SolidWorks menus to close the document.

Tutorial 3

In this tutorial, you will draw the sketch of the model shown in Figure 4-73. You will draw the sketch using the mirror line and then add the required relations and dimensions to it. The sketch is shown in Figure 4-74. The solid model is given only for reference.

(Expected time: 30 min)

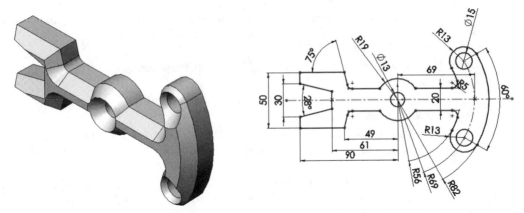

Figure 4-73 *Solid Model for Tutorial 3*   **Figure 4-74** *Sketch of the solid model*

The following steps are required to complete this tutorial:

a. Start a new document file.
b. Create a mirror line.
c. Draw the sketch on one side of the mirror line, refer to Figures 4-75 through 4-80.
d. Trim the arcs and circles and add the fillets, refer to Figures 4-81 through 4-83.
e. Add the required relations.
f. Add the required dimensions and fully define the sketch, refer to Figure 4-84.

Starting a New Document and Invoking the Sketching Environment

1. Choose the **New** button from the Menu Bar; the **New SolidWorks Document** dialog box is invoked.

2. The **Part** button is chosen by default. Choose the **OK** button; a new SolidWorks part document is started.

3. Choose the **Sketch** button from the **Sketch CommandManager** and select the **Front Plane** to invoke the sketching environment.

Drawing the Mirror Line

Similar to the first tutorial, you will draw the sketch of the given model with the help of a mirror line.

1. Increase the display of the drawing area using the **Zoom In/Out** tool and choose **Line > Centerline** from the **Sketch CommandManager**.

2. Move the line cursor to a location whose coordinates are close to -102 mm, 0 mm, 0 mm. You do not need to move the cursor exactly to this location. You can move it to a point close to this location.

3. Specify the start point of the centerline at this point and move the line cursor horizontally toward the right. Specify the endpoint of the centerline when the length of the line

shows a value close to 204. Double-click anywhere in the drawing area to exit the **Line** tool.

4. Choose the **Zoom to Fit** button from the **Heads-up View** toolbar to fit the sketch in the drawing area.

Drawing the Sketch

You will draw the sketch on the upper side of the mirror line, and the same sketch will automatically reflect on the other side of the mirror line.

1. Choose **Straight Slot > Centerpoint Arc Slot** from the **Sketch** **CommandManager**; the arrow cursor is replaced by the arc cursor and the **Slot PropertyManager** is displayed.

2. Move the arc cursor close to the origin. Specify the center point of the slot when the cursor snaps to the origin. Next, move the cursor toward the right and below the horizontal axis to a location, where the radius of the slot above the arc cursor is close to 69, refer to Figure 4-75. Click at this point to specify the start point of the slot.

3. Move the arc cursor in the counterclockwise direction. Specify the endpoint of the arc slot when the value of the angle above the arc cursor is close to 60-degree; a reference slot is attached to the cursor. Specify the point in the drawing area, where the value of width of the slot is close to 26 mm, refer to the Figure 4-76.

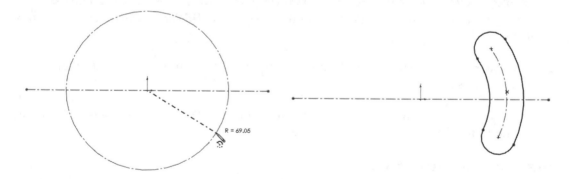

Figure 4-75 *Specifying the start point of the slot*   *Figure 4-76* *The sketch after drawing the slot*

4. Choose the **Display/Delete Relations > Add Relation** from the **Sketch** **CommandManager**; the **Add Relations PropertyManager** is invoked.

5. Right-click in the drawing area and choose the **Clear Selections** option from the shortcut menu to clear the selections from the selection set. Select the centerline and the coordinate point of the slot, as shown in Figure 4-77; the **Coincident** button is highlighted in bold in the **Add Relations** rollout of the **Add Relation PropertyManager**. This indicates that the Coincident relation is the most appropriate relation for the selected entities.

7. Choose the **Coincident** button from the **Add Relations PropertyManager**.

8. Choose the **OK** button from the **Add Relations PropertyManager** or choose **OK** from the confirmation corner. The sketch after applying the coincident relation is shown in Figure 4-78.

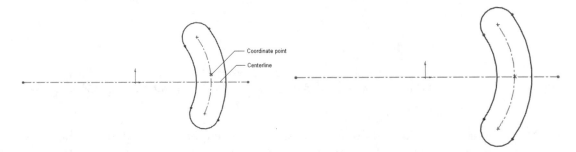

Figure 4-77 The centerline and the coordinate point to be selected

Figure 4-78 The sketch after applying the coincident relation

9. Choose **Tools > Sketch Tools > Dynamic Mirror** from the SolidWorks menus and select the centerline; the centerline is converted into a mirror line.

10. Invoke the **Line** tool from the **Sketch CommandManager** and move the cursor to the point whose coordinates are close to -61, 0, 0.

11. Specify this point as the start point of the line and move the cursor vertically upward to draw a line of length close to 7.

12. Move the cursor toward the left at an angle of 14-degree to the horizontal axis and specify the endpoint of the line where the length of the line is close to 30; the mirrored entities are created on the other side.

13. Move the cursor vertically upward and specify the endpoint of the vertical line where the length of the line is close to 10.

14. Move the cursor horizontally toward the right and specify the endpoint where the length of the line above the line cursor is close to 42.

15. Move the cursor downward at an angle of 105-degree and specify the endpoint of the line where the length is close to 15. The sketch after drawing the inclined line is shown in Figure 4-79.

16. Move the cursor horizontally toward the right and specify the endpoint when the line cursor snaps to the left arc of the slot, as shown in Figure 4-80.

17. Choose the **Circle** button from the **Sketch CommandManager**.

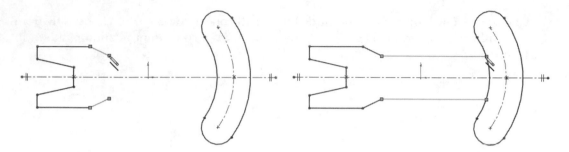

Figure 4-79 *Sketch after drawing the inclined line*   **Figure 4-80** *The line cursor snapping to the slot arc*

18. Move the cursor to the end point of the slot and specify the center point of the circle when the centerpoint is highlighted. Next, move the cursor horizontally toward the right. Now, press the left mouse button when the radius of the circle above the circle cursor is about 7.5. Figure 4-81 shows the sketch after drawing two circles.

19. Right-click and choose **Recent Commands > Dynamic Mirror Entities** to exit the **Dynamic Mirror** tool.

20. Choose the **Circle** button from the **Sketch CommandManager**.

21. Move the cursor to the origin and when it is highlighted, specify the center point of the circle. Next, move the cursor horizontally toward the right and press the left mouse button when the radius of the circle above the circle cursor shows a value close to 6.5.

22. Move the cursor to the origin and when it is highlighted, specify the center point of the circle. Next, move the cursor horizontally toward the right and press the left mouse button when the radius of the circle above the circle cursor displays a value close to 19.

The sketch, after drawing the required slot, circles, and lines is shown in Figure 4-82.

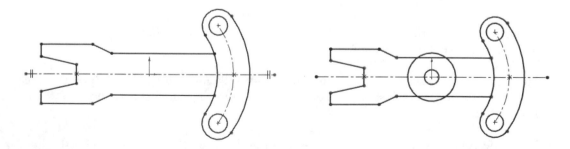

Figure 4-81 *Sketch after drawing two circles*   **Figure 4-82** *Sketch after drawing circles and lines*

Trimming the Unwanted Entities

After drawing the sketch, you need to trim some of the unwanted sketched entities using the **Trim Entities** tool.

1. Choose the **Trim Entities** button from the **Sketch CommandManager** to display the **Trim PropertyManager**.

2. Choose the **Trim to closest** button from the **Options** rollout, if it is not selected by default; the select cursor is replaced by the trim cursor.

3. Select the entities to be trimmed, as shown in Figure 4-83; the entities are dynamically trimmed.

 Note
*While trimming the unwanted sketches of the slot, the **SolidWorks 2009** message box is displayed with the message **This trim operation will destroy the slot entity. Do you want to continue?**. Choose the **OK** button to continue the trimming operation.*

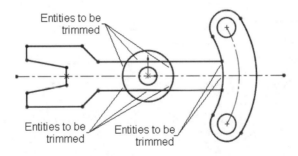

Figure 4-83 The entities to be trimmed

Filleting the Sketched Entities

Next, you need to fillet the sketched entities. The fillets are generally added to avoid the stress concentration at sharp corners.

1. Choose the **Sketch Fillet** button from the **Sketch CommandManager**. Set the value **5** in the **Radius** spinner of the **Sketch Fillet PropertyManager**.

2. Select the entities shown in Figure 4-84 to apply the fillet.

3. Choose the **OK** button from the **Sketch Fillet PropertyManager** to exit the **Fillet** tool. The sketch after adding the fillets is shown in Figure 4-85.

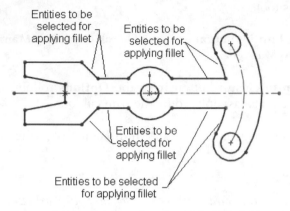

Figure 4-84 *Entities to be selected for filleting*

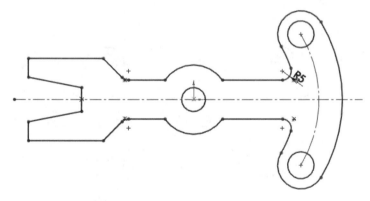

Figure 4-85 *Sketch after adding fillets*

Adding Dimensions to the Sketch

Next, you will apply the required dimensions to the sketch and fully define it.

1. Choose the **Smart Dimension** button from the **Sketch CommandManager** to invoke the dimension tool; the arrow cursor is replaced by the dimension cursor.

2. Select the construction arc of the slot that is displayed as a construction entity; a radius dimension is attached to the cursor. Move the cursor away from the sketch toward the right and place the dimension.

3. Enter the value **69** in the **Modify** dialog box and press ENTER.

4. Select the upper arc of the slot; a radius dimension is attached to the cursor. Move the cursor away from the sketch toward the right and place the dimension.

5. Enter the value **13** in the **Modify** dialog box and press ENTER.

6. Select the origin and the start point of the construction arc of the slot; a dimension is attached to the cursor. Next, select the endpoint of the construction arc; an angular dimension is attached to the cursor. Place the angular dimension outside the sketch.

7. Enter the angular dimension value **60** in the **Modify** dialog box and press ENTER.

8. Select the upper right circle; a diameter dimension is attached to the cursor. Place the dimension outside the sketch.

9. Enter the diameter dimension value **15** in the **Modify** dialog box and press ENTER.

10. Select the upper right horizontal line and the lower right horizontal line that coincides with the trimmed circle, refer to Figure 4-86. A vertical dimension is attached to the cursor. Move the cursor vertically upward and click to place the dimension.

11. Enter the value **20** in the **Modify** dialog box.

12. Select the smaller circle at the origin; a diameter dimension is attached to the cursor. Move the cursor upward and place the dimension outside the sketch.

13. Enter the diameter dimension value **13** in the **Modify** dialog box.

14. Select the outer trimmed circle and place the radius dimension outside the sketch.

15. Enter the radial dimension value **19** in the **Modify** dialog box.

16. Select the upper right inclined line; a dimension is attached to the cursor. Now, select the upper left horizontal line; an angular dimension is attached to the cursor. Place the dimension above the upper left horizontal line, refer to Figure 4-86.

17. Enter the angular dimension value **75** in the **Modify** dialog box.

18. Select the origin and the lower endpoint of the lower right inclined line. Move the cursor vertically downward and place the dimension. Enter the value **49** in the **Modify** dialog box.

19. Select the origin and the middle left vertical line, refer to Figure 4-86. Move the cursor vertically downward and place the dimension below the previous dimension.

20. Enter the value **61** in the **Modify** dialog box.

21. Select the origin and the lower endpoint of the outer left vertical line. Move the cursor vertically downward and place the dimension below the last dimension.

22. Enter the value **90** in the **Modify** dialog box.

23. Select the upper left inclined line and the lower left inclined line, refer to Figure 4-86; an angular dimension is attached to the cursor. Move the cursor horizontally toward the left and place the dimension.

24. Enter the angular dimension value **28** in the **Modify** dialog box.

25. Select the upper left horizontal line and the lower left horizontal line; a linear dimension is attached to the cursor. Move the cursor horizontally toward the left and place the dimension.

26. Enter the value **50** in the **Modify** dialog box.

27. Select the lower endpoint of the upper left vertical line and the upper endpoint of the lower left vertical line; a linear dimension is attached to the cursor. Move the cursor horizontally toward the left and left-click to place the dimension.

28. Enter the value **30** in the **Modify** dialog box.

29. Add the remaining dimensions to the sketch and make a fully defined sketch. The fully defined sketch is shown in Figure 4-86.

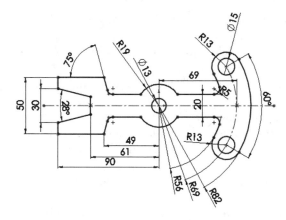

Figure 4-86 *Sketch after applying all relations and dimensions*

Saving the Sketch

1. Choose the **Save** button from the Menu Bar to invoke the **Save As** dialog box.

2. Enter the name of the document as *c04tut3* in the **File name** edit box and choose the **Save** button.

3. Close the document by choosing **File > Close** from the SolidWorks menus.

SELF-EVALUATION TEST

Answer the following questions and then compare them to those given at the end of this chapter:

1. Some relations are automatically applied to the sketch while it is being drawn. (T/F)

2. When you choose the **Add Relation** button, the **Apply Relations PropertyManager** is displayed. (T/F)

3. You can modify the arrowhead style of a selected dimension. (T/F)

4. The dimension favorite created in one document cannot be retrieved in the other document. (T/F)

5. You can make modifications in the read-only file. (T/F)

6. The _____ **PropertyManager** is displayed on invoking the **Dynamic Mirror Entities** tool.

7. The _____ dimension is used to dimension a line that is at an angle with respect to the X-axis or the Y-axis.

8. A _____ defined sketch is the one in which all entities and their positions are described by the relations or dimensions, or both.

9. The _____ dimensions or relations are not able to determine the position of one or more sketched entities.

10. The _____ option is displayed in the **Defined In** column when the entity is defined as placed in the same sketch.

REVIEW QUESTIONS

Answer the following questions:

1. You can invoke the **Display/Delete Relations PropertyManager** using the **Display/Delete Relations** button from _____ **CommandManager**.

2. The linear diameter dimensions are applied to the sketches of _____ features.

3. You can modify the dimension to display the minimum or maximum distance between two circles using the _____ dialog box.

4. The _____ sketch geometry is constrained by too many dimensions and/or relations. Therefore, you must delete the extra and conflicting relations or dimensions.

5. The _____ relation forces two selected lines, arcs, points, or ellipses to remain equidistant from a centerline.

6. In SolidWorks, by default, the dimensioning between two arcs, two circles, or between an arc and a circle is done from _____ .

7. Which relation forces the selected arc to share the same center point with another arc or a point?

    (a) **Concentric**   (b) **Coradial**
    (c) **Merge points**   (d) **Equal**

8. Which type of dimension changes the color of the entities to red?

    (a) Underdefined   (b) Overdefined
    (c) Dangling   (d) None

9. Which dialog box is displayed when you modify a dimension?

    (a) **Modify Dimensional Value**   (b) **Insert a value**
    (c) **Modify**   (d) None

10. Which dialog box is displayed when you add an extra dimension to a sketch or add an extra relation that overdefines the sketch?

    (a) **Over defining**   (b) **Delete relation**
    (c) **Make Dimension Driven?**   (d) **Add Geometric Relations**

EXERCISES

Exercise 1

Create the sketch of the model shown in Figure 4-87. Apply the required relations and dimensions and fully define it. The sketch is shown in Figure 4-88. The solid model is given for reference only.   (**Expected time: 30 min**)

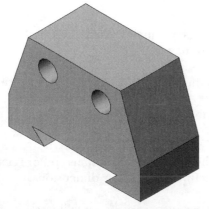

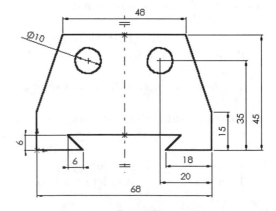

Figure 4-87 Solid model for Exercise 1   *Figure 4-88* Sketch for Exercise 1

Exercise 2

Create the sketch of the model shown in Figure 4-89. Apply the required relations and dimensions and fully define it. The sketch is shown in Figure 4-90. The solid model is given for reference only. **(Expected time: 30 min)**

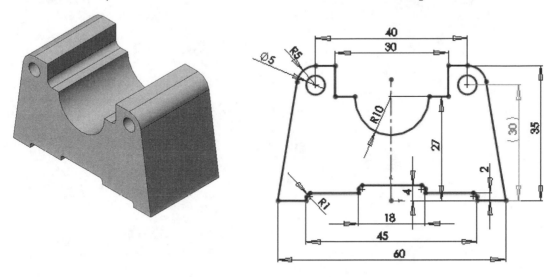

Figure 4-89 *Solid model for Exercise 2*   **Figure 4-90** *Sketch for Exercise 2*

Exercise 3

Create the sketch of the model shown in Figure 4-91. Apply the required relations and dimensions and fully define it. The sketch is shown in Figure 4-92. The solid model is given for reference only. **(Expected time: 30 min)**

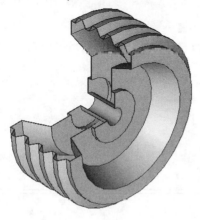

Figure 4-91 *Solid model for Exercise 3*   **Figure 4-92** *Sketch for Exercise 3*

Answers to Self-Evaluation Test
1. T, **2.** F, **3.** T, **4.** F, **5.** T, **6. Mirror**, **7.** aligned, **8.** fully defined, **9.** dangling, **10. All in this sketch**

Chapter 5

Advanced Dimensioning Techniques and Base Feature Options

Learning Objectives

After completing this chapter, you will be able to:

- *Fully define a sketch.*
- *Dimension the true length of an arc.*
- *Measure distances and view section properties.*
- *Create solid base extruded features.*
- *Create thin base extruded features.*
- *Create solid base revolved features.*
- *Create thin base revolved features.*
- *Dynamically rotate the view to display the model from all directions.*
- *Modify the orientation of the view.*
- *Change the display modes of solid models.*
- *Apply materials and textures to models.*

ADVANCED DIMENSIONING TECHNIQUES

In this chapter, you will learn about the advanced dimensioning techniques that are used to dimension the sketches. In SolidWorks, you can apply all possible relations and dimensions to a sketch using a single tool to make the sketch fully defined. The advanced dimensioning techniques are discussed next.

Fully Defining the Sketches

SolidWorks menus:	Tools > Dimensions > Fully Define Sketch
Toolbar:	Dimensions/Relations > Fully Define Sketch

The **Fully Define Sketch** tool is used to apply the relations and dimensions to the sketch automatically. To fully define a sketch, draw the sketch using the standard sketching tools. Choose **Fully Define Sketch** from the **Dimensions/Relations** toolbar; the **Fully Define Sketch PropertyManager** will be displayed, as shown in Figure 5-1. You can also right-click and choose the **Fully Define Sketch** option from the shortcut menu to display this **PropertyManager**. Various rollouts in this **PropertyManager** are discussed next.

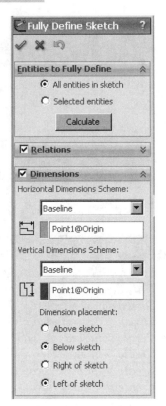

*Figure 5-1 The **Fully Define Sketch PropertyManager***

Entities to Fully Define

The **Entities to Fully Define** rollout is used to specify the entities to which the relations and dimensions need to be applied. The **All entities in sketch** radio button is selected by default. As a result, all entities drawn in the current sketching environment are selected to apply relations and dimensions. If you need to fully define only the selected entities, select the **Selected entities** radio button; the **Selected Entities to Fully Define** selection box will be displayed in the **Entities to Fully Define** rollout. Select the entities to be dimensioned using the select cursor; the names of the selected entities will be displayed in the **Selected Entities to Fully Define** selection box. If you select one or more entities before invoking the **Fully Define Sketch PropertyManager** and then select the **Selected entities** radio button from the **Entities to Fully Define** rollout, the names of the selected entities will be displayed in the **Selected Entities to Fully Define** selection box. After specifying other parameters, choose the **Calculate** button to calculate and place the required number of relations and dimensions to fully define the sketch.

Relations

The **Relations** rollout displays the buttons of all relations. To invoke this rollout, click on the double arrow on the right of the **Relations** rollout; the rollout will expand. All buttons in this rollout are chosen by default. You can disable all buttons by selecting the **Deselect All** radio button from this rollout. You can also choose only those buttons that you want to apply to the sketch from this rollout.

Dimensions

The **Dimensions** rollout is used to specify the type of dimensions to be applied, reference for the dimensions, and the placement of the dimensional value. The options in this rollout are discussed next.

Horizontal Dimensions Scheme and Vertical Dimensions Scheme

The **Horizontal Dimensions Scheme** and **Vertical Dimensions Scheme** drop-down lists in the **Dimensions** rollout are used to specify the dimensioning scheme to be applied to the horizontal and vertical dimensions in the sketch. The dimensioning schemes in this drop-down lists are discussed next.

Chain

The **Chain** option is used for the relative horizontal/vertical dimensioning of the sketch. When you invoke the **Fully Define Sketch PropertyManager** and select this option, the origin will be selected as the reference entity. This reference entity is used as a datum for generating dimensions. The name of the origin will be displayed in the **Datums - Vertical Model Edge, Model Vertex, Vertical Line or Point** selection box and the reference entity will be displayed in pink in the drawing area. You can also specify a user-defined reference entity after clicking in this selection box.

 Note
Chain dimensioning should be avoided if the tolerances relative to a common datum are required in the part.

Baseline

The **Baseline** option is used for the absolute vertical/horizontal dimensioning of the sketch. In this dimensioning method, the dimensions are applied to the sketch with respect to the common datum. When you invoke the **Fully Define Sketch PropertyManager**, this option is selected by default. Also, the origin will be selected as the reference entity and will be used as a datum for generating dimensions. The name of the origin will be displayed in the **Datums - Vertical Model Edge, Model Vertex, Vertical Line or Point** selection box. You can also specify a user-defined reference entity.

Ordinate

The **Ordinate** option is used for the ordinate dimensioning of the sketch. When you invoke the **Fully Define Sketch PropertyManager** and select this option, a point or a vertical line will be selected as the reference entity and will be used as a datum for generating dimensions. The name of the selected reference entity will be displayed in the **Datums - Vertical Model Edge, Model Vertex, Vertical Line or Point** selection box and the reference entity will be displayed in pink in the drawing area. You can also specify a user-defined reference entity.

Dimension placement

The **Dimension placement** area is used to define the position where the generated dimensions will be placed. Four radio buttons are available in this area. The first is the **Above sketch** radio button and if you select this radio button, the horizontal dimensions generated using the **Fully Define Sketch** tool will be placed above the sketch. The **Below sketch** radio button is selected by default and is used to place the dimensions below the sketch. The **Right of sketch** radio button is selected to place the dimensions on the right of the sketch. The **Left of sketch** radio button is selected to place the dimensions on the left of the sketch. This radio button is selected by default.

After specifying all parameters in the **Fully Define Sketch PropertyManager**, choose the **Calculate** button; the sketch will be fully defined. Next, choose the **OK** button or choose the **OK** icon from the confirmation corner. The relations and dimension, with the selected dimension scheme, will be applied to the sketch. Figure 5-2 shows the **Baseline** scheme with the origin as the datum, Figure 5-3 shows the **Ordinate** scheme with the origin as the datum, and Figure 5-4 shows the **Chain** scheme with the origin as the datum.

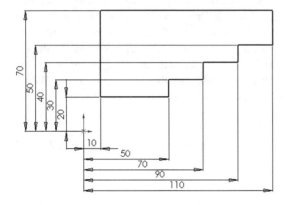

Figure 5-2 *Baseline dimension created using the origin as the reference entity*

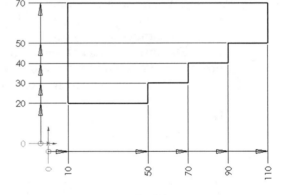

Figure 5-3 *Ordinate dimension created using the origin as the reference entity*

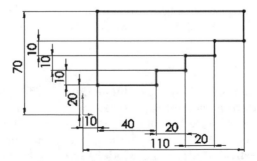

Figure 5-4 *Chain dimension created using the origin as the reference entity*

Dimensioning the True Length of an Arc

In SolidWorks, you can also apply the dimension of the true length of an arc, which is one of the advantages of the sketching environment of SolidWorks. To apply the dimension of the true length, invoke the **Smart Dimension** tool and select the arc using the dimension cursor; a radial dimension will be attached to the cursor. Move the cursor to any of the endpoints of the arc. When the cursor snaps the endpoint, use the left mouse button to specify the first endpoint of the arc; a linear dimension will be attached to the cursor. Move the cursor to the second endpoint of the arc and when the cursor snaps the endpoint, select it; a dimension will be attached to the cursor. Move the cursor to an appropriate place to place the dimension. The dimension of the true length of the arc is shown in Figure 5-5.

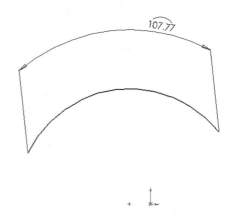

Figure 5-5 *Dimensioning the true length of an arc*

MEASURING DISTANCES AND VIEWING SECTION PROPERTIES

In SolidWorks, you can measure the distance of the entities and view the section properties using various tools that are discussed next.

Measuring Distances

CommandManager:	Evaluate > Measure
SolidWorks menus:	Tools > Measure
Toolbar:	Tools > Measure

The **Measure** tool is used to measure the perimeter, angle, radius, and distance between the lines, points, surfaces, and planes in sketches, 3D models, assemblies, or drawings. To measure an entity, invoke the **Measure** toolbar by choosing the **Measure** button from the **Evaluate CommandManager**; the **Measure** toolbar will be displayed. The name of the document in which you are working will be displayed at the top of the **Measure** toolbar, refer to Figure 5-6. Also, the current cursor will be replaced by the measure cursor. Select the entity or entities to be measured using the measure cursor; the result related to the selected element or elements will be displayed in a callout. You can also view the result in the **Measure** toolbar by expanding it. To expand the toolbar, choose the button with the down arrows on the right of the toolbar. The options in the **Measure** dialog box are discussed next.

Arc/Circle Measurements

The **Arc/Circle Measurements** button is used to specify the technique of measuring the distance between the selected arcs or circles. When you choose the **Arc/Circle Measurements**

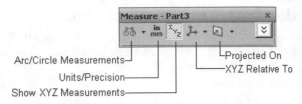

Figure 5-6 *The **Measure** toolbar*

button, a flyout will appear. The **Center to Center** option will be chosen by default in this flyout. So, the center-to-center distance will be measured when you select two arcs or circles. If you choose the **Minimum Distance** option from this flyout, the minimum tangential distance between the two selected arcs or circles will be measured. However, if you choose the **Maximum Distance** option from this flyout, the maximum tangential distance between the selected arcs or circles will be measured.

Units/Precision

The **Units/Precision** button is used to set the type of units and their precision. Choose this button; the **Measure Units/Precision** dialog box will be displayed. The **Use document settings** radio button is selected by default in this dialog box. The default units and precision of the document are used while measuring the entities. You can also set the type of units and their precision for measuring the entities. To do so, select the **Use custom settings** radio button from this dialog box. The other options in this dialog box will be displayed, as shown in Figure 5-7. These options are discussed next.

Figure 5-7 *The **Measure Units/Precision** dialog box*

Length unit Area

The **Length unit** area is used to set the units and the options of linear measurements of the entities. The **Unit** drop-down list is provided at the top left corner of the **Length unit** area. In this drop-down list, you can select any type of unit such as **Angstroms**, **Nanometers**, **Microns**, **Millimeters**, **Centimeters**, **Meters**, **Microinches**, **Mils**, **Inches**, **Feet**, and **Feet and Inches**. The other options in the **Length unit** area are discussed next.

Decimal places
This spinner is used to control the decimal places.

Decimal
The **Decimal** radio button is available only when you select the units as **Microinches**, **Mils**, **Inches**, or **Feet and Inches** from the **Unit** drop-down list. Select this radio button to display the dimension in the decimal form. You can also specify the decimal places using the **Decimal places** spinner provided on the right of the **Decimal** radio button.

Fractions
The **Fractions** radio button is available only when you select the units as **Microinches**, **Mils**, **Inches**, or **Feet and Inches** from the **Units** drop-down list. This radio button is selected to display the dimension in the fraction form. You can also set the value of the denominator by using the **Denominator** spinner provided on the right of the **Fractions** radio button.

Round to nearest fraction
The **Round to nearest fraction** check box is selected to display the value in fractions by rounding the value to the nearest fraction.

Scientific Notation
The **Scientific Notation** check box is selected to display the value in the scientific notation units.

Angular unit Area
The **Angular unit** area is used to set the units for the angular measurement. This area is provided with a drop-down list to specify the angular measurement units such as **Degrees**, **Deg/Min**, **Deg/Min/Sec**, and **Radians**. The **Decimal places** spinner is used to specify the decimal places.

Show XYZ Measurements

The **Show XYZ measurements** button is chosen by default in the **Measure** toolbar so the dx, dy, and dz values of the selected entities are displayed in the drawing area. If you deselect this button, only the minimum distance between the selected entities will be displayed.

XYZ Relative To

The **XYZ Relative To** button is used to define the coordinate system along which the selected entities will be measured. By default, the part origin is selected as the coordinate system. To select any other coordinate system that you created earlier, choose the **XYZ Relative To** button from the **Measure** toolbar; a flyout with all the coordinate systems that you have created along with the part origin will be displayed. Choose the coordinate system from this flyout. You will learn more about creating additional coordinate systems in the later chapters.

Projected On

The **Projected On** button is used to specify the location where the selected entity should be projected. You can project the selected entity on the screen or on a specific plane. The system will then calculate the measurement of the true projection. To specify the location, choose the **Projected On** button from the **Measure** toolbar; a callout will be displayed and you can select the location where you need to project the selected entity.

Determining the Section Properties of Closed Sketches

CommandManager:	Evaluate > Section Properties
SolidWorks menus:	Tools > Section Properties
Toolbar:	Tools > Section Properties

The **Section Properties** tool enables you to determine the section properties of the sketch in the sketching environment or of the selected planar face in the **Part** mode and the **Assembly** mode. Remember that the section properties of only the closed sketches with nonintersecting closed loops can be determined. The section properties include the area, centroid relative to the sketch origin, centroid relative to the part origin, moment of inertia, polar moment of inertia, angle between the principle axes and sketch axes, and the principle moment of inertia.

To calculate the section properties, select a sketch or a face and then choose the **Section Properties** button from the **Evaluate CommandManager**; the **Section Properties** dialog box will be displayed, as shown in Figure 5-8.

When you invoke the **Section Properties** dialog box, a 3D triad will be placed at the centroid of the sketch. The section properties of the sketch are displayed in the **Section Properties** dialog box. The **Selected items** display box is used to display the name of the selected planar face or the sketch whose section properties are to be calculated. When you are in the **Part** mode, select the face to calculate the section properties and choose **Recalculate** to display the properties. To calculate the section properties of some other face, clear the previously selected face from the selection set and then, select the new face and choose the **Recalculate** button.

The **Print** button in the **Section Properties** dialog box is used to print the section properties. The **Copy** button is chosen to copy the section properties to the clip board from where you can copy them to a program such as MS Word. The rest of the options in this dialog box are similar to those discussed earlier.

CREATING BASE FEATURES BY EXTRUDING SKETCHES

CommandManager:	Features > Extruded Boss/Base
SolidWorks Menus:	Insert > Boss/Base > Extrude
Toolbar:	Features > Extruded Boss/Base

The sketches that you have drawn until now can be converted into base features by extruding the sketch using the **Extruded Boss/Base** tool from the **Features CommandManager**. After drawing the sketch, choose the **Features** tab from the **CommandManager** to display the **Features CommandManager**. Choose the **Extruded**

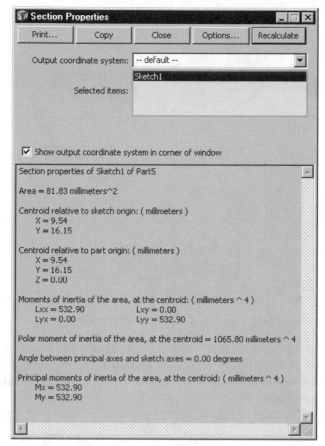

Figure 5-8 *Resized view of the **Section Properties** dialog box*

Boss/Base button from the **Features CommandManager**; the sketching environment will be closed and the part modeling environment will be invoked. Also, the preview of the feature that is created using the default options will be displayed in the trimetric view. The trimetric view gives a better display of the solid feature.

On the basis of the options and the sketch selected for extruding, the resulting feature can be a solid feature or a thin feature. If the sketch is closed, it can be converted into a solid feature or a thin feature. However, if the sketch is open, it will be converted into a thin feature. The solid and thin features are discussed next.

Creating Solid Extruded Features

After you have completed drawing a closed sketch, dimension it to convert the sketch into a fully defined sketch. Next, choose the **Features** tab from the **CommandManager**; the **Features CommandManager** will be displayed. Choose the **Extruded Boss/Base** button; the **Extrude PropertyManager** will be displayed, as shown in Figure 5-9. Also, you will notice that the view is automatically changed to the trimetric view.

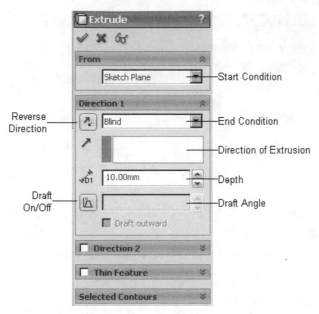

*Figure 5-9 The **Extrude PropertyManager***

You will notice that the preview of the base feature is displayed in temporary graphics. Also, an arrow will appear in front of the sketch. Note that if the sketch consists of some closed loops inside the outer loop, they will automatically be subtracted from the outer loop while extruding, as shown in Figure 5-10.

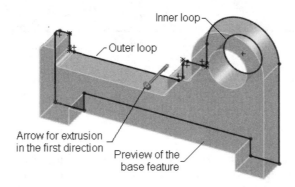

Figure 5-10 Preview of the feature being extruded

The options in the **Extrude PropertyManager** are discussed next.

Direction 1

The **Direction 1** rollout is used to specify the end condition for extruding the sketch in one direction from the sketch plane. The options in the **Direction 1** drop-down list are discussed next.

End Condition

The **End Condition** drop-down list provides the options to define the termination of the extruded feature. Note that when you create the first feature, some of the options in this drop-down list will not be used. Also, some additional options will be available later in this drop-down list. The options that will be used to define the termination of the base feature are discussed next.

Blind

The **Blind** option is selected by default and is used to define the termination of the extruded base feature by specifying the depth of extrusion. The depth of extrusion is specified in the **Depth** spinner that will be displayed in the **Direction 1** rollout on selecting the **Blind** option. To reverse the extrusion direction, select the **Reverse Direction** button provided on the left of this drop-down list. Figure 5-11 shows the preview of the feature being created by extruding the sketch using this option.

You can also extrude a sketch to a blind depth by dragging the feature dynamically using the mouse. To do so, move the mouse to the arrow displayed in the preview; the move cursor will be displayed and the color of the arrow will also be changed. Left-click once on the arrow; a scale will be displayed, as shown in Figure 5-12. Now, move the cursor to specify the depth of extrusion; the value of the depth of extrusion will change dynamically on this scale as you move the cursor. Left-click again to specify the termination of the extruded feature. The select cursor will be replaced by the mouse cursor. Right-click and choose **OK** to complete the feature creation or choose the **OK** button from the **Extrude PropertyManager**.

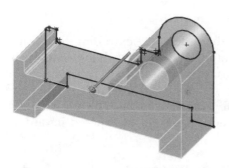

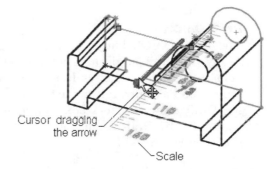

Cursor dragging
the arrow

Scale

Figure 5-11 *Preview of the feature being extruded using the* **Blind** *option*

Figure 5-12 *Preview of the feature being extruded by dynamically dragging the arrow*

Tip. *If you extrude an underdefined or an overdefined sketch. However, if you extrude an underdefined sketch, a (-) sign will be displayed on the left of the sketch in the* **FeatureManager***. Similarly, if you extrude an overdefined sketch, you will find a (+) sign on the left of the sketch in the* **FeatureManager***. To check these signs, click on the (+) sign available on the left of* **Extrude 1** *in the* **FeatureManager***; the sketch will be displayed and you can view the (+) sign.*

Mid Plane

The **Mid Plane** option is used to create the base feature by extruding the sketch equally in both the directions of the plane on which the sketch is drawn. For example, if the total depth of the extruded feature is 30 mm, it will be extruded 15 mm toward the front of the sketching plane and 15 mm toward the back. The depth of the feature can be defined in the **Depth** spinner that is displayed below the **Direction of Extrusion** selection box.

Figure 5-13 shows the preview of the feature being created by extruding the sketch using the **Mid Plane** option.

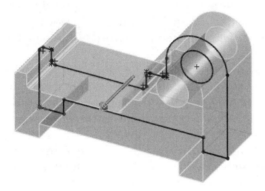

Figure 5-13 *Preview of the feature being extruded using the **Mid Plane** option*

Draft On/Off

The **Draft On/Off** button is used to specify a draft angle while extruding the sketch. Apply the draft angle to taper the resulting feature. This button is not chosen by default. Therefore, the resulting base feature will not have any taper. However, if you want to add a draft angle to the feature, choose this button; the **Draft Angle** spinner and the **Draft outward** check box will be available. You can enter the draft angle for the feature in the **Draft Angle** spinner. By default, the feature will be tapered inward, as shown in Figure 5-14.

If you want to taper the feature outward, select the **Draft outward** check box, which is displayed below the **Draft Angle** spinner. The feature created with the outward taper is shown in Figure 5-15.

Note
*The **Direction of Extrusion** area will be discussed in the later chapters.*

Tip. *You can also choose the termination options using the shortcut menu that is displayed when you right-click in the drawing area.*

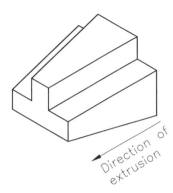

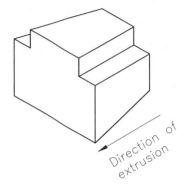

Figure 5-14 *Feature created with inward draft*   **Figure 5-15** *Feature created with outward draft*

Direction 2

The **Direction 2** check box is selected to expand the **Direction 2** rollout. This rollout is used to extrude the sketch with different values in the second direction of the sketching plane. This check box will not be available if you select the **Mid Plane** termination type.

Tip. *As soon as you select the **Direction 2** check box, another arrow will be displayed in the preview of the feature. You can use this arrow to define the depth of extrusion in the second direction.*

The options in this rollout are similar to those in the **Direction 1** rollout. Note that unlike the **Mid Plane** termination option, the depth of extrusion and other parameters in both directions can be different. For example, you can extrude the sketch to a blind depth of 10 mm and an inward draft of 35-degree in front of the sketching plane and to a blind depth of 15 mm and an outward draft of 0-degree behind the sketching plane, as shown in Figure 5-16.

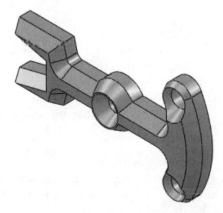

Figure 5-16 *Feature created in two directions with different values*

After setting the values for both directions, choose the **OK** button or choose the **OK** icon from the confirmation corner; the feature will be created with the defined values.

Note
The **Selection Contours** rollout will be discussed in the later chapters.

Creating Thin Extruded Features

The thin extruded features can be created using a closed or an open sketch. If the sketch is closed, the thickness will be specified inside or outside the sketch to create a cavity inside the feature, as shown in Figure 5-17. To convert a closed sketch into a thin feature, choose the **Thin Feature** check box; the **Thin Feature** rollout will be invoked, as shown in Figure 5-18.

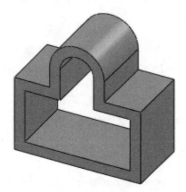

Figure 5-17 *Thin extruded feature created using a closed loop*

Figure 5-18 *The **Thin Feature** rollout*

The options in the **Thin Feature** rollout of the **Extrude PropertyManager** are discussed next.

Type

The options provided in the **Type** drop-down list are used to select the method of defining the thickness of the thin feature. These options are discussed next.

One-Direction

The **One-Direction** option is used to add the thickness on one side of the sketch. The thickness can be specified in the **Thickness** spinner provided below the **Type** drop-down list. For the closed sketches, the direction can be inside or outside the sketch. Similarly, for open sketches, the direction can be below or above the sketch. You can reverse the direction of thickness using the **Reverse Direction** button available on the left of the **Type** drop-down list. This button will be available only when you select the **One-Direction** option from this drop-down list.

Mid-Plane

The **Mid-Plane** option is used to add the thickness equally on both sides of the sketch. The value of the thickness of the thin feature can be specified in the **Thickness** spinner provided below this drop-down list.

Two-Direction

The **Two-Direction** option is used to create a thin feature by adding different thicknesses on both sides of the sketch. The thickness values in direction 1 and direction 2 can be specified in the **Direction 1 Thickness** spinner and the **Direction 2 Thickness** spinner, respectively. These spinners will automatically be displayed below the **Type** drop-down list when you select the **Two-Direction** option from this drop-down list.

Cap ends

The **Cap ends** check box will be displayed only when you select a closed sketch to convert into a thin feature. This check box is selected to cap the two open faces of the thin extruded feature. Both open faces will be capped with a face of the thickness that you specify. When you select this check box, the **Cap Thickness** spinner will be displayed below this check box. The thickness of the end caps can be specified using this spinner.

If the sketch to be extruded is open, as shown in Figure 5-19, the **Thin Feature** rollout will be invoked automatically when you invoke the **Extrude PropertyManager**. The resulting feature is shown in Figure 5-20.

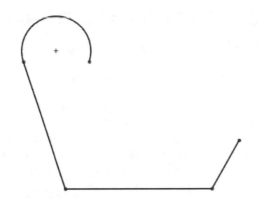

Figure 5-19 *Open sketch to be converted into a thin feature*

Figure 5-20 *Resulting thin feature*

Auto-fillet corners

The **Auto-fillet corners** check box will be displayed only when you select an open sketch to convert into a thin feature. If you select this check box, all sharp vertices in the sketch will automatically be filleted while converting into a thin feature. As a result, the thin feature will have filleted edges. The radius of the fillet can be specified in the **Fillet Radius** spinner, which will be displayed below the **Auto-fillet corners** check box.

Figure 5-21 shows the thin feature created by extruding an open sketch in both directions. Note that a draft angle is applied to the feature while extruding in the front direction and the **Auto-fillet corners** check box is selected while creating this thin feature.

Note
Only the corners of the thin features that can accommodate to the given radius will be filleted; other corners that cannot accommodate to the given radius will not be filleted.

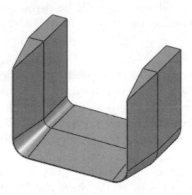

Figure 5-21 *Thin feature created in both directions*

CREATING BASE FEATURES BY REVOLVING SKETCHES

CommandManager:	Features > Revolved Boss/Base
SolidWorks menus:	Insert > Boss/Base > Revolve
Toolbar:	Features > Extruded Boss/Base > Revolved Boss/Base

The sketches that you have drawn until now can also be converted into base features by revolving using the **Revolved Boss/Base** tool. This tool is available in the **Features CommandManager**. Choose this tool to revolve the sketch about a revolution axis. The revolution axis could be an axis, an entity of the sketch, or an edge of another feature to create the revolved feature. Note that whether you use a centerline or an edge to revolve the sketch, the sketch should be drawn on one side of the centerline or the edge.

In SolidWorks, the right-hand thumb rule is followed while determining the direction of revolution. The right-hand thumb rule states that if the thumb of your right hand points in the direction of the axis of revolution, the direction of the curled fingers will determine the default direction of revolution, refer to Figure 5-22.

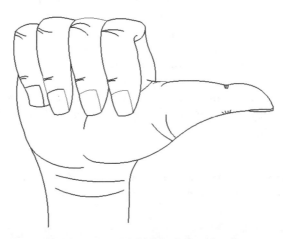

Figure 5-22 *Right-hand thumb rule*

For example, consider a case in which you draw a centerline from left to right (direction of thumb in Figure 5-22) in the drawing area. Now, if you use this centerline to create a revolved feature, the default direction of revolution will be in the direction of the curled fingers.

Note
*You can also reverse the direction of revolution using the **Reverse Direction** button in the **Revolve PropertyManager**.*

Invoke the **Revolved Boss/Base** tool after drawing the sketch; the sketching environment is closed and the part modeling environment is invoked. Similar to extruding the sketches, the resulting feature can be a solid feature or a thin feature, depending on the sketch and the options selected to be revolved. If the sketch is closed, it can be converted into a solid feature or a thin feature. However, if the sketch is open, it can be converted only into a thin feature. The solid and thin features are discussed next.

Creating Solid Revolved Features

After you have completed drawing a closed sketch, dimension it to convert it into a fully defined sketch. Next, choose the **Features** tab above the **FeatureManager design tree**; the **Features CommandManager** will be displayed. Then, choose the **Revolved Boss/Base** button; the **Revolve PropertyManager** will be displayed, as shown in Figure 5-23. Also, the confirmation corner will be displayed and the preview of the base feature, created using the default options, will be displayed in temporary shaded graphics. The direction arrow will also be displayed in gray. If you have not drawn the centerline, you will be prompted to select an axis of revolution. Select an edge or a line as the axis of revolution; the preview will be displayed. The options in the **Revolve Parameters** rollout of the **Revolve PropertyManager** are discussed next.

*Figure 5-23 The **Revolve PropertyManager***

Tip. *Even though you can revolve the sketch using an edge in the sketch, it is recommended to draw a centerline, so that you can create linear diameter dimensions for the revolved features.*

Revolve Type

The **Revolve Type** drop-down list provides the options to define the termination of the revolved feature. The options in this drop-down list are discussed next.

One-Direction

The **One-Direction** option is used to revolve the sketch on one side of the plane on which it is drawn. The angle of revolution can be specified in the **Angle** spinner displayed below this drop-down list. The default value in the **Angle** spinner is **360deg**. Therefore, if you revolve the sketch using this value, a complete round feature will be created. You can also reverse the direction of revolution of the sketch by choosing the **Reverse Direction** button that is displayed on the left of the drop-down list. Figure 5-24 shows the sketch of the piston and Figure 5-25 shows the resulting piston created by revolving the sketch through an angle of 360-degree. Note that the left vertical edge of the sketch that is vertically in line with the origin is used to revolve the sketch.

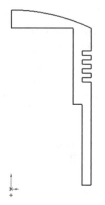

Figure 5-24   *Sketch of the piston to be revolved*

Figure 5-25   *Feature created by revolving the sketch through an angle of 360-degree*

Tip. *You can dynamically modify the angle in a revolved feature by dragging the direction arrows. You can also right-click to display the shortcut menu. The options in the **PropertyManager** will be available in the shortcut menu.*

Figure 5-26 shows a piston created by revolving the same sketch through an angle of 270-degree.

Mid-Plane

The **Mid-Plane** option is used to revolve the sketch equally on both sides of the plane on which it is drawn. The angle of revolution can be specified in the **Angle** spinner. When you select this option, the **Reverse Direction** button will not be available.

Two-Direction

The **Two-Direction** option is used to create a revolved feature by revolving the sketch using different values on both sides of the plane on which it is drawn. The angle values

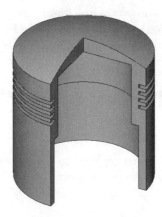

Figure 5-26 *Feature created by revolving the sketch through an angle of 270-degree*

for direction 1 and direction 2 can be specified in the **Direction 1 Angle** spinner and the **Direction 2 Angle** spinner, respectively. These spinners will be displayed below the **Revolve Type** drop-down list automatically when you select the **Two-Direction** option from this drop-down list.

Creating Thin Revolved Features

The thin revolved features can be created using the closed or the open sketches. If the sketch is closed, it will be offset inside or outside to create a cavity inside the feature as shown in Figure 5-27. In this figure, the sketch is revolved through an angle of 180-degree.

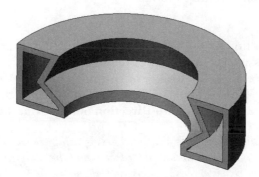

Figure 5-27 *Thin feature created by revolving the sketch through an angle of 180-degree*

To convert a closed sketch into a thin feature, select the **Thin Feature** check box from the **Revolve PropertyManager**; the **Thin Feature** rollout will be invoked, as shown in Figure 5-28. However, if the sketch to be revolved is open and you invoke the **Revolved Boss/Base** tool, the **SolidWorks** information box will be displayed. This information box will inform you that the sketch is currently open and a non-thin revolved feature requires a closed sketch. You will be given an option of automatically closing the sketch. If

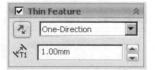

Figure 5-28 *The Thin Feature rollout*

you choose **Yes** from this information box, a line segment will automatically be drawn between the first and the last segment of the sketch and the **Revolve PropertyManager** will be displayed. However, if you choose **No** from this information box, the **Revolve PropertyManager** will be displayed and the **Thin Feature** rollout will be displayed automatically.

The options in the **Thin Feature** rollout of the **Revolve PropertyManager** are discussed next.

Type

The options in the **Type** drop-down list are used to select a method to specify the thickness of the thin feature. These options are discussed next.

One-Direction

The **One-Direction** option is used to add the thickness on one side of the sketch. The thickness can be specified in the **Direction 1 Thickness** spinner provided below this drop-down list. For the closed sketches, the direction can be inside or outside the sketch. Similarly, for open sketches, the direction can be below or above the sketch. You can reverse the direction of thickness using the **Reverse Direction** button available on the right of this drop-down list. This button will be available only when you select the **One-Direction** option from this drop-down list.

Mid-Plane

The **Mid-Plane** option is used to add the thickness equally on both sides of the sketch. The value of the thickness of the thin feature can be specified in the **Direction 1 Thickness** spinner provided below this drop-down list.

Two-Direction

The **Two-Direction** option is used to create a thin feature by adding different thicknesses on both sides of the sketch. The thickness values for direction 1 and direction 2 can be specified in the **Direction 1 Thickness** spinner and the **Direction 2 Thickness** spinner, respectively. These spinners will be displayed below the **Type** drop-down list automatically when you select the **Two-Direction** option from this drop-down list.

> **Tip**. *While defining the wall thickness of a thin revolved feature, remember that the wall thickness should be added such that the centerline does not intersect with the sketch. If the centerline intersects with the sketch, the sketch will not be revolved.*

If the sketch is open, as shown in Figure 5-29, the resulting feature will be similar to that shown in Figure 5-30.

DETERMINING THE MASS PROPERTIES OF PARTS

CommandManager:	Evaluate > Mass Properties
SolidWorks menus:	Tools > Mass Properties
Toolbar:	Tools > Mass Properties

The **Mass Properties** tool enables you to determine the mass properties of the part or assembly that is available in the current session. Note that this tool will not be

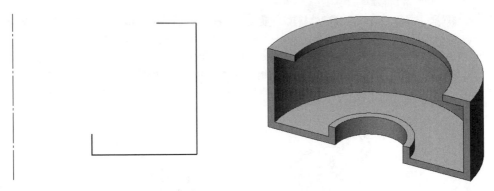

Figure 5-29 *The open sketch to be revolved and the centerline to revolve the sketch*

Figure 5-30 *Thin feature created by revolving the open sketch through an angle of 180-degree*

enabled, if there is no solid model in the current session. Mass properties include density, mass, volume, surface area, center of mass, principal axes of inertia and principal moments of inertia, and moments of inertia.

To calculate the mass properties of the current model, choose the **Mass Properties** button from the **Evaluate CommandManager**; the **Mass Properties** dialog box will be displayed with the mass properties of the model. As soon as you invoke the **Mass Properties** dialog box, a 3D triad will be placed at the center of the model. The other options in this dialog box are the same as discussed in the **Section Properties** dialog box.

DYNAMICALLY ROTATING THE VIEW OF THE MODEL

In SolidWorks, you can dynamically rotate the view in the 3D space so that the solid models in the current document can be viewed from all directions. This allows you to visually maneuver around the model to view all the features clearly. This tool can be invoked even when you are inside some other tool. For example, you can invoke this tool when the **Extrude PropertyManager** is displayed. You can freely rotate the model in the 3D space or rotate it around a selected vertex, edge, or face. Both methods of rotating the model are discussed next.

Rotating the View Freely in 3D Space

Toolbar:	Heads-up View > Rotate View
SolidWorks menus:	View > Modify > Rotate

To rotate the view freely in the 3D space, choose the **Rotate View** button from the **Heads-up View** toolbar. You can also invoke this tool by choosing the **Rotate View** option from the shortcut menu that will be displayed when you right-click in the drawing area. When you are inside some other tool, right-click and choose the **Zoom/Pan/Rotate > Rotate View** from the shortcut menu to invoke the **Rotate View** tool. When you invoke this tool, the cursor will be replaced by the rotate view cursor. Now, press the left mouse button and drag the cursor to rotate the view. Figure 5-31 shows the rotated view of the model.

Rotating the View around a Selected Vertex, Edge, or Face

To rotate the view around a vertex, edge, or face, invoke the **Rotate View** tool and move the rotate view cursor close to the vertex, edge, or the face around which you want to rotate the view. When it is highlighted, select it using the left mouse button; the rotate view cursor will be displayed, as shown in Figure 5-32. Next, drag the cursor to rotate the view around the selected vertex, edge, or face.

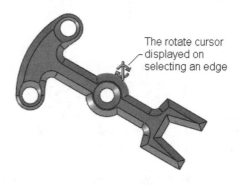

The rotate cursor displayed on selecting an edge

Figure 5-31 *Rotating the view to display the model from different directions*

Figure 5-32 *The rotate cursor displayed on the selecting an edge*

Tip. *To resume rotating the view freely after you have rotated it around a selected vertex, edge, or face, click anywhere in the drawing area. Now when you drag the cursor, you will notice that the view is rotated freely in the 3D space. Invoke the **Select** tool to exit the rotate tool.*

You can also press the middle mouse button and drag the cursor to rotate the model freely in the 3D space. Note that in this case, you cannot rotate the view around the selected vertex, edge, or face.

MODIFYING THE VIEW ORIENTATION

In SolidWorks, you can manually change the view orientation using some predefined standard views or user-defined views. To invoke these standard views, choose the **View Orientation** button from the **Heads-up View** toolbar; a **View Orientation** flyout will be displayed, as shown in Figure 5-33.

You can choose the required view from this flyout and orient the model to standard views. You need to choose the **Normal To** option to reorient the view normal to a selected face or plane. To do so, select the face normal to which you need to reorient the model and choose the **Normal To** option from this flyout. If you have not selected a face before choosing this option, the **Normal To PropertyManager** will be displayed and you will be prompted to select a reference along which the view will be reoriented. In SolidWorks, you can select the **Normal To** option from the pop-up toolbar also, this toolbar will be displayed on selecting an entity.

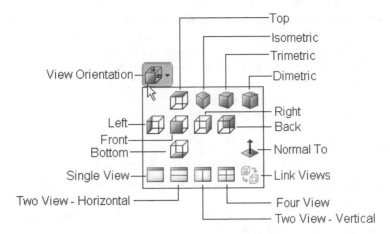

*Figure 5-33 The **View Orientation** flyout*

You can also invoke these standard views using the **Orientation** dialog box, as shown in Figure 5-34. This dialog box can be invoked by choosing **Zoom/Pan/Rotate > View Orientation** from the shortcut menu or by pressing the SPACEBAR on the keyboard. Note that when you invoke this dialog box by pressing the SPACEBAR, the dialog box will be displayed at the location where the cursor is placed currently.

You can invoke a view by double-clicking on the name of the view in this dialog box. The buttons available on this dialog box are discussed next.

*Figure 5-34 The **Orientation** dialog box*

Pin/Unpin the dialog

 You will notice that the **Orientation** dialog box is automatically closed when you select a view and click on the screen or invoke a tool. If you want this dialog box to be retained on the screen, you can pin it at a location by choosing the **Pin/Unpin the dialog** button. This is the last button on this dialog box. Move the dialog box to the desired location and choose this button; the dialog box will be pinned to that location and will not be closed when you perform any operation.

New View

 The **New View** button is chosen to create a user-defined view and save it in the list of views in the **Orientation** dialog box. Modify the current view using the various drawing display tools and the **Rotate View** tool and then choose this button; the **Named View** dialog box will be displayed. Enter the name of the view in the **View name** edit box and then choose the **OK** button. You will notice that a user-defined view is created and it is saved in the list in the **Orientation** dialog box.

Update Standard Views

 The **Update Standard Views** button is chosen to modify the orientation of the standard views. For example, when you select the **Top** option from this dialog box, the top view of a model will be displayed. If you want to make this view as the front view, change the current view to the top view. To do so, double-click on the **Top** option in the **Orientation** dialog box. Now, select the **Front** option from the list of views available in the **Orientation** dialog box and then choose the **Update Standard Views** button. The **SolidWorks** message box will be displayed and you will be informed that if you change the standard view, all other named views in the model will also be changed. Choose the **Yes** button; the views are modified. You will notice that the view that was originally displayed as the top view is now displayed as the front view. Also, all other views will be modified accordingly.

Reset Standard Views

The **Reset Standard Views** button is chosen to reset the standard settings of all standard views in the current drawing. When you choose this button, the **SolidWorks** warning box will be displayed and you will be prompted to confirm whether you want to reset all standard views to their original settings or not. If you choose **Yes**, all the standard views will be reset to their default settings.

Changing the Orientation Using Reference Triad

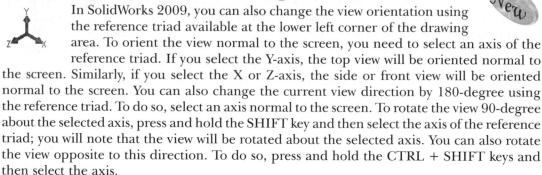

In SolidWorks 2009, you can also change the view orientation using the reference triad available at the lower left corner of the drawing area. To orient the view normal to the screen, you need to select an axis of the reference triad. If you select the Y-axis, the top view will be oriented normal to the screen. Similarly, if you select the X or Z-axis, the side or front view will be oriented normal to the screen. You can also change the current view direction by 180-degree using the reference triad. To do so, select an axis normal to the screen. To rotate the view 90-degree about the selected axis, press and hold the SHIFT key and then select the axis of the reference triad; you will note that the view will be rotated about the selected axis. You can also rotate the view opposite to this direction. To do so, press and hold the CTRL + SHIFT keys and then select the axis.

To rotate the view about the selected axis using the arrow keys, press and hold the ALT key and then select the required axis of the reference triad; the part will rotate to a default angle of 15-degree. Now, holding the ALT key, press the side arrow key; the part will again rotate to an angle of 15-degree. In this way, you can rotate the part at an increment of 15-degree. To change this angle value, choose the **Options** button from the Menu Bar; the **System Options - General** dialog box will be displayed. Choose the **View** option from the area on the left of the dialog box to display the options related to the view. Next, set the required angle value in the **Arrow keys** spinner and choose the **OK** button.

Tip. *To rotate the view using the arrow keys in the opposite direction, press and hold the CTRL + ALT keys and then select the axis.*

RESTORING PREVIOUS VIEW

While working on a model, you need to temporarily change the view of the model to view it from different directions. Once you have finished editing or viewing the model in the current view, choose the **Previous View** button in the **Heads-up View** toolbar to restore the previous view. This tool saves ten previous views of the model.

DISPLAYING THE DRAWING AREA IN VIEWPORTS

In SolidWorks, you can display the drawing area in multiple viewports. The procedure to do so is discussed next.

Displaying the Drawing Area in Two Horizontal Viewports

SolidWorks menus:	Window > Viewport > Two View - Horizontal
Toolbar:	Heads-up View > View Orientation > Two View - Horizontal

The **Two View - Horizontal** option is used to split the drawing view to display the model in two viewports that are placed horizontally. To do so, choose **View Orientation > Two View - Horizontal** from the **Heads-up View** toolbar; the drawing area will be divided into two rows. Figure 5-35 shows the model placed at the top orientation in the upper row and in the front orientation in the lower row. The type of orientation of both the models is displayed on the lower left corner of each viewport.

To switch back to the single viewport, choose **View Orientation > Single View** from the **Heads-up View** toolbar or choose **Window > Viewport > Single View** in the SolidWorks menus.

Displaying the Drawing Area in Two Vertical Viewports

SolidWorks menus:	Window > Viewport > Two View - Vertical
Toolbar:	Heads-up View > View Orientation > Two View - Vertical

The **Two View - Vertical** button is used to split the drawing view to display the model in two viewports that are placed vertically. To display the model in this fashion, choose **View Orientation > Two View - Vertical** from the **Heads-up View** toolbar; the drawing area will be divided into two columns placed vertically. Figure 5-36 shows the model placed at the front orientation in the left column and in the right orientation in the right column.

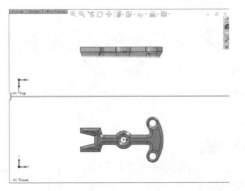

*Figure 5-35 Drawing area divided into two rows horizontally using the **Two View - Horizontal** tool*

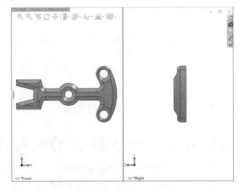

*Figure 5-36 Drawing area divided into two columns vertically using the **Two View - Vertical** tool*

Tip. *On creating multiple viewports, you will notice that the Heads-up View toolbar will be available in the currently active viewport. To activate another viewport, click once in the drawing area in that viewport.*

Displaying the Drawing Area in Four Viewports

SolidWorks menus:	Window > Viewport > Four View
Toolbar:	Heads-up View > View Orientation > Four View

The **Four View** option is used to split the drawing view to display the model in four viewports, as shown in Figure 5-37. To display the model in this fashion, choose **View Orientation > Four View** from the **Heads-up View** toolbar; the drawing area will be divided into four parts. The model is placed in the front, top, right, and trimetric orientations in these four viewports. The type of orientation of all models is displayed at the lower left corner of each viewport.

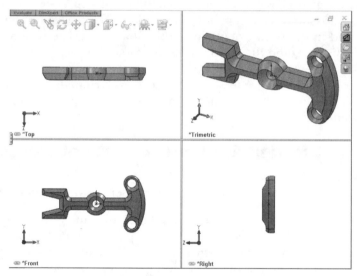

Figure 5-37 *Model displayed in four viewports*

Tip. *Right-click and choose* **Link Views** *from the shortcut menu to link the viewports. Now, if you pan or zoom one view while multiple viewports are being displayed, the model will pan or zoom accordingly in all the other viewports. Note, that this linking is not applicable for the viewport in which the model is displayed in 3D orientation.*

DISPLAY MODES OF THE MODEL

SolidWorks provides you with various predefined modes to display the model. In SolidWorks, the display modes are grouped together in the **Display Style** tool. To invoke a tool, choose the **Display Style** button from the **Heads-up View** toolbar; a flyout consisting of tools that are used for various display modes will be displayed. Choose any of the display modes. These modes are discussed next.

Wireframe

 When you choose the **Wireframe** button, all hidden lines will be displayed along with the visible lines in the model. Sometimes it becomes difficult to recognize the visible lines and the hidden lines if you set this display mode for complex models.

Hidden Lines Visible

 When you choose the **Hidden Lines Visible** button, the model will be displayed in the wireframe and the hidden lines in the model will be displayed as dashed lines.

Hidden Lines Removed

 When you choose the **Hidden Lines Removed** button, the hidden lines in the model will not be displayed. Only the edges of the faces visible in the current view of the model will be displayed.

Shaded With Edges

 The **Shaded With Edges** mode is the default mode in which the model is displayed. In this display mode, the model is shaded and the edges of the visible faces of the model are displayed.

Shaded

 This display mode is similar to the **Shaded With Edges** mode the only difference is that the edges of the visible faces will not be displayed.

 Tip. *Sometimes when you rotate the view of an assembly or a model having large number of features in the **Shaded** or the **Hidden Lines Removed** shading modes, the regeneration of the model takes a lot of time. This can be avoided by choosing the **Draft Quality HLR/HLV** button combined with the other shading modes. This button is not available by default, therefore, you need to customize a toolbar or a **CommandManager**. On choosing this button, you can speed up the regeneration time and easily rotate the view. This is a toggle mode and is turned on when you choose this button.*

ADDITIONAL DISPLAY MODES

In addition to the standard display modes discussed earlier, you can also display a model in the shaded mode, or view a model in the perspective view. The tools for displaying these views are available in the **Heads-up View** toolbar. These tools are discussed next.

Shadows In Shaded Mode

Toolbar: Heads-up View > View Settings > Shadows In Shaded Mode

 The **Shadows In Shaded Mode** button is used to display the shadow of a model. A light appears from the top of the model to display the shadow in the current view.

With this option activated, the performance of the system is affected during the dynamic orientation. Remember that the position of the shadow is not changed when you rotate the model in the 3D space. To change the placement of the shadow, first remove the shadow in the shaded model using the **Shadows In Shaded Mode** button and rotate the model. After rotating the model, use the same button to activate the shadow in the shaded mode. Figure 5-38 shows a T-section in the shadow in the shaded mode.

Perspective

Toolbar:	Heads-up View > View Settings > Perspective

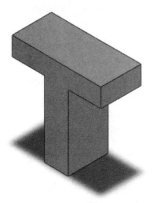 You can display the perspective view of a model by choosing **View Settings > Perspective** from the **Heads-up View** toolbar. Figure 5-39 shows the T-section with shadow in the perspective view. You can also modify the settings of the perspective view. To modify the settings, choose **View > Modify > Perspective** from the SolidWorks menus; the **Perspective View PropertyManager** will be displayed. Use the **Object Sizes Away** spinner of this **PropertyManager** to modify the observer's position.

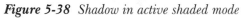

Figure 5-38 *Shadow in active shaded mode*

Figure 5-39 *T-section displayed in perspective view with shadow*

 Tip. *You can also save a perspective view as a named view. To do this, invoke the perspective view and define the orientation by rotating the view. Press the SPACEBAR to invoke the* **Orientation** *dialog box. Choose the* **New View** *button and specify the name of the view in the* **Named View** *dialog box.*

ASSIGNING MATERIALS AND TEXTURES TO MODELS

You can assign materials and textures to models. When you apply a material to a model, the physical properties such as density, young's modulus, and so on will be assigned to the model. When you apply a texture to a model or its face, the image of that texture will be applied to the model or its selected face. Physical properties are not applied to the model when you apply the texture. The method to assign materials and textures is discussed next.

Assigning Materials to the Model

Toolbar:	Standard > Edit Material *(Customize to add)*
SolidWorks menus:	Edit > Appearance > Material

Whenever you assign a material to a model, all physical properties of the selected material are also assigned to the model. As a result, when you calculate the mass properties of the model, they will be based on the physical properties of the material applied. To assign a material to a model, choose the **Edit Material** button from the **Standard** toolbar; the **Material** dialog box will be displayed, as shown in Figure 5-40. You can also right-click on the **Material <not specified>** option in the **FeatureManager design tree** to invoke the **Material** dialog box.

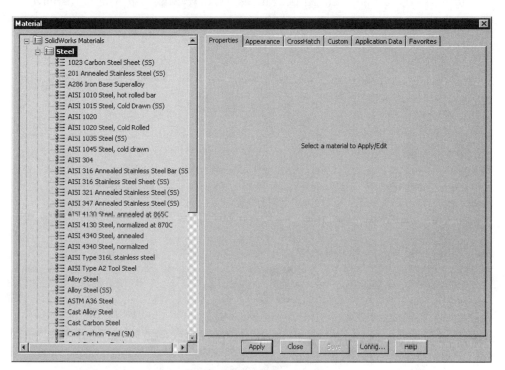

*Figure 5-40 The **Material** dialog box*

A number of material families are available in the left area of the dialog box. Click on the (+) sign located on the left of the material family to display all materials under that family. Select the material from that family.

Assigning Textures to the Model

SolidWorks menus:	Edit > Appearance > Appearance
Toolbar:	View > Edit Appearance

In SolidWorks 2009, you can assign a texture or color to a model, feature, or a selected face. To do so, invoke the **Edit Appearance** tool by choosing the **Edit > Appearance > Appearance** from the SolidWorks menus; the **Appearances PropertyManager** will be displayed, as shown in Figure 5-41. You can also invoke the **Appearances PropertyManager** using another method. In this method, first, you need to select a face; a pop-up toolbar will be displayed. Now, choose the **Appearance Callout** button from this toolbar; a flyout will be displayed with the name of the Face, Extrude, Body, and Part. Select the check box corresponding to the texture; the **Appearances PropertyManager** will be displayed.

*Figure 5-41 The **Appearances PropertyManager***

In this **PropertyManager**, the **Selected Geometry** rollout has four buttons on its left, namely, **Select Faces**, **Select Surfaces**, **Select Bodies**, and **Select Features**. These buttons are used as filters for making a selection to assign the texture or color to a model. For example, if you want to assign the texture or color on the face of a model, clear the existing selection from the **Selected Entities** area and then choose the **Select Faces** button from the **Selected Geometry** rollout. This allows you to select only a specified face of the model. Select the required face from the model; the selected face will be displayed in the **Selected Entities** area.

The **Appearance** rollout is used to display the appearance applied on the model. You can also browse the required appearance by choosing the **Browse** button. The **Transparency** spinner is used to set the transparency level of the appearance.

The **Color** rollout is used to apply required color to the model. The color selected in this rollout will be applied to various entities that are listed in the **Selected Entities** area of the **Selected Geometry** rollout such as face, surface, body, or feature. Set the required color using the **Pick to Color** display area; the selected color will be displayed in the **Color** display area of this rollout. You can also use the **Red Component of Color**, **Green Component of Color**, and **Blue Component of Color** spinners to set the color.

Various texture families that can be selected for applying on the model are available in the **Appearances/Scenes PropertyManager**. To invoke this **PropertyManager**, choose the **Appearances/Scenes** tab from the task pane and then click on the (+) sign located on the left of a texture family to select the texture of that family; the texture of the selected texture family will be listed at the bottom of the **Appearances/Scenes PropertyManager**. Now, select the required texture from it; the selected texture will be displayed in the **Appearances** rollout of the **Appearances PropertyManager**. Figure 5-42 shows the model with the Gravel type of stone applied to its top face.

Figure 5-42 Appearances applied to the top face of a model

The preview of the selected appearances will be displayed on the model or face. If you do not want to keep a particular appearance, you can remove it by choosing the **Remove Appearances** button available below the **Selected Entities** area of the **Selection** rollout.

TUTORIALS

Tutorial 1

In this tutorial, you will open the sketch drawn in Tutorial 3 of Chapter 4. You will then convert that sketch into an extruded model by extruding it in two directions, as shown in Figure 5-43. The parameters for extruding the sketch are given next.

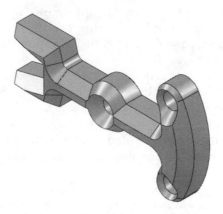

Figure 5-43 Model for Tutorial 1

Direction 1
Depth = 10 mm
Draft angle = 35-degree

Direction 2
Depth = 15 mm
Draft angle = 0-degree

After creating the model, you will rotate the view using the **Rotate View** tool and then modify the standard views such that the front view of the model becomes the top view. You will then save the model with the current settings.   **(Expected time: 30 min)**

The following steps are required to complete this tutorial:

a. Open the document of Tutorial 3 of Chapter 4, refer to Figure 5-44.
b. Save this document in the *c05* folder with a new name.
c. Invoke the **Extruded Boss/Base** tool and convert the sketch into a model, refer to Figures 5-45 and 5-46.
d. Rotate the view using the **Rotate View** tool to view the model from all directions, refer to Figure 5-47.
e. Invoke the **Orientation** dialog box and then modify the standard view, refer to Figure 5-48.

Opening the Document of Tutorial 3 of Chapter 4

As the required document is saved in the *\c04* folder, you need to select this folder and then open the *c04tut3.sldprt* document.

1. Start SolidWorks 2009 by double-clicking on its shortcut icon on the desktop of your computer.

2. Choose the **Open a Document** option from the **SolidWorks Resources** task pane to display the **Open** dialog box.

3. Browse and select the *c04* folder.

4. Select the *c04tut3.sldprt* document and then choose the **Open** button. Close the **SolidWorks Resources** task pane.

    As the sketch was saved in the sketching environment in Chapter 4, it is opened in the sketching environment.

Saving the Document in the c05 Folder

It is recommended that when you open a document of some other chapter, you should save it in the folder of the current chapter with some other name before modifying the document. This is because if you save the document in the folder of the current chapter, the original document of the other chapter will not get modified.

1. Choose **File > Save As** from the SolidWorks menus; the **Save As** dialog box is displayed.

    As the *c04* folder was selected last to open the document, it will be the current folder.

2. Choose the **Up One Level** button available on the right of the **Save in** drop-down list and move to the *\SolidWorks* folder. Create a new folder with the name *c05* using the **Create New Folder** button. Make the *c05* folder as current by double-clicking on it.

3. Enter the new name of the document as *c05tut1* in the **File name** edit box and then choose the **Save** button to save the document.

    The document is saved with the new name and is now opened in the drawing area, as shown in Figure 5-44.

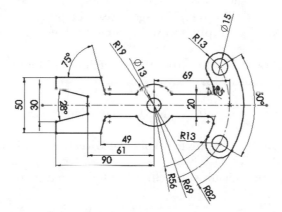

Figure 5-44 *Sketch that will open in the drawing area*

Extruding the Sketch

Next, you need to invoke the **Extruded Boss/Base** tool and extrude the sketch using the parameters given in the tutorial description.

1. Choose the **Features** tab from the **CommandManager** to display the **Features CommandManager**. Then, choose the **Extruded Boss/Base** button; the sketch is automatically oriented to the trimetric view and the **Extrude PropertyManager** is displayed, as shown in Figure 5-45.

Figure 5-45 The Extrude PropertyManager

As you are converting the closed sketch into a feature, only the **Direction 1** rollout is displayed in the **Extrude PropertyManager**. Also, the preview of the feature is displayed in the temporary shaded graphics with the default values.

2. Choose the **Draft On/Off** button from the **Direction 1** rollout and then set the value of the **Draft Angle** spinner to **35**.

   These are the settings for direction 1. Next, you need to specify the settings for direction 2.

3. Select the **Direction 2** check box to invoke the **Direction 2** rollout.

   You will notice that the default values in this rollout are the same as you specified in the **Direction 1** rollout.

4. Choose the **Draft On/Off** button in the **Direction 2** rollout to turn this option off. This is because you do not require the draft angle in the second direction.

5. Set the value in the **Depth** spinner to **15** as the depth in the second direction is 15 mm.

6. Choose the **OK** button to create the feature or choose **OK** from the confirmation corner.

It is recommended that you change the view to isometric after creating the feature so that you can view the feature properly.

7. Choose the **View Orientation** button from the **Heads-up View** toolbar; a flyout is displayed. Then, choose **Isometric** button from it. If the origin is displayed, turn off the display of the origin in the model by choosing **Hide/Show Items > View Origins** from the **Heads-up View** toolbar. The isometric view of the resulting solid model is shown in Figure 5-46.

Rotating the View

As mentioned earlier, you can rotate the view so that you can view the model from all directions.

1. Press the middle mouse button and move the cursor; the arrow cursor is replaced by the rotate view cursor.

2. Press and hold the middle mouse button and drag the cursor in the drawing area to rotate the view, as shown in Figure 5-47.

Figure 5-46 *Isometric view of the solid model*

Figure 5-47 *Rotating the view to display the model from different directions*

You will notice that the model is being displayed from different directions. Remember that when you rotate the view, the model is not being rotated. The camera that is used to view the model is being rotated around the model.

3. After viewing the model from all directions, press CTRL+7 from the keyboard; the model again gets oriented to the isometric view.

Modifying Standard Views

As mentioned in the tutorial description, you need to modify the standard views such that the front view of the model becomes the top view. This is done using the **Orientation** dialog box.

1. Press the SPACEBAR on the keyboard; the **Orientation** dialog box is displayed.

2. Hold the **Orientation** dialog box by selecting it on the title bar of this dialog box and then drag it to the top right corner of the drawing area.

    The **Orientation** dialog box will close automatically if you perform any other operation. Therefore, you need to pin this dialog box.

3. Choose the **Pin/Unpin the dialog** button to pin this dialog box at the top right corner of the drawing area. Pinning the dialog box ensures that the dialog box is not automatically closed when you perform any other operation.

4. Double-click on the **Front** option in the list box of the **Orientation** dialog box; the current view is automatically changed to the front view and the model is now reoriented and displayed from the front.

    Now, you need to modify the standard views such that the front view of the model becomes the top view. Then, you need to save the model with the current settings.

5. Select the **Top** option from the list box by selecting it once.

    Make sure you do not double-click on this option. This is because if you double-click on this option, the model will be reoriented and displayed from the top.

6. Now, choose the **Update Standard Views** button to update the standard views; the **SolidWorks** warning box is displayed and you are warned that modifying the standard views will change the orientation of any named view in this document.

7. Choose **Yes** from this warning box to modify the standard views.

8. Now, double-click on the **Isometric** option in the list box of the **Orientation** dialog box. You will notice that the isometric view is different now, refer to Figure 5-48.

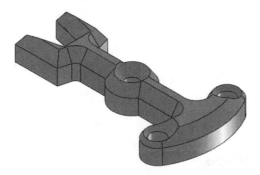

Figure 5-48 Model displayed from the modified isometric view

9. Choose the **Pin/Unpin the dialog** button from the **Orientation** dialog box again and left-click anywhere in the drawing area to close the dialog box.

Saving the Model

As the name of the document was specified at the beginning, you need to choose the save button to save the document.

1. Choose the **Save** button from the Menu Bar to save the document; the model is saved with the name *\My Documents\SolidWorks\c05\c05tut1.sldprt*.

2. Choose **File > Close** from the SolidWorks menus to close the document.

Tutorial 2

In this tutorial, you will create the model shown in Figure 5-49. Its dimensions are shown in Figure 5-50. The extrusion depth of the model is 20 mm. After creating the model, rotate the view and then change the view back to the isometric view before saving the model.

(Expected time: 45 min)

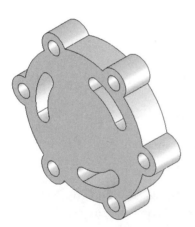

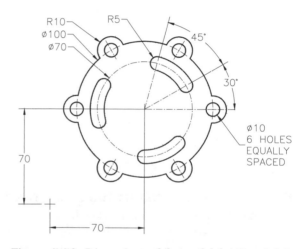

Figure 5-49 *Model for Tutorial 2*   **Figure 5-50** *Dimensions of the model for Tutorial 2*

The following steps are required to complete this tutorial:

a. Start a new SolidWorks part document and then invoke the sketching environment.
b. Create the outer loop and then create the sketch of three inner cavities. Finally, draw the six circles inside the outer loop for the holes, refer to Figures 5-51 through 5-55.
c. Invoke the **Extruded Boss/Base** tool and extrude the sketch through a distance of 20 mm, refer to Figure 5-56.
d. Rotate the view using the **Rotate View** tool.
e. Change the current view to isometric view and then save the document.

Starting a New Part Document

1. Choose the **New** button from the Menu Bar and start a new part document using the **New SolidWorks Document** dialog box.

2. Choose the **Sketch** button from the **Sketch CommandManager** and select the **Front Plane**; the sketching environment is invoked.

Drawing the Outer Loop

This is the same sketch that was created in the Tutorial 3 of Chapter 3. In this tutorial, you will create only the outer loop using the steps that were discussed in Chapter 3. It is recommended that you add relations and dimensions to it to make it fully defined.

1. Follow the steps that were discussed in the Tutorial 3 of Chapter 3 to create the outer loop.

2. Add dimensions to it to fully define the sketch, as shown in Figure 5-51.

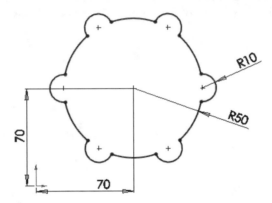

Figure 5-51 Sketch after creating the outer loop

Drawing the Sketch of Inner Cavities

Now, you need to draw the sketch of inner cavities. Draw the sketch of one of the cavities and then add the required relations and dimensions to it. Next, you need to create a circular pattern of this cavity. The number of instances in the circular pattern is 3.

1. Choose the **Centerpoint Arc Slot** button from the **Sketch CommandManager**. Next, draw a slot with its center at the center point of the larger arc having 100 mm diameter. Make sure the start point and endpoint of the slot arc are in the first quadrant.

2. Complete the slot and then add dimension to it, as shown in Figure 5-52. The slot turns black, indicating that it is fully defined.

   Next, you need to create a circular pattern of the inner cavity.

3. Select the slot of the inner cavity and then invoke the **Circular Pattern PropertyManager**.

4. Drag the center of the circular pattern to the center of the circle having 100 mm diameter.

5. Set the value **3** in the **Number** spinner of the **Parameters** rollout and then choose the **OK** button to create the circular pattern, as shown in Figure 5-53.

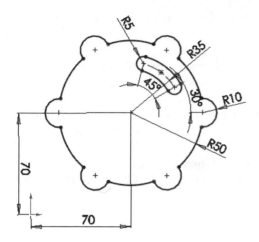

Figure 5-52 *Sketch after drawing the inner cavity*

Figure 5-53 *Sketch after creating the circular pattern of the inner cavity*

6. Draw a circle of 10 mm diameter and create a circular pattern of the circle. Next, fully define the sketch by using the **Fully Define Sketch** tool, if required. This completes the sketch of the model. The final sketch of the model is shown in Figure 5-54.

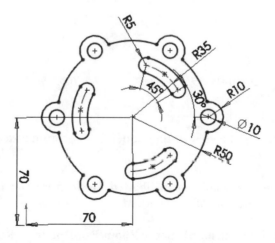

Figure 5-54 *Sketch after drawing the inner cavity*

Extruding the Sketch

The next step after creating the sketch is to extrude it. The sketch is extruded using the **Extruded Boss/Base** tool.

1. Choose the **Features** tab from the **CommandManager** to display the **Features CommandManager** and choose the **Extruded Boss/Base** tool.

The current view is changed to the trimetric view and the **Extrude PropertyManager** is displayed. Also, the preview of the model, created using the default values, is displayed in the drawing area.

2. Set the value of the **Depth** spinner to **20** and then choose the **OK** button to extrude the sketch.

3. Choose **View Settings > Shadows In Shaded Mode** from the **Heads-up View** toolbar to display the model with shadow.

4. Press SPACEBAR and then double-click on the **Isometric** option in the **Orientation** dialog box to change the current view to the isometric view. The complete model for Tutorial 2 is shown in Figure 5-55.

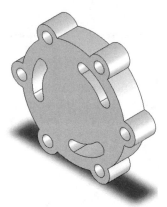

Figure 5-55 Complete model for Tutorial 2

Rotating the View

Before you start rotating the view of the model, it is recommended that you turn off the display of the shadow.

1. Choose **View Settings > Shadows In Shaded Mode** from the **Heads-up View** toolbar to turn off the display of the shadow.

2. Now, right-click on the model and choose **Zoom/Pan/Rotate > Rotate** from the shortcut menu; the arrow cursor is replaced by the rotate view cursor.

3. Press the left mouse button and drag the cursor in the drawing area to rotate the view.

4. Change the current view to the isometric view using the **Orientation** dialog box.

Saving the Model

1. Choose the **Save** button from the Menu Bar and save the model with the name given below.

    \My Documents\SolidWorks\c05\c05tut2.sldprt.

2. Choose **File > Close** from the SolidWorks menus to close the document.

Tutorial 3

In this tutorial, you will open the sketch drawn in Exercise 3 of Chapter 4. You will then create a thin feature by revolving the sketch through an angle of 270-degree, as shown in Figure 5-56. You will offset the sketch outward while creating the thin feature. After creating the model, you will turn on the option to display the shadows and also apply the Copper material to the model. Also, determine the mass properties.   **(Expected time: 30 min)**

Figure 5-56 Revolved model for Tutorial 3

The following steps are required to complete this tutorial:
a. Open the sketch of Exercise 3 of Chapter 4, refer to Figure 5-57.
b. Save it in the folder of the current chapter.
c. Invoke the **Revolved Boss/Base** tool and revolve the sketch through an angle of 270-degree, refer to Figure 5-59.
d. Change the current view to isometric view and then display the model in shadow, refer to Figure 5-60.
e. Assign copper material to the model, refer to Figure 5-61 and then check the mass properties.

Opening the Document of Exercise 3 of Chapter 4

As the required document is saved in the *\My Documents\SolidWorks\c04* folder, you need to select this folder and then open the *c04exr3.sldprt* document.

1. Choose the **Open** button from the Menu Bar to display the **Open** dialog box. The *c05* folder is the current folder in this dialog box.

2. Browse and select the *\My Documents\SolidWorks\c04* folder. All documents that were created in Chapter 4 are displayed in this folder.

3. Select the *c04exr3.sldprt* document; and then choose the **Open** button; the document is opened in the sketching environment.

Saving the Document in the c05 Folder

As mentioned earlier, it is recommended that you need to save the document with a new name in the folder of the current chapter so that the original document is not modified.

1. Choose **File > Save As** from the SolidWorks menus to display the **Save As** dialog box. Because the *c04* folder was selected last to open the document, it is the current folder.

2. Browse and select the *c05* folder and double-click on it to make it current.

3. Enter the name of the document in the **File name** edit box as *c05tut3*. Choose the **Save** button to save the document. The sketch is displayed in the drawing area, as shown in Figure 5-57.

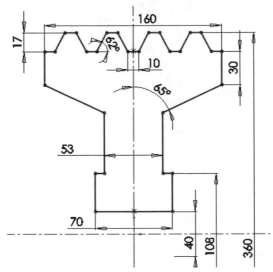

Figure 5-57 *Sketch for the revolved model*

Revolving the Sketch

The sketch consists of two centerlines. The first centerline was used to mirror the sketched entities and the second was drawn to apply linear diameter dimensions. You need to revolve the sketch around the second centerline.

1. Choose the **Features** tab from the **CommandManager** to display the **Features CommandManager**. Choose the **Revolved Boss/Base** button. The sketch is automatically oriented in the trimetric view and the **Revolve PropertyManager** is displayed.

Because the sketch has two centerlines, SolidWorks cannot determine which one to use as an axis of revolution. This is the reason why you are prompted to select the axis of revolution.

2. Select the horizontal centerline that was used to create linear diameter dimensions as the axis of revolution. The preview of a complete revolved feature in temporary shaded graphics is displayed in the drawing area. As the preview of the model is not displayed properly in the current view, you need to zoom the drawing.

3. Choose the **Zoom to Fit** button from the **Heads-up View** toolbar or press the F key on the keyboard.

4. Set the value of the **Angle** spinner in the **Revolve PropertyManager** to **270**; the preview of the revolved model is also modified accordingly. If you enter the value in the **Angle** spinner, you need to click anywhere on the screen to make sure the preview is modified.

    Note that if the horizontal centerline was drawn from left to right, then the direction of revolution has to be reversed to get the required model; refer to the right-hand thumb rule. You can reverse the direction of revolution using the **Reverse Direction** button available on the left of the **Revolve Type** drop-down list.

5. Select the **Thin Feature** check box to invoke the **Thin Feature** rollout, as shown in Figure 5-58. Set the value in the **Direction 1 Thickness** spinner to **5**. You will notice that the preview of the thin feature is shown outside the original sketch.

6. Choose the **OK** button; the revolved feature is created, as shown in Figure 5-59.

7. Choose the **Isometric** option from the flyout that is displayed on choosing the **View Orientation** button from the **Heads-up View** toolbar.

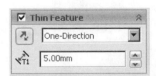

Figure 5-58 The Thin Feature rollout

Figure 5-59 Model created by revolving the sketch

Rotating the View

Next, you need to rotate the view so that you can view the model from all directions. As mentioned earlier, the view can be rotated using the **Rotate View** tool.

1. Press the middle mouse button and move the cursor; the arrow cursor is replaced by the rotate view cursor.

2. Hold the middle mouse button and drag the cursor in the drawing area to rotate the view.

3. Press SPACEBAR to invoke the **Orientation** dialog box. In this dialog box, double-click on the **Isometric** option.

Displaying the Shadow

As mentioned in the tutorial description, you need to display the shadow of the model if it is not displayed by default. You can turn on the display of the shadow using the **Heads-up View** toolbar.

1. Choose **View Settings > Shadows In Shaded Mode** from the **Heads-up View** toolbar to display the model with shadow, as shown in Figure 5-60.

Assigning Materials to the Model

As mentioned earlier, you can invoke this **PropertyManager** using the **Material** option in the **FeatureManager design tree**. Note that you can also assign a material to a model by choosing **Edit > Appearance > Material** from the SolidWorks menus.

1. Right-click on the **Material <not specified>** option in the **FeatureManager design tree** and choose the **Edit Material** option; the **Material** dialog box is displayed.

2. Click on the (+) sign located on the left of the **Copper and its Alloys** option from the list of materials available on the left area of the dialog box; the tree view expands and materials in this family are displayed.

3. Select the **Copper** option and choose **Apply** button from the **Material** dialog box and then choose the **Close** button to exit. The model, after assigning the material, is shown in Figure 5-61.

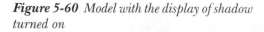

Figure 5-60 Model with the display of shadow turned on

Figure 5-61 Model after assigning the copper material

Determining the Mass Properties of the Model

As discussed earlier, to determine the mass properties of the current model, you need to invoke the **Mass Properties** dialog box.

1. Choose the **Mass Properties** button from the **Evaluate CommandManager**; the **Mass Properties** dialog box will be displayed with the mass properties of the current model, as shown in Figure 5-62.

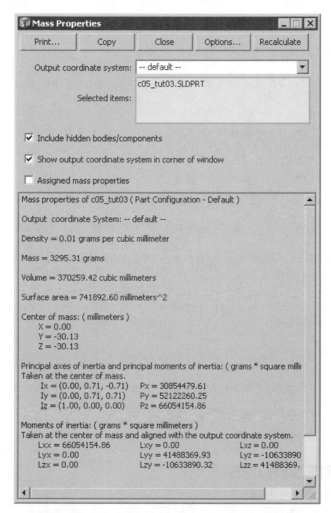

*Figure 5-62 The **Mass Properties** dialog box*

Saving the Model

As the name of the document was specified at the beginning, you just need to choose the save button now to save the document.

1. Choose the **Save** button from the Menu Bar to save the model. If the SolidWorks warning box is displayed, choose **Yes** from it to rebuild the model before saving.

The model is saved with the name *\My Documents\SolidWorks\c05\c05tut3.sldprt*.

2. Choose **File > Close** from the SolidWorks menus to close the document.

SELF-EVALUATION TEST

Answer the following questions and then compare them to those given at the end of this chapter:

1. In SolidWorks, a sketch is revolved using the **Extrude PropertyManager**. (T/F)

2. You can also specify the depth of extrusion dynamically in the preview of the extruded feature. (T/F)

3. You can invoke the drawing display tools such as **Zoom to Fit** while the preview of a model is displayed on the screen. (T/F)

4. If you rotate the view when the current display mode is set to **Hidden Lines Visible**, the hidden lines in the model are automatically displayed. (T/F)

5. The _____ tool is used to display the perspective view of a model.

6. The **Cap ends** check box is displayed in the **Extrude PropertyManager** only when the sketch for the thin base feature is _____.

7. The _____ check box is used to create a feature with different values in both directions of the sketching plane.

8. The _____ check box is used to apply automatic fillets while creating a thin feature.

9. The _____ button is used to display the shadow in the shaded mode.

10. To resume the rotation of the view freely after you have completed rotating it around a selected vertex, edge, or face, _____ anywhere in the drawing area.

REVIEW QUESTIONS

Answer the following questions:

1. You can also invoke the **Rotate View** tool by choosing the **Rotate View** option from the _____ that is displayed when you right-click in the drawing area.

2. When you choose the **Wireframe** button, all _____ lines will be displayed along with the visible lines in the model.

3. You can also modify the parallel view to perspective view by choosing _____ from the SolidWorks menus.

4. When you invoke the **Extruded Boss/Base** tool or the **Revolved Boss/Base** tool, the view is automatically changed to a _____.

5. The thin revolved features can be created using a _____ or an _____ sketch.

6. Which of the following buttons is chosen to modify the orientation of the standard views?

    (a) **Update Standard Views**   (b) **Reset Standard Views**
    (c) None   (d) Both

7. Which of the following buttons is not available in the **View** toolbar by default?

    (a) **Hidden Lines Removed**   (b) **Hidden Lines Visible**
    (c) **Shaded**   (d) **Perspective**

8. Which of the following parameters is not displayed in the preview of the model?

    (a) Depth   (b) Draft angle
    (c) None   (d) Both

9. If the sketch is open, it can be converted into:

    (a) Thin feature   (b) Solid feature
    (c) None   (d) Both

10. In SolidWorks, which tool is used to make a sketch fully defined?

    (a) **Fully Define Sketch**   (b) **Smart Dimension**
    (c) None   (d) Both

EXERCISES

Exercise 1

Create the model shown in Figure 5-63. The sketch of the model is shown in Figure 5-64. Create the sketch and dimension it using the fully define sketch option. The extrusion depth of the model is 15 mm. After creating the model, rotate the view.

(Expected time: 30 min)

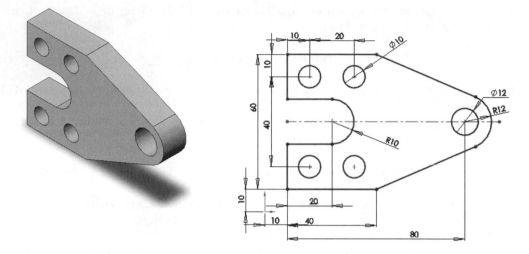

Figure 5-63 *Model for Exercise 1*   **Figure 5-64** *Sketch of the model for Exercise 1*

Exercise 2

Create the model shown in Figure 5-65. The sketch of the model is shown in Figure 5-66. Create the sketch and dimension it using the fully define sketch option. The extrusion depth of the model is 25 mm. Modify the standard view such that the current front view of the model is displayed when you invoke the top view. **(Expected time: 30 min)**

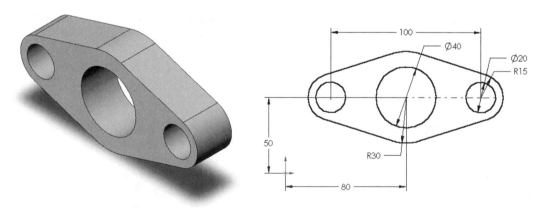

Figure 5-65 *Model for Exercise 2*   **Figure 5-66** *Sketch of the model for Exercise 2*

Answers to Self-Evaluation Test
1. F, **2.** T, **3.** T, **4.** T, **5. Perspective, 6.** closed, **7. Direction 2, 8. Auto-fillet corners, 9. Shadows In Shaded Mode, 10.** double-click

Chapter 6

Creating Reference Geometries

Learning Objectives

After completing this chapter, you will be able to:

- *Create a reference plane.*
- *Create a reference axis.*
- *Create reference points.*
- *Create a reference coordinate system.*
- *Create a model using advanced Boss/Base options.*
- *Create a model using the contour selection technique.*
- *Create a cut feature.*
- *Create multiple disjoint bodies.*

IMPORTANCE OF SKETCHING PLANES

In the earlier chapters, you created basic models by extruding or revolving the sketches. All these models were created on a single sketching plane, the **Front Plane**. But most mechanical designs consist of multiple sketched features, referenced geometries, and placed features. These features are integrated together to complete a model. Most of these features lie on different planes. When you start a new SolidWorks document and try to invoke the sketching plane, you are prompted to select the plane on which you want to draw the sketch. On the basis of the design requirements, you can select any plane to create the base feature. To create additional sketched features, you need to select an existing plane or a planar surface, or you need to create a plane that will be used as a sketching plane. For cxample, consider the model shown in Figure 6-1.

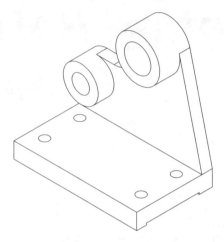

Figure 6-1 A multifeatured model

The base feature of this model is shown in Figure 6-2. The sketch for the base feature is drawn on the **Top Plane**. After creating the base feature, you need to create the other sketched features, placed features, and referenced features, see Figure 6-3. The boss features and cut features are the sketched features that require sketching planes where you can draw the sketch of the features.

It is evident from Figure 6-3 that the features added to the base feature are not created on the same plane on which the sketch for the base feature is created. Therefore, to draw the sketches of other sketched features, you need to define other sketching planes.

REFERENCE GEOMETRY

The reference geometry features are those that are available only to assist you in creating models. The reference geometries in SolidWorks include planes, axes, points, and coordinate systems. These reference geometries act as reference for drawing the sketches for the sketched features, defining the sketch plane, and assembling the components. They also act as references for various placed features and sketched features. These features have no mass or volume. You must have a good understanding of these geometries because they are widely used in creating complex models.

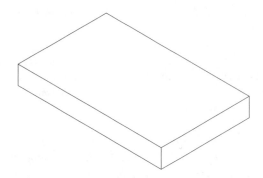

Figure 6-2 *Base feature of the model*   **Figure 6-3** *Model after adding other features*

Reference Planes

Generally, all engineering components or designs are multifeatured models. Also, as discussed earlier, all features of a model are not created on the same plane on which the base feature is created. Therefore, you need to select one of the default planes or create a new plane that will be used as the sketching plane for the second feature. It is clear from the above discussion that you can use the default planes as the sketching plane or you can create a plane that can be used as a sketching plane. The default planes and the creation of a new plane are discussed next.

Default Planes

When you start a new SolidWorks part document, SolidWorks provides you with three default planes: **Front Plane**, **Top Plane**, and **Right Plane**.

The orientation of the component depends on the sketch of the base feature. Therefore, it is recommended that you should select the sketching plane carefully to draw the sketch for the base feature. The sketching plane for drawing the sketch of the base feature can be one of the three datum planes provided by default.

The three default planes will automatically be displayed in the drawing area only if the sketching environment is invoked for the first time to create the sketch. These planes will not be displayed when you invoke the sketching environment again to create the sketch for the additional feature. You need to select the required plane manually.

To select a plane for an additional feature, choose the **Sketch** button; the **Edit Sketch PropertyManager** will be displayed. Whenever the **PropertyManager** is displayed, the **FeatureManager design tree** shifts to the drawing area. Click on the (+) sign located on the left of the part document name in the **FeatureManager design tree**. The tree view will expand and display the names of the planes. Select the required plane from the tree view.

Note
*You can also select a plane before choosing the **Sketch** button to invoke the sketching environment. In this case, the **Edit Sketch PropertyManager** will not be displayed and you will not be prompted to select a plane for sketching. The selected plane will automatically be taken as the sketching plane.*

Tip. *You can turn on the display of the default planes in the drawing area using the following procedure:*

Press and hold the CTRL key, select the **Front Plane**, **Top Plane**, *and* **Right Plane** *one-by-one from the* **FeatureManager design tree**; *a pop-up toolbar will be displayed. Choose the* **Show** *button from the toolbar. Set the view to* **Isometric** *using the* **Orientation** *dialog box; the three default planes will be visible.*

By default, the reference planes are not shaded. To turn on the shade of the planes, choose the **Options** *button from the Menu Bar; the* **System Options - General** *dialog box will be invoked. Select the* **Display/Selection** *option from the left of this dialog box; the name of the dialog box will be changed to* **System Options - Display/Selection**. *Select the* **Display shaded planes** *check box from this dialog box and choose the* **OK** *button.*

When the planes are displayed in the shaded mode, invoke the **Rotate View** *tool and drag the rotate view cursor to rotate the shaded planes. You will observe that both the sides of the plane are displayed in different colors. This is to symbolize the positive side and the negative side of the plane. This means that when you create an extruded feature, the depth of extrusion will be assigned to the positive side of the plane by default. When you create a cut feature, the depth of the cut feature will be assigned to the negative direction by default.*

Creating New Planes

CommandManager:	Features > Reference Geometry > Plane
SolidWorks menus:	Insert > Reference Geometry > Plane
Toolbar:	Reference Geometry > Plane

The default planes or the reference planes are used to draw sketches for the sketched features. These planes are also used to create placed features such as holes; reference an entity or a feature; and so on. You can also select a planar face of a feature that will be used as the sketching plane. Generally, it is recommended that you should use the planar faces of the features as the sketching planes. However, sometimes you have to create a sketch on a plane that is at some offset distance or at an angle from a plane or a planar face. In this case, you have to create a new reference plane at an offset distance from a plane or a planar face. Consider another case, where you have to define a sketching plane tangent to a cylindrical face of a shaft. You have to create a plane tangent to the cylindrical face of the shaft and this plane will be used as a sketching plane.

In SolidWorks, there are six methods for creating planes. To create planes, choose **Reference Geometry > Plane** from the **Sketch CommandManager**; the **Plane PropertyManager** will be displayed, as shown in Figure 6-4. The confirmation corner will also be displayed at the top right corner of the drawing area.

*Figure 6-4 Partial view of **Plane PropertyManager***

The options in the **Plane PropertyManager** to create new planes are discussed next.

Creating a Plane Passing Through Lines/Points

The **Through Lines/Points** option is used to create a plane that passes through an edge and a point, an axis and a point, or a sketch line and a point. You can also use this option to create a plane that passes through three points. The selected point can be a sketched point or a vertex. To create a plane using this option, invoke the **Plane PropertyManager** and choose the **Through Lines/Points** button. Select the required entities from the drawing area; the preview will be displayed in the drawing area and the name of the selected entities will be displayed in the **Reference Entities** selection box. Choose the **OK** button from the **Plane PropertyManager**. Figure 6-5 shows an edge and a vertex selected to create a plane. The resulting plane is displayed in Figure 6-6. The creation of a new plane by selecting three points is displayed in Figures 6-7 and 6-8.

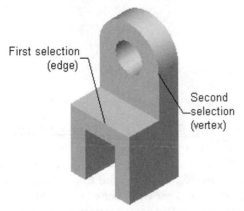

Figure 6-5 Selecting an edge and a vertex

Figure 6-6 Resulting plane

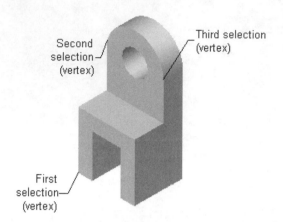

Figure 6-7 *Selecting the vertices*   *Figure 6-8* *Resulting plane*

Creating a Plane Parallel to an Existing Plane or a Planar Face and Passing Through a Point

The **Parallel Plane at Point** option is used to create a plane that is parallel to another plane or a planar face and passes through a point. To create a plane using this option, invoke the **Plane PropertyManager** and then choose the **Parallel Plane at Point** button. Now, select a plane or a planar face to which the new plane will be parallel. Next, select a sketched point, the endpoint of an edge, or the midpoint of an edge. The new plane will pass through this point. Choose the **OK** button. Figure 6-9 shows a planar face and the point selected to create the parallel plane. Figure 6-10 shows the resulting plane.

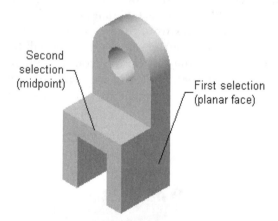

Figure 6-9 *Selecting a planar face and a vertex*   *Figure 6-10* *Resulting plane*

Creating a Plane at an Angle to an Existing Plane or a Planar Face

The **At Angle** option is used to create a plane that is at an angle to the selected plane or a planar face, and also passes through an edge, axis, or a sketched line. To create a plane at an angle, choose the **At Angle** button from the **Plane PropertyManager**; the **Angle** spinner will be enabled. The **Reverse direction** check box and the **Number of Planes to Create** spinner will also appear below the **Distance** spinner in the **Plane PropertyManager**, as shown in Figure 6-11. Now, select an edge, an axis, or a sketched line through which the plane will

*Figure 6-11 The **Plane PropertyManager** with the **At Angle** button chosen*

pass. Next, you have to select a planar face or a plane to define the angle. After selecting the plane or the planar face, set the angle value in the **Angle** spinner. You can reverse the direction of the plane creation by selecting the **Reverse direction** check box. You can also create multiple planes by increasing the value in the **Number of Planes to Create** spinner. Each plane will be incremented by the angle value specified in the **Angle** spinner. Figure 6-12 shows a planar face and an edge selected. Figure 6-13 shows the resulting plane created at an angle of 45-degree to the selected plane.

Tip. *You can also create a plane at an angle dynamically. To do so select an edge or an axis, hold the CTRL key, and click on the boundary of the existing plane and then drag it; the **Plane PropertyManager** will be invoked. Enter the angle value in the **Angle** spinner and choose **OK**; the plane will be created at an angle to the selected planar face.*

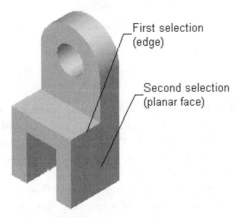

Figure 6-12 A planar face and an edge selected

Figure 6-13 Resulting plane

Creating a Plane at some Offset from an Existing Plane or a Planar Face

The **Offset Distance** option is used to create a plane that is at some offset distance from a selected plane or a planar face. To create a plane using this option, choose the **Offset Distance** button from the **Plane PropertyManager**; the **Distance** spinner will be available. Also, the **Reverse direction** check box and the **Number of Planes to Create** spinner will be displayed below the **Distance** spinner in the **Plane PropertyManager**. Select a plane or a planar face and set the value of the distance in the **Distance** spinner and choose the **OK** button from the **Plane PropertyManager**. You can reverse the direction of the plane creation by selecting the **Reverse direction** check box. You can also create multiple planes by increasing the value in the **Number of Planes to Create** spinner. Each plane will be placed at the offset distance specified in the **Distance** spinner. Figure 6-14 shows a plane selected to create a parallel plane and Figure 6-15 shows the resulting plane created at the required offset.

Tip. *You can also create the planes at an offset distance by dragging the existing plane dynamically. To do so, select the plane from the drawing area by clicking on its boundary by using the left mouse button. Press and hold the CTRL key and drag the cursor; the **Plane PropertyManager** will be displayed. Drag the cursor to the required distance and then release the left mouse button. Alternatively, enter the offset distance in the **Distance** spinner. Right-click and choose the **OK** option or choose the **OK** button from the **Plane PropertyManager**.*

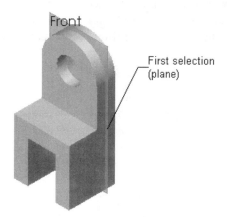

Figure 6-14 Plane to be selected   *Figure 6-15 Resulting plane*

Creating a Plane Normal to Curve

This option is used to create a plane normal to a selected curve. The curve can be a sketched entity or an edge of a feature. To create a plane normal to a curve, choose the **Normal to Curve** button from the **Plane PropertyManager** and select a curve; the preview of the plane will be displayed in the drawing area. By default, the new plane will be created at the endpoint, closest to the point where you selected the curve. If you want to place the curve at the other endpoint or any other point on the curve, select that particular point; the preview of the plane will change accordingly. If you select the curve close to its midpoint, the plane will be displayed in the midpoint of the selected curve. After selecting the plane and the point, choose the **OK** button to create the plane.

When you choose the **Normal to Curve** button from the **Plane PropertyManager**, the **Set origin on curve** check box will be displayed below this button. Select this check box to set the origin of the plane on the curve. Figure 6-16 shows a curve to create the plane and Figure 6-17 shows the resulting plane created normal to the selected curve.

Tip. *If you select an edge of a model or an existing curve and invoke the sketching environment, a reference plane will automatically be created normal to that edge or curve. Also, it will be selected as the sketching plane.*

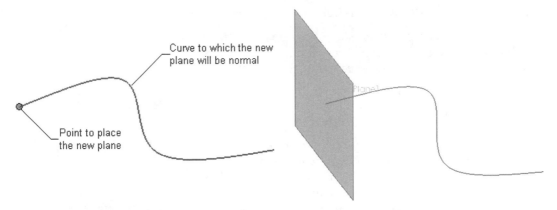

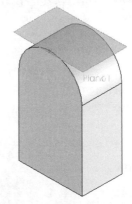

Figure 6-16 *Entities to be selected*   *Figure 6-17* *Resulting plane*

Creating a Plane on Surface

The **On Surface** option is used to create a plane passing through a point on the selected plane or the planar surface. To create a plane on a surface, choose the **On Surface** button from the **Plane PropertyManager** and select the surface on which you want to create the plane. Next, select the sketched point; the preview of the plane will be displayed in the drawing area. Right-click and choose the **OK** option. If the sketch is created on a plane at an offset distance from the selected surface, the **Project to nearest location on surface** and **Project onto surface along sketch normal** radio buttons, and the **Other Solutions** button will be displayed in the **Plane PropertyManager**. Select any of the radio buttons according to the requirement. You can also view the other solutions of the plane creation using the **Other Solutions** button from the **Plane PropertyManager**. Figure 6-18 shows the selection of references for the plane creation and Figure 6-19 shows the resulting plane.

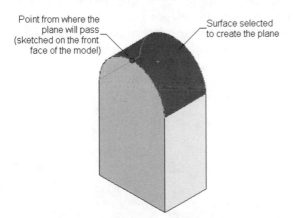

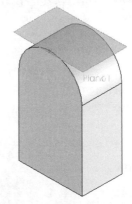

Figure 6-18 *References to be selected*   *Figure 6-19* *Resulting plane*

Tip. *In SolidWorks, if you choose the **Rapid Sketch** button from the **Sketch CommandManager**, you can draw the sketch for the additional features in any existing plane or face without actually selecting the plane.*

Creating Reference Axes

CommandManager:	Features > Reference Geometry > Axis
SolidWorks menus:	Insert > Reference Geometry > Axis
Toolbar:	Reference Geometry > Axis

This tool is used to create a reference axis or a construction axis. These axes are the parametric lines passing through a model, feature, or a reference entity. The reference axes are used to create reference planes, coordinate systems, circular patterns, and for applying mates in the assembly. These are also used as reference while sketching or creating features. The reference axes are displayed in the model as well as in the **FeatureManager design tree**. To create an axis, choose **Reference Geometry > Axis** from the **Features CommandManager**; the **Axis PropertyManager**; will be displayed, as shown in Figure 6-20.

The options in the **Axis PropertyManager** are discussed next.

Figure 6-20 Partial view of the Axis PropertyManager

Creating a Reference Axis Using One Line/Edge/Axis

The **One Line/Edge/Axis** option is used to create a reference axis by selecting a sketched line or a construction line, an edge, or a temporary axis. To use this option, invoke the **Axis PropertyManager** and choose the **One Line/Edge/Axis** button. Select a sketched line, edge, or a temporary axis, as shown in Figure 6-21. The name of the selected entity will be displayed in the **Reference Entities** selection box and the preview of the reference axis will be displayed in the drawing area. Choose the **OK** button to create the reference axis, as shown in Figure 6-22.

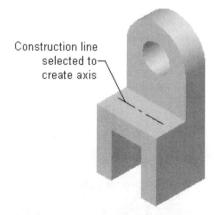

Construction line selected to create axis

Figure 6-21 Line to be selected

Axis1

Figure 6-22 Resulting reference axis

Tip. *If the axis is not displayed in the drawing area, even after you have created it, choose* **Hide/Show Items > View Axes** *from the* **Heads-up View** *toolbar; the axis will be displayed*

Creating a Reference Axis Using Two Planes

You can use the **Two Planes** option to create a reference axis at the intersection of two planes. To create a reference axis using this option, invoke the **Axis PropertyManager** and choose the **Two Planes** button. Now, select two planes, two planar faces, or a plane and a planar face that you want to use to create the axis. The preview of the axis will be displayed in the drawing area. Choose the **OK** button from the **Axis PropertyManager**. Figure 6-23 shows two planes selected and Figure 6-24 shows the resulting reference axis created using the **Two Planes** option.

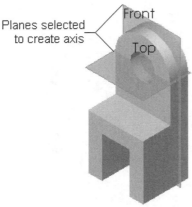

Figure 6-23 Planes to be selected

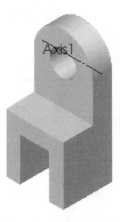

Figure 6-24 Resulting reference axis

Creating a Reference Axis Using Two Points or Vertices

You can use the **Two Points/Vertices** option to create a reference axis that passes through two points or two vertices. To create a reference axis using this option, invoke the **Axis PropertyManager** and choose the **Two Points/Vertices** button. Now, select two points or two vertices through which you want the reference axis to pass; the preview of the reference axis will be displayed in the drawing area. Choose the **OK** button from the **Axis PropertyManager**. Figure 6-25 shows two vertices to be selected and Figure 6-26 shows the resulting reference axis created using the **Two Points/Vertices** option.

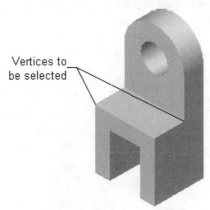

Figure 6-25 Vertices to be selected

Figure 6-26 Resulting reference axis

Creating a Reference Axis Using a Cylindrical or a Conical Face

You can use the **Cylindrical/Conical Face** option to create a reference axis that passes through the center of a cylindrical or a conical face. To create a reference axis using this option, invoke the **Axis PropertyManager** and choose the **Cylindrical/Conical Face** button. Now, select the cylindrical or the conical face through the center of which the axis needs to pass. The preview of the reference axis will be displayed in the drawing area. Choose the **OK** button from the **Axis PropertyManager**. Figure 6-27 shows a cylindrical face selected and Figure 6-28 shows the resulting reference axis created using this option.

Figure 6-27 Cylindrical face to be selected   *Figure 6-28* Resulting reference axis

Creating a Reference Axis on a Face/Plane Passing Through a Point

Use the **Point and Face/Plane** option to create a reference axis that passes through a point and is normal to the selected face/plane. If the face to be selected is a non-planar face, the point should be on the face. To create a reference axis using this option, invoke the **Axis PropertyManager**. Choose the **Point and Face/Plane** button from this **PropertyManager**. Now, select a point, vertex, or a midpoint and then select a face or a plane; the preview of the axis will be displayed in the drawing area. Choose the **OK** button from the **Axis PropertyManager**. The newly created axis will be normal to the selected face or the plane. Figure 6-29 shows the point and the face selected and Figure 6-30 shows the resulting axis created using this option.

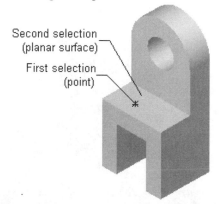

Figure 6-29 Point and face to be selected   *Figure 6-30* Resulting reference axis

Creating Reference Points

CommandManager:	Features > Reference Geometry > Point
SolidWorks menu:	Insert > Reference Geometry > Point
Toolbar:	Reference Geometry > Point

Reference points are created to assist you in designing. They work as an aid for creating another reference geometry or feature. To create a reference point, choose **Reference Geometry > Point** from the **Features CommandManager**; the **Point PropertyManager** will be displayed, as shown in Figure 6-31.

This **PropertyManager** allows you to use five methods for creating reference points. These methods are discussed next.

Creating a Reference Point at the Center of an Arc or a Curved Edge

The **Arc Center** option is used to create a reference point at the center of a sketched arc or a curved edge. When you invoke the **Point PropertyManager** and choose the **Arc Center** button, you will be prompted to select an arc or a circular edge to define the reference point. As soon as you select a sketched arc, circle, or a curved edge, the preview of the reference point will be displayed at its center. Choose **OK** to confirm the creation of the reference point. Figure 6-32 shows a curved edge selected to create the reference point and the preview of the resulting reference point.

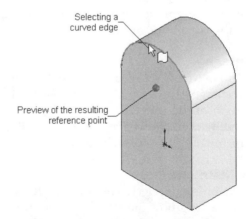

Figure 6-31 *The Point PropertyManager*

Figure 6-32 *Reference point at the center of the selected curved edge*

Creating a Reference Point at the Center of a Face

The **Center of Face** option allows you to create a reference point at the center of a face. When you choose this button, you will be prompted to select a face to define the reference point. You can select a plane or a curved face. The resulting point is automatically placed at the point of the center of gravity of the selected face.

Creating a Reference Point at the Intersection of Two Edges, Sketched Segments, or Reference Axes

The **Intersection** option allows you to create a reference point at the intersection of two edges, sketched segments, or reference axes.

Creating a Reference Point by Projecting an Existing Point

The **Projection** option allows you to create a reference point by projecting a point from some other plane to a specified plane. The point that you can project can be a sketched point, endpoints, center points of the sketched entities, or a reference point.

Creating Single or Multiple Reference Points Along the Distance of a Sketched Curve or an Edge

The **Along curve distance or multiple reference points** option allows you to create single or multiple reference points along the distance of a selected curve. When you choose this button, the **Selections** rollout of the **Point PropertyManager** will expand and provide additional options. These options are discussed next.

Enter the distance/percentage value according to distance

This spinner is used to specify the distance or the percentage value between the individual reference points along the selected curve.

Distance

This radio button is selected to define the distance between the individual points in terms of the distance value. If this radio button is selected, the value entered in the **Enter the distance/percentage value according to distance** spinner will be in terms of linear units of the current document.

Percentage

This radio button is selected to define the gap between the individual points in terms of the percentage of the length of the selected curve. If this radio button is selected, the total length of the selected curve will be taken as 100%. Now, the value entered in the **Enter the distance/percentage value according to distance** spinner will be in terms of the percentage of the selected curve.

Evenly Distribute

This radio button is selected to distribute the specified number of reference points evenly through the length of the selected curve. If this radio button is selected, the **Enter the distance/percentage value according to distance** spinner will not be available.

Enter the number of reference points to be created along the selected entity

This spinner is used to specify the number of reference points to be created. The specified number of reference points will be placed with the gap defined in the **Enter the distance/percentage value according to distance** spinner along the selected curve.

Creating Reference Coordinate Systems

CommandManager:	Features > Reference Geometry > Coordinate System
SolidWorks menu:	Insert > Reference Geometry > Coordinate System
Toolbar:	Reference Geometry > Coordinate System

In SolidWorks, you may need to define some reference coordinate systems other than the default coordinate system for creating features, analyzing the geometry, analyzing the assemblies, and so on. To create a user-defined coordinate system, choose **Reference Geometry > Coordinate System** from the **Features CommandManager**; the **Coordinate System PropertyManager** will be displayed, as shown in Figure 6-33. Also, a coordinate system will be displayed at the origin of the current document.

Figure 6-33 The Coordinate System PropertyManager

To create a new coordinate system, you need to select a point that will be selected as the origin for the new coordinate system, and then define the directions of the X and Y, Y and Z, or Z and X axes. On selecting the point for the origin, the preview of the new coordinate system will be displayed. Define the direction of the axis by selecting an edge, point, or reference axes. You need to specify the direction of any two axes. The direction of the third axis will be automatically determined.

You can reverse the directions of the axes by choosing the corresponding buttons available on the right of their respective selection boxes.

ADVANCED BOSS/BASE OPTIONS

Some of the boss/base extrusion options in the **Extrude PropertyManager** have already been discussed in the previous chapter. The advanced options are discussed next.

From

In the recent/latest release of SolidWorks, then are major enhancements in the **From** rollout of the **Extrude PropertyManager**. The **Start Condition** drop-down list in this rollout is used to specify the position from where the sketch will start to extrude, refer to Figure 6-34. The options in this rollout are discussed next.

Figure 6-34 The From rollout of the Extrude PropertyManager

Sketch Plane

When you invoke the **Extrude PropertyManager**, the **Sketch Plane** option will be selected by default in the **Start Condition** drop-down list of the **From** rollout. So, the extrude feature will start from the sketching plane on which the sketch is drawn. This option is mostly used while creating the extrude features.

Surface/Face/Plane

The **Surface/Face/Plane** option is used to start the extrude feature from a selected surface, face, or a plane, instead of the plane on which the sketch is drawn. To do so, invoke the **Extrude PropertyManager** and select the **Surface/Face/Plane** option from the **Start Condition** drop-down list in the **From** rollout; the **Select A Surface/Face/Plane** selection box will be displayed in the **From** rollout. Select a surface, face, or a plane from where you need to start the extrude feature, as shown in Figure 6-35. Make sure that the sketch is drawn in such a way that all parts of the sketch intersect the selected plane or surface on projection. Figure 6-36 shows the resulting extruded feature from the selected face up to a specified depth.

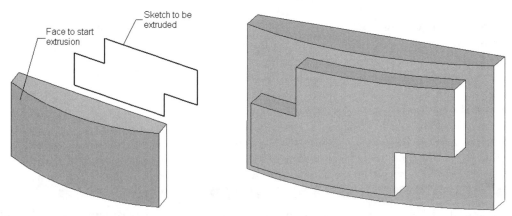

Figure 6-35 Sketch to be extruded and the reference face selected

Figure 6-36 Resulting extruded feature

Vertex

The **Vertex** option is used to specify a vertex as the reference for starting the extrude feature. To do so, invoke the **Extrude PropertyManager** and select the **Vertex** option from the **Start**

Condition drop-down list; the **Select A Vertex** selection box will be displayed. Select a vertex on an existing feature or the endpoint of an existing sketch. Figure 6-37 shows the sketch to be extruded and the vertex to be selected as reference to start the extrude feature. Figure 6-38 shows the resulting extruded feature from the selected vertex to the defined depth.

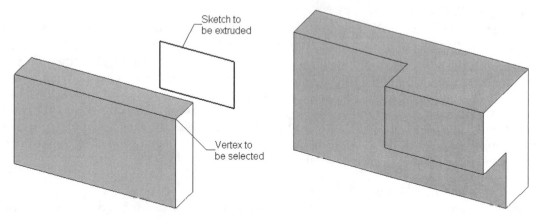

Figure 6-37 Sketch to be extruded and a reference vertex to be selected

Figure 6-38 Resulting extruded feature

Offset

The **Offset** option is used to start the extrude feature at an offset from the plane on which the sketch is drawn. To do so, select the **Offset** option from the **Start Condition** drop-down list; the **Enter Offset Value** spinner will be displayed. Set the value of the offset in this spinner. Figure 6-39 shows the preview of the sketch drawn on the Front Plane being extruded using the **Offset** option. Figure 6-40 shows the resulting extruded feature from an offset distance from the sketching plane to a defined depth.

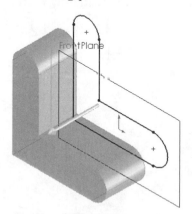

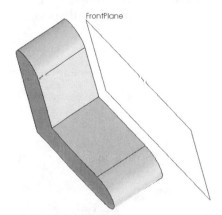

*Figure 6-39 Sketch being extruded using the **Offset** option*

Figure 6-40 Resulting extruded feature

End Condition

The options in the **End Condition** drop-down list of the **Extrude PropertyManager** are discussed next.

Through All

The **Through All** option will be available in the **End Condition** drop-down list only after you create a base feature. After creating a base feature, define a new sketching plane and draw the sketch using the standard sketching tools. Now, choose the **Extruded Boss/Base** button from the **Features CommandManager** to invoke the **Extrude PropertyManager**. The preview of the extruded feature that will be created using the default settings will be displayed in temporary graphics in the drawing area. Select the **Through All** option from the **End Condition** drop-down list; the extrude feature will extend from the sketching plane through all existing geometric entities. You can also reverse the direction of extrusion using the **Reverse Direction** button available on the left of the **End Condition** drop-down list.

When you select the **Through All** option, the sketch will be extruded through all existing geometries. You will observe that the **Merge result** check box is displayed in the **Extrude PropertyManager**. This check box is selected by default. Therefore, the newly created extruded feature will merge with the base feature. If you clear this check box, this extruded feature will not merge with the existing base feature, resulting in the creation of another body. The creation of a new body can be confirmed by observing the **Solid Bodies** folder in the **FeatureManager design tree**. The value of the number of disjoint bodies in the model is displayed in parentheses on the right of the **Solid Bodies** folder. You can click on the (+) sign on the left of the **Solid Bodies** folder to expand the folder. To collapse the folder back, click on the (-) sign.

Figure 6-41 displays a sketch created on the sketching plane at an offset distance from the right planar face of the model. Figure 6-42 displays the feature created by extruding the sketch using the **Through All** option.

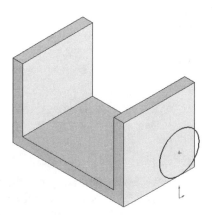

Figure 6-41 A sketch drawn at an offset distance from the right planar surface

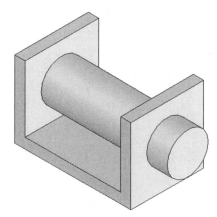

*Figure 6-42 Sketch extruded using the **Through All** option*

Tip. *The feature created from multiple disjoint closed contours results in the creation of disjoint bodies.*

Note

*It is recommended that while creating additional features after the base feature, you should always select the **Merge results** check box in the **Feature PropertyManager**.*

Up To Next

The **Up To Next** option is used to extrude the sketch from the sketching plane to the next surface that intersects the feature. After creating a base feature, create a sketch by selecting or creating a sketching plane. Invoke the **Extrude PropertyManager**; the preview of the new feature will be displayed with the default options. Select the **Up To Next** option from the **End Condition** drop-down list. You can also reverse the direction of feature creation by choosing the **Reverse Direction** button. The preview of the feature will be modified accordingly, and the sketch will be displayed as extruded from the sketching plane to the next surface that completely intersects the feature geometry. Figure 6-43 shows the sketch that will be extruded using the **Up To Next** option and Figure 6-44 shows the resulting feature.

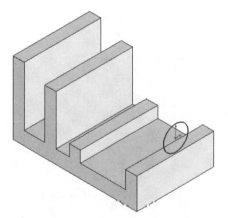

Figure 6-43 A sketch drawn on the Right Plane as the sketching plane

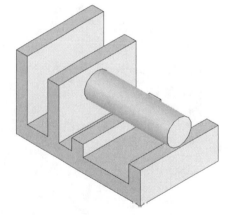

*Figure 6-44 Sketch extruded using the **Up To Next** option*

Up To Vertex

The **Up To Vertex** option is used to define the termination of the extruded feature at a virtual plane that is parallel to the sketching plane and passes through the selected vertex. You can also select a point on an edge, a sketched point, or a reference point. Figure 6-45 shows a sketch drawn on a plane at an offset distance and Figure 6-46 shows the model in which the sketch is extruded up to the selected vertex.

Up To Surface

The **Up To Surface** option is used to define the termination of the extruded feature using a selected surface or a face. To create an extruded feature using this option, draw a sketch and then invoke the **Extrude PropertyManager**. Select the **Up To Surface** option from the **End**

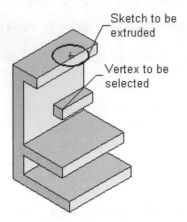
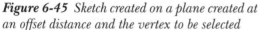

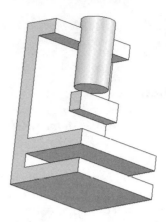

Figure 6-45 Sketch created on a plane created at an offset distance and the vertex to be selected

*Figure 6-46 Sketch extruded using the **Up To Vertex** option*

Condition drop-down list; the **Face/Plane** selection box will be displayed and you will be prompted to select a face or a surface. Select a surface up to which you want to extrude the feature. Figure 6-47 shows the sketch drawn at an offset distance and the surface to be selected. Figure 6-48 shows the resulting feature extruded up to the selected surface.

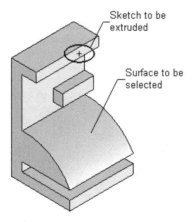

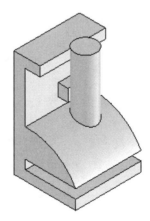

Figure 6-47 Sketch drawn on a plane created at an offset distance and the surface to be selected

*Figure 6-48 Sketch extruded using the **Up To Surface** option*

Offset From Surface

The **Offset From Surface** option is used to define the termination of the extruded feature on a virtual surface created at an offset distance from the selected surface. To create an extruded feature using the **Offset From Surface** option, create a sketch and invoke the **Extrude PropertyManager**. Select the **Offset From Surface** option from the **End Condition** drop-down list; the **Face/Plane** selection box will be displayed along with the **Offset Distance** spinner. You will be prompted to select a face or a surface. Select the surface and set the offset distance in the **Offset Distance** spinner. You can reverse the direction of the offset by selecting the **Reverse offset** check box from the **Direction 1** rollout. If the **Translate surface** check box is cleared from the **Direction 1** rollout, the virtual surface created for the termination of the extruded feature will have a concentric relation with the selected surface. Therefore, it reflects the true offset of the selected surface. If the **Translate surface** check box is selected, the virtual surface will be translated to the distance provided as the offset distance from the reference surface. Therefore, a virtual surface will be created to define the termination of the extruded feature, and it does not reflect the true offset of the selected surface. This concept will be more clear if you refer to Figure 6-49.

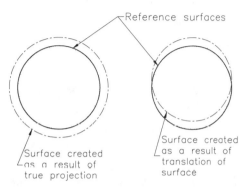

Figure 6-49 Surfaces with true projection and translation

Figure 6-50 shows the front view of the sketch extruded with its termination at an offset distance from the selected cylindrical surface, and the **Translate surface** check box cleared. Figure 6-51 shows the front view of the extruded feature with the **Translate surface** check box selected.

*Figure 6-50 Sketch extruded using the **Offset From Surface** option with the **Translate surface** check box cleared*

*Figure 6-51 Sketch extruded using the **Offset From Surface** option with the **Translate surface** check box selected*

Up To Body

The **Up To Body** option is used to define the termination of the extruded feature to another body. To create an extruded feature using the **Up To Body** option, invoke the **Extrude PropertyManager** and select the **Up To Body** option from the **End Condition** drop-down list; the **Solid/Surface Body** selection box will be displayed. Select the body to terminate the feature and choose the **OK** button. Figure 6-52 shows the sketch for the extruded feature and a body up to which the sketch will be extruded. Figure 6-53 shows the resulting feature.

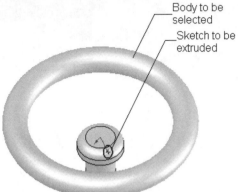

Figure 6-52 Sketch to be extruded and the body to be selected for the extrude feature

*Figure 6-53 Sketch extruded using the **Up To Body** option*

Direction of Extrusion

In SolidWorks, you can define the direction for extruding the sketches. As mentioned in the previous chapter, the direction of extrusion is generally normal to the sketching plane. You can also define the direction of extrusion using a sketched line, an edge, or a reference axis. Note that the entity you want to use for defining the direction of extrusion should not be drawn on the sketch plane parallel to the plane on which the sketch to be extruded is drawn.

To define the direction of extrusion, click on the **Direction of Extrusion** selection box in the **Direction 1** area of the **Extrude PropertyManager**. Next, select an edge, a sketched line segment, or an axis. Figure 6-54 shows a sketch drawn on the top face of a rectangular block and a line sketched on the left face of the block to define the direction of extrusion. Figure 6-55 shows the resulting extruded feature.

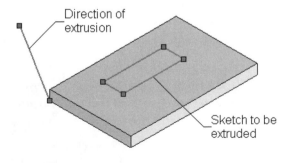

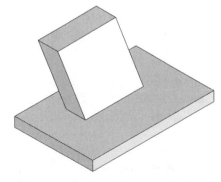

Figure 6-54 Sketch to be extruded and the direction of extrusion

Figure 6-55 Resulting extruded feature

MODELING USING THE CONTOUR SELECTION METHOD

Modeling using the contour selection method allows you to use partial sketches for creating the features. You can use this method to create the model from a single sketch that has multiple contours. To understand this concept, consider the multifeatured solid model shown in Figure 6-56.

For a multifeatured model similar to the one shown in Figure 6-56, ideally you first need to draw the sketch for the base feature and then convert it into the base feature. Next, you need to draw the sketch for the second sketched feature and convert it into feature. In other words, you have to draw separate sketches for each feature. But when you use the contour selection method, you can create the sketch with all contours and select it one-by-one to create the feature. Figure 6-57 shows the sketch to be drawn for modeling using the contour selection method and the procedure to convert it into model is discussed next.

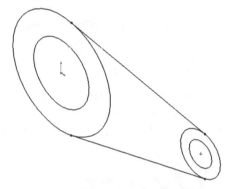

Figure 6-56 *Multifeatured solid model*   *Figure 6-57* *Sketch for creating the model*

After drawing the entire sketch, right-click in the drawing area to invoke the shortcut menu. Make sure you are still in the sketching environment. Choose the **Contour Select Tool** option from the shortcut menu. If this option is not displayed by default, choose the down arrows in the shortcut menu to expand it. When you choose this option, the select cursor will be replaced by the contour selection cursor and contour selection confirmation corner will be displayed. Click the contour selection cursor between the two circles on the left. The area between the two circles will be selected, as shown in Figure 6-58. Invoke the **Extrude PropertyManager** and extrude the selected contour using the **Mid Plane** option. Finally, choose the **OK** button from the **PropertyManager** to exit from it. Figure 6-59 shows the extruded feature using the **Mid Plane** option.

Now, right-click in the drawing area and again choose the **Contour Select Tool** option from the shortcut menu. Select any entity in the sketch using the contour selection cursor and then select the middle contour of the sketch, as shown in Figure 6-60. Invoke the **Extrude PropertyManager** and extrude the selected contour using the **Mid Plane** option. Again, invoke the **Contour Select Tool** and select an entity in the sketch. Next, specify a point between the two circles on the right and extrude the same using the **Mid Plane** option.

After creating the model using this option, you will notice that the sketches are displayed in the model. So, you need to hide them. Click on the **+** sign located on the left of any of the

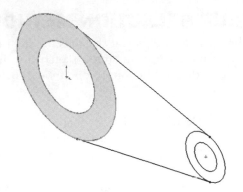

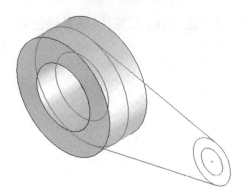

Figure 6-58 *Contour selected for creating the extruded feature*

Figure 6-59 *Isometric view of the feature created by extruding the selected contour*

Tip. *When you move the contour selection cursor in the sketch, the areas where the contour selection is possible are highlighted dynamically.*

extruded features to expand the tree view. Select the sketch icon; a pop-up toolbar will be displayed. Choose the **Hide** option. Figure 6-61 shows the model after creating all features using the contour selection method and after hiding the sketch.

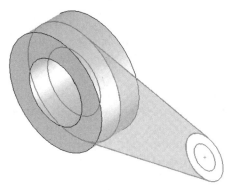

Figure 6-60 *Contour selected for the second feature*

Figure 6-61 *Final model*

In SolidWorks, you can also select the model edges as a part of the contour. For example, consider Figure 6-62. This figure shows a line drawn on the top face of a rectangular block. You can use the edges of the top face that form a contour with the line as the sketch to be extruded, see Figure 6-63.

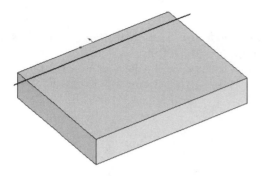

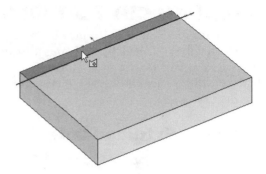

Figure 6-62 *Line drawn on the top face of a rectangular model*

Figure 6-63 *Selecting the contour formed by the line and the model edges*

Figure 6-64 shows the resulting extruded feature.

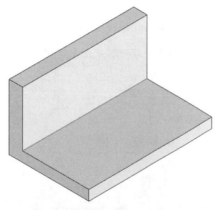

Figure 6-64 *Extruded feature created using the model edges as a part of the contour*

Tip. *When you select the contour using the **Contour Select Tool** option and invoke the **Extrude PropertyManager**, you will observe that the name of the selected contour is displayed in the selection box of the **Contour Selection** rollout.*

You can select the contours for all sketched features such as revolve, cut, sweep, loft, and so on.

*You can also select a single sketched entity from a sketch using the **Contour Select Tool** option instead of selecting the contour for creating the sketched features.*

Note

*If you click on the (+) sign to expand the extruded feature in the **FeatureManager design tree**, you will notice that instead of showing the icon of a simple sketch, it will show the icon of the contour selected sketch.*

CREATING CUT FEATURES

Cut extrude is a material removal process. You can define a cut feature by extruding a sketch, revolving a sketch, sweeping a section along a path, lofting sections, or by using a surface. You will learn more about sweep, loft, and surface in the later chapters. The cut feature can be created only if a base feature exists. The extruded and revolved cut features are discussed next.

Creating Extruded Cuts

CommandManager:	Features > Extruded Cut
SolidWorks menu:	Insert > Cut > Extrude
Toolbar:	Features > Extruded Cut

To create an extruded cut feature, create a sketch for the cut feature and then choose the **Extruded Cut** button from the **Features CommandManager**; the **Extrude PropertyManager** will be displayed, as shown in Figure 6-65. Also, the preview of the cut feature with the default options will be displayed in the drawing area. In SolidWorks, the **Extrude PropertyManager** will be displayed for the extruded cut feature also, but its icon will be different in the **FeatureManager design tree**.

Figure 6-65 The Extrude PropertyManager

Figure 6-66 shows the preview of the cut feature when you invoke the **Extrude PropertyManager** after creating a sketch. Remember that when you create a cut feature, the current view will not change automatically to a 3D view, you need to change it manually. The material to be removed will be displayed in the temporary graphics. Figure 6-67 shows the model after creating the cut feature.

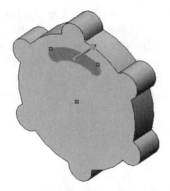

Figure 6-66 *The preview of the cut feature*

Figure 6-67 *Cut feature added to the model*

The options in the **Extrude PropertyManager** are discussed next.

From

In SolidWorks, you are provided with the options for specifying parameters at the start of the extruded cut. These options are in the **Start Condition** drop-down list of the **From** rollout and are the same as those discussed for the **Extrude Boss/Base** tool. Figure 6-68 shows the sketch to be extruded and the curved face selected as the reference face for starting the extrusion. Figure 6-69 shows the resulting extruded cut feature.

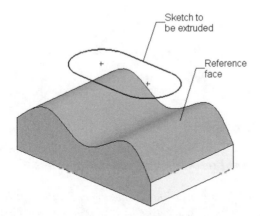

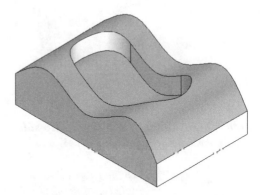

Figure 6-68 *Sketch to be extruded and the reference face*

Figure 6-69 *Resulting extruded cut feature*

Direction 1

The **Direction 1** rollout is used to define the termination of the extrude in the first direction. The options in the **Direction 1** rollout are discussed next.

End Condition

The **End Condition** drop-down list in the **Direction 1** rollout is used to specify the type of termination. The feature termination options in this drop-down list are **Blind, Through**

All, **Up To Next**, **Up To Vertex**, **Up To Surface**, **Offset From Surface**, **Up To Body**, and **Mid Plane**. These options are the same as those discussed for the **Extrude Boss/Base** tool. By default, the **Blind** option is selected in the **End Condition** drop-down list. Therefore, the **Depth** spinner is displayed to specify the depth. If you choose the **Through All** or the **Up to Next** options, the spinner will not be displayed. The type of spinner or the selection box that is displayed depends on the option selected from the **End Condition** drop-down list. The **Reverse Direction** button is used to reverse the direction of the feature creation. If you select the **Mid Plane** option from the **End Condition** drop-down list, the **Reverse Direction** button will not be available.

Flip side to cut

The **Flip side to cut** check box is used to define the side from where the material has to be removed with respect to the profile drawn for the cut feature. By default, the **Flip side to cut** check box is cleared. Therefore, the material enclosed by the profile will be removed. If you select this check box, the material left outside the profile will be removed. Figure 6-70 shows a cut feature with the **Flip side to cut** check box cleared and Figure 6-71 shows a cut feature with the **Flip side to cut** check box selected.

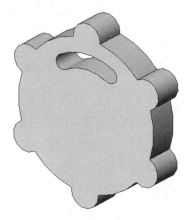

*Figure 6-70 Cut feature with the **Flip side to cut** check box cleared*

*Figure 6-71 Cut feature with the **Flip side to cut** check box selected*

Tip. *You can also flip the direction of cut by clicking on the arrow on the sketch while creating the cut feature. This arrow is available only if you have selected or cleared the **Flip side to cut** check box once.*

Draft On/Off

The **Draft On/Off** button is used to apply the draft angle to the extruded cut feature. The **Draft Angle** spinner on the right of the **Draft On/Off** button is used to set the value of the draft angle. By default, the **Draft outward** check box is cleared. Therefore, the draft is created inward with respect to the direction of feature creation. If you select this check box, the draft added to the cut feature will be created outward with respect to the direction of the feature creation. Figure 6-72 shows the draft added to the cut feature with the **Draft outward** check box cleared and Figure 6-73 shows the draft added to the cut feature with the **Draft outward** check box selected.

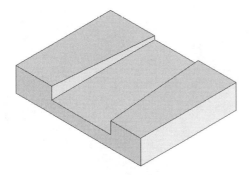

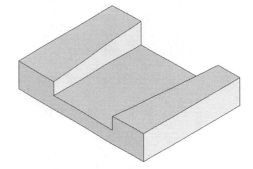

*Figure 6-72 Cut feature with the **Draft outward** check box cleared*

*Figure 6-73 Cut feature with the **Draft outward** check box selected*

The **Direction 2** rollout is used to specify the termination of the feature creation in the second direction. The options in the **Direction 2** rollout are the same as those discussed the **Direction 1** rollout.

The **Selected Contours** rollout is used to select specific contours from the current sketch.

Tip. *The sketch used for the cut feature can be a closed loop or an open sketch. Note that if the sketch is an open sketch, the sketch should completely divide the model into two or more parts.*

Thin Feature

The **Thin Feature** rollout is used to create a thin cut feature. When you create a cut feature, you need to apply the thickness to the sketch in addition to the end condition. This rollout is used to specify the parameters to create the thin feature. To create a thin cut feature, invoke the **Extruded Cut** tool after creating the sketch and specify the end conditions in the **Direction 1** and **Direction 2** rollouts. Now, select the check box in the **Thin Feature** rollout to activate the it. The options in this rollout are the same as those discussed for the thin feature in the **Extruded Boss/Base** tool.

Handling Multiple Bodies in the Cut Feature

While creating the cut feature, sometimes because of the geometric conditions, feature termination, or end conditions, the cut feature results in the creation of multiple bodies. Figure 6-74 shows a sketch created on the top planar surface of the base feature to create a cut feature. Figure 6-75 shows the cut feature created with the end condition as **Through All**. On choosing **OK** from the **Extrude PropertyManager** with this type of sketch and end condition, the **Bodies to Keep** dialog box will be displayed, as shown in Figure 6-76. This dialog box is used to define the part of the model to be kept, as multiple bodies are created while applying the cut feature.

By default, the **All Bodies** radio button is selected in the **Bodies to Keep** dialog box. Therefore, if you choose **OK** from this dialog box, all bodies created after the cut feature will remain in

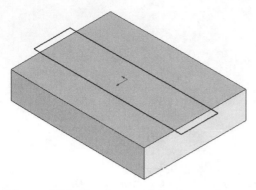

Figure 6-74 *Sketch created for the cut feature*

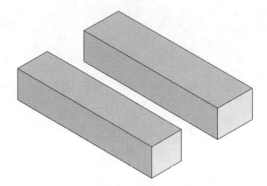

Figure 6-75 *Multiple bodies created using the cut feature*

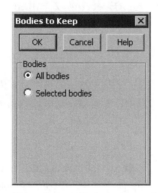

Figure 6-76 *The **Bodies to Keep** dialog box*

the model. If you want the cut feature to consume any of the bodies, select the **Selected bodies** radio button to expand the dialog box, as shown in Figure 6-77.

You can select the check box provided on the left of the name of the body to specify the body to keep. On selecting a check box, the corresponding body will be displayed in different colors in temporary graphics. Choose the **OK** button from the **Bodies to Keep** dialog box. Figure 6-78 shows a sketch created for the cut feature. Figure 6-79 shows the cut feature created using the **Thin Feature** option and the **All bodies** radio button selected in the **Bodies to Keep** dialog box.

 Note
You will learn about configurations in the later chapters.

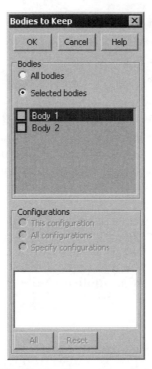

Figure 6-77 *The Bodies to Keep dialog box with the Selected bodies radio button selected*

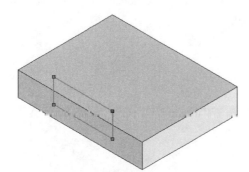

Figure 6-78 *Sketch to create a cut feature using the Thin Feature option*

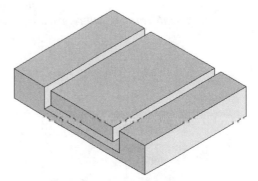

Figure 6-79 *A thin cut feature created with all the resulting bodies retained*

Creating Revolved Cuts

CommandManager:	Features > Revolved Cut
SolidWorks menu:	Insert > Cut > Revolve
Toolbar:	Features > Extruded Cut > Revolved Cut

 Revolved cuts are used to remove the material by revolving a sketch around the selected axis. Similar to the revolved boss/base features, you can define the revolution axis using a centerline or using an edge in the sketch. When you invoke the **Revolved Cut** tool, the **Cut-Revolve PropertyManager** will be displayed, as shown in Figure 6-80.

The options in this **PropertyManager** are similar to those discussed earlier. Figure 6-81 shows a sketch for a revolved cut feature and Figure 6-82 shows the resulting cut feature. Note that in Figure 6-82, a texture is applied to the cut feature.

*Figure 6-80 The **Cut-Revolve** PropertyManager*

 Note

*You can also select the tool first and then the plane to create the sketch. On doing so, the feature tool will be activated automatically after you exit the sketching environment and you can define the parameters in their respective rollouts. For example, you can invoke the **Revolved Cut** tool without creating any sketch. In this case, the **Revolve PropertyManager** will be displayed and you will be prompted to select a plane or a planar face to create a sketch or to select a sketch. As soon as you exit the sketching environment after creating the sketch, the **Cut-Revolve PropertyManager** will be displayed automatically.*

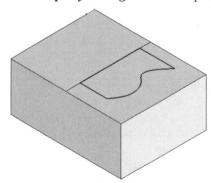

Figure 6-81 Sketch for the revolved cut feature

Figure 6-82 Resulting cut feature with a texture

CONCEPT OF THE FEATURE SCOPE

As discussed earlier, you can create different disjoint bodies in a single part file in SolidWorks. After creating two or more disjoint bodies, when you create another feature, the **Feature Scope** rollout will be displayed in the **Cut-Revolve PropertyManager**. This rollout is used to define the bodies that will be affected by the creation of the feature. The **feature scope** option is used with the Extrude boss and cut, Revolve boss and cut, Sweep boss and cut, Loft boss and cut, Boss thicken, Surface cut, and Cavity features.

In the **Feature Scope** rollout, the **Selected bodies** radio button and the **Auto-select** check box are selected by default. With the **Auto-select** check box selected, all disjoint bodies will be selected and they will be affected by the feature creation. If you clear the **Auto-select** check box, a selection box will be invoked. You can select the bodies that you want to be affected by the feature creation. The name of the selected body will be displayed in the selection box. If you select the **All bodies** radio button, all bodies in the part file will be selected and affected by the creation of the feature.

Tip. *After exiting a tool, you can invoke the same tool immediately by pressing the ENTER key.*

TUTORIALS

Tutorial 1

In this tutorial, you will create the model shown in Figure 6-83 by drawing the sketch of the front view of the model and then select the contours to extrude them. As a result, you will learn the procedure of modeling using the contours selection method. The dimensions of the model are shown in Figure 6-84. **(Expected time: 30 min)**

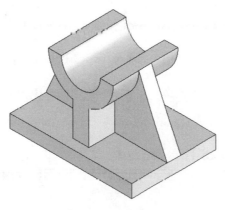

Figure 6-83 Solid model for Tutorial 1

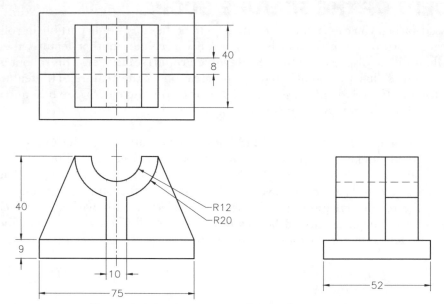

Figure 6-84 *Dimensions and views for Tutorial 1*

It is clear from the above figures that the given model is a multifeatured model. It consists of various extruded features. You first need to draw the sketch for each feature and then convert that sketch into a feature. In conventional methods, you create a separate sketch for each sketched feature. But in this tutorial, you need to use the contour selection method to draw a sketch and then select the contours and share the same sketch for creating all the features.

The following steps are required to complete this tutorial:

a. Create the sketch on the default plane and apply the required relations and dimensions to it, refer to Figure 6-85.
b. Invoke the **Extrude Boss/Base** tool and extrude the selected contour, refer to Figures 6-86 and 6-87.
c. Select the second set of contours and extrude them to the required distance, refer to Figures 6-88 and 6-89.
d. Select the third set of contours and extrude them to the required distance, refer to Figures 6-90 and 6-91.
e. Save and then close the document.

Creating the Sketch of the Model

1. Start a new SolidWorks part document using the **New SolidWorks Document** dialog box.

2. Draw the sketch of the front view of the model on the Front Plane. Apply the required relations and dimensions to the sketch, as shown in Figure 6-85. Make sure that you do not exit the sketching environment.

Selecting and Extruding the Contours of the Sketch

In this tutorial, you need to use the contour selection method to create the model. Therefore, you first need to select one of the contours from the given sketch and extrude it. For a better view, you can also orient the sketch to Isometric view.

1. Choose **View Orientation** > **Isometric** from the **Heads-up View** toolbar; the sketch is displayed in the isometric view.

2. Right-click in the drawing area to invoke the shortcut menu. Expand the shortcut menu, if required. Choose the **Contour Select Tool** option; the select cursor is replaced by the contour selection cursor and the selection confirmation corner is displayed.

3. Move the cursor to the lower rectangle of the sketch; the area of the rectangle is highlighted. This indicates that this rectangle is a closed profile.

4. Click on the highlighted rectangular area; the lower rectangular area is selected as a contour, as shown in Figure 6-86.

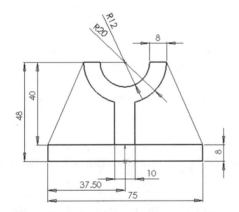

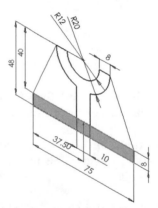

Figure 6-85 *Fully defined sketch for creating the model*

Figure 6-86 *Lower rectangle selected as a contour*

5. Choose the **Extruded Boss/Base** button from the **Features CommandManager**; the **Extrude PropertyManager** is invoked and the preview of the base feature is displayed in the drawing area in temporary graphics.

The name of the selected contour is displayed in the selection box of the **Selected Contours** rollout.

6. Right-click in the drawing area and choose the **Mid Plane** option from the shortcut menu; the preview of the feature is modified dynamically.

7. Set the value of the **Depth** spinner to **52** and choose the **OK** button from the **Extrude PropertyManager**; the selected contour is extruded, as shown in Figure 6-87.

8. Right-click in the drawing area and choose the **Contour Select Tool** option from the shortcut menu; the select cursor is replaced by the contour selection cursor.

9. Select an entity of the sketch using the contour selection cursor to invoke the selection mode of the sketch.

10. Select the middle contour of the sketch using the left mouse button; the selected region is highlighted, as shown in Figure 6-88.

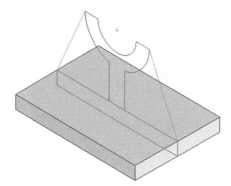

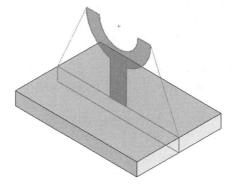

Figure 6-87 *Base feature of the model*

Figure 6-88 *Middle contour is selected using the contour selection tool*

11. Invoke the **Extruded Boss/Base** tool. Right-click in the drawing area and choose the **Mid Plane** option from the shortcut menu.

12. Set the value of the **Depth** spinner to **40** and choose the **OK** button from the **Extrude PropertyManager**. The feature created by selecting the middle contour is shown in Figure 6-89.

13. Again choose the **Contour Select Tool** option and then select a sketched entity. Next, select the contour on the right side. Press and hold the CTRL key and now, select the contour on the left side, see Figure 6-90.

14. Invoke the **Extruded Boss/Base** tool. Right-click and choose the **Mid Plane** option from the shortcut menu.

15. Set the value of the **Depth** spinner to **8** and choose the **OK** button from the **Extrude PropertyManager**.

    The model is completed, but the sketch is displayed in the model. Therefore, you need to hide the sketch.

16. Move the cursor to any of the sketched entities and when the entity turns orange, select it; a pop-up toolbar is displayed. Choose the **Hide** button from the pop-up toolbar.

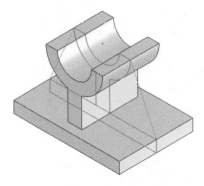

Figure 6-89 Second feature created by extruding the middle contour

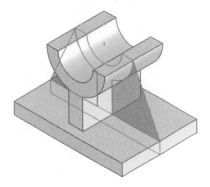

Figure 6-90 The right and the left contours selected

The isometric view of the final model, with the display of the sketch turned off, is shown in Figure 6-91. The **FeatureManager design tree** of the model is shown in Figure 6-92.

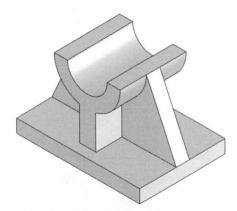

Figure 6-91 Final solid model

Figure 6-92 The FeatureManager design tree

Saving the Model

1. Choose the **Save** button from the Menu Bar and save the model with the name given below:

   \My Documents\SolidWorks\c06\c06tut1.sldprt

2. Choose **File > Close** from the SolidWorks menus to close the document.

Tutorial 2

In this tutorial, you will create the model shown in Figure 6-93. You will use a combination of the conventional modeling method and the contour selection method to create this model. The dimensions of the model are given in Figure 6-94.   **(Expected time: 30 min)**

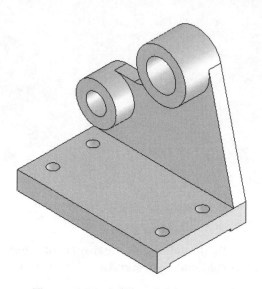

Figure 6-93 *Solid model for Tutorial 2*

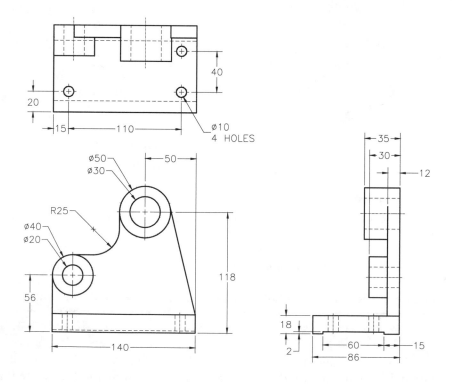

Figure 6-94 *Dimensions for the solid model*

The following steps are required to complete this tutorial:

a. Draw the sketch of the front view of the model, refer to Figure 6-95.
b. Extrude the selected contours, refer to Figures 6-96 through 6-98.
c. Add the recess feature to the model by drawing the sketch on the right planar face, refer to Figures 6-99 and 6-100.
d. Create four holes using the cut feature on the top face of the base feature, refer to Figures 6-101 and 6-102.
e. Save and close the document.

Drawing the Sketch for Contour Selection Modeling

1. Start a new SolidWorks part document. Draw the sketch of the front view of the model on the Front Plane using the sketching tools.

2. Apply the required relations and dimensions to fully define the sketch, see Figure 6-95.

   Orient the view to isometric view because it will help you in the selection of contours.

3. Press the SPACEBAR key and change the current view to the isometric view.

4. Right-click and choose the **Contour Select Tool** option from the shortcut menu; the select cursor is replaced by the contour selection cursor.

5. Select the area enclosed by the lower rectangle using the contour selection cursor, as shown in Figure 6-96.

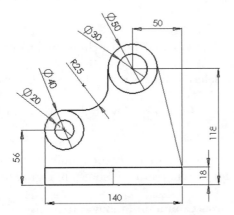

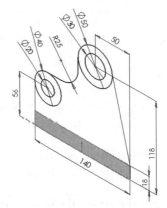

Figure 6-95 *Fully defined sketch*   *Figure 6-96* *Lower rectangle selected as a contour*

6. Choose the **Extruded Boss/Base** button from the **Features CommandManager;** the **Extrude PropertyManager** is displayed.

7. Set the value in the **Depth** spinner to **86** and choose the **OK** button from the **Extrude PropertyManager**. The base feature created after extruding the selected contour is shown in Figure 6-97.

8. Use the **Contour Select Tool** and the **Extruded Boss/Base** tools to create the other features and then hide the sketch. For depth of the extruded features, refer to Figure 6-94. The model created after extruding all contours and hiding the sketch is shown in Figure 6-98.

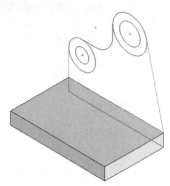
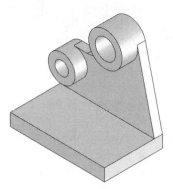

Figure 6-97 *Base feature created after extruding the selected contour*

Figure 6-98 *Model created after extruding all contours*

Creating the Recess at the Base of the Model

After creating the extruded features of the model, you need to create the recess provided at the base of the model. The recess is created by a cut extrude feature. This cut extrude feature is created by drawing a sketch on the right planar face of the model.

1. Select the right planar face of the base feature as the sketching plane; the selected face is highlighted and a pop-up toolbar is displayed.

2. Choose the **Sketch** option from the pop-up toolbar to invoke the sketching environment.

    Now, you need to orient the view such that the selected face is normal to your eye view.

3. Choose **View Orientation > Normal To** from the **Heads-up View** toolbar to orient the selected plane normal to the view.

4. Draw the sketch for the recess using the sketching tools and apply the required relations and dimensions to it. The fully defined sketch for the cut feature is shown in Figure 6-99.

5. Choose the **Extruded Cut** button from the **Features CommandManager** to invoke the **Extrude PropertyManager**. The preview of the cut feature is displayed in the drawing area in temporary graphics.

6. Right-click in the drawing area and choose the **Through All** option from the shortcut menu.

7. Choose **OK** from the **Extrude PropertyManager** to complete the feature creation. The isometric view of the model after creating the cut feature is shown in Figure 6-100.

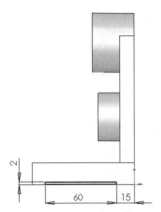

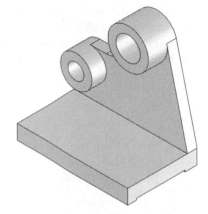

Figure 6-99 *Sketch for the cut feature*   **Figure 6-100** *Cut feature added to the model*

Creating Holes

Next, you need to create the holes at the base of the model. These holes will be created as the extruded cut features. You need to draw the sketch of the hole feature on the top planar face of the base feature of the model. To draw the sketch of the holes, you first need to draw a circle and then create the pattern of remaining circles.

1. Select the top planar face of the base feature; a pop-up toolbar is displayed. Select the **Sketch** tool from the pop-up toolbar.

2. Orient the current view normal to the viewing direction. Draw a circle of 10 mm diameter and pattern it using the **Linear Sketch Pattern** tool. You may need to apply the horizontal relations between the center points of the top circles to fully define the sketch. The fully defined sketch is shown in Figure 6-101.

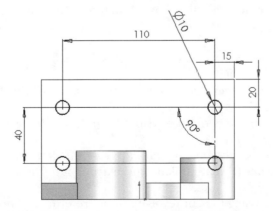

Figure 6-101 *Holes sketched for the cut feature*

3. Change the current view to the isometric view and then choose the **Extruded Cut** button from the **Features CommandManager** to invoke the **Extrude PropertyManager**.

4. Right-click in the drawing area and choose the **Through All** option from the shortcut menu. Choose the **OK** button from the **Extrude PropertyManager**. The isometric view of the final model after hiding the sketch is shown in Figure 6-102. The **FeatureManager design tree** of the model is shown in Figure 6-103.

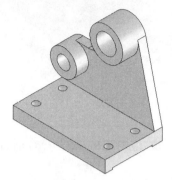

Figure 6-102   *Final solid model*   *Figure 6-103*   *The **FeatureManager** design tree*

Saving the Model

1. Choose the **Save** button from the Menu Bar and save the model with the name given below.

   \My Documents\SolidWorks\c06\c06tut2.sldprt

2. Choose **File > Close** from the SolidWorks menus to close the file.

Tutorial 3

In this tutorial, you will create a model whose dimensions are shown in Figure 6-104. The solid model is shown in Figure 6-105.   **(Expected Time: 30 min)**

The following steps are required to complete this tutorial:

a. Create the base feature by extruding the sketch drawn on the Front Plane, refer to Figures 6-106 and 6-107.
b. Extrude the sketch created on the Top Plane to create a cut feature, refer to Figures 6-108 through 6-110.
c. Create a plane at an offset distance of 150 mm from the Top Plane.
d. Draw a sketch on the newly created plane and extrude it to the selected surface, refer to Figures 6-111 and 6-112.
e. Create a contour bore using the cut revolve option, refer to Figures 6-113 and 6-114.
f. Create the holes using the cut feature, refer to Figures 6-115 and 6-116.
g. Save and close the document.

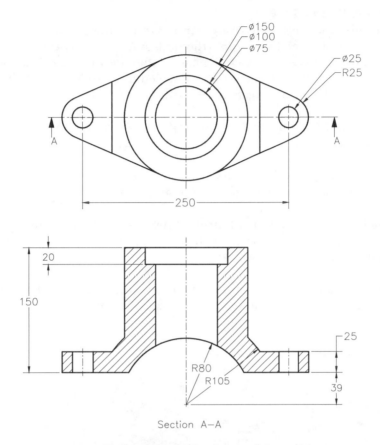

Figure 6-104 *Dimensions of the model*

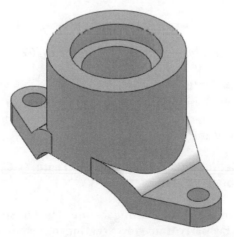

Figure 6-105 *Solid model for Tutorial 3*

Creating the Base Feature

It is evident from the model that its base comprises of a complex geometry. You first need to create the base feature and then apply the cut feature to the base of the model to get the desired shape. You need to create the base feature on the Front Plane which is the sketching plane. After drawing the sketch, you need to extrude it using the mid plane option to complete the feature creation.

1. Start a new SolidWorks part document and invoke the **Extruded Boss/Base** tool; you are prompted to select a plane.

2. Select the Front Plane, draw the sketch of the base feature and then, apply the required relations and dimensions to the sketch, as shown in Figure 6-106.

3. Exit the sketching environment; the **Extrude PropertyManager** and the preview of the base feature is displayed. Right-click in the drawing area and choose the **Mid Plane** option from the shortcut menu displayed.

4. Set the value of the **Depth** spinner to **150** and choose the **OK** button from the **Extrude PropertyManager**. The isometric view of the base feature of the model is shown in Figure 6-107.

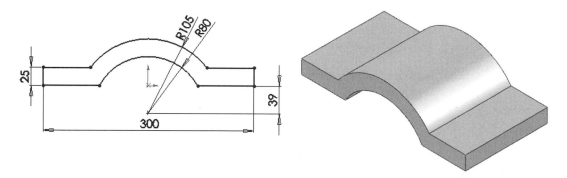

Figure 6-106 *Sketch of the base feature*   ***Figure 6-107*** *Base feature of the solid model*

Creating the Cut Feature

Now, you need to create a cut feature to get the required shape of the base feature. The sketch for this cut feature is created using a reference plane defined tangent to the curved face of the previous feature.

1. Choose **Reference Geometry > Plane** from the **Features CommandManager** to display the **Plane PropertyManager**.

2. Select the upper curved face of the existing feature. The **On Surface** button is automatically chosen in the **Plane PropertyManager**. Now, move the cursor close to the midpoint of the curved edge of the upper curved face; the midpoint is highlighted in orange, see Figure 6-108. Select this point; the preview of the plane tangent to the curved face and

passing through the midpoint of the curved edge is displayed. Choose **OK** to create the reference plane.

3. Draw the sketch for the cut feature using the standard sketching tools and then apply the required relations and dimensions to the sketch, as shown in Figure 6-109.

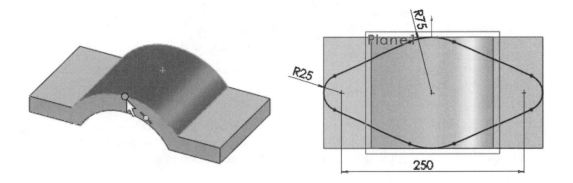

Figure 6-108 Selecting the midpoint to define the tangent plane

Figure 6-109 Fully dimensioned sketch for the cut feature

4. Choose the **Extruded Cut** button from the **Features CommandManager** to invoke the **Extrude PropertyManager**. Change the current view to the isometric view.

    You will observe that the direction of the material removal is not in the required way. Therefore, you need to flip its direction.

5. Select the **Flip side to cut** check box. Notice that the direction of the material removal is also changed in the preview.

6. Right-click in the drawing area and choose the **Through All** option from the shortcut menu and then, choose the **OK** button from the **Extrude PropertyManager**.

    The reference plane is displayed in the drawing area. Therefore, you need to hide it.

7. Left-click on **Plane1** in the drawing area and choose **Hide** from the pop-up toolbar; the display of the reference plane is turned off. The model, after adding the cut feature, is shown in Figure 6-110.

Creating a Plane at an Offset Distance for the Extruded Feature

After creating the base of the model, you need to create a plane at an offset distance of 150 mm from the Top Plane. This newly created plane will be used as a sketching plane for the next feature.

1. Choose **Reference Geometry > Plane** from the **Features CommandManager** to display the **Plane PropertyManager**.

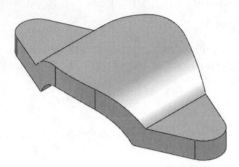

Figure 6-110 *Cut feature added to the base feature*

2. Choose the **Offset Distance** button from the **Plane PropertyManager**; the
   Distance spinner, the **Reverse direction** check box, and the **Number of Planes**
   to Create spinner are displayed in the **Plane PropertyManager**.

3. Click on the (+) sign located on the left of the **FeatureManager design tree**, which is
   now displayed in the drawing area. The tree view expands and the three default planes
   are now visible in the tree view.

4. Select the **Top Plane** from the **FeatureManager design tree**; the preview of the newly
   created plane at a default offset is displayed in the drawing area.

5. Set the value of the **Distance** spinner to **150** and choose the **OK** button from the **Plane**
   PropertyManager; the required plane is created.

Creating the Extruded Feature

After creating the plane at an offset distance from the Top Plane, you need to draw the
sketch for the next feature.

1. Select the reference plane which you just created, if it is not already selected, and invoke
   the sketching environment. Set the current view normal to the eye view.

2. Draw the sketch of the circle and apply the required relations to the sketch, as shown in
   Figure 6-111.

3. Change the current view to isometric view and invoke the **Extruded Boss/Base** tool. You
   will observe in the preview that the direction of the feature creation is opposite to the
   required direction in the preview. Therefore, you need to change the direction of the
   feature creation.

4. Choose the **Reverse Direction** button on the left of the **End Condition** drop-down list to
   reverse the direction of feature creation; the preview of the feature is changed dynamically.

5. Right-click in the drawing area and choose the **Up To Surface** option from the shortcut

menu; you are prompted to select a face or a surface to complete the specification of the first direction. Also, the **Face/Plane** selection box is displayed below the **End Condition** drop-down list in the **Direction 1** rollout.

6. Select the upper curved surface of the model using the left mouse button. You will observe that the preview shows the feature extruded up to the selected surface.

7. Choose the **OK** button from the **Extrude PropertyManager**.

The plane is displayed in the drawing area. Therefore, you need to turn its display off.

8. Select **Plane2** from the **FeatureManager design tree** or from the drawing area and choose **Hide** from the pop-up toolbar. The model created after creating the extruded feature is shown in Figure 6-112.

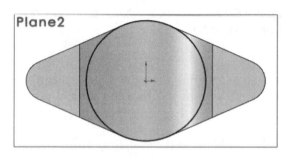

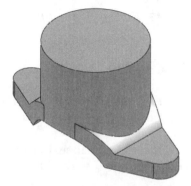

Figure 6-111 Sketch created on the newly created plane

Figure 6-112 Sketch extruded up to a selected surface

Creating the Counterbore Hole

Next, you need to create the counterbore hole. It will be created as a revolved cut feature using a sketch drawn on the Front Plane.

1. Invoke the sketching environment by selecting the Front Plane as the sketching plane and orient the plane normal to the view.

2. Draw the sketch of the counterbore hole using the standard sketching tools. Add the required relations and then add the linear diameter dimensions, as shown in Figure 6-113.

3. Set the current view to the isometric view and then choose the **Revolved Cut** button from the **Features CommandManager**; the **Cut-Revolve PropertyManager** is displayed.

The preview of the cut feature is displayed in the drawing area in temporary graphics. The value of the angle in the **Angle** spinner is set to **360** by default. Therefore, you do not need to set the value of the **Angle** spinner.

4. Choose the **OK** button from the **Cut-Revolve PropertyManager**. Figure 6-114 shows the
    model after creating the revolved cut feature.

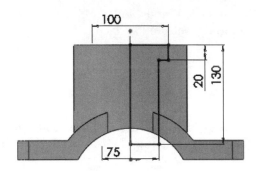

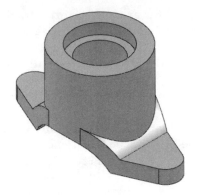

Figure 6-113 *Fully defined sketch for the
counterbore hole*

Figure 6-114 *Counterbore hole added using the
Cut-Revolve tool*

Creating Holes

After creating all features, you need to create the holes using the extruded cut feature to
complete the model. The sketch for the cut feature is to be drawn using the top planar
surface of the base feature as the sketching plane.

1. Select the top planar surface of the base feature and invoke the sketching environment.
    Orient the model so that the selected face of the model is oriented normal to the view.

2. Draw the sketch using the standard sketching tools and apply the required relations and
    dimensions to it, as shown in Figure 6-115.

3. Change the current view to the isometric view. Choose the **Extruded Cut** button
    from the **Features CommandManager**; the **Extrude PropertyManager** is
    displayed.

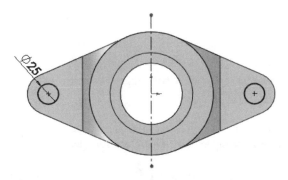

Figure 6-115 *Fully defined sketch for the cut feature*

4. Right-click and choose the **Through All** option from the shortcut menu and choose the **OK** button from the **Extrude PropertyManager**. The final model is shown in Figure 6-116. The **FeatureManager design tree** of the model is shown in Figure 6-117.

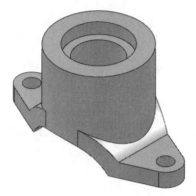

Figure 6-116 *Final model*

Figure 6-117 *The FeatureManager design tree*

Saving the Model

1. Choose the **Save** button from the Menu Bar and save the model with the name given below:

    \My Documents\SolidWorks\c06\c06tut3.sldprt

2. Choose **File** > **Close** from the SolidWorks menus to close the file.

SELF-EVALUATION TEST

Answer the following questions and then compare them to those given at the end of this chapter:

1. When you draw a sketch for the first time in the sketching environment, the sketch is drawn on the default plane, which is the Front Plane. (T/F)

2. When you start a new SolidWorks part document, SolidWorks provides you with two default planes. (T/F)

3. You can choose the **Plane** button from the **Features CommandManager** to invoke the **Plane PropertyManager**. (T/F)

4. You cannot create a plane at an offset distance by dragging a default plane dynamically. (T/F)

5. When you create a circular feature, a temporary axis is automatically displayed. (T/F)

6. The _____ option is used to extrude a sketch from the sketching plane to the next surface that intersects the feature.

7. The _____ option in the **End Condition** drop-down list is used to define the termination of the extruded feature up to another body.

8. The _____ check box is used to merge the newly created body with the parent body.

9. You can use the _____ option to create a reference axis that passes through the center point of a cylindrical or a conical surface.

10. Sometimes multiple bodies are created while applying the cut feature. In such case, the _____ dialog box is displayed, which allows you to specify the body to keep.

REVIEW QUESTIONS

Answer the following questions:

1. If the _____ check box is cleared, the virtual surface created for the termination of the extruded feature will have a concentric relation with the selected surface.

2. The _____ option is chosen from the shortcut menu to select the contours.

3. The _____ option is available in the **End Condition** drop-down list only after you create the base feature.

4. The _____ check box is used to specify the side from where the material will be removed.

5. The _____ check box is used to create an outward draft in a cut feature.

6. Which check box is selected while creating a feature in a single-body modeling?

    (a) **Combine results**   (b) **Fix bodies**
    (c) **Merge results**   (d) **Union results**

7. Which button is used to add a draft angle to a cut feature?

    (a) **Add Draft**   (b) **Create Draft**
    (c) **Draft On/Off**   (d) None of these

8. Which **PropertyManager** is invoked to create a cut feature by extruding a sketch?

    (a) **Extruded Cut**   (b) **Extrude**
    (c) **Extrude-Cut**   (d) **Cut**

9. Which of the following options is used to define the termination of feature creation at an offset distance to a selected surface?

    (a) **Distance To Surface**   (b) **Normal From Surface**
    (c) **Distance From Surface**   (d) **Offset From Surface**

10. Which of the following options is used to define the termination of feature creation to the selected surface?

    (a) **To Surface**   (b) **Selected Surface**
    (c) **Up To Surface**   (d) None of these

EXERCISES

Exercise 1

Create the solid model shown in Figure 6-118. The dimensions of the model are given in Figure 6-119.   (**Expected time: 30 min**)

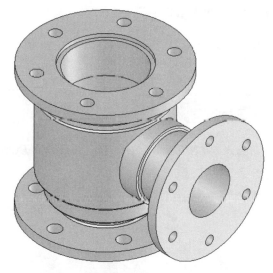

Figure 6-118 *Model for Exercise 1*

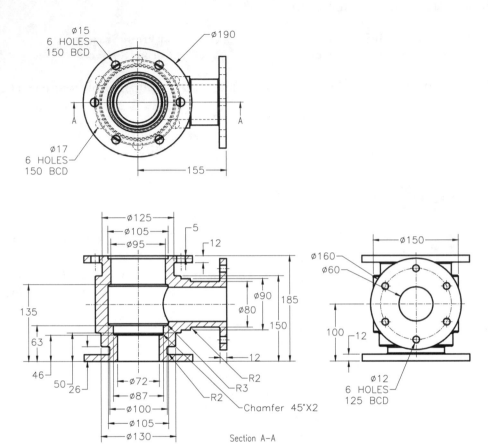

Figure 6-119 *Dimensions of the model for Exercise 1*

Exercise 2

Create the model shown in Figure 6-120. The dimensions of the model are given in the same figure. **(Expected time: 30 min)**

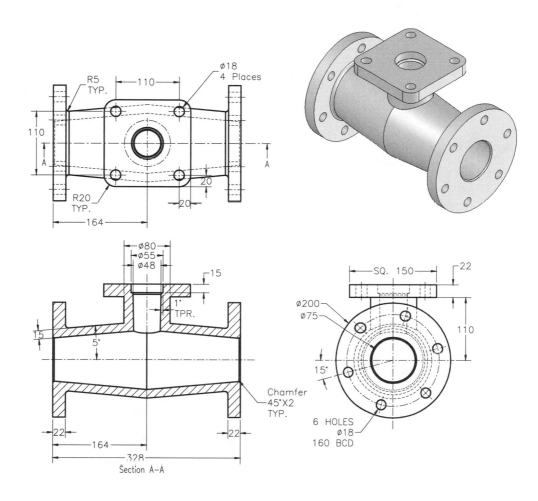

Figure 6-120 *The model and its dimensions for Exercise 2*

Answers to Self-Evaluation Test

1. F, 2. F, 3. T, 4. F, 5. F, 6. Up To Next, 7. Up To Body, 8. Merge results, 9. Cylindrical/Conical Face, 10. Bodies to Keep

Chapter 7

Advanced Modeling Tools-I

Learning Objectives

After completing this chapter, you will be able to:
- *Create holes using the Simple Hole option.*
- *Create standard holes using the Hole Wizard option.*
- *Apply simple and advanced fillets.*
- *Understand various selection methods.*
- *Chamfer the edges and vertices of the model.*
- *Create the shell feature.*
- *Create the wrap feature.*

ADVANCED MODELING TOOLS

This chapter discusses various advanced modeling tools available in SolidWorks that assist you in creating a better and accurate design by capturing the design intent in the model. For example, in the previous chapters, you have learned to create a hole using the **Extruded Cut** tool. In this chapter, you will create holes using the **Simple Hole** option and the **Hole Wizard** option. The hole wizard is used to create standard holes classified on the basis of industrial standard, screw type, and size. The **Hole Wizard** tool of SolidWorks is one of the largest standard industrial virtual hole generation methods available in any CAD package. You will also learn about some other advanced modeling tools such as the fillet, chamfer, shell, and warp in this chapter.

Creating Simple Holes

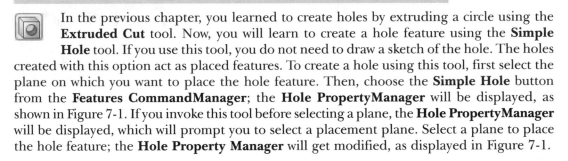

CommandManager:	Features > Simple Hole	*(Customize to add)*
SolidWorks menus:	Insert > Features > Hole > Simple	
Toolbar:	Features > Simple Hole	*(Customize to add)*

In the previous chapter, you learned to create holes by extruding a circle using the **Extruded Cut** tool. Now, you will learn to create a hole feature using the **Simple Hole** tool. If you use this tool, you do not need to draw a sketch of the hole. The holes created with this option act as placed features. To create a hole using this tool, first select the plane on which you want to place the hole feature. Then, choose the **Simple Hole** button from the **Features CommandManager**; the **Hole PropertyManager** will be displayed, as shown in Figure 7-1. If you invoke this tool before selecting a plane, the **Hole PropertyManager** will be displayed, which will prompt you to select a placement plane. Select a plane to place the hole feature; the **Hole Property Manager** will get modified, as displayed in Figure 7-1.

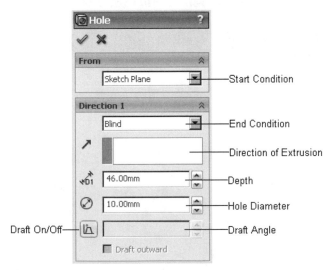

*Figure 7-1 The **Hole PropertyManager***

Also, the preview of the hole feature will be displayed in the drawing area in temporary graphics with the default values, as shown in Figure 7-2.

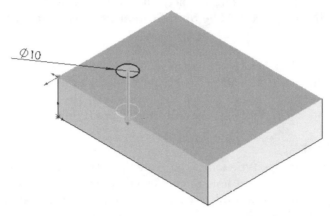

*Figure 7-2 Preview of the hole created using the **Simple Hole** tool*

Specify the termination type of the hole feature using the **End Condition** drop-down list, and set the value of the hole diameter in the **Hole Diameter** spinner. You can also use the **Direction of Extrusion** selection box to specify the direction of extrusion. If the hole feature to be created is a tapered hole, specify a draft angle using the **Draft On/Off** button and set the value of the draft angle using the **Draft Angle** spinner. The preview of the draft angle is displayed in the drawing area in temporary graphics. After setting all parameters, choose the **OK** button from the **Hole PropertyManager**.

The hole feature created using this option is placed on the selected plane but the placement of the hole is not yet defined. Therefore, select the hole feature from the **FeatureManager design tree**; a pop-up toolbar will be displayed. Choose **Edit Sketch** from the pop-up toolbar; the sketching environment will be invoked. Apply the relations and dimensions to define the placement of the hole feature on the selected face and exit the sketching environment.

 Tip. *It is recommended to create placed features such as holes, fillets, and so on after creating all sketch based features. This will help in maintaining the design intent by applying the relations and dimensions with respect to the existing features.*

Creating Standard Holes Using the Hole Wizard

CommandManager:	Features > Hole Wizard
SolidWorks menus:	Insert > Features > Hole > Wizard
Toolbar:	Features > Hole Wizard

 The **Hole Wizard** tool is used to add standard holes such as the counterbore, countersink, drilled, tapped, and pipe tap holes. You can also add a user-defined counterbored drilled hole, simple hole, simple drilled hole, tapered hole, and so on. You can control all parameters of the holes, including the termination options. You can also modify the holes according to your requirement after placing them. Therefore, you can place the standard parametric holes using this tool. You can select a face or a plane to place the hole even before invoking this tool. The placement face can be a planar face or a curved face. After selecting the placement plane or face, choose the **Hole Wizard** button from the **Features CommandManager**; the **Hole Specification PropertyManager** will be displayed, as shown in Figure 7-3.

When you preselect the placement plane and invoke the **Hole Specification PropertyManager**, the preview of the hole feature will be displayed in the graphics area. If you modify the parameters of the hole or change its type, the preview of the hole will also be modified dynamically. The options in the **Hole Specification PropertyManager** are discussed next.

Hole Type Rollout

The **Hole Type** rollout in the **Type** tab of the **Hole Specification PropertyManager** is used to define the type of the standard hole to be created. You will notice that the **Counterbore** button is chosen by default. As a result, a counterbore hole will be created. Figure 7-4 shows the buttons in the **Hole Type** rollout. Each button is used to create a specific type of standard hole. The other options in this rollout are discussed next.

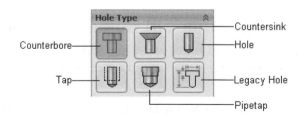

Figure 7-3 The **Hole Specification** *PropertyManager*

Figure 7-4 Buttons in the **Hole Type** rollout

Standard

The **Standard** drop-down list is used to specify the industrial dimensioning and hole standards. By default, the **Ansi Inch** standard is selected. Other dimensioning standards available in this drop-down list are **Ansi Metric**, **BSI**, **DIN**, **ISO**, **JIS**, **DME**, **HASCO Metric**, **PCS**, **GB, Progressive**, **Superior**, and so on.

Type

The **Type** drop-down list is used to define the type of fastener to be inserted in the hole. The standard holes created using the **Hole Wizard** tool depend on the type and the size of the fastener to be inserted in that hole. You can select the screw type from the **Type** drop-down list. The types of screws available in the drop-down list depend on the standard selected from the **Standard** drop-down list.

Hole Specifications Rollout

The **Hole Specifications** rollout, see Figure 7-5, in the **Type** tab of the **Hole Specification PropertyManager** is used to define the size and fit of standard hole to be created. The other options in this rollout are discussed next.

Size

The **Size** drop-down list is used to define the size of the fastener that will be inserted in the hole that is created using the **Hole Wizard** tool. The size of the fasteners in the **Size** drop-down list depend on the standard selected from the **Standard** drop-down list in the **Hole Type** rollout.

Fit

The **Fit** drop-down list is used to specify the type of fit to be applied to the hole. You can apply the **Close**, **Normal**, or **Loose** fit type to the hole.

Show custom sizing

The **Show custom sizing** check box is used to create a user-defined hole feature. On selecting this check box, the parameters to be specified to create a user-defined hole feature will be displayed below the check box, as shown in Figure 7-6. If you change the default values of the various parameters meant for the standard holes, the corresponding spinners will turn yellow. Also, the **Restore Default Values** button will be displayed in this area. You can choose this button to restore the default values of the standard holes.

Figure 7-5 *The* **Hole Specifications** *rollout*

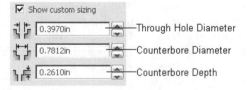

Figure 7-6 *The parameters of the counterbore hole displayed on selecting the* **Show custom sizing** *check*

The options used to create the standard holes, except the **Legacy Hole**, are the same as those discussed above. When you choose the **Legacy Hole** button from the **Hole Type** rollout of the **PropertyManager**, the preview of the hole will be displayed in the preview area below the **Type** drop-down list. Also, the **Section Dimensions** rollout will be displayed. Select the type of hole that you need to create using the **Type** drop-down list; the preview of the hole feature will be updated automatically. You can set the parameters of the hole by double-clicking on the fields in the **Value** column of the **Section Dimensions** rollout.

End Condition Rollout

The **End Condition** rollout, shown in Figure 7-7, is used to specify the hole termination options. By default, the **Through All** option is selected in this drop-down list. The hole termination options are similar to the other feature termination options discussed in earlier chapters. You can also flip the direction of the hole creation using the **Reverse Direction** button.

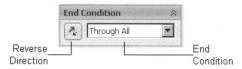

Reverse   End
Direction   Condition

*Figure 7-7 The **End Condition** rollout*

If you are creating a tapped hole or a pipe tapped hole, the additional options will be displayed to specify the termination conditions for threads.

Options Rollout

The options in the **Options** rollout are used to define some of the additional parameters of the hole. These parameters are optional and are specified only if required. Figure 7-8 shows the **Options** rollout with all the check boxes selected. All these options are discussed next.

Head clearance

The **Head clearance** check box is selected to specify the clearance distance between the head of the fastener and the placement plane of the hole feature. If you select this check box, the **Head Clearance** spinner will be displayed. You can set the clearance value in this spinner.

Near side countersink

The **Near side countersink** check box is selected to specify the diameter and the angle for the countersink on the upper face, which is the placement plane of the hole feature. If you select this check box, the **Near Side Countersink Diameter** and **Near Side Countersink Angle** spinners will be displayed. You can set the values of the diameter and angle using their respective spinners.

Under head countersink

The **Under head countersink** check box is selected to specify

*Figure 7-8 The **Options** rollout*

the diameter and the angle for the countersink to be applied at the end of the counterbore head. If you select this check box, the **Under Head Countersink Diameter** and the **Under Head Countersink Angle** spinners will be displayed. You can set the values of the diameter and the angle using the corresponding spinners.

Far side countersink

The **Far side countersink** check box is selected to specify the diameter and the angle for the countersink on the bottom face of the hole feature. If you select this check box, the **Far Side Countersink Diameter** and **Far Side Countersink Angle** spinners will be displayed. You can set the values of the diameter and the angle using their respective spinners.

If you create a user-defined hole using the **Legacy Hole** button, the **Options** rollout will not be displayed. If you are creating a **Tap** hole, some additional options will be displayed in the **Options** rollout. These options are discussed next.

Tap drill diameter

This option is selected if you need to create a hole equal the diameter of the tap.

Cosmetic thread

The **Cosmetic thread** option is selected if you need to create a hole equal to the diameter of the tap, and to display the schematic representation of the thread, as shown in Figure 7-9. When you select this option, the **With thread callout** check box is displayed. If you select this check box, a callout will be attached to the hole feature when you create drawings in the drawing environment.

Figure 7-9 The holes with and without cosmetic thread

Remove Thread

Select this option if you need to create a hole equal to the diameter of the thread.

Thread class

The **Thread class** check box is selected to specify the class of the thread. When you select this check box, the **Thread Class** drop-down list will be displayed. You can select the type of class using this drop-down list.

Tip. *By default, the shaded display mode of the cosmetic thread is off. To turn it on, choose the* **Options** *button in the Menu Bar; the* **Systems Options - General** *dialog box will be displayed. Choose the* **Document Properties** *tab and select the* **Detailing** *option on the left. Next, select the* **Shaded cosmetic threads** *check box and choose* **OK**.

Favorites Rollout

The **Favorites** rollout is used to add the frequently used holes to the favorite list. If you add a hole to the favorite list, you will not have to configure the same settings to add similar types of holes every time. The method of adding a hole setting to the favorite list is the same as that of adding the dimensional settings as discussed in Chapter 4.

Defining the Position for Placing a Hole

If you have selected the placement plane and invoked the **Hole Wizard** tool, the preview of the hole feature will be updated dynamically when you define the parameters of the hole feature using the options in the **Type** tab. If you do not select a placement plane before invoking the **Hole Wizard** tool, the preview of the hole feature will not be displayed in the drawing area. So, after configuring all parameters of the hole feature, you need to define its placement position. To do so, choose the **Positions** tab from the **Hole Specification PropertyManager**; the **Hole Specification PropertyManager** will be changed to **Hole Position PropertyManager**, as shown in Figure 7-10.

Figure 7-10 The Hole Position PropertyManager

The message in the **Hole Position(s)** rollout informs you to use the dimension and other sketch tools to place the hole. The select cursor will be replaced by the placement cursor. Use the placement cursor to place more holes. As discussed earlier, if the placement plane is selected first, the hole will be placed on the selected placement plane. However, if the placement plane is not selected earlier, you can specify a point to place the hole feature and constrain the placement point using the relations and dimensions. Choose the **OK** button to complete the feature creation.

 Note

*If you create a pattern feature of a tapped hole feature, the thread graphic will not be displayed in the other instances of the pattern, except the parent instance. Therefore to add the thread graphic in other pattern instances, use the **Texture PropertyManager**. You will learn more about patterns in the later chapters.*

Figures 7-11 through 7-14 show the models with various types of holes placed using the **Hole Wizard** tool. Figure 7-15 shows a base plate on which various types of holes are created using the **Hole Wizard** tool.

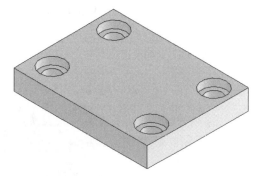

Figure 7-11 Counterbore holes

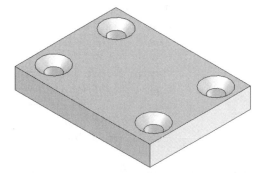

Figure 7-12 Countersink holes

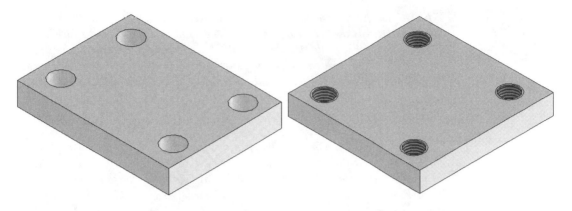

Figure 7-13 *Drilled holes*   *Figure 7-14* *Tapped holes*

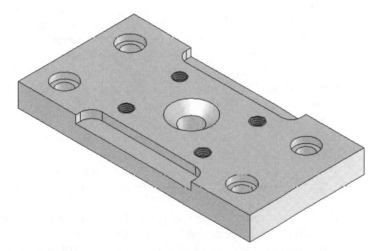

Figure 7-15 *Base plate with holes created using the* ***Hole Wizard*** *tool*

Creating Fillets

CommandManager:	Features > Fillet
SolidWorks menus:	Insert > Features > Fillet/Round
Toolbar:	Features > Fillet

In SolidWorks, you can add fillets as a feature to the model using the **Manual** or the **FilletXpert** option. The **Manual** option is used to fillet an internal or external face or edge of a model. You can preselect the face, edge, or feature to which the fillet has to be applied. You can also select the entity to be filleted after invoking the **Fillet** tool. To add a fillet using the **Manual** option, choose the **Fillet** button from the **Features CommandManager**; the **Fillet PropertyManager** will be displayed. But, if the **FilletXpert PropertyManager** is displayed, choose the **Manual** button to display the **Fillet PropertyManager**, as shown in Figure 7-16. If the entities to be filleted are preselected, the preview of the fillet feature will be displayed in the drawing area. This is because the **Full**

*Tip. The hole feature created using the **Hole Wizard** tool consists of two sketches. The first sketch is the sketch of the placement point and the second sketch is the sketch of the profile of the hole feature. If you select the placement plane before invoking the **Hole Wizard** tool, the resulting placement sketch will be a 2D sketch. However, if you select the placement point after invoking the **Placement Point** dialog box, the resulting placement sketch will be a 3D sketch. You will learn more about 3D sketches in the later chapters.*

In the modern modeling practice, the creation of threads is avoided in model because it results in the creation of a complex geometry. The views that are generated from the models that contain complex geometry are difficult to understand. Therefore, it is better to avoid the creation of threads in the model and add the cosmetic threads. It is recommended to use the cosmetic threads to get the thread convention in the drawing views.

*If a cosmetic thread is added to a tapped hole, the cosmetic thread will also be displayed along with the placement and hole profile sketches. To edit the cosmetic threads, select them from the **FeatureManager design tree**; the pop-up toolbar will be displayed. Choose the **Edit Feature** option from the pop-up toolbar; the **Cosmetic Thread** dialog box will be displayed. The **Cosmetic Thread** dialog box and the cosmetic threads are discussed in the later chapters.*

You can also view the convention of the thread if the cosmetic thread is added to a tapped hole feature. Orient the model to the top view to observe the thread convention from the top view. Similarly, orient the model to the front view, back view, or any side view to observe the thread convention from different side views.

preview radio button will be selected by default in the **Fillet PropertyManager**. If the entities are not preselected, you will be prompted to select the edges, faces, features, or loops to add the fillet feature. Use the select cursor to select the entity to be filleted. A fillet callout will also be displayed along with the preview of the fillet. Figure 7-17 shows the preview of the fillet feature with the fillet callout.

The types of fillets that can be created using the **fillet** tool are given next.

1. Constant radius fillet
2. Variable radius fillet
3. Face fillet
4. Full round fillet

Creating Constant Radius Fillet

Select the **Constant radius** radio button in the **Fillet Type** rollout of the **Fillet PropertyManager** to create a fillet of a constant radius along the selected entity. This radio button is selected, by default. You can set the value of the fillet radius in the **Radius** spinner provided in the **Items To Fillet** rollout or by clicking in the value area of the fillet callout. Enter the value of the radius and press the ENTER key on the keyboard. The preview of the

Figure 7-16 The **Fillet PropertyManager**

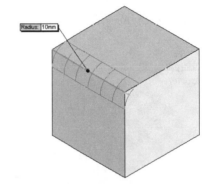

Figure 7-17 *Preview of the fillet feature*

fillet will be changed dynamically on modifying the value of the radius of the fillet. The entities that you can select to add the fillet feature are faces, edges, features, and loops. The names of the selected entities are displayed in the **Edges, Faces, Features, and Loops** selection box. Next, choose the **OK** button from the **Fillet PropertyManager**. Figures 7-18 through 7-23 show the selection of different entities and the resulting fillet from the selected entities.

If you select the **Constant radius** radio button in the **FilletPropertyManager**, various options will be displayed in the **Items To Fillet** rollout, refer to Figure 7-16. These options are discussed next.

Multiple Radius Fillet

By selecting the **Multiple radius fillet** check box provided in the **Items To Fillet** rollout of the **Fillet PropertyManager**, you can specify a fillet of different radii to all the selected edges. To create a fillet feature using the multiple radius option, preselect the edges, faces, or features or select them after invoking the **Fillet PropertyManager**. After invoking the **Fillet** tool, select the **Multiple radius fillet** check box. The preview of the fillet feature with the default values will be displayed in the drawing area. You will notice that you are provided with different callouts for each selected entity. Figure 7-24 shows the preview of the fillet feature with the **Multiple radius fillet** check box selected.

Edges selected
to fillet

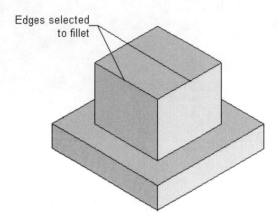

Figure 7-18 *Selecting the edges*

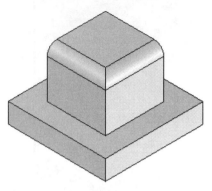

Figure 7-19 *Resulting fillet feature*

Face selected
to fillet

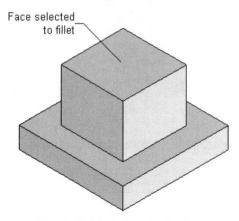

Figure 7-20 *Selecting the face*

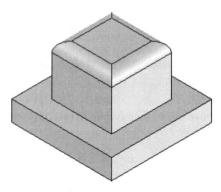

Figure 7-21 *Resulting fillet feature*

Boss feature
selected to
fillet

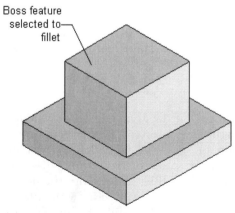

Figure 7-22 *Selecting the feature*

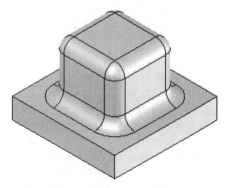

Figure 7-23 *Resulting fillet feature*

Tip. *You can preselect a feature to create a fillet feature or select the feature after invoking the **Fillet** tool. For the post-selection of the feature to be filleted, expand the **FeatureManager** design tree that is displayed in the drawing area, and select the feature. You can also select the feature directly from the drawing area. The preview of the filleted feature will be displayed in the drawing area.*

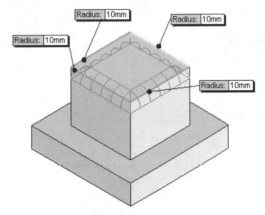

Figure 7-24 Preview of the fillet feature with the
Multiple radius fillet *check box selected*

The names of the selected entities are displayed in the **Edges, Faces, Features and Loops** selection box. The boundaries of the currently selected entity in the selection box are highlighted with a thick line. You can set the value of each selected entity by using the **Radius** spinner or by specifying the value of the fillet radius in the radius callout, as shown in Figure 7-25. As you modify the value of the radius, the preview of the fillet feature will be modified dynamically in the drawing area. Figure 7-26 shows the fillet created using the multiple radius fillets.

Fillet With and Without Tangent Propagation

In SolidWorks, you can add a fillet feature to a model with or without the tangent propagation. When you invoke the **Fillet PropertyManager**, you will observe that the **Tangent propagation** check box is selected by default in the **Items To Fillet** rollout. Therefore, if you select an edge, face, feature, or a loop to fillet, it will automatically select other entities that are tangential to the selected entity. Thus, it will apply the fillet feature to all entities that are tangential to the selected one. If you clear the **Tangent propagation** check box, the fillet will be applied only to the selected entity. Figure 7-27 shows the existing fillet and the edge to be selected to add a fillet feature. Figures 7-28 and 7-29 show the fillet feature created with the **Tangent propagation** check box cleared and selected, respectively.

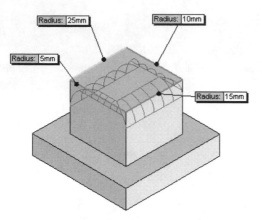

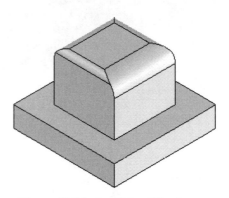

Figure 7-25 *Different radii specified in each radius callout*

Figure 7-26 *Resulting fillet feature*

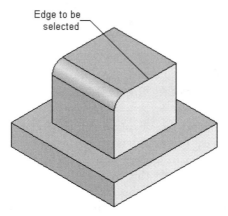

Figure 7-27 *Edge to be selected to apply the fillet feature*

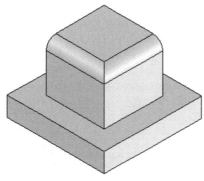

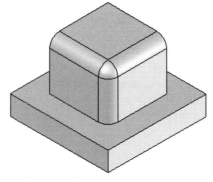

Figure 7-28 *Fillet feature created with the* **Tangent propagation** *check box cleared*

Figure 7-29 *Fillet feature created with the* **Tangent propagation** *check box selected*

Note
*The **Full preview** radio button in the **Fillet PropertyManager** is used to preview the fillet feature before actually creating it. If you select the **Partial preview** radio button, you can view only the partial preview of the fillet feature. If you select a face to add a fillet feature and select the **Partial preview** radio button, you cannot preview the fillet feature created on all edges adjacent to the selected face. You can preview only the fillet on the single edge of the selected face. Press the A key on the keyboard to cycle the preview of the fillet feature on other edges of the selected face. If you select the **No preview** radio button, the preview of the fillet feature will not be displayed.*

Setback Fillets

The setback fillet is created where three or more edges are merged into a vertex. This type of fillet is used to smoothly blend the transition surfaces generated from the edges to the fillet vertex. This smooth transition is created between all selected edges and the vertex selected for the setback type of fillet. To create a setback fillet, invoke the **Fillet PropertyManager** and select three or more edges to apply the fillet. Note that the edges should share the same vertex. The preview of the fillet will be displayed in the drawing area. Now, click on the black arrows in the **Setback Parameters** rollout to expand the rollout; the **Setback Parameters** rollout will be expanded, as shown in Figure 7-30. This rollout will be used to specify the setback parameters. Click once in the **Setback Vertices** selection box to invoke the setback vertex selection command. Now, select the vertex where the edges meet. Figure 7-31 shows the edges selected and the vertex to which the setback parameters are to be assigned.

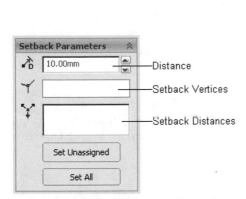

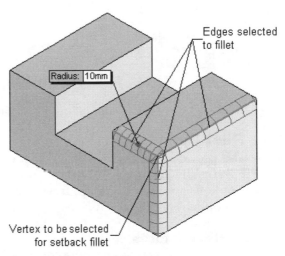

*Figure 7-30 The **Setback Parameters** rollout*

Figure 7-31 Edges and vertex to be selected to apply the setback fillet feature

When you select the vertex for the setback fillet, you will observe that the callouts with unassigned setback distances are displayed in the drawing area. The name of the selected vertex will be displayed in the **Setback Vertices** selection box. The names of the selected edges will be displayed in the **Setback Distances** edit box. Select the name of the edge in this edit box to assign a setback distance to that edge; a magenta arrow will be displayed along that edge. Use the **Distance** spinner to assign a setback distance to the selected edge. Similarly, assign the setback distance to all edges. You can also assign the setback distance directly by specifying the value in the setback callouts displayed in the drawing area. As discussed earlier, the preview of the fillet will be updated automatically when you assign any value. The **Set Unassigned** button in the **Setback Parameters** rollout is used to assign the setback distance displayed in the **Distance** spinner to the unassigned edges, if any. The **Set All** button is used to assign the setback distance displayed in the **distance** spinner to all selected edges. Figure 7-32 shows the preview of the setback fillet and Figure 7-33 shows a setback fillet on one side of the model and a normal fillet on the other side of the model.

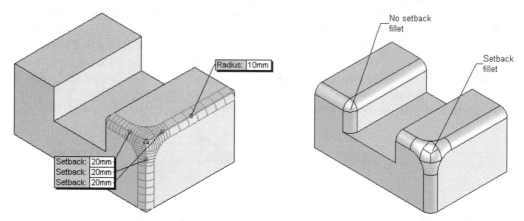

Figure 7-32 Preview of the setback fillet   *Figure 7-33 Simple and setback fillet features*

Other Fillet Options

You are also provided with various other fillet options in the **Fillet Options** rollout of the **Fillet PropertyManager**. These options are used to create an accurate and aesthetic design. The fillet options are **Select through faces**, **Keep features**, **Round corners**, and **Overflow type**. These options are discussed next.

Select through faces

This option allows you to select the edges hidden behind the faces of the model. This is a new feature introduced in the recent release of SolidWorks.

Keep features

If there are boss or cut features in a model and the fillet created is large enough to consume them, it is recommended that you select the **Keep features** check box in the **Fillet Options** rollout. This check box is selected by default, but you should confirm it before creating any fillet feature. If you clear this check box, the fillet feature will consume the features that will obstruct its path. Note that the features that are consumed by the fillet feature are not deleted from the model. They disappear from the model because of some geometric inconsistency. However, if you rollback, suppress, or delete the fillet, the consumed features will reappear. You will learn more about rollback and suppress in the later chapters. Figure 7-34 shows the model and the edge to be selected for applying fillet.

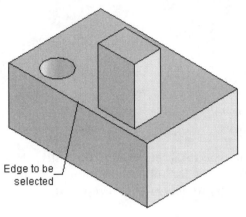

Figure 7-34 Edge to be selected to apply the fillet feature

Figure 7-35 shows the fillet feature created with the **Keep features** check box selected and Figure 7-36 shows the fillet feature created with the **Keep features** check box cleared.

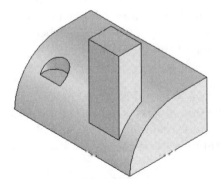 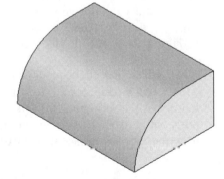

*Figure 7-35 Fillet feature created with the **Keep features** check box selected*

*Figure 7-36 Fillet feature created with the **Keep features** check box cleared*

Round corners

The **Round corners** option is used to round the edges at the corner of the fillet feature. To create a fillet feature with round corners, select the **Round corners** check box from the **Fillet Options** rollout after specifying all parameters of the fillet feature. Figure 7-37 shows a fillet feature created with the **Round corners** check box cleared and Figure 7-38 shows a fillet feature created with the **Round corners** check box selected.

Overflow type

The **Overflow type** area is used to specify the physical condition that the fillet feature should adopt when it extends beyond an area. By default, SolidWorks automatically adopts

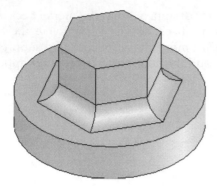 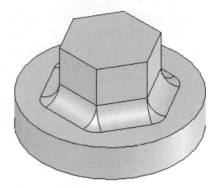

Figure 7-37 *Fillet feature created with the* **Round corners** *check box cleared*

Figure 7-38 *Fillet feature created with the* **Round corners** *check box selected*

the best possible flow type to accommodate the fillet, depending on the geometric conditions. This is because the **Default** radio button is selected by default in the **Overflow type** area. The options in this area are discussed next.

Default
On selecting the **Default** radio button, SolidWorks calculates the best suitable option to create the fillet, when the fillet feature created extends beyond a specified area.

Keep edge
The **Keep edge** radio button is selected when the fillet feature extends beyond a specified area. Therefore, to accommodate the fillet feature, this option will divide the fillet into multiple surfaces and the adjacent edges will not be disturbed, as shown in Figure 7-39. A dip will be created at the top of the fillet feature.

Keep surface
The **Keep surface** radio button in this area is selected to accommodate the fillet feature by trimming it. This will maintain the smoothness of the rounded fillet surface but it will disturb the adjacent edges. As this option maintains the smooth fillet surface, it extends to the adjacent surface, as shown in Figure 7-40.

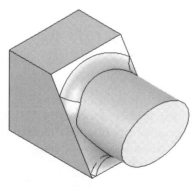 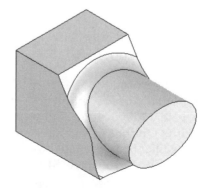

Figure 7-39 *Fillet feature created with the* **Keep edge** *radio button selected*

Figure 7-40 *Fillet feature created with the* **Keep surface** *radio button selected*

Creating Variable Radius Fillet

The variable radius fillet is created by specifying different radii along the length of the selected edge at specified intervals. You can create a smooth transition or a straight transition between the vertices to which the radii are applied by selecting suitable options. To create a variable radius fillet, invoke the **Fillet PropertyManager**. Select the **Variable radius** radio button from the **Fillet Type** rollout; the **Variable Radius Parameters** rollout will be displayed in the **Fillet PropertyManager**, as shown in Figure 7-41.

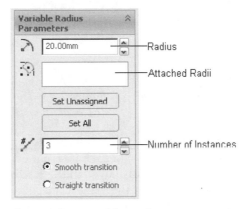

*Figure 7-41 The **Variable Radius Parameters** rollout*

You will be prompted to select the edge to fillet. Use the left mouse button to select the edge or the edges that you want to fillet. The name of the selected edge will be displayed in the **Edges, Faces, Features and Loops** selection box. By default, the radius is applied at the start point and the endpoint. Also, the variable radius callouts will be displayed at the vertices of the selected edge, as shown in Figure 7-42.

The names of the vertices on which the callouts are added are listed in the **Attached Radii** display box in the **Variable Radius Parameters** rollout. You will find three red points on the selected edge because by default, the value of the control points in the **Number of Instances** spinner is set to **3**. You can add additional control points using the **Number of Instances** spinner. These control points are also called movable points because you can change their positions. The additional radii are specified on these points on the selected edge.

Use the left mouse button to select the control points available on the selected edge. As you select the control point, the **Radius and Position** callouts will be displayed for each control point, as shown in Figure 7-43. The name of the selected points will also be displayed in the **Attached Radii** display box.

You will observe that the position of the three points is described in terms of percentage. You can modify the position of the points by modifying the value of percentage in the **Position** area of the **Radius and Position** callout. By following this procedure, you can also modify the placement of the other points. You will also notice that the radius value is not assigned to any of the callouts. Therefore, you need to specify the value of the radius in the callouts. Use the left mouse button to select the name of the vertex in the **Attached Radii** selection list; the name of the selected item will be highlighted in its respective callout. Use the **Radius** spinner

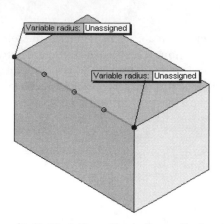

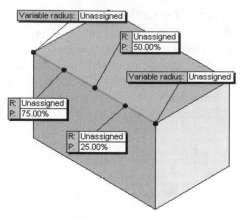

Figure 7-42 *Variable radius callouts displayed at the vertices of the selected edge*

Figure 7-43 *The **Radius and Position** callouts displayed after selecting the control points*

to set the value of the radius for the selected item. You can also specify the value of the radius in the radius area of the callout. Set the value of each unassigned radius. You can also use the **Set Unassigned** button to assign the value displayed in the **Radius** spinner to all unassigned point. The **Set All** button is used to assign the same value that is displayed in the **Radius** spinner to all points. Figure 7-44 shows the preview of the fillet feature with modified positions of the control points and the radius values specified for all points and vertices. Figure 7-45 shows the resulting fillet feature.

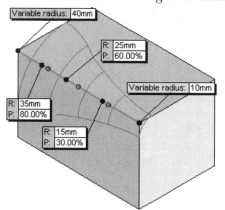

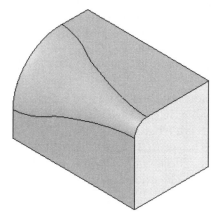

Figure 7-44 *Preview of the variable radius fillet*

Figure 7-45 *Resulting fillet feature*

The other options in this rollout are discussed next.

Smooth transition

Select this radio button to create a smooth transition by smoothly blending the fillets at the points and vertices on which you have defined the radius.

Straight transition

Select this radio button to create a linear transition by blending the fillets at the points and vertices on which you have defined the radius. In this case, the edge tangency is not maintained between one fillet radius and the adjacent face.

Figures 7-46 and 7-47 show the fillets created with the **Smooth transition** and **Straight transition** options selected, respectively.

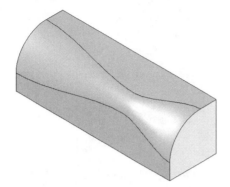

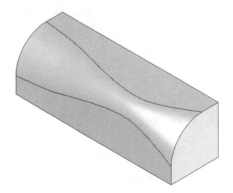

Figure 7-46 *Variable radius fillet with smooth transition*

Figure 7-47 *Variable radius fillet with straight transition*

Creating Face Fillet

In SolidWorks, you can add a fillet between two sets of faces. It blends the first set of faces with the second set of faces. It adds or removes the material according to the geometric conditions. It can also completely or partially remove the faces to accommodate the fillet feature. To create a face fillet feature, invoke the **Fillet PropertyManager** and select the **Face fillet** radio button from the **Fillet Type** rollout; the **Items To Fillet** rollout will be modified and the **Face Set 1** and **Face Set 2** selection boxes will be enabled. The **Fillet PropertyManager** with the **Face fillet** radio button selected is shown in Figure 7-48.

You will be prompted to select the faces to fillet for face set 1 and face set 2. Use the left mouse button to select the first set of faces. You can even select more than one face in a set. The name of the selected faces will be displayed in the **Face Set 1** selection box and the selected faces will be highlighted. The **Face Set 1** callout with radius will be displayed in the drawing area. Click in the **Face Set 2** selection box to invoke the selection tool and select the second set of faces. The second set of selected faces will be displayed in magenta and the **Face Set 2** callout will be displayed in the drawing area. Also, the preview of the face fillet will be displayed in the drawing area. Now, set the value of the radius in the **Radius** spinner. The **Tangent propagation** check box is used to create the face fillet

Figure 7-48 *The **Fillet PropertyManager** with the **Face fillet** radio button selected*

tangent to the adjacent faces. This check box is selected by default. If you clear this check box, the fillet will not be forced to be tangent to the adjacent faces. Figure 7-49 shows the faces to be selected to apply the face fillet. Figure 7-50 displays the resulting fillet feature with three faces of the slot completely eliminated after applying the fillet.

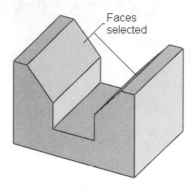

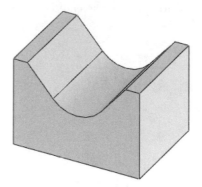

Figure 7-49 *Faces to be selected*   **Figure 7-50** *Resulting fillet feature*

Creating the Face Fillet Using the Hold Line

You can specify the radius and the shape of the fillet by determining a hold line. A hold line can be a set of edges, or a split line projected on a face. You will learn more about split lines in the later chapters. To create a face fillet using the hold line, invoke the **Fillet PropertyManager**. The selection mode will be activated by default in the **Face Set 1** selection box in the **Items To Fillet** rollout and you will be prompted to select the faces to be filleted. Select the faces for the face set 1; the names of the selected faces will be displayed in the **Face Set 1** selection box and the selected faces will be highlighted. Now, click in the **Face Set 2** selection box to activate the selection mode and select the faces to add in the face set 2; the selected faces will be displayed in magenta. Also, the preview of the face fillet with the default settings will be displayed in the drawing area. By default, the **Tangent propagation** check box is selected. Therefore, you do not need to select the tangent faces in both the face sets. Next, click on the double arrow at the right of the **Fillet Options** rollout to expand the rollout, as shown in Figure 7-51.

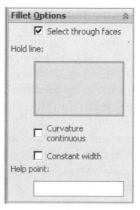

Figure 7-51 *The* **Fillet Options** *rollout*

Now, left-click on the **Hold line** selection box and select the hold line or lines. The preview of the face fillet will be modified automatically. Note that the **Radius** spinner will not be available in the **Items To Fillet** rollout and the radius of the fillet will be determined by the distance between the hold line and the edges or faces selected to be filleted. Now, choose the **OK** button from the **Fillet PropertyManager**. Figure 7-52 shows an example in which the faces and the hold line are selected. Figure 7-53 shows the resulting face fillet using the hold line.

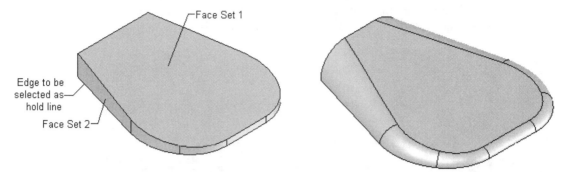

Figure 7-52 *Faces and hold line to be selected*   *Figure 7-53* *Resulting face fillet*

Curvature Continuous in the Face Fillet With Hold Line

The **Curvature continuous** check box in the **Fillet Options** rollout is selected to apply the face fillet feature with continuous curvature throughout the fillet feature. Note that a fillet with continuous curvature is possible only by creating a face fillet feature with the hold line. You need to specify the hold lines on both sets of faces. Figure 7-54 shows a model in which a face fillet is created on both the pillars using the hold line. On the right pillar, the face fillet is created with the **Curvature continuous** check box cleared and on the left pillar, the face fillet is created with the **Curvature continuous** check box selected.

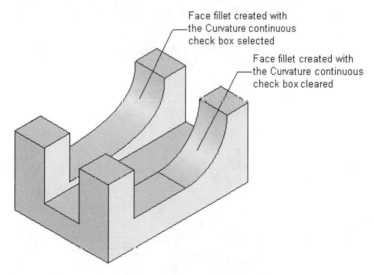

Figure 7-54 *Face fillet created with the **Curvature continuous** check box selected and cleared*

Constant Width

In SolidWorks, the **Fillet** tool is enhanced with the addition of the **Constant width** option. Consider a case in which you have applied a face fillet to the faces that are at an angle other than 90-degree to each other. You will notice that the additional material is added to the fillet on the side that forms an acute angle with the other face, refer to Figure 7-55. However, if you select the **Constant width** check box from the **Fillet Options** rollout, a fillet of constant width will be applied between the selected faces, refer to Figure 7-56.

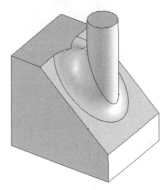

Figure 7-55 Face fillet with the **Constant width** check box cleared

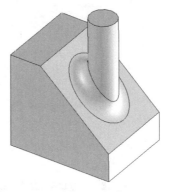

Figure 7-56 Face fillet with the **Constant width** check box selected

Creating Full Round Fillet

The full round fillet is used to add a semi-circular fillet feature. To create a full round fillet, invoke the **Fillet PropertyManager** and select the **Full round fillet** radio button in the **Fillet Type** rollout; the **Items To Fillet** rollout will be displayed, as shown in Figure 7-57. The selection mode will be active in the **Face Set 1** selection box and you will be prompted to

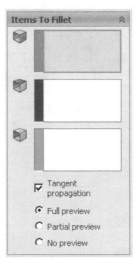

Figure 7-57 The **Items To Fillet** rollout when the **Full round fillet** radio button is selected from the **Fillet Type** rollout

select faces. Select the first face for the side face set 1. Now, click in the **Center Face Set** selection box and select the center face. Next, click in the **Face Set 2** selection box and select the face for the side face set 2; the preview of the full round fillet will be displayed in the drawing area. Choose the **OK** button from the **Fillet PropertyManager**. Figure 7-58 shows the faces to be selected to create the full round fillet. Note that the third face is the left face parallel to the first selected face. Figure 7-59 shows the resulting full round fillet.

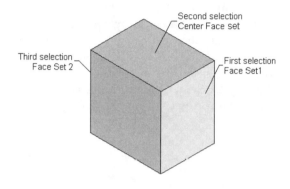

Figure 7-58 *Faces selected to create the full round fillet*

Figure 7-59 *Resulting full round fillet*

Tip. *You can turn on or off the display of the tangent edges of the model. To do so, choose **Options** from the Menu Bar to display the **System Options - General** dialog box. Select the **Display/Selection** option from the area on the left and then select the **As visible** or **Removed** radio button from the **Part/Assembly tangent edge display** area.*

Selection Methods

You have learned about the basic and advanced modeling tools. Now, you will learn about some selection methods that will increase your productivity and speed of modeling. These selection methods are discussed next.

Select Other

The **Select Other** option is the most common tool to cycle through the entities for selection. This option is used when the selection is difficult in a multifeatured complex model. Before invoking any other tool, select an entity and do not move the mouse; a pop-up toolbar will be displayed. Choose the **Select Other** option from the pop-up toolbar to display the **Select Other** list box, as shown in Figure 7-60, and the select cursor will be replaced by the select next cursor. The entities that surround the selected entities will be listed in this list box. Also, the entities that are hidden behind

Figure 7-60 *The **Select Other** list box*

the selected entity will be listed in this list box. When you move the cursor on the name of an entity in the **Select Other** list box, the entity will be highlighted in the drawing area. To select an entity using this list box, you need to select the name of the entity in the list box.

If you select a face and invoke the **Select Other** list box, the display of the selected face will be turned off and you can easily select the face that is behind the selected face. The name of the hidden face will be displayed in the **Select Other** list box.

Select Loop

The **Select Loop** option is used to select the loops. You can also cycle through various loops before confirming the selection. This option is extremely useful when you are working with a complex model and you need to select a loop from that model. Select any of the edges of the loop and right-click to invoke the shortcut menu. Choose the **Select Loop** option from the shortcut menu. The loop that is possible by selecting that edge will be highlighted and an arrow will be displayed in yellow. Move the cursor on that arrow and when the arrow is highlighted in orange, left-click to cycle through the loops. Repeat this until you select the required loop. Figure 7-61 shows a loop selected using the **Select Loop** option. Figure 7-62 shows the second loop selected when the left mouse button is used on the arrow to cycle through the loops.

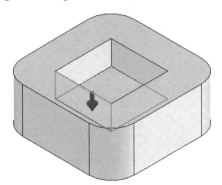   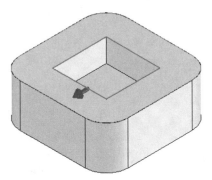

Figure 7-61 Loop selected using the **Select Loop** tool

Figure 7-62 Second loop selected while cycling through the loops

Select Partial Loop

This technique is used to select the partial loop created by joining two edges. To select a partial loop, select two edges, as shown in Figure 7-63. Invoke the shortcut menu and choose the **Select Partial Loop** option from the shortcut menu. Generally, the selection point on the second edge defines the major or minor partial loop selection. Figure 7-64 shows the resulting partial loop selected.

Select Tangency

The **Select Tangency** option is used to automatically select the edges or the faces that are tangent to the selected face. This option will be available in the shortcut menu only when a face or an edge is tangent to the selected face or edge. To use this option, select any face or edge using the **Select** tool and right-click. Choose the **Select Tangency** option from the shortcut menu.

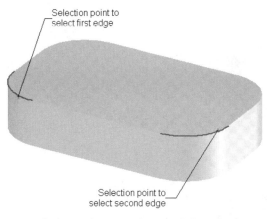

Selection point to
select first edge

Selection point to
select second edge

Figure 7-63 *Selecting edges to define the partial loop*

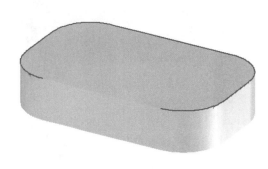

Figure 7-64 *Resulting partial loop that is selected*

Tip. *The **Select Midpoint** option in the shortcut menu is generally used in the sketching environment or while creating 3D sketches. You will learn more about 3D sketches in the later chapters.*

Creating Fillets Using the FilletXpert

CommandManager:	Features > Fillet
SolidWorks menus:	Insert > Features > Fillet/Round
Toolbar:	Features > Fillet

 The **FilletXpert** tool allows you to create single or multiple fillets, change the existing fillet, and create fillets at corners. To create fillets using the **FilletXpert**, invoke the **Fillet PropertyManager** and choose the **FilletXpert** button; the **FilletXpert** options will be displayed, as shown in Figure 7-65.

By default, the **Add** tab is chosen in the **FilletXpert**. This tab provides the options to create single or multiple fillets. To create a single fillet, select an edge, specify the radius, and then choose the **OK** button. To create multiple fillets, create a single fillet, and then choose **Apply** from the **Items To Fillet** rollout. Now, add other fillets. Once a fillet is created, it will be listed in the **Existing Fillets** rollout of the **Change** tab of the **PropertyManager**. You can select the existing fillets from the **Existing Fillets** rollout of this tab to resize or remove them.

In SolidWorks, the **Corner** tab is added to the **FilletXpert PropertyManager**. Choose this tab to modify the shape of the fillets that are formed at the intersection of three fillets, as shown in Figure 7-66. Remember that the fillet at the corner can be modified only if it is created by the combination of concave and convex shaped fillets. To change the shape of a corner fillet, invoke the **FilletXpert PropertyManager**, choose the **Corner** tab; the selection box in the

Tip. *If you select an edge and pause when the **Add** tab is chosen in the **FilletXpert PropertyManager**, a pop-up toolbar will be displayed. Move the cursor on the buttons in this toolbar; the corresponding entities will be highlighted in the model. Left-click when the required entities are highlighted; the entities will be selected.*

Figure 7-65 *The **FilletXpert** options in the Fillet PropertyManager*

Corner Faces rollout will be activated and you will be prompted to select the corner fillet to be modified. Select the corner fillet from the model; the **Show Alternatives** button will be available in the **Corner Faces** rollout. Choose this button; the **Select Alternatives** display box, with all possible alternatives, will be displayed. Select the required shape from the display box; the shape of the corner fillet will be modified in the model.

After modifying the shape of a corner fillet, you can copy the shape of this corner fillet to the other corner fillets. To do so, select the modified corner fillet; it will be displayed in the selection box in the **Corner Faces** rollout. Then, left-click on the selection box in the **Copy**

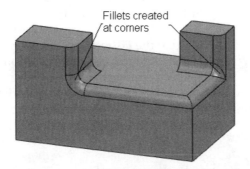

Figure 7-66 *Fillets created at the corners*

Targets rollout. Now, select the corner fillets to be changed; the **Copy to** button will be available in the **Copy Targets** rollout. Choose the **Copy to** button; the shape of the selected fillet will be modified. Also, the **Fillet-Corner** node will be added to the **FeatureManager** design tree. Figure 7-67 shows the fillet to be copied and modified. Figure 7-68 shows the resulting copied fillet.

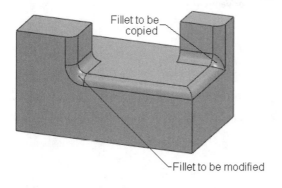

Fillet to be copied

Fillet to be modified

Figure 7-67 Fillets to be copied and changed

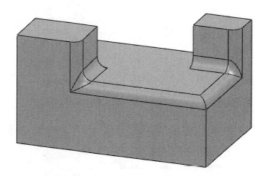

Figure 7-68 Resulting copied fillet

Creating Chamfers

CommandManager:	Features > Fillet > Chamfer
SolidWorks menus:	Insert > Features > Chamfer
Toolbar:	Features > Fillet > Chamfer

 Chamfering is defined as a process in which the sharp edges are beveled in order to reduce the area of stress concentration. This process also eliminates the undesirable sharp edges and corners. In SolidWorks, a chamfer is created using the **Chamfer** tool. This tool is invoked by choosing the **Chamfer** button in the **Features CommandManager**. When you choose **Fillet > Chamfer** in the **Features CommandManager**, the **Chamfer PropertyManager** will be displayed, as shown in Figure 7-69. Various types of chamfers created using the **Chamfer PropertyManager** are discussed next.

Creating Edge Chamfer

The chamfers that are applied to the edges are known as the edge chamfer. To create an edge chamfer, invoke the **Chamfer PropertyManager** and then select the edges to be chamfered. When you select an edge to be chamfered, the preview of the chamfer with a distance and angle callout will be displayed in the drawing area. The name of the selected edge will be displayed in the **Edges and Faces or Vertex** selection box. Also, the selected entity will be highlighted and the preview will be displayed. The **Tangent propagation** check box is selected by default. Therefore, the edges tangent to the selected edge are selected automatically. If the **Partial preview** button is selected, by default, select the **Full preview** button to display the full preview of the chamfer feature. Figure 7-70 shows the edge to be selected for chamfering and Figure 7-71 shows the full preview of the chamfer feature.

By default, the **Angle distance** radio button is selected. Therefore, the distance and angle callout is displayed in the drawing area. You can set the value of the distance and angle using the **Distance** and **Angle** spinners, or you can enter their values directly in the **Distance** and

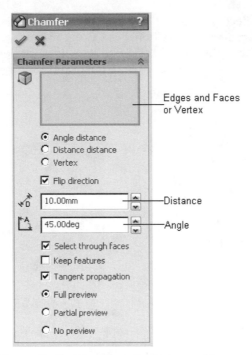

Figure 7-69 The Chamfer PropertyManager

Angle callouts. The **Flip direction** check box is used to specify the direction of the distance measurement. You can also flip the direction by clicking on the arrow in the drawing area.

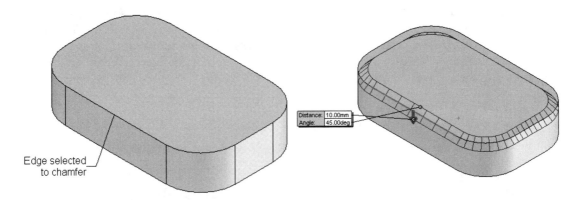

Figure 7-70 Edge selected to chamfer   *Figure 7-71 Preview of the chamfer feature*

Tip. *You can also select a face to apply the chamfer feature. If you do so, the chamfer will be applied to all edges of the selected face.*

If you select the **Distance distance** radio button from the **Chamfer Parameters** rollout, the **Flip direction** check box will be replaced by the **Equal distance** check box. Also, the **Angle** and **Distance** callouts will be replaced by the **Distance 1** and **Distance 2** callouts. By default, the **Equal distance** check box is cleared. Set the value of the chamfer distance in the **Distance 1** spinner or specify the value in the callout. Now, set the value of distance 2 in the respective spinner or callout. If you need to specify the same distance for creating the chamfer, select the **Equal distance** check box. The **Distance 2** spinner will disappear from the **Chamfer Parameters** rollout.

After specifying all parameters, choose the **OK** button from the **Chamfer PropertyManager**. Figure 7-72 shows the chamfer created on a base plate.

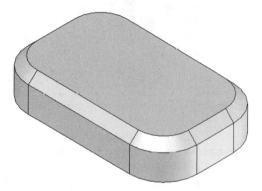

Figure 7-72 Chamfer created on a base plate

Creating Vertex Chamfer

You can also use the **Chamfer** tool to add a chamfer to the selected vertex by chopping the selected vertex to a specified distance. To create the vertex chamfer, invoke the **Chamfer PropertyManager** and select the **Vertex** radio button from the **Chamfer Parameters** rollout. Select the vertex; the preview of the chamfer will be displayed in the drawing area with the **Distance** callouts. Figure 7-73 shows the vertex to be selected and Figure 7-74 shows the preview of the vertex chamfer.

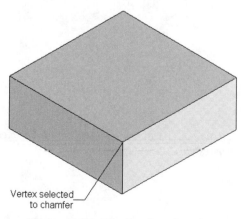

Figure 7-73 Vertex to be selected

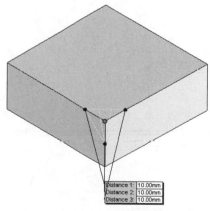

Figure 7-74 Preview of the vertex chamfer

Set the value of the chamfer distance along each edge in the **Distance 1**, **Distance 2**, and **Distance 3** spinners. You can also specify the value of the chamfer distance in the distance callouts. If you want to specify an equal distance for all edges, select the **Equal distance** check box. After specifying all parameters, choose the **OK** button from the **Chamfer PropertyManager**. Figure 7-75 shows the vertex chamfer feature created on a base feature.

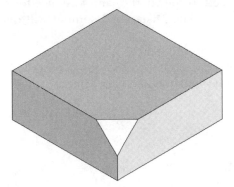

Figure 7-75 *Vertex chamfer created on a base feature*

Chamfer With and Without Keep features Option

If you have boss or cut features in a model and the chamfer created is large enough to consume those features, it is recommended that you select the **Keep features** check box. If this check box is cleared, the chamfer feature will consume the features that will obstruct its path. Note that the features that are consumed by the chamfer feature are not deleted from the model. They are removed from the model because of some geometric inconsistency. When you rollback or delete the chamfer, the consumed features will reappear. Figure 7-76 shows the chamfer feature with the **Keep features** check box cleared and Figure 7-77 shows the chamfer feature with the **Keep features** check box selected.

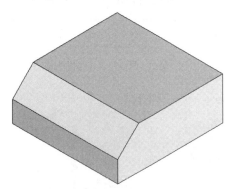

Figure 7-76 *Chamfer feature with the* **Keep features** *check box cleared*

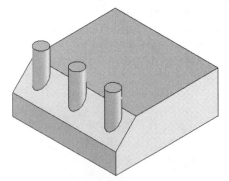

Figure 7-77 *Chamfer feature with the* **Keep features** *check box selected*

Creating Shell Features

CommandManager:	Features > Shell
SolidWorks menus:	Insert > Features > Shell
Toolbar:	Features > Shell

Shelling is defined as a process in which the material is scooped out from a model. The resulting model will be a hollow model with walls of a specified thickness and cavity inside. The selected face or the faces of the model are also removed in this operation. If you do not select any face to be removed, a closed hollow model will be created. You can also specify multiple thicknesses to the walls. To create a shell feature, choose the **Shell** tool from the **Features CommandManager**; the **Shell PropertyManager** will be displayed, as shown in Figure 7-78.

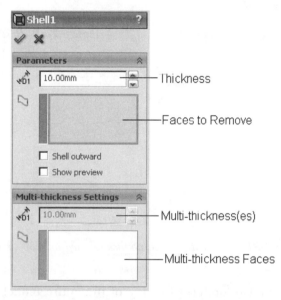

Figure 7-78 The Shell PropertyManager

You will be prompted to select the faces to remove. Select the face or the faces of the model that you want to remove. The selected faces will be highlighted in blue and their names will be displayed in the **Faces to Remove** selection box. Set the value of the wall thickness in the **Thickness** spinner and choose the **OK** button from the **Shell PropertyManager**. Figure 7-79 shows the face selected and Figure 7-80 shows the resulting shell feature created.

If none of the faces are selected to be removed, the resulting model will be hollowed from inside with no face removed. Figure 7-81 shows a model in the **Hidden Line Visible** mode with a shell feature in which no face is selected to be removed.

Based on the geometric conditions, the in-built artificial intelligence of the **Shell** command in SolidWorks enables the shell feature to decide the quantity of the material to be removed. Figure 7-82 shows the shell feature whose wall thickness is small for uniform shelling of the entire model. Figure 7-83 shows the shell feature whose wall thickness is large because of

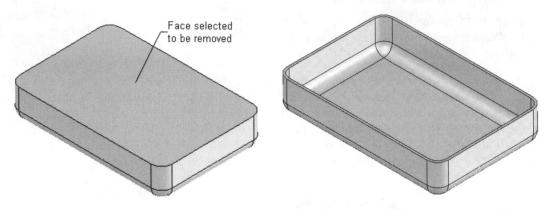

Figure 7-79 *Face selected to be removed*   **Figure 7-80** *Resulting shell feature*

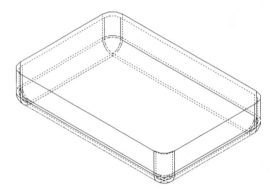

Figure 7-81 *Shell feature with no face selected to be removed*

which it cannot accommodate uniform shelling of the entire model. Therefore, the shell feature will not remove the material from the area where the material removal is not possible. The **Shell outward** check box is selected to create the shell feature on the outer side of the

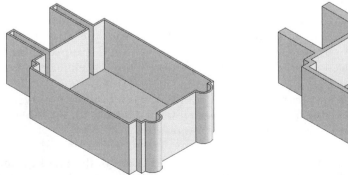

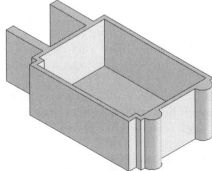

Figure 7-82 *Shell feature with smaller shell thickness*   **Figure 7-83** *Shell feature with larger shell thickness*

model. You can also display the preview of the shell feature by selecting the **Show preview** check box from the **Parameters** rollout of the **Shell PropertyManager**.

Note

If the thickness of the shell feature is more than the radius of the fillet feature, the fillet will not be included in the shell feature. Therefore, it results in sharp edges after adding the fillet. The same is true for the chamfer feature. The face selected to be removed in the shell feature can be a planar face or a curved face. But creating a shell by removing a curved face depends on the geometry of the curved face to adopt the specified shell thickness and other geometric conditions.

Creating Multi-thickness Shell

The **Shell** tool can be used to shell the model by applying different thickness values to the selected faces. To do so, invoke the **Shell PropertyManager**, select the faces to be removed and then specify the thickness in the **Thickness** spinner of the **Parameters** rollout. Click once in the **Multi-thickness Faces** selection box to activate the selection mode. Select the faces for which you want to specify different thicknesses. Set the value of the thickness using the **Multi-thickness(es)** spinner and choose the **OK** button. Note that you can specify different thickness for each face. Figure 7-84 shows the faces selected to create the multi-thickness shell and Figure 7-85 shows the resulting shell feature.

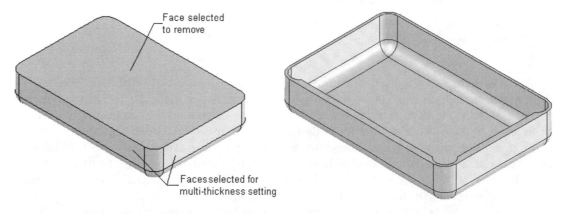

Figure 7-84 Faces selected to create multi-thickness shell

Figure 7-85 Resulting multi-thickness shell

Error Diagnostics

While creating the shell feature, specify all parameters in the **Shell PropertyManager** and choose the **OK** button. If the shell feature creation is failed because of geometric inconsistency, the **Error Diagnostics** rollout will be displayed in the **Shell PropertyManager**, as shown in Figure 7-86. This rollout will be activated automatically if the shell feature creation fails. You can use the options in this rollout to figure out the possible reasons for the failure of the shell feature creation.

Also, the **What's Wrong** dialog box will be displayed, which will inform you about the possible errors due to which the feature creation failed. You will learn more about the **Rebuild Errors** dialog box in the later chapters.

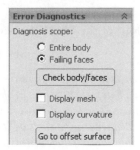

Figure 7-86 The Error Diagnostics rollout

The radio buttons in the **Diagnosis scope** area are used to specify whether the diagnosis has to be done on the entire body or only on the faces that have failed while being shelled. The **Check body/faces** button is used to run the diagnostic tool. When you choose this button, the areas of the model that are responsible for the feature creation failure will be highlighted using callouts. The **Display mesh** check box is used to display the surface curvature mesh. The **Display curvature** check box is selected to display the surface curvature.

Creating Wrap Features

CommandManager:	Features > Wrap
SolidWorks menus:	Insert > Features > Wrap
Toolbar:	Features > Wrap *(Customize to add)*

 The **Wrap** tool is used to emboss, deboss, or scribe a closed multiloop sketch on a selected planar or curved face that is tangent to the plane on which the selected sketch is created. You can also create this type of geometry by extruding the sketch from a selected surface using the **Extruded Boss/Base** or the **Extruded Cut** tool. There are two main differences between the emboss and deboss feature created using the **Wrap** tool, and those created using the **Extruded Boss/Base** or the **Extruded Cut** tool. The first difference is in the method of projection. The projection of the geometry using the **Wrap** tool follows the rule of true length, which means the actual length of the geometry remains the same after projecting it on the surface. The projection of the geometry created using the **From** option of the **Extruded Boss/Base** or the **Extruded Cut** tool follows the rule of true projection. Therefore, the original size of the geometry is distorted. The second difference is the direction of the side faces of the geometry. The side faces of the geometry created using the **Wrap** tool are always normal to the reference surface, while those created using the **From** option of the **Extruded Boss/Base** or the **Extruded Cut** tool are normal to the sketching plane or parallel to the direction vector.

To create a wrap feature, create a closed multiloop or a single loop sketch and then choose the **Wrap** button from the **Features CommandManager**; the **Message PropertyManager** will be displayed and you will be prompted to select a plane or a face on which you need to create a closed counter or select an existing sketch. Select an existing sketch from the **Features CommandManager**; the **Wrap PropertyManager** will be displayed, as shown in Figure 7-87.

You will notice that the **Emboss** radio button is selected by default in the **Wrap Parameters**

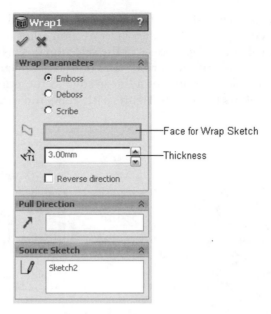

*Figure 7-87 The **Wrap PropertyManager***

rollout. This radio button is selected to create an embossed wrap feature. Next, select the face on which you need to wrap the sketch. As soon as you select the face, the preview of the wrap feature created will be displayed with the default setting in the drawing area. Set the value of the thickness using the **Thickness** spinner. Choose the **OK** button from the **Wrap PropertyManager**. Figure 7-88 shows the sketch and the face selected to create the wrap feature and Figure 7-89 shows the resulting embossed wrap feature.

Figure 7-88 *Sketch and face selected to create the wrap feature*   **Figure 7-89** *Resulting embossed wrap feature*

The **Deboss** radio button in the **Wrap Parameters** rollout can be used to engrave the sketch on a selected planar or curved face. Figure 7-90 shows a wrap feature created using the **Deboss** radio button. The **Scribe** radio button in this rollout is selected to project the selected sketch on a planar or a curved face. The projected sketch will split the face on which it is projected. If you need to project the sketch in a direction other than the normal, then expand the **Pull Direction** rollout and click once in the selection box. Note that, the **Pull Direction** rollout will not be available, if the **Scribe** radio button is selected in the **Wrap Parameters** rollout. Next, select a sketched line or a linear edge as the pull direction along which you need to emboss or deboss the sketch. Figure 7-91 shows the wrap feature created using the **Scribe** option.

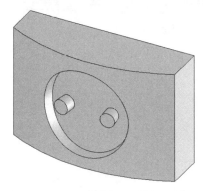

Figure 7-90 *Wrap feature created using the* **Deboss** *radio button*

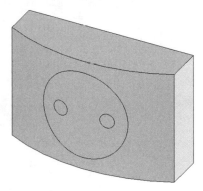

Figure 7-91 *Wrap feature created using the* **Scribe** *radio button*

TUTORIALS

Tutorial 1

In this tutorial, you will create the model of the Plummer Block Casting shown in Figure 7-92. The dimensions of the model are shown in Figure 7-93. **(Expected time: 30 min)**

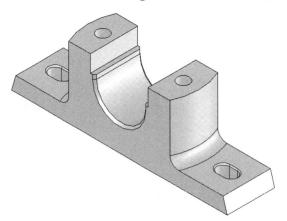

Figure 7-92 *Solid model of the Plummer Block Casting*

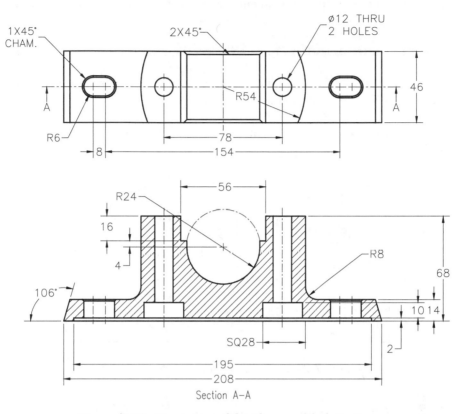

Figure 7-93 *Dimensions of the Plummer Block Casting*

The following steps are required to complete this tutorial:

a. Create the base feature of the model on the Front Plane, refer to Figures 7-94 and 7-95.
b. Create the second feature, which is a cut feature, on the top planar face of the base feature, refer to Figures 7-96 through 7-98.
c. Create the rectangular recess as a cut feature at the bottom of the base, refer to Figure 7-99.
d. Create the square cuts that will act as the recess for the head of the square head bolts, refer to Figure 7-99.
e. Create a hole feature using the **Hole PropertyManager** and modify the placement of the hole feature, refer to Figures 7-100 and 7-101.
f. Create the cut feature on the second top planar face of the base feature, refer to Figure 7-102.
g. Add the fillet feature to the model, refer to Figures 7-103 and 7-104.
h. Add chamfers to the model, refer to Figure 7-105 and 7-106.
i. Save the model.

Creating the Base Feature

1. Start a new SolidWorks part document using the **New SolidWorks Document** dialog box.

2. Invoke the **Extruded Boss/Base** tool and select the Front Plane as the sketching plane.

3. Draw the sketch of the front view of the model. Use the **Dynamic Mirror Entities** tool to capture the design intent of the model.

4. Add the required relations and dimensions to fully define the sketch, as shown in Figure 7-94.

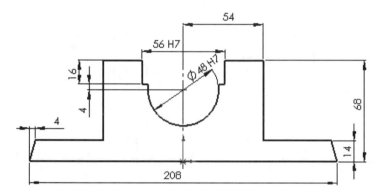

Figure 7-94 *Fully defined sketch of the base feature*

Note
*After adding the dimensions to the sketch, select the dimension and add the tolerance to them using the **Dimension PropertyManager**, as discussed in the earlier chapters. Also, change the radial dimension of the arc to the diameter dimension using the **Leaders** tab of the **Dimension PropertyManager**.*

You need to extrude the sketch to a distance of 46 mm using the **Mid Plane** option so that the parts that are to be assembled should have the default planes in the center of the model.

5. Exit the sketching environment to display the **Extrude PropertyManager**.

6. Right-click in the drawing area and choose the **Mid Plane** option from the shortcut menu to extrude the sketch symmetrically on both the sides of the sketching plane.

Tip. *Sometimes, you may need to apply tolerance to the dimensions. For example, consider a case where the depth of the extruded feature has a tolerance applied to it. In such cases, double-click on the extruded feature in the **FeatureManager design tree** or in the drawing area; all dimensions applied to the model are displayed. Select the dimension that reflects the depth of the extruded feature and apply the tolerance using the **Dimension PropertyManager**.*

7. Set the value in the **Depth** spinner to **46** and choose the **OK** button from the **Extrude PropertyManager**.

8. Change the view orientation to isometric. The resulting base feature created after extruding the sketch to a given depth is shown in Figure 7-95.

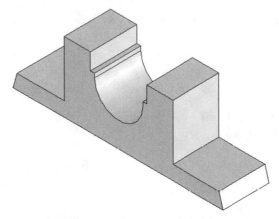

Figure 7-95 Isometric view of the base feature of the model

Creating the Second Feature

The second feature of the model is a cut-extrude feature. The sketch of the cut-extrude feature is drawn on the top planar face of the base feature. This sketch is extruded up to the specified plane to create the resulting cut feature.

1. Invoke the **Extruded Cut** tool and select the top planar face of the base feature as the sketching plane, as shown in Figure 7-96.

2. Orient the model normal to the sketching plane and draw the sketch for the cut feature using the sketching tools. Apply the required relations to the sketch.

The sketch of the cut-extrude feature is shown in Figure 7-96.

Figure 7-96 Sketch of the second feature

3. Exit the sketching environment to display the **Cut-Extrude PropertyManager**.

The preview of the cut feature is displayed in the drawing area with the default values of the **Blind** option. You need to extrude the cut feature up to the selected surface. Therefore, orient the model in the isometric view because the feature termination surface can easily be selected in this view.

4. Change the view orientation to isometric.

You will observe that the preview of the cut feature is inside the model. You need to remove the outer part of the sketch profile. Therefore, you need to change the side of the cut feature.

5. Select the **Flip side to cut** check box; the preview of the cut feature is modified dynamically.

6. Right-click in the drawing area and choose **Up To Surface** from the shortcut menu.

You are prompted to select a face or a surface to complete the specification of direction 1.

7. Select the surface for the feature termination, as shown in Figure 7-97. Right-click and choose **OK** from the shortcut menu to exit the tool.

The model after creating the cut feature is shown in Figure 7-98.

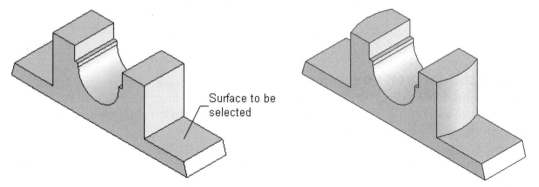

Figure 7-97 Surface to be selected for the cut feature   *Figure 7-98 Model after creating the cut feature*

Creating the Rectangular Recess

The third feature is the rectangular recess. This feature is created using a rectangular cut feature that will be created on the bottom face of the model.

1. Orient the model using the **Rotate View** tool and select the bottom face of the base feature.

2. Invoke the **Extruded Cut** tool to invoke the sketching environment.

3. Use the standard sketching tools to draw a rectangle of 195 mm x 35 mm as the sketch of the rectangular recess. Apply the required relations and dimensions to the sketch.

4. Exit the sketching environment.

5. Set the value in the **Depth** spinner to **2** and choose **OK** from the **Extrude PropertyManager**.

Creating the Recess for the Head of Square-Headed Bolt

It is evident from Figure 7-93 that the bolt to be inserted in the part will be a square-headed bolt. Therefore, you need to create the recess for the head of the square-headed bolt. A square of 26 mm length is used to create this recess.

1. Rotate the model and select the upper face of the recess created in the previous section as the sketching plane. Invoke the **Extruded Cut** tool and orient the model normal to the sketching plane.

2. Draw the sketch using the sketching tools. The sketch includes two squares of 26 mm length and the distance between the centers of the squares is 78 mm, refer to Figure 7-93. Apply the required relations and dimensions to fully define the sketch.

3. Exit the sketching environment and extrude the sketch to a depth of 10 mm. Exit the tool. The rotated model, after adding this cut feature, is shown in Figure 7-99.

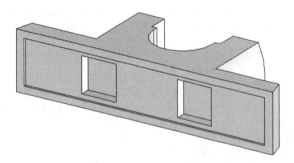

Figure 7-99 Model after creating recess for the square-headed bolts

Creating the Hole Features

After creating the recess for the head of the square-headed bolt, you need to create a hole using the **Hole** tool. You first need to create the hole on the top planar surface of the base feature, as shown in Figure 7-100. But do not need to place a point, it is shown for your reference only.

1. Select the top planar surface of the base feature as the placement plane for the hole feature.

2. Choose **Insert > Features > Hole > Simple** from the SolidWorks menus to invoke the **Hole PropertyManager**; the preview of the hole feature with the default settings is displayed in the drawing area.

3. Right-click in the drawing area and choose the **Through All** option from the shortcut menu to specify the feature termination.ssss

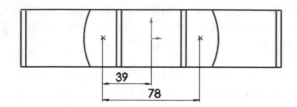

Figure 7-100 *The point created and dimensioned*

4. Set the value in the **Hole Diameter** spinner to **12**.

5. Choose the **OK** button from the **Hole PropertyManager.**

6. Select **Hole1** from the **FeaturesManager design tree**; a pop-up toolbar is displayed.

7. Choose **Edit Sketch** from the pop-up toolbar; the sketching environment is displayed. Apply relations and dimensions to locate the hole feature.

8. Press CTRL+B to rebuild the model.

9. Use the same procedure to create the second hole feature on the left of the model. The model, after creating both hole features, is displayed in Figure 7-101.

10. Similarly, create the cut feature on the second top planar face of the base feature, refer to Figure 7-97, for the surface to be selected and Figure 7-93 for the dimensions of the sketch.

Tip. *You can draw the sketch on one side, mirror it, and create the cut feature. However, you can create a cut feature and mirror the feature also. Mirroring a feature will be discussed in the later chapters.*

The model, after creating the cut features, is shown in Figure 7-102.

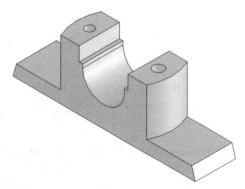

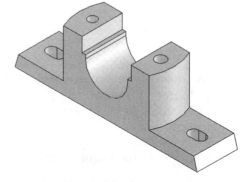

Figure 7-101 *Model after creating the hole features*

Figure 7-102 *Model after creating the cut features*

Adding a Fillet to the Model

After creating all other features, you now need to add the fillet feature to the model.

1. Choose the **Fillet** button from the **Features CommandManager** to invoke the **Fillet PropertyManager**. You need to choose the **Manual** button, if the **Fillet Xpert PropertyManager** is displayed.

   After invoking the **Fillet PropertyManager**, you are prompted to selected edges, faces, features, or loops to be filleted. As evident from the model, you need to select only the edges to apply the fillet feature.

2. Select the edges, as shown in Figure 7-103.

   As soon as you select the edges, the preview of the fillet feature with the default values is shown in the drawing area. A radius callout is also displayed along the selected edge. Now, you need to modify the default radius value of the fillet feature.

Note
*If the preview of the fillet feature is not displayed in the drawing area, select the **Full Preview** radio button available in the **Items To Fillet** rollout of the **Fillet PropertyManager**.*

3. Set the value in the **Radius** spinner to **8** and choose the **OK** button from the **Fillet PropertyManager**.

   The model, after adding the fillet, is shown in Figure 7-104.

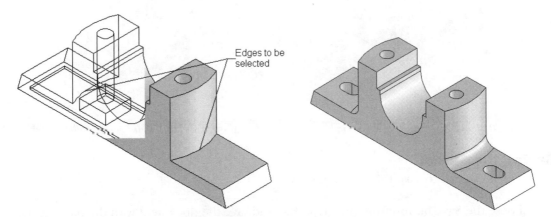

Figure 7-103 Edges to be selected for the fillet feature   *Figure 7-104 Model after adding the fillet*

Adding a Chamfer to the Model

The next feature that you need to add to this model is chamfer.

1. Choose **Fillet > Chamfer** from the **Features CommandManager** to invoke the **Chamfer PropertyManager**.

2. Select the edges of the cut features, as shown in Figure 7-105. The edges that are tangent to the selected edges are selected automatically because the selection mode of the chamfer feature uses the tangent propagation by default.

    As soon as you select the edges, the preview of the chamfer feature is displayed in the drawing area with the default values. The angle and distance callouts are also displayed. Now, you need to set the required value of the chamfer.

    The required values of the chamfer parameters are 1 mm and 45-degree. The **Angle distance** radio button is selected by default in the **Chamfer Parameters** rollout. The value of the angle in the **Angle** spinner is set as 45-degree. Therefore, you do not need to modify this value. You need to set only the value of the distance in the **Distance** spinner.

3. Set the value of the distance in the **Distance** spinner to **1** and choose the **OK** button from the **Chamfer PropertyManager**. Refer to Figure 7-93 for the parameters of the chamfer feature. The final solid model is shown in Figure 7-106.

4. Create the chamfer of dimension 2 X 45° on the base feature, refer to Figure 7-93.

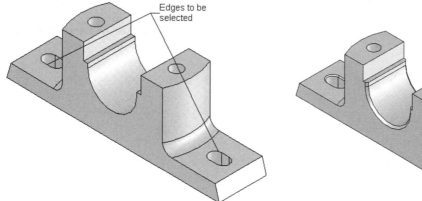

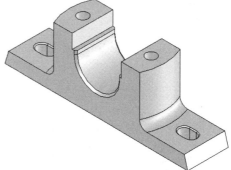

Figure 7-105 *Edges to be selected*   *Figure 7-106* *Final solid model*

Saving the Model

Next, you need to save the document.

1. Choose the **Save** button from the Menu Bar and save the document with the name given below:

    \My Documents\SolidWorks\c07\c07tut1.sldprt

2. Choose **File > Close** from the SolidWorks menus to close the file.

Tutorial 2

In this tutorial, you will create the model shown in Figure 7-107. The section view of the model is shown in Figure 7-108 for a better understanding. The dimensions of the model are shown in Figure 7-109. **(Expected time: 30 min)**

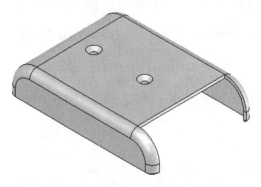

Figure 7-107 Solid model for Tutorial 2

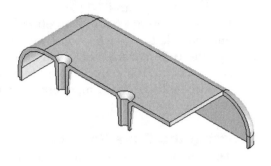

Figure 7-108 Section view of the model

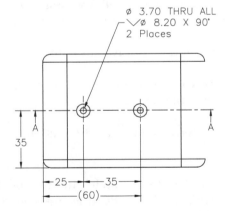

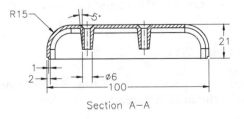

Section A–A

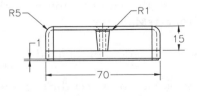

Figure 7-109 Top view, front section view, and right side view with dimensions

The following steps are required to complete this tutorial:

a. Create the base feature of the model by extruding a rectangle of 100 mm x 70 mm to a distance of 20 mm.
b. Add a fillet to the base feature, refer to Figures 7-110 through 7-113.
c. Create the shell feature to create a thin-walled part and remove some of the faces, refer to Figures 7-114 and 7-115.
d. Create a reference plane at an offset distance from the top planar face of the base feature and extrude the sketch created on the new plane, refer to Figure 7-116.
e. Use the **Hole Wizard** tool to add the countersink hole to the model, refer to Figure 7-117.
f. Add a fillet to the extruded feature, refer to Figures 7-118 and 7-119.
g. Create the lip of the component by extruding the sketch, refer to Figure 7-120.
h. Save the model.

Creating the Base Feature

The base feature of the model is created by extruding a rectangle of 100 mm x 70 mm to a distance of 20 mm. It is evident from the model that the sketch of the base feature is created on the **Top Plane**. Therefore, you need to select the Top Plane as the sketching plane.

1. Start a new SolidWorks part document and invoke the **Extruded Boss/Base** tool. Select the **Top Plane** from the **FeatureManager design tree** or from the drawing area.

2. Orient the sketch plane normal to the viewing direction, if it is not oriented by default.

3. Draw a rectangle using the **Rectangle** tool and force it to a dimension of 100 mm x 70 mm. Add the other required dimensions to fully define the sketch.

4. Exit the sketching environment and extrude the rectangle to a depth of 20 mm.

Creating the Fillet Features

After creating the base feature, you need to add fillets to the model. In this model, you need to add three fillet features. Two fillet features will be added at this stage of the design process and the remaining one will be added at a later stage of the design process.

1. Choose the **Fillet** button from the **Features CommandManager** to invoke the **Fillet PropertyManager**.

2. Select the edges of the model, as shown in Figure 7-110.

As soon as you select the edges of the model, the preview of the fillet with the default values and the radius callout are displayed in the drawing area.

3. Set the value in the **Radius** spinner to **15** and choose the **OK** button from the **Fillet PropertyManager**.

Figure 7-111 shows the model, after adding the first fillet feature.

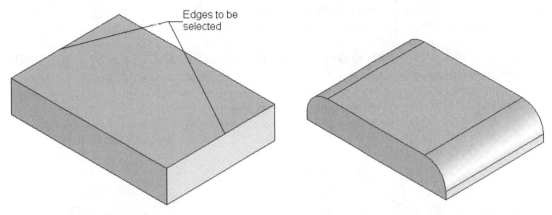

Figure 7-110 *Edges to be selected*   **Figure 7-111** *Fillet added to the base feature*

Now, add the second fillet feature to the model.

4. Invoke the **Fillet PropertyManager** and set the value **5** in the **Radius** spinner.

5. Select the edges of the model, as shown in Figure 7-112. Right-click and choose **OK** from the shortcut menu to complete the feature creation. The model, after adding the second fillet feature, is shown in Figure 7-113.

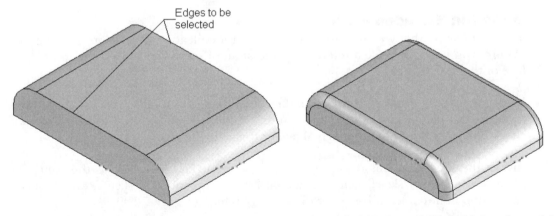

Figure 7-112 *Edges to be selected*   **Figure 7-113** *Second fillet added to the model*

Creating the Shell Feature

It is evident from Figures 7-107 and 7-108 that a shell feature is required to create a thin-walled structure. As discussed earlier, the shell feature is used to scoop out the material from the model, leaving behind a thin-walled hollow part.

1. Choose the **Shell** button from the **Features CommandManager** to invoke the **Shell1 PropertyManager**; you are prompted to select the faces to be removed.

2. Rotate the model and select the faces to be removed, as shown in Figure 7-114; the names of the selected faces are displayed in the **Faces to Remove** selection box.

3. Set the value **2** in the **Thickness** spinner and choose the **OK** button from the **Shell1 PropertyManager**.

    The model, after creating the shell feature, is shown in Figure 7-115.

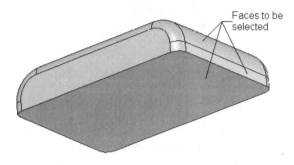

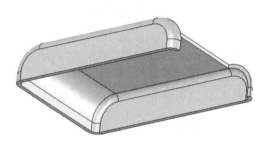

Figure 7-114 *Faces selected to be removed*   *Figure 7-115* *Model after creating the shell feature*

Creating the Extruded Feature

The next feature that you need to create is an extruded feature. But before creating this feature, you need to create a reference plane at an offset distance from the top planar face of the base feature.

1. Invoke the **Plane PropertyManager** and create a plane at an offset distance of 15 mm from the top planar face of the base feature. You need to select the **Reverse direction** check box from the **Plane PropertyManager** to create the plane.

2. Invoke the **Extruded Boss/Base** tool, select the newly created plane as the sketching plane and create the sketch using the standard sketching tools. The sketch consists of two circles of 6 mm diameter. For other dimensions, refer to Figure 7-109.

3. Exit the sketching environment and extrude the sketch using the **Up To Next** option and add an outward draft of 5-degree. Choose the **OK** button from the **Extrude PropertyManager** to close it. Also, hide the reference plane.

    Figure 7-116 shows the rotated model after creating the extruded feature with draft and hiding the reference plane.

Adding the Countersink Hole Using the Hole Wizard Tool

The next feature that you need to create is an **M3.5 Flat Head Machine Screw** countersink hole, refer to Figure 7-109. In SolidWorks, you are provided with one of the largest

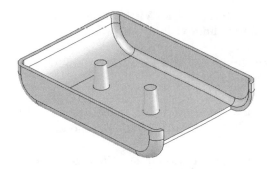

Figure 7-116 *Model after creating the extruded feature*

standard hole-generating tool, known as the **Hole Wizard**. You can use the **Hole Wizard** tool to create the standard holes to the model that can accommodate standard fasteners.

1. Choose the **Hole Wizard** button from the **Features CommandManager**; the **Hole Specification PropertyManager** is displayed.

2. Choose the **Countersink** button from the **Hole Type** rollout.

   Now, set the parameters to define the standard hole.

3. Select the **Ansi Metric** option from the **Standard** drop-down list.

4. Select the **Flat Head Screw - ANSI B18.6.7M** option from the **Type** drop-down list.

5. Select the **M3.5** option from the **Size** drop-down list and the **Normal** option from the **Fit** drop-down list in the **Hole Specifications** rollout.

6. Select the **Through All** option from the **End Condition** rollout.

7. Choose the **Positions** tab from the **Hole Specification PropertyManager**; you are prompted to use the dimensions and other sketching tools to position the hole. Also, the select cursor is replaced by the point cursor.

8. Move the point cursor on the top planar face and specify two points when the concentric relation symbol is displayed.

   If you place the points anywhere in the top planar face, you need to add the required relations and dimensions to define the proper location of these placement points. Before doing that, you need to change the model display from **Shaded With Edges** to **Hidden Lines Visible** for a better display.

9. Right-click in the drawing area and choose the **Select** option.

10. Choose **Display Style > Hidden Lines Visible** from the **Heads-up View** toolbar to display the model with the hidden lines visible.

11. Right-click again and choose the **Add Relation** option from the shortcut menu to display the **Add Relations PropertyManager**.

12. Select the left placement point and then select the upper left hidden circle. Choose the **Concentric** button from the **Add Relations** rollout.

13. Right-click in the drawing area and choose **Clear Selections** from the shortcut menu. Select the right placement point and the upper right hidden circle. Choose the **Concentric** button from the **Add Relations** rollout. Now, choose **OK** from the confirmation corner.

14. Choose the **OK** button from the **Hole Position PropertyManager** and choose the **Shaded With Edges** button from the **View** toolbar.

The isometric view of the model, after adding the hole feature, is shown in Figure 7-117.

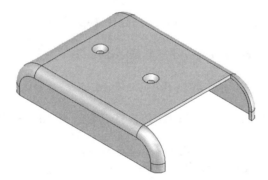

Figure 7-117 *Model after adding the hole feature using the **Hole Wizard** tool*

Adding a Fillet to the Model

Now, you need to add a fillet to the edges of the extruded feature with the draft that was created earlier.

1. Rotate the model and choose the **Fillet** tool; the **Fillet PropertyManager** is displayed.

2. Choose the **FilletXpert** button; the **FilletXpert PropertyManager** is displayed.

3. Choose the **Add** tab and select one of the edges of the draft, as shown in Figure 7-118 and do not move the mouse; a pop-up toolbar is displayed. Remember that if you move the cursor away from the edge after selecting it, the pop-up toolbar will disappear.

4. Move the cursor on the **Alternate loops of right face, 1 Edge** button in the pop-up toolbar; the edge of the other draft that has to be filleted will be highlighted. Refer to Figure 7-118.

5. Click once on the **Alternate loops of right face, 1 Edge** button to select the edge; the name of the edge will be displayed in the selection box in the **Items To Fillet** rollout.

6. Set the value of the **Radius** spinner to **1** and choose the **OK** button to end the feature creation. The model, after adding the fillet, is shown in Figure 7-119.

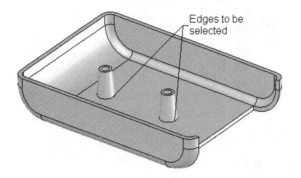

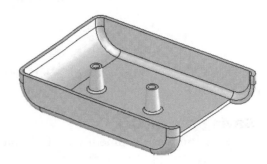

Figure 7-118 *Edges to be selected*   *Figure 7-119* *Model after adding the fillet*

Adding a Lip to the Model

The last feature that you need to add to the model is a lip. It is created by extruding an open sketch using the thin option.

1. Invoke the **Extrude Boss/Base** tool and select the bottom face of the base feature as the sketching plane and invoke the sketching environment.

2. Select any one of the inner edges of the model on the current sketching plane using the select tool and right-click to display the shortcut menu. Now, choose the **Select Tangency** option from the shortcut menu.

If you need to create a sketch similar to that of an existing entity, it is recommended to convert the existing entity to sketch by choosing the **Convert Entities** tool.

3. Choose the **Convert Entities** button from the **Sketch CommandManager**; the selected edges are converted into sketched entities.

4. Exit the sketching environment; the **Extrude PropertyManager** is displayed and the **Thin Feature** rollout is invoked automatically because you are extruding an open sketch.

5. In the **Direction 1** rollout, set the value **1** in both the **Depth** and the **Thickness** spinners of the **Thin Feature** rollout.

6. Choose the **OK** button from the **Extrude PropertyManager**. The rotated view of the final model is shown in Figure 7-120.

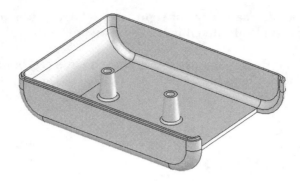

Figure 7-120 *Final model rotated to display maximum features*

Saving the Model

1. Save the part document with the name given below:

    \My Documents\SolidWorks\c07\c07tut2.sldprt

2. Choose **File** > **Close** from the SolidWorks menus to close the document.

Tutorial 3

In this tutorial, you will create the model shown in Figure 7-121. The section view of the model is shown in Figure 7-122 for a better understanding. The views and dimensions of the model are shown in Figures 7-123 and 7-124. The model has a uniform shell thickness of 1 mm. You can also add fillet features to the model with radius of 2 mm and 1 mm using the **FilletXpert**. **(Expected time: 45 min)**

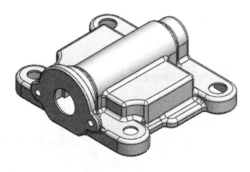

Figure 7-121 *Solid model for Tutorial 3*

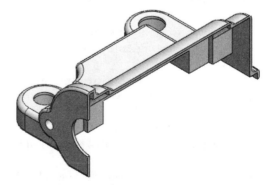

Figure 7-122 *Section view of the model*

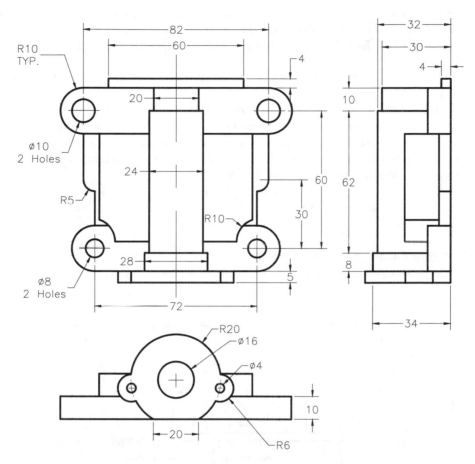

Figure 7-123 Views and dimensions of other components

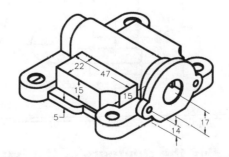

Figure 7-124 Isometric view of the model

The following steps are required to complete this tutorial:

a. Create the sketch of the model on the default plane and apply the required relations and dimensions to it, refer to Figure 7-125.
b. Invoke the **Extrude Boss/Base** tool and extrude the selected contour, refer to Figures 7-126 and 7-127.
c. Select the other set of contours and extrude them to the required distance, refer to Figure 7-128.
d. Create the full round fillets, refer to Figures 7-129 through 7-132.
e. Create the next circular extrude features on the model, refer to Figures 7-133 through 7-134.
f. Create the extrude feature and its mirror image, refer to Figures 7-135 through 7-137.
g. Create the shell feature with a wall thickness of 1 mm, refer to Figure 7-138.
h. Create the cut feature, refer to Figure 7-139.
i. Create the simple hole feature, refer to Figure 7-141.
j. Create the fillet features, refer to Figure 7-142.
k. Save the model.

Creating the Sketch of the Model

1. Start a new SolidWorks part document using the **New SolidWorks Document** dialog box.

2. Draw the sketch of the model on the **Top Plane**. Apply the required relations and dimensions to the sketch, as shown in Figure 7-125. Do not exit the sketching environment.

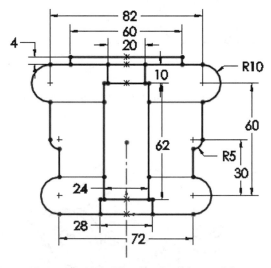

Figure 7-125 The sketch of the model

Selecting and Extruding the Contours of the Sketch

You need to use the Contour selection method to create the model. Therefore, you first need to select one of the contours from the given sketch and extrude it. For a better view, you can also orient the sketch to isometric view.

1. Choose **View Orientation > Isometric** from the **Heads-up View** toolbar; the sketch is displayed in the isometric view.

2. Right-click in the drawing area to invoke the shortcut menu. Expand the shortcut menu, if required. Choose the **Contour Select Tool** option from the shortcut menu; the select cursor is replaced by the contour selection cursor and the selection confirmation corner is displayed.

3. Move the cursor over the 60 x 40 rectangle and select it; the selected area of the rectangle is highlighted. This indicates that this rectangle is a closed profile.

4. Click on the highlighted rectangular area; the area is selected as a contour, as shown in Figure 7-126.

5. Choose the **Extruded Boss/Base** button from the **Features CommandManager**; the **Extrude PropertyManager** is invoked and the preview of the base feature is displayed in the drawing area.

    The name of the selected contour is displayed in the selection box of the **Selected Contours** rollout.

6. Enter the value **4** mm in the **Depth** spinner and choose the **OK** button; the selected contour is extruded, as shown in Figure 7-127.

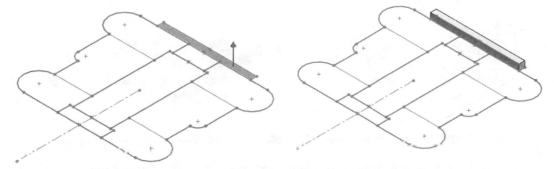

Figure 7-126 The rectangle selected as a contour   *Figure 7-127 The extruded feature of the selected rectangle*

7. Similarly, extrude the other contours of the sketch. The final model, after extruding the other contours of the sketch, is shown in Figure 7-128.

Creating the Fillet Features

After creating the extrude features, you need to add full round fillets to the model.

1. Choose the **Fillet** button from the **Features CommandManager**; the **Fillet PropertyManager** is displayed. Select the **Full round fillet** radio button from the **Fillet Type** rollout of the **PropertyManager**.

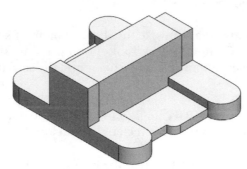

Figure 7-128 *The other extruded features of the model*

2. The **Face Set 1** selection box is activated by default in the **Items to Fillet** rollout. Select the face, as shown in Figure 7-129, as the face set 1. Next, click on the **Center Face Set** selection box of this rollout to activate it. Now, select the top face of the model, refer to Figure 7-129, as the center face set. Next, activate the **Face Set 2** selection box and select the face, refer to Figure 7-129, as the face set 2. The preview of the full round fillet is displayed in the drawing area with the respective callouts, as shown in Figure 7-130.

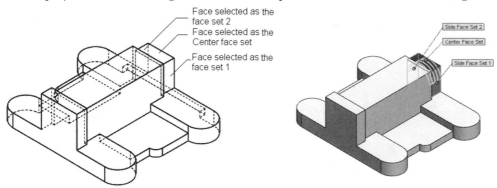

Figure 7-129 *The faces to be selected*   *Figure 7-130* *The preview of the full round fillet*

3. Choose the **OK** button from the **PropertyManager** to exit. The rotated view of the model, after creating the full round fillet, is shown in Figure 7-131.

4. Similarly, create the full round fillets on the other features, as shown in Figure 7-132.

Creating the Next Circular Extrude Feature

1. Choose the **Extruded Boss/Base** button from the **Features CommandManager**; the **Extrude PropertyManager** is invoked.

2. Select the front planar face of the model as the sketching plane and draw the sketch of the extrude feature, as shown in Figure 7-133.

3. Click on the confirmation corner; the **Extrude PropertyManager** is displayed. Enter the value **5** in the **Depth** spinner.

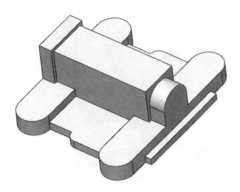

Figure 7-131 *The rotated view after creating the full round fillet*

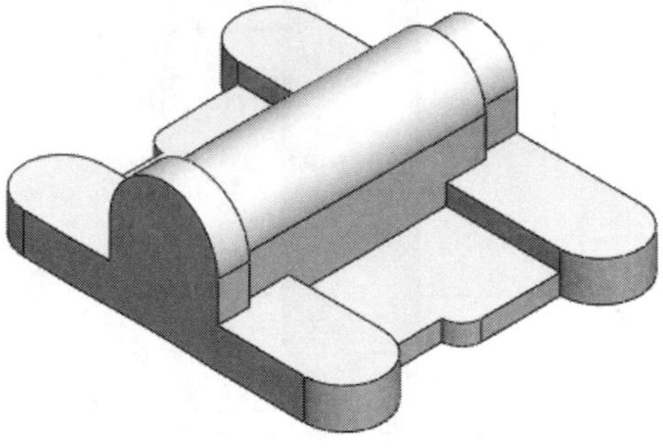

Figure 7-132 *The isometric view after creating other full round fillets*

4. Choose the **OK** button. The isometric view of the model, after creating the circular feature, is shown in Figure 7-134.

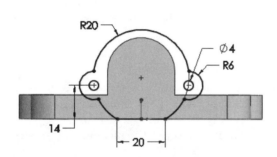

Figure 7-133 *Sketch of the extrude feature*

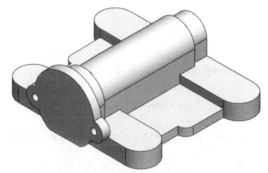

Figure 7-134 *Isometric view after creating the circular feature*

Creating an Extrude Feature and its Mirror Image

To create an extrude feature, you need to create a reference plane at an offset distance from the Top plane. Create the extrude feature on the newly created plane, and then mirror it about the Right Plane.

1. Invoke the **Plane PropertyManager** and create a plane at an offset distance of 20 mm from the Top Plane.

2. Invoke the **Extruded Boss/Base** tool and select the newly created plane as the sketching plane. Orient the sketching plane normal to the viewing direction and create a sketch using the standard sketching tools, as shown in Figure 7-135. Exit from the sketching environment; the **Extrude PropertyManager** is invoked. Choose the **Reverse Direction** button from the **Direction 1** rollout and select the **Up To Next** option from the **End Condition** drop-down list. Figure 7-136 shows the model after creating the extrude feature.

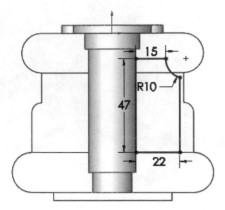

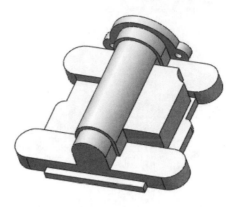

Figure 7-135 *Sketch of the extrude feature*

Figure 7-136 *Rotated view of the model after creating the extrude feature*

3. Select this extrude feature from the **FeatureManager design tree** and then choose the **Mirror** button from the **Features CommandManager**; the **Mirror PropertyManager** is displayed. Select the **Right Plane** from the **FeatureManager design tree**; the preview of the mirror feature is displayed. Choose the **OK** button. Figure 7-137 shows the model after mirroring the extrude feature. You will learn more about the **Mirror** tool in the later chapters.

Creating the Shell Feature

It is evident from Figures 7-121 and 7-122 that a shell feature is required to create a thin-walled structure.

1. Invoke the **Shell1 PropertyManager**; you are prompted to select the faces to be removed.

2. Rotate the model and select the bottom planar face of the model; the selected face is displayed in the **Faces to Remove** selection box.

3. Set the value **1 mm** in the **Thickness** spinner of the **PropertyManager**. Choose the **OK** button to exit.

The rotated view of the model, after creating the shell feature, is shown in Figure 7-138.

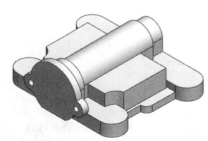

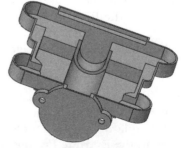

Figure 7-137 *Isometric view after mirroring the extrude feature*

Figure 7-138 *Model after creating the shell feature*

Creating the Cut Feature

1. Invoke the **Extruded Cut** tool and select the front circular face of the model as the sketching plane.

2. Draw the sketch of the cut feature, as shown in Figure 7-139 and extrude it using the **Up To Next** option. Figure 7-140 shows the isometric view of the model after creating the cut feature.

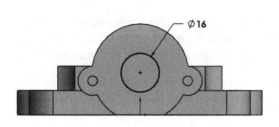

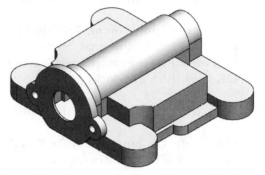

Figure 7-139 Sketch of the cut feature

Figure 7-140 Isometric view of the model after creating the cut feature

Creating the Simple Hole Features

1. Choose the **Simple Hole** button; the **Hole PropertyManager** is invoked.

2. Create simple holes on the model using this **PropertyManager**. Figure 7-141 shows the model after creating the simple hole features. For dimension of the holes, refer to Figure 7-123.

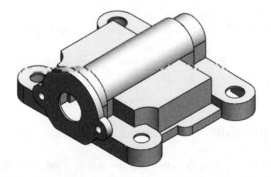

Figure 7-141 Model after creating simple hole features

Creating the Fillet Features

1. Invoke the **Fillet PropertyManager** and choose the **FilletXpert** button, the **FilletXpert PropertyManager** is invoked.

2. Set the value **2 mm** in the **Radius** spinner.

3. Rotate the model and select an edge, as shown in Figure 7-142; the selected edge is displayed in the **Edges, Faces, Features and Loops** selection box. As soon as you select the edge, a pop-up toolbar is displayed near the cursor.

4. Choose the **Connected, 137 Edges** button from the pop-up toolbar; all the related edges are displayed in the **Edges, Faces, Features and Loops** selection box.

5. Choose the **Apply** button; the **FilletXpert** window is displayed and the process of creating fillets is started. Note that, after some time the **SolidWorks** message box is displayed with the message **FeatureXpert has not resolved all the features in this model**. Choose **OK** from the **SolidWorks** message box.

6. Next, set the value **1 mm** in the **Radius** spinner and choose the **Apply** button.

7. Choose the **OK** button from the **FilletXpert PropertyManager**. The fillets are added to the model. The isometric view of the resultant model is shown in Figure 7-143.

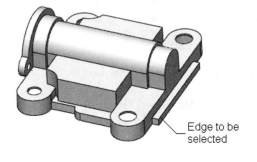

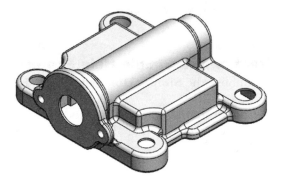

Figure 7-142 *The edge to be selected for adding fillet*   *Figure 7-143* *The final model*

Saving the Model

1. Save the part document with the name given below:

    \My Documents\SolidWorks\c07\c07tut3.sldprt

2. Choose **File** > **Close** from the SolidWorks menus to close the document.

SELF-EVALUATION TEST

Answer the following questions and then compare them to those given at the end of this chapter:

1. You can create counterbore, countersink, and tapped holes using the **Hole PropertyManager**. (T/F)

2. The hole features created using the **Hole Wizard** tool and the **Hole PropertyManager** are not parametric. (T/F)

3. You cannot define a user-defined hole using the **Hole Wizard** tool. (T/F)

4. You cannot preselect the edges or faces for creating a fillet feature. (T/F)

5. In SolidWorks, you can create a multi-thickness shell feature. (T/F)

6. The _____ check box is selected to create the shell feature on the outer side of the model.

7. The _____ is created by specifying different radii along the length of the selected edge at specified intervals.

8. The names of the faces to be removed in the shell features are displayed in the _____ selection box.

9. If you want to specify different distances while creating the chamfer, clear the _____ check box.

10. The _____ check box is selected to apply the face fillet feature with continuous curvature throughout the fillet feature.

REVIEW QUESTIONS

Answer the following questions:

1. The _____ option is used to add standard holes to the model.

2. After specifying all parameters of a hole feature using the **Hole Specification PropertyManager**, the _____ tab is chosen to specify the placement of the hole feature.

3. Invoke the_____ **PropertyManager** to modify the fillets created at corners.

4. The _____ button is chosen from the **Hole Specifications** rollout to define a standard drilled hole.

5. By default, the _____ radio button is selected in the **Chamfer PropertyManager**.

6. If you preselect the placement surface to create a hole feature using the **Hole Wizard** tool, the resulting placement sketch will be a

    (a) 2D sketch   (b) Planar sketch
    (c) Bezier spline   (d) 3D sketch

7. Which one of the following options, when selected, does not require a radius to create a fillet feature?

   (a) **Face fillet with hold line**   (b) **Constant radius fillet**
   (c) **Variable radius fillet**   (d) **Full round fillet**

8. Which radio button in the **Variable Radius Parameters** rollout is used to create a smooth transition while creating a variable radius fillet?

   (a) **Straight transition**   (b) **Parametric transition**
   (c) **Smooth transition**   (d) **Surface transition**

9. What will be the resulting model if you do not select any face to be removed while creating a shell feature ?

   (a) Remains a complete solid model   (b) Thin walled hollow model
   (c) Automatically removes one face   (d) None of these

10. Which **PropertyManager** is displayed by default when you choose the **Hole Wizard** button from the **Features CommandManager**?

   (a) **Hole**   (b) **Hole Definition**
   (c) **Hole Wizard**   (d) **Hole Specification**

EXERCISES

Exercise 1

Create the model shown in Figure 7-144. The dimensions of the model are shown in Figure 7-145.   **(Expected time: 30 min)**

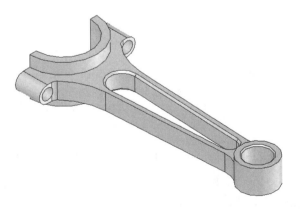

Figure 7-144 Solid model for Exercise 1

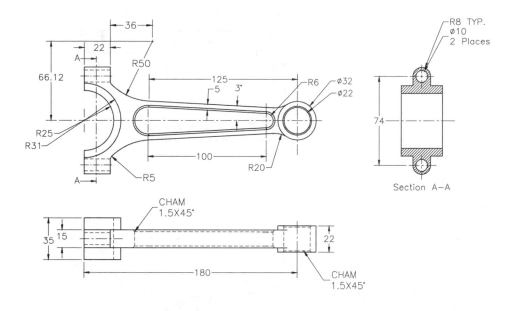

Figure 7-145 *Views and dimensions of the model for Exercise 1*

Exercise 2

Create the model shown in Figure 7-146. The dimensions of the model are shown in Figure 7-147. **(Expected time: 30 min)**

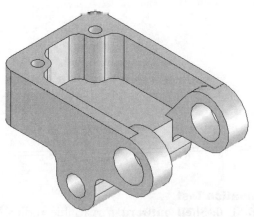

Figure 7-146 *Solid model for Exercise 2*

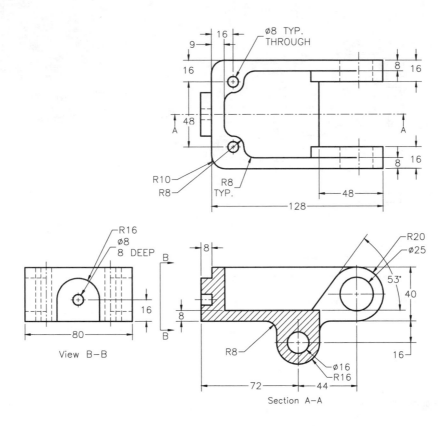

Figure 7-147 *Views and dimensions of the model for Exercise 2*

Answers to Self-Evaluation Test
1. F, 2. F, 3. F, 4. F, 5. T, 6. **Shell outward**, 7. variable radius fillet, 8. **Faces to Remove**,
9. **Equal distance**, 10. **Curvature continuous**

Chapter 8

Advanced Modeling Tools-II

Learning Objectives

After completing this chapter, you will be able to:
* Mirror features, faces, and bodies.
* Create linear patterns.
* Create circular patterns.
* Create sketch driven patterns.
* Create curve driven patterns.
* Create table driven patterns.
* Create rib features.
* Display the section view of the model.

ADVANCED MODELING TOOLS

Some of the advanced modeling options were discussed in Chapter 7, Advanced Modeling Tools-I. In this chapter, you will learn about some more advanced modeling tools that you can use to capture the design intent of the model. The rest of the advanced modeling tools are discussed in the later chapters.

Creating Mirror Features

CommandManager:	Features > Linear Pattern > Mirror
SolidWorks menus:	Insert > Pattern/Mirror > Mirror
Toolbar:	Features > Linear Pattern > Mirror

The **Mirror** tool is used to copy or mirror the selected feature, face, or body about a specified mirror plane, which can be a reference plane or a planar face. To use this tool, choose **Linear Pattern > Mirror** from the **Features CommandManager**, or choose **Insert > Pattern/Mirror > Mirror** from the SolidWorks menus to invoke the **Mirror PropertyManager**, as shown in Figure 8-1. The confirmation corner is also displayed in the drawing area.

The options that are used to mirror features, faces, and bodies are discussed next.

Mirroring Features

You can mirror the selected feature along the specified mirror plane or face by using this feature. To do so, invoke the **Mirror PropertyManager**; you are prompted to select a plane or a planar face about which the features will be mirrored, followed by the features to be mirrored. Select a plane or a planar face that will act as a mirror plane or mirror face. After selecting the mirror plane or face, the selection mode of the **Features to Mirror** selection box will be invoked and you will be prompted to select the features to mirror. Select the feature or features from the drawing area or from the **FeatureManager design tree** which is displayed in the drawing area. When you select the

Figure 8-1 The Mirror PropertyManager

features to be mirrored, the preview of the mirrored image will be displayed in the drawing area. After selecting all the required features, choose the **OK** button from the **Mirror PropertyManager**. Figure 8-2 shows the mirror plane and features to be mirrored and Figure 8-3 shows the resulting mirrored features.

Tip. *You can also preselect the mirror plane or the mirror face and the features to be mirrored before invoking the **Mirror PropertyManager**.*

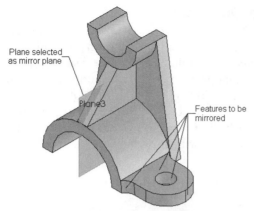
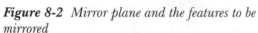

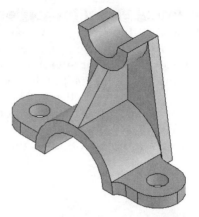

Figure 8-2 *Mirror plane and the features to be mirrored*

Figure 8-3 *The resulting mirrored features*

Mirroring with and without Geometric Pattern

When you create a mirror feature, you are provided with the **Geometry Pattern** option. This option is available in the **Options** rollout, as shown in Figure 8-4.

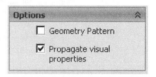

Figure 8-4 *The Options rollout*

By default, the **Geometry Pattern** check box is cleared. Therefore, if you mirror a feature that is related to some other entity, the same relationship will be applied to the mirrored feature. Consider a case in which an extruded cut is created using the **Offset From Surface** option. If you mirror the cut feature along a plane, the same relationship will be applied to the mirrored cut feature. The mirrored cut feature will be created with the same end condition of feature termination. Figure 8-5 shows a hole feature created on the right and mirrored along **Plane 1**, with the **Geometry Pattern** check box cleared.

If you select the **Geometry Pattern** check box, the resulting mirror feature will not depend on the relational references. It will create a replica of the selected geometry, as shown in Figure 8-6. Note that the visual properties will be visible only after you exit this tool.

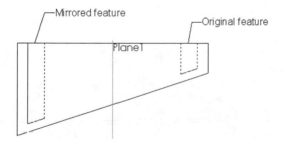
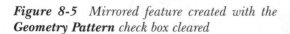

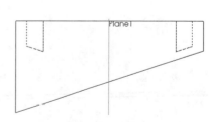

Figure 8-5 *Mirrored feature created with the Geometry Pattern check box cleared*

Figure 8-6 *Mirrored feature created with the Geometry Pattern check box selected*

Propagating Visual Properties While Mirroring

In SolidWorks, the **Propagate visual properties** check box is used to transfer the visual properties assigned to the feature or the parent body to the mirrored instance. This check box is provided in the **Options** rollout and is selected by default. Note that the visual properties will be visible only after you exit this tool. These visual properties include colors and textures applied to the features or the part bodies. If you clear this check box, the color or texture applied on faces, features, or the bodies will be reflected in the resulting mirrored instance. Figure 8-7 shows the mirrored feature with the **Propagate visual properties** check box selected and Figure 8-8 shows the mirrored features with this check box cleared.

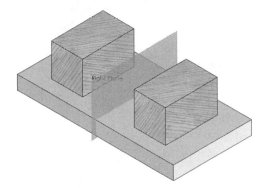 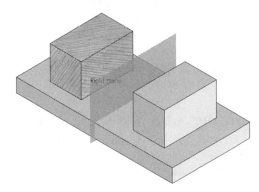

*Figure 8-7 Mirror feature with the **Propagate visual properties** check box selected*

*Figure 8-8 Mirror feature with the **Propagate visual properties** check box cleared*

Mirroring Faces

In SolidWorks, you can mirror faces about a plane or a face. To use this option, invoke the **Mirror PropertyManager**. You are prompted to select a plane or a planar face about which the selected faces will be mirrored. Select the planar face or plane. Next, click once in the **Faces to Mirror** selection box to invoke the selection mode and select the faces to be mirrored. The selected faces must form a closed body. Else, the feature creation is not possible. Choose the **OK** button from the **Mirror PropertyManager** to end the feature creation. Figure 8-9 shows the faces and the mirror plane selected to mirror. Figure 8-10 shows the resulting mirrored feature.

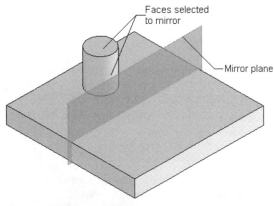 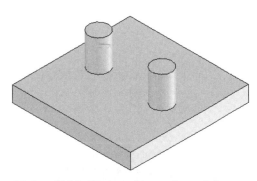

Figure 8-9 Mirror plane and faces selected to mirror

Figure 8-10 The resulting mirrored feature

Note

The following are some of the factors that should be considered while creating a mirror feature by mirroring the faces along the selected plane or the planar face:

1. If the replica of the faces is not coincident to the parent part body, SolidWorks will give an error while creating the mirror feature.

2. If the replica of the faces exists on faces other than the original face, SolidWorks will give an error while creating the mirror feature.

3. If the selected faces form a complex geometry, SolidWorks will give an error while creating the mirror feature.

4. If the mirrored faces exist on more than a face, SolidWorks will give an error while creating the mirror feature.

5. The selected faces should form a closed body. If the selected faces do not form a closed body, SolidWorks will give an error while creating the mirror feature.

Mirroring Bodies

As discussed in the earlier chapters, SolidWorks supports the multibodies environment. Therefore, using the **Mirror** tool, you can also mirror the disjoint bodies. To mirror a body along a plane, invoke the **Mirror PropertyManager** and select a plane or a planar face that will act as a mirror plane. Expand the **Bodies to Mirror** rollout and select the body from the drawing area. Alternatively, you can expand the **FeatureManager design tree** and select the body to be mirrored from the **Solid Bodies** folder; the name of the selected body will be displayed in the **Solid/Surface Bodies to Mirror** selection box. Also, the preview of the mirrored body will be displayed in the drawing area. Choose the **OK** button from the **Mirror PropertyManager**. Figure 8-11 shows the plane and the body selected to be mirrored. Figure 8-12 shows the resulting mirrored feature.

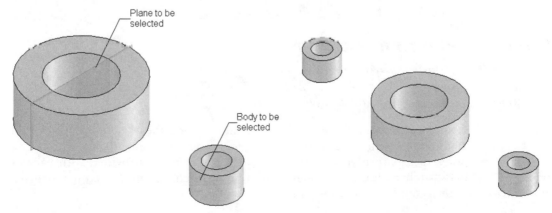

Figure 8-11 Selecting the mirror plane and body to be mirrored

Figure 8-12 Resulting mirrored feature

The options available in the **Options** rollout of the **Mirror PropertyManager** are shown in Figure 8-13 and are discussed next.

*Figure 8-13 The **Options** rollout*

Merge solids

The **Merge solids** check box is used to merge the mirrored body with the parent body. Consider a case, in which you mirror a body along a selected plane or a planar face of the same body and the resulting mirrored body is joined to the parent body. In this case, if you select the **Merge solids** check box, the resulting mirrored body will merge with the parent body to become a single body. If the **Merge solids** check box is cleared, the resulting body will be joined with the parent body, but it will not merge with it. Therefore, it will result in two separate bodies.

Knit surfaces

If you mirror a surface body, the **Knit surfaces** check box is selected to knit the mirrored and the parent body together.

Tip. As discussed earlier, the design intent is captured in the model using the mirror option. Therefore, if you modify the parent feature, face, or body, the same will be reflected in the mirrored feature, face, or body.

*If you want to mirror all the features of the model using the **Features to Mirror** option, you need to select all features. But for using the **Bodies to Mirror** option, you need to select the body from the **Solid Bodies** folder. By selecting the body, all the features will be added to the mirror image.*

Creating Linear Pattern Features

CommandManager:	Features > Linear Pattern
SolidWorks Menus:	Insert > Pattern/Mirror > Linear Pattern
Toolbar:	Features > Linear Pattern

As discussed in the previous chapters, you can arrange the sketched entities in a particular arrangement or pattern. Similarly, you can also arrange the features, faces, and bodies in a particular pattern. In SolidWorks, you are provided with various types of patterns such as linear patterns, circular patterns, sketch driven patterns, curve driven patterns, and table driven patterns.

In this section, you will learn to create linear patterns. The other types of patterns are discussed later in this chapter.

To create a linear pattern, choose the **Linear Pattern** button from the **Features CommandManager**, or choose **Insert > Pattern/ Mirror > Linear Pattern** from the SolidWorks menus. The **Linear Pattern PropertyManager** will be invoked and the confirmation corner will also be displayed. A partial view of the **Linear Pattern PropertyManager** is shown in Figure 8-14. Various options in the **Linear Pattern PropertyManager** are discussed next.

Linear Pattern in One Direction

When you invoke the **Linear Pattern PropertyManager**, the **Direction 1** rollout and the **Features to Pattern** rollout are expanded by default. Also, you will be prompted to select an edge or an axis for the direction reference and face of the feature to pattern. Select an edge or an axis as the direction reference; the name of the selected reference will be displayed in the **Pattern Direction** selection box of the **Direction 1** rollout. The selected reference will be highlighted and the **Direction 1** callout will be attached to it. The **Direction 1** callout has two edit boxes, one to define the number of instances and the other to define spacing. You are also provided with the **Reverse Direction** arrow along with the selected reference. Now, select a face of the feature to be patterned; the name of the selected feature will be displayed in the **Features to Pattern** selection box of the **Features to Pattern** rollout. The preview of the pattern will be displayed in the drawing area with the default values. Set the value of the center to center spacing between the pattern instances in the **Spacing** spinner. Set the value of the number of instances to be patterned in the **Number of Instances** spinner. You can also set these values in the **Direction 1** callout. You can choose the **Reverse Direction** button from the **PropertyManager** or the **Reverse Direction** arrow from the drawing area to reverse the direction of the pattern feature creation. Figure 8-15 shows the feature and edge to be selected for directional reference and Figure 8-16 shows the model after the pattern creation.

*Figure 8-14 Partial view of the **Linear Pattern** PropertyManager*

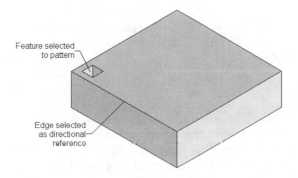

Figure 8-15 Feature and the edge to be selected

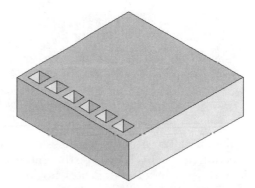

Figure 8-16 Linear pattern created along one direction

Linear Pattern in Two Directions

As discussed earlier, you can create a linear pattern of features, faces, and bodies by defining a single direction using the **Direction 1** rollout. You can also define the parameters in the **Direction 2** rollout to define the pattern in the second direction. The **Direction 2** rollout is shown in Figure 8-17. If the **Direction 2** rollout is not expanded by default in the **Linear Pattern PropertyManager**, click on the arrow in the **Direction 2** rollout to expand it. When you define the pattern in the second direction, the entire row created by specifying the parameters in the first direction will be patterned in the second direction. To create a pattern by specifying the parameters in both the directions, select the feature to be patterned, and invoke the

Figure 8-17　The ***Direction 2*** *rollout*

Linear Pattern PropertyManager. Select the first directional reference. Next, specify the parameters in the **Direction 1** rollout. Now, select the second directional reference and specify the parameters in the **Direction 2** rollout. The options in the **Direction 2** rollout are the same as those discussed in the **Direction 1** rollout. Figure 8-18 shows the directional references and the feature to be selected. Figure 8-19 shows the linear pattern created using the **Direction 1** and **Direction 2** rollouts.

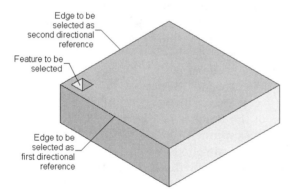

Figure 8-18　References and feature to be selected

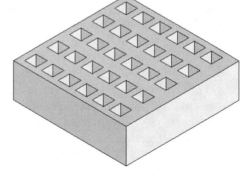

Figure 8-19　Linear pattern created using the ***Direction 1*** *and* ***Direction 2*** *rollouts*

Tip. *When you select the feature to be patterned, its dimensions are also displayed in the drawing area. You can also select the dimensions as the directional reference.*

As discussed earlier, you can mirror the faces and bodies. In addition, you can also pattern them. It should be noted that the selected faces must form a closed body, otherwise the patterning of faces will give an error.

By default, all rows of the instances created in the first direction are patterned in the second direction also. This is because the **Pattern seed only** check box in the **Direction 2** rollout is cleared. You can select this check box to pattern only the original selected feature (also called seed feature) in the second direction. Figure 8-20 shows the pattern created with the **Pattern seed only** check box selected.

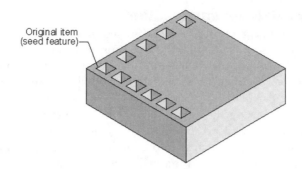

Figure 8-20 *Linear pattern created with the* **Pattern seed only** *check box selected*

Instances to Skip

The **Instances to Skip** option is used to skip some of the instances from the pattern. These instances are not actually deleted but disappear from the pattern feature and you can resume them at any time of your design cycle. To skip the pattern instances, expand the **Instances to Skip** rollout from the **Linear Pattern PropertyManager**. The **Instances to Skip** rollout is displayed, as shown in Figure 8-21.

Figure 8-21 *The* **Instances to Skip** *rollout*

As soon as you expand this rollout, pink dots will be displayed at the center of all pattern instances except the parent instance. Therefore, you cannot skip the parent instance. Now, move the cursor to the pink dot of the instance to be skipped. The cursor will be replaced by the instance to skip cursor and the position of that instance will be displayed in the form of a matrix below this cursor as tooltip. Left-click on the pink dot to skip that instance; the pink dot will be replaced by a red dot, and the preview of that instance will disappear from the pattern. The position of the skipped instance in the form of a matrix will be displayed in the **Instances to Skip** selection box of the **Instances to Skip** rollout. Figure 8-22 shows a pattern created with some instances skipped. You can resume the skipped instances by deleting the name of the instance from the **Instances to Skip** selection box or selecting the red dot from the drawing area.

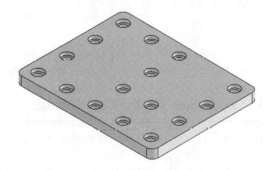

Figure 8-22 *Linear pattern created with some instances skipped*

Creating Pattern Using a Varying Sketch

The **Vary sketch** option in the **Options** rollout is used in a pattern where the shape and size of each pattern instance is controlled by the relations and dimensions of the sketch of that feature. In this type of pattern, the dimension of the sketch of the feature is selected as the directional reference, which then drives the shape and size of the sketch of the feature to be patterned. In Figure 8-23, a cut feature is created on the base feature. Figure 8-24 shows the linear pattern created using the **Vary sketch** option. To create this type of pattern, the sketch of the feature to be patterned should be in relation with the geometry along which it will vary. The dimensions of the sketch should allow it to change its shape and size easily. You should also provide a linear dimension that will drive the entire sketch and will also be the directional reference. Select the feature to be patterned from the **FeatureManager design tree** and then invoke the **Linear Pattern PropertyManager**. Now, select the dimension to specify the directional reference and set the value of spacing and the number of instances. In this case, the horizontal dimension that measures 5 will be selected as the dimensional reference. Next, expand the **Options** rollout and select the **Vary sketch** check box; the preview of the pattern disappears from the drawing area. Choose the **OK** button from the **Linear Pattern PropertyManager** to end the feature creation. In this case, the lower edge of the cut feature will be constrained to the bottom face of the model and top edge varies along the curved edge of the model. Therefore, the pattern instances will be created such that their height varies along with the curved edge of the model.

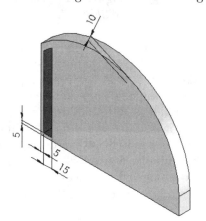

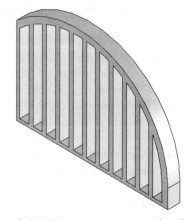

Figure 8-23 Cut feature created on the base feature

*Figure 8-24 Linear pattern created with the **Vary sketch** check box selected*

The **Geometry pattern** check box in the **Options** rollout of the **Linear Pattern PropertyManager** is same as that discussed earlier in the **Mirror PropertyManager**.

Propagating Visual Properties While Patterning

In SolidWorks, the **Propagate visual properties** check box is provided in the **Options** rollout. This check box is selected by default and is used to transfer the visual properties assigned to the feature or the parent body to the patterned instances. These visual properties include colors and textures that are applied to the features or part bodies after you exit this tool. If you clear this check box, then the color or the texture applied to faces, features, or bodies will be not be reflected in the resulting mirrored instance.

Creating Circular Pattern Features

CommandManager:	Features > Linear Pattern > Circular Pattern
SolidWorks menus:	Insert > Pattern/Mirror > Circular Pattern
Toolbar:	Features > Linear Pattern > Circular Pattern

As discussed in the previous chapters, you can arrange the sketched entities in a circular pattern using the **Circular Pattern** tool. In this section, you will learn to create the circular pattern of a feature, face, or body by using the **Circular Pattern** tool. To create a circular pattern, select the features, and choose **Linear Pattern > Circular Pattern** from the **Features CommandManager** or choose **Insert > Pattern/ Mirror > Circular Pattern** from the SolidWorks menus; the **Circular Pattern PropertyManager** will be invoked and the confirmation corner will be displayed. The partial view of the **Circular Pattern PropertyManager** is shown in Figure 8-25.

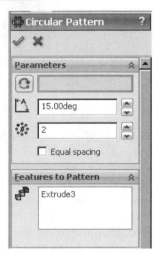

Figure 8-25 Partial view of the **Circular Pattern PropertyManager**

After invoking the **Circular Pattern PropertyManager**, you will be prompted to select an edge or an axis for the direction reference, and a face of the feature to be patterned. If you need to create the circular pattern on a circular feature, select the circular edge; the center of the circular feature will be selected as the pattern axis. You can also select an edge, axis, or a sketched line as the pattern axis. The **Direction 1** callout is also displayed with the **Reverse Direction** arrow in the drawing area. By default, the **Equal spacing** check box is cleared. Therefore, you need to set the value of the incremental angle between the instances in the **Total Angle** spinner. Set the value of number of instances to pattern in the **Number of Instances** spinner. If you select the **Equal spacing** check box, you need to enter the value of the total angle, along which all the instances of the pattern will be placed. The angular spacing between the instances will be automatically calculated.

The **Reverse Direction** button available on the left of the **Pattern Axis** selection box is used to change the direction of rotation. By default, the direction of the pattern creation is clockwise. If you choose this button then the resulting pattern will be created in the counterclockwise direction. You can also change the direction of the pattern creation by clicking on the arrow in the drawing area. Figure 8-26 shows the feature and the temporary axis being selected. Figure 8-27 shows the resulting pattern feature.

Tip. *In SolidWorks, you can pattern a patterned feature. You can also pattern a mirrored feature. It is also possible to mirror a patterned feature.*

Creating Circular Pattern Using a Dimensional Reference

You can also create a circular pattern by selecting an angular dimension. To create a pattern using this option, you need to create an angular dimension in the sketch of the feature that is to be patterned. Invoke the **Circular Pattern PropertyManager** and select the feature to

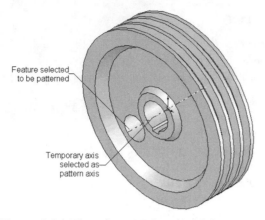

Figure 8-26 *The reference to be selected for creating a circular pattern*

Figure 8-27 *The resulting circular pattern*

be patterned; the dimensions of the feature to be patterned will be displayed in the drawing area, as shown in Figure 8-28. Now, select the angular dimension and set the value of the total angle and spacing in the **Circular Pattern PropertyManager**. Figure 8-29 shows the circular pattern created by selecting the angular dimension as the angular reference. The other options in the **Circular Pattern PropertyManager** are the same as those discussed earlier for the **Linear Pattern PropertyManager**.

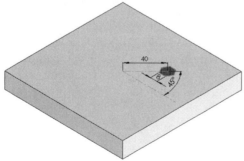

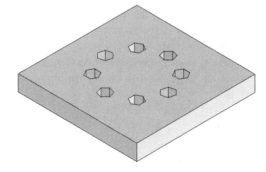

Figure 8-28 *Dimensions displayed after selecting the feature to be patterned*

Figure 8-29 *Circular pattern created by selecting the angular dimension as the angular reference*

Tip. *Instead of setting the value of the angle and the number of instances in the respective spinners, you can also set the values in the callout, as it saves your time.*

It is always a good practice to create patterns of features instead of creating complex sketches or creating the same feature repeatedly. It also helps in capturing the design intent of the model. The patterns created in the **Part** *mode are very useful in the assembly modeling. You will learn more about assemblies in the later chapters.*

Creating Sketch Driven Patterns

CommandManager:	Features > Linear Pattern > Sketch Driven Pattern
SolidWorks menus:	Insert > Pattern/Mirror > Sketch Driven Pattern
Toolbar:	Features > Linear Pattern > Sketch Driven Pattern

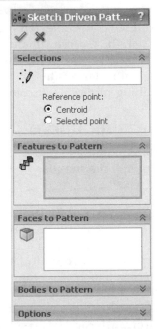

A sketch driven pattern is created when the features, faces, or bodies are to be arranged in a nonuniform manner, which is neither rectangular nor circular. To create a sketch driven pattern, first you need to create an arrangement of the sketch points in a single sketch. This arrangement of the sketch points will drive the instances in the pattern feature. After creating the feature to be patterned and placing the points in the sketch, choose **Linear Pattern > Sketch Driven Pattern** from the **Features CommandManager;** the **Sketch Driven Pattern PropertyManager** will be displayed, as shown in Figure 8-30. You will be prompted to select a sketch for the pattern layout, and the face of the feature to be patterned. Select the feature or the features to be patterned. Now, click in the **Reference Sketch** selection box in the **Selections** rollout. Select any one of the sketched points from the drawing area or from the **FeatureManager design tree**. Choose the **OK** button from the **Sketch Driven Pattern PropertyManager**. Figure 8-31 shows the feature and the sketch point to be selected and Figure 8-32 shows the resulting pattern feature.

Figure 8-30 The Sketch Driven Pattern PropertyManager

The options in the **Sketch Driven Pattern PropertyManager** are discussed next.

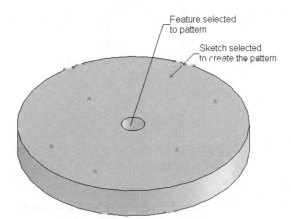

Figure 8-31 The feature and the sketch point to be selected

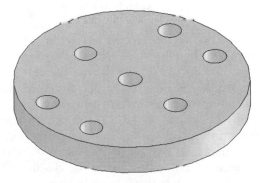

Figure 8-32 The resulting sketch driven pattern feature

Creating Sketch Driven Pattern Using a Centroid

When you invoke the **Sketch Driven Pattern PropertyManager**, the **Centroid** radio button is selected by default in the **Reference point** area of the **Selections** rollout. Therefore, the pattern will be created with the centroid of the instances coinciding with the sketched points.

Creating Sketch Driven Pattern Using a Selected Point

If you select the **Selected point** radio button from the **Reference point** area of the **Selections** rollout, the pattern will be created with reference to the selected point. When you select this radio button, the **Reference Vertex** selection box will be displayed. Select a point in the original instance; the pattern will be created in such a way that the specified vertex in the resulting instance will coincide with the sketched point.

Creating Curve Driven Patterns

CommandManager:	Features > Linear Pattern > Curve Driven Pattern
SolidWorks menus:	Insert > Pattern/Mirror > Curve Driven Pattern
Toolbar:	Features > Linear Pattern > Curve Driven Pattern

 The **Curve Driven Pattern** tool is used to pattern the features, faces, or bodies along a selected reference curve. The reference curve can be a sketched entity, an edge, or an open profile, or a closed loop. To create a pattern using this option, choose **Linear Pattern > Curve Driven Pattern** from the **Features CommandManager** or choose **Insert > Pattern/Mirror > Curve Driven Pattern** from the SolidWorks menus; the **Curve Driven Pattern PropertyManager** will be displayed, as shown in Figure 8-33.

*Figure 8-33 Partial view of the **Curve Driven Pattern PropertyManager***

On invoking the **Curve Driven Pattern PropertyManager**, you will be prompted to select an edge, curve, or a sketch segment for pattern layout and select a face of the feature to be patterned. Select the reference curve along which the feature, face, or body is to be patterned. In SolidWorks, you can also select 3D curves or sketches as the reference curve. You will learn more about 3D curves and sketches in the later chapters. When you select the reference curve, its name will be displayed in the **Pattern Direction** selection box and the **Direction 1** callout will also be displayed. As discussed earlier, the **Direction 1** callout is divided into two areas. Left-click once in the **Features to Pattern** selection box. Then, select the feature to be patterned; the preview of the pattern will be displayed in the drawing area. Set the various parameters in the **Direction 1** callout and choose the **OK** button from the **Curve Driven Pattern PropertyManager**. Figure 8-34 shows the feature and the curve that will be used to create the pattern. Figure 8-35 shows the resulting curve driven pattern.

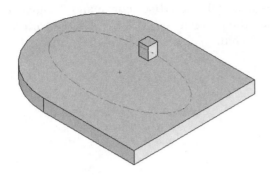

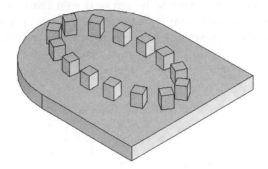

Figure 8-34 *The feature and the curve to be used to create the curve driven pattern*

Figure 8-35 *The resulting curve driven pattern feature*

The options available in the **Direction 1** rollout are discussed next.

Equal Spacing

The **Equal spacing** check box is used to accommodate all the instances of the pattern along the selected curve. By default, this check box is cleared. Therefore, you have to specify the distance between the instances and the total number of instances to be created along the selected curve. When you select this check box, the **Spacing** spinner will not be available and you have to specify only the total number of instances. The distance between the instances is calculated automatically.

Curve method and Alignment method

The **Curve method** area of the **Direction 1** rollout is used to specify the type of curve method to be followed while creating patterns. The two options available in this area are **Transform curve** and **Offset curve**. The **Alignment method** area of the **Direction 1** rollout is used to specify the type of alignment method to be applied. The two alignment methods are the **Tangent to curve** method and the **Align to seed** method. Figure 8-36 shows the curve driven pattern created with the **Transform curve** and the **Tangent to curve** radio buttons selected. Figure 8-37 shows the curve driven pattern created with the **Transform curve** and **Align to seed** radio buttons selected.

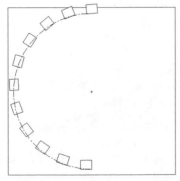

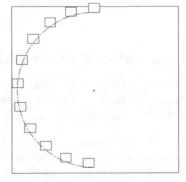

Figure 8-36 *Pattern created with the **Transform curve** and **Tangent to curve** radio buttons selected*

Figure 8-37 *Pattern created with the **Transform curve** and **Align to seed** radio buttons selected*

Figure 8-38 shows the curve driven pattern created with the **Offset curve** and **Tangent to curve** radio buttons selected. Figure 8-39 shows the curve driven pattern created with the **Offset curve** and **Align to seed** radio buttons selected.

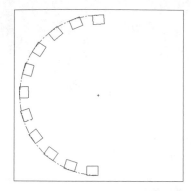
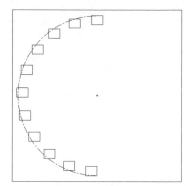

Figure 8-38 *Pattern created with the **Offset curve** and **Tangent to curve** radio buttons selected*

Figure 8-39 *Pattern created with the **Offset curve** and **Align to seed** radio buttons selected*

The other options in the **Curve Driven PropertyManager** are the same as those discussed earlier for the mirror and other pattern features. By selecting the check box in the **Direction 2** rollout, you can also specify the parameters in the second direction. Figure 8-40 shows the curve driven pattern feature created with the pattern defined in the first and second direction.

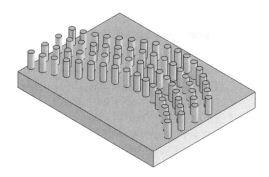

Figure 8-40 *A curve driven pattern created by specifying parameters in both the directions*

Creating Table Driven Patterns

CommandManager:	Features > Linear Pattern >Table Driven Pattern
SolidWorks menus:	Insert > Pattern/Mirror > Table Driven Pattern
Toolbar:	Features > Linear Pattern >Table Driven Pattern

The table driven pattern is created by specifying the X and Y coordinates of the pattern feature with reference to a coordinate system. The instances of the selected features, faces, or bodies are created at the points specified using the X and Y coordinates. To create this pattern, you first need to create a coordinate system using the

Coordinate System button from the **Reference Geometry** toolbar. The coordinate system defines the direction along which the selected feature will be patterned. Choose **Linear Pattern > Table Driven Pattern** from the **Features CommandManager** or choose **Insert > Pattern/Mirror > Table Driven Pattern** from the SolidWorks menus; the **Table Driven Pattern** dialog box will be displayed, as shown in Figure 8-41.

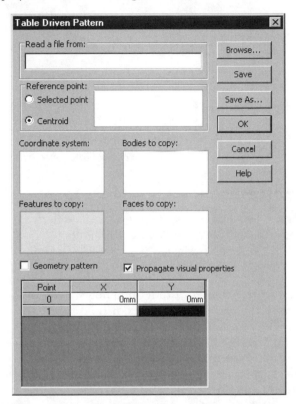

Figure 8-41 *The **Table Driven Pattern** dialog box*

Select the feature to be patterned and the coordinate system from the drawing area or from the **FeatureManager design tree**. Enter the coordinates for creating the instances in the **Coordinate points** area of the **Table Driven Pattern** dialog box. As you enter the coordinates for the instances, the preview of the pattern will be displayed in the drawing area. After entering all the coordinate points, choose the **OK** button from the **Table Driven Pattern** dialog box. Figure 8-42 shows the feature and the coordinate system to be selected. Figure 8-43 shows the table driven pattern created after entering the coordinate values in the **Table Driven Pattern** dialog box.

You can also save the table driven pattern file by choosing the **Save** button. Choose the **Browse** button to retrieve the already saved file. You can also write the coordinates in a text file and browse the same file while creating a table driven pattern. The other options in this dialog box are the same as those discussed earlier.

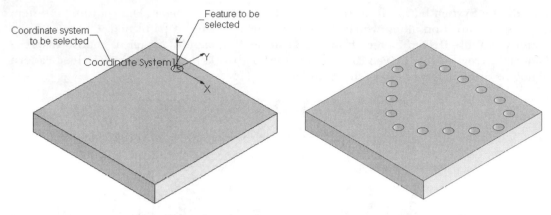

Figure 8-42 *Feature and the coordinate system to be selected*

Figure 8-43 *The resulting table driven pattern created after specifying the coordinate points*

Creating Fill Patterns

CommandManager:	Features > Linear Pattern > Fill Pattern
SolidWorks menus:	Insert > Pattern/Mirror > Fill Pattern
Toolbar:	Features > Linear Pattern > Fill Pattern

The **Fill Pattern** tool is used to fill a defined area with the pattern of the features, faces, bodies, or predefined holes. The area to be filled with the pattern of features or holes can be a sketched entity, face, or a co-planar face. To create a fill pattern, select the feature to be patterned from the drawing area or from the **FeatureManager design tree**. Next, choose **Linear Pattern > Fill Pattern** from the **Features CommandManager**; the **Fill Pattern PropertyManager** will be displayed, as shown in Figure 8-44. Note that the name of the selected feature will be displayed in the **Features to Pattern** selection box and you will be prompted to select the edge or axis for direction reference and the face of feature to define the area of fill pattern. Select the sketched entity, a face, or a co-planar face to define the area of fill pattern; the preview of the fill pattern will be displayed in the drawing area. Choose the **OK** button from the **PropertyManager**. Figure 8-45 shows the feature and the planar face to be selected and Figure 8-46 shows the resulting pattern feature.

The procedures to create different fill patterns using **Fill Pattern PropertyManager** are discussed next.

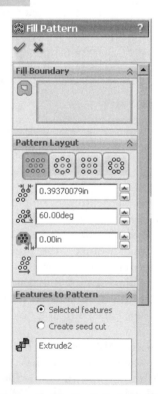

Figure 8-44 *Partial view of the Fill Pattern PropertyManager*

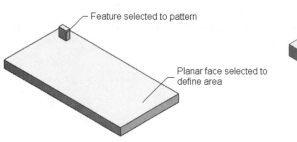

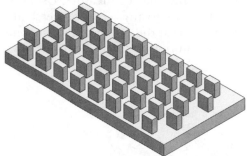

Figure 8-45 *The feature and planar face to be selected*

Figure 8-46 *Resulting pattern feature*

Creating a Fill Pattern of the Selected Features

When you invoke the **Fill Pattern PropertyManager**, the **Selected features** radio button is selected by default in the **Features to Pattern** rollout. Therefore, you need to select a feature from the drawing area to create a fill pattern.

Creating a Fill Pattern of the Predefined Holes

Select the **Create seed cut** radio button from the **Features to Pattern** rollout of the **Fill Pattern PropertyManager** to create a pattern of the predefined holes. The predefined cut shapes available are circle, square, diamond, and polygon. On selecting this radio button, the **Circle**, **Square**, **Diamond**, and **Polygon** buttons will be enabled below it. The **Circle** button is chosen by default, therefore, a pattern of circular holes will be created. Figure 8-47 shows the planar face to be selected and Figure 8-48 shows the resultant fill pattern with the **Circle** button chosen.

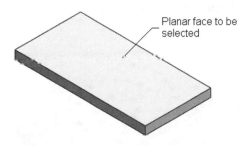

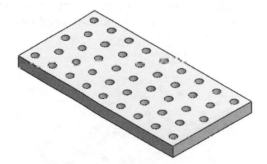

Figure 8-47 *The planar face to be selected*

Figure 8-48 *The resultant fill pattern*

Creating a Fill Pattern by Specifying a Vertex or Sketch Point

The **Vertex or Sketch Point** selection box will be available, when the **Create seed cut** radio button is selected in the **Features to Pattern** rollout of the **PropertyManager**. By default, the seed feature is located at the center of the fill boundary and the pattern feature is created around the seed feature. Using this selection box, you can change the location of the seed feature to any vertex or sketched point. Figure 8-49 shows the fill pattern when the seed feature is at the center of the fill boundary and Figure 8-50 shows the fill pattern when the seed feature is at the right vertex of the fill boundary.

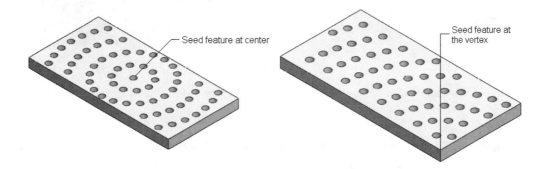

Figure 8-49 *The fill pattern with seed feature at the center of the fill boundary*

Figure 8-50 *The fill pattern with seed feature at the right vertex of the fill boundary*

Creating a Fill Pattern of Different Layouts

You can define the layout of the instances within the fill boundary using the **Perforation**, **Circular**, **Square**, and **Polygon** buttons available in the **Pattern Layout** rollout of the **PropertyManager**. The **Perforation** button is chosen by default in this rollout. Using this button, you can create a perforated style pattern. To create a circular shape pattern, choose the **Circular** button from the **Pattern Layout** rollout. Similarly, the **Square** and **Polygon** buttons are used to create a square and polygon shape pattern, respectively. Figures 8-51 through 8-54 show different pattern layouts created using the buttons available in the **Pattern Layout** rollout, when the **Create seed cut** radio button is selected.

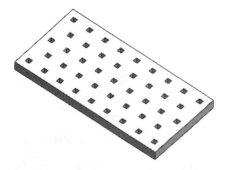

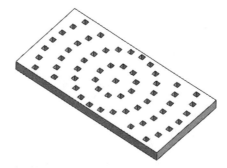

Figure 8-51 *The perforated style fill pattern*

Figure 8-52 *The circular shape fill pattern*

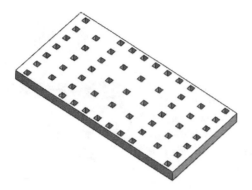

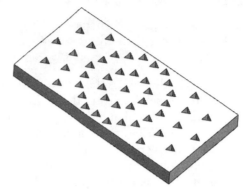

Figure 8-53 *The square shape fill pattern*   *Figure 8-54* *The polygon shape fill pattern*

Creating a Fill Pattern by Specifying Target Spacing and Instances Per Side

When you choose the **Circular**, **Square**, or **Polygon** button from the **Pattern Layout** rollout of the **Fill Pattern PropertyManager**, the **Target Spacing** and **Instances Per Side** radio buttons will be enabled below these buttons. The **Target Spacing** radio button is selected by default. Therefore, you need to specify the spacing between the instances in the **Instance Spacing** spinner. On selecting this radio button, the number of instances are calculated such that the instances fit evenly. If you select the **Instances Per Side** radio button from the **Pattern Layout** rollout, you need to specify the number of instances in each loop of the fill pattern in the **Number of Instances** spinner. Figure 8-55 shows the circular shape fill pattern created when the **Target Spacing** radio button is selected. Figure 8-56 shows the circular shape fill pattern created when the **Instances Per Side** radio button is selected, with 8 instances in each loop.

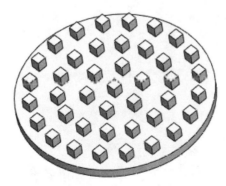

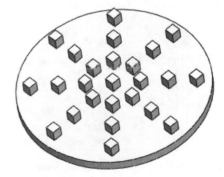

Figure 8-55 *Fill pattern with the* **Target Spacing** *radio button selected*   *Figure 8-56* *Fill pattern with the* **Instances Per Side** *radio button selected*

Creating Rib Features

CommandManager:	Features > Rib
SolidWorks menus:	Insert > Features > Rib
Toolbar:	Features > Rib

 Ribs are defined as the thin-walled structures that are used to increase the strength of the entire structure of the component so that it does not fail under an increased load. In SolidWorks, the ribs are created using an open sketch as well as a closed sketch. To create a rib feature, draw a sketch and exit the sketching environment. Invoke the **Rib** tool by choosing the **Rib** button from the **Features CommandManager** or by choosing **Insert > Features > Rib** from the SolidWorks menus; the **Rib PropertyManager** will be displayed and you will be prompted to select a plane, a planar face, or an edge to sketch the feature, or an existing sketch to use for the feature. Select the sketch from the drawing area; the **Rib PropertyManager** will be modified, as shown in Figure 8-57 and the preview of the rib feature with the direction arrow and the confirmation corner will be displayed in the drawing area. You can also invoke the **Rib** tool, select a plane, draw a sketch, and then exit the sketching environment to display the **Rib PropertyManager** and the preview of the rib feature.

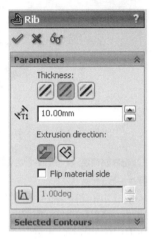

*Figure 8-57 The **Rib** PropertyManager*

Specify the rib parameters in the **Rib PropertyManager** and view the detailed preview using the **Detailed Preview** button. Figure 8-58 shows the sketch drawn for the rib feature and Figure 8-59 shows the resulting rib feature.

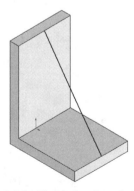

Figure 8-58 Sketch for the rib feature

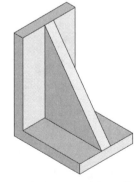

Figure 8-59 Resulting rib feature

The options in the **Rib PropertyManager** are discussed next.

Thickness

The **Thickness** area in the **Parameters** rollout is used to specify the side of the sketch where the material is to be added and the thickness of the rib feature. The buttons in the **Thickness** area are used to control the side on which you want to add the rib thickness. By default, the **Both Sides** button is chosen. Therefore, the rib is created on both sides of the sketch. You can choose the **First Side** or the **Second Side** button to create ribs on either sides of the sketch. The **Rib Thickness** spinner in this area is used to specify the rib thickness.

Extrusion direction

The **Extrusion direction** area in the **Parameters** rollout is used to specify the method of extruding the closed or the open sketch. When you invoke the **Rib PropertyManager**, the option that is suitable for creating the rib feature will be activated, by default, depending on the geometric conditions. The options in this area are discussed next.

Parallel to Sketch

The **Parallel to Sketch** button is used to extrude the sketch in a direction that is parallel to both the sketch and sketching plane. When the sketch created for the rib feature is a open sketch and continuous single entity, this button is selected by default in the **Rib PropertyManager**. Figure 8-60 shows an open sketch suitable for creating a rib by choosing the **Parallel to Sketch** button. Figure 8-61 shows the rib feature created using the sketch.

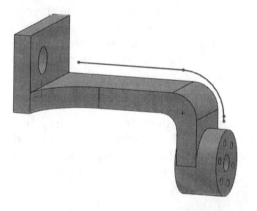
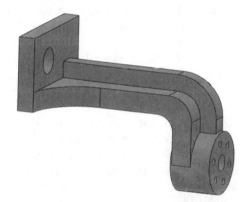

Figure 8-60 An open sketch for the rib feature   *Figure 8-61* The resulting rib feature

Note
You will observe that the endpoints of the sketched lines drawn in Figure 8-60 do not merge with the edges of the model. However, the rib created using this sketch merges with the edges of the model. This is because while creating the sketch for the rib feature, the ends of the rib feature automatically extend to the next surface; you do not need to create a complete sketch.

Normal to Sketch

The **Normal to Sketch** option is used to extrude the sketch in a direction that is normal to both the sketch and the sketching plane. This button is used when the sketch of the rib feature is a closed loop sketch, or it consists of multiple sketched entities. The sketch with multiple entities can be a closed loop or an open profile. If you draw a sketch with a closed loop or with multiple sketched entities and invoke the **Rib** tool, the **Normal to Sketch** button will be chosen by default. You can also choose the **Normal to Sketch** button from the **Extrusion direction** area to use this option. Figure 8-62 shows a multiple sketch entities for the rib feature. Figure 8-63 shows the resulting rib feature.

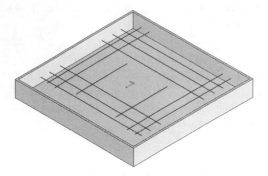

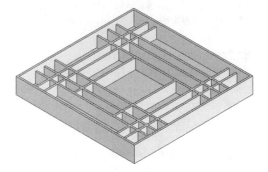

Figure 8-62 *Multiple sketch entities for the rib feature*

Figure 8-63 *The resulting rib feature*

When you choose the **Normal to Sketch** button, the **Type** area is displayed under the **Draft Angle** spinner. The **Type** area is provided with two radio buttons, **Linear** and **Natural**. These radio buttons are used if the endpoints of the open sketch for the rib are not coincident with the faces of the existing feature. If the **Linear** radio button is selected, the rib will be created by extending the sketch normal to the sketched entity direction. The sketch will be extended up to a point where it meets the boundary. On the other hand, if the **Natural** radio button is selected, the rib feature will be created by extending the sketch along the same curvature of the sketched entities.

For example, consider the sketch shown in Figure 8-64, which shows a multiple entities sketch created for the rib feature. Figure 8-65 shows a rib feature created by extending the sketch normal to the arc and the line on selecting the **Linear** radio button. Similarly, in Figure 8-66, the feature is created by extending the sketch along the line and arc by selecting the **Natural** radio button.

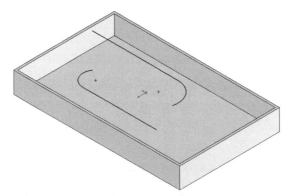

Figure 8-64 *Sketch for the rib feature*

Flip material side

The **Flip material side** check box is selected to reverse the direction for adding material, while creating the rib feature. You can also left-click on the arrow displayed in the preview to reverse the direction.

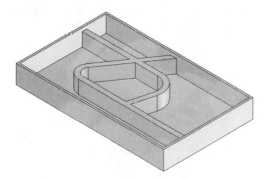

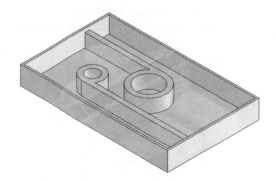

Figure 8-65 Rib feature created with the
Linear radio button selected from the Type
area of the Rib PropertyManager

Figure 8-66 Rib feature created with the
Natural radio button selected from the Type
area of the Rib PropertyManager

Draft On/Off

The **Draft On/Off** button is used to add taper to the faces of the rib feature. When you choose the **Draft On/Off** button, the **Draft Angle** spinner will be available. If you are creating a rib feature using multiple sketched entities, you can add only a simple draft to it. Figure 8-67 shows the draft angle added to the rib feature.

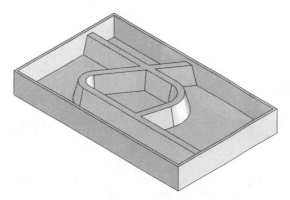

Figure 8-67 Draft angle added to the rib feature

By default, the draft is added inward to the rib feature. You need to choose the **Draft outward** check box to add the draft outwards. If the rib feature to be created consists of single continuous sketch and if you choose the **Draft On/Off** button, the **Next Reference** button will be displayed below the **Draft Angle** spinner. A reference arrow will also be displayed in the drawing area. Choose the **Next Reference** button to cycle through the reference along which you want to add the draft angle.

When you choose the **Draft On/Off** button, the **At sketch plane** and **At wall interface** radio buttons will be displayed below the **Rib Thickness** spinner. The **At sketch plane** radio button is selected by default. Therefore, the rib thickness will be applied at the sketch plane. On selecting the **At wall interface** radio button, rib thickness will be applied at the point, where the rib meets the wall.

Figure 8-68 shows the sketch and the preview of rib feature and Figure 8-69 shows the resulting rib feature created with the **Draft outward** check box selected.

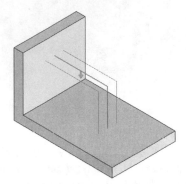

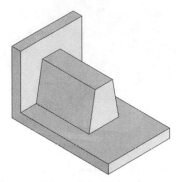

Figure 8-68 *The sketch and the preview of the rib feature*

Figure 8-69 *The resulting rib feature created with the **Draft outward** check box selected*

Figure 8-70 shows the sketch and the preview of the rib feature and Figure 8-71 shows the resulting rib feature created with the **Draft outward** check box cleared.

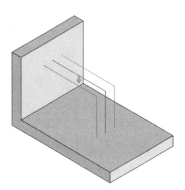

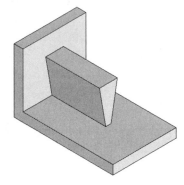

Figure 8-70 *The sketch and the preview of the rib feature*

Figure 8-71 *Resulting rib feature*

Displaying the Section View of the Model

SolidWorks menus:	View > Display > Section View
Toolbar:	Heads-up View > Section View

The **Section View** tool is used to display the section view of the model by cutting it using a plane or a face. You can also save the section view with a name to generate the section view directly on the drawing sheet in the drawing mode. To display the section view of a model, choose the **Section View** button from the **Heads-up View** toolbar. On invoking this tool, the **Section View PropertyManager** will be displayed, as shown in Figure 8-72.

By default, the **Front Plane** is automatically selected in the **Section View PropertyManager** and the section view of the model created using the **Front Plane** as the section plane is displayed in the drawing area. If you need to select the Right Plane or Top Plane as the section plane, choose the respective buttons in the **Section 1** rollout. You can also select a face or a user-defined plane as the section plane. To do so, clear the reference plane selected in the **Reference Section Plane/Face** selection box and select the face or the plane from the drawing area.

A drag handle is provided at the center of the section plane to drag and dynamically adjust the offset distance of the section plane, as shown in Figure 8-73. You can also specify the offset distance using the **Offset Distance** spinner. You will observe that as you modify the offset distance, the preview of the section view is automatically modified. You can also rotate the section plane along the X-axis and the Y-axis using the **X Rotation** and **Y Rotation** spinners, respectively. Alternatively, move the cursor on the edge of the plane; the **Rotate** cursor will be displayed. Left-click and drag the cursor to rotate the section plane dynamically.

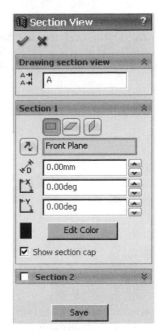

Figure 8-72 The Section View PropertyManager

The **Edit Color** button is used to modify the color of the preview of the section cap. However, the color of the section cap will be displayed only when the **Section View PropertyManager** is active. When you exit the **PropertyManager**, the color will not be displayed in the section view.

To create a half section view, you need to expand the **Section 2** rollout and specify the section plane in it. You can also specify the offset distance and the rotation of the plane in this rollout, as discussed earlier for **Section 1**. After setting all the parameters, choose the **OK** button from the **Section View PropertyManager**. Figure 8-74 shows the preview of the model after defining the second section plane.

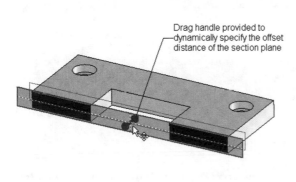

Drag handle provided to dynamically specify the offset distance of the section plane

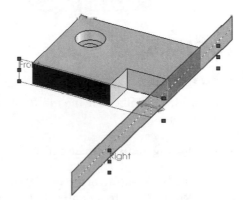

Figure 8-73 Drag handle for dynamically specifying the offset

Figure 8-74 Section preview after selecting the second section plane

You can also define the third section plane using the **Section 3** rollout. This rollout is displayed only if you expand the **Section 2** rollout. The **Show section cap** check box is selected by default. If you clear this check box, the preview of the section view will not be capped. Figure 8-75 shows the section view of a model.

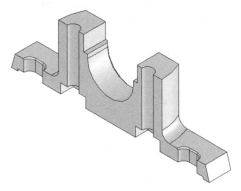

Figure 8-75 *Section view of a model*

You can save the sectioned view and retrieve it later at any stage during the design cycle. To save a sectioned view, choose the **Save** button from the **Section View PropertyManager**; the **Save As** dialog box will be displayed. Specify the name of the view and choose the **OK** button from this dialog box. On invoking the **Orientation** dialog box, you can notice that the saved section view will be listed along with the default views.

Tip. *To switch back to the full view mode, you need to choose the **Section View** button from the **Heads-up View** toolbar. You can also select any face of the sectioned model and then right-click to invoke the shortcut menu. Choose the **Section View** option from the shortcut menu; you will be switched back to the full view mode.*

*To modify the section view, select any face of the sectioned model and invoke the shortcut menu. Choose the **Section View Properties** option from it; the **Section View PropertyManager** will be displayed and you can modify the section view.*

TUTORIALS

Tutorial 1

In this tutorial, you will create the model shown in Figure 8-76. The dimensions of the model are shown in Figure 8-77.   **(Expected time: 30 min)**

The following steps are required to complete this tutorial:

a.   Create the base feature of the model by extruding a rectangle of 69 mm x 45 mm, created on the Right Plane to a depth of 10 mm, refer to Figure 8-78.
b.   Create the second feature, which is created by extruding the sketch created on the back face of the base feature, refer to Figure 8-79.
c.   The third feature of the model is a circular feature, refer to Figure 8-80.

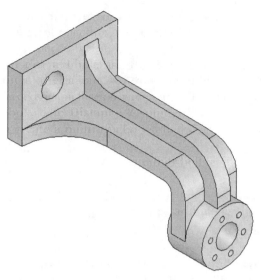

Figure 8-76 Solid model for Tutorial 1

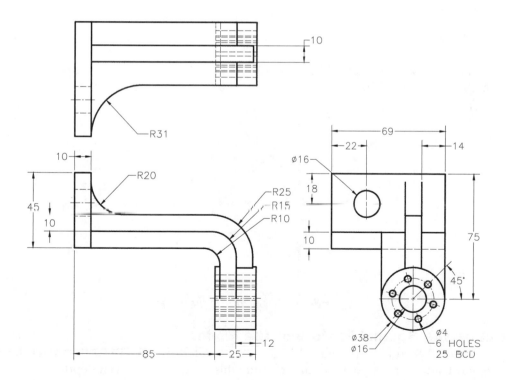

Figure 8-77 Views and dimensions of the model for Tutorial 1

d. Create a hole feature placed concentric to the circular feature.
e. Create a hole on the specified BCD and pattern the hole feature using the circular pattern option.
f. Create a hole feature on the base feature, refer to Figure 8-81.
g. Create a fillet feature to add the required fillets, refer to Figures 8-80 and 8-83.
h. Create a rib feature, refer to Figures 8-84 and 8-85.

Creating the Base Feature

1. Start SolidWorks and then start a new part document from the **New SolidWorks Document** dialog box.

   It is evident from the model that the sketch of its base feature is drawn on the Right Plane. Therefore, you need to select the **Right Plane** from the **FeatureManager design tree** to create the base feature.

2. Select the **Right Plane** from the **FeatureManager design tree** and choose the **Extruded Boss/Base** button from the **Features CommandManager**; the sketching environment is invoked and the **Right Plane** is oriented normal to the view.

3. Draw the sketch of the base feature of the model, which consists of a rectangle having dimensions 69 mm x 45 mm.

4. Add the required relations and dimensions to the sketch. Exit the sketching environment.

5. Set the value of the **Depth** spinner to **10 mm** and exit the **Extrude PropertyManager**. The base feature of the model is created, as shown in Figure 8-78.

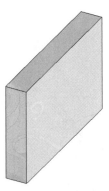

Figure 8-78 *Base feature of the model*

Creating the Second Feature of the Model

The second feature of the model is also an extruded feature. Draw the sketch for the second feature on its front face and extrude this sketch to the given depth.

1. Choose the **Rapid Sketch** button from the **Sketch CommandManager**, if it is not chosen by default.

2. Choose the **Line** tool and move the cursor on the back face of the base feature; the sketch plane is displayed in the temporary graphics. Select the back face to invoke the sketching environment.

3. Draw the sketch of the second feature, add the required relations and dimensions. Then exit the sketching environment.

Note

*Before drawing a sketch, make sure that the **Rapid Sketch** button is chosen, so that you can sketch the profile on the existing plane or face without actually selecting it.*

4. Choose the **Extruded Boss/Base** tool and select the **Reverse Direction** button from the **Extrude PropertyManager**.

5. Set the value of the **Depth** spinner to **38** and end the feature creation.

The model after creating the second feature is shown in Figure 8-79.

Creating the Third Feature

The third feature of this model is a circular extruded feature. The sketch for this feature is drawn on the right planar face of the second feature and extruded on both sides of the sketching plane.

1. Choose the **Circle** tool and select the right planar face of the second feature. As the **Rapid Sketch** button is already chosen, the sketching environment will be displayed automatically.

2. Draw the sketch using the **Circle** tool. Add the required relations and dimensions to it.

3. Invoke the **Extruded Boss/Base** tool and set the value of the **Depth** spinner in the **Direction 1** rollout to **12**. Since you have to extrude the sketch in both the directions with variable values, you need to invoke the **Direction 2** rollout. Set the value of the **Depth** spinner available in the **Direction 2** rollout to **13**, and end the feature creation. Figure 8-80 shows the model, after adding the third feature.

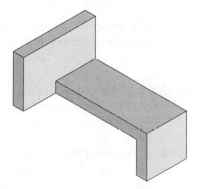

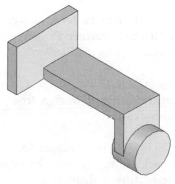

Figure 8-79 Second feature added to the model   *Figure 8-80* Third feature added to the model

Creating the Fourth Feature

The fourth feature of this model is a hole feature. You need to create a hole arbitrarily on the right face of the third feature using the **Simple Hole** option and position it later.

1. Select the right face of the third feature and choose the **Simple Hole** button from the **Features CommandManager**, or choose **Insert > Features > Hole > Simple** from the SolidWorks menus to invoke the **Hole PropertyManager**.

2. Select the **Up To Next** option from the **End Condition** drop-down list and set the value of the **Hole Diameter** spinner to **16**.

3. Choose the **OK** button from the **Hole PropertyManager**; the hole feature is placed arbitrarily on the selected face.

    Now, you need to position the hole feature concentric to the circular feature.

4. Select the hole feature from the **FeatureManager design tree**; a pop-up toolbar will be displayed.

5. Choose **Edit Sketch**; the sketching environment is displayed.

6. Apply **Concentric** relation between the circle and the circular edge of the face.

7. Press CTRL+B on the keyboard to rebuild the model; the hole feature is positioned.

Creating the Fifth Feature

1. Use the procedure given in the previous section to create the fifth feature, which is also a hole feature placed on the same placement plane. The hole feature is created using the **Through All** option, with the diameter of the hole as 4 mm. Next, define the placement of the feature by adding the required relations and dimensions to it.

Patterning the Hole Feature

After creating the fifth feature, which is a hole feature, you will pattern it using the **Circular Pattern** tool.

1. Choose **Linear Pattern > Circular Pattern** from the **Features CommandManager**; the **Circular Pattern PropertyManager** is invoked and you are prompted to select the features to pattern.

2. Select the hole feature created in the previous step from the drawing area, or expand the **FeatureManager design tree**, which is displayed in the drawing area, and select the **Hole2** feature.

3. Left-click on the **Pattern Axis** selection box in the **Circular Pattern PropertyManager** and select the circular edge of the hole feature; the preview of the circular pattern of the hole feature is displayed.

4.   Select the **Equal spacing** check box, if it is not selected and set the value in the **Number of Instances** spinner to **6**. Choose the **OK** button from the **PropertyManager**.

Creating the Hole Feature

1.   The next feature to be created is also a hole feature. You will create this hole feature using the procedure given to create the fourth feature. This hole feature will be placed on the right planar face of the base feature. Therefore, after selecting the right planar face of the base feature, place the hole feature. Next, define the placement of the hole feature by adding the required relations and dimensions. Figure 8-81 shows the model after adding all hole features.

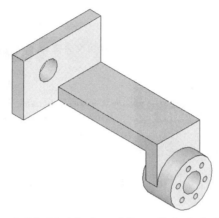

Figure 8-81 Model after adding all the hole features

Creating the Fillet Feature

Next, you need to create the fillet feature. It is evident from the model that the fillets to be added to the model are of different radii. In SolidWorks, you can specify different radii to the individual selected edges, faces, or loops in a single fillet feature.

1.   Choose the **Fillet** button from the **Features CommandManager**; the **Fillet PropertyManager** is displayed. If the **FilletXpert PropertyManager** is displayed, choose the **Manual** button from it to display the **Fillet PropertyManager**.

2.   Select the **Multiple radius fillet** check box from the **Items To Fillet** rollout in the **Fillet PropertyManager**.

3.   Select the edges to be filleted, as shown in Figure 8-82. As the **Multiple radius fillet** check box is selected, each selected edge has a separate **Radius** callout.

4.   Modify the values of the radii, as required in their respective **Radius** callouts.

5.   Choose the **OK** button from the **Fillet PropertyManager**.

The isometric view of the model, after adding the fillet feature, is shown in Figure 8-83.

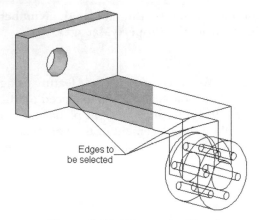

Figure 8-82 *Edges to be filleted*   *Figure 8-83* *Model after adding the fillet feature*

Creating the Rib Feature

The next feature that you need to create is a rib feature. The sketch of the rib feature needs to be drawn on a sketching plane at an offset distance from the back planar face of the model. Therefore, first you need to create a reference plane at an offset distance from the back planar face of the model.

1. Choose **Reference Geometry > Planes** from the **Features CommandManager** to invoke the **Plane PropertyManager**.

2. Rotate the model and select its back planar face. Choose the **Reverse direction** check box below the **Distance** spinner and set the value in the **Distance** spinner to **19**.

3. Choose the **OK** button from the **Plane PropertyManager** to end the feature creation; a new plane is created at an offset distance from the back planar face of the model.

4. Choose the **Rib** button from the **Features CommandManager**.

5. Create the sketch for the rib feature on the newly created plane and add the required relations and dimensions to the sketch, as shown in Figure 8-84.

6. Exit the sketching environment; the **Rib PropertyManager** is displayed.

    The preview of the rib feature is displayed in the drawing area and you will observe that the direction of material addition is displayed by an arrow in the drawing area. The direction of material addition is opposite to the required direction. Therefore, you need to flip its direction.

7. Select the **Flip material side** check box to flip the direction of the material addition.

    The default value of the rib thickness is **10**, which is the required value. So, you do not need to change it.

8. Choose **OK** from the **Rib PropertyManager**. Also, hide the newly created plane.

The last feature of the model is the fillet feature. Add the fillet feature on the left edge of the rib using the **Fillet** tool. Figure 8-85 shows the isometric view of the final model.

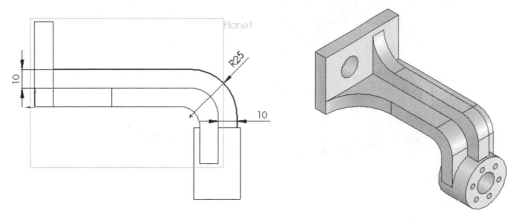

Figure 8-84 *Sketch for the rib feature*   *Figure 8-85* *The final solid model*

Saving the Model

1. Create a *c08* folder in the *SolidWorks* folder and choose the **Save** button from the Menu Bar. Save the model with the name and location given below:

    \My Documents\SolidWorks\c08\c08tut1.sldprt

2. Choose **File** > **Close** from the SolidWorks menus to close the document.

Tutorial 2

In this tutorial, you will create the model shown in Figure 8-86. The dimensions of the model are shown in Figure 8-87.   **(Expected time: 30 min)**

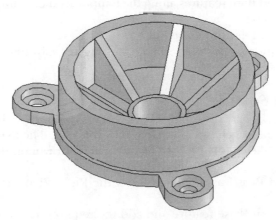

Figure 8-86 *Model for Tutorial 2*

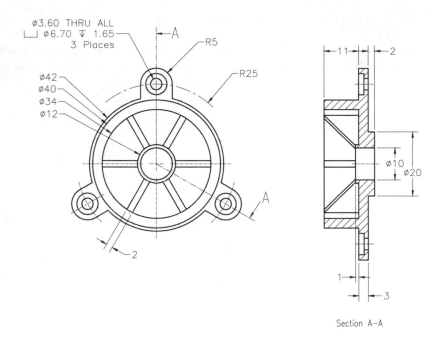

Figure 8-87 *Front view and aligned section view with dimensions*

The following steps are required to complete this tutorial:

a. Create the base feature of the model by revolving the sketch along a centerline, refer to Figures 8-88 and 8-89.
b. Create the second feature by extruding the sketch from the sketch plane to the selected surface, refer to Figures 8-90 through 8-93.
c. Place a counterbore hole feature on the top face of the second feature using the **Hole Wizard** tool.
d. Pattern the second and third features along the temporary axis using the **Circular Pattern** tool, refer to Figure 8-94.
e. Create the rib feature, refer to Figure 8-95.
f. Pattern the rib feature along a temporary axis using the **Circular Pattern** tool, refer to Figure 8-96.

Creating the Base Feature

Start a new SolidWorks part document. First you need to create the base feature of the model by revolving the sketch along the axis of revolution. The axis of revolution will be a centerline and the sketch for the base feature will be drawn on the Right Plane.

1. Invoke the **Revolved Boss/Base** tool and select the Right Plane as the sketching plane.

2. Create the sketch for the base feature and add the required relations and dimensions to the sketch, as shown in Figure 8-88.

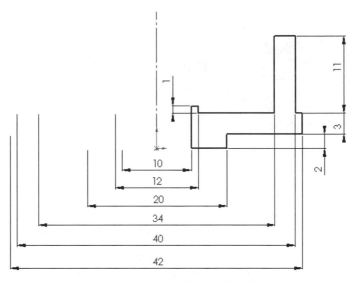

Figure 8-88 *Sketch for the base feature*

3. Exit the sketching environment and set the value in the **Angle** spinner to **360**.

4. Choose the **OK** button from the **Revolve PropertyManager**; the base feature is created as shown in Figure 8-89.

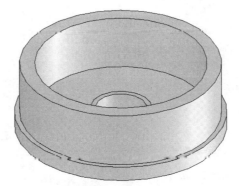

Figure 8-89 *Base feature of the model*

Creating the Second Feature

The second feature is created by extruding the sketch up to the selected surface.

1. Invoke the **Extruded Boss/Base** tool and select the face, as shown in Figure 8-90 as the sketching plane.

2. Create the sketch of the second feature and add the required relations and dimensions to it, as shown in Figure 8-91.

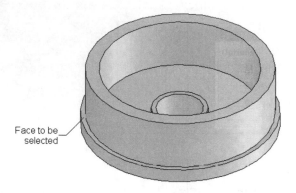

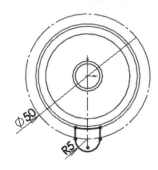

Figure 8-90 *Face to be selected*

Figure 8-91 *Sketch created for the second feature*

3. Exit the sketching environment. Use the **Up To Surface** option to extrude the sketch. The surface to be selected is shown in Figure 8-92.

4. Choose the **OK** button from the **Extrude PropertyManager**; the second feature is created, as shown in Figure 8-93.

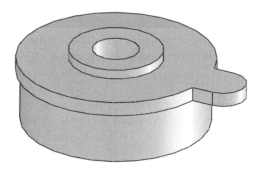

Figure 8-92 *Surface to be selected*

Figure 8-93 *Second feature created*

Creating the Hole Feature

It is evident from Figure 8-87 that a counterbore hole needs to be added to the model by using the **Hole Wizard** tool. Before invoking this tool, select the placement plane for the hole feature.

1. Select the top face of the second feature as the placement plane for the hole feature and press **S** on the keyboard; a pop-up toolbar is displayed.

2. Choose **Hole Wizard** from the pop-up toolbar to invoke the **Hole Specification PropertyManager**.

The preview of the hole feature with the default settings in the **Hole Specification PropertyManager** is displayed in the drawing area.

3. Choose the **Counterbore** button from the **Hole Type** rollout, if it is not chosen by default. Select the **Ansi Metric** option from the **Standard** drop-down list.

4. Select the **Socket Button Head Cap Screw - ANSI B18.3.4M** option from the **Type** drop-down list to specify the type of screw.

5. Select the **M3** option from the **Size** drop-down list to specify the size of the fastener to be used in the hole.

6. Choose the **Positions** tab from the **Hole Specification PropertyManager**; you will be prompted to use dimensions and other sketching tools to position the center of the holes.

7. Choose **Display/Delete Relation > Add Relation** from the **Sketch CommandManager** and apply a concentric relation between the center point of the hole feature and the circular edge of the second feature.

8. Choose **OK** from the **Hole Specification PropertyManager** to end the feature creation.

Patterning the Features

After creating the second and third features, you need to pattern them using the **Circular Pattern** tool.

1. Choose **Linear Pattern > Circular Pattern** from the **Features CommandManager** to invoke the **Circular Pattern PropertyManager**.

2. Select the second and third features from the drawing area or from the **FeatureManager design tree** that is displayed in the drawing area.

3. Left-click on the **Pattern Axis** selection box in the **Circular Pattern PropertyManager** and select the circular edge of the base feature; the preview of the circular pattern of the hole feature is displayed.

4. Set the value in the **Number of Instances** spinner to **3** and make sure the **Equal spacing** check box is selected. Clear the **Geometry pattern** check box from the **Options** rollout, if it is selected.

5. Choose the **OK** button from the **Circular Pattern PropertyManager**; the features are patterned, as shown in Figure 8-94.

Creating the Rib Feature

The next feature is a rib. The sketch for the rib feature will be created on the Front Plane.

1. Choose the **Rib** button from the **Features CommandManager** and select the **Front Plane** from the **FeatureManager design tree**.

2. Set the display model to wireframe, create the sketch for the rib feature, and add the required relations, as shown in Figure 8-95.

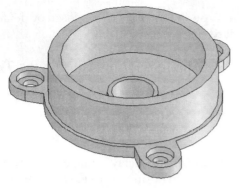

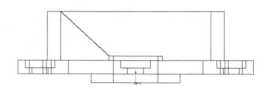

Figure 8-94 *Model after patterning the features*   **Figure 8-95** *Sketch for the rib feature*

3. Exit the sketching environment and set the value of the **Rib Thickness** spinner to **2**. Reverse the direction of material, if required using the **Flip material side** check box. Use the default values for other options and choose the **OK** button from the **Rib PropertyManager**.

4. Change the model display mode to shaded with edges.

5. Use the **Circular Pattern** tool to create six instances of the rib feature. The final model, after creating all features, is shown in Figure 8-96.

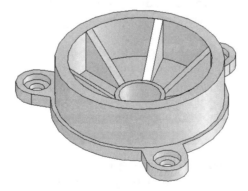

Figure 8-96 *Final solid model*

Saving the Model

1. Save the model in the *c08* folder with the name and location given below:

   \My Documents\SolidWorks\c08\c08tut2.sldprt

2. Choose **File > Close** from the SolidWorks menus to close the document.

Tutorial 3

In this tutorial, you will create the cylinder head of a two-stroke automobile engine. The dimensions of the model are shown in Figure 8-97. The model is shown in Figure 8-98. You will also create a section view of the model using the **Section View** tool.

(Expected time: 1 hr)

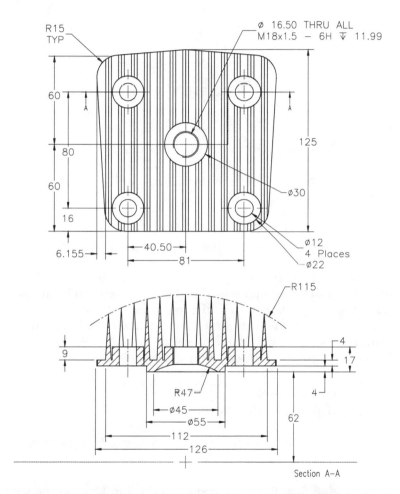

Figure 8-97 *Top view and the section front view with dimensions*

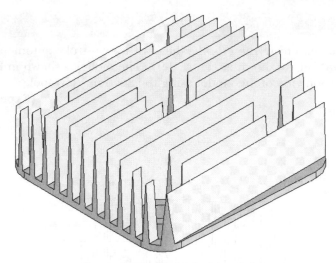

Figure 8-98 *Model for Tutorial 3*

The following steps are required to complete this tutorial:

a. Create the base feature of the model by extruding a polygon to the given depth, refer to Figure 8-99.
b. Add a fillet to the base feature.
c. Create a circular feature at the bottom face of the base feature.
d. Create the revolve cut feature to create the dome of the cylinder head, refer to Figures 8-100 and 8-101.
e. Create the left fin of the cylinder head by extruding the sketch. The sketch for this feature should be carefully dimensioned and defined, refer to Figure 8-102.
f. Use the **Vary sketch** option to pattern the fins, refer to Figure 8-103.
g. Create other cut and extrude features to complete the model, refer to Figure 8-104.
h. Create a tap hole using the hole wizard, refer to Figure 8-105.
i. Create the section view of the model, refer to Figure 8-106.

Creating the Base Feature

1. Create a new SolidWorks part document.

    The base feature of the model will be created by extruding the sketch created on the Top plane.

2. Invoke the **Extruded Boss/Base** tool and select the Top Plane as the sketching plane.

3. Create the sketch for the base feature and add the required relations and dimensions to the sketch, as shown in Figure 8-99.

4. Exit the sketching environment and extrude the sketch to a depth of 4 mm.

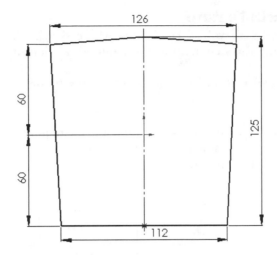

Figure 8-99 *Sketch for the base feature*

Creating the Second Feature

The second feature of the model is a fillet feature. You need to fillet all the vertical edges of the base feature using the given radius.

1. Invoke the **Fillet** tool and choose the **FilletXpert** button to display the **FilletXpert PropertyManager**.

2. Choose one of the vertical edges and do not move the mouse; a pop-up toolbar is displayed.

3. Choose the **Connected to start face, 4 edges** button from the pop-up toolbar; all the vertical edges of the base feature are selected.

4. Set the value in the **Radius** spinner to **15**.

5. Choose the **OK** button from the **FilletXpert PropertyManager**; the fillets are created.

Creating the Third Feature

After creating the base feature and adding fillet at its vertical edges, you will create the third feature of the model, which is a circular extruded feature. The sketch of the feature will be drawn on the bottom face of the base feature and it will be extruded to the given depth.

1. Select the bottom face of the base feature as the sketching plane and press S on the keyboard. Invoke the **Extruded Boss/Base** tool from the pop-up toolbar.

2. Create a circle of 55 mm diameter with its center point at the origin.

3. Exit the sketching environment and extrude the sketch to a depth of 4 mm.

Creating the Fourth Feature

The fourth feature is a revolved cut feature whose sketch will be drawn on the Front Plane. After drawing the sketch, apply the required relations and dimensions to it.

1. Invoke the **Revolved Cut** tool and select the **Front Plane** from the **FeatureManager design tree**.

2. Draw the sketch for the revolved cut feature and add the required relations and dimensions, as shown in Figure 8-100. You need to apply the vertical relation between the center point of the arc and the origin to fully define it.

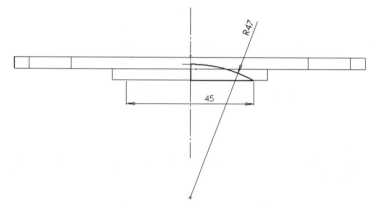

Figure 8-100 Sketch for the revolved cut feature

Note

When you draw a sketch for the revolved cut feature for this tutorial, draw a horizontal centerline, such that the start point of the centerline is merged with the upper endpoint of the arc. Also, ensure that the tangent relation exists between the arc and the centerline to maintain the tangency of the arc.

3. Select the vertical centerline and exit the sketching environment. Make sure that the value in the **Angle** spinner is **360**.

4. Choose the **OK** button from the **Cut-Revolve PropertyManager**.

The rotated model, after creating the fourth feature, is shown in Figure 8-101.

Creating the Fifth Feature

Next, you will create the left fin of the cylinder head. It will be created by extruding a sketch in both the directions using the **Through All** option. The sketch of this feature, drawn on the Front Plane, will be dimensioned and defined such that the length of the fin is driven by a construction arc and a horizontal dimension. The detailed step by step procedure of drawing, dimensioning, and defining the sketch is discussed next.

Figure 8-101 *Cut revolve feature added to the model*

1. Invoke the **Extruded Boss/Base** tool and select the **Front Plane** from the **FeatureManager design tree**.

2. Use the **Line** tool to draw the triangle and then draw a vertical centerline that passes through the upper vertex to the triangle, refer to Figure 8-102.

3. Invoke the **3 Point Arc** tool and draw the arc, as shown in Figure 8-102. Select the arc and select the **For construction** check box from the **Options** rollout of the **Arc PropertyManager**.

4. Invoke the **Add Relations PropertyManager** and add the coincident relation between the upper vertex of the triangle and the centerline.

5. Add the midpoint relation between the lower endpoint of the centerline and the horizontal line of the triangle. Make sure that the **Coincident** relation exists between the upper vertex of the triangle and the centerline. Also, add the vertical relation to the centerline, if it is missing.

6. Add the coincident relation between the upper vertex of the triangle and the arc.

7. Add the required dimensions and relations to fully define the sketch, as shown in Figure 8-102.

 Tip. *It is evident from Figure 8-102 that one of the horizontal dimensions is 6.155. By default, the primary unit precision is set to two decimal places. Therefore, for defining a dimension value with more number of decimal places, you need to select the dimension and set the precision value to the required decimal places from the **Primary Unit Precision** drop-down list of the **Dimension PropertyManager**.*

8. Exit the sketching environment and extrude the sketch in both the directions using the **Mid Plane** option and enter the value **130** in the **Depth** spinner. Choose the **OK** button from the **PropertyManager**. You will notice that the fin extends out of the base feature at both the ends. You will learn how to remove the unwanted material of the fin later in this tutorial.

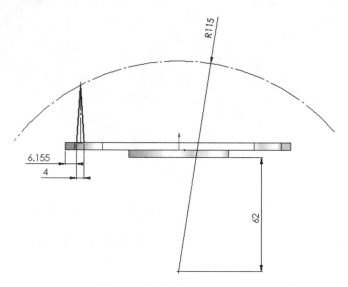

Figure 8-102 Sketch for the fin of the cylinder head

Patterning the Fifth Feature

You will pattern the fin using the **Vary sketch** option from the **Linear Pattern** tool. On using the **Vary sketch** option, the geometry of each instance of the pattern varies according to the driven dimension and the relation added to the sketch of the feature to be patterned.

1. Select the fifth feature, if it is not already selected and choose the **Linear Pattern** button from the **Features CommandManager** to invoke the **Linear Pattern PropertyManager**.

   You are prompted to select the directional reference.

2. Select the horizontal dimension with the value of 6.155 as the directional reference from the drawing area.

3. Set the value of the **Spacing** spinner to **9**. Set the value of the **Number of Instances** spinner to **13**. Choose the **Reverse Direction** button, if required.

4. Expand the **Options** rollout and clear the **Geometry Pattern** check box.

5. Select the **Vary sketch** check box from this rollout; the preview of the pattern is not displayed in the drawing area.

6. Choose the **OK** button from the **Linear Pattern PropertyManager**.

   The model, after adding the pattern feature, is shown in Figure 8-103.

Creating the Cut Feature

The next feature that you will create is a cut feature. Rotate the solid model using the **Rotate View** tool. You will observe that the fins of the cylinder head that you patterned in

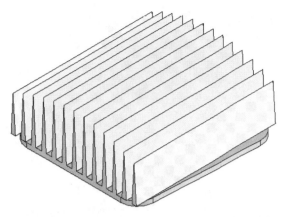

Figure 8-103 *Model after patterning the fin of the cylinder head*

the last feature extend beyond the boundary of the base feature. Therefore, to trim the extended portion of the fins, you need to create a cut feature.

1. Select the top planar face of the base feature as the sketching plane and press S on the keyboard. Invoke the **Extruded Cut** tool from the pop-up toolbar.

2. Draw the sketch using the standard sketch tools. The sketch for this feature will be the outer profile of the base feature.

 Tip. *You can draw the outer profile of the base feature using the **Convert Entities** tool. To do so, select the lower flat face of the base feature and choose the **Convert Entities** button from the **Sketch** toolbar. You will notice that the sketch similar to the outer boundary of the base feature will be placed on the sketching plane.*

3. Exit the sketching environment and choose the **Reverse Direction** button from the **Direction 1** rollout and select the **Through All** option from the **End Condition** drop-down list.

    Since the direction of the side from which the material is to be removed is opposite to the required direction, therefore, you need to flip the direction of material removal.

4. Select the **Flip side to cut** check box from the **Direction 1** rollout and choose the **OK** button from the **Extrude PropertyManager**.

5. Use the **Extruded Cut** and **Extruded Boss/Base** tools to create the model, as shown in Figure 8-104.

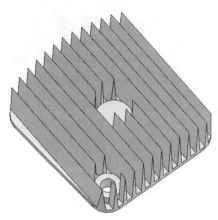

Figure 8-104 *Model after adding other extrude*
and cut features

Patterning the Remaining Features

After creating all the features, you need to pattern the cut, extrude, and hole features created at the lower left corner of the model.

1. Invoke the **Linear Pattern PropertyManager** and select the cut, extrude, and hole features created on the lower left corner of the model.

2. Select the two directional references to pattern the features in both the directions and set the values of the distances between the instances and the number of instances, refer to Figure 8-97.

3. Choose the **OK** button from the **Linear Pattern PropertyManager**.

Creating a Tapped Hole

The last feature of the model is a hole feature. You will create a tapped hole using the **Hole Wizard** tool and then specify the location of the hole.

1. Select the top face of the middle circular extrude feature as the plane for the hole feature.

2. Invoke the **Hole Specification PropertyManager** by choosing the **Hole Wizard** button from the **Features CommandManager**. Choose the **Tap** button from the **Hole Type** rollout. Select **ANSI Metric** from the **Standard** drop-down list.

3. Select the **M18x1.5** option from the **Size** drop-down list to define the size of the tap hole.

4. Select the **Through All** option from the **End Condition** drop-down list in the **End Condition** rollout. Also, select the **Through All** option from the **Thread** drop-down list.

5. Choose the **Cosmetic thread** button from the **Options** rollout. Also, select the **With thread callout** check box.

6. Choose the **Position** tab from the **Hole Specification PropertyManager**.

The tapped hole will be placed by default on the placement plane. This default location is not the required position to place the hole. You need to relocate the tapped hole concentric with the center circular feature.

7. Invoke the **Add Relations PropertyManager** and add the **Concentric** relation between the center point of the tapped hole and the circular extruded feature of diameter 30 mm.

Tip. *If the graphic thread is not displayed in the tapped hole, invoke the **Document Properties - Detailing** dialog box. Choose the **Annotations Display** subnode and select the **Shaded cosmetic threads** check box.*

On orienting the model in the top view, you will observe that the thread convention is visible. However, on orienting the model in the front, back, right, or left views, you can view the side convention of the thread.

*You can also hide the cosmetic thread. To do so, move the cursor on the cosmetic thread; the cosmetic thread cursor will be displayed. Select the cosmetic thread; a pop-up toolbar is displayed. Choose **Hide** to hide the cosmetic thread.*

8. Choose the **OK** button from the **Hole Specification PropertyManager** to end the tapped hole feature creation. The rotated final model is shown in Figure 8-105.

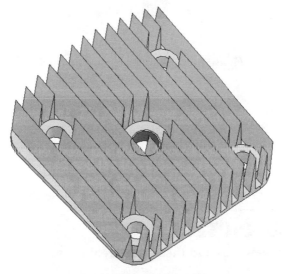

Figure 8-105 Final solid model

Displaying the Section View of the Model

Next, you will display the section view of the model. The section view of the model is created using the **Section View PropertyManager**.

1. Orient the model to the isometric view.

2. Choose the **Section View** button from the **Heads-Up View** toolbar.

    By default, the **Front** view is selected as the section plane in the **Section View PropertyManager**. The preview of the section view, using the **Front Plane** as the section plane, is displayed in the drawing area.

3. Choose the **OK** button from the **Section View PropertyManager** to display the section view of the model.

    The section view of the model is shown in Figure 8-106.

4. Choose the **Section View** button again from the **Heads-Up View** toolbar to return to the full view mode.

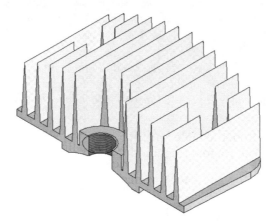

Figure 8-106 *Section view of the model*

Saving the Model

1. Save the model in the *c08* folder with the name given below.

    \My Documents\SolidWorks\c08\c08tut3.sldprt

2. Choose **File > Close** from the SolidWorks menus to close the document.

SELF-EVALUATION TEST

Answer the following questions and then compare them to those given at the end of this chapter:

1. To invoke the **Mirror PropertyManager**, choose **View > Pattern/Mirror > Mirror** from the SolidWorks menus. (T/F)

2. If you modify the parent feature, then the same change will not be reflected in the mirrored feature. (T/F)

3. You cannot preselect the mirror plane and the feature to be patterned before invoking the **Mirror** tool. (T/F)

4. You can mirror a single face using the **Mirror** tool. (T/F)

5. You can pattern a patterned feature. (T/F)

6. The _____ **PropertyManager** is used to view the section view.

7. A _____ is provided in the drawing area to adjust the offset distance of the section plane dynamically.

8. The _____ option is used to create a pattern by specifying the coordinates.

9. The _____ option is used to create a pattern with respect to the sketched points.

10. The _____ rollout is used to delete the pattern instances.

REVIEW QUESTIONS

Answer the following questions:

1. The _____ check box is used to accommodate all instances of a pattern along the selected curve.

2. Enter the coordinates for creating the instances in the _____ area of the **Table Driven Pattern** dialog box.

3. You need to invoke the _____ to create a rib feature.

4. The _____ check box is used to transfer the visual properties assigned to the feature or the parent body to the mirrored instance.

5. Select the _____ check box from the **Section View PropertyManager** to create a section using an invisible plane normal to the eye view as the section plane.

6. Which **PropertyManager** is displayed, when you choose the **Mirror** button from the **Features** tool?

    (a) **Mirror Feature PropertyManager**   (b) **Mirror All PropertyManager**
    (c) **Mirror PropertyManager**   (d) **Copy/Mirror PropertyManager**

7. Which option is used to mirror the exact geometry of the feature independent of the relationships between the geometries?

    (a) **Same Mirror**   (b) **Geometry Pattern**
    (c) **Geometry Copy**   (d) **Copy Geometry**

8. Which pattern is created along the sketched lines, arcs, or splines?

    (a) Curve driven pattern   (b) Sketch driven pattern
    (c) Geometry driven pattern   (d) Linear pattern

9. Which dialog box is invoked to create a pattern by specifying the coordinate points?

    (a) **Sketch Driven Pattern**   (b) **Table Driven Pattern**
    (c) **Mirror**   (d) None of these

10. Which plane is selected by default when you invoke the **Section View PropertyManager** to view a section of the model?

    (a) **Right**   (b) **Top**
    (c) **Front**   (d) **Plane 1**

EXERCISES

Exercise 1

Create the model shown in Figure 8-107. The dimensions of the model are given in Figure 8-108.   **(Expected time: 1 hr)**

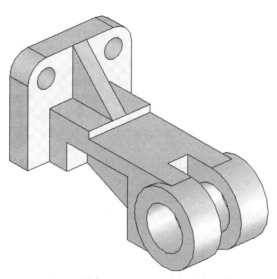

Figure 8-107 *Solid model for Exercise 1*

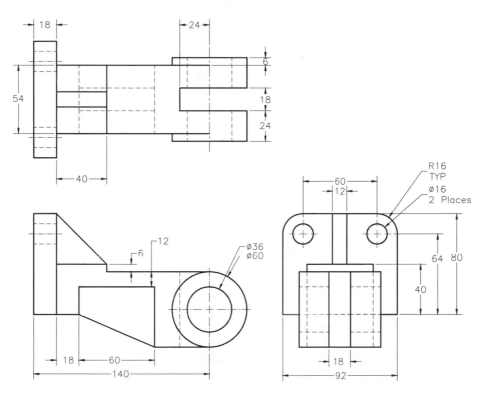

Figure 8-108 *Views and dimensions of the model for Exercise 1*

Exercise 2

Create the model shown in Figure 8-109. The dimensions of the model are given in Figure 8-110. **(Expected time: 1 hr)**

Figure 8-109 *Solid model for Exercise 2*

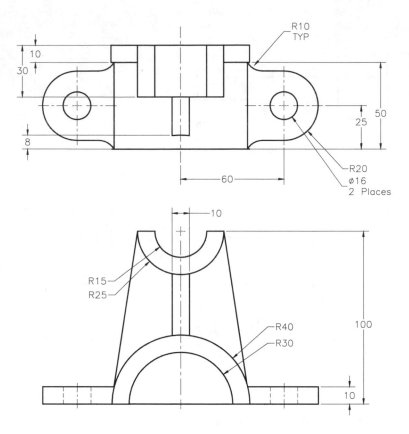

Figure 8-110 *Views and dimensions of the model for Exercise 2*

Exercise 3

Create the model shown in Figure 8-111. Next, create the section view of the model using the Right Plane. Figure 8-112 shows the section view of the model whose dimensions are given in Figure 8-113. **(Expected time: 45 min)**

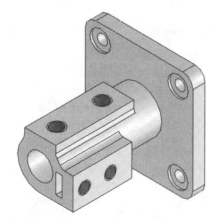

Figure 8-111 *Solid model for Exercise 3*

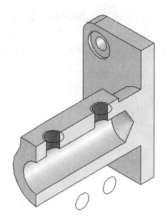

Figure 8-112 *Section view of the model*

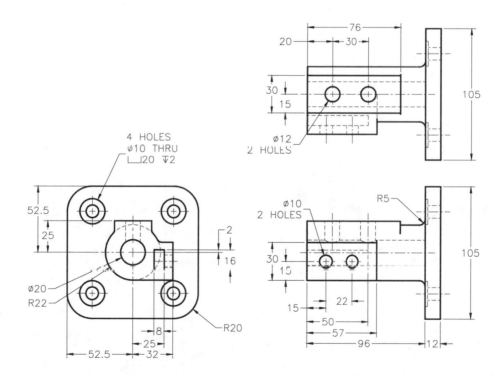

Figure 8-113 *Views and dimensions of the model for Exercise 3*

Answers to Self-Evaluation Test

1. F, **2.** F, **3.** F, **4.** F, **5.** T, **6. Section View**, **7.** drag handle, **8. Table Driven Pattern**, **9. Sketch Driven Pattern**, **10. Instances to Skip**

Chapter 9

Editing Features

Learning Objectives

After completing this chapter, you will be able to:

- *Edit features.*
- *Edit sketches of the sketch based features.*
- *Edit the sketch plane of the sketch based features.*
- *Edit features using the Move/Size Features option.*
- *Cut, copy, and paste features and sketches.*
- *Copy features using the drag and drop method.*
- *Delete features.*
- *Delete bodies.*
- *Suppress and unsuppress features.*
- *Move or copy bodies.*
- *Reorder features.*
- *Roll back the model.*
- *Rename features.*
- *Create folders.*
- *Use the What's Wrong functionality.*

EDITING FEATURES OF THE MODEL

Editing is one of the most important aspect of the product design cycle. Almost all designs require editing during or after their creation. As discussed earlier, SolidWorks is a feature-based parametric software. Therefore, the design created in SolidWorks is a combination of individual features integrated together to form a solid model. All these features can be edited individually.

For example, Figure 9-1 shows a base plate with some drilled holes. To replace the four drilled holes with four counterbore holes, you need to perform an editing operation. For editing the holes, you need to select the hole feature and right-click; the shortcut menu will be displayed. Choose **Edit Feature** from the shortcut menu to invoke the **Hole Specification PropertyManager**. Alternatively, select the hole feature and do not move the mouse; a pop-up toolbar will be displayed. Choose **Edit Feature** from the pop-up toolbar to display the **Hole Specification PropertyManager**. Set the new parameters in the **Hole Specification PropertyManager** and end the feature modification. The drilled holes will be automatically replaced by the counterbore holes, as shown in Figure 9-2.

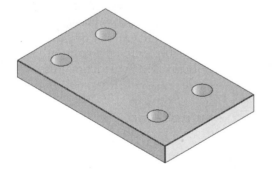
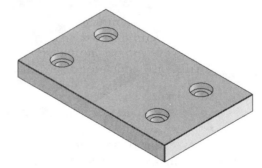

Figure 9-1 *Base plate with drilled holes*   *Figure 9-2* *Modified base plate with counterbore holes*

Similarly, you can also edit the reference geometry and the sketches of the sketch based features. When you modify the reference geometry, the feature created using the reference geometry is also modified. For example, if you create a feature on a plane at some angle and then edit the angle of the plane, the resulting feature will be automatically modified. In SolidWorks, you can perform editing tasks using various methods, which are discussed next.

Editing Using the Edit Feature Option

In SolidWorks, the **Edit Feature** option is the most commonly used method for editing. To edit a feature of the model using this option, select the feature from the **FeatureManager design tree** or from the drawing area. Next, right-click on it to invoke the shortcut menu and choose the **Edit Feature** option, as shown in Figure 9-3; a **PropertyManager** or dialog box will be invoked depending on the feature selected. Alternatively, select the feature and do not move the mouse; a pop-up toolbar will be displayed. Choose **Edit Feature** from the pop-up toolbar to display the **PropertyManager.** You can modify the parameters of that feature using the **PropertyManager**. The **PropertyManager** will also have the sequence number of the feature, as shown in Figure 9-4. After editing the parameters, choose the **OK** button to complete the feature creation; the feature will be modified automatically.

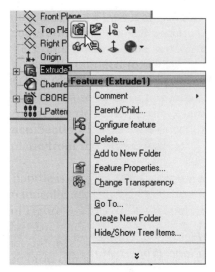

Figure 9-3 *Choosing the* **Edit Feature** *option from the shortcut menu*

Figure 9-4 *The partial view of the* **Extrude PropertyManager**

Editing Sketches of the Sketch Based Features

In SolidWorks, you can also edit the sketches of the sketch based features. To do so, select the feature from the **FeatureManager design tree** or from the drawing area and right-click to invoke the shortcut menu. Choose the **Edit Sketch** option from it; the sketching environment will be displayed. Alternatively, select the feature and do not move the mouse, a pop-up toolbar will be displayed. Choose **Edit Sketch** from the pop-up toolbar to display the sketching environment. Edit the sketch of the sketched feature using the sketching tools and exit the sketching environment. Choose CTRL+B to rebuild the model. You can also select the **Rebuild** button from the Menu Bar to exit the sketching environment and rebuild the model.

Tip. *You can also use the (+) sign available on the left of the sketched feature to expand the sketched feature in the **FeatureManager design tree**. The sketch icon will be displayed. Select the sketch icon and invoke the shortcut menu. Choose the **Edit Sketch** option from it to enter the sketching environment to edit the sketch.*

Changing the Sketch Plane of the Sketches

You can also change the sketch plane of the sketches of the sketch based features. To do so, expand the sketched feature by clicking on the (+) sign on its left in the **FeatureManager design tree**. Select the sketch icon in the **FeatureManager design tree**. Right-click to invoke the shortcut menu and choose the **Edit Sketch Plane** option from it, as shown in Figure 9-5. Alternatively, choose **Edit Sketch Plane** from the pop-up toolbar as discussed earlier.

On choosing the **Edit Sketch Plane** option, the **Sketch Plane PropertyManager** will be displayed, as shown in Figure 9-6. The name of the current sketch plane will be displayed in the **Sketch Plane/Face** selection box. Now, select any other plane or face as the sketching plane and choose **OK** from the **Sketch Plane PropertyManager**; the sketch plane will be modified.

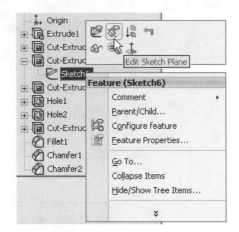

Figure 9-5 *Choosing the **Edit Sketch** **Plane** option from the shortcut menu*

Figure 9-6 *Partial view of the **Sketch** **Plane PropertyManager***

Tip. *While modifying the sketch plane, if you select a sketch plane on which the relations and dimensions do not find any reference to be placed, the **What's Wrong** dialog box will be displayed. So, you need to undo the last step. After this, invoke the **Sketch Plane PropertyManager** again and select an appropriate plane. You will learn more about the **What's Wrong** dialog box later in this chapter.*

Editing by Selecting an Entity or a Feature

You can also edit a feature, reference geometry, or a sketch by selecting the feature either from the **FeatureManager design tree** or from the drawing area. To do so, ensure that the **Instant 3D** tool is invoked and then left-click on a feature in the **FeatureManager design tree** or in the drawing area; all dimensions of the feature and the sketch used for creating it are displayed. Remember that the dimensions of the sketch will be displayed in black and the dimensions of the feature will be displayed in blue. Double-click on the dimension that you need to modify; the **Modify** dialog box will be invoked. Set the new value in the **Modify** dialog box and press the ENTER key or choose the **Save the current value and exit the dialog** button from the dialog box. You will notice that the value of the dimension is modified but the model is not modified with respect to the modified value. Therefore, you need to rebuild the model using the **Rebuild** option. To rebuild the model, choose the **Rebuild** button from the Menu Bar or press CTRL+B.

Editing Using the Instant3D Tool

| **CommandManager:** | Features > Instant3D |
| **Toolbar:** | Features > Instant3D |

In SolidWorks 2009, you can modify the feature and the sketch of the sketched feature dynamically without invoking the sketching environment. To edit the feature or its sketch, choose the **Instant3D** button from the **Features CommandManager**, if it is not chosen by default, and select any face of the feature to be modified in the drawing area; the selected face will be highlighted. Also, the handles to resize and relocate the feature will be displayed, as shown in Figure 9-7.

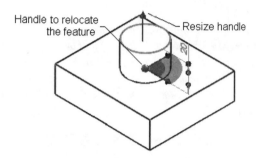

Figure 9-7 *Resize and relocate handles displayed on the selected feature*

To resize the feature, move the cursor to the resize handle, press and hold the left mouse button at this location and drag the cursor; a scale will be displayed. Drag the cursor further to resize the feature. You will notice that the feature is dynamically resized. Release the left mouse button after resizing the feature. Note that while dragging the cursor, if you move the cursor on the scale, the values will be integers. If you move the cursor away from the scale, the values will be rational numbers. Figure 9-8 shows the resize handle being dragged to resize the feature and Figure 9-9 shows the resulting feature.

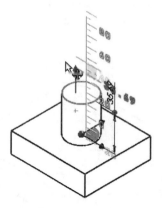

Figure 9-8 *Cursor dragging the resize handle to resize the feature*

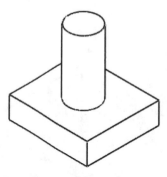

Figure 9-9 *Resulting feature*

To rotate the feature, move the cursor to the bubble on the handle and right-click; the shortcut menu will be displayed. Choose the **Show Rotate Handle** option; the cursor changes to the rotate cursor and a circular path will be displayed. Drag the cursor to rotate the feature. You can drag the cursor clockwise or counterclockwise. If you drag the cursor inside the circular path, you can rotate the model in multiples of 90-degree. However, if you drag the cursor outside the circular path, you can rotate the model at any angle. The feature will be rotated dynamically in the drawing area. Release the left mouse button after rotating the feature to a required angle.

Note
*If you rotate the sketched feature whose sketch is fully or partially defined using the relations and dimensions, the **Move Confirmation** dialog box will be displayed, as shown in Figure 9-10. This dialog box informs you that the external constraints in the feature are being moved and prompts whether you want to delete those constraints or keep them by recalculating or make them dangling. The relations or the dimensions that do not find the external reference after the placement are made dangling.*

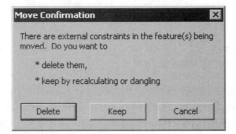

*Figure 9-10 The **Move Confirmation** dialog box*

While rotating the feature, if the **Move Confirmation** dialog box is displayed, you need to choose either the **Delete** or the **Keep** button, based on the geometric and dimensional conditions. Click anywhere in the drawing area to exit the rotate handle. Figure 9-11 shows the preview of the rotating feature. Figure 9-12 shows the resulting rotated feature.

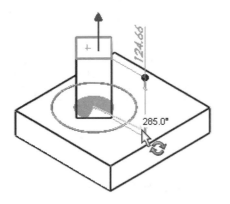

Figure 9-11 Preview of the feature being rotated

Figure 9-12 Resulting rotated feature

You can also change the placement plane or the sketch plane of the feature by choosing the bubble in the relocating handle. To do so, select a face of the feature and move the cursor to the bubble on the relocate handle. Press and hold the left mouse button on the bubble, drag the cursor and release the left mouse button on another face. If the feature has some external reference, the **Move Confirmation** dialog box will be displayed. Choose the appropriate button in this dialog box; the feature will be relocated. Figure 9-13 shows the feature being moved to another face. Figure 9-14 shows the resulting moved feature.

Tip. *In SolidWorks 2009, you can also modify the cut feature and the sketch of the cut feature dynamically, as you did for the extrude feature.*

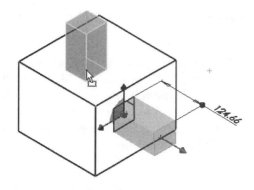

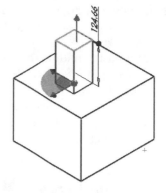

Figure 9-13 *The feature being moved*   ***Figure 9-14*** *Resulting moved feature*

To translate the feature on the same plane, select a face of the feature and move the cursor to the move handle. Press and hold the left mouse button on the arrow and drag the cursor.

You can also view the cross-section of a model without sectioning it. To view the cross-section of a model, choose the feature and right-click. Choose the **Live Section Plane** option from the shortcut menu; the rings and a section plane parallel to the selected face will be displayed. Move the cursor toward the red colored ring; the cursor will change to the rotate cursor. Press and hold the left mouse button and move the cursor along the red colored ring; the section plane will be rotated about the horizontal axis and you can view the cross-section at different angles. Similarly, move the cursor about the green colored ring to view the cross-section about the vertical axis. Select the vertical arrow inside the rings and drag the cursor to relocate the live section plane vertically upward or downward. Choose the cross mark on the section plane to exit the live section.

Editing Features and Sketches by Cut, Copy, and Paste

SolidWorks allows you to adapt the windows functionality of cut, copy, and paste to copy and paste the features and sketches. The method of using this functionality is the same as used in other windows-based applications. To cut a feature, select the feature to cut, and then choose **Edit > Cut** from the SolidWorks menus or use the shortcut keys, CTRL+X; the **Confirm Delete** dialog box will be displayed. Choose the **Yes** button from this dialog box; the selected feature will be cut, but the sketch will be still displayed in the plane. This is because when you cut the feature only the selected feature

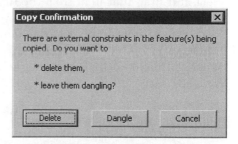

Figure 9-15 *The **Copy Confirmation** dialog box*

will be deleted from the document. You will learn more about deleting later in this chapter. After you cut a feature, select the placement plane or the placement reference to place the feature. Choose **Edit > Paste** from the SolidWorks menus or use the shortcut keys, CTRL+V. If you cut and paste a feature that has some external reference, the **Copy Confirmation** dialog box will be displayed, prompting you to delete the external constraints or leave them dangling, as shown in Figure 9-15. You need to choose the appropriate button to paste the feature.

If you copy and paste an item, the selected item will remain at its position and its copy will be pasted on the selected reference. To copy an item, select the feature or sketch. Choose **Edit > Copy** from the SolidWorks menus, or press CTRL+C. Select the reference where you want to paste the selected item and choose **Edit > Paste** from the SolidWorks menus, or press CTRL+V to paste it. You can paste the selected item any number of times. If you select another item and copy it on the clipboard, the last copied item will be deleted from the memory of the clipboard.

 Tip. *For pasting a sketched feature, a simple hole, or a hole created using the hole wizard, you have to select a plane or a planar face as the reference. For pasting chamfers and fillets, you have to select an edge, edges, or a face as the reference.*

Cutting, Copying, and Pasting Features and Sketches from One Document to the Other

You can also cut or copy the features and sketches from one document and paste them in another document. For example, if you need to copy a sketch created in the current document and paste it in a new document, then select the sketch and press CTRL+C to copy the item to the clipboard. Then, create a new document in the **Part** mode and select the plane on which you want to paste the sketch. Press CTRL+V to paste the sketch on the selected plane. Use the same procedure to copy features from one document to the other.

Copying Features Using Drag and Drop

SolidWorks also provides you with the drag and drop functionality of Windows to copy and paste the item within the document. Press and hold the CTRL key on the keyboard. Next, select and drag that item from the drawing area or from the **FeatureManager design tree**. Drag the cursor to a location where you want to paste the item and release the left mouse button. If the item to be pasted is defined using the dimensions or the relations, the **Copy Confirmation** dialog box will be displayed to delete or make those constraints dangle. Figure 9-16 shows the feature being dragged and Figure 9-17 shows the resulting pasted feature.

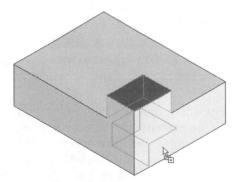

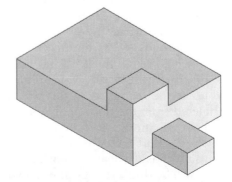

Figure 9-16 *Feature being dragged*   *Figure 9-17* *Resulting pasted feature*

Dragging and Dropping Features from One Document to the Other

You can also drag and drop features and sketches from one document to the other. To do so, you should open both the documents in the SolidWorks session. Choose **Windows > Tile Vertical/Tile Horizontal** from the SolidWorks menus; both the documents are displayed at the same time in the SolidWorks window. Press and hold the CTRL key on the keyboard. Select the feature or the sketch in the **Feature Manager design tree** in one document, drag and place it on the other document on the required entity, as shown in Figure 9-18. Note that you cannot drag and drop the base feature.

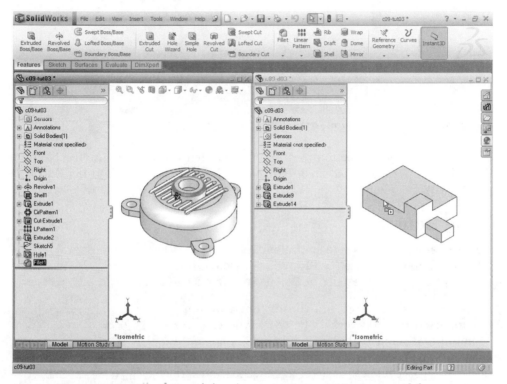

Figure 9-18 Fillet feature being dragged to be pasted in the second document

Deleting Features

You can delete the unwanted features from the model by selecting the feature from the **FeatureManager design tree** or from the drawing area. After selecting the feature to be deleted, choose the DELETE key on the keyboard, or right-click to invoke the shortcut menu and choose **Delete** from the **Feature** area; the **Confirm Delete** dialog box will be displayed, as shown in Figure 9-19. The features that are dependent on the feature to be deleted are also displayed in the **Confirm Delete** dialog box, which informs you that all the dependent features of the parent feature will also be deleted. If the **Also delete all child features** check box is selected, all the child features related to the parent feature will be also deleted. But when you delete a sketched feature, the sketches related to it will not be deleted. These sketches are known as absorbed features. To delete the absorbed features along with the parent feature, select the **Also delete absorbed features** check box from the **Confirm Delete**

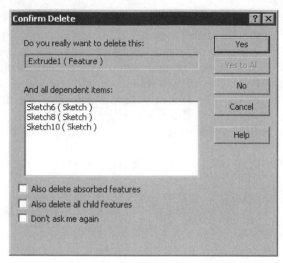

Figure 9-19 The **Confirm Delete** dialog box

dialog box. Choose the **Yes** button to delete the selected features, choose the **No** button to cancel the delete operation. You can also delete a selected feature by choosing **Edit** > **Delete** from the SolidWorks menus.

Deleting Bodies

CommandManager:	Features > Delete Solid/Surface *(Customize to add)*
SolidWorks menus:	Insert > Features > Delete Body
Toolbar:	Features > Delete Solid/Surface *(Customize to add)*

As discussed earlier, multibody environment is supported in SolidWorks. Therefore, you can create multiple disjoint bodies in SolidWorks. You can also delete the unwanted bodies. The bodies to be deleted can be solid bodies or surface bodies. To delete a body, choose **Insert** > **Features** > **Delete Body** from the SolidWorks menus. You can also invoke this tool by choosing the **Delete Solid/Surface** button from the **Features CommandManager** after customizing the **CommandManager**; the **Delete Body PropertyManager** will be displayed, as shown in Figure 9-20. You are also prompted to select the solid and/or surface bodies to be deleted.

Figure 9-20 The Delete Body PropertyManager

Select the body or the bodies to be deleted from the drawing area or from the **Solid Bodies** folder available in the **FeatureManager design tree**, which is displayed in the drawing area; the selected body will be displayed in blue and its name will be displayed in the **Solid/Surface Bodies to Delete** selection box. Choose the **OK** button from the **Delete Body PropertyManager**; a new item with the name **Body-Delete1** will appear in the **FeatureManager design tree**. This item will store the deleted bodies. Therefore, at any point of your design cycle, you can delete or suppress this item to resume the deleted body back in your design. You will learn more about suppressing features later in this chapter.

Tip. *You can also choose the* **Delete Body** *option from the shortcut menu. To do so, select the body and right-click. Choose the* **Delete** *option from the* **Body** *area of the shortcut menu; the* **Delete Body PropertyManager** *will be displayed. Choose the* **OK** *button from the* **Delete Body PropertyManager** *to delete the body.*

Suppressing Features

CommandManager:	Features > Suppress *(Customize to add)*
SolidWorks menus:	Edit > Suppress > This Configuration
Toolbar:	Features > Suppress *(Customize to add)*

Sometimes, you do not want a feature to be displayed in the model or in its drawing views. Instead of deleting those features, they can be suppressed. When you suppress a feature, it is neither visible in the model nor in the drawing views. Also, if you create an assembly using that model, the suppressed feature will not be displayed even in the assembly. You can resume such suppressed features at anytime by unsuppressing them. When you suppress a feature, the features that are dependent on it are also suppressed. To suppress a feature, select it from the **FeatureManager design tree** or from the drawing area. Choose the **Suppress** button from the **Features CommandManager** after customizing it, or right-click and choose the **Suppress** option from the shortcut menu. You can also choose **Suppress** from the pop-up toolbar that will be displayed on selecting a feature. The suppressed feature will be removed from the display of the model and the icon of the feature will be displayed in gray in the **FeatureManager design tree**.

Unsuppressing the Suppressed Features

CommandManager:	Features > Unsuppress *(Customize to add)*
SolidWorks menus:	Edit > Unsuppress > This Configuration
Toolbar:	Features > Unsuppress *(Customize to add)*

The suppressed features can be unsuppressed using the **Unsuppress** tool. To resume the suppressed feature, select the suppressed feature from the **FeatureManager design tree** and choose the **Unsuppress** button. You can also choose this option from the shortcut menu or from the pop-up toolbar after selecting the suppressed feature. Note that when you resume a suppressed feature using this tool, the dependent features remain suppressed. Therefore, you need to unsuppress all the features independently.

Unsuppressing Features With Dependents

CommandManager:	Features > Unsuppress with Dependents *(Customize to add)*
SolidWorks menus:	Edit > Unsuppress with Dependents > This Configuration
Toolbar:	Features > Unsuppress with Dependents *(Customize to add)*

As discussed earlier, when you suppress a feature, the dependent features are also suppressed. You can resume the suppressed feature along with the dependents of the suppressed parent feature in a single-click using the **Unsuppress with Dependents** tool. To do so, select the suppressed feature from the **FeatureManager design tree**. Choose the **Unsuppress with Dependents** button from the **Features** toolbar. You will observe that the dependent suppressed features are also unsuppressed.

Hiding Bodies

While working in the multibody environment, you can also hide the bodies. The hidden body is not displayed in the model, assembly, or in the drawing views. The display of the dependent bodies is also turned off when you hide a body. To hide a body, expand the **Solid Bodies** folder in the **FeatureManager design tree**, and select the body to be hidden. Right-click to invoke the shortcut menu and choose the **Hide Solid Body** option from it. The selected body will disappear from the drawing area. The icon of the hidden body is displayed in wireframe in the **Solid Bodies** folder. To turn on the display of the hidden body, select it from the **Solid Bodies** folder and choose the **Show Solid Body** option from the shortcut menu.

Moving and Copying Bodies

CommandManager:	Features > Move/Copy Bodies *(Customize to add)*
SolidWorks menus:	Insert > Features > Move/Copy Bodies
Toolbar:	Features > Move/Copy Bodies *(Customize to add)*

In the multibody environment, you can also move or copy the bodies by choosing the **Move/Copy Bodies** button from the **Features CommandManager** after customizing it, or choosing **Insert > Features > Move/Copy Bodies** from the SolidWorks menus; the **Move/Copy Body PropertyManager** will be displayed. By default, it shows the **Mates Settings** rollout. Choose the **Translate/Rotate** button below the **Options** rollout; the **Translate** and **Rotate** rollouts will be displayed, as shown in Figure 9-21.

The **Bodies to Move/Copy** rollout is used to define the body to copy or move. On invoking the **Move/Copy Body PropertyManager**, you will be prompted to select the bodies to move/copy and set the options. Move the cursor on the body to be selected; the cursor will be replaced by the body selection cursor and the edges of the body will be highlighted. The name of the body will also be displayed in the tooltip. Select the body; it will be highlighted and a 3D triad is displayed. The name of the body will be displayed in the **Solid and Surface or Graphics Bodies to Move/Copy** selection box. You can also select the body from the **Solid Bodies** folder after expanding the **FeatureManager design tree**.

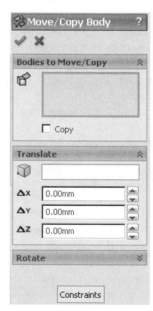

Figure 9-21 The Move/Copy Body PropertyManager

The **Copy** check box is cleared by default. Select the **Copy** check box to create multiple copies of the selected body. When you select this check box, the **Number of Copies** spinner will be displayed below the **Copy** check box. Set the number of copies in this spinner.

On selecting a body, you will notice that a 3D triad is displayed at the centroid of the selected body. It is used to dynamically rotate or move the selected body. The three arrows of this triad are the X, Y, and Z axes along which the body can be moved. This triad also has three rings around which the body can be rotated, see Figure 9-22.

To move a body dynamically, move the cursor close to any one of the arrows of the triad; the arrow will be highlighted and the select cursor will be replaced by the move cursor. Press and hold the left mouse button and drag the cursor to move the body. You can also move the cursor on the plane displayed between two arrows and drag the cursor to move the body in that plane.

Figure 9-22 *3D triad to move and rotate the body*

To rotate the body, move the cursor over one of the rings; the ring will be highlighted and the cursor will be replaced by the rotate cursor. Press and hold the left mouse button and drag the cursor to rotate the body.

Other rollouts in the **Move/Copy Body PropertyManager** are discussed next.

Translate Rollout

The **Translate** rollout in the **Move/Copy Body PropertyManager** is used to define the translational parameters to move the selected body. Set the value of the destination in the **Delta X**, **Delta Y**, and **Delta Z** spinners. When you set the values, the preview of the moved body will be displayed in temporary graphics in the drawing area. You can also move or copy the selected body with respect to two points. To move or copy a body by specifying two points, select the **Translation Reference (Linear Entity, Coordinate System, Vertex)** selection box. The selection mode in this area becomes active. Select the vertex from which you want the translation to start. When you select the first vertex as the translation reference, the **Delta X**, **Delta Y**, and **Delta Z** spinners will be replaced by the **To Vertex** selection box. Now, the selection mode in the **To Vertex** selection box will be activated. Select the second translation reference. You will observe the preview of the translated body with respect to the selected points. The placement of the body also depends on the sequence of selection of the vertices. Therefore, you need to be very careful, while selecting the two vertices. Figure 9-23 shows the sequence for the selection of references and Figure 9-24 shows the resulting copied body.

You can also move the body freely in 3D space. To do so, move the cursor on the spherical ball where the three arrows meet. The cursor will be replaced by the move cursor. Drag it to move the body to a desired location in the 3D space.

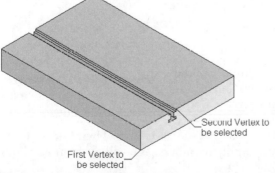

First Vertex to be selected

Second Vertex to be selected

Figure 9-23 *Sequence of selection of the references*

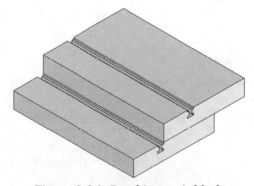

Figure 9-24 *Resulting copied body*

Rotate Rollout

The **Rotate** rollout in the **Move/Copy Body PropertyManager** is used to define the parameters to rotate the body. To expand this rollout, click once on the black arrow provided on the right of this rollout. The expanded **Rotate** rollout is shown in Figure 9-25.

Figure 9-25 The Rotate rollout

A filled square is placed at the origin when you invoke the **Move/ Copy Body PropertyManager**. It is clearly visible, when you hide the origin by choosing **Hide/Show Items > View Origins** from the **Heads-up View** toolbar. It indicates the origin along which the selected body will be rotated. You can adjust the position of this temporary moveable origin using the **X Rotation Origin**, **Y Rotation Origin**, and **Z Rotation Origin** spinners. The **X Rotation Angle** spinner is used to set the value of the angular increment to rotate or copy the body along the X-axis, the **Y Rotation Angle** spinner is used to rotate or copy the body along the Y-axis, and the **Z Rotation Angle** spinner is used to rotate or copy the body along the Z-axis. You can also dynamically rotate the model. To do so, press and hold the left mouse button on the bubble, drag the cursor, and relocate the triad. Now, left-click on a ring and drag the cursor to rotate the model. You can drag the cursor clockwise or counterclockwise. The model will be rotated dynamically in the drawing area. Release the left mouse button after rotating the feature to the required angle.

To rotate or copy the selected body along an edge, click once in the **Rotation Reference (Linear Entity, Coordinate System, Vertex)** selection box to invoke the selection. Select the edge about which you want to rotate the selected body. When you select an edge, all the other spinners will disappear from the rollout, and the **Angle** spinner will be enabled in the **Rotate** rollout. Set the value of the angular increment in this spinner.

Instead of selecting an edge, you can also select a vertex along which the body will rotate or copy. Next, you need to specify the axis along which you want to rotate it.

Figure 9-26 The Property Manager after choosing the Constraints button

Constraints

In SolidWorks, you can apply mates between the multiple bodies to place them at an appropriate location. Choose the **Constraints** button from the **Move/Copy Body PropertyManager**; the **Bodies to Move** and the **Mate Settings** rollouts will be displayed, as shown in Figure 9-26. You need to select the body that you want to move. The **Mate Settings** rollout helps you to position the selected body by applying mates. You will learn more about mates in the later chapters.

Reordering the Features

Reordering the features is defined as a process of changing the sequence of the features created in the model. Sometimes after creating a model, it may be required to change the order in which its features were created. For reordering the features, the features are dragged and placed before or after other features in the **FeatureManager design tree**.

To reorder a feature, select the feature in the **FeatureManager design tree**, and drag it; a bend arrow pointer will be displayed, which suggests that feature dragging is possible. Drop the feature at the required position. If you try to drag and drop the child feature above the parent feature, the reorder error pointer will be displayed and the **SolidWorks** warning box will be displayed. Choose **OK** from this warning box.

Consider a case in which you have created a rectangular block and a pattern of through holes created on its base feature, as shown in Figure 9-27. Now, if you create a shell feature and remove the top face, the front face, and the right face of the model, it will appear, as shown in Figure 9-28.

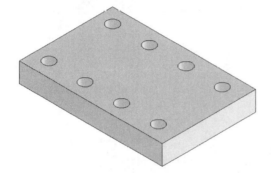

Figure 9-27 Model created with a pattern of through holes on the base feature

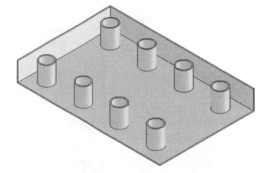

Figure 9-28 Shell feature added to the model

But this was not the desired result. Therefore, you need to reorder the shell feature before the holes. Select the shell feature in the **FeatureManager design tree** and drag it above the holes; all the features will be automatically adjusted in the new order, as shown in Figure 9-29.

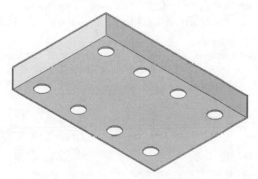

Figure 9-29 Model after reordering the features

Rolling Back the Feature

Rolling back the feature is defined as a process, in which you rollback the feature to an earlier stage. When you rollback a feature, it will be suppressed and you can add new features to the model in the rollback state. The newly added features are added before the features that are rolled back. While working with a multifeatured model, if you want to edit a feature that was created at the starting stage of the design cycle, it is recommended that you rollback the feature up to that stage. This is because after each editing operation, the time of regeneration will be minimized. Rolling back is done by shifting the **Rollback Bar** in the **FeatureManager design tree**.

To rollback a feature, select the **Rollback Bar**; it will be changed to blue and the select cursor will be replaced by the hand pointer, as shown in Figure 9-30. Drag the hand pointer to the feature up to the stage you want to rollback, and then release it. To resume the model, drag the **Rollback Bar** to the last feature of the model. You can also rollback the features using the SolidWorks menus. To do so, select the feature up to which you want to rollback the model and choose **Edit > Rollback** from the SolidWorks menus.

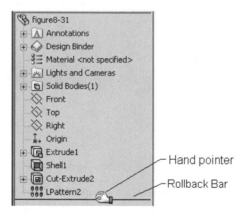

Figure 9-30 The **Rollback Bar** of the *FeatureManager design tree*

Tip. *If you want to rollback the feature to the previous step, choose **Edit > Roll to Previous** from the SolidWorks menus. To rollback the entire model to its original position, choose **Edit > Roll to End** from the SolidWorks menus.*

*You can also choose the **Roll Forward**, **Roll to Previous**, or **Roll to End** options from the shortcut menu invoked by selecting the features placed below the **Rollback Bar**. These options are used to control the roll and rollback of the feature.*

*You can also rollback the feature using the keyboard. To do so, select the **Rollback Bar** and press the CTRL+ALT+Up arrow keys to roll forward. Similarly, use the CTRL+ALT+Down arrow keys to roll backward.*

Renaming Features

The names of the features are displayed in the **FeatureManager design tree**. By default, the naming of the features is done according to the sequence in which they are created. You can also rename the features according to your convenience by selecting the feature from the **FeatureManager design tree** and then clicking once on the selected feature; an edit box will be displayed in the **FeatureManager design tree**. Enter the name of the feature and press the ENTER key or click anywhere on the screen.

Creating Folders in the FeatureManager design tree

You can also add folders in the **FeatureManager design tree** and the features displayed in the **FeatureManager design tree** are added in the folder. This is done to reduce the length of the **FeatureManager**. Consider a case, in which the base of the model consists of more than one feature. You can add a folder named Base Feature, and add all the features used to create the base in that folder. To add a folder in the **FeatureManager design tree**, select any feature in the **FeatureManager design tree**, right-click to invoke the shortcut menu, and choose the **Create New Folder** option; a new folder will be created above the selected feature. Specify the name of the folder and click anywhere on the screen. Now, you can drag and drop the features to the newly created folder. You can also rename the folder by selecting it and then clicking on it once. Now, enter its name in the edit box and press the ENTER key.

To add the selected feature in a new folder, choose **Add to New Folder** from the shortcut menu; a new folder will be created in the **FeatureManager design tree** and the selected feature will be added to the newly created folder. To delete the folder, select it, right-click and choose the **Delete** option from the shortcut menu. Use the options in this shortcut menu to rollback and suppress the features in the selected folder.

What's Wrong Functionality

Sometimes a model may not be rebuilt properly after you modify a sketch or a feature because of the errors resulting from the modification. Therefore, you are provided with the **What's Wrong** dialog box, as shown in Figure 9-31. The possible errors in the feature are displayed in this dialog box along with their detailed description.

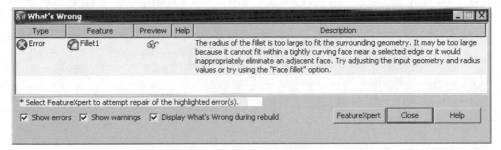

*Figure 9-31 The **What's Wrong** dialog box*

The **Show errors** check box is selected by default to display the errors in the **What's Wrong** dialog box. The **Show warnings** check box is selected by default to display the warning messages. The **Display What's Wrong during rebuild** check box is selected by default and is used to display the errors at every rebuild of the model, unless the error is fixed. After reading the description of the errors from this dialog box, choose the **Close** button to exit it. The errors will also be displayed in the **FeatureManager design tree**. The **FeatureManager design tree** with errors in a feature is displayed in Figure 9-32.

Down arrow error symbol displayed at the left of the document name indicates an error in the part or assembly

Cross symbol indicates the features responsible for the error

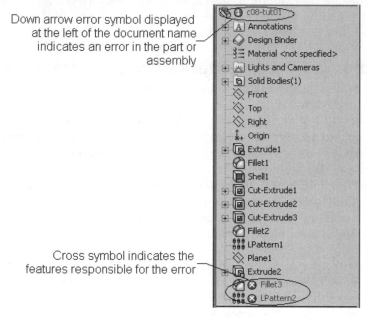

Figure 9-32 The **FeatureManager design tree** *with a feature having errors*

If there is an error in a model or in an assembly, the down arrow symbol will appear on the left of the name of the model or the assembly in the **FeatureManager design tree**. If a feature has an error, then the cross symbol will appear on the left of the feature in the **FeatureManager design tree**. If there is an error in the child feature, the error symbol will appear on the left of the parent feature and also on the name of the document in the **FeatureManager design tree**. If a warning message appears for a feature, then a triangle with an exclamation mark will appear on the left of that feature in the **FeatureManager design tree**.

Tip. *You can also invoke the* **What's Wrong** *dialog box by selecting the feature having errors from the* **FeatureManager design tree** *and choosing the* **What's Wrong?** *option from the shortcut menu.*

TUTORIALS

Tutorial 1

In this tutorial, you will create the model shown in Figure 9-33. After creating some of its features, you will dynamically modify it, and then undo the modification. The dimensions of the model are shown in Figure 9-34.   **(Expected time: 30 min)**

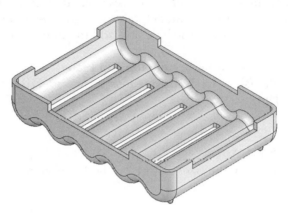

Figure 9-33 *Model for Tutorial 1*

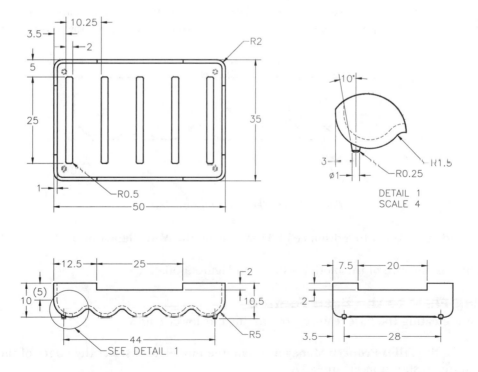

Figure 9-34 *Views and dimensions of the model for Tutorial 1*

The following steps are required to complete this tutorial:

a.   Create the base feature of the model by extruding the profile to a given distance, refer to Figures 9-35 and 9-36.
b.   Add the fillets to the base feature, refer to Figures 9-37 and 9-38.
c.   Add the shell feature to the model and remove the top face of the base feature, refer to Figures 9-39 and 9-40.
d.   Dynamically modify the model, refer to Figures 9-41 through 9-43.
e.   Create the cuts on the sides of the model, refer to Figure 9-44 and 9-45.
f.   Create slots on the lower part of the base and add the fillet to the slots feature, refer to Figure 9-46.
g.   Create a plane at an offset distance from the **Top Plane**.
h.   Create the standoffs using the **Extrude Boss/Base** and **Fillet** tool, and pattern the standoffs, refer to Figure 9-47.
i.   Save the model.

Creating the Base Feature

You will draw the sketch of the base feature on the Front Plane and extrude it using the **Mid Plane** option.

1.   Start SolidWorks and start a new SolidWorks Part document using the **New SolidWorks Document** dialog box.

2.   Invoke the **Extruded Boss/Base** tool and draw the sketch of the base feature on the Front Plane. Add the required relations and dimensions to the sketch, as shown in Figure 9-35.

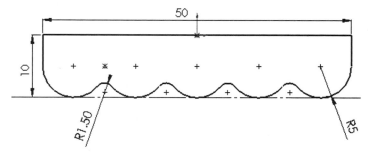

Figure 9-35 *Sketch for the base feature*

3.   Extrude the sketch to a distance of 35 mm using the **Mid Plane** option.

The base feature of the model is shown in Figure 9-36.

Adding Fillet to the Base Feature

After creating the base feature, you will fillet its lower edges.

1.   Invoke the **Fillet PropertyManager**, rotate the model, and select the edges of the base feature, as shown in Figure 9-37.

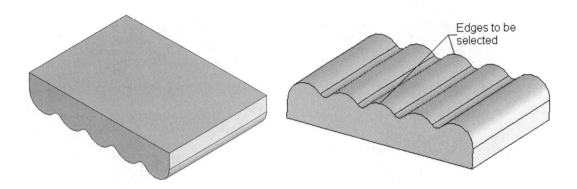

Figure 9-36 *Base feature of the model*   *Figure 9-37* *Edges to be selected*

2. Set the value in the **Radius** spinner to **2.5** and choose the **OK** button from the **Fillet PropertyManager**.

    The model, after adding fillet to its edges, is shown in Figure 9-38.

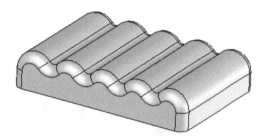

Figure 9-38 *Fillet added to the model*

Adding Shell to the Model

After creating the fillet feature, you need to shell the model using the **Shell** tool.

1. Orient the model in the isometric view and invoke the **Shell1 PropertyManager**.

2. Select the top planar face of the model, as shown in Figure 9-39.

3. Set the value in the **Thickness** spinner to **1**, and choose the **OK** button from the **Shell1 PropertyManager**.

    The model, after adding the shell feature, is shown in Figure 9-40.

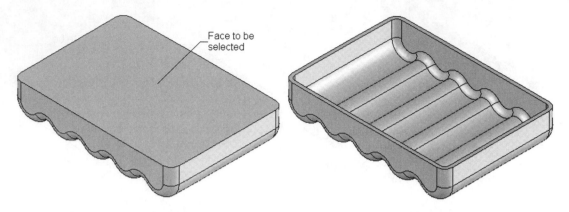

Figure 9-39 *Face to be selected*　　　　　　　**Figure 9-40** *Shell feature added to the model*

Dynamically Editing the Features

After adding the shell feature to the base of the model, you will edit the features dynamically using the **Instant3D** tool.

1. Choose the **Instant3D** button from the **Features CommandManager**, if it is not chosen already.

2. Select the front planar face of the base feature from the drawing area; the selected face is highlighted in blue and a green colored arrow is displayed.

3. Move the cursor to the green colored arrow and press and hold the left mouse button; the move cursor is displayed, as shown in Figure 9-41. Drag the cursor to resize the feature.

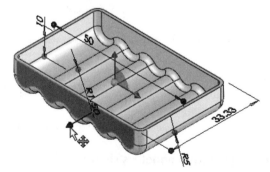

Figure 9-41 *Editing handles for editing the base feature*

The preview of the resized feature and its dimensions are displayed in the drawing area. As you drag the cursor, the preview and the dimensions update automatically.

4. Release the left mouse button after dragging the cursor to some distance. Figure 9-42 shows the preview of the dragged feature and Figure 9-43 shows the edited feature.

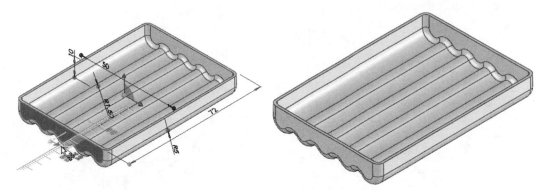

Figure 9-42 *Preview of the feature while dragging*   **Figure 9-43** *Resulting edited feature*

You have edited the model dynamically by dragging, but the original depth value of the feature was 35 mm. To bring the base feature back to its original size, you need to edit the feature.

5. Select the base feature from the **FeatureManager design tree** or from the drawing area; all dimensions of the feature are displayed in the drawing area.

6. Double-click on the dimension that reflects the depth of the base feature and is displayed in blue; the selected dimension is displayed in the text edit box.

7. Set the value in the **Dimension** spinner to **35** and press the ENTER key on the keyboard.

8. Choose the **Rebuild** button from the Menu Bar or press CTRL+B to rebuild the model.

Creating the Cut Feature

You need to create a cut feature on the front face. Next, you need to copy the cut feature on the right planar face.

1. Use the **Extruded Cut** tool to create the cut feature on the front face, as shown in Figure 9-44.

2. Select the feature in the **FeatureManager design tree**, press and hold the CTRL key, drag the selected feature, and place it on the right planar face; the **Copy Confirmation** dialog box is displayed.

3. Choose the **Delete** button; the cut feature will be created on the right planar face.

4. Select the newly created cut feature from the **FeatureManager design tree**; a pop-up toolbar is displayed. Choose **Edit Sketch** from the pop-up toolbar.

5. Apply the suitable constraints and dimensions to make it a fully defined sketch.

6. Choose the **Rebuild** button from the Menu Bar or press CTRL+B to rebuild the model; the model is displayed, as shown in Figure 9-45.

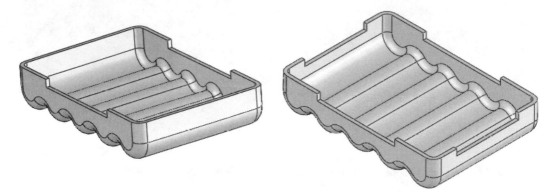

Figure 9-44 *The cut feature created on the front face*   **Figure 9-45** *The model after copying the feature*

7. Create slots, add fillet, and pattern the features. The model, after creating the other features, is shown in Figure 9-46.

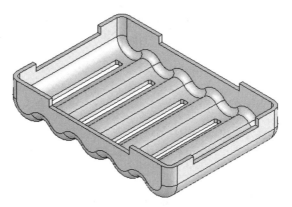

Figure 9-46 *Model after creating other features*

Tip. *To create a fillet, invoke the **Fillet** tool and choose the **Add** tab in the **FilletXpert** PropertyManager. Now, choose an edge of the slot; a pop-up toolbar will be displayed. Choose **Connected to start loop, 3 edges** from the pop-up toolbar to select all vertical edges of the slot.*

Creating the Standoff

Now, you need to create the standoff for the model. It is created by extruding a sketch drawn on a sketch plane at an offset distance from the Top Plane. You also need to specify a draft angle while creating this feature.

1. Create a reference plane at an offset distance of 10.5 mm from the Top Plane. You need to select the **Reverse direction** check box from the **Plane PropertyManager**.

2. Select the newly created sketching plane, draw the sketch of the standoff, and apply the required relations and dimensions. The sketch consists of a circle of 1 mm diameter. For other dimensions, refer to Figure 9-34.

3. Extrude the sketch using the **Up To Next** option with an outward draft angle of 10-degree. Hide the newly created plane; the standoffs of the model are created.

4. Rotate the model and add a fillet of radius 0.25 to the base of the standoff.

    The rotated and zoom view of the complete standoff is displayed in Figure 9-47.

5. Pattern the filleted standoff feature using the **Linear Pattern** tool. The isometric view of the final model is shown in Figure 9-48.

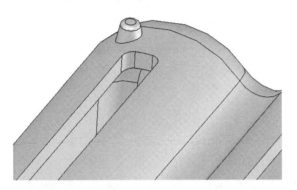

Figure 9-47 Rotated and zoom view of the model to show the standoff

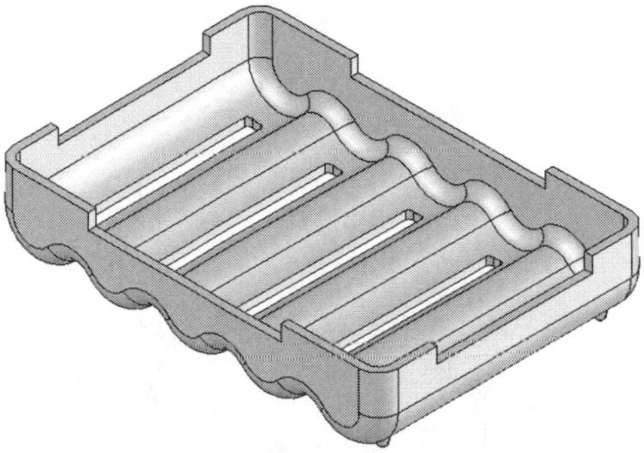

Figure 9-48 Final model

Saving the Model

1. Save the model with the name and location given below:

    \My Documents\SolidWorks\c09\c09tut1.sldprt

2. Choose **File > Close** from the SolidWorks menus to close the document.

Tutorial 2

In this tutorial, you will create the model shown in Figure 9-49, and then edit it using the **Move/Size Features** option. The views and dimensions of the model are shown in the same figure. **(Expected time: 45 min)**

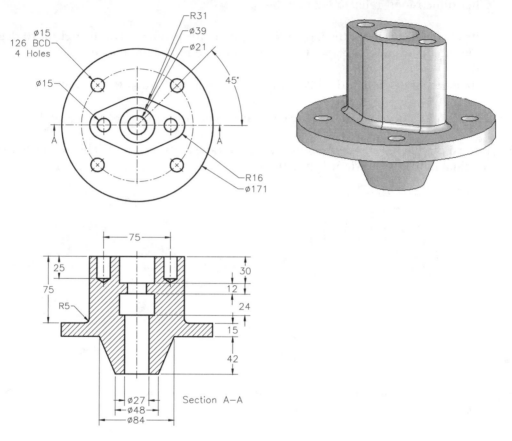

Figure 9-49 *Views and dimensions of the model for Tutorial 2*

The following steps are required to complete this tutorial:

a. Create the base feature of the model by revolving the sketch along the central axis of the sketch, refer to Figures 9-50 and 9-51.
b. Draw the sketch of the second feature on the top face of the base feature and extrude it to a given dimension, refer to Figures 9-52 and 9-53.
c. Create the revolve cut feature, refer to Figures 9-54 and 9-55.
d. Create the hole using the **Simple Hole** tool, and then pattern it using the **Circular Pattern** tool, refer to Figure 9-55.
e. Create a drilled hole feature using the **Hole Wizard** tool, refer to Figure 9-55.
f. Mirror the hole feature about the Right Plane, refer to Figure 9-55.
g. Apply the fillet, refer to Figure 9-55.
h. Perform the live sectioning of the model, refer to Figure 9-56.
i. Save the model.

Creating the Base Feature

First, you will create the base feature of the model by revolving the sketch created on the Front Plane.

1. Start a new SolidWorks Part document using the **New SolidWorks Document** dialog box.

2. Invoke the **Revolved Boss/Base** tool and draw the sketch of the base feature on the Front Plane. Add the required relations and dimensions to the sketch, as shown in Figure 9-50.

3. Exit the sketching environment.

   You do not need to set any parameters in the **Revolve PropertyManager** because the default value in the **Angle** spinner is 360-degree, as required.

4. Choose the **OK** button from the **Revolve PropertyManager**.

   The base feature created after revolving the sketch is shown in Figure 9-51.

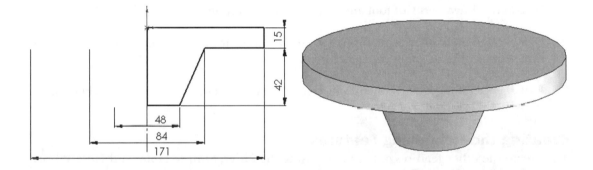

Figure 9-50 *Sketch for the base feature*   **Figure 9-51** *The Dimetric view of the base feature*

Creating the Second Feature

The second feature of this model is an extruded feature. It is created by extruding a sketch created on the top planar face of the base feature.

1. Invoke the **Extruded Boss/Base** tool and select the top planar face of the base feature as the sketching plane.

2. Draw the sketch of the second feature and apply the required relations and dimensions to it, as shown in Figure 9-52. Make sure that the sketch is symmetrical about the centerline. If it is not, the sketch will not be properly mirrored.

3. Extrude the sketch to a distance of 75 mm.

   The isometric view of the model after creating the second feature is displayed in Figure 9-53.

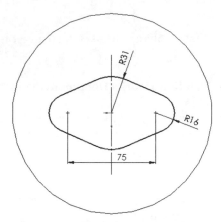

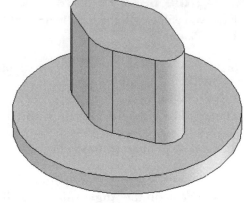

Figure 9-52 *Sketch for the second feature*   **Figure 9-53** *Second feature added to the model*

Creating the Third Feature

The third feature of the model is created by revolving a sketch using the cut option. The sketch for this feature will be created on the Front Plane.

1. Invoke the **Revolved Cut** tool and select the **Front Plane** as the sketching plane.

2. Draw the sketch for the revolved cut feature and apply the required relations and dimensions to it, as shown in Figure 9-54.

3. Exit the sketching environment and create a revolved cut feature with a default angle value of 360-degree.

Creating the Remaining Features

1. Create the other features of the model using the **Fillet, Simple Hole,** and **Hole Wizard** tools, refer to Figure 9-54.

The isometric view of the model, after creating all the other features, is displayed in Figure 9-55.

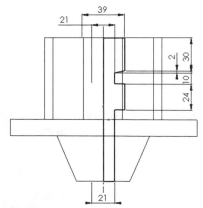

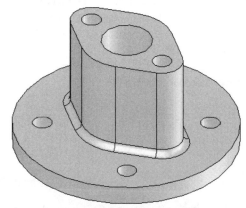

Figure 9-54 *Sketch for the revolved cut feature*   **Figure 9-55** *Isometric view of the final model*

Sectioning the Model

1. Choose the top planar surface of the base feature and right-click; the shortcut menu is displayed.

2. Choose the **Live Section Plane** option from the shortcut menu; a sectioning plane is displayed with two rings at the centre.

3. Move the cursor to the red colored ring, press and hold the left mouse down and drag the cursor to section the model along the vertical plane. Figure 9-56 shows the live section of the model when the sectioning plane is at an angle of 90-degree.

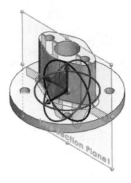

Figure 9-56 *Model with the sectioning plane*

4. Similarly, you can rotate the sectioning plane using the green colored ring.

5. Choose the cross mark in the section plane to close the live section.

Saving the Model

Now, you need to save the model.

1. Save the model with the name and location given below:

    \My Documents\SolidWorks\c09\c09tut2.sldprt.

2. Choose **File** > **Close** from the SolidWorks menus to close the document.

Tutorial 3

In this tutorial, you will create the model shown in Figure 9-57. While creating it, you will also perform some editing operations on it. The views and dimensions of the model are displayed in Figure 9-58. **(Expected time: 45min)**

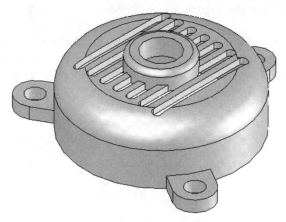

Figure 9-57 *Model for Tutorial 3*

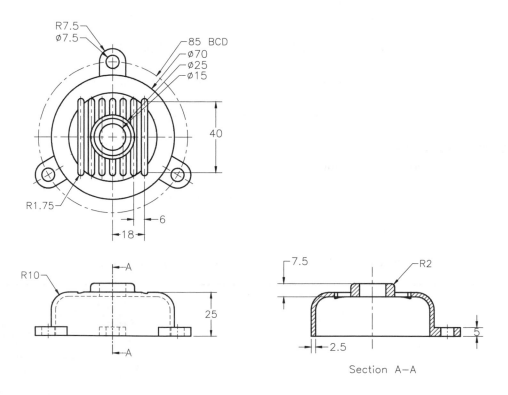

Figure 9-58 *Views and dimensions of the model for Tutorial 3*

The following steps are required to complete this tutorial:

a. Create a base feature of the model by revolving the sketch drawn on the **Front Plane**, refer to Figures 9-59 and 9-60.
b. Shell the model using the **Shell** tool, refer to Figure 9-61.
c. Draw the sketch on the Top Plane and extrude it to the given distance, refer to Figure 9-62.
d. Pattern the extrude feature using the **Circular Pattern** tool, refer to Figure 9-63.
e. Edit the circular pattern, refer to Figure 9-64.
f. Create the features on the top planar face, refer to Figures 9-63 and 9-65.
g. Create the slot on the top planar face and pattern it, refer to Figures 9-67 and 9-68.
h. Unsuppress the suppressed features and create the remaining features of the model, refer to Figures 9-67 and 9-68.
i. Save the model.

Creating the Base Feature

First, you need to create the base feature of the model by revolving the sketch created on the Front Plane.

1. Start a new SolidWorks Part document using the **New SolidWorks Document** dialog box.

2. Invoke the **Revolved Boss/Base** tool and draw the sketch of the base feature on the Front Plane. Add the required relations and dimensions to it, as shown in Figure 9-59.

3. Exit the sketching environment and create the base feature of the model, as shown in Figure 9-60.

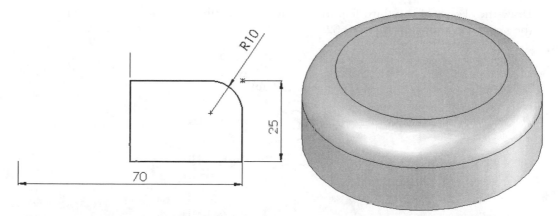

Figure 9-59 *Sketch for the base feature*   **Figure 9-60** *Base feature of the model*

Shelling the Base Feature

After creating the base feature, you need to shell the model using the **Shell** tool. You will also remove the bottom face of the base feature, leaving behind a thin walled model.

1. Invoke the **Shell1 PropertyManager** and set the value in the **Thickness** spinner to **2.5**.

2. Rotate the model and select its bottom face to remove it.

3. Choose the **OK** button from the **Shell1 PropertyManager**. The model, after adding the shell feature, is displayed in Figure 9-61.

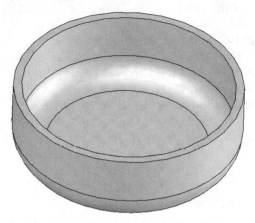

Figure 9-61 *Shell feature added to the model*

Creating the Third Feature

After adding the shell feature to the model, you need to create its third feature, which is an extruded feature. The sketch for this feature will be drawn on the Top Plane.

1. Invoke the **Extruded Boss/Base** tool and select the Top Plane as the sketching plane.

2. Orient the model in the top view.

3. Draw the sketch of the third feature and add the required relations and dimensions to the sketch, as shown in Figure 9-62.

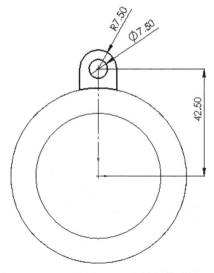

Figure 9-62 *Sketch of the third feature*

4. Exit the sketching environment and extrude the sketch to a depth of 5 mm.

Patterning the Third Feature

You need to pattern the third feature after creating it. This feature will be patterned using the **Circular Pattern** tool.

1. Invoke the **Circular Pattern PropertyManager.**

2. Select the third feature from the drawing area, if it is not selected in the **Features to Pattern** selection box.

3. Left-click once in the **Pattern Axis** selection box and select the circular edge of the base feature; the preview of the pattern feature is displayed.

4. Set the value in the **Number of Instances** spinner to **6** and choose **OK** from the **Circular Pattern PropertyManager**.

The model, after creating the pattern feature, is displayed in Figure 9-63.

Editing the Pattern Feature

The pattern created is not the same as required, refer to Figure 9-57. As a result, you need to skip the instances that are not required.

1. Select **CirPattern1** from the **FeatureManager design tree** or any one of the pattern instances other than the parent instance from the drawing area. Right-click and choose the **Edit Feature** option from the shortcut menu.

    The **CirPattern1 PropertyManager** is displayed. Currently, the number of instances in the pattern feature is 6, but the required number of instances is 3. Therefore, you need to edit the number of instances.

2. Expand the **Instances to Skip** rollout and left-click in the selection box in this rollout; a pink colored dot is displayed in the patterned feature.

3. Move the cursor to the pink colored dot; the numbers of the instance is displayed. Left-click on the second, fourth, and sixth instances.

4. Choose the **OK** button from the **CirPattern1 PropertyManager**.

The model, after editing the features, is shown in Figure 9-64.

Suppressing the Features

As discussed earlier, sometimes you may need to suppress some features to reduce the complications in the model. The suppressed features are not actually deleted, but their display is turned off. When you suppress a feature, the child features associated with that feature are also suppressed.

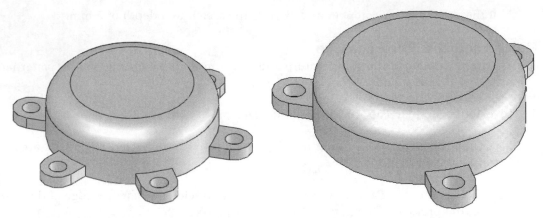

Figure 9-63 *Pattern feature added to the model*   **Figure 9-64** *The edited pattern feature*

1. Select the **Extrude1** feature, which is the third feature of the model, from the **FeatureManager design tree**; a pop-up toolbar is displayed. Choose **Suppress** from the pop-up toolbar.

    The circular pattern feature is the child feature of the extrude feature. Therefore, it is also suppressed. Both features are not displayed in the drawing area. The **Extrude1** and the **CirPattern1** features are displayed in gray in the **FeatureManager design tree**, indicating that both of them are suppressed.

Creating the Protrusion

The next feature that you are need to create is the protrusion on the top face of the base feature using the **Extruded Base/Boss** tool.

1. Invoke the **Extruded Boss/Base** tool and draw the sketch of the feature on the bottom face of the base feature and extrude it to a distance of 7.5mm, as shown in Figure 9-65.

2. Create the remaining features using the **Simple Hole** and **Fillet** tool, as shown in Figure 9-66.

Figure 9-65 *The extrude feature*   **Figure 9-66** *Model after creating other features*

Note

The protrusion should be created after creating the slot. But for the purpose of tutorial, it has been created earlier. Now, you will rollback this feature and create the slot.

Rollback the Feature

1.   Select the **Rollback Bar** and drag it before the **Extrude2** feature using the hand pointer.

Creating the Slots

Next, you need to create the slots. The sketch for this feature will be drawn on the top planar face of the base feature.

1.   Invoke the **Extruded Cut** tool and select the top planar face of the base feature as the sketching plane.

2.   Draw the sketch of the cut feature and add the required relations and dimensions to the sketch, as shown in Figure 9-67.

3.   Exit the sketching environment and specify the end condition as **Through All** from the **PropertyManager**.

4.   Choose the **OK** button from the **PropertyManager**.

5.   Now, using the **Linear Pattern** tool, create a linear pattern of the cut feature. You can select the dimension 18 as the directional reference. The model, after creating the linear pattern, is shown in Figure 9-68.

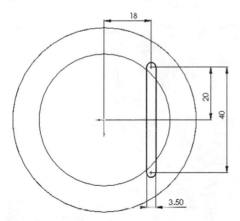
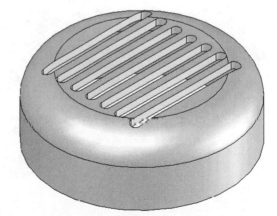

Figure 9-67 Sketch for the cut feature   *Figure 9-68 Model after patterning the cut feature*

Rollforward the Feature

1.   Select the **CirPattern1** feature from the **FeatureManager design tree** and right-click; the shortcut menu is displayed.

2.   Choose the **Roll to End** option from the shortcut menu.

Unsuppressing the Features

After completing the model, you need to unsuppress the features that you suppressed earlier.

1. Press and hold the CTRL key and select all the suppressed features from the **FeatureManager design tree**.

2. Right-click and choose the **Unsuppress** option from the shortcut menu.

Note

On selecting only the parent suppressed feature and unsuppressing it, the child features will not be unsuppressed. Therefore, you have to select both the parent feature as well as the suppressed child features.

*Instead of selecting all the parent and child suppressed features from the **FeatureManager design tree**, select only the parent feature, and choose **Edit > Unsuppress with Dependents > All Configurations** from the SolidWorks menus. You will learn more about the configurations in the later chapters.*

On unsuppressing the child feature, the parent feature will be unsuppressed automatically.

The suppressed features will be restored in the model. The final model, after unsuppressing the features, is shown in Figure 9-69.

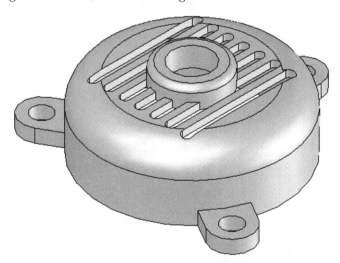

Figure 9-69 The final model

Saving the Model

1. Save the model with the name *c09tut3* in the location *\My Documents\SolidWorks\c09*.

2. Choose **File > Close** from the SolidWorks menus to close the document.

SELF-EVALUATION TEST

Answer the following questions and then compare them to those given at the end of this chapter:

1. You cannot edit the sketch of a sketched feature. (T/F)

2. The **Edit Feature** option is used to edit any feature. (T/F)

3. You cannot rename a feature in the **FeatureManager design tree**. (T/F)

4. You cannot edit the sketch plane of the sketch of a sketched feature. (T/F)

5. You cannot edit the sketches using the **Move/ Size Features** option. (T/F)

6. The _____ dialog box is displayed when you edit a dimension.

7. The process of changing the position of a feature in the **FeatureManager design tree** is known as _____.

8. To edit the feature or the sketch dynamically, choose the _____ button.

9. The _____ **PropertyManager** is used to move or copy the bodies.

10. The _____ dialog box is displayed when there is any error in a feature.

REVIEW QUESTIONS

Answer the following questions:

1. The _____ **PropertyManager** is invoked to delete a body.

2. You can rotate a body using the _____ **PropertyManager**.

3. The _____ key is used to copy a feature or a sketch.

4. The _____ key is used to cut a feature or a sketch.

5. When the _____ tool is active, the preview of the feature is displayed in temporary graphics while editing the sketches.

6. The _____ **PropertyManager** is displayed to edit the sketch plane of a sketch.

7. To add the selected feature in a new folder, you need to choose **Add to New Folder** from the shortcut menu. (T/F)

8. For reordering the features, select the feature in the **FeatureManager design tree** and drag the feature to the required position. (T/F)

9. The **Modify** dialog box is invoked using a single-click on the dimension to modify it. (T/F)

10. If you want to modify the sketch by dragging the fully or partially defined sketch, the **Override Dims on Drag/Move** option should be selected. (T/F)

EXERCISES

Exercise 1

Create the model that is sectioned and shown in Figure 9-70. The other views and dimensions of the model are also given in the same figure. The complete model is shown in Figure 9-71.

(Expected time: 45 min)

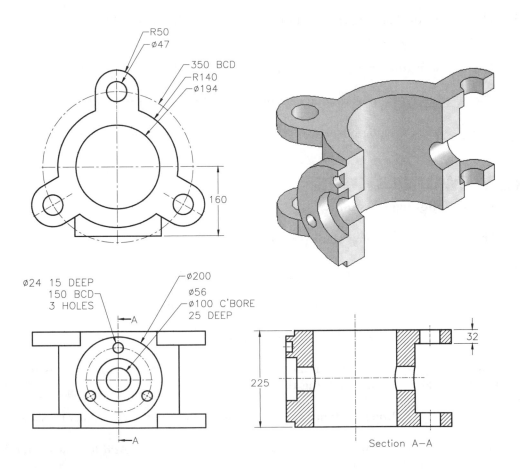

Figure 9-70 *Views and dimensions of the model for Exercise 1*

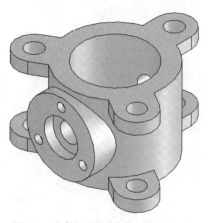

Figure 9-71 *Model for Exercise 1*

Exercise 2

Create the model shown in Figure 9-72. Its dimensions are shown in Figure 9-73.

(Expected time: 30 min)

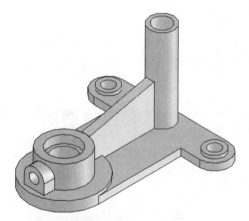

Figure 9-72 *Model for Exercise 2*

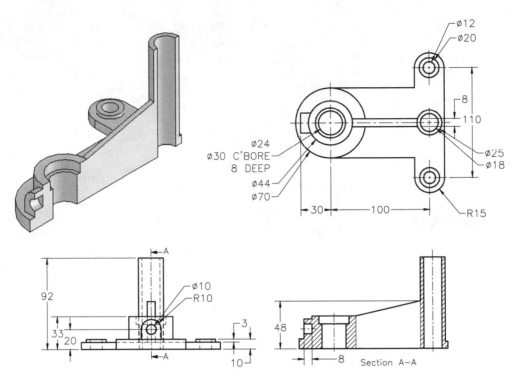

Figure 9-73 *Views and dimensions of the model for Exercise 2*

Chapter *10*

Advanced Modeling Tools-III

Learning Objectives

After completing this chapter, you will be able to:
- *Create sweep features.*
- *Create loft features.*
- *Create 3D sketches.*
- *Edit 3D sketches.*
- *Create various types of curves.*
- *Extrude 3D sketches.*
- *Create draft features using the manual method and the DraftXpert.*

ADVANCED MODELING TOOLS

Some of the advanced modeling tools were discussed in the earlier chapters. In this chapter, you will learn about some more advanced modeling tools such as sweep, loft, draft, curves, 3D sketches, and so on.

Creating Sweep Features

CommandManager:	Features > Swept Boss/Base
SolidWorks menus:	Insert > Boss/Base > Sweep
Toolbar:	Features > Extruded Boss/Base > Swept Boss/Base

One of the most important advanced modeling tools is the **Swept Boss/Base** tool. This tool is used to extrude a closed profile along an open or a closed path. Therefore, you need a profile and a path to create a sweep feature. A profile is a section for the sweep feature and a path is the course taken by the profile while creating the sweep feature. The profile has to be a sketch, but the path can be a sketch, curve or an edge. You will learn more about the procedure to create the curves later in this chapter. An example of the profile and the path for creating sweep feature is shown in Figure 10-1.

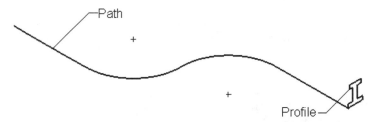

Figure 10-1 *Profile and path to create a sweep feature*

Choose the **Swept Boss/Base** button from the **Features CommandManager** to invoke the **Sweep PropertyManager**, as shown in Figure 10-2.

After invoking the **Sweep PropertyManager**, you will be prompted to select the sweep profile. Select the sketch that is drawn as the profile from the drawing area; the sketch will be highlighted and the **Profile** callout will be displayed. Now, you will be prompted to select the path for the sweep feature. Select the sketch or an edge to be used as the path; it is highlighted in magenta and the **Path** callout will be displayed. The sweep feature will also be displayed in temporary graphics in the drawing area. Choose the **OK** button from the **Sweep PropertyManager** to end the feature creation. Figure 10-3 shows a sweep feature.

Tip. *You can also use the **Contour Select Tool** to select a contour as the section for the sweep feature. To do so, invoke the **Sweep PropertyManager** and choose **SelectionManager** from the shortcut menu. Choose the **Select Region** button, select the contour, and choose OK from the **Selection Manager**. If you need to select multiple contours, press the CTRL key and select the contours. If you pin the **SelectionManager**, it will be displayed by default whenever you invoke the **Sweep PropertyManager**. You can also use a shared sketch as the section of the sweep feature.*

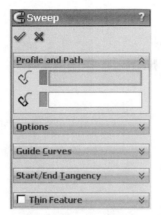

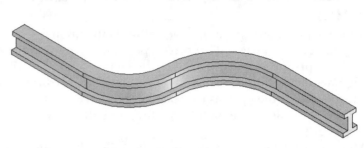

Figure 10-2 *The Sweep PropertyManager*

Figure 10-3 *Sweep feature*

It is not necessary that the sketch drawn for the profile of the sweep feature will intersect its path. However, the plane on which the profile is drawn should lie at one of the endpoints of the path. Figure 10-4 shows the nonintersecting sketches of a profile and a path. Figure 10-5 shows the resulting sweep feature. Figure 10-6 shows the sketch of a profile and a closed path. Remember, the plane on which the profile is drawn should intersect the closed path. Figure 10-7 shows the resulting sweep feature.

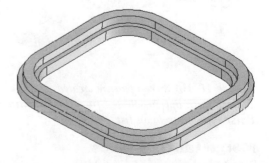

Figure 10-4 *Nonintersecting sketches of a profile and a path*

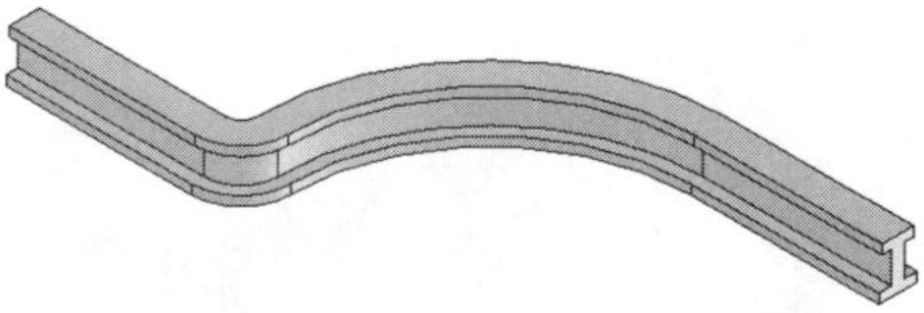

Figure 10-5 *Resulting sweep feature*

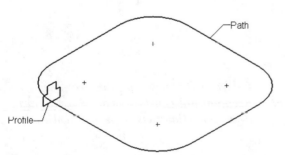

Figure 10-6 *Sketch of a profile and a closed path*

Figure 10-7 *Resulting sweep feature*

The other options available in the **Sweep PropertyManager** to create the advanced sweep features are discussed next.

Creating Sweep Using the Follow Path and Keep Normal Constant Options

While creating a sweep feature, the **Follow Path** option is selected by default in the **Orientation/twist type** drop-down list available in the **Options** rollout, as shown in Figure 10-8. The **Path alignment type** drop-down list is also displayed. In this drop-down list, you can set the options to create an even sweep feature when the curvature along the path fluctuates unevenly.

*Figure 10-8 The **Options** rollout*

While creating a sweep feature using the **Follow Path** option, the section will follow the path to create it. If you select the **Keep normal constant** option from the **Orientation/twist type** drop-down list, the section will be swept along the path with a normal constraint and will not change its orientation along the sweep path. Therefore, the start and the end face of the sweep feature will be parallel. Figure 10-9 shows the sketches of the path and the profile for creating the sweep feature. Figure 10-10 shows the sweep feature created using the **Follow Path** option. Figure 10-11 shows the sweep feature created using the **Keep normal constant** option. The other options in the **Orientation/twist type** drop-down list are discussed later in this chapter.

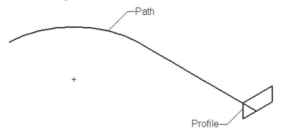

Figure 10-9 Sketches of the path and the profile

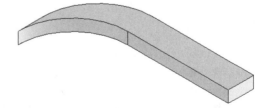

*Figure 10-10 Sweep feature created with the **Follow Path** option selected from the **Orientation/ twist type** drop-down list*

*Figure 10-11 Sweep feature created with the **Keep normal constant** option selected from the **Orientation/twist type** drop-down list*

Merge tangent faces

The **Merge tangent faces** check box in the **Options** rollout is used to merge the tangent faces of the profile throughout the swept feature.

Show preview

The **Show preview** check box in the **Options** rollout is used to display the preview of the sweep feature in the drawing area. This check box is selected by default. If you clear it, the preview of the sweep feature will not be displayed in the drawing area.

Merge result

The **Merge result** check box selected by default and is available only when you have at least one feature in the current document. If you clear this check box, it will result in the creation of the sweep feature as a separate body.

Align with end faces

The **Align with end faces** check box is available in the **Options** rollout only when at least one feature has already been created in the current document. When this check box is selected, the sweep feature is extended or trimmed to align with the end faces. Figure 10-12 shows the profile and path for creating sweep feature. Figure 10-13 shows the resulting sweep feature created with the **Align with end faces** check box cleared. Figure 10-14 shows the resulting sweep feature created with the **Align with end faces** check box selected.

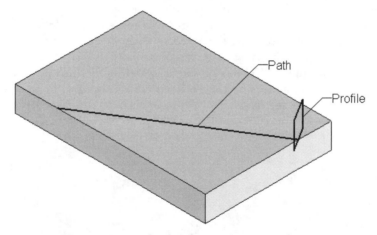

Figure 10-12 Sketches for creating sweep feature

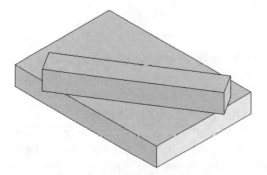

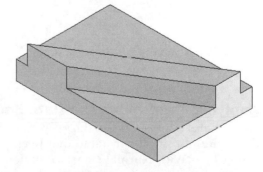

*Figure 10-13 Resulting sweep feature created with the **Align with end faces** check box cleared*

*Figure 10-14 Resulting sweep feature created with the **Align with end faces** check box selected*

Tip. *On selecting a model edge as the sweep path, the **Tangent Propagation** check box is displayed in the **Options** rollout. If this check box is selected, the edges tangent to the selected edge will be selected automatically as the path of the sweep feature.*

Note
If the sweep feature does not merge, you need to reduce the size of the profile.

Applying Twist to the Sweep Feature

While creating a sweep feature, you can also apply a twist to it. To do so, select the **Twist Along Path** option from the **Orientation/twist type** drop-down list; the **Define by** drop-down list and the **Twist Angle** spinner will be displayed below the **Orientation/twist type** drop-down list, as shown in Figure 10-15.

*Figure 10-15 The **Options** rollout*

You can apply a twist to the sweep feature by using the option in the **Define by** drop-down list. By default, the **Degrees** option is selected in this drop-down list. With this option selected, you need to specify the twist angle in the **Twist Angle** spinner. You can reverse the direction of twist using the **Reverse Direction** button. You can also specify the twist in terms of radians or turns by selecting the **Radians** or **Turns** option in the **Define by** drop-down list. Figure 10-16 shows the sweep feature created using the **Follow Path** option and Figure 10-17 shows the sweep feature after applying the twist.

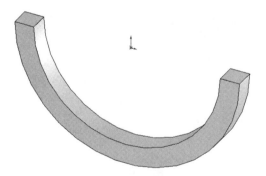

*Figure 10-16 Sweep feature created using the **Follow Path** option*

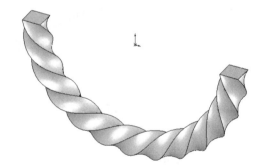

Figure 10-17 Sweep feature after applying the twist

Applying Twist along the Path Keeping the Normal Constant

You can also apply a twist to the swept feature keeping its end face parallel to the profile and the entire transition normal to the sweep path. To apply this type of twist, select the **Twist Along Path With Normal Constant** option from the **Orientation/twist type** drop-down list and then set the twist parameters. Figure 10-18 shows the twist applied using the **Twist Along Path** option and Figure 10-19 shows the twist applied using the **Twist Along Path With Normal Constant** option.

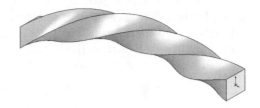

Figure 10-18 *Twist applied using the* **Twist Along Path** *option*

Figure 10-19 *Twist applied using the* **Twist Along Path With Normal Constant** *option*

Sweep with Guide Curves

The sweep with guide curves is the most important option in the advanced modeling tools. In this sweep feature, the section of the sweep profile varies according to the guide curves along the sweep path. To create this type of feature, you need a profile, a path, and the guide curves. After drawing the sketch of the profile, path, and guide curve, apply the coincident relation between the guide curves and the profile. You need to make sure that the guide curves intersect the profile. Now, invoke the **Sweep PropertyManager**. Select the profile and the path; the preview of the sweep feature will be displayed in the drawing area. Click on the arrow on the left of the **Guide Curves** rollout to expand this rollout. The **Guide Curves** rollout is shown in Figure 10-20.

Figure 10-20 *The* **Guide Curves** *rollout*

Select the sketch of the guide curve; the selected guide curve will be highlighted with a **Guide Curve** callout. The preview of the sweep feature will also be displayed in the drawing area. Choose the **OK** button from the **Sweep PropertyManager**. Figure 10-21 shows the sketch for creating the sweep feature with the guide curve. Figure 10-22 shows the resulting sweep feature.

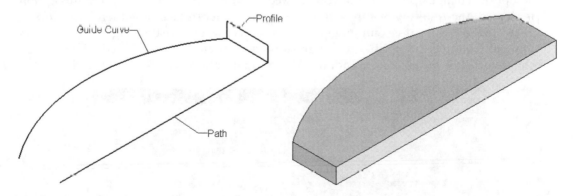

Figure 10-21 *Sketch for creating the sweep feature with the path and guide curve*

Figure 10-22 *Resulting sweep feature*

In the previous case, the path of the sweep feature was a straight line and the guide curve was an arc. In the next case, an arc is selected as the path of the sweep feature and a straight line will be selected as the guide curve. Figure 10-23 shows the sketches for creating sweep feature. Figure 10-24 shows the resulting sweep feature.

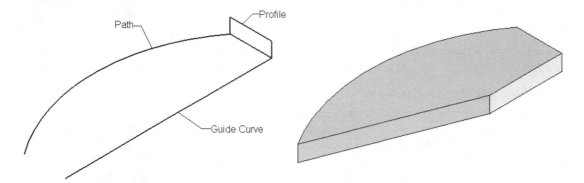

Figure 10-23 *Sketch for creating sweep feature with the path and guide curve*

Figure 10-24 *Resulting sweep feature*

Move Up and Move Down

The **Move Up** button and the **Move Down** button on the left of the **Guide Curves** selection box are used to change the sequence of the selected guide curves.

Merge smooth faces

In the **Guide Curves** rollout, the **Merge smooth faces** check box is selected by default. This option is used to merge all the smooth faces together, resulting in a smooth sweep feature. After creating the sweep feature, when you edit it and clear the **Merge smooth faces** check box, the **Sweep Preview Warning** dialog box will be displayed, as shown in Figure 10-25. This dialog box warns that the feature you are creating may fail because of the change in the smooth face option. Choose the **Yes** button from this dialog box to accept the change option. If you create a sweep feature with guide curves and this option is cleared, the resulting feature will not merge the smooth faces together. Therefore, a sweep feature with a noncontinuous curvature surface will be created. Figure 10-26 shows a sweep feature created with the **Merge smooth faces** check box selected. Figure 10-27 shows the same sweep feature with the **Merge smooth faces** check box cleared.

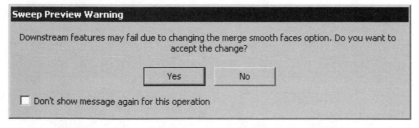

Figure 10-25 *The **Sweep Preview Warning** dialog box*

Figure 10-26 *Sweep feature created with the* **Merge smooth faces** *check box selected*

Figure 10-27 *Sweep feature created with the* **Merge smooth faces** *check box cleared*

Note

Remember that if you create the sweep feature with the **Merge smooth faces** *check box cleared, the resulting feature will be generated faster.*

Show Sections

The **Show Sections** button in the **Guide Curves** rollout is used to display the intermediate sections while creating the sweep feature with the guide curves. To display the intermediate profiles or the sections along the sweep path, choose the **Show Sections** button from the **Guide Curves** rollout; the **Section Number** spinner will be available. This spinner is used to view the sections of the profile along the sweep path. The maximum value of the spinner goes up to the number of sections that fit inside the sweep feature. Figure 10-28 shows a section being displayed using the **Show Sections** option and constrained by the guide curves.

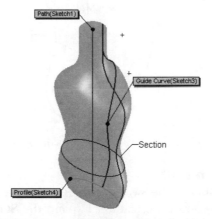

Figure 10-28 *Section displayed on choosing the* **Show Sections** *button*

Creating Sweep Feature Using the Follow path and 1st guide curve Option

When you create a sweep feature with a guide curve using the **Follow path and 1st guide**

curve option from the **Options** rollout, the profile will follow the path and the first guide curve to create the feature. To create a sweep feature using this option, invoke the **Sweep PropertyManager** and select the profile, path, and guide curve(s). By default, the **Follow path** option is selected in the **Orientation/twist type** drop-down list of the **Options** rollout. Select the **Follow path and 1st guide curve** option from the **Orientation/twist type** drop-down list. Choose the **OK** button from the **Sweep PropertyManager** to end the creation of the feature.

Creating Sweep Feature Using the Follow 1st and 2nd guide curves Option

You can also create a sweep feature by sweeping the profile along a path and also by following the two guide curves. To create this type of sweep feature, select the **Follow 1st and 2nd guide curves** option from the **Orientation/twist type** drop-down list in the **Options** rollout. Choose the **OK** button from the **Sweep PropertyManager** to end the creation of the feature.

Figure 10-29 shows the sketches of the profile, path, and guide curves for creating a sweep feature. Figures 10-30 and 10-31 show the sweep features created using the **Follow path and 1st guide curve** and **Follow 1st and 2nd guide curves** options, respectively.

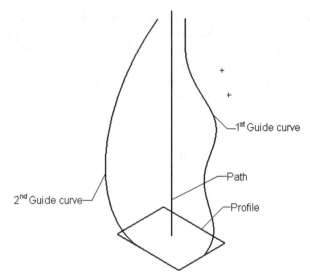

Figure 10-29 Sketches of the profile, path, and guide curves

Start/End Tangency Rollout

The **Start/End Tangency** rollout in the **Sweep PropertyManager** is used to define the tangency conditions at the start and end of the feature. Expand the **Start/End Tangency** rollout, as shown in Figure 10-32. The various options in the **Start/End Tangency** rollout are discussed next.

Start tangency type

The **Start tangency type** drop-down list is used to specify the options to define the tangency at the start of the sweep feature. The various options in this drop-down list are discussed next.

Figure 10-30 Sweep feature created using the
Follow path and 1st guide curve *option*

Figure 10-31 Sweep feature created using the
Follow 1st and 2nd guide curves *option*

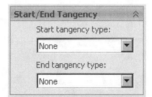

*Figure 10-32 The **Start/End Tangency** rollout*

None

The **None** option is selected by default and is used to create a sweep feature without applying any start tangency.

Path Tangent

The **Path Tangent** option is used to maintain the sweep feature normal to the profile at the start.

Direction Vector

If you select the **Direction Vector** option, the starting of the sweep feature will be tangent to a virtual normal created from the selected entity. When you select this option, the **Direction Vector** selection box is also displayed and you need to select a linear edge, axis, planar face, or plane to specify the direction of sweep.

All Faces

The **All Faces** option is used to sweep the feature tangent to the adjoining faces of the existing geometry at the start.

The options in the **End tangency type** drop-down list are the same as those discussed above, except the **All Faces** option. The only difference is that the options in this drop-down list are applied to the end of the sweep feature. Figure 10-33 shows the sketches and references to create sweep feature with the start and end tangency, using the **Direction Vector** option. Figure 10-34 shows the resulting sweep feature.

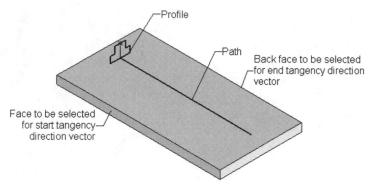

Figure 10-33 *Profile, path, and references for tangency using the*
Direction Vector *option*

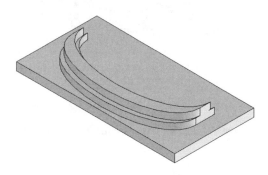

Figure 10-34 *Resulting sweep feature*

Creating a Thin Sweep Feature

You can also create a thin sweep feature by specifying the thickness of the sweep feature. To
do so, expand the **Thin Feature** rollout by selecting the check box on the left of the **Thin
Feature** rollout. The **Thin Feature** rollout is shown in Figure 10-35. The options in this
rollout are the same as those discussed in the earlier chapters, where extruding and revolving
of the thin features were discussed. Figure 10-36 shows a thin sweep feature.

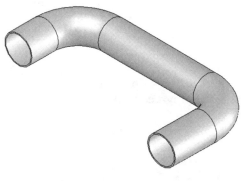

Figure 10-35 *The* ***Thin***
Feature *rollout*

Figure 10-36 *Thin sweep feature*

Creating Cut-Sweep Features

CommandManager: Features > Swept Cut
SolidWorks menus: Insert > Cut > Sweep
Toolbar: Features > Extruded Cut > Swept Cut

You can also remove material from an existing feature or a model by creating a cut-sweep feature. To create it, choose the **Swept Cut** button from the **Features CommandManager**; the **Cut-Sweep PropertyManager** will be displayed, as shown in Figure 10-37. In SolidWorks, you can create the cut-sweep feature by sweeping a profile or a solid body along the specified path. If you need to create a cut-sweep feature by using a profile, select the **Profile sweep** radio button from the **Profile and Path** rollout. The options that will be displayed in the **Cut-Sweep PropertyManager** on selecting the **Profile Sweep** radio button are the same as those discussed in the **Sweep PropertyManager**, with the only difference that the options in this case are meant for the cut operation. Figure 10-38 shows the profile and the path for creating the cut-sweep feature. Figure 10-39 shows the resulting cut-sweep feature created by selecting the **Profile sweep** radio button from the **Profile and Path** rollout.

*Figure 10-37 The **Cut-Sweep** PropertyManager*

If you need to create a cut-sweep feature by using a disjoint body, select the **Solid sweep** radio button in the **Profile and Path** rollout. Select the solid body from the drawing area as the tool body. Note that the solid body should be of a revolved feature and should be tangent to the path. Then, select the path along which the cut-sweep feature is to be created. The options in the **Options** rollout are similar to those discussed earlier. Figure 10-40 shows the solid body and the path for creating the cut-sweep feature. Figure 10-41 shows the cut-sweep feature created using the disjoint solid body.

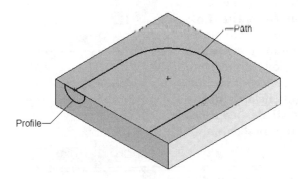

Figure 10-38 Profile and path for creating the cut-sweep feature

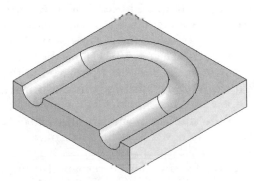

Figure 10-39 Resulting cut-sweep feature

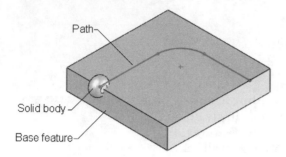

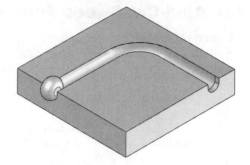

Figure 10-40 *Solid body and the path*   **Figure 10-41** *Resulting cut-sweep feature*

Creating Loft Features

CommandManager:	Features > Lofted Boss/Base
SolidWorks menus:	Insert > Boss/Base > Loft
Toolbar:	Features > Extruded Boss/Base > Lofted Boss/Base

 The loft features are created by blending more than one similar or dissimilar sections together to get a free form shape. These similar or dissimilar sections may or may not be parallel to each other. Note that the sections for the solid lofts should be the closed sketches.

To create a loft feature, draw the sketches and invoke the **Loft PropertyManager** by choosing the **Lofted Boss/Base** button from the **Features CommandManager**. A partial view of the **Loft PropertyManager** is shown in Figure 10-42.

On invoking the **Loft PropertyManager**, you will be prompted to select at least two profiles. Select the profiles from the drawing area; the preview of the loft feature along with a connector is displayed in it. Choose the **OK** button from the **Loft PropertyManager** to end the creation of the loft feature. Figure 10-43 shows the preview of the loft feature along with a connector and Figure 10-44 shows the resulting loft feature. Note that by default, a mesh is displayed in the preview of the loft feature. You can turn off this mesh by right-clicking on the preview and choosing **Mesh Preview > Clear All Meshed Faces** from the shortcut menu. In this textbook, the mesh from all faces are removed for a better display.

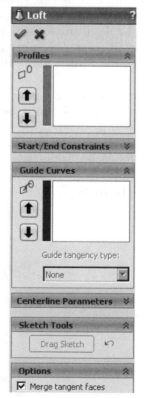

Figure 10-42 *Partial view of the Loft PropertyManager*

The loft feature can be reshaped using the handles of the connector that appear as the filled circle in the preview. To do so, press and hold the left mouse button on a handle, drag the cursor to specify a new location and release the left mouse button to place the connector on it. The process of controlling the loft shape using the connectors is

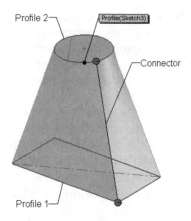

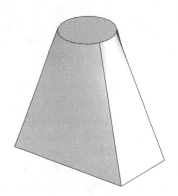

Figure 10-43 *Preview of the loft feature along with a connector*

Figure 10-44 *Resulting loft feature*

known as Loft Synchronization. Figure 10-45 shows the preview of the loft feature after modifying the location of the handle of the connector. Figure 10-46 shows the resulting loft feature.

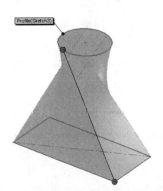

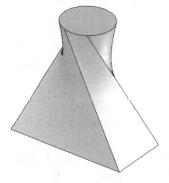

Figure 10-45 *Preview of the loft feature after modifying the location of the connector*

Figure 10-46 *Resulting loft feature*

Note

The reshaping or twisting using the default connector while creating the loft feature is known as global twisting. Global twisting means if you change the location of one connecting point of the profile, other connecting points of the profile will automatically change their positions with respect to the modified connecting point.

In global twisting of non-tangent profiles, the handles of the connectors move only from vertex to vertex.

Tip. *You can also use the **Contour Select** tool to select a contour that will be used as the profile to create the loft feature. You can also use a shared sketch as a profile that is currently in use by some other sketched feature.*

To display all connectors, right-click and choose the **Show All Connectors** option from the shortcut menu. The number of connectors displayed using this option depends on the maximum number of vertices in the start or the end loft section. If the start and end loft sections are circular, elliptical, or closed spline sections, then only one controller will be displayed.

You can also add more connectors to manipulate the loft feature. Connectors can be added to the straight profiles or the curved profiles. To add a connector, right-click on the location in the sketch, where you need to add the connector to invoke the shortcut menu. Choose the **Add Connector** option from the shortcut menu; a connector will be added to the loft feature. Similarly, you can add more connectors using this option. You can also modify them by dragging their handles. Figure 10-47 shows the preview of the loft feature after modifying all additional connectors and Figure 10-48 shows the resulting loft feature.

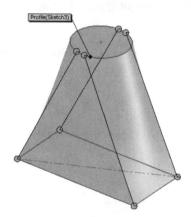   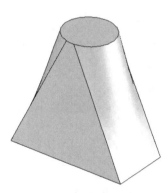

Figure 10-47 *Preview after modifying all connectors*   *Figure 10-48* *Resulting loft feature*

Note
Reshaping or twisting using additional connectors is known as local twisting, because the twisting using one connector does not affect the other connecting points of the profile. Therefore, you can independently modify all connectors simply by dragging the handles along the profile.

Start/End Constraints Rollout
The **Start/End Constraints** rollout in the **Loft PropertyManager** is used to define the constraints at the start and end sections of the loft feature. You can define the normal, tangency, or continuity constraints for the loft feature. Expand this rollout to define the tangency. By

Tip. *Invoke the shortcut menu and choose **Hide All Connectors** to hide all connectors. The connectors will not be displayed in the preview, but the settings made by them remain in the loft feature. To hide a specific connector, select it and invoke the shortcut menu. Then, choose the **Hide Connector** option.*

*If you choose the **Reset Connectors** option from the shortcut menu, all connectors and the settings related to them will be deleted from the memory of the feature. Also, the default connector will be displayed with the default connection points lying between the profiles of the loft feature.*

default, the **None** option is selected in the **Start constraint** and the **End constraint** drop-down lists. This implies that no constraint is applied to the loft feature. The other options available in these drop-down lists are discussed next.

Normal To Profile

The **Normal To Profile** option is used to define the tangency normal to the profile. When you select this option from the **Start constraint** and **End constraint** drop-down lists, an arrow will be displayed at the start and end sections. Also, some additional options will be displayed in the **Start/End Constraints** rollout, as shown in Figure 10-49. You can set the length of the tangency by dragging the tangency arrows attached to the sections or by setting the values in the **Start Tangent Length** and **End Tangent Length** spinners provided in this rollout. You can also specify a draft angle using the **Draft angle** spinners. You will notice that the **Apply to all** check boxes are selected by default, which implies that the tangency is applied evenly to all the vertices of the sections. However, on clearing these check boxes, you can apply the values of tangencies individually to all the vertices. Figure 10-50 shows the preview of the loft feature with the tangency arrows attached to the end

Figure 10-49 The ***Start/End Constraints*** *rollout with the* ***Normal To Profile*** *option selected*

sections of the loft feature. Figure 10-51 shows the tangency arrows attached to all vertices of the end sections of the loft feature. Figure 10-52 shows the resulting loft feature after specifying the length of tangency.

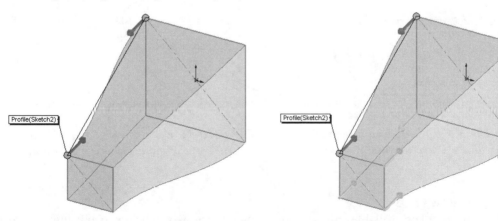

Figure 10-50 Two arrows attached to the sections   *Figure 10-51 Arrows attached to all vertices*

Direction Vector

The **Direction Vector** option is used to define the tangency at the start and end of the loft feature by defining a direction vector. On selecting this option, you will be provided with the **Direction Vector** selection box and the spinners to define the length of the tangents and the draft angle. You need to select the direction vectors to specify the

Figure 10-52 Resulting loft feature

tangent direction at the start and end of the loft feature. Specify the length of the tangents using the spinners provided in the **Start/End Constraints** rollout. The **Start/End Constraints** rollout with the **Direction Vector** option selected, is shown in Figure 10-53.

Figure 10-54 shows the sections for the loft feature. Figure 10-55 shows the initial preview of the loft feature. Figure 10-56 shows the preview of the loft feature with tangent at the start section of the loft feature and Figure 10-57 shows the tangent at the start and at the end sections of the loft feature. Figure 10-58 shows the final loft feature.

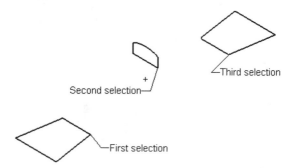

*Figure 10-53 The **Start/End Constraints** rollout with the **Direction Vector** option selected*

Figure 10-54 Sections, selection points, and sequence of selection to create the loft feature

Tangency To Face

This option will be available only if the resulting loft feature will lie on an existing feature. If you select the **Tangent To Face** option from the **Start constraint** or the **End constraint** drop-down list, the resulting loft feature will maintain the tangency along the adjacent curved faces. The face, along which the tangency is to be maintained, will be highlighted. You can also switch between the faces along which you need to maintain the tangency using the **Next Face** button. The spinners below the **Next Face** button can be used to specify the length of the start and end tangencies.

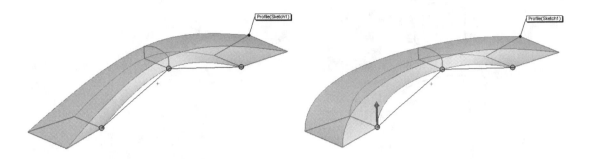

Figure 10-55 *Initial preview of the loft feature*   **Figure 10-56** *Tangent applied at the start section*

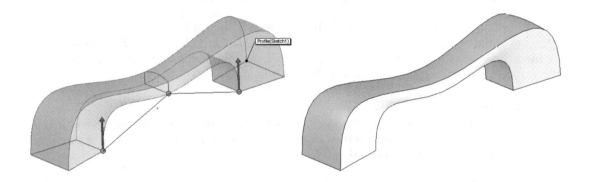

Figure 10-57 *Tangent applied at the start and end sections of the loft feature*

Figure 10-58 *The final loft feature*

Curvature To Face
This option will be available only if the resulting loft feature lies on an existing feature. If you select the **Curvature To Face** option from the **Start constraint** or the **End constraint** drop-down list, the resulting loft feature will maintain the curvature along the adjacent curved faces. The face, along which the curvature is to be maintained, will be highlighted. You can also switch between the faces along which you need to maintain the tangency, using the **Next Face** button.

Guide Curves Rollout
You can create the loft feature by specifying the guide curves between the profiles to define the path of transition of the loft feature as you created the sweep feature. The sketches drawn for the guide curve must coincide with the sketches that define the loft sections.

Figure 10-59 shows the profiles and guide curves for creating a loft feature. Figure 10-60 shows the resulting loft feature created using guide curves.

Centerline Parameters Rollout
The **Centerline Parameters** rollout is used to create a loft feature by blending two or more

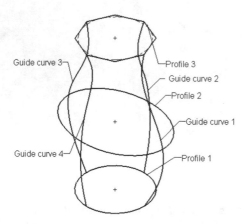

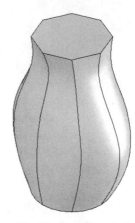

Figure 10-59 *Profiles and guide curves*   ***Figure 10-60*** *Resulting loft feature*

than two sections along a specified path. You can specify the centerline and the guide curves to the loft feature created by using the centerline. Note that the path that specifies the transition is called the centerline and the profile that defines the external shape are the guide curves. The options available in this rollout are discussed next.

Centerline

You need to specify the centerline after invoking the **Centerline Parameters** rollout. On selecting the sketch that defines the centerline for the loft feature, the name of the sketch will be displayed in the **Centerline** selection box.

Number of sections

The **Number of sections** slider bar provided in the **Centerline Parameters** rollout is used to define the number of intermediate sections, which further defines the accuracy and the smoothness of the loft feature.

The **Show Sections** button and the **Section Number** spinner in this rollout are used to display the intermediate sections, as discussed earlier. Figure 10-61 shows the sketches of the profiles and the centerline used to create the loft feature. Figure 10-62 shows the resulting loft feature.

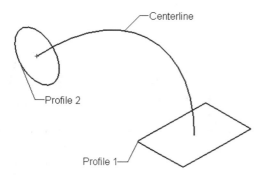

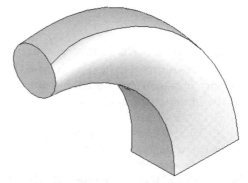

Figure 10-61 *Profiles and centerline*   ***Figure 10-62*** *Resulting loft feature*

Sketch Tools

You can also select the 3D sketches as the profile or the guide curves for the loft feature. If you create the loft feature using the 3D sketches, the sketches or the guide curves can be from the same sketch. So, use the **Selection Manager** to select the individual loops as the sketch profiles and create the loft feature. The button in the **Sketch Tools** rollout is used to edit the loft features that are created using the 3D sketch. This button will be enabled only when you edit the loft feature created using the 3D sketches. While editing choose the **Drag Sketch** button to drag the 3D sketch. Choose the **Undo sketch drag** button to undo the dragging of the 3D sketch. You will learn more about the 3D sketches later in this chapter.

Options Rollout

The **Options** rollout in the **Loft PropertyManager** provides the options to improve the creation of the loft feature. These options are the same as those discussed in the sweep option. An additional option in with this rollout is discussed next.

Close loft

A closed loft feature is one in which the end and start of the loft features are joined together. The **Close loft** check box is selected to create a closed loft feature. Note that the angle between the start and end sections should be more than 180 degrees to create the closed loft. Figure 10-63 shows a loft feature created with the **Close loft** check box cleared. Figure 10-64 shows the loft feature created with the **Close loft** check box selected.

Figure 10-63 Loft feature created with the **Close loft** *check box cleared*

Figure 10-64 Loft feature created with the **Close loft** *check box selected*

You can also create a thin loft feature by defining the thin parameters using the **Thin Feature** rollout. The options available in this rollout are the same as those discussed in the earlier chapters. Figure 10-65 shows a thin loft feature created using the options in the **Thin Feature** rollout of the **Loft PropertyManager**.

Tip. *To create a smooth loft feature between a circle and a polygon, it is a good practice to split the circle into a number of arcs. The number of arcs that form the circle should be the same as the number of sides of the polygon. Now, when you create the loft feature, the number of connecting points in both the sections will be predefined, which results in a smoother loft feature.*

Figure 10-65 *A thin loft feature*

Adding a Section to the Loft Feature

After creating a loft feature, you can also add a section to it by selecting one of the side faces of the loft feature and then right-clicking to invoke the shortcut menu. Choose the **Add Loft Section** option from it; the **Add Loft Section PropertyManager** will be displayed. You will be provided with a plane that can be moved or rotated dynamically. To move the plane, place the cursor on the arrows displayed on it, press and hold the left mouse button and drag the cursor to move the plane. To rotate the plane, select one of its edges and drag the cursor. Set the position of the plane by dynamically moving and rotating it to specify the position to add the sketch. Figures 10-66 and 10-67 show the planes being moved and rotated. After specifying the position of the plane, choose the **OK** button from the **Add Loft Section PropertyManager**. Figure 10-68 shows the section added to the loft feature. This is a closed section created using a spline.

Expand the **Loft1** feature and select the sketch that is added using the **Add Loft Section** tool. Right-click and choose the **Edit Sketch** option from the shortcut menu. Edit the sketch, as shown in Figure 10-69, and rebuild the part. Figure 10-70 shows the modified loft feature.

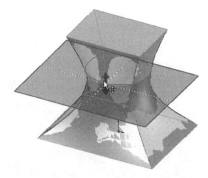

Figure 10-66 *Moving the plane*

Figure 10-67 *Rotating the plane*

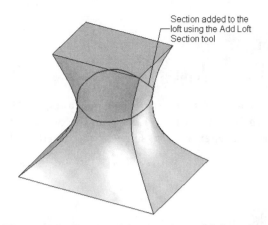

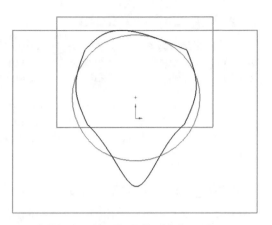

Section added to the loft using the Add Loft Section tool

Figure 10-68 *Resulting section added to the loft feature*

Figure 10-69 *Edited loft section*

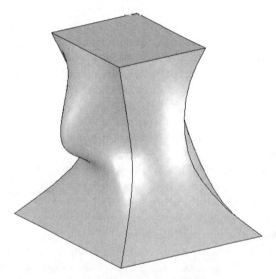

Figure 10-70 *Resulting loft feature after modification*

Tip. *You can also display a mesh in the preview of the loft feature by right-clicking to invoke the shortcut menu and choosing **Mesh Preview > Mesh All Faces**. The mesh preview will only be displayed on the non-planar faces and not on the planar faces. To display a mesh preview on all faces of the loft preview, you need to change the planar faces to non-planar faces by manipulating the connectors.*

Creating Lofted Cuts

CommandManager:	Features > Lofted Cut
SolidWorks menus:	Insert > Cut > Loft
Toolbar:	Features > Extruded Cut > Lofted cut

 You can remove the material in a part using the **Cut Loft PropertyManager**. This **PropertyManager** is invoked by choosing **Insert > Cut > Loft** from the SolidWorks menus and the options in this **PropertyManager** are the same as discussed in the previous tool.

Creating 3D Sketches

CommandManager:	Sketch > Sketch > 3D Sketch
SolidWorks menus:	Insert > 3D Sketch
Toolbar:	Sketch > Sketch > 3D Sketch

 In the earlier chapters, you have learned to draw 2D sketches in the sketching environment. In this chapter, you will learn to draw 3D sketches. These are mostly used to create 3D paths for the sweep features, 3D curves, and so on. Figure 10-71 shows a chair frame created by sweeping a profile along a 3D path.

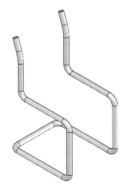

Figure 10-71 A chair frame created by sweeping a profile along a 3D path

To draw a 3D sketch, choose the **3D Sketch** button from the **Sketch CommandManager**; the 3D sketching environment will be invoked and the origin will be displayed in red color. You do not need to select a sketching plane to draw a 3D sketch. On invoking the 3D sketching environment, some of the sketching tools are activated in the **Sketch CommandManager**. These tools can be used in the 3D sketching environment and are discussed next.

Line

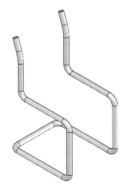 It is better to orient the view to isometric for drawing lines in the 3D sketching environment. Choose the **Line** button from the **Sketch CommandManager**; the **Insert Line PropertyManager** will be displayed. The **As sketched** radio button is selected in the **Orientation** rollout, while the other options are frozen. The select cursor is replaced by the line cursor with **XY** displayed at its bottom. This implies that by default, the sketch will be drawn in the XY plane. The coordinate system is also displayed in the current plane. You can toggle between the default planes using the TAB key. On doing so, the orientation of the coordinate system also modifies with respect to the current plane. Move the cursor to the location from where you want to start sketching. On specifying the start point of the line, you are provided with a space handle.

You can also toggle the plane after specifying the start point of the line. The coordinate system will also change with respect to the current plane. Move the cursor to specify the endpoint of the line. Its length will be displayed above the line cursor. Specify the endpoint of the line at this location. You will notice that a rubber-band line segment is attached to the cursor. Toggle the plane using the TAB key, if required. Move the cursor to draw another line and specify its endpoint at the desired location. Right-click to invoke the shortcut menu and choose the **Select** option to end drawing the line. Figures 10-72 through 10-74 show sketching in different planes in the 3D sketching environment. Figure 10-75 shows an example of a 3D sketch.

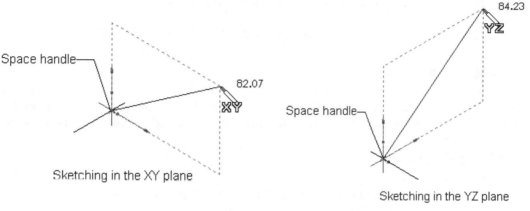

Figure 10-72 *Sketching in the XY plane*

Figure 10-73 *Sketching in the YZ plane*

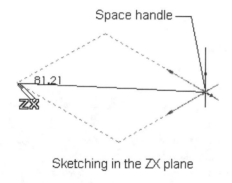

Figure 10-74 *Sketching in the ZX plane*

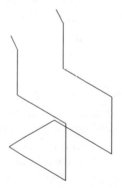

Figure 10-75 *3D sketch created using the Line tool*

Spline

 You can also draw a spline in the 3D sketching environment by choosing the **Spline** button from the **Sketch CommandManager**. The select cursor will be replaced by the spline cursor. Move it to the desired location to start the sketch. Specify the start point of the spline; the space handle will be displayed. You can toggle between the default planes using the TAB key. Move the cursor and specify the second point of the spline. Follow the same procedure to continue drawing the spline. To end the spline creation, right-click and choose the **Select** or the **End Spline** option from the shortcut menu.

Point

Choose the **Point** button from the **Sketch CommandManager**; the select cursor will be replaced by the point cursor. Use the left mouse button to place the points.

Centerline

You can also draw centerlines in the 3D sketching environment. Invoke the 3D sketching environment and orient the view to isometric. Choose **Line > Centerline** from the **Sketch CommandManager** to draw a centerline; the select cursor will be replaced by the line cursor. The procedure of drawing the centerline is the same as that discussed for drawing lines in the 2D sketching environment.

The dimensioning of 3D sketches is the same as the dimensioning of 2D sketches.

Editing 3D Sketches

You can perform a number of editing operations on 3D sketches including **Convert Entities**, **Sketch Chamfer**, **Trim Entities**, **Fit Spline**, **Sketch Fillet**, **Extend Entities**, **Construction Geometry**, and **Split Entities**. All these tools have been discussed in the previous chapters.

Creating Curves

You can also create various types of curves in SolidWorks. These curves are mostly used to create complex shapes using the **Swept Boss/Base** and **Lofted Boss/Base** tools. The types of curves that can be created in SolidWorks are discussed next.

Creating a Projection Curve

CommandManager:	Features > Curves > Project Curve
SolidWorks menus:	Insert > Curve > Projected
Toolbar:	Curves > Project Curve

This option allows you to project a single closed/open sketched entity on one or more than one planar or curved faces. You can also project a sketched entity on another sketched entity to create a 3D curve. To create a projected curve, draw at least two sketches or a single sketch and at least one feature that are not on the same plane. Next, choose **Curves > Project Curve** from the **Features CommandManager**; the **Projected Curve PropertyManager** will be displayed, as shown in Figure 10-76. The confirmation corner will also be displayed in the drawing area. The two different options used to create projected curves are discussed next.

Figure 10-76 The Projected Curve PropertyManager

Sketch on Sketch

Invoke the **Projected Curve PropertyManager** and then select the **Sketch on Sketch** radio button in the **Projection Type** area, if it is not selected by default. You will be prompted to select two sketches to project onto one another. Select two sketches that do not lie on the same plane. When you select the sketches, their names are displayed in the **Sketches to Project** selection box. The preview of the projected curve will also be displayed in the drawing area. Choose the **OK** button from the **Projected Curve PropertyManager** or choose **OK** from the confirmation corner. Figure 10-77 shows the two sketches selected to create a projected curve. Figure 10-78 shows the preview of the projected curve. Figure 10-79 shows the resulting projected curve.

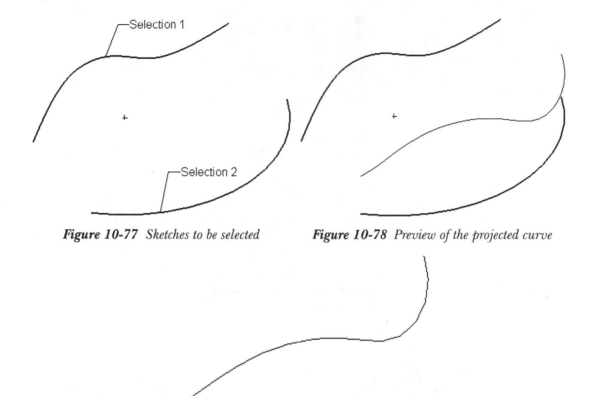

Figure 10-77 *Sketches to be selected*   **Figure 10-78** *Preview of the projected curve*

Figure 10-79 *Resulting projected curve*

Sketch on Faces

Select the **Sketch on Faces** radio button in the **Projection Type** area to project a sketch on a planar or curved faces. The **Projected Curve PropertyManager** with the **Sketch on Faces** radio button selected is shown in Figure 10-80. On selecting this option, the **Sketch to Project** and the **Projection Faces** selection boxes will be displayed in the **Selections** rollout. Select the sketch from the drawing area and the face or faces on which you want to project the sketch. The selected sketch will be highlighted in blue and the selected face will be highlighted in magenta. The arrow provided in the drawing area is used to reverse the direction of the projection. You can also reverse the direction of projection using the **Reverse Projection** check box. Choose the **OK** button from the **Projected Curve PropertyManager** or choose **OK** from the confirmation corner. Figure 10-81 shows the sketch to be selected for projection and also the face to be selected on which the sketch will be projected. Figure 10-82 shows the resulting projected curve.

*Figure 10-80 The **Projected Curve** **PropertyManager** with the **Sketch onto Face(s)** option selected*

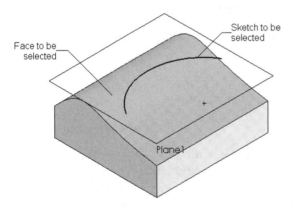

Figure 10-81 Sketch and face to be selected

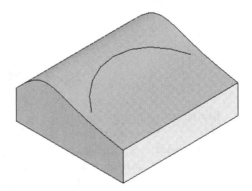

Figure 10-82 Resulting projected curve

Creating Split Lines

CommandManager:	Features > Curves > Split Line
SolidWorks menus:	Insert > Curve > Split Line
Toolbar:	Curves > Split Line

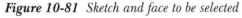

The **Split Line** tool is generally used to project a sketch on a planar or curved face, which in turn splits or divides the single face into two or more than two faces. Choose **Curves > Split Line** from the **Features CommandManager**; the **Split Line PropertyManager** will be displayed, as shown in Figure 10-83. The three methods to create a split line are discussed next.

> **Tip**. *You can also use the **Contour Select Tool** to select the contours for creating a projected curve or a split line.*

Silhouette

You can split a curved face by creating a silhouette line at the intersection of the projection of direction entity and the curved face. Invoke the **Split Line PropertyManager**; the **Silhouette** radio button in the **Type of Split** rollout will be selected by default. You need to select an edge, line, or a plane that defines the direction of pull. Select the direction of pull; the selected entity will be highlighted. Next, select the curved face; the selected face will be highlighted. Choose the **OK** button from the **Split Line PropertyManager** or choose the **OK** option from the confirmation corner. The curved face will be divided into two or more faces. The **Angle** spinner in the **Selections** rollout is used to define the draft angle for creating the silhouette line. By default, the value in this spinner is set to 0-degree.

Consider a case in which you need to split a circular face using this option. The plane will be selected to define the direction of pull. Figure 10-84 shows the plane and the face to be selected. Figure 10-85 shows the resulting split line created to split the selected face.

*Figure 10-83 The **Split Line PropertyManager***

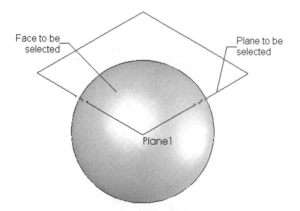

Figure 10-84 Plane and face to be selected

Figure 10-85 Resulting split line

Projection

You can project a sketched entity onto a planar or curved face to create a split line on it. The split line splits the selected face on which the sketch is projected. To use this option, invoke the **Split Line PropertyManager**, and select the **Projection** radio button from the **Type of Split** rollout, as shown in Figure 10-86.

Figure 10-86 *The* **Split Line PropertyManager**
with the **Projection** *option selected*

You will be prompted to change the type of split, or select the sketch to project, direction, and faces to be split. First select the sketch and then select the face to be split. Choose the **OK** button from the **Split Line PropertyManager**; the selected face will be split into two or more than two faces, depending on the sketch that is used to project it. Figure 10-87 shows the sketch and the face to be selected. Figure 10-88 shows the resulting split line created to split the selected face.

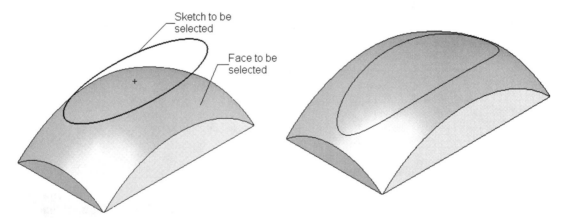

Figure 10-87 *Sketch and face to be selected*   **Figure 10-88** *Resulting split line*

The other options in the **Selections** rollout of the **Split Line PropertyManager** are discussed next.

Single direction

If the sketching plane on which the sketch is created lies within the model, the split line will be created on its two sides. Select the **Single direction** check box in the **Selections** rollout to create the split line only in one direction.

Reverse direction

The **Reverse direction** check box will be available only if the **Single direction** check box is selected. This option is used to reverse the direction of the split line created. Figure 10-89 shows the split line created on both sides of the model. Figure 10-90 shows the split line created on a single side of the model.

Figure 10-89 Split line created on both sides   *Figure 10-90* Split line created on single side

Intersection

The **Intersection** radio button is used to split the selected bodies or faces using the tool bodies, faces, or planes. Invoke the **Split Line PropertyManager** and select the **Intersection** radio button from the **Type of Split** rollout; the selection mode in the **Splitting Bodies/Faces/Planes** selection box will be active. Select the bodies, faces, or planes that will be used as tool bodies. Next, click in the **Faces/Bodies to Split** selection box and select the bodies to be split.

The **Split all** check box in the **Surface Split Options** rollout is used to split almost all areas of surfaces using the current selection set. You can also select the **Natural** or **Linear** radio button to define the shape of the split. Figure 10-91 shows the plane to be selected as a split tool and also faces to be split. Figure 10-92 shows the resulting split faces.

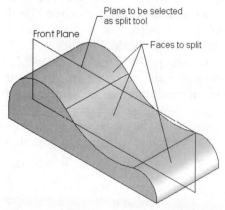

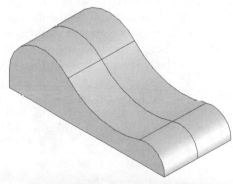

Figure 10-91 Plane and faces to be split   *Figure 10-92* Resulting split faces

Creating a Composite Curve

CommandManager:	Features > Curves > Composite Curve
SolidWorks menus:	Insert > Curve > Composite
Toolbar:	Curves > Composite Curve

The **Composite Curve** tool is used to create a curve by combining 2D or 3D curves, sketched entities, and part edges into a single curve. You need to ensure that the selected entities form a continuous chain. The composite curve is mainly used while creating a sweep or loft feature. To create a composite curve, choose **Curves > Composite Curve** from the **Features CommandManager**; the **Composite Curve PropertyManager** will be displayed, as shown in Figure 10-93.

Figure 10-93 The Composite Curve PropertyManager

On invoking the **Composite Curve PropertyManager**, you will be prompted to select a continuous set of sketches, edges, and/or curves. Select the continuous edges, curves, or sketched entities to create a composite curve. Choose the **OK** button to end its creation.

Creating a Curve Through XYZ Points

CommandManager:	Features > Curves > Curve Through XYZ Points
SolidWorks menus:	Insert > Curve > Curve Through XYZ Points
Toolbar:	Curves > Curve Through XYZ Points

The **Curve Through XYZ Points** option is used to create a curve by specifying the coordinate points. To create a curve using this option, choose **Curves > Curve Through XYZ Points** from the **Features CommandManager**; the **Curve File** dialog box will be displayed, as shown in Figure 10-94. Double-click in the cell under the **X** column to enter the X coordinate as the start point for the curve. Similarly, double-click in the **Y** and **Z** cells to enter the respective Y and Z coordinates of the start point of the curve. Double-click in the cell below the first cell to enter the coordinates for the second point to create the curve. Similarly, specify the coordinates of other points of the curve, as shown in Figure 10-95.

When you enter the coordinates of the points, the preview of the curve will be displayed in the drawing area. Choose the **OK** button from the **Curve File** dialog box to complete the feature creation, as shown in Figure 10-96.

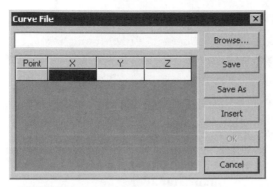

Figure 10-94 The **Curve File** *dialog box*

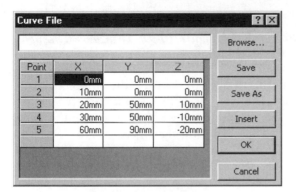

Figure 10-95 Coordinates entered in the **Curve File** dialog box

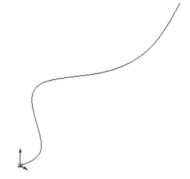

Figure 10-96 Resulting 3D curve

You can also save the current set of coordinates using the **Save** button in the **Curve File** dialog box. On choosing this button, the **Save As** dialog box will be displayed. Browse to the folder where you need to save the coordinates, enter the name of the file in the **File name** edit box and choose the **Save** button. The curve file will be saved with the *.sldcrv* extension. Choose **Save As** to save the current set of coordinates in a file with some other name.

On choosing the **Browse** button; the **Open** dialog box will be displayed. You can browse to the previously saved curve file to specify the coordinate points. You can also write the coordinates in a text (notepad) file and save it. In the **Open** dialog box, select the **Text Files (*.txt)** option from the **Files of type** drop-down list and browse the text file to specify the coordinates.

Tip. *To delete row from the* **Curve File** *dialog box, select row by using the SHIFT key and then press the DELETE key to delete the selected row. To insert a new row in the* **Curve File** *dialog box, select the row and then choose the* **Insert** *button; the new row will be inserted above the selected row.*

Creating a Curve Through Reference Points

CommandManager:	Features > Curves > Curve Through Reference Points
SolidWorks menus:	Insert > Curve > Curve Through Reference Points
Toolbar:	Curves > Curve Through Reference Points

The **Curve Through Reference Points** option enables you to create a curve by selecting the sketched points, vertices, origin, endpoints, or center points. To create a curve through reference points, choose **Curves > Curve Through Reference Points** from the **Features CommandManager**; the **Curve Through Reference Points PropertyManager** will be displayed, as shown in Figure 10-97.

*Figure 10-97 The **Curve Through Reference Points** PropertyManager*

On invoking this tool, you will be prompted to select the vertices to define the through points for the curve. Select the points to define the curve. On defining the points, the preview of the resulting curve will be displayed in the drawing area. After specifying all the points, choose the **OK** button. You can select the **Closed curve** check box to create a closed curve. Figure 10-98 shows the vertices to be selected to create the curve through the reference points. Figure 10-99 shows the 3D resulting curve.

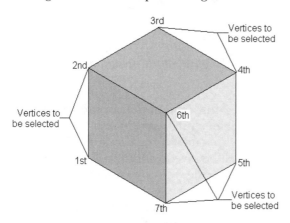

Figure 10-98 Vertices to be selected

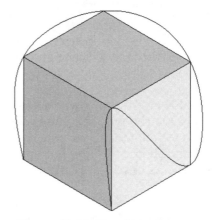

Figure 10-99 Resulting 3D curve

Creating a Helical/Spiral Curve

CommandManager:	Features > Curves > Helix and Spiral
SolidWorks menus:	Insert > Curve > Helix/Spiral
Toolbar:	Curves > Helix and Spiral

The **Helix and Spiral** tool is used to create a helical curve or a spiral curve. This curve is generally used as the sweep path to create springs, threads, spiral coils, and so on. Figure 10-100 shows a spring created by sweeping a circular profile along a helical path. Figure 10-101 shows a spiral coil created by sweeping a rectangular profile along a spiral path.

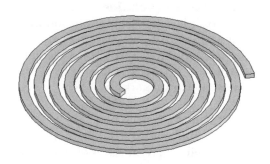

Figure 10-100 *Spring created*   *Figure 10-101* *Spiral coil created*

To create a helix, choose **Curves > Helix and Spiral** from
the **Features CommandManager**; the **Helix/Spiral**
PropertyManager will be displayed. Also, you will be
prompted to select a plane, a planar face, or an edge to
sketch a circle to define helix cross-section or to select a
single circle. The circle will define the diameter of the spring.
If you are creating a spiral, the sketch will define the starting
diameter of the spiral curve. The **Helix/Spiral**
PropertyManager disappears on selecting a plane and you
enter the sketching environment to draw the cross-section
sketch for the helix or spiral. Exit the sketching environment
after drawing the sketch. The **Helix/Spiral**
PropertyManager will be displayed again, as shown in
Figure 10-102.

When the **Helix/Spiral PropertyManager** will be displayed
again, set the view to isometric. You will notice that two arrows
are displayed. One emerging from the center of the circle
and it defines the direction of the helix. The second arrow is
tangent to the circle and it defines the start point of the helix,
either clockwise or counterclockwise. The preview of the helix
curve, with the default values, will be displayed in the drawing
area. Various methods to specify the parameters of the helical
curve are discussed next.

Figure 10-102 *The **Helix/***
Spiral PropertyManager

Pitch and Revolution
The **Pitch and Revolution** option selected by default from the **Type** drop-down list in
the **Defined By** rollout, is used to specify the pitch of the helical curve and the number
of revolutions. When this option is selected, the **Pitch** spinner and the **Revolutions** spinner
in the **Parameters** rollout will be used to define the value of pitch and the number of
revolutions. You can also select the **Reverse direction** check box available in the
Parameters rollout to reverse the direction of the helix creation. You can specify the start
angle of the helical curve using the **Start angle** spinner. The **Clockwise** and
Counterclockwise radio buttons in this rollout are used to define the direction of rotation
of the helix.

Height and Revolution

The **Height and Revolution** option in the **Type** drop-down list is used to define the parameters of the helix curve in the form of total helix height and the number of revolutions. On choosing this option, the **Height** and **Revolutions** spinners will be displayed in the **Parameters** rollout along with the other options to specify the required parameters.

Height and Pitch

The **Height and Pitch** option in the **Type** drop-down list is used to define the parameters of the helix curve in terms of height and pitch of the helix. When you select this option, the **Height** and **Pitch** spinners will be displayed in the **Parameters** rollout along with other options to specify the required parameters.

After you specify all parameters to create the helix curve, the preview in the drawing area will be modified automatically. Figure 10-103 shows a helix curve.

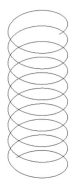

Figure 10-103 Helix Curve

If you want to create a helix of variable pitch, select the **Variable Pitch** radio button in the **Parameters** rollout and specify the number of revolutions, diameter, and pitch in the table displayed in the **Region Parameters** area.

Taper Helix

You can create a tapered helix using the **Taper Helix** rollout. Select the check box available at the left of the **Taper Helix** rollout; the **Taper Angle** spinner and the **Taper outward** check box will be available. Specify the angle between the central axis of the helix and the periphery of the helix using the **Taper Angle** spinner. The **Taper outward** check box is selected by default and is used to create an outward taper. When you specify the parameters to create a tapered helical curve, the preview of the helical curve will update automatically in the drawing area. Figure 10-104 shows a tapered helical curve. Figure 10-105 shows a tapered helical curve created with the **Taper outward** check box selected.

By default, the helical curve is created in the clockwise direction because the **Clockwise** radio button is selected in the **Parameters** rollout of the **Helix/Spiral PropertyManager**. Select the **Counterclockwise** radio button to create the helical curve in the counterclockwise direction. After setting the parameters, choose the **OK** button from the **Helix/Spiral PropertyManager**.

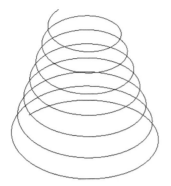

Figure 10-104 *Tapered helical curve*

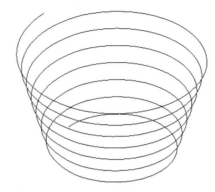

Figure 10-105 *Tapered helical curve with the* ***Taper outward*** *check box selected*

Creating a Spiral Curve

To create a spiral curve, select the **Spiral** option from the **Type** drop-down list in the **Defined By** rollout. The preview of the spiral curve will be displayed in the drawing area. You can define the pitch and the number of revolutions in the **Pitch** and **Revolutions** spinners, respectively. The other options in the **Parameters** rollout are the same as those discussed earlier. After specifying all the required parameters, choose the **OK** button. Figure 10-106 shows a spiral curve.

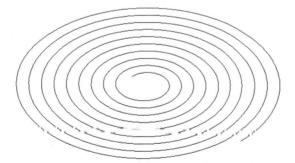

Figure 10-106 *Spiral curve*

Extruding a 3D Sketch

You can also extrude a 3D sketch drawn on the 3D sketching environment. A 3D sketch is always extruded along a direction vector, which can be a line, edge, planar face, or a plane. Invoke the **Extrude PropertyManager** and select the 3D sketch that you need to extrude. Also, you need to select a direction vector along which the sketch will be extruded. Set the parameters at the start of the extrude feature using the **From** rollout. Now, set the value of the depth of the extrude feature and choose the **OK** button from the **Extrude PropertyManager**. Figure 10-107 shows a 3D sketch and the direction vector along which it will be extruded. Figure 10-108 shows the resulting extruded feature.

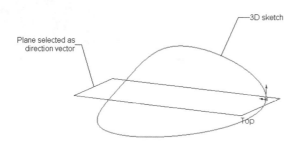

Figure 10-107 *3D sketch and the direction vector*   **Figure 10-108** *Resulting extruded feature*

Creating Draft Features

CommandManager:	Features > Draft
SolidWorks menus:	Insert > Features > Draft
Toolbar:	Features > Draft

The **Draft** tool is used to add taper to the selected faces of the model. Draft feature is mostly added to the model that are to be molded or casted as it will be easier to remove them from the mold or die. To apply draft, choose the **Draft** button from the **Features CommandManager**; the **Draft PropertyManager** will be displayed. In SolidWorks, you can create drafts manually or by using the **DraftXpert**. The process of creating the draft using the manual method is discussed next.

To create a manual draft, choose the **Manual** tab, as shown in Figure 10-109; you will be prompted to select a neutral plane and faces to add draft. On doing so, you will notice that the **Neutral Plane** radio button is selected by default in the **Type of Draft** rollout. Select a neutral plane to create the draft feature. Select a planar face or a plane that acts as a neutral plane. Neutral plane is the plane with respect to which the draft angle is measured. The name of the selected entity will appear in the **Neutral Plane** rollout. The **Reverse Direction** arrow is also displayed in the drawing area. The selection mode in the **Faces to Draft** selection box of the **Faces to Draft** rollout will be activated. Select the faces to apply the draft. The selected faces will be displayed with the **Draft Face** callout. Next, set the value of the draft angle in the **Draft Angle** spinner available in the **Draft Angle** rollout. Choose the **OK** button from the **Draft PropertyManager** or choose **OK** from the confirmation corner.

Figure 10-109 *The Draft PropertyManager*

Figure 10-110 shows the neutral face and the faces to be selected to add draft. Figure 10-111 shows the resulting draft feature.

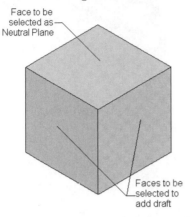

Face to be selected as Neutral Plane

Faces to be selected to add draft

Figure 10-110 Faces to be selected   *Figure 10-111 Resulting draft feature*

You can draft a portion of the selected faces using parting line. The parting line is a line that divides the faces of a feature. You need to create a parting line by using the **Split Line** tool or by using the edges of an existing model. To apply draft using the parting line, invoke the **Draft PropertyManager** and select the **Parting Line** radio button from the **Type of Draft** rollout; you will be prompted to select the pulling direction and the parting line. Select a planar face or a plane that act as a pulling direction; the **Reverse Direction** arrow will be displayed in the drawing area. Also, the selection mode in the **Parting Lines** selection box will be activated. Select the parting lines from the drawing area; the arrows will be displayed in the drawing area. These arrows specify different draft directions for each segment of the parting line. To change the direction of these arrows, select the respective parting line from the **Parting Lines** selection area and then choose the **Other Face** button available below the **Parting Lines** selection area. Next, specify the angle of the draft in the **Draft Angle** spinner and choose the **OK** button from the **Draft PropertyManager**. Figure 10-112 shows the pulling direction and parting lines to be selected and Figure 10-113 shows the resulting draft feature.

The **Step Draft** radio button in the **Type of Draft** rollout is used to apply step draft. To do so, invoke the **Draft PropertyManager** and then select the **Step Draft** radio button; the **Tapered steps** and **Perpendicular steps** radio buttons will be displayed. The **Tapered steps** radio button is selected by default. So that, surfaces will be generated in the same manner as the tapered surfaces. On selecting the **Perpendicular steps** radio button, surfaces will be generated perpendicular to original faces. Select the pulling direction and then the parting line from the drawing area. Next, specify the draft angle in the **Draft Angle** spinner and choose the **OK** button from the **Draft PropertyManager**. Figure 10-114 shows the pulling direction and the parting lines to be selected. Figures 10-115 and 10-116 show the resulting step draft features using the **Tapered steps** and **Perpendicular steps** radio buttons selected.

The other options in the **Draft PropertyManager** are discussed next.

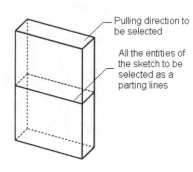

Figure 10-112 *Pulling direction and parting lines to be selected*

Figure 10-113 *The resulting draft feature*

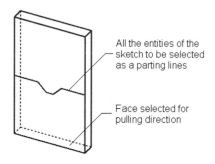

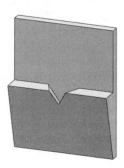

Figure 10-114 *Parting lines and pulling direction to be selected*

Figure 10-115 *The resulting draft feature using the **Tapered steps** radio button selected*

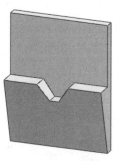

Figure 10-116 *The resulting draft feature using the **Perpendicular steps** radio button selected*

Reverse Direction

The **Reverse Direction** button on the left of the **Neutral Plane** selection box in the **Neutral Plane** rollout is used to reverse the direction of creation of the draft. You can also reverse the direction of the draft creation by selecting the **Reverse Direction** arrow in the drawing area.

Face propagation

The options in the **Face propagation** drop-down list in the **Faces to Draft** rollout are used to extend the draft feature to the other faces. These options are discussed next.

None

The **None** option is selected by default. This option is used when you do not need to apply any type of face propagation.

Along Tangent

The **Along Tangent** option is used to apply the draft to the faces tangent to the selected face.

All Faces

The **All Faces** option is used to apply the draft to all the faces attached to the neutral plane or face.

Inner Faces

This option is used to draft all the faces inside the model such as holes, slots, and so on that are attached to the neutral plane or face.

Outer Faces

This option is used to draft all the outside faces of the model that are attached to the neutral plane or face.

The **DraftXpert** is used to create or modify an existing draft feature. To create the draft using the **DraftXpert**, choose this tab; the **DraftXpert PropertyManager** will be displayed, as shown in Figure 10-117. Also, the **Add** tab will be chosen by default and the related options will be displayed in the **DraftXpert PropertyManager**. Most of the options to create the draft feature are the same as those discussed in the manual draft. The options in the **Draft Analysis** rollout are different and are discussed next.

Auto paint

Select the **Auto paint** check box to enable the draft analysis options. These options are discussed next.

Figure 10-117 The options in the DraftXpert Property Manager

Show/hide faces with positive draft

This is the first button below the **Auto paint** check box. If this button is chosen, the faces with the positive draft are highlighted with the color shown in the color box on the right of this button. Note that the faces will be highlighted only after you select the faces to add the draft and choose the **Apply** button from the **Items to Draft** rollout.

Show/hide faces requiring draft

While analyzing the draft, SolidWorks highlights the faces that require a draft. These faces are highlighted if this button is chosen.

Show/hide faces with negative draft

Choose this button to highlight the faces with the negative draft with the color shown in the color box on the right of this button. Note that the faces will be highlighted only after you select the faces to add the draft and choose the **Apply** button from the **Items to Draft** rollout.

To modify or remove an existing draft, choose the **Change** tab and select the draft faces to be changed. If you need to remove the draft, choose the **Remove** button. If you need to change the draft angle, set the new draft angle in the **Draft Angle** spinner and choose the **Change** button; the draft angle will be changed. If there are multiple drafts, you can filter the drafts using the options in the **Existing Drafts** rollout. To do so, select an option from the **Sort List by** drop-down list in this rollout; the items related to the options in the **Sort List by** drop-down list will be listed in the **Filtered face groups** list box. On selecting an item from this list box, the corresponding face, neutral plane, and the draft angle will be displayed in the **Drafts to change** rollout. Now you can change or remove the selected draft face. Choose the **OK** button after creating or modifying the feature.

Tip. *After choosing the **Apply** button and selecting the **Auto paint** check box in the **DraftXpert PropertyManager**, if you move the cursor over any faces of the model other than the neutral plane, the draft angle of that face will be displayed above the cursor.*

TUTORIALS

Tutorial 1

In this tutorial, you will create the model shown in Figure 10-118. The dimensions of the model are shown in the same figure. The hidden lines in the top and side views are suppressed for clarity.   **(Expected time: 45 min)**

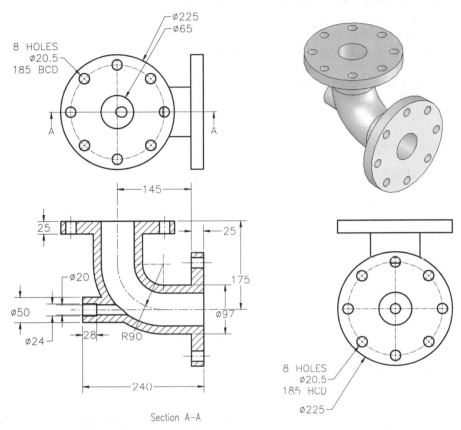

Figure 10-118 *Views and dimensions of the model for Tutorial 1*

The following steps are required to complete this tutorial:

a. The base feature of the model is a sweep feature. First, you need to create the path for
    the sweep feature on the Front Plane. Next, you need to create a plane normal to this
    path. Select the newly created plane as the sketching plane and create the profile for the
    sweep feature. You will create a thin sweep feature because the base feature of the model
    is a hollow feature, refer to Figures 10-119 through 10-121.
b. Create the remaining features, refer to Figure 10-122.
c. Save the model.

Creating the Path for the Sweep Feature

As discussed earlier, the base feature of the model is a sweep feature. To create the sweep
feature, you first need to create its path. This path will be created on the Front Plane.

1. Start a new SolidWorks part document using the **New SolidWorks Document** dialog box.

2. Draw the sketch of the path for the sweep feature on the Front Plane and add the required
    relations and dimensions to the sketch, as shown in Figure 10-119. Exit the sketching
    environment and change the view to isometric.

Creating the Profile of the Sweep Feature

After creating the path for the sweep feature, you will create its profile. To create the profile, first you need to create a reference plane normal to the path. The newly created plane will be selected as the sketching plane for creating the profile for the sweep feature.

1. Invoke the **Plane PropertyManager** and create a plane normal to the path using the **Normal to Curve** option, as shown in Figure 10-120.

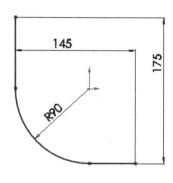

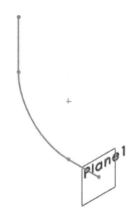

Figure 10-119 *Sketch of the path*   **Figure 10-120** *Plane created normal to the path*

2. Invoke the sketching environment by selecting the newly created plane as the sketching plane.

3. Draw the sketch of the profile of the sweep feature using the **Circle** tool. The center of the circle is at the origin and the diameter of the circle is 97 mm.

4. Exit the sketching environment after drawing the profile of the sweep feature.

Creating the Sweep Feature

The sweep feature that you are going to create is a thin sweep feature. You will use the **Thin Feature** rollout to specify its parameters.

1. Choose the **Swept Boss/Base** button from the **Features CommandManager**; the **Sweep PropertyManager** is displayed and you are prompted to select the profile.

2. Select the circle as the profile for the sweep feature; the circle is highlighted and the **Profile** callout is also displayed. Also, you are prompted to select the sweep path after selecting the profile.

3. Select the path for the sweep feature; the selected path is highlighted and the **Path** callout is also displayed. The preview of the sweep feature is also displayed.

4. Select the check box on the left of the **Thin Feature** rollout; the **Thin Feature** rollout is invoked.

5. Set the value of thickness in the **Thickness** spinner to **16**.

Since the wall thickness added to the model is reverse to the required direction, therefore, you need to reverse the direction to create the thin feature.

6. Choose the **Reverse Direction** button from the **Thin Features** rollout. Choose the **OK** button from the **Sweep PropertyManager** or choose **OK** from the confirmation corner.

The base feature created by sweeping a profile along a path is shown in Figure 10-121.

 Tip. *Instead of creating a thin sweep feature, you can also create a solid sweep feature and then add a shell feature to hollow the base feature.*

Creating Remaining Features

1. Create the features on both the ends of the sweep feature using the **Extruded Boss/Base** tool, refer to Figure 10-122.

2. Create the hole using the **Simple Hole** tool and create the circular pattern of the hole feature.

3. Create a plane at an offset distance from the right face of the model. Then, create the circular feature by extruding it using the **Up To Next** option.

4. Create the custom sized counterbore hole using the **Hole Wizard** tool on the extruded feature created in the previous step. The final solid model for Tutorial 1 is shown in Figure 10-122.

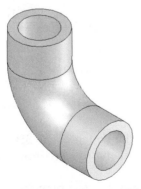

Figure 10-121 Base feature of the model   *Figure 10-122 Final model for Tutorial 1*

Saving the Model

1. Save the model with the name and the location given below:

   \My Documents\SolidWorks\c10\c10tut1.sldprt

2. Choose **File > Close** from the SolidWorks menus to close the file.

Tutorial 2

In this tutorial, you will create the chair frame shown in Figure 10-123. The dimensions of the chair frame are also shown in the same figure.   **(Expected time: 30 min)**

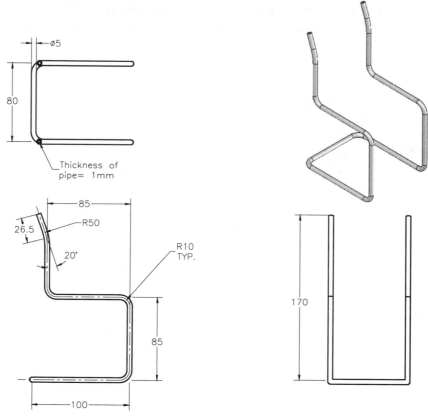

Figure 10-123 *Views and dimensions of the model for Tutorial 2*

The following steps are required to complete this tutorial:

a. Invoke the 3D sketching environment and then draw the sketch of the 3D path. You will create only the left half of the 3D path in the 3D sketching environment, refer to Figure 10-124.
b. Create a plane normal to the 3D path. Select the newly created plane as the sketching plane and draw the sketch of the profile.
c. Sweep the profile along the 3D path using the **Thin Feature** option, refer to Figure 10-125.
d. Mirror the sweep feature using the Front Plane, refer to Figure 10-126.
e. Save the model.

Creating the Path for the Sweep Feature Using the 3D Sketching Environment

It is evident from Figure 10-118 that the model is created by sweeping a profile along a 3D path. Therefore, you need to create a path for the sweep feature in the 3D sketching environment.

1. Start a new SolidWorks part document.

2. Create a plane at an offset distance of 40 mm from the Front Plane.

3. Change the current view to isometric.

4. Choose **Insert > 3D Sketch** from the SolidWorks menus to invoke the 3D sketching environment. You can also choose **Sketch > 3D Sketch** from the **Sketch CommandManager** to invoke the 3D sketching environment.

   The 3D sketching environment is invoked and the sketch origin is displayed in red. You are also provided with the confirmation corner on the top right corner of the drawing area. The sketching tools that can be used in the 3D sketching environment are also highlighted.

   You need to draw the left half of the sketch as the path of the sweep profile.

5. Invoke the **Line** tool; the select cursor is replaced by the line cursor. The **XY** symbol displayed below the line cursor suggests that the line will be sketched in the XY plane, by default.

   You need to draw the first line in the ZX plane. Therefore, you need to toggle the plane before you start creating the sketch.

6. Press the TAB key twice to switch to the ZX plane.

7. Move the line cursor to the origin. When a red dot is displayed, specify the start point of the line.

8. Move the cursor in the positive Z direction of the triad; a small triad with Z appears below the cursor indicating that you are drawing the line in the **Z** direction. Specify the endpoint of the line, when a value close to 40 is displayed above the cursor; a rubber-band line is attached to the cursor.

9. Move the cursor toward the right along the infinite line indicating the X-axis. Specify the endpoint of the line when a value close to 100 is displayed above the cursor.

10. Press the TAB key to switch over to the XY plane. Move the cursor vertically upward.

11. Specify the endpoint of the line when the value above the cursor shows a value close to 85.

12. Similarly, draw the remaining sketch and add the required relations and dimensions to it.

13. Add the **On Plane** relation between the upper endpoint of the 3D sketch and Plane1. The final sketch is displayed in Figure 10-124.

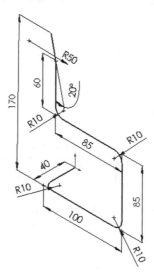

Figure 10-124 *Sketch of the 3D path*

14. Exit the 3D sketching environment using the confirmation corner.

Creating the Profile of the Sweep Feature

As discussed earlier, the sweep feature will be created by sweeping the profile along the 3D path. After creating the path, you need to create the profile of the sweep feature.

You do not need to create a reference plane because the Front Plane is normal to the 3D path.

1. Select the Front Plane as the sketching plane and invoke the sketching environment.

2. Draw a circle of diameter 5 mm with origin as center. This sketch will be used as the sketch of the profile of the sweep feature, refer to Figure 10-125.

3. Exit the sketching environment.

Sweeping the Profile along the 3D Path

After creating the 3D path and the profile for the sweep feature, you need to sweep the profile along the 3D path using the **Swept Boss/Base** tool.

1. Choose the **Swept Boss/Base** button from the **Features CommandManager**; the **Sweep PropertyManager** is displayed.

2. Select the circle as the profile; the name of the selected profile is displayed in the selection box. The profile callout is also displayed.

   You are prompted to select the path for the sweep feature.

3. Select the 3D sketch as the path for the sweep feature. The name of the path will be displayed in the selection box. The path callout is also displayed. The preview of the sweep feature is also displayed in the drawing area.

   As is evident from Figure 10-123, the frame of the chair is made up of a hollow pipe. Therefore, you need to create a thin sweep feature to create a hollow chair frame.

4. Expand the **Thin Feature** rollout and set the value in the **Thickness** spinner to **1**.

5. Choose the **Reverse Direction** button from the **Thin Features** rollout to reverse the direction of the thin feature creation.

6. Choose the **OK** button from the **Sweep PropertyManager** to end the creation of the feature.

   The model, after creating the sweep feature, is displayed in Figure 10-125.

7. Mirror the sweep feature about the Front Plane using the **Mirror** tool. The model, after mirroring, is shown in Figure 10-126.

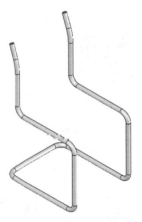

Figure 10-125 Sweep feature created by sweeping a profile along the 3D path

Figure 10-126 The final model

Saving the Model

1. Save the model with the name and the location given below:

   \My Documents\SolidWorks\c10\c10tut2.sldprt

2. Close the document.

Tutorial 3

In this tutorial, you will create a spring shown in Figure 10-127. The views and dimensions of the spring are shown in Figure 10-128. **(Expected time: 45 min)**

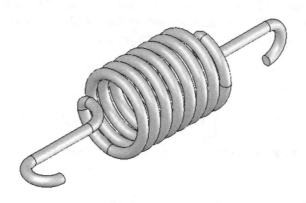

Figure 10-127 *Model for Tutorial 3*

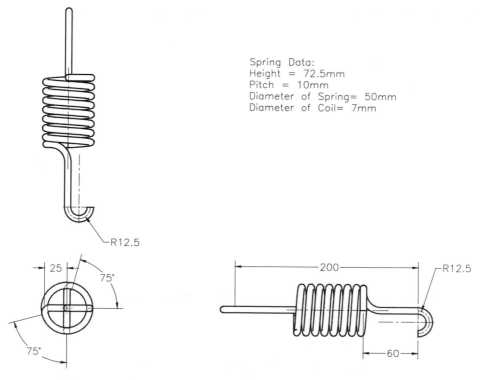

Spring Data:
Height = 72.5mm
Pitch = 10mm
Diameter of Spring= 50mm
Diameter of Coil= 7mm

Figure 10-128 *Views and dimensions of the model for Tutorial 3*

The following steps are required to complete this tutorial:

a. Create the helical path of the spring, refer to Figure 10-129.
b. Create the end clips of the spring, refer to Figure 10-132.
c. Combine the end clips and the helical curve to create a single curve using the **Composite Curve** option, refer to Figure 10-133.
d. Create the profile on the plane normal to the curve and sweep it along the curve, refer to Figures 10-134 and 10-135.

Creating the Helical Curve

To create this model, you first need to create the helical curve of the spring. For creating the helical curve, you first need to create a circular sketch. This sketch will define the diameter of the spring.

1. Start a new SolidWorks Part document.

2. Choose **Curves > Helix and Spiral** from the **Curves CommandManager** and select the Front Plane as the sketching plane.

3. Draw a circle of diameter 50 mm. Change its view to isometric and exit the sketching environment; the **Helix/Spiral Curve PropertyManager** is displayed and the preview of the helical curve with the default values is displayed in the drawing area.

4. Select the **Height and Pitch** option from the **Type** drop-down list in the **Define By** rollout.

5. Set the value in the **Height** spinner to **72.5** and the value in the **Pitch** spinner to **10**. You will observe that the preview of the helical curve is updated automatically when you modify the values in the spinners.

6. Set the value of the **Start angle** spinner to **0** and choose the **OK** button from the **Helix/Spiral PropertyManager**; the helical curve is created, as shown in Figure 10-129.

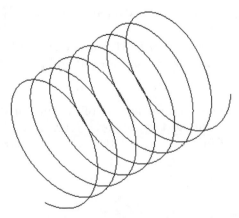

Figure 10-129 Helical curve

Drawing the Sketch of the End Clips of the Spring

After creating the helical curve, you need to draw the sketch that defines the path of the end clips. There are two end clips in this spring, and each end clip is created using two sketches. First, you will create the right end-clip and then the left end-clip.

1. Select the Front Plane as the sketching plane and invoke the sketching environment.

    The first sketch of the right end-clip consists of two arcs. The first arc will be drawn using the **Centerpoint Arc** tool and the second arc will be drawn using the **3 Point Arc** tool.

2. Choose the **Centerpoint Arc** button from the **Sketch CommandManager** and specify the centerpoint of the arc at the origin.

3. Move the cursor toward the right and specify the start point of the arc when the radius of the reference circle shows a value close to **25**.

4. Move the cursor in the counterclockwise direction. Specify the endpoint of the arc when the value of the angle above the cursor shows a value close to **75**.

5. Set the view to the front view.

6. Choose the **3 Point Arc** button from the **Arc PropertyManager**. Specify the start point of the arc on the upper endpoint of the previous arc. Create the arc, as shown in Figure 10-130.

7. Add the **Pierce** relation between the lower endpoint of the first arc and the helical curve. Add the other relations and the dimensions to fully define the sketch. The fully defined sketch is shown in Figure 10-130.

8. Exit the sketching environment.

    After drawing the first sketch of the right end-clip, you need to draw the second sketch of the right end-clip. The second sketch of the right end-clip is drawn on the Right Plane.

9. Select the Right Plane and invoke the sketching environment.

10. Draw the sketch, as shown in Figure 10-131. You need to apply the **Pierce** relation between the upper arc of the previous sketch and the left end point of the left arc of the current sketch.

11. Add a **Tangent** relation between the left arc of the current sketch and the upper arc of the sketch previously drawn. Add the required relations and dimensions to the current sketch. The sketch, after applying all the relations and dimensions, is shown in Figure 10-131.

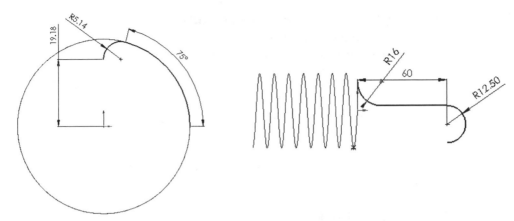

Figure 10-130 First sketch of right end-clip   *Figure 10-131* Second sketch of right end-clip

12. Similarly, draw the sketch of the left end-clip. Figure 10-132 shows the path for the spring after creating the helical curve, right end-clip, and the left end-clip.

Creating the Composite Curve

After creating all the required sketches and the helical curve, you need to combine them so that they form a single curve. This is done because the path of the sweep feature has to be a single curve or sketch.

1. Choose **Curves > Composite Curve** from the **Feature CommandManager** or choose **Insert > Curve > Composite** from the SolidWorks menus; the **Composite Curve PropertyManager** is displayed and the confirmation corner is also available.

2. Select both the end-clips and the helical curve from the drawing area or from the **FeatureManager design tree**.

3. Choose the **OK** button from the **Composite Curve PropertyManager** or choose **OK** from the confirmation corner; the composite curve is created, as shown in Figure 10-133.

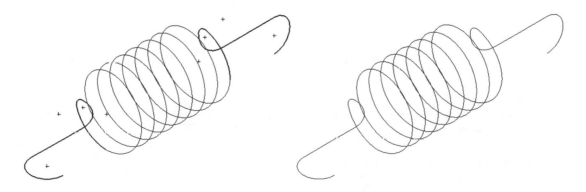

Figure 10-132 Path for the spring   *Figure 10-133* Composite curve

Creating the Profile for the Sweep Feature

Next, you need to create the profile for the sweep feature. The sketch of the profile will be drawn on a plane normal to the curve on the endpoint of the right end-clip.

1. Create a plane normal to the path and at the endpoint of the right end-clip.

2. Draw the profile of the sweep feature and add the **Pierce** relation between the center of the circle and the composite curve. Add the required dimensions to the sketch.

3. Exit the sketching environment. Figure 10-134 shows the profile and the path for the sweep feature.

Creating the Sweep Feature

You will create a sweep feature to complete the creation of the spring.

1. Invoke the **Sweep PropertyManager**; you are prompted to select the sweep profile.

2. Select the sweep profile from the drawing area; you are prompted to select the sweep path.

3. Select the composite curve as the path and choose the **OK** button from the **Sweep PropertyManager**.

    The spring created, after sweeping the profile along the path, is shown in Figure 10-135.

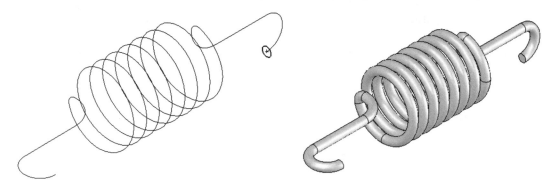

Figure 10-134 *Profile and path for the sweep feature*   ***Figure 10-135*** *Final model*

Saving the Model

1. Choose the **Save** button from the Menu Bar and save the model with the name and the location given below:

    \My Documents\SolidWorks\c10\c10tut3.sldprt

2. Close the document.

SELF-EVALUATION TEST

Answer the following questions and then compare them to those given at the end of this chapter:

1. You need a profile and a path to create a sweep feature. (T/F)

2. At least two sections are required to create a loft feature. (T/F)

3. You cannot sweep a closed profile along a closed path. (T/F)

4. You cannot create a thin sweep feature. (T/F)

5. You can create a loft feature using open sections. (T/F)

6. The _____ **PropertyManager** is used to create a loft feature.

7. The _____ option is used to create a single curve by joining the continuous chain of existing sketches, edges, or curves.

8. You need to apply the _____ relation between the sketch and the guide curve while sweeping a profile along a path using guide curves.

9. The _____ option is used to create a curve by defining coordinates.

10. The _____ **PropertyManager** is invoked to create a cut-sweep feature.

REVIEW QUESTIONS

Answer the following questions:

1. In the _____ rollout, you can define the tangency at the start and end sections in the sweep feature.

2. The _____ rollout is used to create a thin loft feature.

3. You need to invoke the _____ dialog box to create a spiral curve.

4. The _____ **PropertyManager** is invoked to create a curve projected on a surface.

5. The _____ dialog box is used to specify coordinates to create a curve.

6. Which button is chosen to invoke the 3D sketching environment?

    (a) **2D Sketch**   (b) **3D Sketching Environment**
    (c) **3D Sketch**   (d) **Sketch**

7. Which rollout in the **Sweep PropertyManager** is used to define the tangency?

    (a) **Start/End Tangency**   (b) **Tangency**
    (c) **Options**   (d) None of these

8. Which button in the **Features PropertyManager** is used to invoke the **Draft PropertyManager**?

    (a) **Draft**   (b) **Taper Angle**
    (c) **Draft Feature**   (d) **Draft Angle**

9. Which **PropertyManager** is used to change an existing draft feature?

    (a) **DraftXpert**   (b) **Draft**
    (c) Both a and b   (d) None of these

10. Which button in the **Guide Curves** rollout is used to display sections while creating the sweep feature with guide curves?

    (a) **Preview Sections**   (b) **Show Sections**
    (c) **Sections**   (d) **Preview**

EXERCISE

Exercise 1

Create the model of the Upper Housing shown in Figure 10-136. The dimensions of the model are shown in Figure 10-137.   **(Expected time: 1 hr)**

Tip. *This model is divided into three major parts. The first part is the base and is created by extruding the sketch to a distance of 80 mm using the **Mid Plane** option.*

The second part of this model is the right portion of the discharge venturi and is created using the sweep feature. The path of the sweep feature will be created on the Right Plane. You need to create this plane at the left endpoint of the path and also normal to the path.

The third part of this model is the left portion of the discharge venturi created using the loft feature. You need to create the first section of the loft feature on the planar face of the sweep feature created earlier. The second section will be created on a plane at an offset distance from the planar face of the sweep feature created earlier. Create a loft feature using the two sections created earlier. The other features needed to complete the model are fillets, hole, circular pattern, and so on.

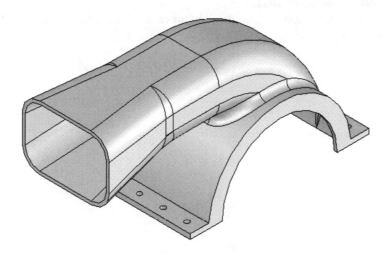

Figure 10-136 *Model of the Upper Housing*

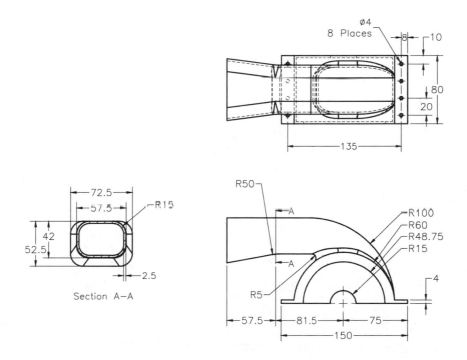

Figure 10-137 *Dimensions of the Upper Housing*

Answers to Self-Evaluation Test

1. T, 2. T, 3. F, 4. F, 5. T, 6. **Loft**, 7. **Composite Curve**, 8. **Coincident**, 9. **Curve Through Free Points**, 10. **Cut-Sweep**

Chapter 11

Advanced Modeling Tools-IV

Learning Objectives

After completing this chapter, you will be able to:
- *Create dome features.*
- *Create shape features.*
- *Create indent features.*
- *Create deform features.*
- *Create flex features.*
- *Create fastening features.*
- *Create freeform features.*

ADVANCED MODELING TOOLS

Some of the advanced modeling options have already been discussed in Chapters 7, 8, and 10. In this chapter, you will learn about some more advanced modeling tools that you can use to enhance your ability to style your concept of product designing.

Creating Dome Features

CommandManager:	Features > Dome	
SolidWorks menus:	Insert > Features > Dome	
Toolbar:	Features > Dome	*(Customize to add)*

The **Dome** tool can be used to create a dome feature on the selected face. Depending on the direction of feature creation, a dome can be of a convex or concave shape. To create a dome feature, choose the **Dome** button from the **Features CommandManager**, or choose **Insert > Features > Dome** from the SolidWorks menus; the **Dome PropertyManager** will be displayed, as shown in Figure 11-1. Also, you will be prompted to select a face or faces on which you want to add the dome feature. The face to be selected can be a planar or a non-planar face. Select the face on which you need to create the dome feature; the name of the selected face will be displayed in the **Faces to Dome** selection box. The preview of the dome feature, with the default values, will be displayed in the drawing area. Set the height of the dome feature in the **Distance** spinner. You can also move the cursor on the thumbwheel below the **Distance** spinner and drag the cursor to modify its value. If you drag the thumbwheel to the

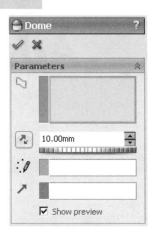

*Figure 11-1 The **Dome** PropertyManager*

right, the value will increase and if you drag it to the left, the value will decrease. The preview of the dome feature will modify dynamically when you modify the height using the **Distance** spinner. The height of the dome feature is calculated from the centroid of the selected face to the top of the dome feature. After specifying the height of the dome feature, choose the **OK** button from the **Dome PropertyManager**. Figure 11-2 shows the planar face to be selected for the dome feature. Figure 11-3 shows the resulting dome feature.

If the selected planar face belongs to a circular or an elliptical feature, the **Elliptical dome** check box will be displayed in the **Dome PropertyManager**. You can create an elliptical dome feature by selecting this check box. If you select two planar faces of a circular feature, an elliptical dome will be created, by default. Figure 11-4 shows a circular dome created by selecting a circular planar face. Figure 11-5 shows an elliptical dome created by first selecting the **Elliptical dome** check box and then a circular planar face.

You can also create a concave shaped dome by removing the material and creating a cavity in the form of a dome. To do so, choose the **Reverse Direction** button on the left of the **Distance** spinner; a concave shaped dome will be created, as shown in Figure 11-6.

Other options in the **Dome PropertyManager** are discussed next.

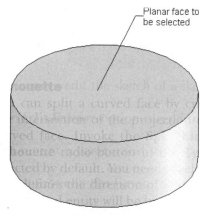

Planar face to
be selected

Figure 11-2 *Planar face to be selected*

Figure 11-3 *Resulting dome feature*

Figure 11-4 *Circular dome*

Figure 11-5 *Elliptical dome*

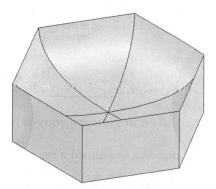

Figure 11-6 *A dome feature created with the*
Reverse Direction *button chosen*

Constraint Point or Sketch

The **Constraint Point or Sketch** option is provided in the **Dome PropertyManager** to constrain the dome creation to the selected reference. The selected reference can be a point, sketched point, or an endpoint of an entity. To create a dome feature using the **Constraint Point or Sketch** option, invoke the **Dome PropertyManager** and select the face on which you need to add the dome feature. Now, click once in the **Constraint Point or Sketch** selection box and select the constraint point from the drawing area and choose the **OK** button from the **Dome PropertyManager**. Figure 11-7 shows the face on which you need to add the dome feature and the point to be selected as the constraint point. Figure 11-8 shows the resulting dome feature.

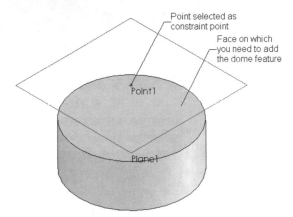

Figure 11-7 Face and the point to be selected

Figure 11-8 Resulting dome feature

Note
The dome feature will be created depending on the height of the dome and the position of the constraint point.

Direction

The **Direction** option in the **Dome PropertyManager** is used to specify the direction vector in which you need to create the dome feature. To create the dome feature by defining the direction vector, invoke the **Dome PropertyManager**. Select the face on which you need to create the dome feature. Now, click once in the **Direction** selection box and select an edge as the directional reference from the drawing area. The selected edge will be highlighted. Set the value of the height of the dome and choose the **OK** button from the **Dome PropertyManager**. Figure 11-9 shows the face on which you need to add the dome feature and the edge to be selected as the direction vector. Figure 11-10 shows the resulting dome.

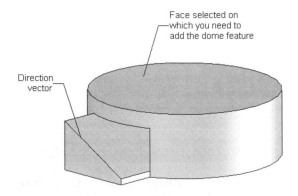

Figure 11-9 Face and direction vector to be selected

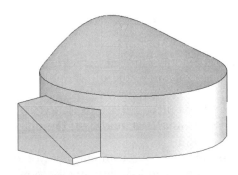

Figure 11-10 Resulting dome feature

Creating Shape Features

CommandManager:	Features > Shape	*(Customize to add)*
SolidWorks menus:	Insert > Features > Shape	
Toolbar:	Features > Shape	*(Customize to add)*

SolidWorks provides you with a styling tool named as the **Shape** tool. You can use this tool to create shapes by manipulating the faces of the models. On using the **Shape** tool, the selected face acts like a rubber membrane on which the pressure is applied. As a result, the face inflates or deflates like a balloon. You can also adjust the shape of the membrane by changing its stretch and bend characteristics. To create a shape feature, choose **Insert > Features > Shape** from the SolidWorks menus; the **Shape Feature** dialog box will be displayed, as shown in Figure 11-11.

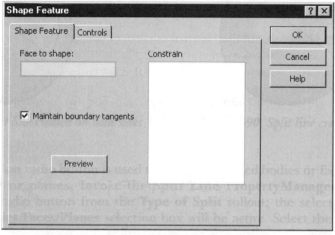

*Figure 11-11 The **Shape Feature** dialog box*

After invoking the **Shape Feature** dialog box, select the face that you need to manipulate; the selected face will be highlighted and its name will be displayed in the **Face to shape** selection box. You can also constrain the selected face along a curve, sketch, or an edge. To select the constraining curve, click once in the **Constrain** selection box and select the constraining reference from the drawing area. The **Maintain boundary tangents** check box is selected by default and is used to maintain the tangency between the shape feature and the boundary of the selected face. Choose the **Preview** button to display the preview of the shape feature. The preview of the shape feature in the form of a surface mesh will be displayed in the drawing area. Figure 11-12 shows the face to be manipulated and the sketch that will constrain the shape feature. Figure 11-13 shows the preview in the form of a mesh.

Tip. *The constraint that will constrain the shape feature can be a point, sketch point, endpoint, vertex, sketch, edge, or a curve. The constrain can be created on the same face or another face at an offset or angle.*

Next, you need to set the controls to manipulate the shape feature. Choose the **Controls** tab to set its parameters. The options in the **Controls** tab are discussed next.

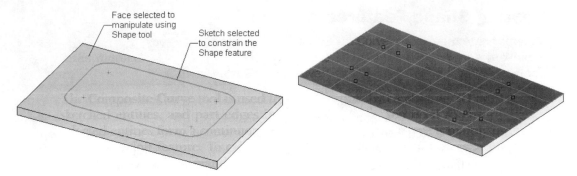

Figure 11-12 *Face to be manipulated and the sketch to constrain the shape feature*

Figure 11-13 *Preview in the form of a mesh*

Gains

The options in the **Gains** area of the **Control** tab are used to set the pressure and value of the curve influence while creating the shape feature. These options are discussed next.

Pressure

The **Pressure** slider in the **Gains** area is used to specify the pressure on the selected face. By default, the slider is set at **0**. The positive pressure inflates and the negative pressure deflates the surface.

Curve Influence

The **Curve Influence** slider is used to specify the percentage of influence of the constraining curve on the shape feature creation.

Characteristics

The smoothness of the shape feature can be adjusted by using the options in the **Characteristics** area. The options available in this area are, **Stretch** and **Bend**.

Advanced controls

The **Advanced controls** area is used to set the resolution of the mesh. By using the **Resolution** slider in the **Advanced controls** area, you can set the value of the resolution. The higher the resolution, the better will be the shape of the feature and more time it will take to rebuild the feature.

Figure 11-14 shows the model with the top face manipulated using the shape feature.

Figure 11-14 *Shape feature added on the top face of the model*

Creating Indents

CommandManager:	Features > Indent	*(Customize to add)*
SolidWorks menus:	Insert > Features > Indent	
Toolbar:	Features > Indent	*(Customize to add)*

The **Indent** tool is extremely useful for the packaging industries, industrial designers, and product designers. You will learn about its benefits while going through the examples in this section. The **Indent** tool is used in the multibody environment. This tool is used to add or scoop out material from a target body. The body that is used to add or scoop out the material is known as the tool body. Depending on the geometry, the tool is used to add or scoop out the material from the target body.

To create an indent feature, choose **Insert > Features > Indent** from the SolidWorks menus; the **Indent PropertyManager** will be displayed, as shown in Figure 11-15. The rollouts in this **PropertyManager** are discussed next.

Figure 11-15 The Indent PropertyManager

Selections Rollout

The options in the **Selections** rollout are used to select the target body, tool body, and set some parameters. These options are discussed next.

Target body

After invoking the **Indent PropertyManager**, you need to select the body that will be deformed using this tool. This selected body is known as the target body. The name of the selected body is displayed in the **Target body** selection box.

Tool body region

After selecting the target body, you need to select a body that will be used as the tool for deforming the target body. This body is known as the tool body. Select the body that needs to be defined as the tool body. The selected portion of the body will be highlighted and its name will be displayed in the **Tool body region** selection box. You will notice that by default, the **Keep selections** radio button is selected. Therefore, the selected portion of the tool body will be retained and the other portion will be removed. If you select the **Remove selections** radio button, the selected portion of the tool body will be removed and the remaining portion will be retained.

Cut

The **Cut** check box is selected to create a cut in the target body. This cut is defined by the geometry of the tool body.

Parameters Rollout

The **Parameters** rollout is used to define the value of clearance and thickness in the **Clearance** and **Thickness** spinners, respectively. Refer to Figure 11-16 to understand more about clearance and thickness. On selecting the **Cut** check box from the **Selections** rollout, the **Thickness** spinner is frozen.

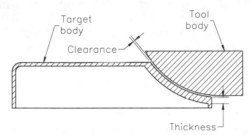

Figure 11-16 *The parameters to create an indent feature*

Figure 11-17 shows two different bodies, with the smaller rectangular body placed inside the main body. Figure 11-18 shows the target body and the portion of the tool body to be selected. Figure 11-19 shows the resulting body after removing the material using the **Indent** tool. In this figure, the display of the tool body is turned off. To turn off the display of a body, select it in the **FeatureManager design tree** and choose **Hide** from the pop-up toolbar. You will learn more about toggling the display of the bodies in the later chapters. Figure 11-20 shows the resulting body after rotating the view of the model.

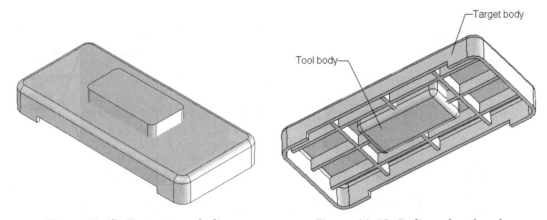

Figure 11-17 *Two separate bodies*   *Figure 11-18* *Bodies to be selected*

Figure 11-21 shows the target body and the tool body to be selected. Figure 11-22 shows the resulting body created using the **Indent** tool with the **Cut** check box selected. The display of the tool body is turned off in this figure.

Figure 11-23 shows the eggs created by revolving the sketch, and then patterned using the **Linear Pattern** tool. Figure 11-24 shows the base plate created for the egg tray as a separate body and then eggs are placed in it. In this example, the base plate is selected as the target body and all eggs are selected from the bottom portion as tool bodies. Figure 11-25 shows the egg tray created using the **Indent** tool with the **Remove selections** radio button selected. The display of all eggs is turned off in this figure.

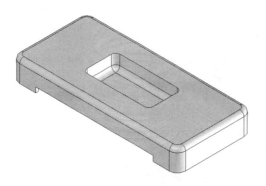

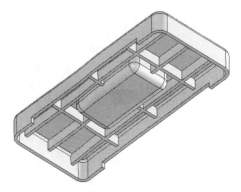

Figure 11-19 *Resulting body after removing the*
material

Figure 11-20 *Resulting body after rotating its view*

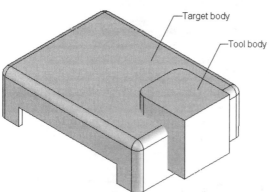

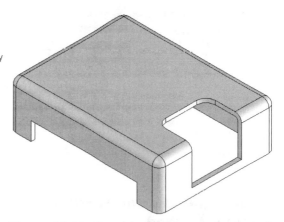

Figure 11-21 *Bodies to be selected*

Figure 11-22 *Resulting body created using the*
Indent tool with the Cut check box selected

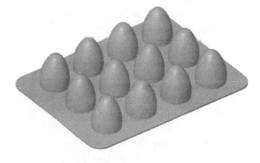

Figure 11-23 *Eggs patterned using the*
Linear Pattern tool

Figure 11-24 *Base plate created for the egg*
tray

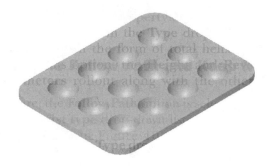

Figure 11-25 Resulting egg tray

Creating Deform Features

CommandManager:	Features > Deform	*(Customize to add)*
SolidWorks menus:	Insert > Features > Deform	
Toolbar:	Features > Deform	*(Customize to add)*

 The **Deform** tool is used to create free-style designs by manipulating the shape of the entire model or a particular portion of it. Choose the **Deform** button from the **Features CommandManager** after customizing it; the **Deform PropertyManager** will be displayed. Its partial view is shown in Figure 11-26. There are three methods to create a deform feature and these are discussed next.

Creating the Deform Features Using the Curve to curve Method

To create a deform feature using the **Curve to curve** method, invoke the **Deform PropertyManager**. Select the **Curve to curve** radio button, if it is not selected by default. The options to create the deform feature using this method are discussed next.

Deform Curves Rollout

The **Deform Curves** rollout is used to define the curves that are used to deform the shape of the model. On invoking this tool, you will be prompted to select the geometry to define the deformation and the fixed geometry for the deform operation. Select an edge, a chain of edges, or curves to define the initial curve. The initial curve defines the reference from where the deformation will start. Next, you need to select the target curves. Click once in the **Target Curves** selection box and select the target curve, which can be a sketch, an edge, or a curve. The profile of the target curve will define the shape of the deform feature, refer to Figure 11-27 and 11-28.

*Figure 11-26 Partial view of the **Deform PropertyManager***

When you select the initial curve and the target curve, a connector connecting both the curves is displayed. You can position the connector by using the handles provided at its sides. To define additional connectors, invoke the shortcut menu and choose the **Add Connector** option from it.

Deform Region Rollout

The **Deform Region** rollout is used to define the options to deform a specific area of the model. By default, the entire model is deformed when you specify the initial curves and the target curves. The **Fixed edges** check box is selected by default. Therefore, the **Fixed Curves/Edges/Faces** selection box is invoked. Using this selection box, you can select the curves, edges, or faces that you need to keep fixed while creating the deform feature. The **Additional Faces to be Deformed** selection box is used to specify the additional faces that you need to deform. If you clear the **Fixed edges** check box, the **Fixed Curves/Edges/Faces** and **Additional Faces to be Deformed** selection boxes will not be displayed.

The **Uniform** check box in the **Deform Region** rollout is used to deform the model uniformly. If you clear the **Fixed edges** check box and select the **Uniform** check box from the **Deform Region** rollout, the **Deform Radius** spinner will be displayed. The **Bodies to be Deformed** selection box is used to define the bodies that you need to deform. This option is used in a multibody model.

Shape Options Rollout

The options in this rollout are used to define the intensity of stiffness, shape accuracy, and intensity of weight along the fixed reference or moving reference.

Note

*If the **Uniform** check box is selected in the **Deform Region** rollout, the **Weight** slider bar in the **Shape Options** rollout will not be available.*

Figure 11-27 shows the references to be selected and Figure 11-28 shows the preview of the deform feature.

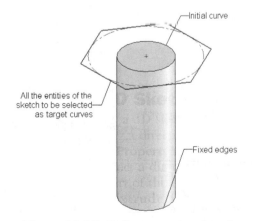

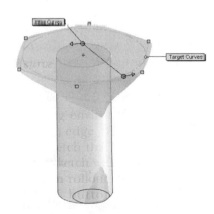

Figure 11-27 References to be selected   *Figure 11-28 Preview of the deform feature*

After setting all the parameters, choose the **OK** button from the **Deform PropertyManager**. Figure 11-29 shows the resulting deform feature.

Figure 11-29 Resulting deform feature

Creating the Deform Feature Using the Point Method

To create the deform feature using the **Point** method, select the **Point** radio button from the **Deform Type** rollout, as shown in Figure 11-30; you will be prompted to select the geometry to define the region, deformation point, and fixed geometry for the deform operation. Select a point on the model face, vertex, or edge from where you need to deform the model. On selecting any of the above mentioned entities from the model, the model will be deformed at the selected point using the default value of the deform distance and deform radius. You can set the value of the deform distance and the deform radius by using the **Deform Distance** and **Deform Radius** spinners from the **Deform Point** and **Deform Region** rollouts, respectively. You can reverse the direction of the deform feature by using the **Reverse deform direction** button in the **Deform Point** rollout.

You can also specify a deform direction to create a deform feature by clicking once in the **Deform Direction** selection box and selecting the direction to create the deform feature. By default, the entire model is deformed using this tool. You can also specify a particular portion by selecting the **Deform region** check box. The options to specify a region for deformation are the same as discussed earlier.

Figure 11-30 The Deform PropertyManager

Figure 11-31 shows the point where you need to select the face of the model. Figure 11-32 shows the resulting deform feature. Figure 11-33 shows the deform feature created with the **Point** radio button and the **Deform region** check box selected. Figure 11-34 shows the deform feature with the **Deform region** check box selected and the front face of the base feature selected as the additional face to be deformed.

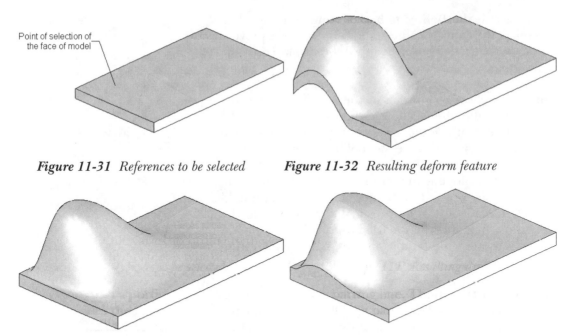

Figure 11-31 References to be selected   *Figure 11-32* Resulting deform feature

Figure 11-33 Deform feature with the **Point** radio   *Figure 11-34* Deform feature with front face
button and the **Deform region** check box selected   selected as the additional face to be deformed

You can also define the deform axis for deforming the entire model by specifying it in the **Deform axis** selection box in the **Shape Options** rollout. Other options are the same as discussed earlier.

Creating the Deform Feature Using the Surface push Method

This option can be used to deform the selected body or bodies by pushing the tool bodies inside them. To deform a body using this option, invoke the **Deform PropertyManager** and select the **Surface push** radio button from the **Deform Type** rollout. The partial view of the **Deform PropertyManager** is shown in Figure 11-35.

A 3D triad along with the axes rings will be placed coincident to the part origin. A transparent spherical ball will also be placed coincident to the 3D triad. This spherical ball is the default tool by which the selected bodies will be deformed. You can also use the other types of geometries as the tool body using the options in the **Tool Body** drop-down list. Other types of geometries that can be used as the tool body are ellipse, ellipsoid, polygon, rectangle, and sphere. You can also select a separately created body as the tool body by selecting the **Select Body** option from the **Tool Body** drop-down list and then selecting the body required as the tool body. You will notice that with each type of default tool body, a callout is displayed. This callout can be used to modify the shape and size of the geometry of the tool body.

Next, you need to select the direction in which you need to push the target body. Select an edge, sketched line, or a face to define the push direction reference. Choose the **Reverse Direction** button to flip the default push direction, if required.

Click once in the **Bodies to be Deformed** selection box and select the body or bodies to be deformed; the preview of the resulting deformed body will be displayed in the drawing area.

You can modify the position of the tool body using the triad. To modify the location of the tool body, move the cursor close to any of the arrows of the triad along which you need to move or rotate the tool body. The cursor will be replaced by the modify cursor. Press and hold the left mouse button and drag the cursor in the direction pointing toward the arrow to move the tool body. Press and hold the left mouse button and drag the cursor along the direction of the arrow of the triad to rotate the tool body. You can also use the options in the **Tool Body Position** rollout to modify the position of the tool body.

The **Deform Deviation** spinner provided in the **Deform Region** rollout is used to define the fillet radius where the tool body intersects the face of the target body. Figure 11-36 shows a deformed feature with a lower value of deviation and Figure 11-37 shows a deformed feature with a higher value of deviation.

*Figure 11-35 The **Deform PropertyManager** with the **Surface push** radio button selected*

Figure 11-36 Deform feature with a lower value of deviation

Figure 11-37 Deform feature with a higher value of deviation

Creating Flex Features

CommandManager:	Features > Flex	*(Customize to add)*
SolidWorks menus:	Insert > Features > Flex	
Toolbar:	Features > Flex	*(Customize to add)*

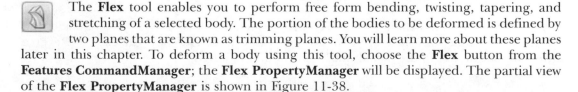

The **Flex** tool enables you to perform free form bending, twisting, tapering, and stretching of a selected body. The portion of the bodies to be deformed is defined by two planes that are known as trimming planes. You will learn more about these planes later in this chapter. To deform a body using this tool, choose the **Flex** button from the **Features CommandManager**; the **Flex PropertyManager** will be displayed. The partial view of the **Flex PropertyManager** is shown in Figure 11-38.

The **Bending** radio button is selected by default in the **Flex Input** rollout and you are prompted to select the bodies for flex and set the options. Select the body from the drawing area. You will notice that the selected body turns transparent and placed between the two trimming planes. A bending axis will also be displayed passing through the selected body along which the body will be bent. A 3D triad along with the axes rings will be placed coincident to the part origin. Figure 11-39 shows the selected body along with the trimming planes, 3D triad, axes rings, and the bending axis.

You can modify the position and location of the trimming planes and the bending axis using the 3D triad and the axes rings. To do so, move the cursor on the triad arrow along which you need to move the bending axis or the ring about which you need to rotate the trimming plane; the select cursor will be replaced by the move or rotate cursor. Press and hold the left mouse button on the arrow to move the location of the bending axis. Figure 11-40 shows the preview of the flex feature after modifying the value of the bending axis and the trimming planes.

You can also modify the location of the 3D triad. To do so, move the cursor to the origin of the triad, press and hold the left mouse button and drag the cursor to change the location of the triad. You can also use the **Triad** rollout to modify the position of the triad and rotation angle of the bending axis and the trimming planes.

Figure 11-38 The Flex PropertyManager

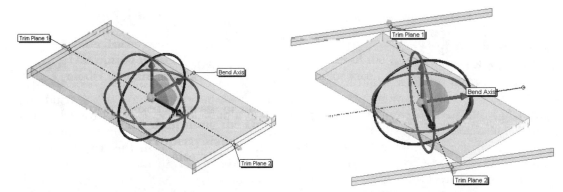

Figure 11-39 Selected body along with the trimming planes, 3D triad, and the bending axis

Figure 11-40 Body after modifying the bending axis and the trimming planes

As discussed earlier, by default, the 3D triad is placed coincident to the part origin. Therefore, the body is deformed about the part origin. If you need to fix a face of the body while deforming it, move the cursor to the origin of the triad and press and hold the left mouse button. Drag the cursor and place it on the face that you need to fix. Release the left mouse button when the boundary of the face on which the cursor moves is displayed in red. You can also set the position of the triad using the **Triad** rollout. Note that you can coincide the origin of the triad with an existing geometry such as a vertex, an edge, or a sketched entity.

The **Trim Plane 1** and the **Trim Plane 2** rollouts are used to specify an offset value of the current trimming planes. You can modify the gap between the trimming planes by dragging them using the arrows attached to them. The **Select a reference entity for Trim Plane 1** and the **Select a reference entity for Trim Plane 2** selection boxes are used to select a vertex along which you need to align the trimming planes. The slider bar provided in the **Flex Options** rollout is used to increase the accuracy of the **Flex** tool.

Next, move the cursor on the boundary of any of the trimming planes; the select cursor will be replaced by a double-sided arrow cursor. Drag the cursor to dynamically define the bending angle and radius of the bend. You can also define them using the **Angle** and **Radius** spinners, respectively. Figure 11-41 shows the preview of a body being bent and Figure 11-42 shows the body after bending using the **Flex** tool.

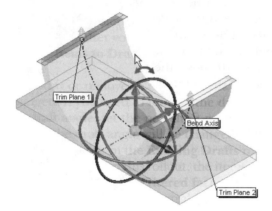

Figure 11-41 Body being bent dynamically

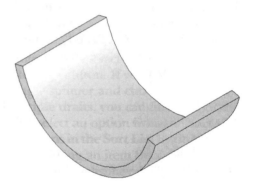

Figure 11-42 Body after bending

Twisting a Body

To twist a body using the **Flex** tool, invoke the **Flex PropertyManager** and select the **Twisting** radio button from the **Flex Input** rollout. Select the body or bodies that you need to twist; the 3D triad and the trimming planes will be displayed. Set the location of the trimming planes and the triad, if required. Move the cursor on the boundary of any of the trimming planes. The select cursor will be replaced by the twist cursor. Drag the cursor to twist the selected body dynamically, or set the value of the twisting angle in the **Angle** spinner. Figure 11-43 shows the body being twisted with the triad placed coincident to the left face of the body and Figure 11-44 shows the resulting twisted body.

Tip. *While creating a flex feature, you can right-click and choose* **Reset Flex** *from the shortcut menu to restore the original shape of the model.*

Tapering a Body

To taper a body using the **Flex** tool, invoke the **Flex PropertyManager**, and select the **Tapering** radio button from the **Flex Input** rollout. Select the body and set the position of the 3D triad and the trimming planes, if required. Move the cursor close to the boundary of any of the trimming planes. The select cursor will be replaced by the taper cursor. Drag the cursor to

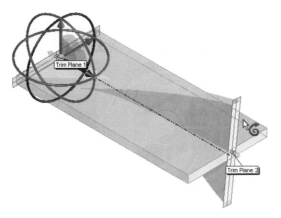

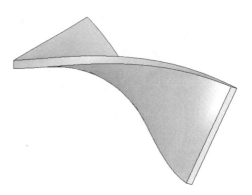

Figure 11-43 *Twisting the body*   *Figure 11-44* *The resulting twisted body*

specify the taper factor. You can also set the taper factor using the **Taper factor** spinner in the **Flex Input** rollout. Figure 11-45 shows the body being tapered and Figure 11-46 shows the resulting tapered body.

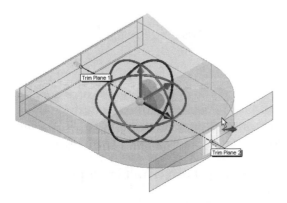

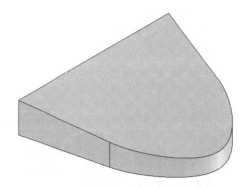

Figure 11-45 *Tapering the body*   *Figure 11-46* *Resulting tapered body*

Stretching a Body

You can also stretch a selected body using the **Flex** tool. To do so, invoke the **Flex PropertyManager** and select the **Stretching** radio button. Select the body and move the cursor on the boundary of any one of the trimming planes. The select cursor will be replaced by the stretch cursor. Drag the cursor to specify the stretching distance. You can also specify it using the **Stretch distance** spinner. Figure 11-47 shows the body being stretched and Figure 11-48 shows the resulting stretched body.

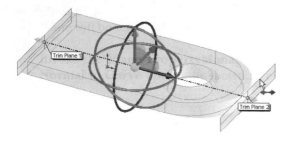

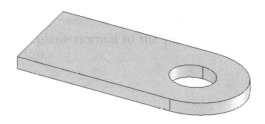

Figure 11-47 Body being stretched   *Figure 11-48 Resulting stretched body*

CREATING FASTENING FEATURES

SolidWorks has a set of tools that are used to design the plastic products. These tools are known as fastening feature tools and are discussed next.

Creating the Mounting Boss

CommandManager:	Features > Mounting Boss	*(Customize to add)*
SolidWorks menus:	Insert > Fastening Feature > Mounting Boss	
Toolbar:	Fastening Feature > Mounting Boss	

 The **Mounting Boss** tool allows you to create mounting boss features, which are used in the plastic components to accommodate fasteners while assembling them. Figure 11-49 shows mounting boss features created on a component. In a mounting boss, the central cylindrical feature is termed as boss and the side features are termed as fins.

When you invoke this tool, the **Mounting Boss PropertyManager** will be displayed. The options in this **PropertyManager** are discussed next.

Position Rollout

The options in this rollout (Figure 11-50) are used to specify the location of the mounting boss. When you invoke the **Mounting Boss PropertyManager**, the **Select a face or a 3D point** selection box will be highlighted in this area. The face that you select will be taken as the

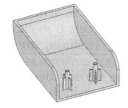

Figure 11-49 Component
with the mounting boss

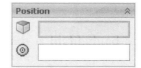

Figure 11-50 The
***Position** rollout*

placement face for the mounting boss and the preview of the mounting boss, created with the default parameters, will be displayed. If the mounting boss is placed at a face that has a circular or filleted edge, you can make the center of the mounting boss concentric with the circular edge. To do so, click once in the **Select circular edge to position the mounting boss** selection box and then select the circular edge; the preview of the mounting boss will be repositioned such that it is concentric with the circular edge.

When you specify the location of the mounting boss, a 3D point will be placed at that point. After creating the mounting boss, you can edit the 3D point to define its exact location using the dimensions.

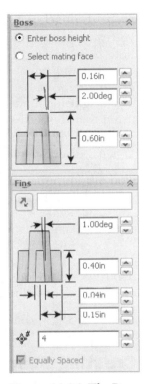

Boss Rollout

The options in this rollout (Figure 11-51) are used to specify the dimensions of the cylindrical feature (boss) in the mounting boss. You can set the values of the diameter, height, and the draft angle of the outer cylindrical face of the boss using the spinners in this rollout. By default, the **Enter boss height** radio button is selected in this area. As a result, you can specify the value of the height. If you select the **Select mating face** radio button, the **Select mating face** selection box will be displayed below this radio button. This selection box allows you to select a mating face that will determine the height of the boss.

Fins Rollout

The options in this rollout (Figure 11-51) are used to specify the dimensions of the fins in the mounting boss. The selection box in this rollout allows you to select a vector to define the orientation of the fins. You can specify the height, width, length, and the draft angle of the fins using the spinners in this rollout. You can also specify the number of fins using the last spinner in this rollout. Figures 11-52 and 11-53 show the mounting boss with different numbers of fins and with different boss and fins parameters.

Figure 11-51 The Boss and Fins rollouts

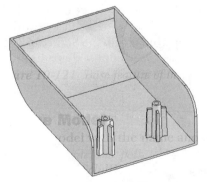

Figure 11-52 Mounting boss with 4 fins

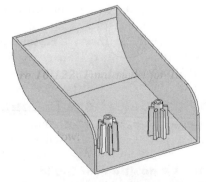

Figure 11-53 Mounting boss with 6 fins

Mounting Hole/Pin Rollout

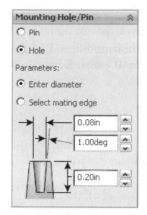

The options in this rollout (Figure 11-54) are used to specify the dimensions of the hole or the pin on top of the boss. The **Pin** and **Hole** radio buttons allow you to specify whether you want to create a hole or a pin in the boss. Figure 11-55 shows the mounting boss with a hole and Figure 11-56 shows the mounting boss with a pin.

If the **Enter diameter** radio button is selected in this rollout, you can specify the diameter, length, and the draft angle of the hole or pin using their respective spinners. However, if the **Select mating edge** radio button is selected, you can specify an existing edge to determine the diameter of the hole or pin. The height and draft of the hole or pin case can also be specified using their respective spinners.

Figure 11-54 *The **Mounting** Hole/Pin rollout*

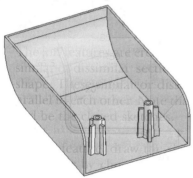

Figure 11-55 *Mounting boss with hole in the boss*

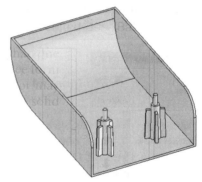

Figure 11-56 *Mounting boss with pin in the boss*

Creating Snap Hooks

CommandManager:	Features > Snap Hook (Customize to add)
SolidWorks menus:	Insert > Fastening Feature > Snap Hook
Toolbar:	Fastening Feature > Snap Hook

The snap hooks are generally created in small plastic boxes to create a push fit type arrangement to close and open the box. Figure 11-57 shows a plastic box with a snap hook. Choose **Insert > Fastening Features > Snap Hook** from the SolidWorks menus; the **Snap Hook PropertyManager** will be displayed. The rollouts and the options in this **PropertyManager** are discussed next.

Snap Hook Selections Rollout

The options available in this rollout (Figure 11-58) are used to specify the location and orientation of the snap hook. These options are discussed next.

Select a position for the location of the hook

This selection box is active by default when you invoke the **Snap Hook PropertyManager**. You can select a face or an edge to define the location of the snap hook. On selecting

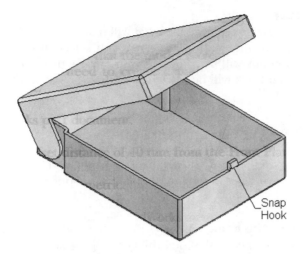

Figure 11-57 *Box with a snap hook*

the location, the preview of the snap hook, created using the default values, will be
displayed.

Define the vertical direction of the hook

This selection box is used to define the vertical direction of
the hook. You can select a planar face or an edge to define
the direction. You can select the **Reverse direction** check
box below this selection box to reverse the vertical direction
of the hook.

Define the direction of the hook

This selection box is used to define the direction of the hook.
The front face of the body of the snap hook will be made
parallel to the face that you select. You can select the **Reverse
direction** check box below this selection box to reverse the
direction of the hook.

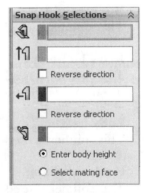

Figure 11-58 *The Snap
Hook Selections rollout*

Select a face to mate the body of the hook

This selection box is used to select a face that will mate with the front face of the body of
the snap hook.

Enter body height

This radio button is selected to specify the height of the body of the snap hook. If this
radio button is selected, the **Body height** spinner will be enabled in the **Snap Hook Data**
rollout and you can specify the height in this spinner.

Tip. *After placing the snap hook, you can edit its sketch to modify its location on
the placement face.*

Select mating face

This radio button is used to select a face that will mate with the bottom face of the hook to define the height of the snap hook. When you select this radio button, the **Select mating face** selection box will be displayed. You can use this selection box to specify the mating face; the snap hook will be resized such that the bottom face of the hook mates with the selected face.

Snap Hook Data Rollout

The options in this rollout (Figure 11-59) will be used to specify the parameters of the snap hook. As you modify these values, you can dynamically view the changes in the snap hook. These options are discussed next.

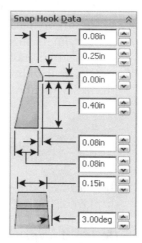

Depth at the top of the hook

This spinner is used to specify the total thickness of the snap hook at its top. Note that the depth at the top should always be equal to or less than that at the bottom. If the depth at the top is less than that at the bottom, the back face of the snap hook will be tapered.

Hook height

This spinner is used to specify the height of the hook.

Figure 11-59 The Snap Hook Data rollout

Hook lip height

This spinner is used to specify the height of the lip of the hook. By default, this value is 0. This value should always be less than that of the hook height.

Body height

This spinner is used to specify the height of the body of the snap hook.

Hook overhang

This spinner is used to specify the distance by which the hook overhangs from the front face of the body of the snap hook.

Depth at the base of the hook

This spinner is used to specify the total thickness of the snap hook at its base. Note that the base of the hook is the face that is aligned with the face that you selected as a position for the location of the hook using the first selection box in the **Snap Hook Selections** rollout.

Total width

This spinner is used to specify the total width of the top edge of the snap hook. Note that the width of the bottom edge of the snap hook is determined by the draft angle, which is also specified using the **Top draft angle** spinner in this rollout.

Top draft angle

This spinner is used to specify the draft angle from the top of the hook. This angle will determine the width of the hook at its bottom. Figure 11-60 shows a snap hook without a lip and Figure 11-61 shows the snap hook with a lip.

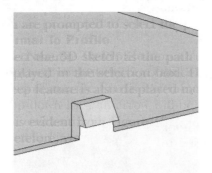

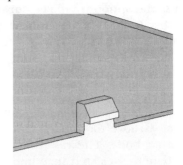

Figure 11-60 *Snap hook without a lip*   **Figure 11-61** *Snap hook with a lip*

Creating Snap Hook Grooves

CommandManager:	Features > Snap Hook Groove *(Customize to add)*
SolidWorks menus:	Insert > Fastening Features > Snap Hook Groove
Toolbar:	Fastening Features > Snap Hook Groove

The snap hook grooves are the cut features that are created to accommodate the snap hook in order to create a push fit type arrangement to close and open the box. Note that this feature works only in the case of multibody models. This is because you need to take reference from the snap hook created in one of the bodies to create the snap hook groove in the other body. Figure 11-62 shows the cap of a plastic box with the snap hook groove. Note that to create the snap hook groove, the two bodies should be placed such that the snap hook intersects with the body in which you want to create the snap hook groove. In Figure 11-62, the display of the body with the snap hook is turned off to make the snap hook groove visible.

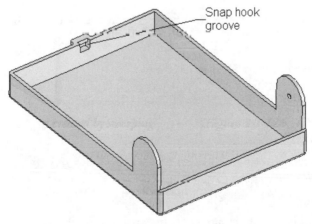

Snap hook
groove

Figure 11-62 *Box with a snap hook groove*

When you invoke this tool, the **Snap Hook Groove PropertyManager** will be displayed, as shown in Figure 11-63. You can use the options in the **Feature and Body Selections** rollout of this **PropertyManager** to create a snap hook groove. These options are discussed next.

Select a snap hook feature from the feature tree

This selection box is active by default when you invoke the **Snap Hook Groove** tool and is used to select a snap hook from another body. The resulting groove will be used to accommodate the selected snap hook.

Select a body

This selection box is used to select the body in which the snap hook groove will be created.

Offset height from Snap Hook

This spinner is used to specify the offset height between the top face of the snap hook and the top face of the snap hook groove when the hook is inserted inside the groove.

Gap Height

This spinner is used to specify the gap height of the snap hook groove.

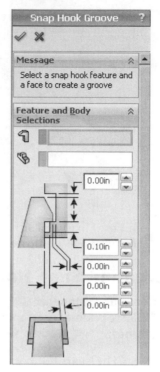

Figure 11-63 The Snap Hook Groove PropertyManager

Groove Clearance

This spinner is used to specify the clearance between the snap and the groove.

Gap Distance

This spinner is used to specify the distance between the body of the snap hook and the groove.

Offset width from Snap Hook

This spinner is used to specify the offset width between the side face of the snap hook and the side face of the groove when the hook is inserted inside the groove.

Creating Vents

CommandManager:	Features > Vent *(Customize to add)*
SolidWorks menus:	Insert > Fastening Features > Vent
Toolbar:	Fastening Features > Vent

The **Vent** tool is used to create vents in existing models. This tool uses a closed sketch as the boundary of the vent and the open or closed sketched segments inside the closed sketch as the ribs and spars of the vent. Figure 11-64 shows a sketch created at an offset plane and the parameters required to create a vent and Figure 11-65 shows the resulting vent. To invoke this tool, choose **Insert > Fastening Features > Vent** from the SolidWorks menus; the **Vent PropertyManager** will be displayed. The options in this **PropertyManager** are discussed next.

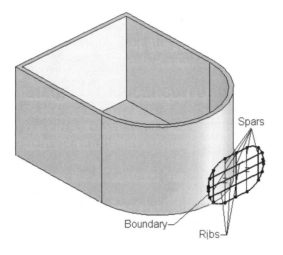

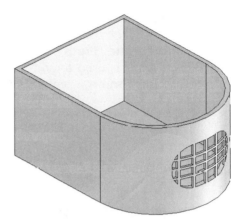

Figure 11-64 *Parameters required to create a vent*   *Figure 11-65* *Resulting vent*

Boundary Rollout

The selection box in this rollout allows you to select a closed sketch that will act as the boundary of the vent. You need to select the segments of the sketch individually to make sure that the result is a closed loop.

Geometry Properties Rollout

The options in this rollout (Figure 11-66) are used to specify the face on which the vent will be created and the draft angle for the ribs and spars in the vent. These options are discussed next.

Figure 11-66 *The Geometry Properties rollout*

Select a face on which to place the vent

This selection box is used to specify the face on which you want to create the vent. In Figure 11-65, the non-planar face was selected as the face to place the vent. After selecting the boundary, select the face; the preview of the vent will be displayed if the **Show preview** check box is selected.

Draft On/Off

This button is chosen to add a draft angle to the ribs and spars. Note that before adding the draft angle, you need to select the segments to define the ribs and spars. When you choose this button, the **Draft Angle** spinner on the right of this button will be enabled. You can specify the draft angle in this spinner.

Neutral Plane

This selection box is displayed below the **Draft Angle** spinner when you choose the **Draft On/Off** button. Note that this selection box will be available only after you select a face for placing the vent. This selection box allows you to select a neutral plane to define the draft angle direction.

Draft inward

This check box is used to reverse the direction of the draft.

Radius for the fillets

This spinner is used to add fillets between the boundary, ribs, and spars in the vent. Figure 11-67 shows a vent without a fillet and Figure 11-68 shows a vent with a fillet.

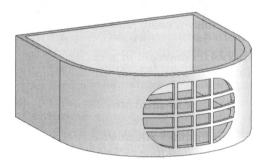   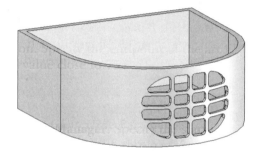

Figure 11-67 Vent without fillet   *Figure 11-68* Vent with fillet

Show preview

If this check box is selected, the preview of the vent will be displayed while it is being created. The changes made in the parameters will also be dynamically reflected in the preview.

Note

*If you have selected the **Show preview** check box and still the preview of the vent is not displayed, this indicates that there is an error in the selections or in the dimensions of the ribs and spars. Then, you need to modify these values to create the vent.*

Flow Area Rollout

This rollout displays the total area of the vent and the unfilled area in the vent. As you increase the number of ribs and spars, the open area in the vent reduces.

Ribs Rollout

The options in this rollout (Figure 11-69) are used to specify the segments that define the ribs and the dimensional and offset values of ribs. These options are discussed next.

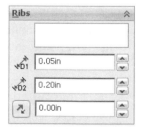

Figure 11-69 The **Ribs** rollout

Select 2D sketch segments that represent ribs of the vent

This selection box is used to select the sketch segments that will create ribs in the vent. If you select the segments for the ribs after selecting the **Show preview** check box, then you can preview the vent with the ribs.

Enter the depth of the ribs

This spinner is used to specify the depth of the ribs in the vent. Figures 11-70 and 11-71 show the ribs with different depths.

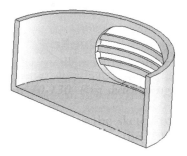
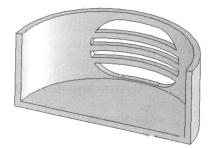

Figure 11-70 *Depth of rib less than the thickness of the component*

Figure 11-71 *Depth of rib equal to the thickness of the component*

Enter the width of the ribs

This spinner is used to specify the width of the ribs in the vent.

Enter the offset of the ribs from the surface

This spinner is used to specify the value by which the ribs will be offset from the face on which the vent will be created. Figure 11-72 shows the ribs of a vent created at an offset. You can reverse the offset direction by choosing the **Select Direction** button, as shown in Figure 11-73.

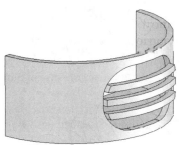
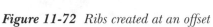
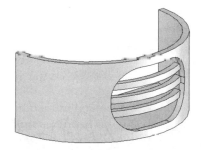

Figure 11-72 *Ribs created at an offset*

Figure 11-73 *After reversing the offset direction*

Spars Rollout

The options in this rollout (Figure 11-74) are used to specify the segments that define the spars and the dimensional and offset values of spars. These options are discussed next.

Select 2D sketch segments that represent spars of the vent

This selection box is used to select the sketch segments that will create spars in the vent.

If you select the segments for the spars after selecting the **Show preview** check box, then you can preview the vent with the spars.

Spars

0.05in
0.08in
0.00in

Enter the depth of the spars
This spinner is used to specify the depth of the spars in the vent.

Figure 11-74 The **Spars** rollout

Enter the width of the spars
This spinner is used to specify the width of the spars in the vent.

Enter the offset of the spars from the surface
This spinner is used to specify the value by which the spars will be offset from the face on which the vent will be created. Figure 11-75 shows a model with a vent having ribs and spars. Note that in this model, the spars are created at an offset. You can reverse the offset direction by choosing the **Select Direction** button.

Fill-In Boundary Rollout
The options in this rollout are used to specify a support boundary for the vent. These options are discussed next.

Select 2D sketch segments that form a closed profile to define a support boundary for the vent
This selection box is used to select the sketch segments that will create a filled feature inside the vent. Note that at least one segment of the rib should intersect the closed profile. Figure 11-76 shows the preview of a filled feature created inside the vent using the closed profile shown in the preview.

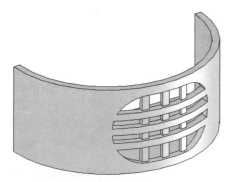

Figure 11-75 Vent with ribs and spars

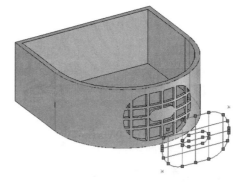

Figure 11-76 Preview of the filled feature

Enter the depth of the support area
This spinner is used to specify the depth of the filled area.

Enter the offset of the support area
This spinner is used to specify the offset value for the filled area. You can reverse the offset direction by choosing the **Select Direction** button on the right of this spinner.

Creating a Lip/Groove Feature

CommandManager:	Features > Lip / Groove *(Customize to add)*
SolidWorks menus:	Insert > Fastening Features > Lip / Groove
Toolbar:	Fastening Features > Lip / Groove

The **Lip/Groove** tool is used to create lip and groove features on a component. These features are mainly used in plastic boxes in which they create a push-fit type arrangement. This arrangement is used for opening and closing the box. In a groove feature, the material is removed from the component and in case of lip feature, the material is added to the component.

On invoking this tool, the **Lip/Groove PropertyManager** will be displayed. The options in this **PropertyManager** are discussed next.

Body/Part Selection Rollout

The options available in this rollout (Figure 11-77) are used to specify the components to create lip and groove features. The options in this rollout are discussed next.

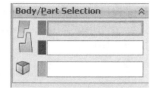

Figure 11-77 The Body/Part Selection rollout

Select body/component on which to create the Groove
This selection box is active by default when you invoke the **Lip/Groove PropertyManager**. This selection box is used to specify the body or component on which you want to create the groove feature.

Select body/component on which to create the lip
This selection box is used to select the body or component on which you want to create the lip feature.

Select a plane, a planar face or a straight edge to define the direction of the lip/groove
This selection box is used to define the direction of the lip/groove. You can select a planar face, plane, or a straight edge to define the direction.

On selecting the body or component on which you need to create a groove, the **Groove Selection** rollout will be displayed, as shown in Figure 11-78. The options in this rollout are discussed next.

Select faces on which to create the groove
This selection box is used to select the faces on which you want to create the groove.

Select inner or outer edge for groove to remove material
This selection box is used to define the edge along which the material is to be removed from the selected faces.

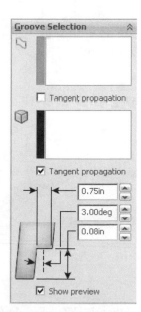

Figure 11-78 The Groove Selection rollout

The **Tangent propagation** check boxes available in this rollout are used to extend the selection to tangent faces. You can specify the groove width, groove draft angle, and groove height in the **Groove Width**, **Groove draft angle**, and **Groove Height** spinners, respectively.

On selecting the body or component on which you want to create a lip, the **Lip Selection** rollout will be displayed, as shown in Figure 11-79. The options in this rollout are similar to those as discussed in the **Groove Selection** rollout.

Figure 11-80 shows the direction, face, and edges to be selected for creating a groove feature and Figure 11-81 shows the resultant groove feature.

Figure 11-82 shows the direction, face, and edges to be selected for creating a lip feature and Figure 11-83 shows the resultant lip feature.

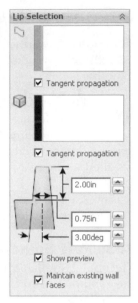

Figure 11-79 The **Lip Selection** rollout

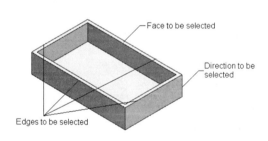

Figure 11-80 Selection for creating a groove

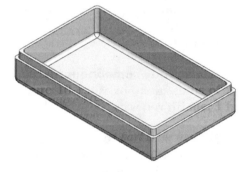

Figure 11-81 The resultant groove feature

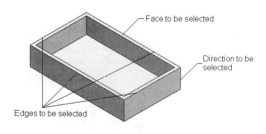

Figure 11-82 Selection for creating a lip

Figure 11-83 The resultant lip feature

CREATING FREEFORM FEATURES

CommandManager:	Features > Freeform	*(Customize to add)*
SolidWorks menus:	Insert > Features > Freeform	
Toolbar:	Features > Freeform	*(Customize to add)*

The **Freeform** tool is used to deform a face to get the required shape. This tool allows you to create the freeform features using the n-sided face of an existing feature. You can select the face of an existing feature and then deform it to any freeform shape. Figure 11-84 shows the model of the tube before deforming the faces and Figure 11-85 shows the same tube after deforming the face using the **Freeform** tool.

Figure 11-84 *Model before deforming the face*   ***Figure 11-85*** *Model after deforming the face*

To create the freeform feature, use the following steps:

1. Create the base feature and then invoke the **Freeform** tool; the **Freeform PropertyManager** will be displayed and the **Face to deform** selection area will be active in the **Face Settings** rollout.

2. Select the face that you want to deform; the grid lines mesh will be displayed on the face.

    Next, you need to define a curve and add points to it. These points will be used to hold the curve and deform it. The same deformation will then be applied to the selected faces.

3. Choose the **Add Curves** button from the **Control Curves** rollout in the **Freeform PropertyManager**. Alternatively, you can right-click and choose **Add Curves** from the shortcut menu. Next, move the cursor over the selected face; a preview of the curve, parallel to the direction of one set of mesh grid lines, will be displayed.

4. Choose the **Flip Direction (Tab)** button from the **Control Curves** rollout, if you want to add curves parallel to the other set of mesh grid lines.

5. Place one or more curves to deform the face, as shown in Figure 11-86.

6. Next, choose the **Add Points** button from the **Control Points** rollout. Alternatively, you can right-click and choose the **Add Points** option from the shortcut menu.

7. Move the cursor on the curve added and then add control points to the curve, as shown in Figure 11-87. Note that more the number of points, more precise the deformation that can be added to the face.

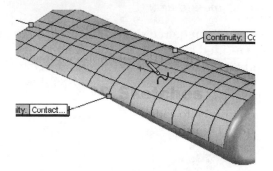

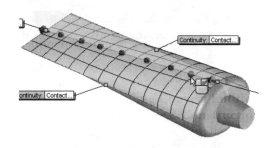

Figure 11-86 *Partial display of the model with a curve being added*

Figure 11-87 *Partial display of the model with points being added*

8. Right-click and choose **Add Points** again from the shortcut menu to clear this option.

9. Move the cursor over any of the points and then drag it; the selected face will be deformed.

10. Similarly, you can drag the other points to deform the face. You can also use the axes of the triad displayed on the selected control point to deform the face. Figure 11-88 shows the points being dragged to deform the face.

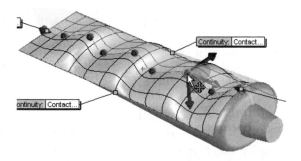

Figure 11-88 *Dragging the points to deform the face*

Whenever you select a face to deform, four callouts will be displayed on it. These callouts control the continuity of the face. After dragging the points and deforming the face, you can click on the white portion of these callouts to modify the continuity of the face.

The rollouts and the options in the **Freeform PropertyManager** are discussed next.

Face Settings Rollout

The options in this rollout are discussed next.

Face to deform

This selection box is used to select the face to be deformed. It is active by default when you invoke the **Freeform** tool. Note that the selected face should have only four sides.

Direction 1 Symmetry

This check box will be available only when the face selected to be deformed is symmetric in one direction. If you select this check box, the preview of the symmetry plane will be displayed on the selected face. Now, if you add a curve, a similar curve will be added on the other side of the symmetry plane. Also, the points added to one of the curves will be added automatically to the symmetric curve. You can drag the points on any of the symmetric curves to deform the face.

Direction 2 Symmetry

This check box will be available only when the face selected to be deformed is symmetric in both the directions. If you select this check box, the preview of the symmetry plane in the second direction will be displayed on the selected face. This option works similar to the **Direction 1 Symmetry** option.

Control Curves Rollout

The options in this rollout are discussed next.

Control type

This area is used to set the type of control to deform the face. The **Through points** option is selected, by default. Therefore, the points are added to the curve and you can use these points to deform the face. If you select the **Control polygon** option, polygons will be displayed on all control points on the curve and you can use these polygons to deform the face.

Add Curves

This button is chosen to add a curve to deform the selected face.

Flip Direction (Tab)

This button is chosen to add the curve in the other direction. You can also press the TAB key to add the curve in the other direction.

Control Points Rollout

The options available in this rollout are discussed next.

Add Points

This button is chosen to add points to the control curve. After creating the control curve, choose this button and add the control points. After adding the required control points, choose this button again to start dragging the points.

Snap to geometry

You can also create a sketched curve to match the shape of the deformed face before invoking the **Freeform** tool. If this check box is selected and you drag the control points to the points of the sketched curve, the cursor snaps to the control points of the sketched curve. In this way, you can match the shape of the face with that of the sketched curve. Note that to use this option, the control curve should be added close to the sketched curve. Figure 11-89 shows the control point of the curve being dragged to the control point of a spline curve.

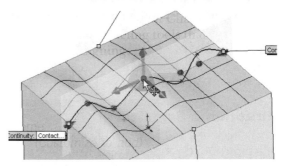

Figure 11-89 *Dragging the points to the control point of a spline curve*

Triad orientation

This area is used to specify whether the triad will be oriented with the reference to the current part file, selected surface, or the control curve. You can select the corresponding radio button of the required option.

Triad follows selection

This check box is selected to move the triad to the selected control point. If this check box is cleared, the triad will remain at its current position, even if you select some other control point on the curve.

Triad X/Y/Z Direction

These spinners will be available in the **Control Points** rollout only when you select a point to drag. These spinners are used to move the selected control point along the X, Y, and Z directions. You can also use the thumbwheel provided below these spinners to modify the value.

Display Rollout

The options in this rollout are discussed next.

Face transparency

This slider is used to set the transparency of the face selected to deform.

Mesh preview

This check box is used to turn on the display of the mesh on the selected surface. If this check box is selected, you can control the density of this mesh by using the slider given below this check box.

Zebra stripes

This check box is selected to display the zebra stripes on the selected face. The zebra stripes are used to check the change in the curvature of the face.

Curvature combs

This check box is selected to display the curvature combs on the grid lines of the mesh to check the curvature of the face. You can specify the directions, curvature type, scale, and density of the grid curvature combs using the available options.

DIMENSIONING THE PART USING DIMXPERT

The **DimXpert CommandManager** and the **DimXpertManager** have been introduced in SolidWorks 2008. The set of tools in the **DimXpert CommandManager** are used to specify the dimension and tolerances of the feature. This helps in checking the design intent and providing an exact information to the production team about the parts. Note that the dimensions created using the **DimXpert** tools are not parametric in nature. These dimensions are only for the display purpose. You can create the dimensions on the parts manually or automatically. The **DimXpertManager** keeps a track of the dimensions placed on the model. The tools in the **DimXpert CommandManager** that are used to dimension the part are discussed next.

Specifying the Datum

CommandManager:	DimXpert > Datum
SolidWorks menus:	Tools > DimXpert > Datum
Toolbar:	DimXpert > Datum

To dimension a part manually, you need to specify the datum using the **Datum** tool. A datum is specified on a face, as shown in Figure 11-90, so that the other features are measured with respect to the datum. To specify a datum, invoke the **Datum** tool from the **DimXpert** toolbar; the **Datum Feature PropertyManager** will be displayed, as shown in Figure 11-91. Also, a datum feature symbol with default parameters will be attached to the cursor. The options in the **Datum Feature PropertyManager** are discussed next.

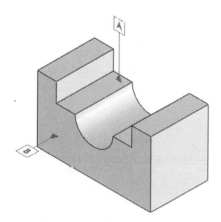

Figure 11-90 Model with datum

*Figure 11-91 The partial view of **Datum Feature PropertyManager***

Label

The **Label** edit box in the **Label Settings** rollout is used to define the label to be used in the datum feature symbol. You can use alphabets or numeric characters as labels.

Use document style

This check box is selected in the **Leader** rollout to use the datum feature style that is defined in the document to display the datum feature symbol.

Square

The **Square** button will be displayed when you clear the **Use document style** check box. This button is used to place the text of the datum feature inside a square. By default, the text of the datum feature is placed using this option. Therefore, by using the buttons available below the **Square** button, you can set the style of placing the datum feature such as filled triangle, filled triangle with shoulder, empty triangle, and empty triangle with shoulder.

Round (GB)

The **Round (GB)** button will be displayed when you clear the **Use document style** check box. This button is used to place the text of the datum feature inside a circle. To do so, you first need to clear the **Use document style** check box and then choose the **Round (GB)** button. On choosing this button, additional buttons will be displayed below the **Round (GB)** button. These buttons are used to set the style of the datum feature.

After defining all parameters of the datum feature symbol, specify a point on an existing entity in the drawing area. Next, move the cursor to define the length and the placement of the datum feature symbol. As soon as you place a datum feature symbol, another datum feature symbol will be attached to the cursor. Therefore, you can place as many datum feature symbols as you want using the **Datum Feature PropertyManager**. As you place multiple datum feature symbols, the sequence of the names of the datum feature symbols automatically follows the order based on the labels.

Pop-up Toolbar

When you invoke a **DimXpert** tool from the **DimXpert CommandManager** and select a feature, a pop-up toolbar will be displayed with the possible options that are applicable for that tool, as shown in Figure 11-92. Select an option from this toolbar to filter the features. Some of the options that will be displayed in the pop-up toolbar are discussed next.

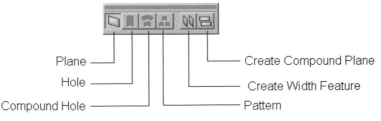

Figure 11-92 The pop-up toolbar displayed while selecting a plane as datum feature

Plane

Select this option to select a plane. By default, this option will be selected when you invoke the **Datum** tool and select a face.

Hole

Select this option to specify the circular feature as a hole.

Cylinder

Select this option to specify the circular feature as a cylinder.

Compound Hole

On selecting this option, you will be prompted to select the holes that are coaxial and coradial. Select the holes from the drawing area and choose **OK** from the pop-up toolbar.

Create Compound Plane

On selecting this option, you will be prompted to select the coplanar planes. Select the planes from the drawing area and choose **OK** from the pop-up toolbar.

Pattern

Select this option if you need to select the features that are created as pattern features.

Create Width Feature

This option is selected to specify the width between the two selected faces. On selecting this option, you will be prompted to select two parallel faces. Select it from the drawing area and choose **OK** from the pop-up toolbar.

Note
The options in the pop-up toolbar depend upon the tool and the feature selected. Therefore, all options in this toolbar are not discussed here.

Adding Dimensions

CommandManager:	DimXpert > Size Dimension
SolidWorks menus:	Tools > DimXpert > Size Dimension
Toolbar:	DimXpert > Size Dimension

 After specifying the datum, you need to add dimensions to the part. You need to add dimensions with respect to the datums to make the feature fully defined. To add a dimension, choose the **Size Dimension** button from the **DimXpert CommandManager**; the select cursor will change to the dimension cursor. Select a face or placed feature; a pop-up toolbar will be displayed. Select an option from the pop-up toolbar and place the dimension, as shown in Figure 11-93.

When you add dimension to a feature, you can notice that the name of the feature is displayed in the **DimXpertManager**. The name will be displayed in blue color with a minus sign, if the feature is under defined. The name will be displayed in black, if the feature is fully defined and the name will be displayed in red color with a plus sign, if the feature is overdefined. You can also choose the **Show Tolerance Status** button to check the status of the feature. If the feature is fully defined, its name is displayed in green. An under defined feature is displayed in yellow color and an over defined feature is displayed in red color. Besides adding a dimension to a feature, you can make a feature fully defined by locating it using the **Location Dimension** tool.

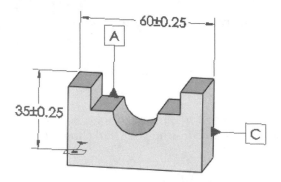

Figure 11-93 Dimensions created on a model

As mentioned earlier, these dimensions are not parametric in nature. They are added for the purpose of display. However, you can display these dimensions while creating the drawing of the model in the drafting environment.

Note
*If you do not want a particular dimension to be displayed in the drafting environment, select the dimension, right-click, and choose the **Mark For Drawing** option to clear the check mark displayed on the left of this option.*

Locating a Feature

CommandManager:	DimXpert > Location Dimension
SolidWorks menus:	Tools > DimXpert > Location Dimension
Toolbar:	DimXpert > Location Dimension

After adding the dimension, you may need to specify the location of a feature with respect to a datum to make the feature fully defined. To specify the location, choose the **Location Dimension** button from the **DimXpert CommandManager**; the select cursor will be changed to the dimension cursor. Select the feature; a pop-up toolbar will be displayed. Select an option from the pop-up toolbar, if required, and also select the datum with respect to which the feature has to be located; the dimension will be attached to the cursor. Place the dimension, as shown in Figure 11-94.

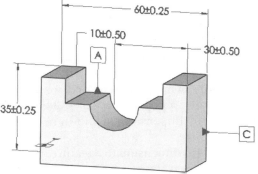

Figure 11-94 Model with location dimension

Adding a Geometric Tolerance to the Features

Command Manager:	DimXpert > Geometric Tolerance
SolidWorks menus:	Tools > DimXpert > Geometric Tolerance
Toolbar:	DimXpert > Geometric Tolerance

In a shop floor drawing, you need to provide various other parameters, along with the dimensions and dimensional tolerance. These parameters can be geometric condition, surface profile, material condition, and so on. All these parameters are defined using the **Geometric Tolerance** tool. To add the geometric tolerance to the features, choose the **Geometric Tolerance** button from the **DimXpert CommandManager**; the **Properties** dialog box will be displayed, as shown in Figure 11-95. Also, the **Geometric Tolerance PropertyManager** will be displayed. You will also observe that a geometric tolerance of default parameter is attached to the cursor.

The two rows in this dialog box are separate frames. You can add additional frames using the **Frames** spinner provided on the right of the **Tertiary** edit box. The parameters that can be added to these frames are geometric condition symbols, diameter symbol, value of tolerance, material condition, and datum references. The options in the **Properties** dialog box are used to add the geometric tolerances to the drawing views and are discussed next.

Symbol

The **Symbol** edit box is used to define the geometric condition symbol. When you choose the down arrow button on the right of this edit box, the **Symbols** flyout will be displayed, as shown in Figure 11-96. This is used to define the geometric condition symbols in the geometric tolerance. Select the standard of the geometric condition symbol from this flyout. On selecting a symbol, the flyout will disappear and the selected symbol will be displayed in the **Symbol** edit box. Also, the preview of the geometric tolerance is displayed in the preview area.

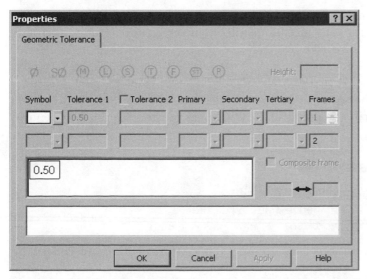

*Figure 11-95 The **Properties** dialog box used to apply the geometric tolerance*

*Figure 11-96 The **Symbols** flyout used to define the geometric condition symbols*

Tolerance 1

The **Tolerance 1** edit box is used to specify the tolerance value with respect to the geometric condition that is defined using the **Symbols** flyout. You can use the buttons available above the rows of the frames to add symbols such as diameter, spherical diameter, material conditions, and so on.

Tolerance 2

The use of the **Tolerance 2** edit box is the same as that of **Tolerance 1**. This edit box is used to define the second geometric tolerance, if required.

Primary

The **Primary** edit box is used to specify the characters to define the datum reference that is added to the entities in the drawing view using the **Datum** tool.

Similarly, you can define the **Secondary** datum reference and the **Tertiary** datum reference.

Frames

The **Frames** spinner is used to increase the number of frames for applying more complex geometric tolerances.

Projected tolerance

The **Projected tolerance** button is the last button available above the frame rows. This button is chosen to define the height of the projected tolerance. When you choose this button, the **Height** edit box will be enabled and you can specify the projected tolerance zone height in this edit box.

Composite frame

The **Composite frame** check box is selected to use a composite frame to add the tolerance. When you select this check box, the tolerance frame will be converted into a composite frame and the preview will be modified accordingly.

Between two points

The **Between two points** edit boxes are used to apply a geometric tolerance between two points or entities. To do so, specify the points in the edit boxes provided in the **Between two points** area.

Collecting Pattern Features

CommandManager:	DimXpert > Pattern Feature
SolidWorks menus:	Tools > DimXpert > Pattern Feature
Toolbar:	DimXpert > Pattern Feature

While applying the dimensions and tolerances, it is recommended to collect the patterned features. You can also collect the identical features that are not created using the pattern tool. To collect the feature, choose the **Pattern Feature** button from the **DimXpert CommandManager**; the **DimXpert Pattern/Collection PropertyManager** will be displayed. Select the **Linked Patterns** radio button, if you want to collect the features created by using the pattern tools. Select the **Manual Patterns** radio button, if you want to collect the features that are similar but not created using the pattern tools. Select the **Collection** radio button to collect and group the dissimilar features. After selecting the appropriate radio button from the **Create Pattern** rollout and selecting the feature from the drawing area, choose the **OK** button; the features will be collected and it will be displayed in the **DimXpert PropertyManager**.

 Tip. *If you have generated the dimensions of two features with respect to a datum and both have the same values, you can combine the dimensions. To do so, select the dimensions and right-click to invoke the shortcut menu. Choose the **Combine Dimensions** option from the shortcut menu.*

Adding Dimensions Automatically

CommandManager:	DimXpert > Auto Dimension Scheme
SolidWorks menus:	Tools > DimXpert > Auto Dimension Scheme
Toolbar:	DimXpert > Auto Dimension Scheme

 You can also add the dimensions in a part automatically. To add dimensions to a part automatically, choose the **Auto Dimension Scheme** button from the **DimXpert CommandManager**; the **Auto Dimension Scheme PropertyManager** will be displayed, as shown in Figure 11-97. The rollouts and options in this **PropertyManager** are discussed next.

Settings Rollout

The options in this rollout are selected based on the method used for manufacturing a part and the tolerance type that has to be specified for the part.

Reference features Rollout

The options in this rollout are used to specify the datum. You need to specify three non-parallel datums.

Scope Rollout

The options in this rollout are used to specify whether the dimension has to be created for the selected features or the whole part.

Feature Filters Rollout

If you do not want to add dimension to a particular category of features using the **DimXpert** tool, then clear the corresponding check box from this rollout.

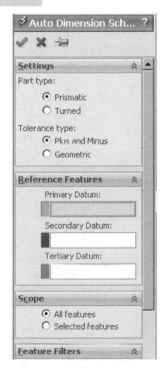

Figure 11-97 The Auto Dimension Scheme PropertyManager

 Tip. *To break the combined dimension, select the combined dimension, right-click and choose the **Break Combined Dimension** option from the shortcut menu.*

Note

*To delete the DimXpert dimensions, invoke the **DimXpertManager**, select the name of the part, right-click, and choose **Delete** from the shortcut menu.*

TUTORIALS

Tutorial 1

In this tutorial, you will create the plastic cover shown in Figure 11-98. The dimensions of this cover are shown in Figure 11-99. Note that a draft angle of 1-degree has to be applied to the side faces of the cover. The parameters of the mounting boss are: Boss diameter = 4.8 mm, Boss height = 14 mm, Draft angle of the main boss = 2-degree, Height of fins = 12 mm, Width of fins = 1.5 mm, Length of fins = 4 mm, Draft angle of fins = 1-degree, Number of fins = 4, Diameter of the inside hole = 2 mm, Height of the inside hole = 5 mm, Draft angle of the inside hole = 1-degree.   **(Expected time: 30 min)**

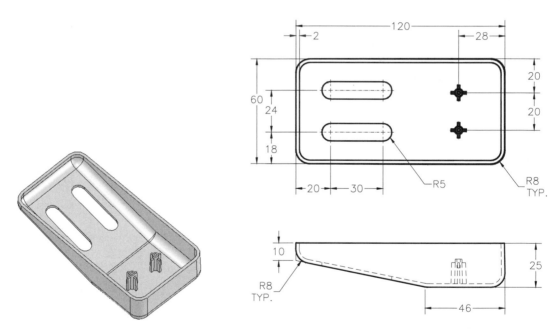

Figure 11-98 *Plastic cover for Tutorial 1*   **Figure 11-99** *Dimensions of the plastic cover*

The following steps are required to complete this tutorial:

a. Create the base feature of the model on the Front Plane and extrude it using the **Mid Plane** option, see Figure 11-100.
b. Add the face draft to the side faces of the model and then create the fillets, as shown in Figure 11-101.
c. Create the shell feature and remove the top face, as shown in Figure 11-102.
d. Create the cut feature, as shown in Figure 11-103.

e. Add one of the mounting bosses and then edit its sketch to locate it using dimensions, refer to Figure 11-105.

f. Mirror the mounting boss feature on the other side, refer to Figure 11-106.

Creating the Base Feature

1. Start SolidWorks and then start a new part file.

2. Create the extruded base feature of the model on the Front Plane and use the **Mid Plane** option to extrude the sketch. The base feature is shown in Figure 11-100.

Adding Draft and Creating Fillets

1. Invoke the **Draft** tool and add a draft of 1-degree to all the four vertical side faces of the model.

2. Add a fillet of 8 mm radius to all the sharp edges of the model excluding that of the bottom face, as shown in Figure 11-101.

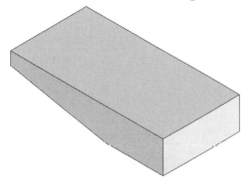

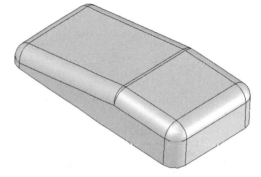

Figure 11-100 *Base feature of the model*   *Figure 11-101* *Base feature with draft and fillet*

Creating the Shell and Cut Features

1. Create the shell feature of a wall thickness of 2 mm and remove the top face of the model, as shown in Figure 11-102.

2. Create the extruded cut feature, as shown in Figure 11-103.

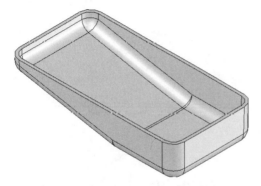

Figure 11-102 *Model after shelling*   *Figure 11-103* *Model after creating the cut feature*

Creating the Mounting Boss

Next, you need to create the two mounting bosses. You will create only one mounting boss and then mirror it to create the other instance. After creating the mounting boss, you need to edit its sketch to place it at the exact location using the dimensions.

1. Invoke the **Mounting Boss** tool from the **Fastening Feature** toolbar; the **Mounting Boss PropertyManager** is displayed and the **Select a face or a 3D point** selection box in the **Position** rollout is highlighted.

2. Click on the horizontal face, close to the top edge, as the face to place the mounting boss; the preview of the mounting boss feature is displayed, as shown in Figure 11-104.

3. Modify the mounting boss parameters based on the values given in the tutorial statement.

4. Click in the **Select a vector to define orientation of the fins** selection box of the **Fins** rollout and then select one of the bottom horizontal edges to reorient the fins in the mounting boss.

5. Choose the **OK** button from the **Mounting Boss PropertyManager**; the mounting boss is created.

    You will notice that by default, the mounting boss is created at the point where you have selected the plane. You need to modify this position to locate the mounting boss. This is done by editing the sketch of the mounting boss, which is automatically created when you create the mounting boss.

6. Click on the (+) sign located on the left of the **Mounting Boss** in the tree view to expand it. Now, right-click on the 3D sketch and choose **Edit Sketch** from the shortcut menu.

7. Locate the 3D sketch to its actual position using the **Smart Dimension** tool. Refer to Figure 11-99 for dimensions.

8. Exit the sketching environment; the mounting boss will be created and located at its proper location, as shown in Figure 11-105.

Figure 11-104 *Preview of the mounting boss*

Figure 11-105 *Model after creating the mounting boss*

9. Use the **Mirror** tool to create the mirror image of the mounting boss. Select the **Front Plane** as the mirroring plane. The final model of the plastic cover is shown in Figure 11-106.

Figure 11-106 *Final model of the plastic cover*

Saving the Model

1. Save this model with the name and the location given below:

    My Documents\SolidWorks\c11\c11tut1.sldprt

Tutorial 2

In this tutorial, you will create the plastic cover shown in Figure 11-107. The dimensions of this cover are shown in Figure 11-108. The fillets in Figure 11-108 are suppressed for clarity. In the lower vent, the vertical lines are ribs and the horizontal lines are spars. The other parameters of this vent are given below:

Depth of ribs = 1 mm, Width of ribs = 2 mm, Depth of spars = 0.5 mm, Width of spars = 2 mm, Offset of spars from surface = 0.5 mm.   **(Expected time: 30 min)**

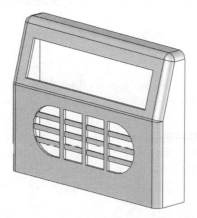

Figure 11-107 *Model for Tutorial 2*

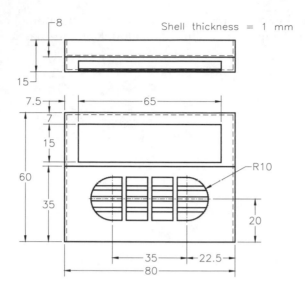

Figure 11-108 *Dimensions of the cover for Tutorial 2*

The following steps are required to complete this tutorial:

a.   Create the base feature of the model on the Right Plane and extrude it using the **Mid Plane** option, see Figure 11-109.
b.   Add the required fillets, as shown in Figure 11-110.
c.   Create the shell feature and remove the back and bottom faces, as shown in Figure 11-111.
d.   Create the first vent, as shown in Figure 11-113.
e.   Create the second vent, as shown in Figure 11-115.
f.   Save the model.

Creating the Base Feature

1.   Start a new part file using the **New SolidWorks Document** dialog box.

2.   Create the base feature of the model on the Right Plane, as shown in Figure 11-109.

Adding Fillets

1.   Add fillets of radius 3 mm to all the sharp edges of the model, except for the edges on the bottom face. The model after adding the fillets is shown in Figure 11-110.

Creating the Shell Feature

1.   Next, create the shell feature with a shell thickness of 1 mm. Remove the back face and the bottom face of the model, as shown in Figure 11-111.

Figure 11-109 *Base feature of the model*

Figure 11-110 *Model after adding fillets*

Figure 11-111 *Model after shelling*

Creating Vents

In the given model, you need to create two vents. The first vent, which has arcs at the two ends, also has fins and spars. However, the upper vent consists of only the boundary. You will first create the lower vent.

1. Define a new work plane at an offset of 20 mm from the front face of the model.

2. Select this plane as the sketching plane and draw the sketch of the vent, as shown in Figure 11-112.

3. Exit the sketching environment and then invoke the **Vent** tool; the **Vent PropertyManager** is displayed and the selection box in the **Boundary** rollout is active.

4. Select the outer loop as the boundary of the vent and then select the front face of the model as the face on which the vent will be placed.

5. Select the vertical lines as ribs and then set the parameters of the ribs based on the information given in the tutorial statement.

6. Select the horizontal lines as spars and then set the parameters of the spars based on the information given in the tutorial statement.

7. Choose **OK** to exit the **Vent PropertyManager**. The model after creating the lower vent is shown in Figure 11-113.

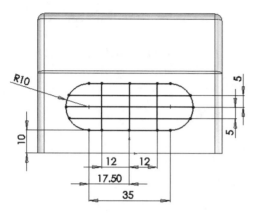

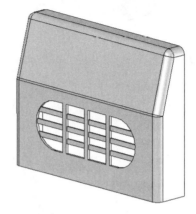

Figure 11-112 *Sketch for the vent*   ***Figure 11-113*** *Model after creating the lower vent*

8. Again, select **Plane1** as the sketching plane and draw the sketch for the upper vent in the inclined face, as shown in Figure 11-114.

9. Exit the sketching environment and then invoke the **Vent** tool. Select the sketch as the boundary of the vent and then select the inclined face to create the vent.

10. Exit the **Vent** tool. The final model after creating the vent is shown in Figure 11-115.

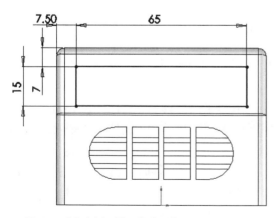

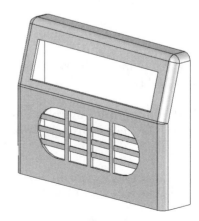

Figure 11-114 *Sketch for the upper vent*   ***Figure 11-115*** *Final model*

Saving the Model

1. Save this model with the name and the location given below:

   My Documents\SolidWorks\c11\c11tut2.sldprt

Tutorial 3

In this tutorial, you will create the model of the tube shown in Figure 11-116. The three sections to be used to create the base loft feature are shown in Figure 11-117. The total spacing between Sections 1 and 2 is 200 mm and between Sections 2 and 3 is also 200 mm. Assume the remaining dimensions.   **(Expected time: 30 min)**

Figure 11-116 *Model for Tutorial 3*

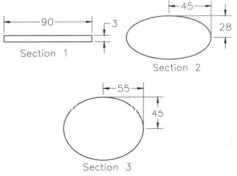

Figure 11-117 *Sections for the base feature*

The following steps are required to complete this tutorial:

a. Create the first section for the base feature of the model on the Front Plane.
b. Create a plane at an offset of 200 mm from the Front Plane and create the second section on this plane, refer to Figure 11-118.
c. Create a plane at an offset of 200 mm from the previous plane and create the third section on this plane, refer to Figure 11-118.

d. Create the loft feature using these three sections, refer to Figure 11-119.
e. Create an extruded feature with a draft on the front face of the base feature, refer to Figure 11-120.
f. Create the freeform feature on the top and bottom faces of the loft feature, as shown in Figures 121 through 123.
g. Create the fillet and the shell feature to complete the model, refer to Figure 11-124.

Creating the Base Feature

1. Start a new part file and draw the first section for the loft feature on the Front Plane, as shown in Figure 11-118.

2. Create a plane at an offset of 200 mm from the Front Plane and create the second section on it, as shown in Figure 11-118.

3. Create a plane at an offset of 200 mm from the previous plane and create the third section on it, as shown in Figure 11-118.

4. Create the loft feature using these three sections, as shown in Figure 11-119.

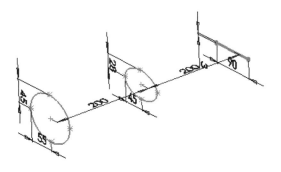

Figure 11-118 *Sections for the loft feature*   *Figure 11-119* *The resulting loft feature*

Creating the Extruded Feature

1. Draw a circle of 50 mm diameter on the front face of the base feature and extrude it through a distance of 50 mm with a draft angle of 6-degree. The model after creating this feature is shown in Figure 11-120.

Figure 11-120   *Model after creating the extruded feature*

Creating the Freeform Feature

It is recommended that you draw a spline first and then use it to create the freeform feature by snapping to the control points of the spline.

1. Select the Right Plane as the sketching plane and draw a spline, as shown in Figure 11-121.

2. Choose **Insert > Features > Freeform** from the SolidWorks menus to invoke the **Freeform PropertyManager**.

3. Select the top face of the loft feature as the face to be deformed; the grid mesh is displayed on the face, as shown in Figure 11-122.

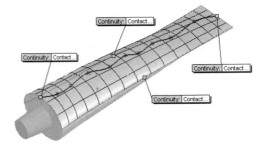

Figure 11-121 Spline drawn to deform the face

Figure 11-122 The grid mesh displayed on the face

4. Right-click and choose **Add Curves** from the shortcut menu. Add a curve below the spline curve drawn earlier.

5. Right-click and choose **Add Points** from the shortcut menu. Add the same number of control points on the curve as in the spline.

6. Right-click and choose **Add Points** again to turn off this option. Make sure the **Snap to geometry** check box is selected in the **Control Points** rollout of the **Freeform PropertyManager**.

7. Drag one of the control points to the corresponding control point of the spline; the cursor snaps to the control point of the spline. Also, observe that the face is deformed.

8. Similarly, drag all the control points to their respective control points on the spline. The model, after dragging all the control points, is shown in Figure 11-123.

9. Choose **OK** from the **PropertyManager** and then hide the display of the spline.

10. Similarly, deform the other side of the base feature. In this case, you can drag the control points arbitrarily in the 3D space. You do not need to draw the spline for this. The model, after deforming the other face, is shown in Figure 11-124.

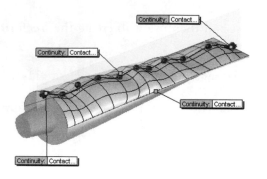

Figure 11-123 *Dragging the control points*

Figure 11-124 *Model after deforming the other side of the base feature*

Creating the Remaining Features

1. Create the fillet feature of radius 10 mm on the front edge of the base feature.

2. Create a shell feature of thickness 0.25 and remove the front face of the extruded feature. The final model of the tube is shown in Figure 11-125.

3. You can also add a twist flex and a bend flex to the tube, as shown in Figure 11-126.

Figure 11-125 *Final model of the tube*

Figure 11-126 *Model after adding a twist and a bend flex*

Saving the Model

1. Save this model with the name and the location given below:

My Documents\SolidWorks\c11\c11tut3.sldprt

Tutorial 4

In this tutorial, you will open the model created in Exercise 1 of Chapter 5. You will apply dimension to the features using the **DimXpert** tool. The model after applying the dimensions is shown in Figure 11-127.   **(Expected time: 30 min)**

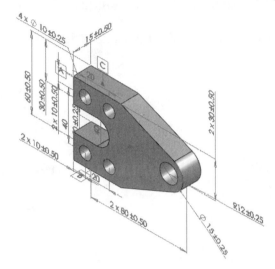

Figure 11-127 Model and the dimensions to be specified

The following steps are required to complete this tutorial:

a. Open the model created in Exercise 1 of Chapter 5.
b. Save it in a new folder.
c. Specify the datum, add dimensions, and locate the features. Refer to Figures 11-129 through 11-136.
d. Save the model

Open and Save the Model Created in Exercise 1 of Chapter 5

1. Choose the **Open** button from the Menu Bar; the **Open** dialog box is displayed. Browse to the c05 folder and open the model created in Exercise 1.

2. Choose **File > Save As** from the SolidWorks menus and save the model in the c11 folder. The location for saving is *My Documents\SolidWorks\c11*. The saved model is shown in Figure 11-128.

Specifying the Datum

When you are applying the dimensions manually using the **DimXpert** toolbar, you need to specify the datum.

1. Choose the **Datum** button from the **DimXpert CommandManager**; the **Datum Feature PropertyManager** is displayed.

2. Enter **A** in the **Label** edit box, if it is not displayed by default.

3. Specify the datum **A** in one of the left faces; a pop-up toolbar is displayed.

4. Choose **Create Compound Plane** from the pop-up toolbar; the pop-up toolbar expands and the name of the selected face is displayed in the selection box.

5. Select the other face on the left side; the name of the selected face is displayed in the selection box. Refer to Figure 11-129.

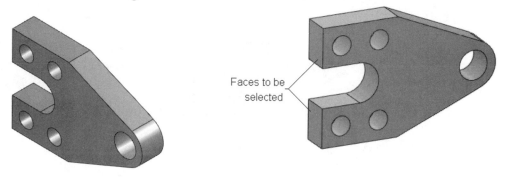

Figure 11-128 *The model created in Chapter 5*   *Figure 11-129* *Faces to be selected for Datum A*

6. Choose **OK** from the selection box and place the datum A at a suitable location, as shown in Figure 11-130.

7. Specify the front face as Datum B and top face as Datum C. The model, after specifying the datums, is shown in Figure 11-131.

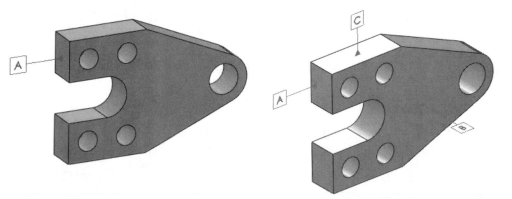

Figure 11-130 *Datum A specified*   *Figure 11-131* *All datums specified in the model*

Adding Dimension to the Features

Next, you need to add dimension to the features.

1. Choose the **Size Dimension** button from the **DimXpert CommandManager** and select the top face that is selected for the Datum C; a pop-up toolbar is displayed.

2. Choose the **Create Width Feature** button; the pop-up toolbar expands with the selection box and **Face <1>** is selected already.

3. Select the bottom face and choose **OK**; the dimension value 60 along with the default tolerance is displayed. Place the dimension at a suitable location.

4. Choose the **Size Dimension** button from the **DimXpert CommandManager** and select the front face selected as Datum B; a pop-up toolbar is displayed.

5. Choose the **Create Width Feature** button; the pop-up toolbar expands with the selection box and **Face <1>** is already selected.

6. Select the back face and choose **OK**; the dimension value 15 with the default tolerance is displayed. Place the dimension at a suitable place.

7. Select the dimension value 15 and right-click.

8. Choose **Change Annotation View (Top) > Left** from the **Selected Entity (Dimension)** area.

The model, after adding two dimensions, is shown in Figure 11-132.

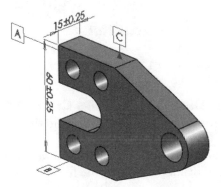

Figure 11-132 Model after adding two dimensions

Adding Dimension to the Notch

Next, you will add the dimension to the notch and locate it.

1. Choose the **Size Dimension** button from the **DimXpert CommandManager** and select the curved face in the slot; a pop-up toolbar is displayed.

2. Choose the **Notch** button, if it is not selected by default, in the pop-up toolbar; the length and width of the notch are displayed.

3. Place it at a suitable location and choose **OK** from the **DimXpert PropertyManager**.

    You can notice that the **Notch1** in the **DimXpertManager** is displayed in blue color with minus sign. This indicates that it is underdefined. You need to locate the notch with respect to a datum to fully define it.

4. Choose the **Location Dimension** button from the **DimXpert CommandManager** and select the cylindrical face of the notch; a pop-up toolbar is displayed with the **Notch** button chosen.

5. Select the top face that is selected for the Datum C; the dimension is displayed. Place it at a suitable location; the notch is fully defined.

6. Orient the model to the front view. The notch and its dimension is shown in Figure 11-133. Note that the other dimensions are suppressed for clarity.

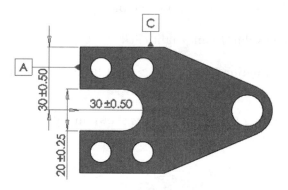

Figure 11-133 *The notch and its dimension*

Adding Dimension to the Hole and the Curved Surface

Next, you need to add the dimension to the hole and the curved surface on the right-side.

1. Select the hole feature and choose the **Size Dimension** button from the **DimXpert CommandManager**; the diameter of the hole feature is displayed.

2. Place the dimension at a suitable location and choose **OK** from the **DimXpert PropertyManager**.

3. Press and hold the CTRL key, select the hole feature and face that is selected for the Datum A. Then, choose the **Location Dimension** button from the **DimXpert CommandManager**. Place the horizontal dimension at a suitable location.

4. Press and hold the CTRL key, select the hole feature and Datum C. Then, choose the **Location Dimension** button from the **DimXpert CommandManager**. Place the vertical dimension at a suitable location.

5. Similarly, add the three dimensions to the curved face that is concentric to the hole feature. The model, after placing all dimensions, is shown in Figure 11-134. Note that the other dimensions are suppressed for clarity.

    Next, you will combine the two dimensions that are measured from the same datum.

6. Select the two horizontal dimensions by pressing the CTRL key and then right-click.

7. Choose the **Combine Dimension** option from the shortcut menu; the horizontal dimensions are combined together.

8. Similarly, combine the vertical dimensions. The model, after combining the dimensions, is shown in Figure 11-135.

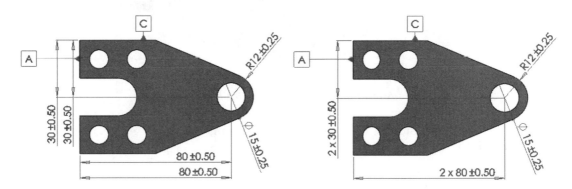

Figure 11-134 *Model after placing the horizontal and vertical dimensions*

Figure 11-135 *Model after combining the dimensions*

Adding Dimension to the Patterned Holes

Next, you need to add the dimension to the hole and the curved surface at the right-side.

1. Choose the **Pattern Feature** button from the **DimXpert CommandManager**; the **DimXpert Pattern/Collection PropertyManager** is displayed.

2. Select the **Linked Patterns** radio button, if it is not selected by default.

3. Then, select one of the holes; all the hole features will be selected.

4. Choose **OK** from the **PropertyManager**; the **Hole Pattern1** node is created in the **DimXpertManager**.

5. Select the left most hole feature and choose the **Size Dimension** button from the **DimXpertCommandManager**; the dimension of the hole feature is displayed. Place it at a suitable location.

6. Locate the hole feature using the **Location Dimension** tool. Refer to Figure 11-136.

7. Locate the other hole features with respect to the left most hole, Datum A and Datum C. Refer to Figure 11-136.

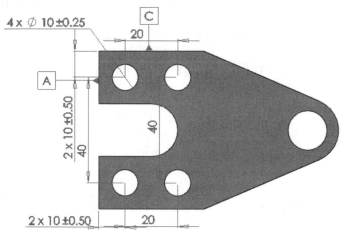

Figure 11-136 *Dimension for the hole features*

8. Set the view to isometric. The dimensions are displayed in the model, as shown in Figure 11-137.

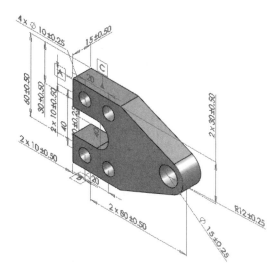

Figure 11-137 *Dimensions displayed in the model*

Saving the Model

1. Choose the **Save** button to save this model with the name and the location given below:

My Documents\SolidWorks\c11\c11tut4.sldprt

SELF-EVALUATION TEST

Answer the following questions and then compare them to those given at the end of this chapter:

1. A concave dome is the one in which the material is removed by creating a cavity in the form of a dome. (T/F)

2. The **Shape** tool is used to create freeform shapes by manipulating the faces of the models. (T/F)

3. The **Deform** tool is used to create free-style designs by manipulating the shape of the entire model or a particular portion of it. (T/F)

4. Mounting boss features cannot be used in the plastic components to accommodate fasteners. (T/F)

5. The vents may or may not have ribs and spars. (T/F)

6. The _____ tool allows you to create vents in a solid model.

7. Using the _____ option, you can deform the selected body or bodies by pushing the tool bodies inside them.

8. The _____ are generally created in small plastic boxes to create a push fit type arrangement to close and open the box.

9. The _____ check box is selected to create an elliptical dome feature.

10. The _____ are the cut features that are created to accommodate the snap hook.

REVIEW QUESTIONS

Answer the following questions:

1. Using the _____ rollout, you can define spars in the vent feature.

2. The _____ tool allows you to create lip/groove in a component.

3. The total thickness of the snap hook at its base can be defined using the _____ rollout.

4. The _____ tool is extremely useful for the packaging industry, industrial designers, and product designers.

5. You can modify the position and location of the trimming planes and the bending axis in the **Flex** tool using the _____.

6. Which tool enables you to perform the freeform bending, twisting, tapering, and stretching of a selected body?

    (a) **Flex**   (b) **Indent**
    (c) **Snap Hook**   (d) **Vent**

7. Which tool is used to create a feature to accommodate the snap hook?

    (a) **Snap Hook**   (b) **Snap Groove**
    (c) **Hook**   (d) **Snap Hook Groove**

8. Which option in the **Dome PropertyManager** is used to specify the direction vector in which you need to create the dome feature?

    (a) **Direction**   (b) **Side**
    (c) **Tangent**   (d) None

9. In the **Flex** tool, which radio button is selected to twist a body?

    (a) **Rotate**   (b) **Twist**
    (c) **Move**   (d) None

10. Which one of the following operations cannot be performed using the **Flex** tool?

    (a) Twisting   (b) Stretching
    (c) Tapering   (d) Aligning

EXERCISE

Exercise 1

Open the model created in Tutorial 1 and then use the **Flex** tool to twist, bend, and stretch it. Figure 11-138 shows the model after twisting. **(Expected time: 15 min)**

Figure 11-138 *Twisted body of the plastic cover*

Answers to Self-Evaluation Test
1. T, **2.** T, **3.** T, **4.** F, **5.** T, **6. Vent**, **7. Surface push**, **8.** Snap hooks, **9. Elliptical dome**, **10.** Snap hook grooves

Chapter 12

Assembly Modeling-I

Learning Objectives

After completing this chapter, you will be able to:
- *Create bottom-up assemblies.*
- *Add mates to assemblies.*
- *Create top-down assemblies.*
- *Move individual components.*
- *Rotate individual components.*

ASSEMBLY MODELING

An assembly design consists of two or more components assembled together at their respective work positions using parametric relations. In SolidWorks, these relations are called mates. These mates allow you to constrain the degrees of freedom of the components at their respective work positions. To start the **Assembly** mode of SolidWorks, invoke the **New SolidWorks Document** dialog box and choose the **Assembly** button, as shown in Figure 12-1.

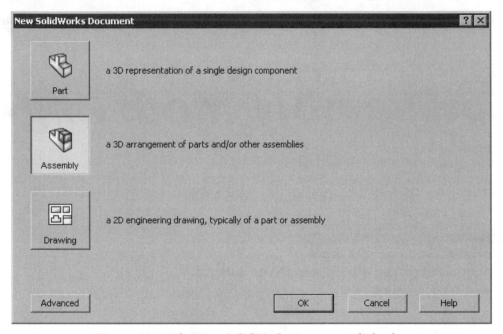

*Figure 12-1 The **New SolidWorks Document** dialog box*

Choose the **OK** button to create a new assembly document; a new SolidWorks document will be started in the **Assembly** mode and the **Begin Assembly PropertyManager** will be invoked, as shown in Figure 12-2.

Types of Assembly Design Approaches

In SolidWorks, assemblies are created using two types of design approaches, the bottom-up approach and the top-down approach. These design approaches are discussed next.

Bottom-up Assembly Design Approach

The bottom-up assembly design approach is the traditional and the most widely preferred approach of assembly design. In this assembly design approach, all components are created as separate part documents, and then they are placed and referenced in the assembly as external components. In this type of approach, the components are created in the **Part** mode and saved as the *.sldprt* documents. After creating and saving all components of the assembly, you need to start a new assembly document (*.sldasm*) and insert the components in it using the tools provided in the **Assembly** mode. After inserting the components, you can assemble them using the assembly mates.

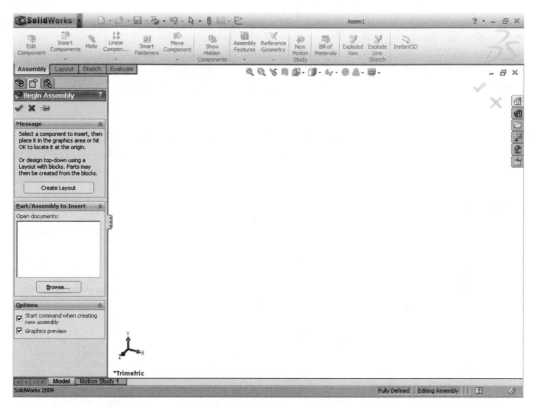

Figure 12-2 *The* **Assembly** *mode with the* **Begin Assembly PropertyManager**

The main advantage of this assembly design approach is that the view of the part is not restricted because there is only a single part in the current file. Therefore, this approach allows you to concentrate on the complex individual features. This approach is preferred while handling large assemblies or the assemblies with complex parts.

Top-down Assembly Design Approach

In the top-down assembly design approach, the components are created in the same assembly document, but saved as separate part files. Therefore, the top-down assembly design approach is entirely different from the bottom-up design approach. In this approach, you will start your work in the assembly document and the geometry of one part will help in defining the geometry of the other.

Note
You can also create an assembly with a combination of the bottom-up and top-down assembly approaches.

CREATING BOTTOM-UP ASSEMBLIES

As mentioned earlier, the bottom-up assemblies are those in which the components are created as separate part documents in the **Part** mode. After creating the components, they are inserted in the assembly and then assembled using the assembly mates. To start an assembly design with this approach, you first need to insert the components in the assembly. It is recommended to place the first component at the origin of the assembly document. By doing this, the default planes of the assembly and the part will coincide and the component will be in the same orientation as it was in the **Part** mode. When you place the first component in the assembly, that component will be fixed at its placement position. The techniques used to place the components in the assembly file are discussed next.

Placing Components in the Assembly Document

In SolidWorks, there are various options to place the components in the assembly. These options are discussed next.

Placing Components Using the PropertyManager

CommandManager:	Assemble > Insert Components
SolidWorks menus:	Insert > Component > Existing Part/Assembly
Toolbar:	Assembly > Insert Components

 When you start a new SolidWorks document in the **Assembly** mode, the **Begin Assembly PropertyManager** will be displayed, as shown in Figure 12-3. Note that this **PropertyManager** will be displayed only when you start a new assembly document. The **Message** rollout in the **Begin Assembly PropertyManager** prompts you to select a part or an assembly and then place the component in the graphics area or to choose the **Create Layout** button to create the top-down assembly. When you choose the **Browse** button in the **Part/Assembly to Insert** rollout, the **Open** dialog box will be displayed. Browse to the location where the component is saved and then select the component and choose the **Open** button. The cursor will be replaced by the component cursor and the graphic preview of the component will also be displayed. The name of the selected component will be displayed in the **Open documents** selection box of the **Part/Assembly to Insert** rollout. It is recommended to align the origin of the first component with the assembly origin. To place the component origin on the assembly origin, choose the **OK** button from the **Begin Assembly PropertyManager**.

*Figure 12-3 The **Begin Assembly PropertyManager***

To place the other components in the assembly document, choose the **Insert Components** button from the **Assemble CommandManager**; the **Insert Component PropertyManager** will be displayed. Choose the **Browse** button from the **Part/Assembly to Insert** rollout. Select the component from the **Open** dialog box; the cursor will be replaced by the component cursor and the preview of the component will also be displayed in the drawing area. Left-click anywhere in the drawing area to place the component.

If the component to be inserted is opened in another window, then it will be listed in the **Open documents** selection box of the **Begin Assembly PropertyManager** or the **Insert Component PropertyManager**. You can insert the component by selecting and dragging it to the drawing area. To preview the selected component, expand the **Thumbnail Preview** rollout.

The **Start command when creating new assembly** check box in the **Options** rollout of the **Begin Assembly PropertyManager** is selected by default. So, the **Begin Assembly PropertyManager** is invoked automatically when you start a new SolidWorks assembly document. The **Graphics preview** check box in the **Options** rollout is also selected by default and is used to display the graphic preview of the component selected to be inserted.

Tip. *To place multiple components or multiple instances of the same component, choose the **Keep Visible** button at the top of the **Begin Assembly PropertyManager** and select the placement points in the drawing area to place the multiple components.*

Starting an Assembly from the Part Document

SolidWorks menus:	File > Make Assembly from Part
Toolbar:	Menu Bar > New > Make Assembly from Part/Assembly

You can also start an assembly document from the part document. If the part document of the base component of the assembly is opened, choose **New** > **Make Assembly from Part/Assembly** from the Menu Bar or choose **File > Make Assembly from Part** from the SolidWorks menus. If the **New SolidWorks Document** dialog box is invoked, choose the **OK** button from this dialog box; an assembly document will be started and the **Begin Assembly PropertyManager** will be invoked. Choose the **OK** button from this **PropertyManager** to place the component at the origin.

Note

*If you invoked the **New SolidWorks Document** dialog box last time in the **Novice** mode, the **Begin Assembly PropertyManager** will be displayed while creating an assembly from a part document. If you invoked the **New SolidWorks Document** dialog box last time in the **Advanced** mode, you first need to select the assembly template and then choose the **OK** button. When you choose the **Make Assembly from Part/Assembly** button and if a **SolidWorks** warning box is displayed, choose **No** from the warning box. The **New SolidWorks Document** dialog box will be displayed in the advanced mode.*

Placing Components Using the Opened Document Window

Another most widely used method of placing components in the assembly is the use of currently opened part documents. For example, if the assembly that you need to create consists of three components, open the part document that you want to insert and then start a new assembly document. Close the **Begin Assembly PropertyManager**. Now, choose **Window** > **Tile Horizontally** or **Tile Vertically** from the SolidWorks menus; all SolidWorks document windows will be tiled horizontally or vertically, depending on the option chosen.

You need to place the first component in the assembly document, at the origin. If the origin is not displayed by default in the assembly document, choose **Hide/Show Items > View Origins** from the **Heads-up View** toolbar. Now, move the cursor on the component in the other window. Press and hold the left mouse button on the name of the component in the **FeatureManager design tree** and drag the cursor to the assembly origin in the assembly window, as shown in Figure 12-4. When the coincident symbol appears below the component cursor, release the left mouse button. If the **Mate** pop-up toolbar is displayed, choose the **Add/Finish Mate** button to place the component in the assembly. Similarly, place the other

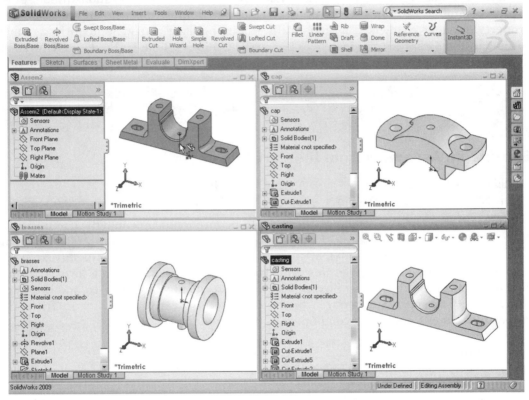

Figure 12-4 *Placing a component in the assembly file by dragging from an existing window*

Tip. *When you insert a component in the assembly, it will be displayed in the* ***FeatureManager design tree***. *The convention of naming the first component is* **(f) *Name of Component* <1>**. *In this convention,* **(f)** *denotes that the component is fixed. You cannot move a fixed component. You will learn more about the fixed and floating components later in this chapter. Next, the name of the component will be displayed. The* **<1>** *symbol denotes the serial number of the same component in the entire assembly.*

The **(-)** *symbol before the name of the component implies that the component is floating and under-defined. You need to apply the required mates to the component to fully define it. You will learn more about assembly mates later in this chapter. The* **(+)** *symbol implies that the component is over-defined. If no symbol appears before the name of the component, then the component is fully defined.*

components in the assembly. If another existing assembly document is opened, you can also drag and drop the part from that assembly document.

Placing Components by Dragging from the Windows Explorer

You can also place components in the assembly document by dragging them from the Windows Explorer. Open Windows Explorer and browse to the location where the part documents are saved. Tile the Windows Explorer window and the SolidWorks window such that you can view both the windows. Move the cursor on the icon of the part document in the Windows Explorer. Press and hold the left mouse button on it, then drag the cursor to the assembly document window. Release the left mouse button at the origin of the assembly document to coincide the origin of the part with that of the assembly document. Figure 12-5 shows the part being dropped in the assembly window.

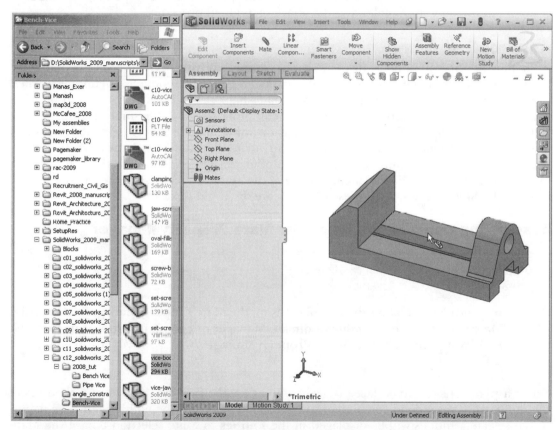

Figure 12-5 *Dropping the part from Windows Explorer to the assembly window*

Tip. *Only the information about the mates is stored in the assembly file. The feature information of parts is stored in the individual part files. Therefore, the size of the assembly file is small.*

It is recommended that all parts of an assembly should be saved in the folder in which the assembly is saved. If you do not save the parts and the assembly in the same folder, the part will not be displayed in the assembly and it will show errors.

Placing Components from the Internet Explorer

You can also place the components from Internet Explorer. You need Internet Explorer 4.0 or a later version. Browse to the location of the SolidWorks part file link on the Web. Drag the hyperlink and drop it in the drawing area of the assembly document; the **Save As** dialog box will be displayed. Save the part document at the desired location.

Placing Additional Instances of an Existing Component in the Assembly

Sometimes you need more than one instance of the component to be placed in the assembly document. To do so, press and hold the CTRL key on the keyboard. Now, select the component in the **FeatureManager design tree** and drag the cursor to the location where you want to place the instance of the selected component. Release the left mouse button to drop the new instance of the component. Similarly, you can place as many copies of the existing component as you want by following the above mentioned procedure.

Assembling Components

After placing the components in the assembly document, you need to assemble them. By assembling the components, you can constrain their degrees of freedom. As mentioned earlier, the components are assembled using mates. Mates help you to precisely place and position the component with respect to the other components and the surroundings in the assembly. You can also define the linear and rotatory movement of the component with respect to the other components. Additionally, you can create a dynamic mechanism and check its stability by precisely defining the combination of mates. There are two methods for adding mates to the assembly. The first method is using the **Mate PropertyManager** and the second is using the **Smart Mates**. Both these methods are discussed next.

Assembling Components Using the Mate PropertyManager

CommandManager:	Assemble > Mate
SolidWorks menus:	Insert > Mate
Toolbar:	Assembly > Mate

 In SolidWorks, mates can be applied using the **Mate PropertyManager**. Choose the **Mate** button in the **Assemble CommandManager** or choose **Insert > Mate** from the SolidWorks menus; the **Mate PropertyManager** will be invoked, as shown in Figure 12-6.

Select a planar face, curved face, axis, or a point on the first component and then select the entity from the second component; the selected entities will be highlighted. The names of the selected entities will be displayed in the **Entities to Mate** selection box of the **Mate Selections** rollout. The **Mate** pop-up toolbar will be invoked, as shown in Figure 12-7. The most suitable mates to be applied to the current selection set are displayed in the **Mate** pop-up toolbar. Also, in the **Standard Mates** rollout of the **Mate PropertyManager**, the most appropriate mate is selected, by default. The preview of the assembly using the most appropriate mate is displayed in the drawing area. You can also select the mates from the given list of the mates that can be applied to the current selection set. As you select some other mate from the **Mate** pop-up toolbar, the preview of the assembly will be displayed using the newly selected mate. Now, choose the **Add/Finish Mate** button from the **Mate** pop-up toolbar; the **Mate PropertyManager** will still be displayed, and you can add other

Figure 12-6 The **Mate**
PropertyManager

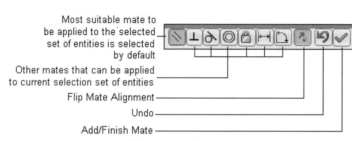

Figure 12-7 *The **Mate** pop-up toolbar*

mates to the assembly. After adding all the mates, choose the **OK** button from the **Mate PropertyManager**. Various types of mates that can be applied are discussed next.

Coincident

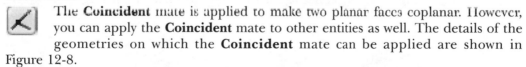

The **Coincident** mate is applied to make two planar faces coplanar. However, you can apply the **Coincident** mate to other entities as well. The details of the geometries on which the **Coincident** mate can be applied are shown in Figure 12-8.

When you choose the **Coincident** button from the **Mate** pop-up toolbar, the preview of the model will be displayed according to the current selection of the mate. Also, the model will be assembled in the aligned or the anti-aligned direction, depending on the current orientation of the model. You can modify the orientation of the assembled component by choosing the **Aligned** or the **Anti-Aligned** button from the **Standard Mates** rollout. You can also choose the **Flip Mate Alignment** button from the **Mate** pop-up toolbar to modify the mate alignment. Figure 12-9 shows the faces to be selected to apply the **Coincident** mate. Figure 12-10 shows the resulting mate applied with the **Anti-Aligned** button chosen. Figure 12-11 shows the **Coincident** mate applied with the **Aligned** button chosen.

ASSEMBLY MATE COMBINATIONS (USING COINCIDENT MATE)		Second Component									
		Cone	Cylinder	Line	Point	Sphere	Circular/Arc Edge	Extrusion	Surface	Plane	Cam
First Component	Cylinder	✗	✗	✓	✓	✗	✓	✗	✗	✗	✗
	Sphere	✗	✗	✗	✓	✗	✗	✗	✗	✗	✗
	Cone	✓	✗	✗	✓	✗	✓	✗	✗	✗	✗
	Circular/Arc Edge	✗	✓	✗	✗	✗	✓	✗	✗	✓	✗
	Line	✗	✓	✓	✓	✗	✗	✗	✗	✓	✗
	Point	✗	✓	✓	✓	✓	✗	✓	✓	✓	✓
	Extrusion	✗	✗	✗	✓	✗	✗	✗	✗	✗	✗
	Surface	✗	✗	✗	✓	✗	✗	✗	✗	✗	✗
	Plane	✗	✗	✓	✓	✗	✓	✗	✗	✓	✗

Figure 12-8 Table displaying the combinations for applying the **Coincident** mate

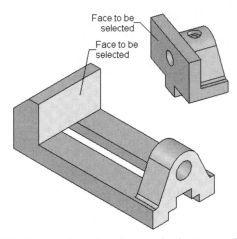

Figure 12-9 Faces to be selected to apply the **Coincident** mate

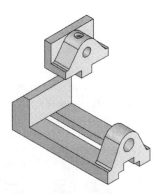

Figure 12-10 The **Coincident** mate applied with the **Anti-Aligned** button chosen

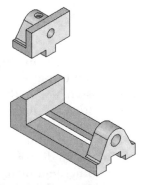

Figure 12-11 The **Coincident** mate applied with the **Aligned** button chosen

Concentric

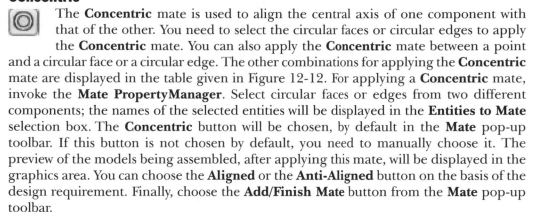

The **Concentric** mate is used to align the central axis of one component with that of the other. You need to select the circular faces or circular edges to apply the **Concentric** mate. You can also apply the **Concentric** mate between a point and a circular face or a circular edge. The other combinations for applying the **Concentric** mate are displayed in the table given in Figure 12-12. For applying a **Concentric** mate, invoke the **Mate PropertyManager**. Select circular faces or edges from two different components; the names of the selected entities will be displayed in the **Entities to Mate** selection box. The **Concentric** button will be chosen, by default in the **Mate** pop-up toolbar. If this button is not chosen by default, you need to manually choose it. The preview of the models being assembled, after applying this mate, will be displayed in the graphics area. You can choose the **Aligned** or the **Anti-Aligned** button on the basis of the design requirement. Finally, choose the **Add/Finish Mate** button from the **Mate** pop-up toolbar.

ASSEMBLY MATE COMBINATIONS (USING CONCENTRIC MATE)		Second Component									
		Cone	Cylinder	Line	Point	Sphere	Circular/Arc Edge	Extrusion	Surface	Plane	Cam
First Component	Cylinder	✓	✓	✓	✓	✓	✓	✗	✗	✗	✗
	Sphere	✗	✓	✓	✓	✓	✗	✗	✗	✗	✗
	Cone	✓	✓	✓	✓	✗	✓	✗	✗	✗	✗
	Circular/Arc Edge	✗	✓	✓	✗	✗	✓	✗	✗	✗	✗
	Line	✓	✓	✗	✗	✓	✓	✗	✗	✗	✗
	Point	✓	✓	✗	✗	✓	✗	✗	✗	✗	✗
	Extrusion	✗	✗	✗	✗	✗	✗	✗	✗	✗	✗
	Surface	✗	✗	✗	✗	✗	✗	✗	✗	✗	✗
	Plane	✗	✗	✗	✗	✗	✗	✗	✗	✗	✗

*Figure 12-12 Table displaying the combinations for applying the **Concentric** mate*

Figure 12-13 shows the faces to be selected to apply the concentric mate. Figure 12-14 shows the **Concentric** mate applied with the **Aligned** button chosen and Figure 12-15 shows the **Concentric** mate applied with the **Anti-Aligned** button chosen.

Distance

The **Distance** button is chosen to apply the **Distance** mate between two components. To apply this mate, invoke the **Mate PropertyManager** and select the entities from both components. Choose the **Distance** button from the **Mate** pop-up toolbar; the **Distance** spinner will be displayed in the **Mate** pop-up toolbar. Set the value of the distance in the **Distance** spinner. The preview of the assembly will be updated automatically after you set the value of the distance. Use the **Flip dimension** check box available below this spinner to reverse the direction of the mate. If needed, you can choose the **Aligned** button or the **Anti-Aligned** button. Figure 12-16 shows the combinations of components to apply the **Distance** mate. Figure 12-17 shows the faces to be selected and Figure 12-18 shows the **Distance** mate applied between two components.

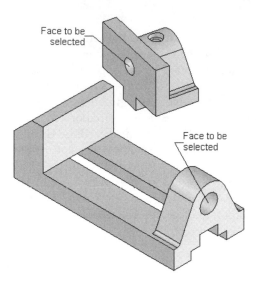

Figure 12-13 *Faces to be selected to apply the **Concentric** mate*

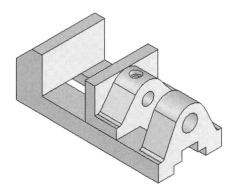

Figure 12-14 *The **Concentric** mate applied with the **Aligned** button chosen*

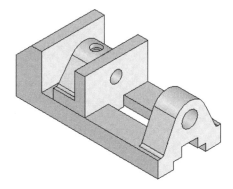

Figure 12-15 *The **Concentric** mate applied with the **Anti-Aligned** button chosen*

Angle

The **Angle** button is used to apply the **Angle** mate between two components. This mate is used to specify the angular position between the selected plane, planar face, or edges of the two components. To apply this mate, invoke the **Mate PropertyManager** and select the entities from the two components. Choose the **Angle** button from the **Mate** pop-up toolbar; the preview of the models will be modified according to the default value of the angle. Also, the **Angle** spinner will be invoked and you can set the value of the angle in this spinner. You can also change the angle direction using the **Flip Dimension** button provided on the right of the angle spinner. You can choose the **Aligned** button or the **Anti-Aligned** button on the basis of the design requirement. After adding the mate, choose the **Add/Finish Mate** button from the **Mate**

ASSEMBLY MATE COMBINATIONS (USING DISTANCE MATE)		Second Component									
		Cone	Cylinder	Line	Point	Sphere	Plane	Extrusion	Surface	Circular/Arc Edge	Cam
First Component	Cylinder	✗	✓	✓	✓	✗	✓	✗	✗	✗	✗
	Sphere	✗	✗	✓	✓	✓	✗	✗	✗	✗	✗
	Cone	✓	✗	✗	✗	✗	✗	✗	✗	✗	✗
	Plane	✗	✓	✓	✓	✓	✓	✗	✗	✗	✗
	Line	✗	✓	✓	✓	✓	✓	✗	✗	✗	✗
	Point	✗	✓	✓	✓	✓	✓	✗	✗	✗	✗
	Extrusion	✗	✗	✗	✗	✗	✗	✗	✗	✗	✗
	Surface	✗	✗	✗	✗	✗	✗	✗	✗	✗	✗
	Circular/Arc Edge	✗	✗	✗	✗	✗	✗	✗	✗	✗	✗

Figure 12-16 *Table displaying the combinations for applying the* ***Distance*** *mate*

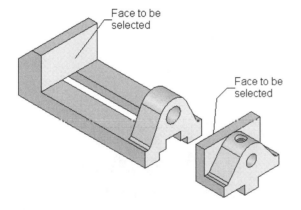

Figure 12-17 *Selecting the faces to apply the* ***Distance*** *mate*

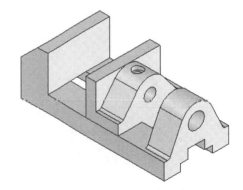

Figure 12-18 *The* ***Distance*** *mate applied to the selected faces*

pop-up toolbar. Various combinations for applying the **Angle** mate are shown in Figure 12-19.

Figure 12-20 shows the faces to be selected to apply the **Angle** mate and Figure 12-21 shows the assembly after applying the **Angle** mate with the angle value of 90-degree.

Parallel

The **Parallel** button in the **Mate** pop-up toolbar is used to apply the **Parallel** mate between two components. To apply the **Parallel** mate, invoke the **Mate PropertyManager** and select two entities from two components. Choose the **Parallel** button from the **Mate** pop-up toolbar to apply the mate. You can also choose the **Align** button or the **Anti-Aligned** button. After applying the mate, choose the **Add/ Finish Mate** button from the **Mate** pop-up toolbar. Figure 12-22 shows the combinations

ASSEMBLY MATE COMBINATIONS (USING ANGLE MATE)		Second Component									
		Cylinder	Extrusion	Line	Plane	Sphere	Circular/Arc Edge	Cone	Surface	Point	Cam
First Component	Cylinder	✓	✓	✓	✗	✗	✗	✗	✗	✗	✗
	Extrusion	✓	✓	✓	✗	✗	✗	✗	✗	✗	✗
	Line	✓	✓	✓	✗	✗	✗	✗	✗	✗	✗
	Plane	✗	✗	✗	✓	✗	✗	✗	✗	✗	✗
	Sphere	✗	✗	✗	✗	✗	✗	✗	✗	✗	✗
	Circular/Arc Edge	✗	✗	✗	✗	✗	✗	✗	✗	✗	✗
	Cone	✓	✓	✓	✗	✗	✗	✓	✗	✗	✗
	Point	✗	✗	✗	✗	✗	✗	✗	✗	✗	✗
	Surface	✗	✗	✗	✗	✗	✗	✗	✗	✗	✗

Figure 12-19 *Table displaying the combinations for applying the **Angle** mate*

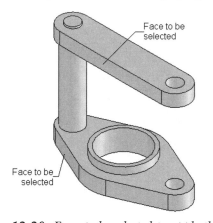

Figure 12-20 *Faces to be selected to apply the **Angle** mate*

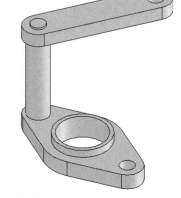

Figure 12-21 *Assembly after applying the **Angle** mate*

of components on which you can apply the **Parallel** mate. Figure 12-23 shows the entities to be selected to apply the **Parallel** mate and Figure 12-24 shows the assembly after applying the **Parallel** mate.

Perpendicular

The **Perpendicular** button in the **Standard Mate** rollout is used to apply the **Perpendicular** mate between the two components. Invoke the **Mate PropertyManager** and select two entities from two components. Choose the **Perpendicular** button from the **Mate** pop-up toolbar. You can also choose the **Aligned** button or the **Anti-Aligned** button. Choose the **Add/Finish Mate** button from the **Mate** pop-up toolbar. Figure 12-25 shows the table displaying the combinations for applying

ASSEMBLY MATE COMBINATIONS (USING PARALLEL MATE)		Second Component									
		Cylinder	Extrusion	Line	Plane	Sphere	Circular/Arc Edge	Cone	Surface	Point	Cam
First Component	Cylinder	✓	✓	✓	✗	✗	✗	✗	✗	✗	✗
	Extrusion	✓	✓	✓	✗	✗	✗	✗	✗	✗	✗
	Line	✓	✓	✓	✓	✗	✗	✗	✗	✗	✗
	Plane	✗	✗	✓	✓	✗	✗	✗	✗	✗	✗
	Circular/Arc Edge	✗	✗	✗	✗	✗	✗	✗	✗	✗	✗
	Sphere	✗	✗	✗	✗	✗	✗	✗	✗	✗	✗
	Cone	✓	✓	✓	✗	✗	✗	✓	✗	✗	✗
	Surface	✗	✗	✗	✗	✗	✗	✗	✗	✗	✗

*Figure 12-22 Table displaying the combinations for applying the **Parallel** mate*

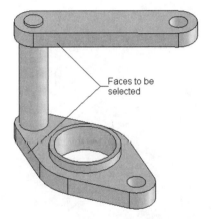

Faces to be selected

*Figure 12-23 Faces to be selected to apply the **Parallel** mate*

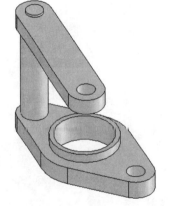

*Figure 12-24 Assembly after applying the **Parallel** mate*

the **Perpendicular** mate. Figure 12-26 shows the entities to be selected and Figure 12-27 shows the **Perpendicular** mate applied to the assembly.

ASSEMBLY MATE COMBINATIONS (USING PERPENDICULAR MATE)		Second Component									
		Cylinder	Extrusion	Line	Plane	Sphere	Circular/Arc Edge	Cone	Surface	Point	Cam
First Component	Cylinder	✓	✓	✓	✗	✗	✗	✗	✗	✗	✗
	Extrusion	✓	✓	✓	✗	✗	✗	✗	✗	✗	✗
	Line	✓	✓	✓	✓	✗	✗	✗	✗	✗	✗
	Plane	✗	✗	✓	✓	✗	✗	✗	✗	✗	✗
	Circular/Arc Edge	✗	✗	✗	✗	✗	✗	✗	✗	✗	✗
	Sphere	✗	✗	✗	✗	✗	✗	✗	✗	✗	✗
	Cone	✓	✓	✓	✗	✗	✗	✓	✗	✗	✗
	Surface	✗	✗	✗	✗	✗	✗	✗	✗	✗	✗

*Figure 12-25 Table displaying the combinations for applying the **Perpendicular** mate*

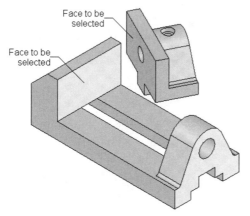

*Figure 12-26 Faces to be selected to apply the **Perpendicular** mate*

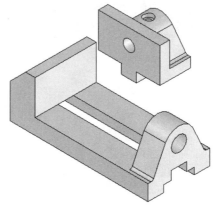

*Figure 12-27 Assembly after applying the **Perpendicular** mate*

Tangent

The **Tangent** button available in the **Mate** pop-up toolbar is used to apply the **Tangent** mate between two components. To apply the **Tangent** mate between two components, invoke the **Mate PropertyManager** and select two components. Choose the **Tangent** button from the **Mate** pop-up toolbar. Figure 12-28 shows the table displaying the combinations for applying the **Tangent** mate. Figure 12-29 shows the entities to be selected to apply the **Tangent** mate and Figure 12-30 shows the **Tangent** mate applied to the assembly.

 Note
*The **Advanced Mates** are discussed in the next chapter.*

ASSEMBLY MATE COMBINATIONS (USING TANGENT MATE)		Second Component								
		Cone	Cylinder	Line	Point	Sphere	Plane	Surface	Cam	Extrusion
First Component	Cylinder	✓	✓	✓	✗	✓	✓	✓	✓	✓
	Sphere	✓	✓	✓	✗	✓	✓	✗	✗	✗
	Cone	✗	✗	✗	✗	✓	✓	✗	✗	✗
	Plane	✗	✓	✗	✗	✓	✗	✓	✓	✓
	Line	✗	✓	✓	✓	✓	✓	✓	✓	✓
	Extrusion	✗	✓	✗	✗	✗	✓	✗	✗	✗
	Surface	✗	✓	✗	✗	✗	✓	✗	✗	✗
	Cam	✗	✗	✗	✗	✗	✗	✗	✗	✗

Figure 12-28 *Table displaying the combinations for applying the* **Tangent** *mate*

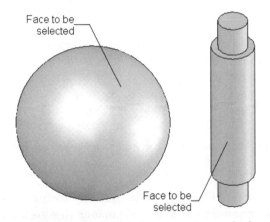

Figure 12-29 *Entities to be selected to apply the* **Tangent** *mate*

Figure 12-30 *Assembly after applying the* **Tangent** *mate*

Creating Multiple Mates

SolidWorks allows you to create multiple mates to a common reference. For example, refer to the Base Plate shown in Figure 12-31. There are four Bolts to be assembled with the Base Plate. After applying the **Concentric** mate, you need to apply a **Coincident** mate to the bottom face of the heads of the Bolts and the top face of the Base Plate. You can apply all these mates together using the **Multiple mate mode** option. To use this option, choose the **Multiple mate mode** button available on the left of the **Entities to Mate** selection box in the **Mate Selections** rollout. When you choose this button, the **Common reference** and **Component references** selection areas will be displayed. The **Common reference** selection area will be highlighted by default. Therefore, you need to select the common reference. In this case,

select the top face of the Base Plate. As soon as you select the common reference, the
Component references selection area will be highlighted. Next, select the bottom face of the
head of one of the Bolts; the **Mate** pop-up toolbar will be displayed. You can select the
required mate type from this toolbar. Similarly, select the faces of the other Bolts to apply the
mate with the common face. Figure 12-31 shows the top face of the Base Plate selected as the
common reference and the four Bolts to be assembled. Figure 12-32 shows the assembly after
applying the **Coincident** mate to the bottom faces of the heads of all Bolts and the top face of
the Base Plate.

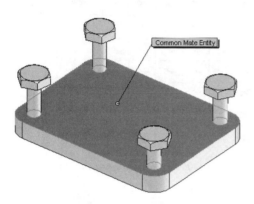 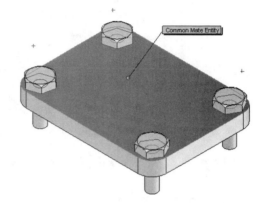

Figure 12-31   *Top face of the Base Plate*
selected as the common reference

Figure 12-32   *Assembly after applying the*
Coincident *mate between the Bolts and the Base Plate*

The remaining options in the **Mate PropertyManager** are discussed next.

Mates

The **Mates** rollout is used to display the mates that are applied between the selected entities.

Options

The **Add to new folder** check box in this rollout is used to add the currently applied mate in
a folder. This folder is placed in the **Mates** mategroup in the **FeatureManager design tree**.
You can also drag and drop the other mates from the **Mates** mategroup in the newly created
folder. The **Show popup dialog** check box is selected by default and is used to display the
Mate pop-up toolbar. The **Show preview** check box is selected by default and is used to
display the dynamic preview of the assembly as you apply the mates to the components. The
Use for positioning only check box is used to define the position of the component only by
applying the mate. This mate is displayed in the **Mates** rollout, but when you exit the **Mate
PropertyManager**, this mate will not be displayed in the **Mates** mategroup in the
FeatureManager design tree.

Assembling Components Using the Smart Mates

CommandManager:	Assemble > Move Component
Toolbar:	Assembly > Move Component

Smart Mates is the most attractive feature of the assembly design environment in SolidWorks. The Smart Mates technology speeds up the design process in the assembly environment of SolidWorks. To add smart mates to the components, choose the **Move Component** button from the **Assemble CommandManager**; the **Move Component PropertyManager** will be displayed. Now, choose the **SmartMates** button available in the **Move** rollout; the **Move Component PropertyManager** will be replaced by the **SmartMates PropertyManager**, as shown in Figure 12-33.

Also, the select cursor will be replaced by the move cursor. Next, double-click on the entity of the first component to add a mate; the component will appear transparent and the cursor will be replaced by the smart mates cursor. Press and

Figure 12-33 The SmartMates PropertyManager

hold the left mouse button on the selected entity and drag the cursor to the entity with which you want to mate the previously selected entity. The symbol of the constraint that can be applied between the two entities will be displayed below the smart mates cursor. You can use the TAB key to toggle between the aligned and anti-aligned options while applying **Smart Mates**. When the symbol of the mate is displayed below the cursor, release the left mouse button; the **Mate** pop-up toolbar will be displayed. Choose the **Add/Finish Mate** button from this toolbar. Figure 12-34 shows the face to be selected to apply a smart mate and Figure 12-35 shows the component being dragged.

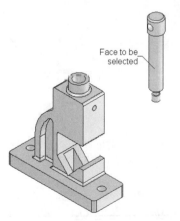

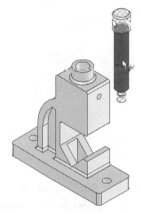

Figure 12-34 Face to be selected to apply a smart mate

Figure 12-35 Component being dragged to apply a smart mate

When the smart mates cursor is placed near a circular face of the other component the concentric symbol appears below the cursor, as shown in Figure 12-36.

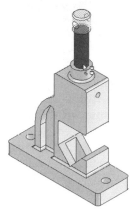

Figure 12-36 *Concentric symbol appears below the smart mates cursor*

Figure 12-37 shows a planar face selected to apply a **Smart Mate**. You can use the TAB key to toggle between the aligned and anti-aligned mates. Figure 12-38 shows that the coincident symbol appears below the cursor and Figure 12-39 shows the assembly after applying the **Coincident** mate using the **Smart Mate**.

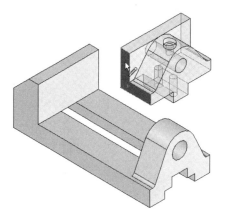

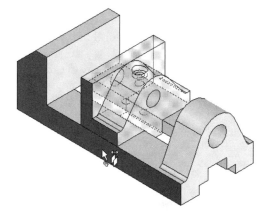

Figure 12-37 *Planar face to be selected to apply* **Smart Mates**

Figure 12-38 *Coincident symbol appears after dragging the component near another planar face*

Tip. *You can also add* **Smart Mates** *without dragging the component. To add a smart mate without dragging, invoke the* **Smart Mates** *tool. Double-click on the entity of the first component; the component will be displayed as transparent. Now, select an entity of the second component; the preview with the most appropriate mate will be displayed and the* **Mate** *pop-up toolbar is invoked.*

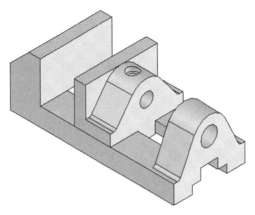

Figure 12-39 *The* **Coincident** *mate applied to the assembly using smart mates*

 Note
To apply smart mates without invoking the **SmartMates** *tool, press and hold the ALT key and select the first component. Drag the component to the entity of the other component to which you need to apply the mate. As you release the left mouse button, the* **Mate** *pop-up toolbar will be displayed. Choose the* **Add/Finish Mate** *button from this toolbar.*

When you drag a component for applying a smart mate, the selected entity of the first component will snap all corresponding entities of the second component. You can press the ALT key to exit the snap. To enter the snap mode, press the ALT key again.

Geometry-based Mates

In the assembly design environment of SolidWorks, you can also add geometry-based mates. Geometry-based mates are also a type of smart mates and are applied while you are placing a component in the assembly environment. Consider a case in which the first component is already placed in the assembly environment. Now, open the part document of the second component. Choose **Window > Tile Horizontal** or **Tile Vertical** from the SolidWorks menus.

Suppose, you need to insert the revolved feature of the second component in the circular slot of the first component and at the same time align the larger bottom face of the second component with the upper face of the first component. To do so, press and hold the left mouse button on the edge of the second component, as shown in Figure 12-40. Drag the cursor to the assembly window near the upper edge of the circular slot of the first component; the second component mated with the first component will be displayed in temporary graphics, as shown in Figure 12-41. The coincident symbol will also be displayed below the smart mates cursor.

You can also toggle the direction of placement of the component. Figure 12-42 shows the direction of placement flipped using the TAB key. Press the TAB key again to return to the default direction. Release the left mouse button to place the component. On expanding the **Mates** option from the **FeatureManager design tree**, you will notice that two mates are applied

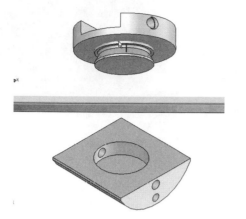

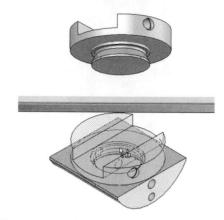

Figure 12-40 *Edge of the second component to be selected*

Figure 12-41 *Component being dragged into the assembly window for applying geometry-based mates*

to the assembly; one is the coincident mate and the other is the concentric mate. Figure 12-43 shows the assembly after adding the geometry-based smart mates.

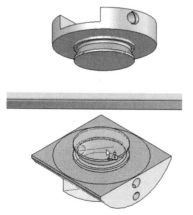

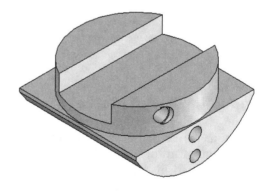

Figure 12-42 *The placement direction of component is flipped using the TAB key*

Figure 12-43 *Assembly after adding a geometry-based mate*

Tip. *You can add the geometry-based mates between two linear edges, two planar faces, two vertices, two conical faces, two axes, between an axis and a conical face, and between two circular edges.*

Feature-based Mates

In the assembly mode of SolidWorks, you can also add feature-based mates. For adding feature-based mates, one of the features of the first component must have a circular base or a boss feature, and the second component must have a hole or a circular cut feature. The feature can be an extruded or a revolved feature. Also, in the assembly document, one of the parts must be placed earlier. Open the part document of the component to be placed using the feature-based mates and tile both document windows. In the **FeatureManager design tree** of the part document, select the extruded or revolved feature and drag it to the assembly window. Place the cursor at a location where you need to place the component. You can also change the alignment or direction of placement using the TAB key. Release the left mouse button to drop the component. Figure 12-44 shows the component being dragged by selecting the revolved feature from the **FeatureManager design tree** of the part document. Figure 12-45 shows the resulting component assembled using the feature-based mates.

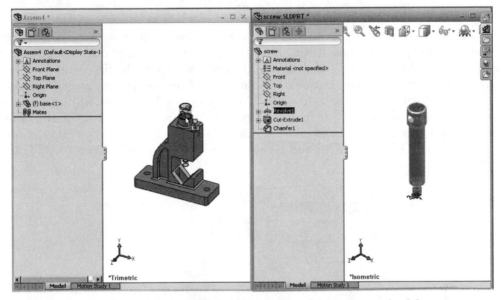

Figure 12-44 Component being dragged by selecting the revolved feature

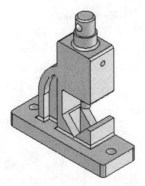

Figure 12-45 Component assembled using the feature-based mates

Pattern-based Mates

Pattern-based mates are used to assemble the components that have a circular pattern created on the circular feature. The best example for these types of components is a flange or a shaft

> **Tip**. *The feature-based mates are applied only to the components having cylindrical or conical features. You cannot add feature-based mates using features other than cylindrical or conical geometry. If you are adding feature-based mates to a component having a conical face, the second component also must have a conical face. You cannot add a feature-based mate if the geometry of the feature of one component is cylindrical and that of the other is conical.*
>
> *If you are adding feature-based mates using the features having conical geometry, there must be a planar face adjacent to the conical face of both features.*

coupling. Note that all components that will be assembled for creating pattern-based mates must have circular pattern on the mating faces. To create pattern-based mates, select the outer edge of the second component and drag it to the circular edge of the first component that is already placed in the assembly document; the preview of the component assembled with the first component will be displayed. Use the TAB key to switch the part with respect to the pattern instances. Release the left mouse button to drop the part. Figure 12-46 shows the component being dragged to the assembly document window. Figure 12-47 shows the preview of the component being assembled and Figure 12-48 shows the component assembled using pattern-based mates.

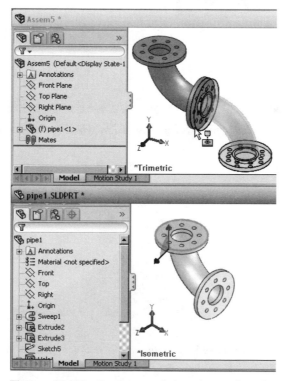

Figure 12-46 *Component being dragged to the assembly document*

Figure 12-47 *Preview of the component being assembled using pattern-based mates*

Figure 12-48 *Component assembled using pattern based mates*

Assembling Components Using the Mate Reference

CommandManager:	Assemble > Reference Geometry > Mate Reference
SolidWorks menus:	Insert > Reference Geometry > Mate Reference
Toolbar:	Reference Geometry > Mate Reference

In SolidWorks, you can define the mate reference for the part in the **Part** mode or in the **Assembly** mode. The mate references allow you to define the mating references such as planar surfaces, axes, edges, and so on before assembling the component.

To define the mate references, choose **Reference Geometry > Mate Reference** from the **Assemble CommandManager**; the **Mate Reference PropertyManager** will be displayed, as shown in Figure 12-49.

The **Mate Reference Name** text box is used to define the name of the mate reference. The **Primary Reference Entity** rollout is used to define the primary mate reference. The **Mate Reference Type** drop-down list is used to define the type of mate. The **Mate Reference Alignment** drop-down list is used to define the type of alignment.

The **Secondary Reference Entity** rollout is used to define the secondary mate reference and the **Tertiary Reference Entity** rollout is used to define the tertiary mate reference.

On adding the mate reference, you will notice that the **MateReference** node will be displayed in the **FeatureManager design tree**.

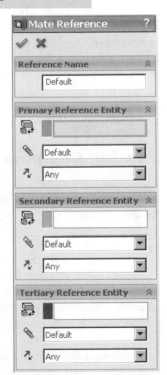

Figure 12-49 *The Mate Reference PropertyManager*

To assemble a component using the mate reference, you need to define the mate references for two components. Also, the names of the mate references should be the same for both the components. After defining the mate references for both the components, place the first component coincident with the origin in the assembly document. Now, drag the second component in the assembly document. You will notice that the second component is aligned to the references that were defined as mate references. Therefore, you do not need to apply mates in the assembly environment.

Note

*As discussed earlier, when you place the first component in the assembly in the bottom-up assembly design approach, it is fixed by default. Therefore, you cannot apply any mates to a fixed component. To add some mates to the fixed component, you first need to float the component. To do so, select the component from the drawing area or from the **FeatureManager design tree**. Right-click to invoke the shortcut menu and choose the **Float** option.*

*By default, the components placed after the first component are floating components. If you need to fix a floating component, select the component and invoke the shortcut menu. Choose the **Fix** option from the shortcut menu.*

CREATING TOP-DOWN ASSEMBLIES

As mentioned earlier, the top-down assemblies are the assemblies in which all components are created in the same assembly file. However, to create the components, you require an environment in which you can draw the sketches of the sketched features and then convert them into features. In other words, you need a sketching environment and a part modeling environment in the assembly file. In SolidWorks, you can invoke the sketching environment and the part modeling environment in the assembly document itself. The basic procedure for creating the components in the assembly, or in other words, the procedure for creating the top-down assembly is discussed next.

Creating Components in the Top-down Assembly

CommandManager:	Assemble > Insert Components > New Part
SolidWorks menus:	Insert > Component > New Part
Toolbar:	Assembly > Insert Components > New Part

Before creating the first component in the top-down assembly, you first need to save the assembly document. To do so, choose the **Save** button from the Menu Bar after starting a new assembly document; the **Save As** dialog box will be displayed and you will be prompted to save the parts internally or externally. It is recommended to save the file externally. So, select the **Save externally (specify paths)** radio button and specify a new folder to save the assembly file and the other referenced file in the same folder.

Now, choose **Insert Components > New Part** from the **Assemble CommandManager**; you will be prompted to select the plane or face to position the new part. To create the base feature, select the default planes; the **Sketch CommandManager** will be displayed with the

Edit Component button chosen. This means that the part modeling environment is invoked in the assembly document. Draw the sketch of the feature in the current sketching environment and create the feature using the **Features CommandManager**. Save the part file and choose the **Edit Component** button from the **Features CommandManager** to exit the part modeling environment. The newly created component will have an **Inplace** mate with the default assembly plane on which it was placed earlier. Therefore, the newly created component is fixed.

Similarly, create the remaining features in the model. Whenever you create a component in a top-down assembly, the component will be fixed using the **Inplace** mate. To delete this mate, expand the **Mates** node in the **FeatureManager design tree** and select the **Inplace** mate. Then, press the DELETE key; the **Inplace** mate will be deleted. Now, this component is floating and you can move it. You can also assemble this component according to your requirement. You will learn more about fixed and floating components later in this chapter.

MOVING INDIVIDUAL COMPONENTS

In SolidWorks, you can move the individual unconstrained components in the assembly document without affecting the position and location of the other components. There are three methods of moving an individual component. Two of these methods are discussed next. The third method is discussed later in this chapter.

Moving Individual Components by Dragging

In the assembly environment of SolidWorks, you can move the component placed in an assembly without invoking any tool. To move an individual component, select the component and drag the cursor to move the component. Release the left mouse button to place the component at the desired location.

Moving Individual Components Using the Move Component Tool

CommandManager:	Assemble > Move Component
Toolbar:	Assembly > Move Component

 You can also move an individual component using the **Move Component** tool. Choose the **Move Component** button from the **Assemble CommandManager** to invoke the **Move Component PropertyManager**; the **Free Drag** option is selected from the **Move** drop-down list in the **Move** rollout, by default. You will be prompted to select a component and drag it. The select cursor will be replaced by the move cursor. Select the component and drag the cursor to move the component. Release the left mouse button to place the component at the desired location. The other options available in the **Move** drop-down list to move the component are discussed next.

Along Assembly XYZ

The **Along Assembly XYZ** option in the **Move** drop-down list is used to move the component dynamically along the X, Y, and Z axes of the assembly document. Select the **Along Assembly**

XYZ option from the **Move** drop-down list; an assembly coordinate system will be displayed in the drawing area and you will be prompted to select a component and drag the cursor parallel to an assembly axis to move the component along that axis. Select the component and drag the cursor to move the component along any one of the assembly axes.

Along Entity

The **Along Entity** option is used to move the component along the direction of the selected entity. When you select this option, the **Selected item** selection box will be displayed. You will be prompted to select an entity to drag along, and a component to drag. Select an entity to define the direction to move the component; the name of the selected entity will be displayed in the **Selected item** selection box. Now, select the component and drag the cursor to move the component along the defined direction.

By Delta XYZ

The **By Delta XYZ** option in the **Move** drop-down list is used for moving the selected component to a given distance in a specified direction. When you select this option, the **Delta X**, **Delta Y**, and **Delta Z** spinners will be invoked and you will be prompted to select a component and enter the distance in the **PropertyManager**. An assembly coordinate system will also be displayed. Select the component to move and specify the distance in the respective direction spinners. Choose the **Apply** button to move the component.

To XYZ Position

The **To XYZ Position** option is used to specify the coordinates of the origin of the part where the component will be placed after moving. When you select this option, the **X Coordinate**, **Y Coordinate**, and **Z Coordinate** spinners will be invoked and you will be prompted to select a component and enter the X, Y, Z coordinates for the part's origin. An assembly coordinate system will also be displayed. Select the component and enter the respective coordinates of the part origin in the spinners and choose the **Apply** button to place the component.

ROTATING INDIVIDUAL COMPONENTS

In SolidWorks, you can rotate an individual unconstrained component in the assembly document without affecting the position and location of the other components. The **Rotate Component** tool is used to rotate the component. There are three methods of rotating an individual component. Two of these methods are discussed next and the third method is discussed later in this chapter.

Rotating Individual Components by Dragging

You can rotate the component placed in the assembly without invoking any tool. To rotate an individual component, select the component, press and hold the right mouse button and then drag the cursor to rotate the component. Release the right mouse button after attaining the desired orientation of the individual component.

 Tip. *You can toggle between the **Move**, **Rotate**, and **SmartMates** PropertyManagers. Invoke the PropertyManager and then choose the **Move**, **Rotate**, or the **SmartMates** button to invoke the corresponding PropertyManager*.

Rotating Individual Components Using the Rotate Component Tool

CommandManager:	Assemble > Move Component > Rotate Component
Toolbar:	Assembly > Rotate Component

You can also rotate an individual component using the **Rotate Component** tool. To rotate an individual component using this tool, choose **Move Component > Rotate Component** from the **Assemble CommandManager**; the **Rotate Component PropertyManager** will be invoked. You will notice that the **Free Drag** option is selected from the **Rotate** drop-down list in the **Rotate** rollout. Therefore, you will be prompted to select a component and drag it to rotate. The select cursor will be replaced by the rotate cursor. Select the component and drag the cursor to rotate the component. The other options in the **Rotate** drop-down list are discussed next.

About Entity

The **About Entity** option in the **Rotate** drop-down list is used to rotate the component with respect to a selected entity. The selected entity is defined as the rotational axis. When you select this option, the **Selected item** selection box will be displayed and you will be prompted to select an axis to rotate about. Select an entity to define the rotational axis; the name of the selected entity will be displayed in the **Selected item** selection box. Now, select the component and drag the cursor to rotate the component about the selected axis.

By Delta XYZ

The **By Delta XYZ** option available in the **Rotate** drop-down list is used to rotate the selected component by a given incremental angle along the specified axis. When you select this option, the **Delta X**, **Delta Y**, and **Delta Z** spinners will be enabled and you will be prompted to select a component and enter the desired rotation in the **PropertyManager**. Select the component to rotate and set the rotation angle in the respective spinners to specify the direction in which you need to rotate the component. Choose the **Apply** button to rotate the component.

MOVING AND ROTATING INDIVIDUAL COMPONENTS USING THE TRIAD

To move an individual component using the triad, you first need to select the component and then right-click to invoke the shortcut menu. Choose the **Move with Triad** option from the shortcut menu; the component will become transparent and the triad along with the rings will be displayed on it. You can move the component using this triad and rotate the component using the rings. The different components of the triad and rings are displayed in Figure 12-50.

To move a component along the X direction, press and hold the left mouse button on the X arm; the select cursor will be replaced by the move cursor. Use the left mouse button to drag the selected component in the X direction. Similarly, you can select the Y or the Z arm and drag the cursor to move the component in the Y or Z direction.

To rotate the component about the X-axis, move the cursor on the rotate around the X-axis

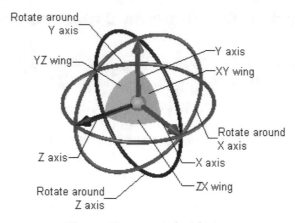

Figure 12-50 *Triad with rings*

ring and drag the cursor; the component will be rotated through an angle of 90-degree. To rotate the component through an angle less than 90-degree, press and hold the left mouse button on the ring, drag the cursor away from the triad and again drag the cursor to rotate the component.

You can also move a component in the XY plane. To do so, select the XY wing of the triad and drag the cursor to move the component. To move the component in the YZ plane, select the YZ wing of the triad and drag the cursor to move the component. Similarly, by selecting the ZX wing and dragging the cursor, you can move the component in the ZX plane.

If you select the sphere in the center of the triad and invoke the shortcut menu, various options will be available. These options are discussed next.

Show Translate XYZ Box

The **Show Translate XYZ Box** option available in the shortcut menu is used to display the **Translate XYZ** box. You can use this box to specify the value of the X, Y, and Z coordinates of the destination where you need to place the selected component. Specify the X, Y, and Z coordinates in the respective edit boxes and then choose **OK** from the box. When you move the component by dragging, the values of the X, Y, and Z spinners will change automatically.

Show Translate Delta XYZ Box

The **Show Translate Delta XYZ Box** option available in the shortcut menu is used to display the **Translate Delta XYZ** box. Use this box to specify the incremental value by which you need to move the selected component in the X, Y, or Z direction. Set the incremental value in the X, Y, or Z edit box and then choose **OK** from the box.

Show Rotate Delta XYZ Box

The **Show Rotate Delta XYZ Box** option available in the shortcut menu is used to display the **Rotate Delta XYZ** box. You can use this box to specify the incremental value by which the selected component will rotate in the X, Y, or Z direction. Set the incremental value in the X, Y, or Z edit box and then choose **OK**.

Align with Component Origin

This option is used to align the triad and the rings to the origin of the selected component.

Align with Assembly Origin

This option is used to align the triad and the rings to the origin of the assembly.

Align to

This option is used to align the triad and the rings to a selected component or a feature.

TUTORIALS

Tutorial 1

In this tutorial, you will create all components of the Bench Vice and then assemble them. The Bench Vice assembly is shown in Figure 12-51. The dimensions of various components of the assembly are given in Figures 12-52 through 12-55.   **(Expected time: 2 hrs 45 min)**

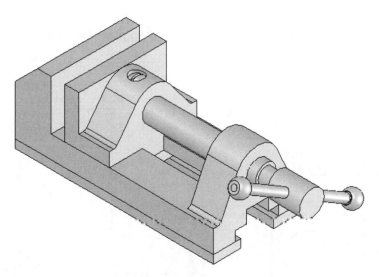

Figure 12-51 *Bench Vice assembly*

The following steps are required to complete this tutorial:

a.   Create all components in individual part documents and save them. The part documents will be saved in the *My Documents\SolidWorks\c12\Bench Vice* folder.
b.   Open the Vice Body and Vice Jaw part documents and define the mate references in both part documents, refer to Figures 12-56 and 12-57
c.   Create a new assembly document and open all part documents. Place the first component, which is the Vice Body. Now, drag and drop the Vice Jaw in the assembly document. It

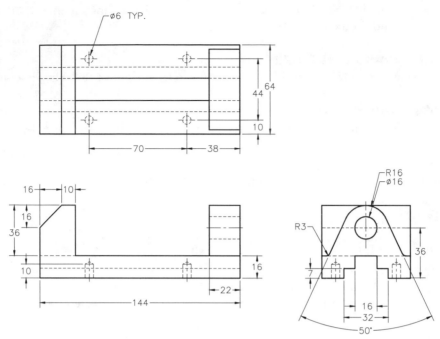

Figure 12-52 *Views and dimensions of the Vice Body*

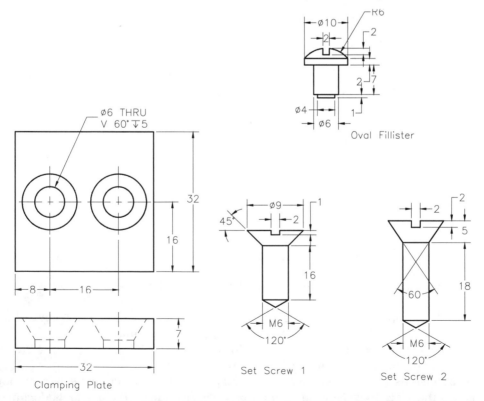

Figure 12-53 *Views and dimensions of Clamping Plate, Oval Fillister, Set Screw 1, and Set Screw 2*

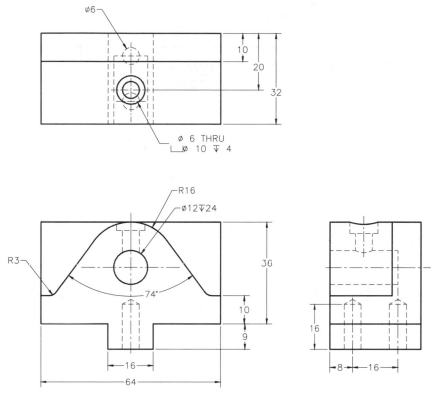

Figure 12-54 *Views and dimensions of the Vice Jaw*

will automatically assemble with the Vice Jaw because the mate references are already defined in both part documents, refer to Figures 12-58 and 12-59.

d.   Drag and drop the Jaw Screw in the assembly document and apply the required mates, refer to Figures 12-61 through 12-66.

e.   Next, analyze the assembly for degrees of freedom of the components.

f.   After analyzing the assembly, apply the required mates to constrain all degrees of freedom, refer to Figures 12-67 and 12-68.

g.   Next, assemble the Clamping Plate, refer to Figures 12-69 through 12-72.

h.   Next, assemble the Oval Fillister using the feature-based mates, refer to Figure 12-73.

i.   Similarly, assemble the other components.

j.   Save the model.

Creating the Components

1.   Create all the components of the Bench Vice assembly as separate part documents. Specify the names of the documents, as shown in Figures 12-52 through 12-55. The files should be saved in the folder *My Documents\SolidWorks\c12\Bench Vice*. Make sure that the *Bench Vice* is your current folder.

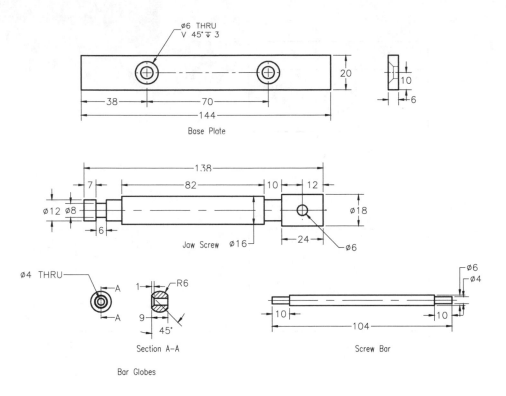

Figure 12-55 *Views and dimensions of Base Plate, Jaw Screw, Screw Bar, and Bar Globes*

Creating the Mate References

In this tutorial, you need to assemble the first two components of the assembly using the mate references. For assembling the components using the mate references, first you need to create the mate reference. Therefore, you need to open the part documents in which you will add the mate references.

1. Choose the **Open** button from the Menu Bar.

2. Double-click on the Vice Body; the vice-body part document is opened in the SolidWorks window.

3. Choose **Reference Geometry > Mate Reference** from the **Sketch CommandManager**; the **Mate Reference PropertyManager** is invoked. The selection mode in the **Primary Reference Entity** selection box is active.

4. Select the planar face of the model, as shown in Figure 12-56, as the primary reference; the selected planar face is highlighted.

5. Select the **Coincident** option from the **Mate Reference Type** drop-down list in the **Primary Reference Entity** rollout; the selection mode in the **Secondary Reference Entity** selection box is active.

6. Select the planar face of the model, as shown in Figure 12-56, as the secondary reference; the selected face is highlighted.

7. Select the **Coincident** option from the **Mate Reference Type** drop-down list in the **Secondary Reference Entity** rollout; the selection mode in the **Tertiary Reference Entity** selection box is active.

8. Select the planar face of the model, as shown in Figure 12-56, as the tertiary reference. The selected face is highlighted.

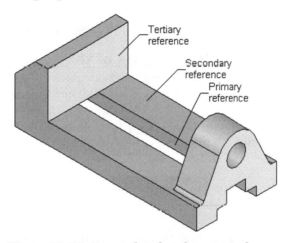

Figure 12-56 Faces to be selected as mate references

9. Select the **Parallel** option from the **Mate Reference Type** drop-down list in the **Tertiary Reference Entity** rollout.

10. Enter **Vice Mate Reference** as the name of the mate reference in the **Mate Reference Name** edit box available in the **Reference Name** rollout.

11. Choose the **OK** button from the **Mate Reference PropertyManager**.

12. Open the Vice Jaw part document.

13. Similarly, create the mate reference in the Vice Jaw part document. The faces to be selected as reference are shown in Figure 12-57. For both the part documents, enter the same name in the **Reference Name** rollout.

14. Close all part documents, except *Vice Body.sldprt* and *Vice Jaw.sldprt*, if they are opened.

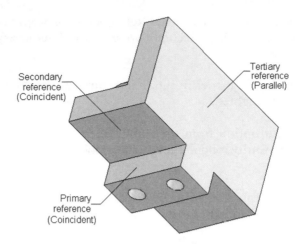

Secondary reference (Coincident)

Tertiary reference (Parallel)

Primary reference (Coincident)

Figure 12-57 Faces to be selected as mate references

Assembling the First Two Components of the Assembly

After creating the mate references in the part documents, you need to assemble the components. To do so, you need to start a new SolidWorks assembly document.

1. Start a new SolidWorks assembly document; the **Begin Assembly PropertyManager** is invoked automatically and the names of components that were opened, are displayed in the **Open documents** selection box.

2. Select the Vice Body from the **Open documents** selection box; the preview of the Vice Body is displayed along with the component cursor.

   It is recommended to place the first component of the assembly at the assembly origin.

3. Choose the **OK** button from the **Begin Assembly PropertyManager;** the first component is placed coincident to the origin.

4. Change the current view to isometric.

   Next, you need to place the second component in the assembly. As discussed earlier, the second component of the assembly, which is the Vice Jaw, is assembled with the Vice Body using the mate references.

5. Choose the **Insert Components** button from the **Assemble CommandManager**; the **Insert Component PropertyManager** is invoked and the names of components, which were opened, are displayed in the **Open documents** selection box.

6. Select the Vice Jaw from the **Open documents** selection box; the preview of the Vice Jaw is displayed in the drawing area.

When you move the cursor close to the Vice Body in the assembly document, the preview of the Vice Jaw assembled after applying the mates with the Vice Body is displayed in the assembly document.

7. Place the component at the required location. The mates specified in the mate references are applied between the Vice Jaw and the Vice Body.

   Figure 12-58 shows the second component being placed in the assembly document and Figure 12-59 shows the isometric view of the Vice Jaw assembled with the Vice Body.

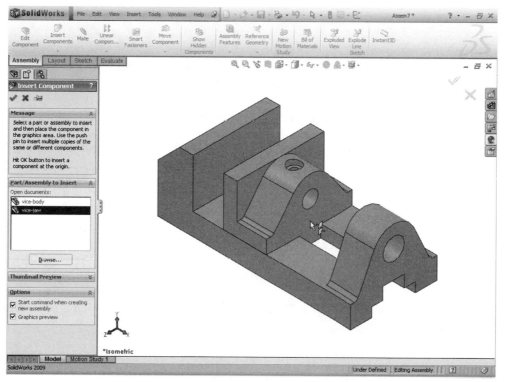

Figure 12-58 Second component being placed

8. Before proceeding further, close the part document windows of all the parts that are placed in the assembly document.

Tip. *The mates that are defined in the mate reference are applied to the components when you place the components in the assembly. You can view the mates applied to both components by expanding the **Mates** node from the **FeatureManager design tree** of the assembly document.*

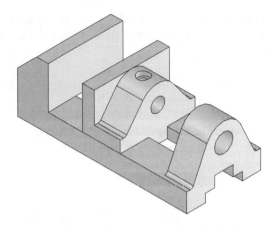

Figure 12-59 Vice Jaw assembled with the Vice Body

Assembling the Jaw Screw

Now, you need to place the Jaw Screw in the assembly document.

1. Choose the **Insert Components** button from the **Assemble CommandManager**.

2. Choose the **Browse** button in the **Part/Assembly to Insert** rollout; the **Open** dialog box is displayed.

3. Double-click on the Jaw Screw to open its part document; the preview of the Jaw Screw is displayed in the drawing area.

4. Click anywhere in the drawing area to place the Jaw Screw, as shown in Figure 12-60.

    Next, you need to add the assembly mates to assemble the components placed in the assembly.

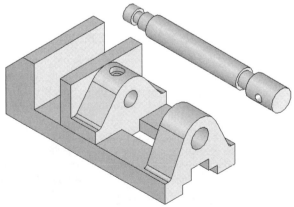

Figure 12-60 Jaw Screw placed in the assembly document

5. Press and hold the ALT key and then select the face from the location shown in Figure 12-61.

6. Drag the Jaw Screw to the hole in the Vice Body, as shown in Figure 12-62; the Jaw Screw appears transparent and the select cursor is replaced by the smart mates cursor. Also, the symbol of the **Concentric** mate is displayed below the cursor.

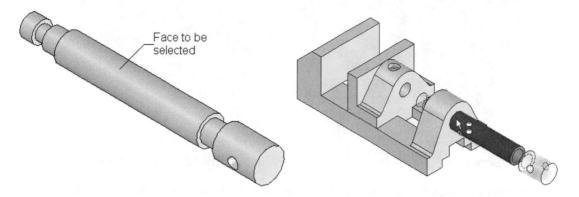

Figure 12-61 *Face to be selected*   Figure 12-62 *Jaw Screw being dragged*

7. Release the left mouse button at this location; the **Mate** pop-up toolbar is displayed and the **Concentric** button is chosen by default, which suggests that the **Concentric** mate is the most appropriate mate to be applied. Choose the **Add/ Finish Mate** button from the **Mate** pop-up toolbar. Figure 12-63 shows the Jaw Screw assembled in the Vice Body.

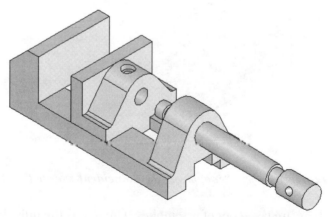

Figure 12-63 *The **Concentric** mate applied between the Jaw Screw and the Vice Body*

Next, you need to apply the **Coincident** mate between the planar faces of the Jaw Screw and the Vice Jaw.

8. Choose the **Mate** button from the **Assemble CommandManager** to invoke the **Mate PropertyManager**.

9. Rotate the assembly view and select the face of the Vice Jaw, as shown in Figure 12-64. Next, select the face of the Jaw Screw, as shown in Figure 12-65.

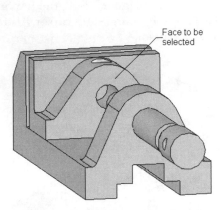

Figure 12-64 *Face to be selected*

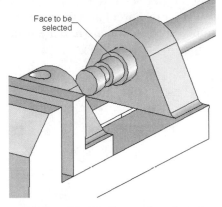

Figure 12-65 *Face to be selected*

As soon as you select the faces, the **Mate** pop-up toolbar is invoked with the **Coincident** button chosen and the preview of the assembly with the coincident mate is displayed in the drawing area.

10. Choose the **Add/Finish Mate** button from the **Mate** pop-up toolbar. The assembly after adding the **Coincident** mate is displayed in Figure 12-66.

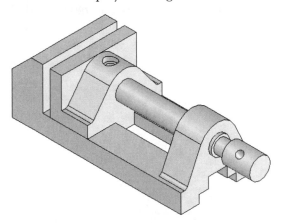

Figure 12-66 *Assembly after applying the **Coincident** mate to the Jaw Screw*

In real world, there are two types of assemblies. The first is the fully defined assembly in which all degrees of freedom of all components are restricted. The other type of assembly is that in which some degrees of freedom of the components are left free so that they can be moved or rotated. These types of assemblies are used for the mechanism, about which you will learn in the next chapter.

After adding the **Coincident** mate, you need to move the assembly to analyze the degree of freedom of the components in the assembly. After analyzing the components of an assembly, you need to add the mates to constrain that degree of freedom.

11. Select the circular face of the Jaw Screw using the left mouse button and drag the cursor. You will notice that the Jaw Screw is rotating about its axis and is moving along the X axis. Also, it is forcing the Vice Jaw to move along the X axis. Although, this degree of freedom of the Vice Jaw and Jaw Screw needs to be left free so that the assembly can function in the mechanism, but in this chapter, you need to restrict this degree of freedom so as to create a fully defined assembly.

12. Select the two faces, one of the Vice Body and the other of the Jaw Screw, as shown in Figures 12-67 and 12-68.

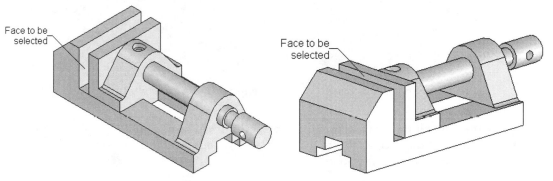

Figure 12-67 Face to be selected   *Figure 12-68* Face to be selected

13. Choose the **Distance** button from the **Standard Mates** rollout; the **PropertyManager** changes to the **Distance 1 PropertyManager**. Set the value in the **Distance** spinner to **10**.

14. Choose the **OK** button from the **Distance 1 PropertyManager** to again display the **Mate PropertyManager**.

15. Expand the **FeatureManager design tree** displayed in the drawing area and select the **Top Plane**. Now, expand the **Jaw Screw** node from the **FeatureManager design tree** and select the **Top Plane**; the **Mate** pop-up toolbar is displayed.

16. Choose the **Angle** button from the **Mate** pop-up toolbar.

17. Set the value in the **Angle** spinner to **45** and choose the **Add/Finish Mate** button from the **Mate** pop-up toolbar.

18. Choose the **OK** button from the **Mate PropertyManager** to exit.

Assembling the Clamping Plate

Next, you need to assemble the Clamping Plate with the assembly.

1. Invoke the **Insert Component PropertyManager** and choose the **Browse** button to invoke the **Open** dialog box. Open and place the Clamping Plate in the drawing area.

2. Rotate the assembly such that the bottom face of the assembly is displayed, as shown in Figure 12-69.

3. Select the Clamping Plate using the right mouse button and drag the cursor to rotate it, as shown in Figure 12-70.

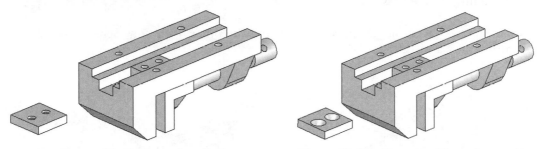

Figure 12-69 *Rotated assembly*   *Figure 12-70* *Clamping Plate after rotating*

4. Apply the **Concentric** mate between the two cylindrical faces of the clamping plate and the two holes of the Vice Jaw, refer to Figure 12-71. You may have to move the Clamping Plate after applying the first mate.

5. Move the Clamping Plate by dragging. Now, apply the **Coincident** mate between the faces of the Clamping Plate and the Vice Jaw, as shown in Figure 12-72.

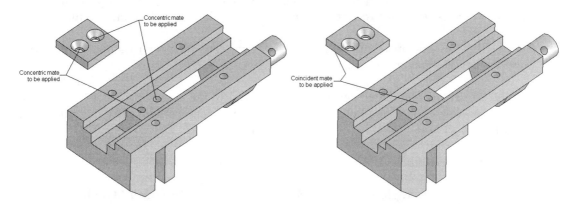

Figure 12-71 *Faces to be selected to apply mate*   *Figure 12-72* *Faces to be selected to apply mate*

6. Similarly, assemble the Screw Bar, Base Plates, and Bar Globes. The assembly after assembling all these components is shown in Figure 12-73.

Assembling the Remaining Components

Next, you need to assemble the Oval Fillister, Set Screw 1, and Set Screw 2. These fasteners are assembled using the feature-based mates.

1. Open the part documents of Oval Fillisters, Set Screw 1, and Set Screw 2.

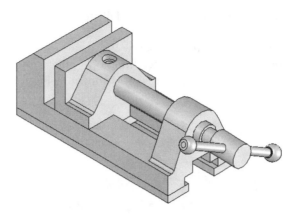

Figure 12-73 *Assembly after assembling the Vice Body, Vice Jaw,*
Jaw Screw, Screw Bar, Clamping Plate, Base Plate, and Bar Globes

2. Choose **Window > Tile Horizontally** from the SolidWorks menus to rearrange the windows.

3. Select the **Revolve1** feature from the **FeatureManager design tree** of the Oval Fillister part document. Drag the cursor to place the component in the assembly, as shown in Figure 12-74.

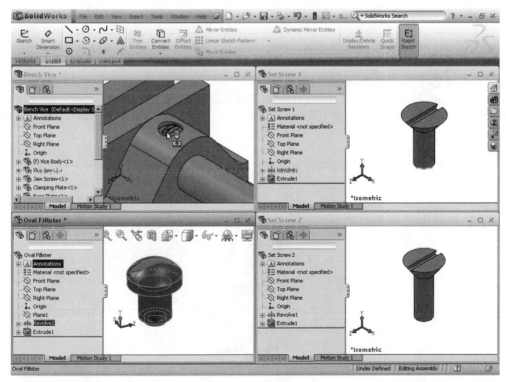

Figure 12-74 *Dragging the Oval Fillisters in the assembly using the feature-based mates*

4. Drop the component at the hole for the Oval Fillister.

    Similarly, assemble Set Screw 1 and Set screw 2 using the feature-based mates. Use the
    TAB key on the keyboard to reverse the direction. The rotated view of the assembly
    after assembling Set Screw 1 and Set Screw 2, is shown in Figure 12-75.

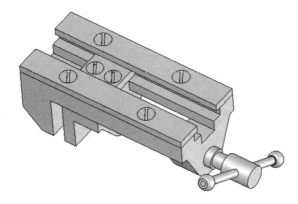

Figure 12-75 Viewing the final assembly from the bottom

5. Choose the **Save** button to save the assembly with the name *Bench Vice* in the folder *My
    Documents\SolidWorks\c12\Bench Vice*.

Tutorial 2

In this tutorial, you will create all components of the Pipe Vice and then assemble them. The
Pipe Vice assembly is shown in Figure 12-76. The dimensions of various components of this
assembly are given in Figures 12-77 and 12-78.   **(Expected time: 2 hrs 45 min)**

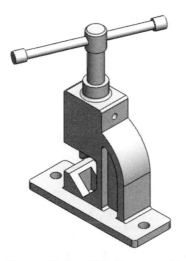

Figure 12-76 Pipe Vice assembly

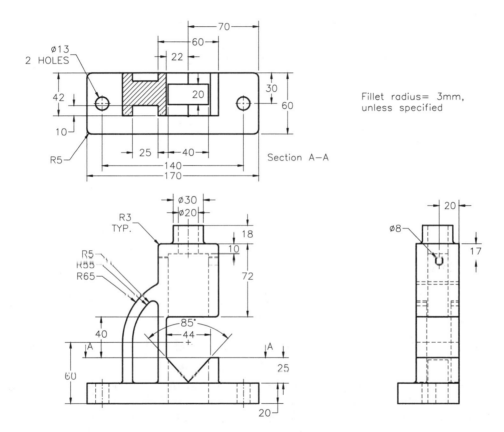

Figure 12-77 *Views and dimensions of the base*

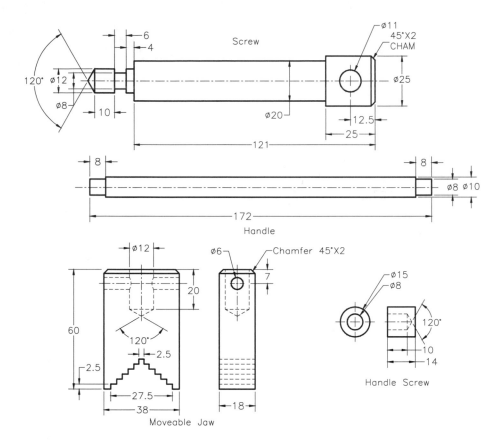

Figure 12-78 *Views and dimensions of the Screw, Handle, Moveable Jaw, and Handle Screw*

You need to create all components of the Pipe Vice assembly as separate part documents. After creating the parts, you will assemble them in the assembly document. Therefore, in this tutorial, you need to use the bottom-up approach for creating the assembly.

The following steps are required to complete this tutorial:

a. Create all components in the individual part documents and save them. The part documents will be saved in *My Documents\SolidWorks\c12\Pipe Vice*.
b. Place the base at the origin of the assembly.
c. Place the Moveable Jaw and the Screw in the assembly. Apply the mates between Moveable Jaw and the Screw, refer to Figures 12-79 through 12-81.
d. Assemble the Screw with the Base.
e. Place the other components in the assembly and apply the required mates to the assembly, refer to Figure 12-82.

Creating the Components

1. Create all components of the Pipe Vice assembly as separate part documents. Specify the names of the files, as shown in Figures 12-77 and 12-78. The documents should be saved in the folder *\My Documents\SolidWorks\c12\Pipe Vice*.

Inserting the First Component in the Assembly

After creating all components of the Pipe Vice assembly, you need to start a new SolidWorks assembly document.

1. Start a new SolidWorks assembly document; the **Begin Assembly PropertyManager** is displayed, by default.

2. Choose the **Browse** button from the **Part/Assembly to Insert** rollout to display the **Open** dialog box. Double-click on the Base.

3. Choose the **OK** button from the **Begin Assembly PropertyManager** to place the Base origin coincident to the origin of the assembly document.

4. Change the view orientation to isometric.

Inserting and Assembling the Moveable Jaw and the Screw

After placing the first component in the assembly document, you need to place the Moveable Jaw and the Screw in the assembly document. After placing these components, you need to apply the required mates.

1. Choose the **Insert Components** button from the **Assemble CommandManager**. Then, choose the **Keep Visible** button from the **PropertyManager**. Now, invoke the **Open** dialog box by choosing the **Browse** button from the **Part/Assembly to Insert** rollout.

2. Double-click on the Moveable Jaw. Place the component anywhere in the assembly document such that it does not interfere with the existing component.

3. Similarly, place the Screw in the assembly document and choose the **OK** button from the **Insert Component PropertyManager**. Figure 12-79 shows the Moveable Jaw, Screw, and Base placed in the assembly document.

    First, you need to assemble the Screw with the Moveable Jaw. Therefore, you need to fix the Moveable Jaw.

4. Select the Moveable Jaw from the drawing area or from the **FeatureManager design tree**. Right-click to invoke the shortcut menu.

5. Choose the **Fix** option from the shortcut menu; the Moveable Jaw is fixed and you cannot move or rotate it.

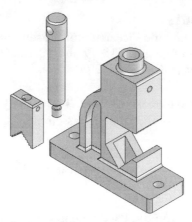

Figure 12-79 *The Moveable Jaw, Screw, and Base placed in the assembly document*

6. Invoke the **Move Component PropertyManager** and choose the **SmartMates** button from the **Move** rollout. Double-click on the lower most cylindrical face of the Screw; the Screw appears transparent.

7. Drag the cursor to the hole located on the top of the Moveable Jaw. Release the left mouse button as soon as the concentric symbol is displayed below the cursor. Choose the **Add/Finish Mate** button from the **Mate** pop-up toolbar.

8. Select the Screw and move it up so that it is not inside the Moveable Jaw.

9. Right-click in the drawing area and choose **Clear Selections** to clear the current selection.

10. Rotate the assembly and double-click on the lower flat face of the Screw; the Screw appears transparent.

11. Again, rotate the model and select the top planar face of the Moveable Jaw. The **Coincident** mate is applied between the two selected faces. Choose the **Add/Finish Mate** button from the **Mate** pop-up toolbar.

12. Choose the **OK** button from the **SmartMates PropertyManager**. Figure 12-80 shows the Screw after applying the mates.

    Next, you need to assemble the Screw and the Moveable Jaw with the Base.

13. Select the Moveable Jaw, invoke the shortcut menu and then choose the **Float** option from it; the Moveable Jaw and the Screw assembled to it can be moved.

14. Press the ALT key, select the cylindrical face of the Screw and move toward the hole created on the top face of the Base to add the **Concentric** mate.

15. Invoke the **Mate PropertyManager** and select the front planar face of the Moveable Jaw and the front planar face of the Base.

16. Choose the **Parallel** button from the **Mate** pop-up toolbar and choose the **Add/Finish Mate** button to add a **Parallel** mate between the selected faces.

17. Next, select the faces. as shown in Figure 12-81.

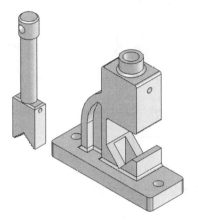

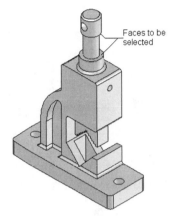

Figure 12-80 *The Screw assembled with the Moveable Jaw*

Figure 12-81 *Faces to be selected*

18. Choose the **Distance** button from the **Mate** pop-up toolbar and set the value in the **Distance** spinner to **35**.

19. Choose the **Add/Finish Mate** button from the **Mate** pop-up toolbar and then choose the **OK** button from the **Mate PropertyManager**.

20. Similarly, assemble the other components of the Pipe Vice. Figure 12-82 shows the final Pipe Vice assembly.

21. Choose the **Save** button to save the assembly document in the *My Documents*\ *SolidWorks**c12**Pipe Vice* folder.

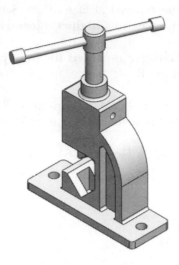

Figure 12-82 *Final Pipe Vice assembly*

SELF-EVALUATION TEST

Answer the following questions and then compare them to those given at the end of this chapter:

1. The bottom-up assembly design approach is the traditional and the most widely preferred approach of assembly design. (T/F)

2. In the top-down assembly design approach, all components are created in the same assembly document. (T/F)

3. The **Coincident** mate is generally applied to make two planar faces coplanar. (T/F)

4. The most suitable mates that can be applied to the current selection set are displayed in the **Mate Selections** rollout in the **Mate PropertyManager**. (T/F)

5. Feature-based mates are applied only to the components that have cylindrical features. (T/F)

6. Pattern-based mates are used to assemble the components that have a circular pattern created on the circular feature. (T/F)

7. Choose the _____ button from the **Assemble CommandManager** to invoke the **Rotate Component PropertyManager**.

8. The _____ option available in the **Rotate** drop-down list is used to rotate the selected component by an incremental angle about the specified axis.

9. The _____ mate is generally used to align the central axis of one component with that of the other.

10. The _____ option available in the **Move** drop-down list is used to move the component along the direction of the selected entity.

REVIEW QUESTIONS

Answer the following questions:

1. The names of the selected entities are displayed in the _____ selection box of the **Mate Component PropertyManager**.

2. Choose _____ from the Menu Bar to place a component in the assembly document.

3. Select the _____ option from the **Move** drop-down list to move the component dynamically along the X, Y, and Z axes of the assembly document.

4. The _____ button available in the **Standard Mates** rollout is used to make the two selected entities normal to each other.

5. The _____ option is used to specify the coordinates of the origin of the part where the component will be placed after moving.

6. If you are adding the feature-based mates using the features that have a conical geometry, then there must be a _____ face adjacent to the conical face of both the features.

7. In SolidWorks, which of the following is the most widely used method of adding the mates to the components in the assembly?

    (a) Smart Mates   (b) **Mate PropertyManager**
    (c) By dragging from part document   (d) None of these

8. Which button is used to make the **Mate Component PropertyManager** available after applying a mate to the selected entities?

    (a) **Help**   (b) **OK**
    (c) **Keep Visible**   (d) **Cancel**

9. Which of the following options in the **Rotate** drop-down list is used to rotate the component with respect to the selected entity?

    (a) **Along Entity**   (b) **Selected Edge**
    (c) **Reference Entity**   (d) None of these

10. Which option is used to specify the coordinates of the origin of the part where the component will be placed after moving?

    (a) **To XYZ Position**   (b) **Reference Position**

    (c) **Along Entity**   (d) None of these

EXERCISE

Exercise 1

Create the Plummer Block assembly, as shown in Figure 12-83. The dimensions of the components of this assembly are shown in Figures 12-84 through 12-86

(Expected time: 1 hr)

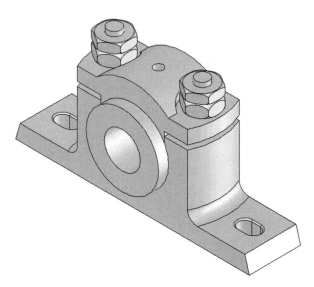

Figure 12-83 Plummer Block assembly

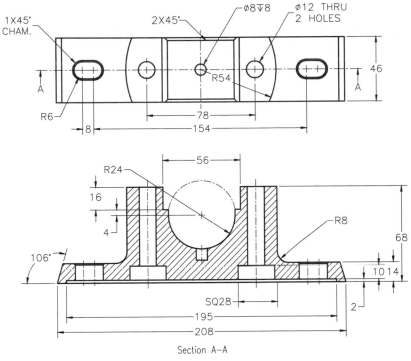

Figure 12-84 *Views and dimensions of Casting*

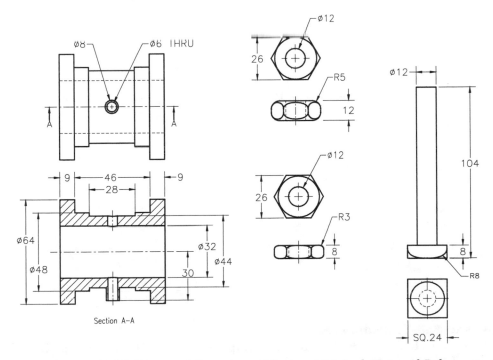

Figure 12-85 *Views and dimensions of Brasses, Nut, Lock Nut, and Bolt*

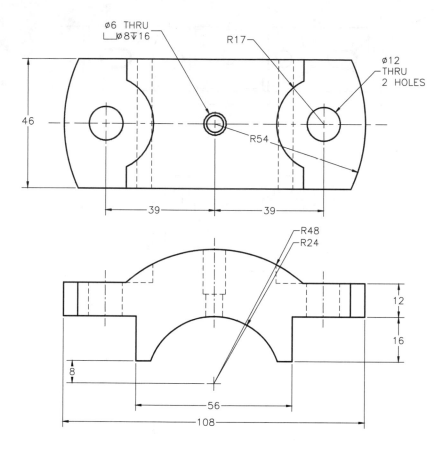

Figure 12-86 *Views and dimensions of Cap*

Chapter **13**

Assembly Modeling-II

Learning Objectives

After completing this chapter, you will be able to:
- *Apply advanced mates.*
- *Create subassemblies.*
- *Delete components and subassemblies.*
- *Edit assembly mates.*
- *Replace mate entities.*
- *Edit components and subassemblies.*
- *Dissolve subassemblies.*
- *Replace components in assemblies.*
- *Create patterns of components in an assembly.*
- *Create mirrored components.*
- *Hide and suppress components in assemblies.*
- *Change the transparency condition of an assembly.*
- *Check the interference in an assembly.*
- *Create assemblies for mechanism.*
- *Detect collision while the assembly is in motion.*
- *Create the exploded state of an assembly.*
- *Create the explode line sketch.*

ADVANCED ASSEMBLY MATES

In the previous chapter, you learned to place the components in an assembly document and also to apply the assembly mates to them. In this chapter, you will learn to apply the advanced mates to the components by invoking the **Mate PropertyManager** and then the **Advanced Mates** rollout available in it. The **Advanced Mates** rollout is displayed in Figure 13-1.

Figure 13-1 The Advanced Mates rollout

The **Symmetric**, **Width**, **Distance**, and **Angle** mates in the **Mate PropertyManager** are discussed next.

Applying the Symmetric Mate

The **Symmetric** mate is applied to create a symmetric relation between two components. To apply this mate, choose the **Symmetric** button available in the **Advanced Mates** rollout; the **Symmetry Plane** selection box will be displayed in the **Mate Selections** rollout. Select a plane or a planar face that will act as the symmetry plane; the **Symmetry Plane** callout will be attached to the selected plane. Next, you need to select two similar entities from the two components to which you need to apply the **Symmetric** mate. The similar entities can be edges, vertices, planar faces, and so on. Click once in the **Entities to Mate** selection box to invoke the selection mode and select the entities, as shown in Figure 13-2. Choose the **OK** button from the **Mate PropertyManager**; the **Symmetric** mate will be applied, as shown in Figure 13-3.

Applying the Width Mate

This mate is used to align a component at an equal distance between the two faces of another component. The faces between which you want to align another component should be planar faces. However, to align the component, you can select a nonplanar face also. To apply this mate, choose the **Width** button from the **Advanced Mates** rollout in the **Mate PropertyManager**; the **Width selections** and **Tab selections** selection boxes will be displayed in the **Mate Selections** rollout. Left-click in the **Width selections** selection box and select the two planar faces between which you want to align the second component; a

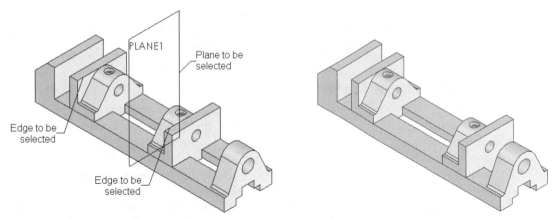

Figure 13-2 *Entities and the plane to be selected to apply the **Symmetric** mate*

Figure 13-3 *Assembly after applying the **Symmetric** mate*

callout will be displayed on the selected faces. Next, left-click in the **Tab selections** selection box and select the planar or the curved faces of the second component that you want to align between the selected width references; the component will be automatically aligned at an equal distance between the two faces of the first component. Figure 13-4 shows the faces of the first component selected as the width reference and the cylindrical face of the second component being selected as the tab reference. Figure 13-5 shows the preview of the resulting position of the second component.

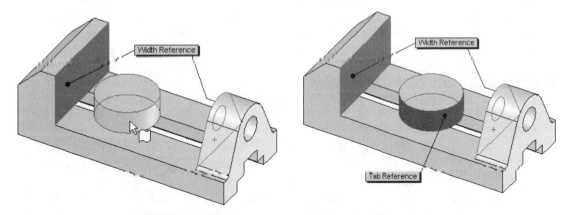

Figure 13-4 *Selecting the faces for the width and tab references*

Figure 13-5 *Preview of the location of the second component*

Applying the Distance Mate

The **Distance** mate is applied to create a to and fro motion between the components. To apply this mate, choose the **Distance** button in the **Advanced Mates** rollout; the **Distance**, **Maximum Value**, and **Minimum Value** spinners will be enabled. Select the two faces between which you need to apply the **Distance** mate. The maximum distance by which the two selected faces can be moved apart is specified in the **Distance** spinner; this value will be displayed in both the **Maximum Value** spinner and the **Minimum Value** spinner.

However, if you want the selected faces to be moved in a to and fro motion, specify the minimum distance in the **Minimum Value** spinner. Choose the **OK** button twice. On moving one of the components, you will notice that it can be moved to and fro.

Applying the Angle Mate

The **Angle** mate is applied to create a swinging motion between the components. To apply this mate, choose the **Angle** button in the **Advanced Mates** rollout; the **Angle**, **Maximum Value**, and **Minimum Value** spinners will be enabled. Select the two faces between which you need to apply the **Angle** mate. The maximum angle by which one of the selected faces has to be moved will be specified in the **Angle** spinner; this value will be displayed in both the **Maximum Value** and **Minimum Value** spinners. The minimum angle between the selected faces is specified in the **Minimum Value** spinner. Choose the **OK** button twice. Now, if you move the floating component, it will swing.

Applying the Path Mate

The **Path Mate** is used to apply a mate such that the part moves along a path. To apply this mate, choose the **Path Mate** button in the **Advanced Mates** rollout; the **Path Constraint**, **Pitch/Yaw Control**, and **Roll Control** drop-down lists will be enabled. In addition, the **Components Vertex** and **Path Selection** selection boxes will be displayed in the **Mate Selections** rollout. Select the vertex of the component that travels along the path. Next, left-click in the **Path Selection** selection box and select the contiguous curves, edges, or sketch entities as path. The **Selection Manager** button available in the **Mate Selections** rollout is used to facilitate the selection. Select the required options from the **Path Constraint**, **Pitch/Yaw Control**, and **Roll Control** drop-down lists in the **Advanced Mates** rollout and then choose the **OK** button. The options in these drop-down lists are discussed next.

Path Constraint Drop-down List

The options in the **Path Constraint** drop-down list are discussed next.

Free

This option allows you to drag the component freely along the selected path.

Distance Along Path

This option is used to constrain the vertex of the component that travels along the path to a specified distance. Specify the dimension using the **Dimension** spinner available below this drop-down list. You can flip the direction of path using the **Flip dimension** check box.

Percent Along Path

This option is used to constrain the vertex of the component that travels along the path to a specified distance. The distance is specified as a percentage along the path. Specify the percentage using the **Percent** spinner available below this drop-down list.

Pitch/Yaw Control Drop-down List

The options in the **Pitch/Yaw Control** drop-down list are discussed next.

Free

On selecting this option, the pitch/Yaw of the component that travels along the path will not be constrained.

Follow Path

This option allows one of the axes of the component to be tangent along the path.

Roll Control Drop-down List

The options in this drop-down list are discussed next.

Free

On selecting this option, the roll of the component that travels along the path will not be constrained.

Up Vector

This option allows you to constrain one of the axes of the component to align with the vector. You can select the linear edge or planar face to define the vector.

MECHANICAL MATES

In SolidWorks, the mates that are applied to create mechanical drives and joints are grouped in the **Mechanical Mates** rollout. These mates are discussed next.

Applying the Cam Mate

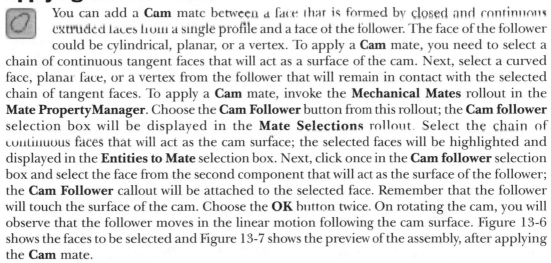

You can add a **Cam** mate between a face that is formed by closed and continuous extruded faces from a single profile and a face of the follower. The face of the follower could be cylindrical, planar, or a vertex. To apply a **Cam** mate, you need to select a chain of continuous tangent faces that will act as a surface of the cam. Next, select a curved face, planar face, or a vertex from the follower that will remain in contact with the selected chain of tangent faces. To apply a **Cam** mate, invoke the **Mechanical Mates** rollout in the **Mate PropertyManager**. Choose the **Cam Follower** button from this rollout; the **Cam follower** selection box will be displayed in the **Mate Selections** rollout. Select the chain of continuous faces that will act as the cam surface; the selected faces will be highlighted and displayed in the **Entities to Mate** selection box. Next, click once in the **Cam follower** selection box and select the face from the second component that will act as the surface of the follower; the **Cam Follower** callout will be attached to the selected face. Remember that the follower will touch the surface of the cam. Choose the **OK** button twice. On rotating the cam, you will observe that the follower moves in the linear motion following the cam surface. Figure 13-6 shows the faces to be selected and Figure 13-7 shows the preview of the assembly, after applying the **Cam** mate.

Note

For a better understanding of this mate, make sure that the front faces of the cam and follower are coplanar. Also, ensure that a proper degree of freedom for the components of the cam and follower assembly is kept free.

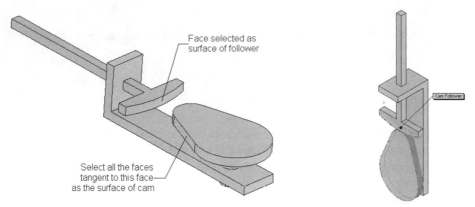

Figure 13-6   *Faces selected to apply the* ***Cam***

Figure 13-7   *Preview of the assembly with the* ***Cam*** *mate*

Applying the Gear Mate

The **Gear** mate allows you to rotate two components such as gears with respect to each other about a selected axis. You can also define a specific gear ratio between the selected components. To apply this mate between the two components, expand the **Mechanical Mates** rollout in the **Mate PropertyManager**. Choose the **Gear** button from the **Mechanical Mates** rollout; the **Ratio** edit boxes and the **Reverse** check box will be displayed. You need to select the references about which the two components will be rotated. These references can be cylindrical faces, conical faces, axes, circular edges, or linear edges. Select the required references (Figure 13-8); the names of selected references will be displayed in the **Entities to Mate** selection box. The **Teeth/Diameter** callouts will also be displayed attached to the selected references, as shown in Figure 13-9. You can set the ratio of rotation using the **Ratio** edit boxes or using the **Teeth/Diameter** callouts. The **Reverse** check box is selected to change the direction of rotation of one component with respect to the other. After applying the mate, choose the **OK** button twice. After adding this mate, rotate any one of the components and you will observe the other component rotating as per the specified gear ratio. Generally, this mate is used to display the rotation of the gears and direction.

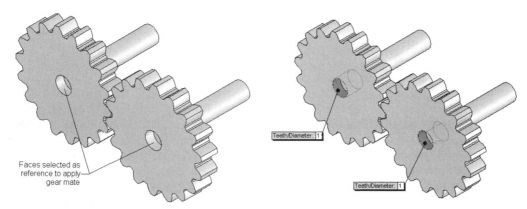

Figure 13-8   *Faces to be selected to apply the* ***Gear*** *mate*

Figure 13-9   *The* ***Teeth/Diameter*** *callouts attached to the selected faces*

Applying the Rack Pinion Mate

The **Rack Pinion** mate allows you to create a rack and pinion relationship between two components. As a result, the rack undergoes translation motion and the pinion undergoes rotational motion. To apply this mate, choose the **Rack Pinion** button in the **Mechanical Mates** rollout; the **Rack** and **Pinion/Gear** selection boxes will be displayed in the **Mate Selections** rollout. Select the linear edge of the rack and then select the circular edge of the pinion; the **Rack Pinion** mate will be applied to the two components. You can specify the pinion pitch diameter or the distance to be traveled by the rack per revolution of the pinion using the options in the **Mechanical Mates** rollout.

Applying the Screw Mate

The **Screw** mate allows you to create a mate for the threaded features. If you rotate the head of the male part after applying this mate, the male part will advance over the female part. To apply this mate, choose the **Screw** button from the **Mechanical Mates** rollout; two radio buttons will be available. Select the **Revolutions/mm** radio button if you need to specify the number of revolutions required by the male part to advance 1 mm over the female part. Specify the number of revolutions in the edit box. Select the **Distance/ revolutions** radio button, if you need to specify the distance by which the male part needs to advance in one revolution. Then, specify the distance to be advanced in the edit box and choose **OK** twice. By default, the left hand thread (counterclockwise direction) will be applied. Select the **Reverse** check box to change the direction of thread to the right hand thread.

Applying the Hinge Mate

The **Hinge** mate is applied to create a swinging motion between two parts about an axis. To apply this mate between two components, expand the **Mechanical Mates** rollout in the **Mate PropertyManager** and choose the **Hinge** button from the **Mechanical Mates** rollout; two selection boxes will be displayed in the **Mate Selections** rollout, **Concentric Selections** and **Coincident Selections**. The **Concentric Selections** selection box is selected by default. Next, select the two circular faces that are to be concentric, as shown in Figure 13-10; the names of the selected faces will be displayed in the **Concentric Selections** selection box. Left-click in the **Coincident Selections** selection box and then select the planar faces to apply the coincident relation, as shown in Figure 13-11; the names of the selected faces will be displayed in the **Coincident Selections** selection box. If you need to swing the selected components within a specific angle, then select the **Specify angle limits** check box; the **Angle**, **Maximum Value**, and **Minimum Value** spinners will be displayed. Select the two planar faces that can be rotated, as shown in Figure 13-12. Set the maximum and minimum angular limits in the corresponding spinners. The maximum angle by which the two selected faces can be rotated apart is specified in the **Angle** spinner and this value will be displayed in both the **Maximum Value** and **Minimum Value** spinners. The minimum angle between the selected faces is specified in the **Minimum Value** spinner. Choose the **OK** button twice. Figure 13-13 shows the resulting assembly, after applying the **Hinge** mate. Now, if you drag the floating component, it will rotate.

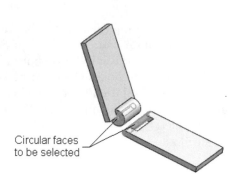

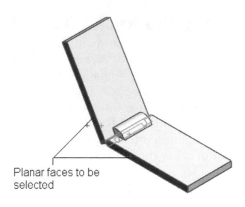

Figure 13-10 *Faces to be selected to apply the* **Concentric** *relation*

Figure 13-11 *Faces to be selected to apply the* **Coincident** *relation*

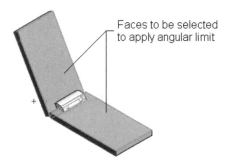

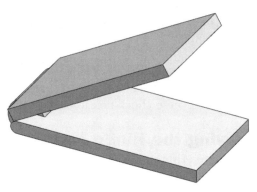

Figure 13-12 *Faces to be selected to apply the angular rotation*

Figure 13-13 *The resulting assembly after applying the* **Hinge** *mate*

CREATING SUB-ASSEMBLIES

In the previous chapter, you learned to place the individual parts in the assembly document and apply the assembly mates to them to create an assembly. However, this method will not be effective if you create a large assembly like assembling a machine tool, car, and so on. In such cases, you need to create the assemblies of smaller units. These are called as sub-assemblies. Then, you need to assemble the parts and the subassemblies to create the main assembly. Different methods to create the subassemblies in the main assembly are discussed next.

Bottom-up Sub-assembly Design

In the bottom-up sub-assembly design approach, the subassemblies are created separately and then saved as an individual assembly file. To place a sub-assembly in the main assembly, open the main assembly document and invoke the **Insert Component PropertyManager**. On choosing the **Browse** button, the **Open** dialog box will be displayed. Select **Assembly** (**.asm, *.sldasm*) from the **Files of type** drop-down list; all assemblies saved in the current location will be displayed in the selection box. Select the sub-assembly from the selection box and choose the **Open** button from the **Open** dialog box. Select a point in the drawing area to place the sub-assembly. Now, assemble the sub-assembly with the parts in the main assembly using the assembly mates. You can also place an assembly in the other assembly using the drag and drop method that was discussed in the previous chapter. In this case, the assembly that was dragged and dropped will be a sub-assembly. Figure 13-14 shows a sub-assembly of a piston and an articulated rod. Figure 13-15 shows the main assembly of the piston and master rod.

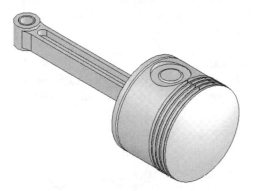

Figure 13-14 The sub-assembly *Figure 13-15* The main assembly

Top-down Sub-assembly Design

The top-down sub-assembly design approach is the most flexible sub-assembly design approach. In this approach, you create a new sub-assembly in the main assembly document. The approach is generally used in the conceptual design or while managing a large assembly. To create a new sub-assembly in the assembly document, choose **Insert Components > New Assembly** from the **Assembly CommandManager**; a new node with the default name will be added to the **FeatureManager design tree**. To open this sub-assembly, select it from the **FeatureManager design tree** and choose **Open Assembly** from the pop-up toolbar; the sub-assembly document will be opened. Create the sub-assembly and choose the **Save As** button to save the assembly as different a assembly file. To revert back to the main assembly, choose the **Window** button in the SolidWorks menus and select the assembly document. Alternatively, press CTRL+TAB keys to cycle through the documents opened. You can drag and place the components in the new sub-assembly from the **FeatureManager design tree**. You will learn more about this approach, while discussing the editing of assemblies and sub-assemblies.

Inserting a New Sub-assembly

You can also create a sub-assembly by grouping the parts in the existing assembly. To do so, select a component or components, then right-click on a component in the **FeatureManager design tree**, and choose the **Form New Sub-assembly Here** option from the shortcut menu; a new sub-assembly node will be displayed in the **Feature Manager design tree**. You need to expand the shortcut menu, if the option is not displayed by default. You can also select the component and choose **Insert > Component > Assembly from Selected Components** from the SolidWorks menus to insert a sub-assembly.

DELETING COMPONENTS AND SUB-ASSEMBLIES

After creating the assembly, at a certain stage of your design cycle, you may need to delete a component or a sub-assembly. To delete a component of the assembly, select the component from the drawing area or from the **FeatureManager design tree**. Invoke the shortcut menu and choose the **Delete** option. You can also delete the selected component by pressing the DELETE key. When you delete a component, the **Confirm Delete** dialog box will be displayed. The name of the component and the items dependent on it will be displayed in this dialog box. Choose the **Yes** button from the **Confirm Delete** dialog box.

To delete a sub-assembly, select it from the **FeatureManager design tree** and press the DELETE key. The **Confirm Delete** dialog box will be displayed; choose the **YES** button from it. Note that on deleting the sub-assembly, all the components of the sub-assembly are also deleted.

EDITING ASSEMBLY MATES

After creating the assembly or during the process of assembling the components, you may need to edit the assembly mates. The editing operations that can be performed include modifying the type of the assembly mate or angle and offset values, changing the component to which the mate was applied, and so on. To edit the mates in an assembly, you first need to expand the **Mates** option at the end of the **FeatureManager design tree**. Next, select the mate that you need to modify; a pop-up toolbar will be displayed. Choose the **Mate** option from the pop-up toolbar; the **Mate PropertyManager** will be displayed. The name of the **Mate PropertyManager** will depend on the name and sequence of the mate applied. Note that the pop-up toolbar will not be displayed if you select a mate of a sub-assembly in the sub-assembly node of the **FeatureManager design tree.** So, you need to select the mate to be edited, right-click and choose the **Mate** option to invoke the **Mate PropertyManager** from the shortcut menu. Figure 13-16 shows a partial view of the **Mate PropertyManager** to edit the **Coincident** mate. You can edit the entities to mate, type of mate, value of offset, value of angle, and so on using this **PropertyManager**.

Figure 13-16 Partial view of the **Mate PropertyManager** to edit the **Coincident** mate

Tip. *When you move the cursor on a mate in the **FeatureManager design tree**, the edges of the entities used in the mate will be highlighted in the drawing area. On selecting the mate from the **FeatureManager design tree**, the surfaces of the entities used in the selected mate will be highlighted in the drawing area.*

Replacing Mated Entities

As discussed, you can edit the mate entities using the **Mate PropertyManager**. They can also be modified using the **Mated Entities PropertyManager**. Select the **Mates** option from the **FeatureManager design tree**, invoke the shortcut menu, expand the shortcut menu, and choose the **Replace Mate Entities** option; the **Mated Entities PropertyManager** will be displayed, as shown in Figure 13-17. On invoking the **Mated Entities PropertyManager**, you will be prompted to select the entity to be replaced. Select the entity from the **Mate Entities** selection box. You can also expand the entity tree to edit an individual mate. On selecting a mate, the corresponding face will be highlighted in the drawing area and its name will be displayed in the **Replacement Mate Entity** selection box. You will be prompted to select the entity to be mated. Select the entity that will replace the previously selected entity. The **SolidWorks** message box will be displayed informing the possible cause of error, if the selected entity over defines the mate or if the mating is not possible between the entities.

The **Flip Mate Alignment** button is used to flip the direction of the mate. The **Disable Preview** button is used to disable the preview of the assembly after replacing the mate entity. The **Show all mates** check box is used to display all the mated entities.

Figure 13-17 The Mated Entities PropertyManager

EDITING COMPONENTS

CommandManager:	Assembly > Edit Component
Toolbar:	Assembly > Edit Component

At some stage of your design cycle, you may need to edit the components after placing and mating them in the assembly document. This may include editing the features, sketches, and sketch planes. To edit the components, you first need to select the component and invoke the part modeling environment in the assembly document. To do so, select the component from the drawing area or from the **FeatureManager design tree** and choose the **Edit Component** button from the **Assembly CommandManager**. The part modeling environment will be invoked and the entire assembly, except the component to be edited, will turn transparent. If not, choose the **Assembly Transparency** button in the **Assembly CommandManager**; a flyout will be invoked and the options in it can be used to set the transparency of the assembly. On choosing the **Opaque** option, all components of the assembly will be set to opaque. The **Maintain Transparency** option retains the default

Tip. *Select the **Mates** option from the **FeatureManager design tree** and invoke the shortcut menu. Choose the **Parent/Child** option from the shortcut menu; the **Parent Child Relationship** dialog box will be displayed. You can display the child and parent relationship of any component placed in the assembly using the **Parent Child Relationship** dialog box.*

transparency settings of the individual components. If the **Force Transparency** option is chosen, all components of the assembly, except the component being edited, will be set as transparent. The name of the component to be edited will be displayed in blue in the **FeatureManager design tree**. Left-click on the + (plus) sign to expand the component node, select the feature to be edited and invoke the respective **PropertyManager**. If required, you can also add new features to the component. This type of editing is technically termed as **Editing in the Context of Assembly**. After editing the component, again choose the **Edit Component** button from the **Assembly CommandManager** to return to the assembly environment.

Tip. *You can also modify the dimensions of an assembled component or those placed in the assembly by double-clicking on the desired feature of that component. All dimensions of that feature will be displayed in the drawing area. Invoke the* **Modify** *dialog box by double-clicking on the dimension to be modified. Enter the new dimension in the* **Modify** *dialog box and press the ENTER key; the dimension will be modified, but the geometry of the feature will not be changed. You need to rebuild the assembly to reflect the modifications. To do so, choose the* **Rebuild** *button from the Menu Bar or use the CTRL+B keys.*

While editing the part in the assembly document, you can use the **Move/Size Features** *or the* **Instant3D** *tool to edit the features dynamically.*

Note

To edit the components separately in their part documents, select the component, and then choose the **Open Part** *option from the pop-up toolbar; the part document of the selected component will be opened. You can edit the component individually in the part document. After editing, save the part, close the part document and return to the assembly document; the* **SolidWorks 2009** *message box will be displayed, which will inform you that the models contained within the assembly have changed. It will further prompt you to specify whether you would like to rebuild the assembly. Choose the* **Yes** *button from this message box.*

EDITING SUB-ASSEMBLIES

CommandManager:	Assembly > Edit Component
Toolbar:	Assembly > Edit Component

To edit sub-assemblies, select them from the **FeatureManager design tree** and choose the **Edit Component** button from the **Assembly CommandManager**. You can set the transparency setting using the **Assembly Transparency** button in the **Assembly CommandManager**. You can add components in the sub-assembly, modify the mates, and replace the components while in the editing mode. After editing the sub-assembly, choose the **Edit Component** button again to exit the editing mode.

Note

To edit a component of the sub-assembly, select the component from the drawing area, invoke the pop-up toolbar, and choose the **Edit Part** *option; the part editing mode will be invoked in the assembly document.*

*You need to expand the desired sub-assembly from the **FeatureManager design tree** to select its components. All the components assembled in that sub-assembly will be displayed once the sub-assembly is expanded.*

DISSOLVING SUB-ASSEMBLIES

Dissolving the sub-assembly means the components of the selected sub-assembly will become the components of the next higher level sub-assembly. When you dissolve a sub-assembly, it will be removed from the assembly and the components of the sub-assembly will become the components of the assembly or the sub-assembly in which it was inserted. To dissolve a sub-assembly, select the sub-assembly from the **FeatureManager design tree**. Invoke the shortcut menu and choose the **Dissolve Sub-assembly** option from it; the sub-assembly will be removed from the **FeatureManager design tree** and its components will be displayed as the components of an assembly or a sub-assembly in the **FeatureManager design tree**.

REPLACING COMPONENTS

Sometimes in the assembly design cycle, you may need to replace a component of the assembly with some other component. To replace a component, select the component to be replaced, invoke the shortcut menu, expand the shortcut menu, if required, and choose the **Replace Components** option to display the **Replace PropertyManager**, as shown in Figure 13-18. You can also invoke this **PropertyManager** by choosing the **Replace Components** button from the **Assembly CommandManager** after customizing it.

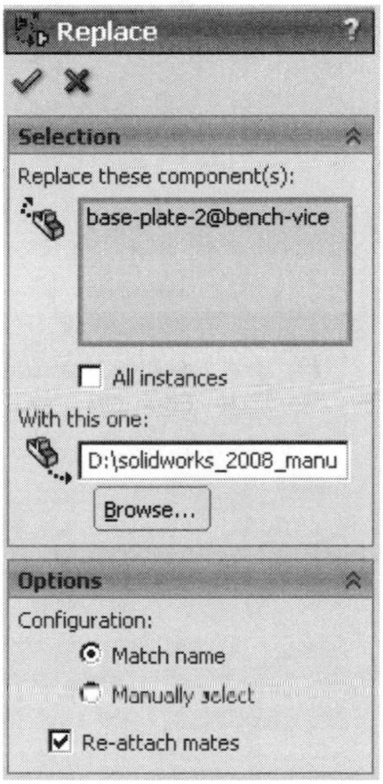

On invoking the **Replace PropertyManager**, you will be prompted to select the components to be replaced; the name of the selected component will be displayed in the **Components to be Replaced** selection box. Next, you need to specify the replacement component. Choose the **Browse** button from the **Selection** rollout; the **Open** dialog box will be displayed. Select the replacement component and choose the **Open** button from the **Open** dialog box; the name and location of the replacement component will be displayed in the **Replacement Component** area.

Figure 13-18 The Replace PropertyManager

The **All instances** check box available in the **Selection** rollout is used to replace all the instances of the selected component.
The options in the **Configuration** area of the **Options** rollout are used to define the selection procedure of the configurations. You will learn more about configurations in the later chapters.

The **Re-attach mates** check box is selected in the **Options** rollout, by default. On exiting the **Replace PropertyManager** with this check box selected, the **What's Wrong** dialog box will be displayed. Choose **Close** from this dialog box; the **Mated Entities PropertyManager** will be displayed. You can replace the mate entities by using this **PropertyManager**.

If the **Re-attach mates** check box is cleared, the **What's Wrong** dialog box will be displayed after you exit the **Replace PropertyManager**. This dialog box displays the name of the mates that contain errors. Therefore, you need to redefine the mates. To do so, expand the **Mates** node from the **FeatureManager design tree**. Select the mate that has an error symbol on the left; invoke the shortcut menu and choose the **Edit Feature** option; the **Mate PropertyManager** of the corresponding mate will be displayed and you can edit the mate entities.

Figure 13-19 shows the assembly in which the bolt is to be replaced by a pin. Figure 13-20 shows the faces of the pin to be used as mate entities, after replacing the component. Figure 13-21 shows the isometric view of the assembly after the bolts are replaced by pins.

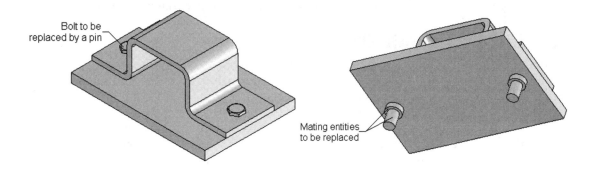

Figure 13-19 *Bolt to be replaced by a pin*   *Figure 13-20* *Mating entities to be replaced*

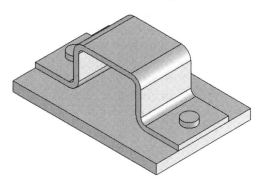

Figure 13-21 *Bolt replaced by pin in the assembly*

Tip. *The exclamation symbol displayed on the **Mates** option in the **FeatureManager design tree** indicates that the mates has errors in it. Expand the mates group. The mate that displays an exclamation sign will have some errors. Select that mate and invoke the shortcut menu. Choose the **What's Wrong?** option; the **What's Wrong** dialog box will be displayed. The possible cause of the error will be displayed in it.*

*If you choose the **MateXpert** option from the shortcut menu, the **MateXpert PropertyManager** will be displayed. The **Diagnose** button in this **PropertyManager** is used to display the entities that are the cause of errors in the mate. Right-click on the mate and choose the **Edit Mates** option from the shortcut menu to edit the mate with errors.*

CREATING PATTERNS OF COMPONENTS IN AN ASSEMBLY

CommandManager:	Assembly > Linear Component Pattern > Circular Component Pattern/ Feature Driven Component Pattern
SolidWorks menus:	Insert > Component Pattern > Linear Pattern/ Circular Pattern/ Feature Driven

While working on a complex assembly, you may need to assemble more than one instance of the component about a specified arrangement. For example, consider the case of a flange coupling where you have to assemble eight instances of nuts and bolts to fasten the coupling. If you assemble eight instances of the nuts and bolts with the couplings individually, it will be very tedious and time-consuming process. Therefore, to reduce the time, SolidWorks has provided a tool to create the patterns of the components. The three types of component patterns provided in SolidWorks are discussed next.

Feature Driven Pattern

The feature driven pattern is used to pattern the instances of the components to be used in an existing pattern feature created while creating the component. To create this type of pattern, choose **Linear Component Pattern > Feature Driven Component Pattern** from the **Assembly CommandManager**; the **Feature Driven PropertyManager** will be displayed, as shown in Figure 13-22.

On invoking the **Feature Driven PropertyManager**, you will be prompted to select the components to be patterned. Select the components to be patterned from the drawing area; the name of the selected components will be listed in the **Components to Pattern** selection box. Left-click in the **Driving Feature** selection box; the **Driving Feature** selection box will be highlighted. Select a pattern feature that will drive the component pattern; the preview of the resulting pattern will be displayed in the drawing area.

Figure 13-22 The Feature Driven PropertyManager

This driving feature is called as seed feature. If the driving feature is created using the **Hole Wizard** tool, the resulting feature may not align with the existing hole feature, as shown in Figure 13-23. Choose the **Select Seed Position** button and select the new seed feature to align the resulting feature, as shown in Figure 13-24. Choose the **OK** button from the **Feature Driven PropertyManager**; the pattern will be created, as shown in Figure 13-25.

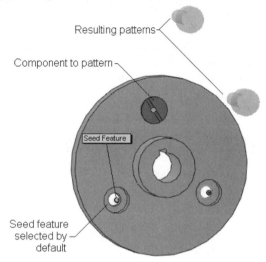

Figure 13-23 *The default seed feature selected and the resulting patterns*

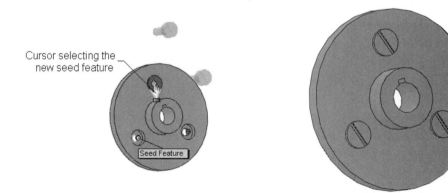

Figure 13-24 *The cursor selecting the new seed feature*

Figure 13-25 *Assembly after creating the feature driven pattern*

In order to skip some of the instances of the pattern after creating it, select the derived pattern feature from the **FeatureManager design tree** and invoke the shortcut menu. Choose the **Edit Feature** option from the shortcut menu; the resulting **PropertyManager** will be displayed. Click once in the **Instances to Skip** selection box; the preview of the instances of the pattern will be displayed with the filled dots in magenta. Select the dot on the instance that you need to skip; the selected instances will disappear from the display and the color of the dot will change to red. To retain the instances again, select the corresponding red colored dot. After selecting the instances to skip, choose the **OK** button from the **PropertyManager**.

Note
The number of instances of the component pattern are automatically modified when you change the number of instances of the pattern feature that was used to derive the component pattern. This indicates the associative nature of the derived component pattern.

*You may have to choose the **Rebuild** button after editing the number of entities in the pattern feature.*

Remember that you need to modify the mates if the feature that was used to assemble the seed component is deleted while reducing the number of features in the pattern. This is because the original feature on which the mates were applied does not exist anymore and so there is an error in associating the elements to mate.

Tip. *You will observe that after creating a derived circular pattern, the **DerivedCirPattern1** feature will be displayed in the **FeatureManager design tree**. If the derived pattern creates a rectangular pattern of the components, the name of the feature will be **DerivedLPattern1**. The number at the end of the feature name indicates the sequence number of the derived pattern feature.*

*To skip a pattern instance, expand the component pattern feature, all instances of the patterned component will be displayed. Select the instance to be skipped from the **FeatureManager design tree** and press the DELETE key; the **Confirmation** dialog box will be displayed. Choose the **Yes** button from it.*

*To restore the skipped pattern instance, select the derived pattern from the **FeatureManager design tree** and choose the **Edit Feature** option from the pop-up toolbar. Select the skipped instance from the **Instances to Skip** rollout and invoke the shortcut menu. Choose the **Delete** option; the instance will be restored.*

Local Pattern

You can also create the patterns of the components individually, even if there is no existing pattern feature. This type of component pattern is known as local pattern. You can create two types of local patterns, the linear pattern and the circular pattern. Both the types of local patterns are discussed next.

Linear Pattern

To create the local linear pattern, choose the **Linear Component Pattern** button from the **Assembly CommandManager**; the **Linear Pattern PropertyManager** will be displayed. Also, you will be prompted to select an edge or an axis for the direction reference and the components to be patterned. Select the direction reference and then the component to pattern from the drawing area. Other options in this **PropertyManager** are the same as those discussed while creating a linear pattern of features, faces, and bodies in the earlier chapters.

Tip. *If one instance of the component pattern is modified or edited, the other instances of the component will also be modified.*

You can also create the component pattern of a component patterned feature.

Circular Pattern

To create the local circular pattern, choose **Linear Component Pattern > Circular Component Pattern** from the **Assembly CommandManager**; the **Circular Pattern PropertyManager** will be displayed and you will be prompted to select an edge or an axis for the direction reference and the components to pattern. Select the direction reference and then the component to be patterned from the drawing area. Other options in this **PropertyManager** are the same as those discussed while creating the circular pattern of the features, faces, and bodies in the earlier chapters.

COPYING AND MIRRORING COMPONENTS

CommandManager:	Assembly > Linear Pattern Component > Mirror Components
SolidWorks menus:	Insert > Mirror Components

In the assembly mode of SolidWorks, you can copy or mirror a component and place the new instance in the assembly document. If you create a copy of a component, then its orientation can be different from the original component. But the mirrored component will have the same orientation as that of the original component. To copy or mirror a component, choose **Linear Pattern Component > Mirror Components** from the **Assembly CommandManager**; the **Mirror Components Property Manager** will be displayed, as shown in Figure 13-26.

Select the planar face or plane that will act as a mirror plane, as shown in Figure 13-27. Next, select the component to be mirrored; you will observe that the name of the component is displayed with a check box in the **Components to Mirror** area. If you are creating the copy of the original component, leave the check box cleared and choose the **Next** button from the **PropertyManager**; the **Step:3 Orientation** rollout will be displayed. Also, the preview of the copied component will be displayed, as shown in Figure 13-25. Select the component and choose the **Reorient Component** button if you need to change the orientation of the new component. After setting the parameters, choose the **OK** button from the confirmation corner. The copy of the selected component will be displayed in the drawing area, as shown in Figure 13-29.

If you are mirroring the original component, select the check box next to the name of the selected component in the **Components to Mirror** area. Then, choose the **Next** button from the **Mirror Components PropertyManager**; **Step: 2 Filenames** rollout will be displayed. The mirrored component must be given a name and the part should be

*Figure 13-26 The **Mirror Components PropertyManager***

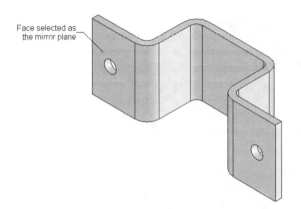

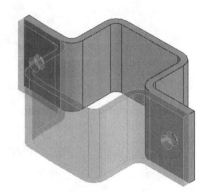

Figure 13-27 *Face to be selected as mirror plane*

Figure 13-28 *Preview of the copied component*

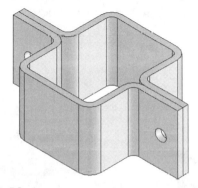

Figure 13-29 *Instance created by copying the component*

saved in a location. To do so, select the component from the list box, specify a name in the edit box, and then specify the location where the mirrored part has to be saved using the swatch button and choose the **OK** button; the component will be mirrored. Also, the new part will be created in the document where you have saved the original component.

COPYING WITH MATES

CommandManager:	Assembly > Insert Components > Copy with Mates
SolidWorks menus:	Insert > Component > Copy with Mates

In SolidWorks, you can copy a component with the mates. This will reduce the time in assembling the components that have similar mates. To copy a component that is already assembled, choose **Insert Components > Copy with Mates** from the CommandManager; the **Copy with Mates PropertyManager** will be displayed, as shown in Figure 13-30. Also, you will be prompted to select the components to copy. Select the component from the drawing area; the name of the selected component will be listed in the selection box in the **Selected Components** rollout and the corresponding mates will be listed in the **Mates** rollout. Click once in the **New Entity to Mate to** edit box and select the face or

Figure 13-30 The **Copy with Mates** *PropertyManager*

the plane as the location for the new mates. Then, specify the new location for all mates and choose the **OK** button in the **Copy with Mates PropertyManager**. If you need to copy more components, follow the same procedure. Select the **Repeat** check box, if you need to use the same reference for all the copied instances. Else, choose the **OK** button in the **Copy with Mates PropertyManager**. Figure 13-31 shows the component to be copied with the mates and Figure 13-32 shows the resulting copied components.

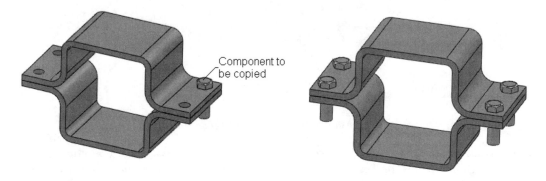

Figure 13-31 Component to be copied   *Figure 13-32* Component copied with the mates

Note
While specifying the mates, it is not necessary to specify all the mates that are in the original component. You can specify few mates of the original component and add new mates later, if required.

SIMPLIFYING ASSEMBLIES USING THE VISIBILITY OPTIONS

When you assemble the components in a large assembly or a small assembly, you may need to simplify the assembly using the visibility options. By simplifying, you can hide the components or set their transparency at any stage of the design cycle. You can also suppress and unsuppress the components at any stage of the design cycle. Various methods of simplifying the assembly are discussed next.

Hiding Components

CommandManager:	Assembly > Hide/Show Components (*Customize to add*)
SolidWorks menus:	Edit > Hide > Current Display State
Toolbar:	Assembly > Hide/Show Components (*Customize to add*)

In order to hide a component placed in the assembly, select the component from the drawing area or from the **FeatureManager design tree**. You can select more than one component to hide by using the CTRL key. Choose the **Hide Components** option from the pop-up toolbar; the display of the component will be turned off and its icon will be displayed in gray in the **FeatureManager design tree**. To display the hidden component, select the icon of the component from the **FeatureManager design tree** and choose **Show Components** from the pop-up toolbar; the hidden component will be displayed again in the drawing area. You can also choose the **Show Hidden Components** button from the **Assembly CommandManager** to temporarily turn on the display of the hidden components.

Suppressing and Unsuppressing the Components

CommandManager:	Assembly > Change Suppression State (*Customize to add*)
SolidWorks menus:	Edit > Suppress > This Configuration

You can also suppress the components placed in the assembly to simplify the assembly representation. To do so, select the component from the drawing area or from the **FeatureManager design tree**, choose **Suppress** from the pop-up toolbar; the component will not be displayed in the assembly document and the icon of the suppressed component will be displayed in gray in the **FeatureManager design tree**. Alternatively, you can also select the component to be suppressed and choose the **Change Suppression State** button from the **Assembly CommandManager**; a flyout will be displayed. Choose the **Suppress** option to suppress the component in the assembly.

To unsuppress the suppressed component, select the component to be resolved from the **FeatureManager design tree**, choose the **Unsuppress** option from the pop-up toolbar.

You can also suppress the component using the **Change Suppression State** button from the **Assembly CommandManager**. To do so, select the component and choose the **Change Suppression State** button from the **Assembly CommandManager**, a flyout will be displayed. Choose the **Resolve** option. The **Resolve** option is used to set the suppressed or the lightweight components to the resolve state.

Changing the Transparency Conditions

In SolidWorks, you can change the transparency of the components or the selected faces to simplify the assembly. To change the transparency, select a component and then choose the **Change Transparency** option from the pop-up toolbar; the transparency of the selected component will be changed.

You can also set the transparency of the selected components or faces using the **Transparency** slider. To do so, select the components or faces and choose the **Edit Appearance** button from the **Heads-up View** toolbar; the **Appearances PropertyManager** will be displayed. Set the transparency of the selected components or faces using the **Transparency** slider available in the **Appearances** rollout of the **PropertyManager**.

Tip. *You will observe that the **Lightweight** check box is provided in the **Open** dialog box. On selecting this check box before opening the assembly file, the assembly will be opened only with the lightweight components.*

*A lightweight component is the one in which the feature information is available in the part document and only the graphical representation of the component is displayed in the assembly document. Therefore, the assembly environment becomes light. An icon of a lightweight component is displayed as a feather attached to the component icon in the **FeatureManager design tree**.*

*To get the feature information of the lightweight component, you need to resolve the component to the normal state. To do so, select the component from the drawing area or from the **FeatureManager design tree** and invoke the shortcut menu. Choose the **Set to Resolved** option from this shortcut menu. To set a resolved component to a lightweight component, select the component and invoke the shortcut menu. Choose **Set to Lightweight** from the shortcut menu.*

CHECKING INTERFERENCES IN AN ASSEMBLY

CommandManager:	Evaluate > Interference Detection
SolidWorks menus:	Tools > Interference Detection
Toolbar:	Assembly > Interference Detection

After creating the assembly design, the first and the most essential step is to check the interference between the components of an assembly. If there is an interference, the components may not assemble properly after they roll out from the machine shop or the tool room. Therefore, before sending the part and assembly files for detailing and drafting, it is essential to check the interference. To do so, choose the **Interference Detection** button from the **Evaluate CommandManager**; the **Interference Detection PropertyManager** will be displayed. Select the assembly from the **FeatureManager** design tree; the name of the current assembly will be displayed in the **Components to Check** selection box in the **Selected Components** rollout. You can also check the interference between two or more than two components. To do so, first clear the current selection set and select the components from the assembly. Next, choose the **Calculate** button from this **Selected Components** rollout to check the interference. If there is any interference between the components in the assembly, it will be displayed in the assembly and also the interfering components will be displayed in the **Results** rollout, as shown in Figure 13-33. Expand the names of the interfering components to view the cause of interference.

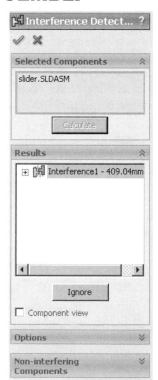

Figure 13-33 Interference Detection PropertyManager

You can select a component/interference from the **Results** rollout and choose the **Ignore** button to ignore that particular component/interference while calculating the interference.

If you select the **Treat coincidence as interference** check box in the **Options** rollout, then the **Coincident** mates are also considered as interference. The **Show ignored interferences** check box is selected to display the interferences that you ignored while using the **Ignore** button in the **Results** rollout. If you select the **Treat subassemblies as components** check box, all subassemblies in the current assembly will be treated as single component and any interference in the sub-assembly will be ignored. The **Include multibody part interferences** check box is selected to analyze the multibody parts for interference. If the **Make interfering parts transparent** check box is selected, the interfering parts are made transparent in the drawing window. The **Create Fasteners Folder** check box is selected to place the interfering fasteners in a separate folder in the **Results** rollout.

The **Non-interfering Components** rollout is used to select the display option for the non-interfering parts. After analyzing the assembly, you can edit or modify the part.

CHECKING HOLE ALIGNMENT

CommandManager:	Evaluate > Hole Alignment	
SolidWorks menus:	Tools > Hole Alignment	
Toolbar:	Assembly > Hole Alignment	*(Customize to add)*

 While assembling the components that have hole features, it is recommended to the apply concentric mates between the two holes. Sometimes based on the requirement or the criticality of the components, their side walls may be given constraints. As a result, the hole features may not align properly. In SolidWorks, you can find the deviation of the centerpoints of the two hole features using the **Hole Alignment** tool. To check the hole alignment in an assembly, invoke the **Hole Alignment** tool from the **Evaluate CommandManager**; the **Hole Alignment PropertyManager** will be displayed, as shown in Figure 13-34. Specify the permissible deviation of the centerpoints in the **Hole center deviation** spinner and choose the **Calculate** button; the centerpoints that deviate more than the permissible limits will be listed with their deviation values in the list box in the **Results** rollout, refer to Figure 13-34. Figure 13-35 shows an assembly of two plates in the **Hidden Lines Visible** display state. Figure 13-36 shows the misalignment of the hole in the top

Figure 13-34 The Hole Alignment PropertyManager

view and the Figure 13-37 shows the misalignment of the holes in the right side view.

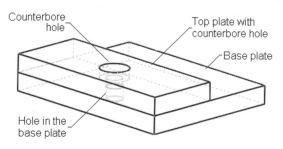

Figure 13-35 An assembly of two plates

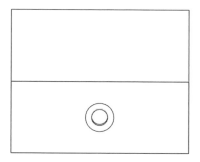

Figure 13-36 Top view of the assembly

Figure 13-37 Right side view of the assembly

Tip. *In SolidWorks 2009, you can check the clearance between the selected components or faces in an assembly. To do so, invoke the* **Clearance Verification PropertyManager** *by choosing the* **Clearance Verification** *button from the* **Evaluate CommandManager**. *Next, select the components or faces; the name of the selected components or faces will be displayed in the* **Components to check** *selection box. Specify the clearance value in the* **Minimum Acceptable Clearance** *spinner and choose the* **Calculate** *button. If the clearance between the selected components or faces is less than or equal to the minimum acceptable clearance you specified, then the result is displayed in the* **Results** *rollout.*

CREATING ASSEMBLIES FOR MECHANISM

As mentioned earlier, there are two types of assemblies. The first one is the fully defined assembly in which the relative movement of all the components is constrained. The second type of assembly is the one in which the components are not fully defined and some degrees of freedom are kept unconstrained. As a result, they can move in a certain direction with respect to the surroundings of the assembly. This flexibility in turn helps you to create mechanisms so that you can move the assembly to check the mechanisms that you have designed. Consider the case of a Bench Vice in which you are assembling the Vice Jaw with the Vice Body. For this assembly to work, the linear movement of the Vice Jaw should be free when placed on the Vice Body. Therefore, while creating this assembly for mechanism, you should not apply the mates for constraining the linear motion of the Vice Jaw with respect to the Vice Body. Figure 13-38 shows the degree of freedom that is required to be free to create an assembly for motion.

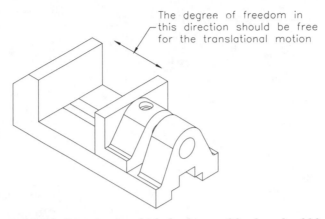

The degree of freedom in this direction should be free for the translational motion

Figure 13-38 *Direction in which the degree of freedom should be free*

After creating the assembly for mechanism by defining minimum mates, invoke the **Move Component** tool. Select one of the faces of the component that you need to move and drag the cursor to move the assembly. The options available for analyzing the assembly while moving the assembly for mechanism design are discussed next.

Analyzing Collisions Using the Collision Detection Tool

In SolidWorks, you can also analyze any collision between the components of the assembly while the assembly is in motion. Invoke the **Move Component PropertyManager** and then the **Options** rollout. Select the **Collision Detection** radio button, as shown in Figure 13-39; the **Check between** area will be displayed. The options in this area are used to specify the components between which the collision will be detected. The options in the **Check between** area are discussed next.

All components

This radio button is selected to check the collision between the components of the assembly.

These components

The **These components** radio button is selected to check the collision only between the selected components when the assembly is in motion. On selecting this radio button, the **Components for Collision Check** selection box and the **Resume Drag** button will be displayed in the **Options** rollout, as shown in Figure 13-40. The name of the components, between which the collision is to be detected, will be displayed in the **Components for Collision Check** selection box. After selecting the components, choose the **Resume Drag** button from the **Options** rollout and drag the cursor to move the assembly.

Stop at collision

The **Stop at collision** check box is selected to stop the motion of the assembly when one of the components collides with another component during the assembly motion.

Dragged part only

Select the **Dragged part only** check box if you need to detect the collision only between the

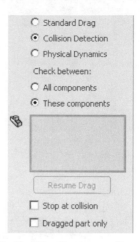

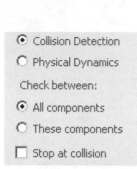

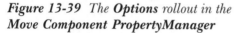

Figure 13-39 *The **Options** rollout in the Move Component PropertyManager*

Figure 13-40 *The **Options** rollout with the **These components** radio button selected*

components that you have selected to move. If this check box is cleared, the collision will be determined between the components that you have selected to move and any other component that moves because of the mates with the selected components.

After setting the options in the **Options** rollout, drag the assembly using the **Move Component** tool or the **Rotate Component** tool. If a component of the assembly collides with another component while the assembly is in motion, the faces of the components that collide with each other will be displayed in green. If the **Stop at collision** check box is selected, the motion of the assembly will be stopped when one of the components collides with another component of the assembly.

Consider the assembly shown in Figure 13-41. In this assembly, you need to move the slider in the given direction. Invoke the **Move PropertyManager** and select the **Collision Detection** radio button in the **Options** rollout. Drag the slider to move it in the given direction. Figure 13-42 shows that the slider collides with the extrusion feature created in the vertical column of the base component. The faces of the components that collide will be highlighted.

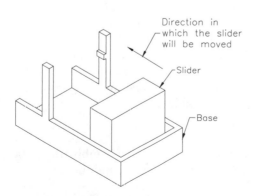

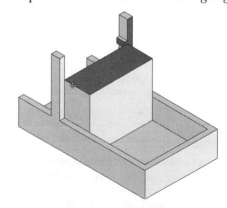

Figure 13-41 *Direction in which the slider will be moved inside the base*

Figure 13-42 *The faces of the components highlighted in green after the collision*

If the **Stop at collision** check box is selected, you cannot move the component further after it collides with one of the components of the assembly.

Once the collision is detected in the assembly, you can edit and modify the components that collide during the assembly motion.

CREATING THE EXPLODED STATE OF AN ASSEMBLY

CommandManager:	Assembly > Exploded View
SolidWorks menus:	Insert > Exploded View
Toolbar:	Assembly > Exploded View

 In SolidWorks, you can create an exploded state of the assembly using the **Explode PropertyManager**. To invoke this **PropertyManager**, choose the **Exploded View** button from the **Assembly CommandManager**. Alternatively, invoke the **ConfigurationManager**, select the **Default** option from the **ConfigurationManager** and right-click. Choose the **New Explode View** option from the shortcut menu. The **Explode PropertyManager** is shown in Figure 13-43.

The **Explode PropertyManager** allows you to explode an assembly using the manipulator. After invoking the **Explode PropertyManager**, select the component to be exploded; the manipulator will be displayed on the component and the name of the component will be displayed in the **Component(s) of the explode step** selection box of the **Settings** rollout. Now, to explode the component along any of the axes of the manipulator, move the cursor over the arrowhead of that axis. When the cursor changes into the move cursor, press and hold the left mouse button and drag the cursor to explode the component. You can also set the exact numeric value of the explode distance. To do so, select the direction from the manipulator and set the value

*Figure 13-43 The **Explode PropertyManager***

of the explosion distance in the **Explode distance** spinner of the **Settings** rollout. Next, choose the **Apply** button below this spinner. You can select an edge or a face to define the direction of explosion.

If the **Auto-space components after drag** check box is selected in the **Options** rollout, the explosion will be displayed as **Chain 1** in the **Existing explode steps** area of the **Explode Steps** rollout. However, if the **Auto-space components after drag** check box is cleared, the explosion will be displayed as **Explode Step 1**. You will learn more about the **Auto-space components after drag** check box later in this chapter. To edit the **Chain 1** or **Explode Step 1**, select it and invoke the shortcut menu. Choose the **Edit Step** option from the shortcut menu. Edit the position of the selected component.

You can delete an explode step by selecting it and choosing the **Delete** option from the shortcut menu. After exploding a component, select another component to be exploded. Similarly, you can create as many explode steps as you want.

You can also perform the auto-explosion by selecting all the components of the assembly together. You can drag a window across the assembly to select all its components. Now, select the direction from the manipulator, along which you need to explode all the components. Set the value of the explode distance in the **Explode distance** spinner. Choose the **Apply** button.

The options available in the **Options** rollout, as shown in Figure 13-44, are used to specify the explode options. The **Auto-space components after drag** check box is used to specify an automatic spacing between the components, after exploding them using the auto-explode method. The **Adjust the spacing between the chain components** slider bar is used to adjust the spacing between the chain of components in order to define the automatic spacing between the components after dragging. The **Select sub-assembly's parts** check box is used to select the components of the sub-assembly also for exploding.

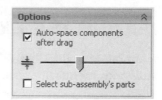

*Figure 13-44 The **Options** rollout in the **Explode PropertyManager***

The **Re-use Sub-assembly Explode** button is chosen to reuse the explode steps of a sub-assembly also in the current assembly.

Figure 13-45 shows the assembly exploded using the auto-explode method. Figure 13-46 shows the systematic exploded state of an assembly.

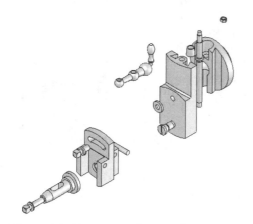
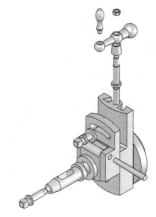

Figure 13-45 Auto-explosion of an assembly   *Figure 13-46 A systematic exploded state of an assembly*

To collapse an exploded view, right-click and choose the **Collapse** option from the shortcut menu. To view the exploded view again, invoke the **ConfigurationManager** and double-click on the **ExplView1** option. To view the animated view of the exploded view, invoke the **ConfigurationManager**, select the **ExplView1** option and right-click. Then, choose the **Animate explode** option; the exploded view will be animated and you can control its speed using the **Animation Controller** toolbar. To delete the exploded view, invoke the **ConfigurationManager**, select the **ExplView1** option and right-click. Choose the **Delete** option from the shortcut menu.

Creating the Explode Line Sketch

CommandManager:	Assembly > Explode Line Sketch
SolidWorks menus:	Insert > Explode Line Sketch
Toolbar:	Assembly > Explode Line Sketch

The explode lines are the parametric axes that display the direction of explosion of the components in an exploded state. Figure 13-47 shows an exploded assembly with the explode lines. To create an explode line sketch, explode an assembly and choose the **Explode Line Sketch** button from the **Assembly CommandManager**; the sketching environment will be invoked and the **Explode Sketch** toolbar will be displayed. Also, the **Route Line PropertyManager** will be displayed, as shown in Figure 13-48.

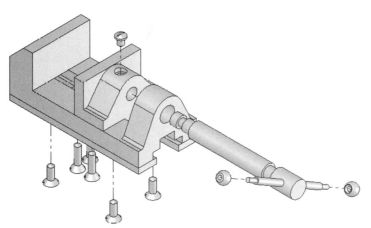

Figure 13-47 Explode line sketch created on an exploded assembly

*Figure 13-48 The **Route Line PropertyManager***

You will be prompted to select a cylindrical face, planar face, vertex, point, arc, or line entities. Select the cylindrical faces of the two components in succession to create an explode line between them. For example, in order to create an explode line between the Oval Fillister and the Vice Jaw, select the cylindrical face of the Oval Fillister that goes inside the Vice Jaw. Now, select the cylindrical hole of the Vice Jaw; the preview of the explode line will be displayed. Choose **OK** to create the explode line. The names of the selected faces are displayed in the **Items To Connect** selection box in the **Route Line PropertyManager**. When you select an entity to create an explode line, an arrow is also displayed with the line. You can use that arrow or select the **Reverse** check box from the **Options** rollout to reverse the direction of the explode line creation. Next, choose the **OK** button from the **Route Line PropertyManager** and exit the sketching environment.

TUTORIALS

Tutorial 1

In this tutorial, you will create the radial engine assembly shown in Figure 13-49. This assembly will be created in two parts: the sub-assembly and the main assembly. You will also create the exploded state of the assembly and then create the explode line sketch. The exploded state of the assembly is displayed in Figure 13-50. The views and dimensions of all the components of this assembly are displayed in Figures 13-51 through 13-54.   **(Expected time: 3 hrs)**

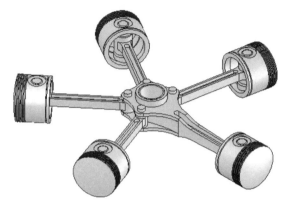

Figure 13-49 *The radial engine assembly*

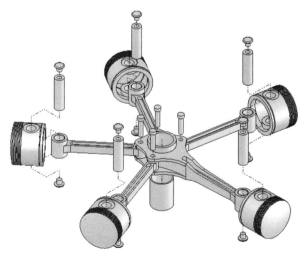

Figure 13-50 *Exploded view of the assembly*

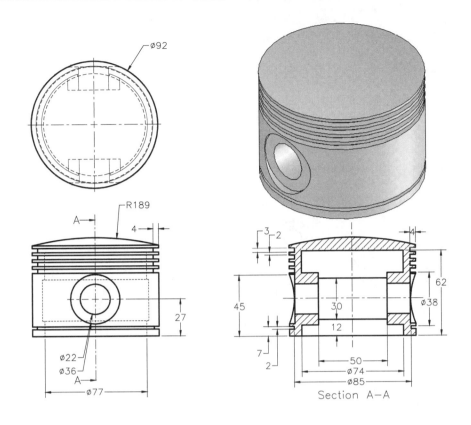

Figure 13-51 *Views and dimensions of the Piston*

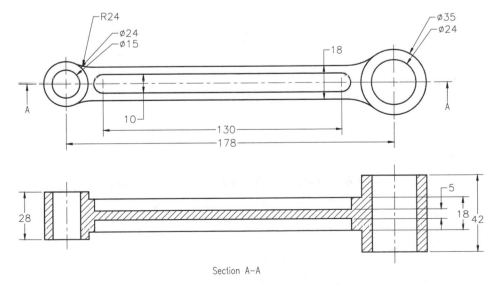

Figure 13-52 *Views and dimensions of the Articulated Rod*

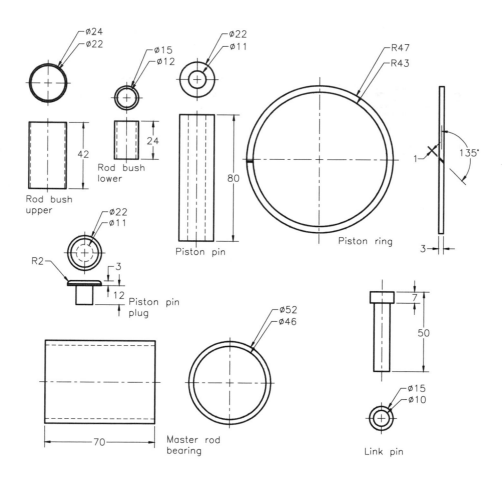

Figure 13-53 *Views and dimensions of other components*

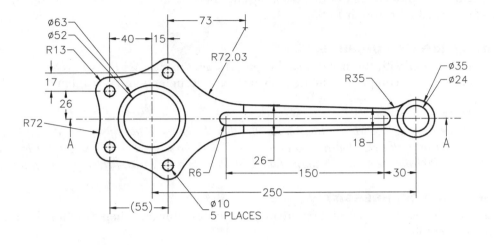

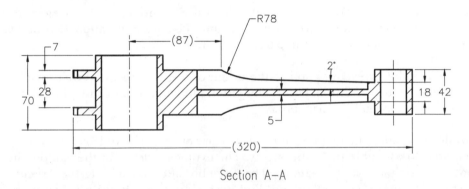

Section A–A

Figure 13-54 *Views and dimensions of the Master Rod*

You need to break this assembly in two steps because it is a large assembly. One will be the sub-assembly and the other will be the main assembly. First, you need to create the sub-assembly consisting of Articulated Rod, Piston, Piston Rings, Piston Pin, Rod Bush Upper, Rod Bush Lower, and Piston Pin Plug. Next, create the main assembly by assembling the Master Rod with the Piston, Piston Rings, Piston Pin, Rod Bush Upper, and Piston Pin Plug. Finally, you will assemble the sub-assembly with the main assembly.

The following steps are required to complete this tutorial:

a. Create all components of the assembly in the **Part** mode and save it in the *Radial Engine Assembly* folder .
b. Start a new assembly document and assemble the components to complete the sub-assembly, refer to Figures 13-55 through 13-57.
c. Start a new assembly document and assemble the components of the main assembly, refer to Figure 13-58.

d.   Assemble the sub-assembly in the main assembly, refer to Figures 13-59 through 13-63.

e.   Create the exploded view of the assembly and then create the explode line sketch, refer to Figures 13-64 through 13-65.

Creating the Components

1.   Create a folder with the name *Radial Engine Assembly* in the *My Documents\SolidWorks\c13* folder. Create all components in the individual part documents and save them in this folder.

Note
While creating the Master Rod, make sure that the holes on the left of the Master Rod are created using the sketch-driven pattern. This is done because while assembling the Link Pin, you will create the derived pattern of the Link Pin using the sketch-driven pattern feature.

Creating the Sub-assembly

As discussed earlier, you will first create the sub-assembly and then assemble it with the main assembly.

1.   Start a new SolidWorks assembly document and exit the **Begin Assembly PropertyManager**. Next, save it with the name **Piston Articulation Rod Sub-assembly** in the same folder in which the parts are created.

2.   First place the Articulated Rod at the origin of the assembly and then place the other components such as Piston, Piston Pin, Piston Pin Plug, Rod Bush Upper, and Rod Bush Lower in the assembly document.

3.   Apply the required mates to assemble these components. Figure 13-55 shows the sequence required to assemble the components. The exploded view and the explode line sketch are given only for your reference. The assembly, after assembling the Articulated Rod, Piston, Piston Pin, Piston Pin Plug, Rod Bush Upper, and Rod Bush Lower, is shown in Figure 13-56.

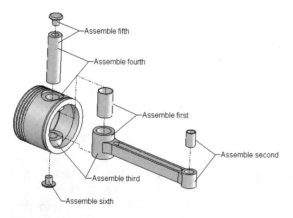

Figure 13-55 *Assembly of the Articulated Rod, Piston, Piston Pin, Piston Pin Plug, Rod Bush Upper, and Rod Bush Lower*

Figure 13-56 *First instance of the Piston Ring assembled with the Piston*

It is clear from the assembly that you need to assemble four instances of the Piston Ring. You will assemble only one instance of the Piston Ring at the uppermost groove of the ring and then create a local linear pattern.

4. Insert the Piston Ring in the assembly document and assemble the Piston Ring at the uppermost groove of the Piston using the assembly mates, refer to Figure 13-56. In this assembly, the color of the Piston Ring is changed by selecting it. Select the Piston Ring; the pop-up toolbar is displayed. Choose the **Appearances** button from the pop-up toolbar; the **Appearances PropertyManager** will be displayed. Set the color using the option available in this **PropertyManager**.

    Next, you need to create the local linear pattern of the Piston Ring.

5. Choose the **Linear Component Pattern** button from the **Assembly CommandManager**; the **Linear Pattern PropertyManager** is displayed.

6. Select any one of the horizontal edges of the Articulated Rod to define the direction of pattern creation.

7. Click once in the **Components to Pattern** selection box and select the Piston Ring from the drawing area; the preview of the linear pattern with the default settings is displayed in the drawing area.

8. Select the **Reverse Direction** button to reverse the direction of the pattern creation, if required.

9. Set the value **5** in the **Spacing** spinner and the value **4** in the **Number of Instances** spinner.

10. Choose the **OK** button from the **Linear Pattern PropertyManager**; the sub-assembly, after patterning the Piston Ring, is shown in Figure 13-57.

11. Save and close the assembly document.

Creating the Main Assembly

Next, you will create the main assembly and then assemble the sub-assembly with it.

1. Start a new SolidWorks assembly document and exit the **Begin Assembly PropertyManager**. Now, save it with the name **Radial Engine Sub-assembly** in the same folder in which the parts are created.

2. First, place the Master Rod at the origin of the assembly and then place the Piston, Piston Pin, Piston Pin Plug, Piston Ring, Rod Bush Upper, and Master Rod Bearing in the current assembly document.

3.   Assemble all components of the main assembly using the assembly mates.

     The components after assembling in the main assembly are displayed in Figure 13-58.

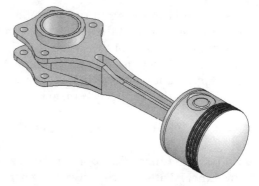

Figure 13-57 *Sub-assembly after patterning the Piston ring*

Figure 13-58 *Components assembled in the main assembly*

Assembling the Sub-assembly with the Main Assembly

Next, you will place the sub-assembly in the main assembly and then assemble them together.

1.   Choose the **Insert Components** button from the **Assembly CommandManager**; the **Insert Component PropertyManager** is displayed.

2.   If the sub-assembly document is not opened, choose the **Browse** button in the **Part/ Assembly to Insert** rollout; the **Open** dialog box is displayed.

3.   Select **Assembly** (**.asm, *.sldasm*) from the **Files of type** drop-down list.

4.   Double-click on *Piston Articulated Rod Sub-assembly* and place the sub-assembly in the main assembly. Figure 13-59 shows the sub-assembly and the main assembly placed together.

5.   Assemble the sub-assembly with the main assembly using the assembly mates. Refer to Figure 13-60, which shows the assembly structure to help you in assembling the instances of the sub-assembly.

     Figure 13-61 shows all instances of the sub-assembly assembled with the main assembly.

Tip. *You can create more than one instance of the sub-assembly by holding down the CTRL key; select and drag the sub-assembly from the **FeatureManager design tree**. Release the left mouse button to place the assembly in the current assembly document.*

Figure 13-59 *Sub-assembly and the main assembly placed together*

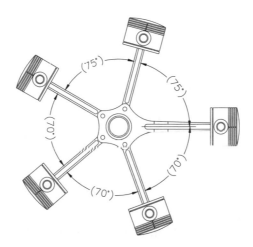

Figure 13-60 *Assembly structure*

Assembling the Link Pin

After assembling the sub-assembly with the main assembly, you need to assemble the Link Pin with the main assembly.

1. Place the Link Pin in the current assembly document. Assemble the Link Pin with the main assembly using the assembly mates. Figure 13-62 shows the first instance of Link Pin assembled with the main assembly.

    As discussed earlier, the other instances of the Link Pin will be assembled using the sketch-driven pattern feature of the holes created on the left of the master rod.

Figure 13-61 *Sub-assembly assembled with the main assembly*

Figure 13-62 *First instance of the Link Pin assembled with the main assembly*

2. Choose **Linear Component Pattern** > **Feature Driven Component Pattern** from the **Assembly CommandManager**; the **Feature Driven PropertyManager** is displayed.

3. Select the Link Pin from the main assembly; its name is displayed in the **Components to Pattern** selection box.

4. Click once in the **Driving Feature** selection box to activate the selection mode.

5. Select any one of the hole instances from the master rod; the name of the sketch pattern feature is displayed in the **Driving Feature** selection box and the preview of the resulting pattern is also displayed.

6. If the instances are not placed properly, choose the **Select Seed Position** button and select the correct seed feature.

7. Choose the **OK** button from the **Feature Driven PropertyManager**.

   Figure 13-63 displays the final assembly.

Exploding the Assembly

After creating the assembly, you need to explode it using the **Exploded View** tool. You can explode the subassembly and it will be reflected in the main assembly. So, you need to open the Piston Articulate Rod Subassembly.

1. Open the Piston Articulate Rod Subassembly assembly document.

2. Choose the **Exploded View** button from the **Assembly CommandManager**; the **Explode PropertyManager** is displayed.

3. Ensure that all check boxes are cleared.

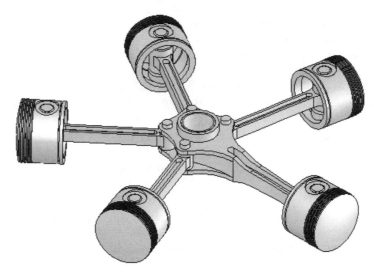

Figure 13-63 The final assembly

4. Select the top face of the piston pin plug; the triad is displayed.

5. Select the arrow of the triad that is normal to the selected plane.

6. Set the value of the **Explode distance** spinner to **170**, choose the **Apply** button; the selected instances of the piston pin plug are exploded and the components are removed from the selection set. Also, the sequence of explosion is displayed as **Explode Step1** in the **Existing explode steps** list box of the **Explode Steps** rollout.

7. If the piston pin plug is moved downward, choose the **Reverse direction** button on the left of the **Explode direction** edit box in the **Settings** rollout and then choose **Done**.

8. Select the piston pin in the drawing area; the triad is displayed.

9. Select the arrow of the triad that is normal to the selected plane.

10. Set the value of the **Explode distance** spinner to **150**, choose the **Apply** button; the selected instances of the Piston Pin are exploded and the components are removed from the selection set. Also, the sequence of explosion is displayed as **Explode Step2** in the **Existing explode steps** list box of the **Explode Steps** rollout.

11. If the piston pin is moved downward, choose the **Reverse direction** button on the left of the **Explode direction** edit box in the **Settings** rollout and then choose **Done**.

    When the triad is displayed on selecting the face, you can select an arrow to specify the direction and drag the arrow to relocate the component.

12. Explode all the components of the sub-assembly.

13. Save the sub-assembly and open the main assembly document; the **SolidWorks** message box will be displayed stating that the models in the assembly have changed and would you like to rebuild it. Choose **OK**.

14. Choose the **Exploded View** button from the **Assembly CommandManager**; the **Explode PropertyManager** is displayed. Ensure that all check boxes are cleared.

15. Explode only the components of the main assembly as discussed earlier.

Next, you need to explode the parts the remaining sub-assemblies.

16. Select all sub-assemblies from the drawing area and choose the **Reuse Sub-assembly Explode** button in the **Explode PropertyManager**; all the sub-assemblies are exploded.

17. Choose **OK** to exit the **Explode PropertyManager**. The assembly, after exploding the components, is shown in Figure 13-64.

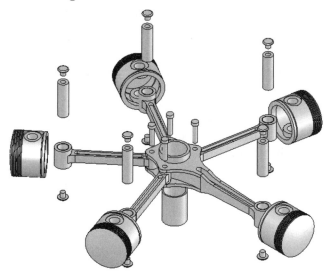

Figure 13-64 *Final exploded assembly*

Creating the Explode Line Sketch

After exploding the assembly, you need to create the explode line sketch of the exploded state of the assembly.

1. Choose the **Explode Line Sketch** button from the **Assembly CommandManager**; the **Route Line PropertyManager** is displayed and you are prompted to select a cylindrical face, planar face, vertex, point, arc, or line entities.

2. Choose the **Keep Visible** button, if not chosen automatically, from the **Route Line PropertyManager**, to keep the **PropertyManager** visible on the screen.

3. Select the cylindrical face, as shown in Figure 13-65, as the first selection; the name of

the selected face is displayed in the **Items To Connect** selection box. Also, the preview of the explode line sketch is displayed at the center of the selected face.

4.   Refer to Figure 13-65 and select the other cylindrical faces to create the explode line sketch.

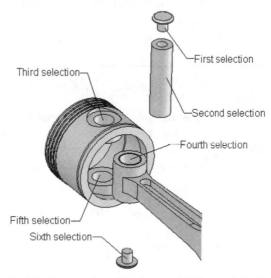

Figure 13-65   *Faces to be selected to create the explode line sketch*

5.   Next, choose the **OK** button; an exploded line is created.

6.   Similarly, create explode lines between the other parts of the exploded assembly. Figure 13-66 shows the assembly after creating the explode line sketch.

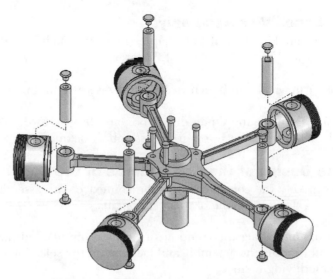

Figure 13-66   *Explode line sketch created for the exploded state of the assembly*

7. Invoke the **ConfigurationManager** and expand the **Default** node. Select
   ExplView1 and invoke the shortcut menu.

8. Choose the **Animate explode** option to view the animation of the exploded view.

9. Right-click and choose the **Collapse** option from the shortcut menu to switch back to the
   collapsed state of the assembly.

10. Save and close the assembly document.

Tutorial 2

In this tutorial, you will modify the assembly created in Tutorial 1 (Bench Vice) of Chapter 12.
You will modify the design of the components of the assembly and then suppress some mates
that enable it to move along a particular degree of freedom. Next, check the assembly for
collision detection when the assembly is in motion and then modify the assembly and check
the interference.   **(Expected time: 1 hr)**

The following steps are required to complete this tutorial:

a. Copy and save the Bench Vice assembly folder in the *c13* directory and then open the
   Bench Vice assembly.
b. Modify the design of the components within the context of the assembly, refer to
   Figures 13-67 through 13-71.
c. Suppress the mate to enable the Vice Jaw to move along the slide ways of the Vice Body.
d. Check the new assembly design for the collision detection when the assembly is in motion.
   Modify the design, if there is any collision between the components, refer to
   Figures 13-72 and 13-73.
e. Check the interference in the modified assembly.

Opening the Bench Vice Assembly

The assembly created in Tutorial 1 of Chapter 12 is the Bench Vice assembly. You need to
copy and save it in the current folder of Chapter 13.

1. Copy the folder in which the Bench vice assembly is saved and paste it in the *c13* folder.

2. Start SolidWorks, invoke the **Open** dialog box and browse to the Bench Vice assembly
   document. Double-click on it to open the assembly document.

Modifying the Design of the Components of the Bench Vice Assembly

You need to modify the components in the context of the assembly because of some
alteration in the design of some of the components.

Before you start modifying the components, it is recommended that you hide some of
them. This will simplify the assembly and facilitate in the selection of components while
editing and modifying them.

1. Press and hold the CTRL key and select the Clamping Plate, Base Plate, all four Set Screw 1, both Set Screw 2, Oval Fillister, Screw Bar, Bar Globes, and Jaw Screw from the **FeatureManager design tree**.

2. When you release the CTRL key; the pop-up toolbar is displayed. Choose the **Hide components** from the pop-up toolbar; the display of the selected components is turned off.

   The design alteration includes creating a through slot on the right face of the Vice Jaw. To modify its design, you first need to enable the part editing environment.

3. Select the Vice Jaw from the assembly and choose the **Edit Component** button from the **Assembly CommandManager**. The part modeling environment is invoked in the assembly document.

4. Make sure that the Vice Body is transparent. If not, choose the **Assembly Transparency** button from the **Assembly CommandManager**; a flyout is displayed. Choose the **Force Transparency** option from the flyout. The Vice Body becomes transparent, as shown in Figure 13-67.

5. Select the right face of the Vice Jaw and invoke the sketching environment.

6. Create the sketch of the slot, as shown in Figure 13-68.

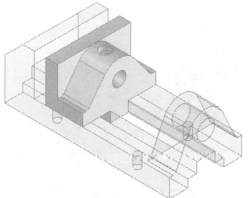

Figure 13-67 *Vice Jaw in the part edit mode in the assembly document*

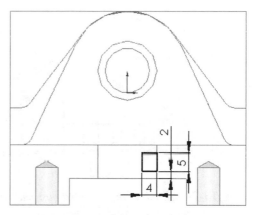

Figure 13-68 *Sketch of the slot*

7. Invoke the **Cut-Extrude PropertyManager**.

8. Create the cut feature using the **Through All** option.

9. Choose the **Edit Component** button to exit the part editing environment.

   Figure 13-69 shows the assembly after modifying the design of the Vice Jaw.

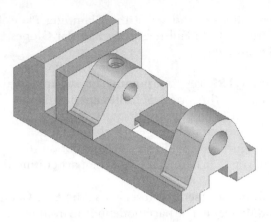

Figure 13-69 *Modified Vice Jaw*

10. Similarly, modify the design of the Vice Body. You need to create a blind extruded boss feature up to 60 mm depth on the right face of the component. You also need to reverse the direction of feature creation.

The sketch of the feature is shown in Figure 13-70. Figure 13-71 shows the assembly, after exiting the part editing environment.

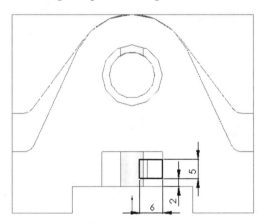

Figure 13-70 *Sketch of the extruded boss feature*

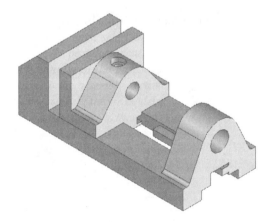

Figure 13-71 *Modified assembly*

11. Choose the **Save** button from the Menu Bar. The **SolidWorks** information box is displayed and you are informed that some models referenced in the document are modified and they must be saved. Choose **Yes** to save the referenced models also.

Suppressing the Mate to Make the Movement of Vice Jaw Free in a Specified Direction

To analyze the movement of the Bench Vice assembly, you need to make the movement of the Vice Jaw free in the X direction. By doing so, the Vice Jaw will slide on the sideways of the Vice Body.

1. Expand the **Mates** node from the **FeatureManager design tree** and select the **Distance1** mate; the planar faces of the Vice Jaw and the Vice Body, to which this mate is applied, are highlighted and the pop-up toolbar is displayed.

2. Choose **Suppress** from the pop-up toolbar.

   Now, the degree of freedom in the X direction is free.

3. Select a horizontal edge of the Vice Jaw and choose the **Move Component** button from the **Assembly CommandManager**. On dragging the cursor, you will observe that you can move the Vice Jaw in the X direction.

4. Drag the Vice Jaw back to its original position and choose the **OK** button from the **Move Component PropertyManager**.

Analyzing the Collision between the Components when the Assembly is in Motion

Next, you will analyze the collision between the components of the assembly when the assembly is in motion.

1. Choose the **Move Component** button from the **Assembly CommandManager**. Select the **Collision Detection** radio button and the **Stop at collision** check box from the **Options** rollout.

2. Select the Vice Jaw and drag the cursor to move it in the direction shown in Figure 13-72.

3. On moving the Vice Jaw in the specified direction, you will observe that the right face of the Vice Jaw and the newly created extrusion feature of the Vice Body are highlighted in different color, as shown in Figure 13-73; this indicates that the Vice Jaw collides with the Vice Body. Leave the assembly at this location.

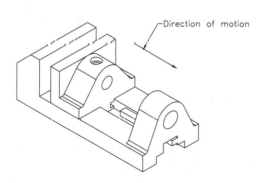
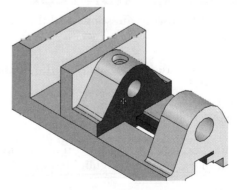

Figure 13-72 Direction in which the Vice Jaw will be moved

Figure 13-73 Faces of the Vice Jaw and the Vice Body highlighted in different color

4. Choose the **OK** button from the **Move Component PropertyManager**.

The collision is detected in the assembly, and so you need to modify the design of one of the components. In this case, you will modify the dimensions of the extruded boss feature.

5. Double-click on the newly created extrusion feature of the Vice Body; the dimensions of the newly created feature are displayed.

6. Double-click on the dimension having the value **6**; the **Modify** dialog box is displayed; set the value of the dimension to **4** and press the ENTER key.

7. Press CTRL+B on the keyboard to rebuild the entire assembly.

8. Choose the **Interference Detection** button from the **Evaluate CommandManager**; the **Interference Detection PropertyManager** is displayed.

9. You will observe that **No Interferences** is displayed in the **Interference Results** selection box in the **Results** rollout of this **PropertyManager**.

10. Choose the **Cancel** button from the **Interference Detection PropertyManager**.

Next, you need to show all the components of this assembly.

11. Press and hold the CTRL key, select the hidden components from the **FeatureManager design tree,** and choose **Show components** from the pop-up toolbar.

12. Expand the **Mates** node from the **FeatureManager design tree**, select the **Distance1** mate that is suppressed, and choose **Unsuppress** from the pop-up toolbar.

13. Save the assembly document and all the referenced part documents.

SELF-EVALUATION TEST

Answer the following questions and then compare them to those given at the end of this chapter:

1. You can create subassemblies in the assembly environment of SolidWorks. (T/F)

2. You cannot create a sub-assembly of the components that are already placed in an assembly document. (T/F)

3. When you move the cursor on a mate in the **FeatureManager design tree**, the entities used in the mate are highlighted in red in the drawing area. (T/F)

4. You cannot edit the assembly mates. (T/F)

5. While in the part editing mode in the assembly document, you can use the **Move/Size Features** tool to edit the features dynamically using the editing handles. (T/F)

6. The component patterns created individually without the use of any existing pattern feature are known as _____ patterns.

7. The component patterns created using an existing pattern feature are known as _____ patterns.

8. In a _____ component, the feature information is available in the part document and only the graphical representation of the component is displayed in the assembly document.

9. After selecting the component, choose the _____ option from the shortcut menu to change the transparency condition of the selected component.

10. To create the explode line sketch, choose the _____ button from the **Assembly CommandManager**.

REVIEW QUESTIONS

Answer the following questions:

1. Which option is used to open a component separately in the part document?

    (a) **Modify**   (b) **Edit**
    (c) **Open Part**   (d) None of these

2. Which option is used to define whether a component collides with another component of the assembly or not?

    (a) **Collision Detection**   (b) **Interference Detection**
    (c) **Mass Properties**   (d) None of these

3. Which check box is selected in the **Open** dialog box to open an assembly with lightweight parts?

    (a) **Lightweight**   (b) **Open Lightweight**
    (c) **Lightweight parts**   (d) **Lightweight assembly**

4. Which button available in the **Assembly CommandManager** is used to suppress a component?

    (a) **Change Suppression State**   (b) **Suppress**
    (c) **Hide/Show Component**   (d) **Move Component**

5. The exploded state of the assembly is created using the _____ dialog box.

6. The _____ radio button is used to create a local linear pattern.

7. To show the hidden component, select the icon of the component from the **FeatureManager design tree,** invoke the shortcut menu, and choose the _____ option from it.

8. The _____ option is used to pattern the instances of the components using an existing pattern feature.

9. Which button is chosen from the **Assembly CommandManager** to create an exploded view?

   (a) **Exploded View**   (b) **Assembly Exploder**
   (c) **Mate**   (d) None of these

10. The _____ check box is selected to stop the motion of the assembly, when one of the component collides with another component, when the assembly is in motion.

EXERCISE

Exercise 1

Create the assembly shown in Figure 13-74. Ensure that the back plate is fixed and the entire assembly can move in the Y direction with respect to the back plate. Keep the rotational degree of freedom of the screw rod free, so that it can also rotate on its axis. After creating the assembly, explode it and create the explode line sketch. The exploded view of the assembly with the explode line sketch is shown in Figure 13-75. The dimensions of the model are given in Figures 13-76 through 13-80. Assume the missing dimensions.   **(Expected time: 4 hrs)**

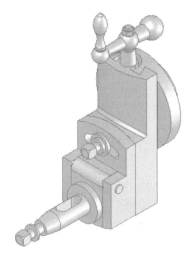

Figure 13-74 Shaper tool holder assembly

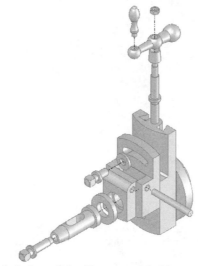

Figure 13-75 *Exploded view of the Shaper tool holder assembly with explode lines*

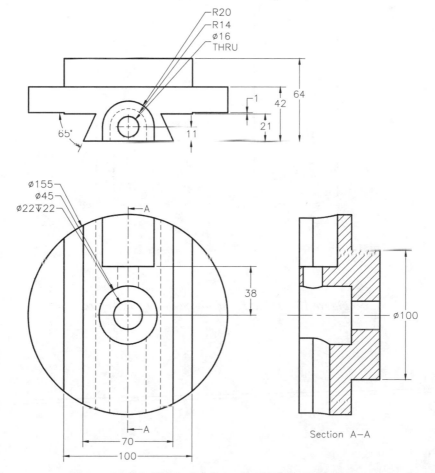

Figure 13-76 *Views and dimensions of the Back Plate*

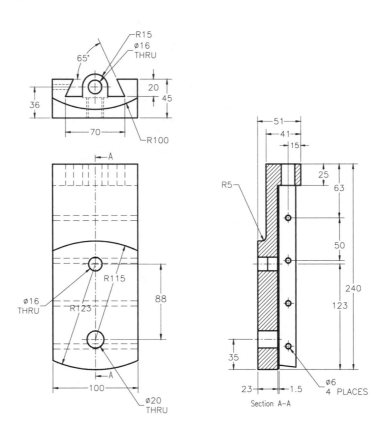

Figure 13-77 *Views and dimensions of the Vertical Slide*

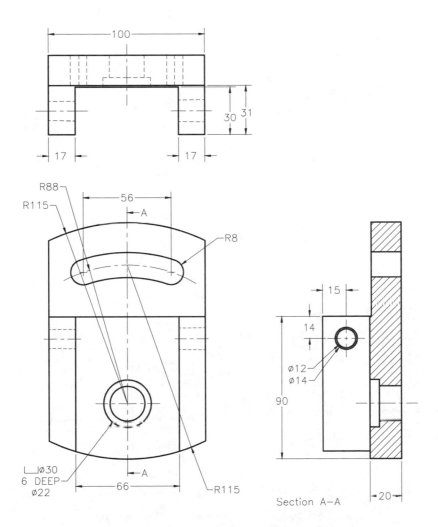

Figure 13-78 *Views and dimensions of the Swivel Plate*

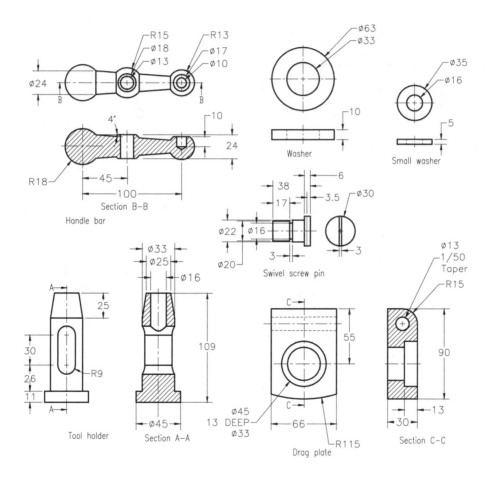

Figure 13-79 *Views and dimensions of other components*

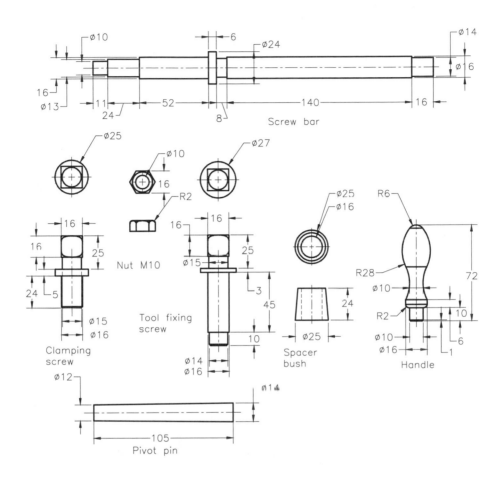

Figure 13-80 *Views and dimensions of the components*

Answers to Self-Evaluation Test

1. T, **2.** F, **3.** T, **4.** F, **5.** F, **6.** Local, **7.** Derived, **8.** Lightweight, **9. Component Properties**, **10. Explode Line Sketch**

Chapter 14

Working with Drawing Views-I

THE DRAWING MODE

After creating the solid models or the assemblies, you need to generate the two-dimensional (2D) drawing views. These views are the lifeline of all manufacturing systems because at the shop floor or the machine floor, the machinist mostly needs the 2D drawing for manufacturing. SolidWorks provides a specialized environment, known as the **Drawing** mode, which has all the tools required to generate and modify the drawing views and add dimensions and annotations to them. In other words, you can get the final shop floor drawing using this mode of SolidWorks. You can also sketch the 2D drawings in the **Drawing** mode of SolidWorks using the sketching tools provided in this mode.

In other words, there are two types of drafting methods available in SolidWorks, Generative drafting and Interactive drafting. Generative drafting is a technique of generating the drawing views using a solid model or an assembly. Interactive drafting is a technique of using the sketching tools to sketch a drawing view in the **Drawing** mode. In this chapter, you will learn about generating the drawing views of parts or assemblies.

One of the major advantages of working in SolidWorks is that this software is bidirectionally associative property. This property ensures that the modifications made in a model in the **Part** mode are reflected in the **Assembly** and **Drawing** modes, and vice versa.

STARTING A DRAWING DOCUMENT

To generate the drawing views, you need to start a new drawing document. There are two methods of starting a drawing document in SolidWorks. You can use the **New SolidWorks Document** dialog box or the option available in the part or assembly document to start a drawing document. Both these methods are discussed next.

Starting a New Drawing Document Using the New SolidWorks Document Dialog Box

To start a new drawing document for generating the drawing views, invoke the **New SolidWorks Document** dialog box. Choose the **Drawing** button, as shown in Figure 14-1, and choose the **OK** button; a new drawing document will be started and the **Sheet Format/Size** dialog box will also be displayed. Figure 14-2 shows the initial screen of the drawing document with the **Sheet Format/Size** dialog box. Double-click on a drawing template file available in this dialog box; a new drawing document will be started.

The **Model View PropertyManager** will be invoked automatically when you start a new drawing document. Its appearance will depend on whether any part or assembly document was opened or not when you started the new drawing document.

Tip. *If you are in the practice of using the advanced form of the New SolidWorks Document dialog box, the New SolidWorks Document dialog box will be displayed every time you choose Make Drawing from Part/Assembly. Select the drawing template from the Template tab of the New SolidWorks Document dialog box and choose OK.*

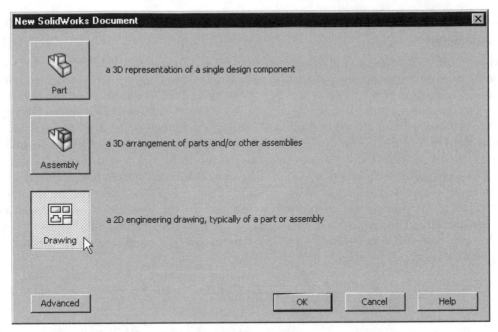

Figure 14-1 *The* **New SolidWorks Document** *dialog box*

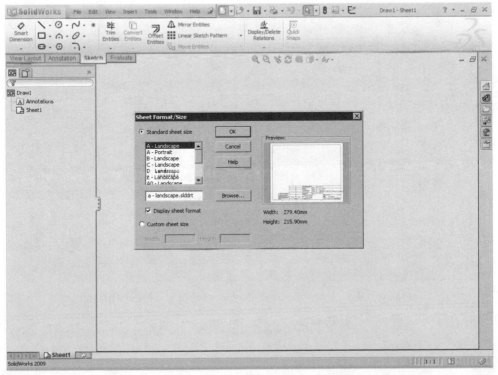

Figure 14-2 *The initial screen of the drawing document with the* **Sheet Format/Size** *dialog box*

Starting a New Drawing Document from the Part/Assembly Document

This method of starting a new drawing document is recommended when the part or the assembly document for which you want to generate the drawing views is opened in another window. In this case, choose **File** > **Make Drawing from Part/Assembly** from the SolidWorks menus of the part or the assembly document; the **New SolidWorks Document** dialog box will be displayed, if you are using it in the advanced mode. Select the drawing template and choose the **OK** button; a new drawing document will be started and the **Sheet Format/Size** dialog box will be displayed. You can select the required format and size of the sheet from this dialog box. A new drawing document will be started and the **View Palette** will be displayed on the right of the drawing window, as shown in Figure 14-3. The **View Palette** displays the preview of all the views of the component in the part file that was used to start this drawing file. You can drag the required view from this window to the drawing sheet. As soon as you drag a view to the drawing sheet, the **View Palette** will be closed and the **Projected View PropertyManager** will be displayed to create the projected views.

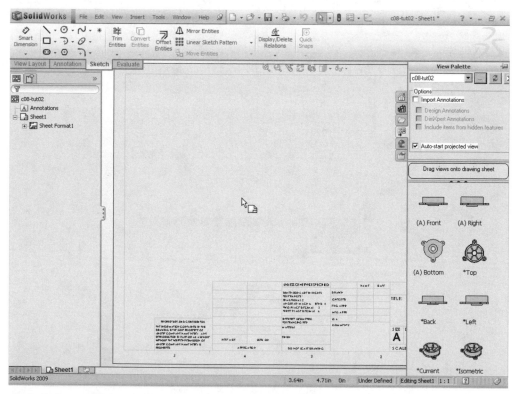

Figure 14-3 *A new drawing document with the* ***View Palette***

Tip. *If you choose the **Cancel** button from the **Sheet Format/Size** dialog box, a blank custom sheet of size 431.80 mm x 279.40 mm will be inserted in the drawing document.*

TYPES OF VIEWS

You can generate nine types of views in SolidWorks. You first need to generate a standard view, such as the top view or the front view, and then use it to derive the remaining views from the standard view. You can generate the following types of drawing views:

Model View

The model view is used to create the base view in the drawing sheet. You can generate orthogonal views such as the front, top, left, and so on as the model view. You can also generate an isometric, trimetric, or dimetric views as the model view.

Projected View

The projected view is generated by taking an existing view as the parent view. It is generated by projecting the lines normal to the parent view or at an angle. The resulting view will be an orthographic view or isometric view.

Section View

A section view is generated by chopping a part of an existing view using a plane and then viewing the parent view from a direction normal to the section plane. In SolidWorks, the section plane is defined using one or more sketched line segments.

Aligned Section View

An aligned section view is used to section the features that are created at a certain angle to the main section planes. Align sections straighten these features by revolving them about an axis that is normal to the view plane. Remember that the axis about which the feature is straightened should lie on the cutting planes.

Auxiliary View

An auxiliary view is generated by projecting the lines normal to a specified edge of an existing view.

Detail View

A detail view is used to display the details of a portion of an existing view. You can select the portion whose detailing has to be shown in the parent view. The portion that you have selected will be magnified and placed as a separate view. You can control the magnification of the detail view.

Broken View

A broken view is the one in which a portion of the drawing view is removed from the existing view, keeping the ends of the drawing view intact. This type of view is used to display the components whose length to width ratio is very high. This means that either the length is very large as compared to the width or the width is very large as compared to the length. The broken view will break the view along the horizontal or vertical direction such that the drawing view fits the required area.

Broken-out Section View

A broken-out section view is used to remove a part of the existing view and display the area of the model or the assembly that lies behind the removed portion. This type of view is generated using a closed sketch associated with the parent view.

Crop View

A crop view is used to crop an existing view enclosed in a closed sketch associated to that view. The portion of the view that lies inside the associated sketch is retained and the remaining portion is removed.

Alternate Position View

The alternate position view is used to create a view in which you can show both the maximum and minimum range of motion of the assembly. The main position is displayed in the drawing view in continuous lines and the alternate position of the assembly is displayed in the same view in dashed lines (phantom lines).

GENERATING STANDARD DRAWING VIEWS

A standard view is generally the first view that you generate in the current drawing sheet. There are a number of methods for generating the standard drawing views. All these methods are discussed next.

Generating Model Views

CommandManager:	View Layout > Model View
SolidWorks menus:	Insert > Drawing View > Model
Toolbar:	Drawing > Model View

As mentioned earlier, the model views can be used to generate the base view in the drawing sheet. Invoke the **Model View PropertyManager** by choosing the **Model View** button from the **View Layout CommandManager**, if it is not invoked by default.

If you start the new drawing document from within the part or the assembly document, the part or the assembly will automatically be selected and you can place the view using the **View Palette**. However, if you start the new drawing document using the **New SolidWorks Document** dialog box, a message will be displayed in the **Model View PropertyManager** and you will be prompted to select a part or an assembly to generate the drawing view. If any part or assembly document is opened, it will be displayed in the selection box of the **Part/Assembly to Insert** rollout. You can preview the part or the assembly document by expanding the **Thumbnail Preview** rollout, as shown in Figure 14-4.

You can also choose the **Browse** button and use the **Open** dialog box to select the document; the **Model View PropertyManager** will automatically be modified and the options related to generating the

Figure 14-4   Selecting the document to generate the model views

standard views will be displayed, as shown in Figure 14-5. The rollouts in this **PropertyManager** are discussed next.

Number of Views Rollout

The radio buttons available in this rollout allow you to specify whether you want to generate only a single view or multiple views. To generate multiple views, select the **Multiple views** radio button and then choose the buttons of the required views from the **Orientation** rollout.

Orientation Rollout

The buttons available in the **Orientation** rollout are used to specify the orientation of the view. You can select the additional orientations by selecting the required check box from the **More views** list box. Select the **Preview** check box to preview the drawing view before it is placed.

> **Note**
> *You can change the orientation of the model view even after placing it. To do so, double-click on the required view; the **Model View PropertyManager** will be displayed. Select the required view from the **Orientation** rollout; the orientation of the view will be automatically modified.*

Figure 14-5 Partial view of the Model View PropertyManager after selecting the model to generate the drawing views

Import options Rollout

If you have dimensioned the model using the **DimXpert** tool in the part or the assembly mode, then on selecting the **Import annotations** check box and the other check boxes in this rollout, the dimensions will be generated automatically.

Options Rollout

The **Auto-start projected view** check box available in this rollout is used to invoke the **Projected View** tool to generate the projected view immediately after placing the model view. The model view that you generate will automatically be taken as the parent view to generate the projected view. Note that this rollout will not be displayed if you generate the isometric view of the model.

Display Style Rollout

The options in this rollout are used to specify the display styles for the model view. These display styles are similar to those available in the **View** toolbar to display the parts or the assemblies in the part document or the assembly document.

Scale Rollout

The **Use sheet scale** radio button is selected, by default in the **Scale** rollout. Therefore, when you select a template to start a new drawing sheet, a default scale is automatically defined to generate the drawing views. To define a custom scale for the model view, select the **Use**

custom scale radio button and select the scale factor from the drop-down list below this radio button. On selecting the **User Defined** option from this drop-down list, you need to specify the scale factor in the edit box that will be displayed below the drop-down list.

Dimension Type Rollout

The radio buttons available in this rollout are used to specify whether the model view will have true dimensions or projected dimensions. The true dimensions are the exact model dimensions that were specified while creating the model. The projected dimensions are the reduced dimensions that are used in case of the isometric, dimetric, or trimetric view. Generally, the value of the projected dimension is about 81.6% of the value of true dimension.

Cosmetic Thread Display Rollout

If the model has cosmetic threads, then the visibility of the threads can be controlled by selecting the **High quality** or **Draft quality** radio button from this rollout.

Using the View Palette to Place the Drawing Views

In SolidWorks, the **View Palette** is automatically displayed when you start a new drawing file from the part or the assembly document. You can also display the **View Palette** manually by displaying the task pane and choosing the **View Palette** tab. The **View Palette** is shown in Figure 14-6.

To place a view using the **View Palette**, select the preview of the view in the **View Palette** and then drag it to the drawing sheet at the desired location; the **Projected View** tool will be invoked. Now, create the projected views from the view placed earlier. You can choose the **Browse to select a part/assembly** button from the **View Palette** to browse and select a part or an assembly file to generate the drawing views.

If you have dimensioned the model using the **DimXpert** tool in the part or the assembly mode, then on selecting the **Import Annotations** check box and the other check boxes in the **Options** area, the dimensions will be generated automatically. The **Auto-start projected view** check box in the **Options** area is used to invoke the **Projected View** tool automatically to generate the projected view immediately after placing the model view.

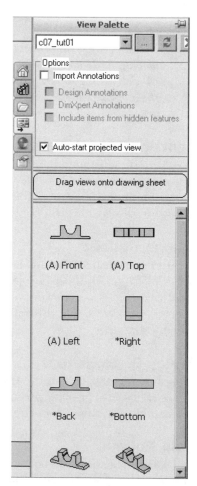

Figure 14-6 The View Palette

Generating the Three Standard Views

CommandManager: View Layout > Standard 3 View
SolidWorks menus: Insert > Drawing View > Standard 3 View
Toolbar: Drawing > Standard 3 View

You can generate three default orthographic views of the specified part or the assembly by using the **Standard 3 View** tool. To create the standard views, choose the **Standard 3 View** tool from the **View Layout CommandManager**; the **Standard 3 View PropertyManager** will be displayed. If any part or assembly document is opened in the current session of SolidWorks, it will be displayed in the list box reduce gap in the **Part/Assembly to Insert** rollout, as shown in Figure 14-7.

Figure 14-7 The Standard 3 View PropertyManager

You can select the document from this list box or choose the **Browse** button to select the part or the assembly document, if no documents are opened. As soon as you select a document, three standard views will be generated based on the default scale of the current sheet. Figure 14-8 shows the three standard views of a model generated in the third angle projection by using the **Standard 3 View** tool.

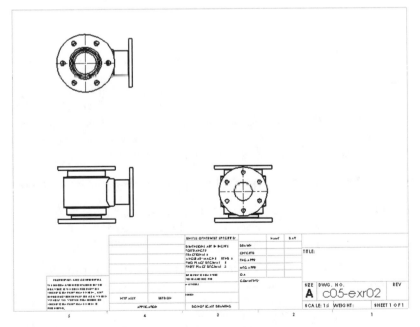

*Figure 14-8 Three standard views generated using the **Standard 3 View** tool*

Tip. *The drawing views that are generated depend on the default projection type of the current sheet. If the sheet is configured for the first angle projection, the drawing views will be generated according to that. If the drawing sheet is configured for the third angle projection, the views will be generated accordingly.*

To change the projection type of the current sheet, right-click on **Sheet Format1** *in the* **FeatureManager design tree** *and choose* **Properties** *from the shortcut menu; the* **Sheet Properties** *dialog box will be displayed. Set the required projection type using the options in the* **Type of projection** *area.*

Note
You will observe that the name of the part document whose drawing views are generated is displayed in the **DWG NO.** *text box of the title block. The size of the sheet is also displayed at the lower right corner of the title block. Try changing the sheet format, if these parameters are not displayed.*

You will observe that the center marks are automatically created on generating the drawing views. If they are not generated automatically, you can set the option to do so. Invoke the **System Options** *dialog box and choose the* **Document Properties** *tab; the* **Drafting Standard** *option is chosen by default. Choose the* **Detailing** *option from the area available on the left of the dialog box. Select the* **Center marks-holes** *check box from the* **Auto insert on view creation** *area. You can also set auto-insertion of centerlines, balloons, and so on using the options provided in this dialog box.*

Tip. *If the view generated using the* **Standard 3 View** *tool overlaps the title block, then you need to move this view. To do so, place the cursor over the view; the bounding box of the view is displayed in dashed red lines. At this point, click to select the view. Next, move the cursor to the boundary of the selected view; the cursor will be replaced by the move cursor. Press and hold the left mouse button and drag the cursor to move the view. Remember that on moving the parent view, all the views generated using this tool will also be moved.*

Generating Standard Views Using the Relative View Tool

CommandManager:	View Layout > Relative View *(Customize to add)*
SolidWorks menus:	Insert > Drawing View > Relative To Model
Toolbar:	Drawing > Relative View *(Customize to add)*

The **Relative View** tool is used to generate an orthographic view such that the orientation of the view is defined by selecting two reference planes or the planar faces of the model. This option is very useful if you need the orientation of the parent view other than the default orientations.

Open the part or the assembly document and tile it vertically or horizontally with the drawing document in order to create a relative view. Invoke the **Relative View** tool and click once in the part or the assembly document; the **Relative View PropertyManager** will be displayed in that document, as shown in Figure 14-9, and you will be prompted to select a planar face of the model.

Select the orientation for the first plane or the planar face from the drop-down list available in the **First** area. Then, select the plane or the planar face of the model to be oriented in that direction. For example, if you select the **Top** option from this drop-down list and then select a planar face, then the selected face will be displayed in the top view.

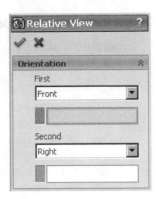

Figure 14-9 *The Relative View PropertyManager*

Select the orientation for the second reference from the drop-down list and then select a plane or a planar face. Next, choose **OK** from the **Relative View PropertyManager**. You will return to the drawing document. Place the view at the required location. Figure 14-10 shows the faces of the model selected to generate a standard view and Figure 14-11 shows the resulting view.

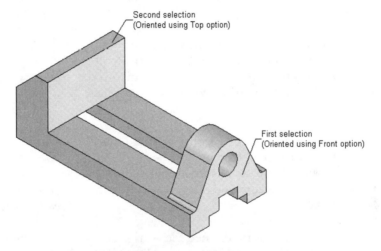

Figure 14-10 *Faces to be selected*

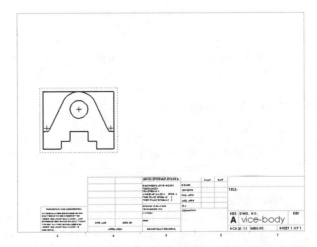

Figure 14-11 *Resulting view*

Generating Standard Views Using the Predefined View Tool

CommandManager:	View Layout > Predefined View *(Customize to add)*
SolidWorks menus:	Insert > Drawing View > Predefined
Toolbar:	Drawing > Predefined View *(Customize to add)*

 The **Predefined View** tool is used to create empty views with the predefined orientation. After their creation, you can populate the view by inserting the component. To create the predefined views, invoke the **Predefined View** tool from the **View Layout CommandManager**; an empty view will be attached to the cursor. Specify a point in the drawing document to place the predefined view; a rectangle defining the boundary of the view will be placed in the drawing document and the **Drawing View PropertyManager** will be displayed, as shown in Figure 14-12.

Select the view orientation from the **Standard views** area in the **Orientation** rollout and choose the **OK** button from the **Drawing View PropertyManager**. To create additional predefined views, invoke the **Predefined View** tool and place the view in the drawing sheet.

After creating all the predefined views, click once in a predefined view; the **Drawing View PropertyManager** will be displayed. Choose the **Browse** button from the **Insert Model** rollout in the **Drawing View PropertyManager** and insert the model; the drawing will be created.

*Figure 14-12 The **Drawing View1 PropertyManager***

If you need to align the multiple predefined views, right-click inside a bounding box and choose **Alignment > Align Horizontal by Center/Align Vertical by Center**. Next, select the previous predefined view to align the corresponding view. Similarly, align the other predefined views using this option.

Figure 14-13 shows the selected predefined views with the orientation in which the views are created. Figure 14-14 shows the drawing document after populating the drawing views.

 Note
*The views generated in the **Drawing** mode of SolidWorks are automatically scaled on the basis of the size of the sheet.*

The views will also be scaled automatically if the drawing contains more than one predefined view.

*A predefined view placed in the drawing document will be scaled with respect to the **Custom Scale** value, if specified. Otherwise, it will be scaled with the default scale factor of the drawing sheet. You can change the view scale using the **Sheet Properties** dialog box. You will learn more about scaling the views in the next chapter.*

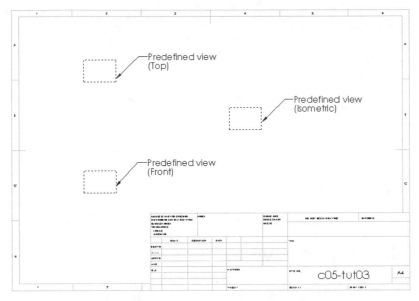

Figure 14-13 Various predefined views

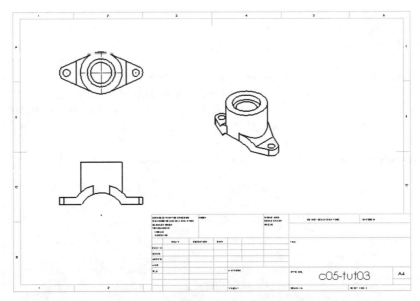

Figure 14-14 Views created after populating the predefined views

GENERATING DERIVED VIEWS

All views generated from a view that is already placed in the drawing document are known as derived views. These include:

1. Projected view
2. Section view
3. Aligned Section view
4. Broken-out Section view
5. Auxiliary view
6. Detail view
7. Crop view
8. Broken view
9. Alternate Position view

The methods of generating various derived drawing views are discussed next.

Generating Projected Views

CommandManager:	View Layout > Projected View
SolidWorks menus:	Insert > Drawing View > Projected
Toolbar:	Drawing > Projected View

 As mentioned earlier, the projected views are generated by projecting the normal lines from an existing view or at an angle from an existing view. To generate a projected view, choose the **Projected View** button from the **View Layout CommandManager**; the **Projected View PropertyManager** will be displayed. If there are multiple views on the sheet, you will be prompted to select a drawing view to project the normal lines. If there is only one view, it will be automatically selected as the parent view. Select the parent view and move the cursor vertically to generate the top view or the bottom view or move the cursor horizontally to generate the right or the left view. If you move the cursor at an angle, a 3D view will be generated. Specify a point on the drawing sheet to place the view. To generate more than one projected views, choose the **Keep Visible** button to pin the **Projected View PropertyManager**. Figure 14-15 shows the front view generated from the top view.

 Tip. *When you generate a projected drawing view, it is aligned to the parent view. To place the projected view that is not in alignment with the parent view, press and hold the CTRL key before placing it. Next, move the cursor to the desired location and place the view.*

All the standard and derived views such as projected views, section view, detailed view, and so on are linked to their parent view by a Parent-Child relationship. If you select the child view, the bounding box of the parent view will also be displayed.

*Select the child view, invoke the shortcut menu, and choose the **Jump to Parent View** option from it; the parent view will be selected automatically.*

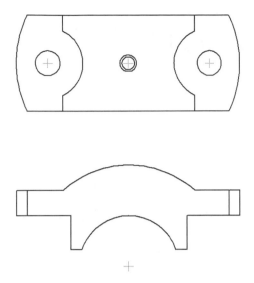

Figure 14-15 *Front view generated from the top view*

Generating Section Views

CommandManager:	View Layout > Section View
SolidWorks menus:	Insert > Drawing View > Section
Toolbar:	Drawing > Section View

 As mentioned earlier, section views are generated by chopping a portion of an existing view using a cutting plane (defined by the sketched lines) and then viewing the parent view from a direction normal to the cutting plane.

In SolidWorks, you can use the **Section View** tool to create a full section view or a half section view, as shown in Figures 14-16 and 14-17. A full section view is defined using a single line segment but a half section view is defined using three line segments. Note that the section plane for a full section view can be defined after invoking the **Section View** tool. But to generate a half section view, you need to draw the line segments to define the section plane before invoking the **Section View** tool. To do this, select the drawing view that you want to use as the parent view and choose the **Sketch** button from the **CommandManager**; the sketching environment will be invoked. You can use the inferencing lines to draw the lines for the section plane.

To create a full section view, activate the view in which you need to draw the section line. The view symbol will be displayed below the cursor and the bounding box of the view will also be displayed. Now, choose the **Section View** button from the **View Layout CommandManager**; the **Section View PropertyManager** will be displayed and you will be prompted to sketch a line to continue the view creation.

After activating the view, draw a line that will define the section plane. On specifying the endpoint of the section line, the view will be defined and attached to the cursor. Also, the other options in the **Section View PropertyManager** will be displayed.

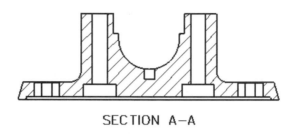

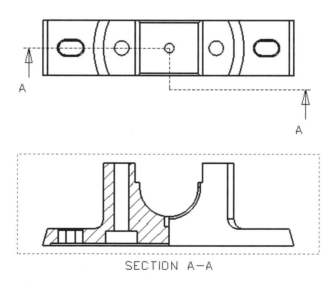

Figure 14-16 *Full section view*

Figure 14-17 *Half section view*

To generate a half section view, select all the line segments that define the section plane and then invoke the **Section View** tool; the section view will be attached to the cursor. Move the

Tip. *On creating a section view and moving the cursor to place the section view, you will observe that the view is aligned to the direction of arrows on the section line. To remove this alignment, press and hold the CTRL key and move the view to the desired location. Now, select a point in the drawing sheet to place the view.*

cursor and specify a point on the drawing sheet to place the section view; the name and the scale factor of the drawing view will be displayed below the section view and the **Section View PropertyManager** will be invoked, as shown in Figure 14-18.

You can use the **Flip direction** check box to flip the direction of the section view. The view will automatically be modified in the drawing sheet. The **Scale with model** check box is used to scale the drawing view, if the model is scaled in the part document. You will learn more about scaling the model in the next chapter.

Note

The default hatch pattern in the section view depends on the material assigned to the model. Also, you may need to increase the spacing of the hatch pattern, if it is not correct. You will learn more about editing the hatch pattern later in this chapter.

You can create a partial section view and the surface section view using the options in the **Section View PropertyManager** as discussed next.

Creating the Partial Section View

If the section line does not cut through the model, the **SolidWorks** information box will be displayed. This dialog box informs you that the section line does not completely cut through the bounding box of the model in this view. It then prompts you whether you want this to be a partial section cut? To create the partial section view, choose the **Yes** button from this dialog box. If you choose the **No** button from this dialog box, a full section view will be created. Figure 14-19 shows a partial section view generated from the top view.

Figure 14-18 Partial view of the Section View PropertyManager

Creating the Surface Section View

A surface section view is the one in which only the sectioned surface is displayed in the section view. To create a surface section view, you first need to create the section view and then select the **Display only cut face(s)** check box from the **Section View** rollout of the **Section View PropertyManager**. Figure 14-20 shows a surface section view.

Tip. *Sometimes the sectioned view is generated upside down even if you have set the projection type to the third angle. In such cases, you need to flip the direction of the section line by selecting the **Flip direction** check box from the **Section View PropertyManager**.*

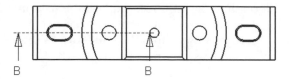

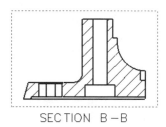

SECTION B—B

Figure 14-19 *A partial section view*

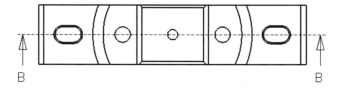

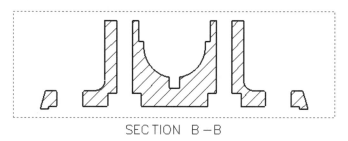

SECTION B—B

Figure 14-20 *A surface section view*

Generating the Section View of an Assembly

According to the drawing standards, when you create the section view of an assembly, some components such as fasteners, shafts, keys, and so on should not be sectioned. Therefore, when you create the section view of an assembly, the **Section View** dialog box will be displayed, as shown in Figure 14-21.

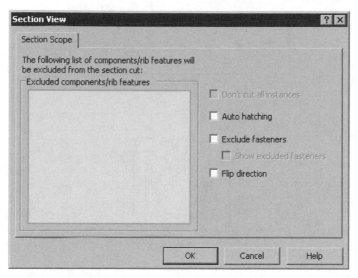

Figure 14-21 The **Section View** *dialog box*

This dialog box allows you to select the components that will be excluded from the section cut. You can also select the components from the parent view. But if the components are not visible in the parent view, you can invoke the **FeatureManager design tree** and expand the parent drawing view. Next, expand the assembly tree view to display all the components of the assembly. Select the components that are not required to be sectioned; the name of the selected component will be displayed in the **Excluded components/rib features** selection box.

The **Auto hatching** check box is used to define the hatch patterns automatically. You can even change them if required. The method of changing the hatch patterns is discussed later. SolidWorks provides you with an option to exclude the fasteners that are inserted in the assembly using the **Toolbox** application. Toolbox, one of the add-ins of SolidWorks, is used to insert standard fasteners to the assembly. To exclude the fasteners that are inserted using this option, select the **Exclude fasteners** check box from the **SectionView** dialog box.

The **Flip direction** check box is used to flip the direction of viewing the section view.

In case you have more than one instance of the component in the assembly and you need to exclude all the instances of the component from the section view, select the component from the drawing sheet and also the name of the component from the **Exclude components/rib features** selection box. Select the **Don't cut all instances** check box from the **Section View** dialog box; all instances of the selected component will be excluded from the section view. Figure 14-22 shows an assembly section view with the fasteners excluded from the cut.

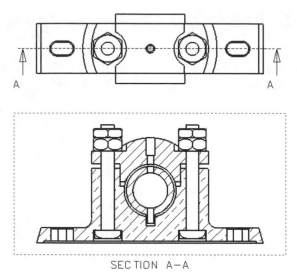

SECTION A—A

Figure 14-22 *Section view of an assembly with some of the components excluded from the cut*

Tip. *To add or remove the components that are sectioned, right-click on the drawing view and choosing **Properties** from the shortcut menu; the **Properties** dialog box. Next, choose the **Section Scope** tab and add or remove the components.*

Generating Aligned Section Views

CommandManager:	View Layout > Section View > Aligned Section View
SolidWorks menus:	Insert > Drawing View > Aligned Section
Toolbar:	Drawing > Aligned Section View

 This tool is used to generate a section view of the component in which at least one of the features is at an angle. In the aligned section view, the sectioned portion revolves about an axis normal to the view such that it is straightened.

Figure 14-23 explains the concept of an aligned section view of a model. Notice that the inclined feature sectioned in this view is straightened. As a result, the section view is longer than the parent view. Activate the view to create the aligned section view. Choose **Section View > Aligned Section View** from the **View Layout CommandManager**. Draw the sketch that defines the section plane; the aligned section view will be attached to the cursor. Place the view at an appropriate location in the drawing sheet. Note that the resulting view will be projected normal to the line drawn at the end in the section sketch. Therefore, to get the aligned section view similar to that shown in Figure 14-23, the inclined line in the section sketch should be drawn first, followed by the vertical line. Figure 14-24 shows the aligned section view in which the vertical line in the section sketch is drawn first. This is the reason the section view is projected normal to the inclined line that was drawn last. On the other hand, Figure 14-25 shows the view in which the inclined line is drawn first.

You can also create a section view and aligned section views from a crop view, detail view, and an orthogonal exploded view.

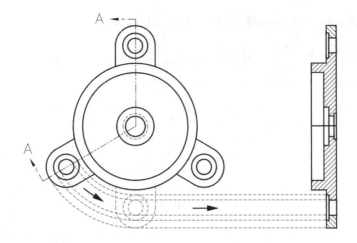

Figure 14-23 *Aligned section view*

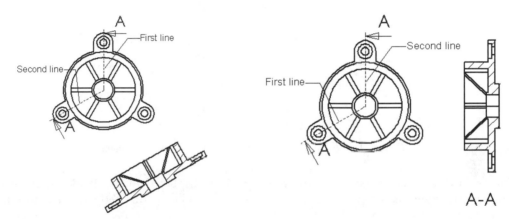

Figure 14-24 *Aligned section view*   **Figure 14-25** *Aligned section view*

Note

*You can also create a sketch associated to a view. This sketch can be selected as the section plane for generating the section view. To create an associated sketch, activate the view and draw the sketch that defines the section plane using the **Line** tool.*

*If you create a sketch to define the section plane for the aligned section view before invoking the **Aligned Section View** tool, the view will be projected normal to the line that you select last. However, if you select the sketch by dragging a window around it, the view will be projected normal to the line that was drawn last.*

Tip. *In SolidWorks, you can also use more than two lines to create an aligned section view. To do so, you need to draw the lines prior to invoking the **Aligned Section View** tool.*

Generating Broken-out Section Views

CommandManager:	View Layout > Broken-out Section
SolidWorks menus:	Insert > Drawing View > Broken-out Section
Toolbar:	Drawing > Broken-out Section

This tool is used to create a broken-out section view that is used to remove a part of the existing view and display the area of the model or the assembly behind the removed portion. This view is generated using a closed sketch that is associated with the parent view. To create a broken-out section view, activate the view on which you need to create the broken-out section view. Choose the **Broken-out Section** button from the **View Layout CommandManager**; the **Broken-out Section PropertyManager** will be displayed and it will prompt you to create a closed spline to continue the section creation. The cursor will be replaced by the spline cursor. Draw a closed sketch using the spline cursor. If you do not want a spline profile, select a closed profile before choosing the **Broken-out Section** button. Figure 14-26 shows an associated sketch created for creating a broken-out section view.

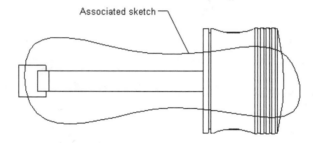

Associated sketch

Figure 14-26 Sketch for creating a broken-out section view

When you draw a closed sketch, the options will be displayed in the **Broken-out Section PropertyManager**, as shown in Figure 14-27, and you will be prompted to specify the depth of the broken-out section.

*Figure 14-27 The **Broken-out Section PropertyManager***

Select the **Preview** check box to preview the broken-out section view. The **Auto hatching** check box, is available only for assemblies and is used to define the hatch pattern automatically to section the drawing view of the assembly. The **Exclude fasteners** check box, which will be available only for assemblies, is used to exclude fasteners from getting sectioned in the broken-out section view. Figure 14-28 shows the preview of the broken-out section view of a part.

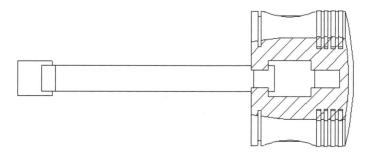

Figure 14-28 Preview of the broken-out section view

Set the value of the depth of the broken-out section in the **Depth** spinner; the preview of the section will be modified dynamically in the drawing view. After setting the value of the depth of the broken-out section, choose the **OK** button from the **Broken-out Section PropertyManager**. Figure 14-29 shows a broken-out section view with a different depth value.

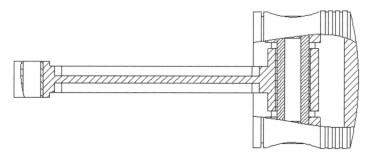

Figure 14-29 Broken-out section view

Generating Auxiliary Views

CommandManager:	View Layout > Auxiliary View
SolidWorks menus:	Insert > Drawing View > Auxiliary
Toolbar:	Drawing > Auxiliary View

An auxiliary view is a drawing view that is generated by projecting the lines normal to a specified edge of an existing view. SolidWorks also allows you to create a line segment associated with the view that can be used to generate the auxiliary view. For this, the associated line segment needs to be created before invoking this tool.

To create an auxiliary view, choose the **Auxiliary View** button from the **View Layout CommandManager**; the **Auxiliary View PropertyManager** will be displayed and you will be prompted to select a reference edge to continue. Select the edge or the associated sketch; a view will be attached to the cursor and some options will be displayed in the **Auxiliary View PropertyManager**, as shown in Figure 14-30. Also, you will be prompted to specify the location to place the view.

Select the check box in the **Arrow** rollout to display the arrow of the viewing direction in the drawing views. The name of the auxiliary view is specified in the **Label** edit box. You can flip the viewing direction for creating the auxiliary view by selecting the **Flip direction** check box. Figure 14-31 shows the reference edge to be selected to create the auxiliary view.

Figure 14-32 shows the auxiliary view created with the default viewing direction. Figure 14-33 shows the auxiliary view created with the **Flip direction** check box selected.

Figure 14-30 Partial view of the ***Auxiliary View PropertyManager***

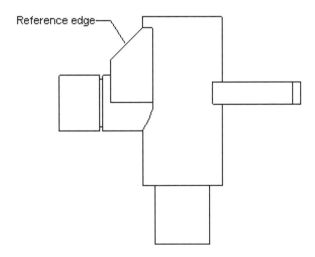

Figure 14-31 Reference edge to be selected to create the auxiliary view

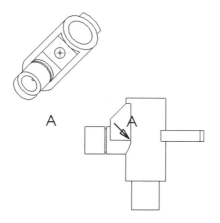

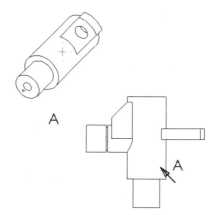

Figure 14-32 Auxiliary view created with the **Flip direction** *check box cleared*

Figure 14-33 Auxiliary view created with the **Flip direction** *check box selected*

While generating the auxiliary view of an assembly, the **Display Style** rollout will be displayed. This rollout allows you to select the display state whose auxiliary view will be generated.

Generating Detail Views

CommandManager:	View Layout > Detail View
SolidWorks menus:	Insert > Drawing View > Detail
Toolbar:	Drawing > Detail View

A detail view is used to display the details of a portion of an existing view. You can select the portion whose detailing needs to be shown in the parent view. The portion that you select will be magnified and placed as a separate view. You can control the magnification of the detail view. To create a detail view, activate the view from which you will generate the detail view. Next, choose the **Detail View** button from the **View Layout CommandManager**; the **Detail View PropertyManager** will be displayed and you will be prompted to sketch a circle to continue the view creation. The cursor will be replaced by a circle cursor.

Create the circle on the portion of the view that is to be displayed in the detail view; the detail view will be attached to the cursor and the options will be displayed in the **Detail View PropertyManager**, as shown in Figure 14-34. You will also be prompted to select a location for the new view. Specify a point on the drawing sheet to place the view. To use a profile other than the circle, you need to create the profile in a view. Then, select the profile and invoke the **Detail View** tool. The rollouts in the **Detail View PropertyManager** are discussed next.

Detail Circle Rollout

This rollout is used to define the options to display the circle of the detail view. You can also apply the leader to the detail view using the options in the rollout. These options are discussed next.

Style Area

The **Style** area has the **Style** drop-down list to specify the style of a closed profile. By default, the **Circle** radio button is selected below the **Style** drop-down list. Therefore, the portion of the parent view that is shown in the detail view is highlighted in the circle. Select the **Profile** radio button, if you have already created a closed profile for defining the portion to be shown in the detail view. The options in the **Style** drop-down list are discussed next.

Per Standard. The **Per Standard** option is used to create the detail view as per the default standards.

Broken Circle. The **Broken Circle** option is used to display the area of the parent view to be displayed in the detailed view in a broken circle.

With Leader. The **With Leader** option is used to add the leader to the callout of the detail view.

Figure 14-34 The Detail View PropertyManager

No Leader. The **No Leader** option is used to remove the leader from the callout of the detail view.

Connected. This option is used to create a line that connects the detail view with the closed profile in the parent view.

Detail View Rollout

This rollout is used to set the parameters of the detail view. The various options available in this rollout are discussed next.

Full outline

The **Full outline** check box is used to display the complete outline of the closed profile in the detail view.

Pin position

The **Pin position** check box is used to pin the position of the detail view.

Scale hatch pattern

While creating a detail view of a section view, the **Scale hatch pattern** check box is used to scale the hatch pattern with respect to the scale factor of the detail view.

If you create a detail view with another detail view or a crop view as the parent view, the default scale factor of the resulting detail view will be twice the immediate parent view. Figure 14-35 shows the detail view created using the **Detail View** tool.

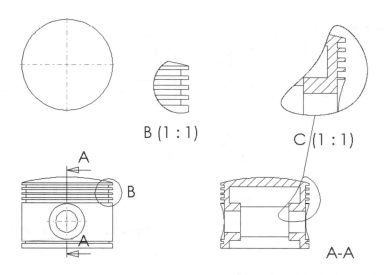

Figure 14-35 *Detail views generated using the existing views*

Tip. *When you create a detail view, by default it is scaled as 1:1. You can define the default scale factor in the **System Options** dialog box so that the detail view is be created with the scaling factor specified by you. To specify the scale factor for the detail view, invoke the **System Options** dialog box and select the **Drawings** option from its left. Set the value of the scale factor of the detail view in the **Detail view scaling** edit box and choose the **OK** button; the detail view will be created with the scale factor defined in the **System Options** dialog box.*

Cropping Drawing Views

CommandManager:	View Layout > Crop View
SolidWorks menus:	Insert > Drawing View > Crop
Toolbar:	Drawing > Crop View

This tool is used to crop an existing view using a closed sketch associated to it. The portion of the view that lies inside the associated sketch is retained and the remaining portion is removed. To crop the view, you first need to create a closed profile that defines the area of the view to be displayed. Select the closed profile and choose the **Crop View** button from the **View Layout CommandManager**; the area of the view outside the closed profile will not be displayed. Figure 14-36 shows the closed profile used to crop the view and Figure 14-37 shows the cropped view.

Tip. *To remove the crop view, invoke the shortcut menu and choose **Crop View** > **Remove Crop** from the shortcut menu.*

*To edit the closed profile of the crop view, select the crop view and right-click. Choose **Crop View** > **Edit Crop** from the shortcut menu. The sketch of the closed profile and the complete view are displayed in the drawing sheet. Edit the closed profile and choose the **Rebuild** button.*

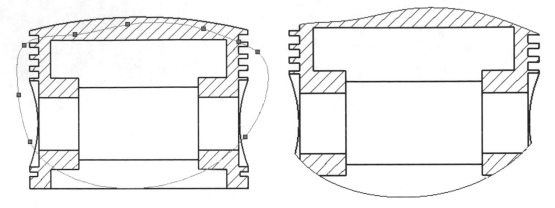

Figure 14-36 *Closed profile to crop the view*   ***Figure 14-37*** *Resulting crop view*

Generating Broken Views

CommandManager:	View Layout > Break
SolidWorks menus:	Insert > Drawing View > Break
Toolbar:	Drawing > Break

A broken view is the one in which a portion of the drawing view is removed between the ends, keeping the ends of the drawing view intact. This view is used to display the component whose length to width ratio is very high. This means that either the length is very large as compared to the width, or the width is very large as compared to the length. The **Break** tool will break the view along the horizontal or the vertical direction such that the drawing view fits the area you require. To create a broken view, choose the **Break** button from the **View Layout CommandManager** and then select the view; the **Broken View PropertyManager** will be displayed. Depending on the direction in which you need to break the view, choose the **Add vertical break line** or the **Add horizontal break line** button in the **Broken View Settings** rollout; a break line will be displayed on the selected view. Place the first break line and then the second break line; the model will be broken between the two break lines, as shown in Figure 14-38.

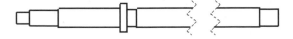

Figure 14-38 *Break lines added to the view*

Similarly, you can continue adding the break lines to create multiple breaks in the drawing view, as shown in Figure 14-39. You can define the gap between the broken lines using the

Gap Size spinner in the **Broken View PropertyManager**. You can also modify the style of the break line using the **Break line style** drop-down list in the **Broken View PropertyManager**. Figure 14-40 shows a view with the curved break lines.

Figure 14-39 *Multiple break lines*   *Figure 14-40* *Curved break lines*

You can also break an isometric view; the procedure of breaking an isometric view or any 3D view is the same as discussed earlier. Figure 14-41 shows a broken isometric view.

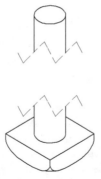

Figure 14-41 *A broken isometric view*

In SolidWorks, you can lock the position of the break lines. To do so, after placing the two break lines, exit the **Broken View PropertyManager**. Invoke the **Smart Dimension** tool from the **Sketch CommandManager** and dimension both the break lines with respect to an entity in the drawing view. Click anywhere in the drawing area; the dimension will disappear. To view the dimension that is use to lock the break lines, select the break lines.

If you change the dimension of the model in the part document after locking the break lines, the gap between the break lines will not change. Remember that this dimension is not displayed when you print the drawing document.

To unbreak the broken view, select the view, invoke the shortcut menu, and choose the **Un-Break View** option from it.

Note

If the break lines are not locked, you can select and drag the break lines to dynamically modify the gap between the broken view.

If you generate a projected view from a broken view, the resulting projected view is also a broken view.

If you break the isometric view of a component placed horizontally, the two parts of the view will lose their alignment because of the break.

Tip. *You can also change the style of the break line by selecting it and invoking the shortcut menu, which consists of various break line styles such as straight cut, curve cut, and small zig zag cut.*

*Select the view, invoke the shortcut menu and choose **Drawing Views > Break** to break the view again.*

If you select the break lines and press the DELETE key, the broken view will be replaced by the parent view.

Generating Alternate Position Views

CommandManager:	View Layout > Alternate Position View
SolidWorks menus:	Insert > Drawing View > Alternate Position
Toolbar:	Drawing > Alternate Position View

The alternate position view is used to create a view in which you can show the maximum and minimum range of the motion of an assembly. The main position of the assembly is displayed with continuous lines in the drawing view, while the alternate position of the assembly is shown in the same view with the dashed (phantom) lines. To create an alternate position view, activate and select the view of the assembly drawing on which you need to create the alternate position view. Choose the **Alternate Position View** button from the **View Layout CommandManager**; the **Alternate Position PropertyManager** will be displayed, as shown in Figure 14-42.

The **Alternate Position PropertyManager** prompts you to select a new configuration, choose **OK** or enter and define the new configuration parameters. If you have not created any configurations, the **New Configuration** radio button will be automatically selected to create one. Enter the name of the configuration in the edit box given below and choose the **OK**

Figure 14-42 The Alternate Position PropertyManager

button from the **Alternate Position PropertyManager**. Choose **OK** from the **Tangent Edge Display** dialog box, if displayed.

The assembly document will be opened and the **Move Component PropertyManager** will be displayed in the assembly document. The **Move Component PropertyManager** will prompt you to move the desired components to the position to be shown in the alternate view. Note that the component or components that you need to move should have that particular degree of freedom free. These components should not be fully defined in the assembly. Select and drag the cursor to move the components to the desired location. After defining the alternate position of the components, choose the **OK** button from the **Move Component PropertyManager**. You will return to the drawing document automatically. The alternate position of the components that are moved will be displayed in the phantom lines in the drawing view, as shown in Figure 14-43.

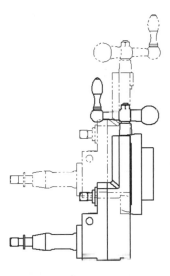

Figure 14-43 *Alternate position view*

You can also create the alternate position view of an isometric view or any 3D view. The procedure of creating the alternate position view of a 3D view is the same as that discussed earlier. Figure 14-44 shows the alternate position view of an isometric view.

Note

*On creating an alternate view of an assembly, a new configuration will be created inside the assembly document with the same name that is specified to the configuration while creating the alternate position view. Open the assembly document and invoke the **ConfigurationManager**; you will observe that a new configuration has been created along with the default configuration. By default, the newly created configuration is selected. Therefore, the assembly is displayed with the components moved to their extreme positions. To switch back to the default configuration, select **Default** from the **ConfigurationManager**, invoke the shortcut menu and choose the **Show Configuration** option from it. You will observe that the assembly is displayed with the moved components back to their original positions. If the **Show Configuration** option is not available in the shortcut menu, the assembly will be at the default configuration.*

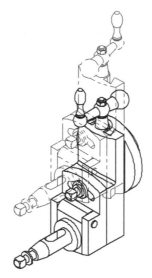

Figure 14-44 *Alternate view of an isometric view.*

Generating Drawing Views of the Exploded State of an Assembly

You can create the drawing views of the exploded state of an assembly. To do so, you need to have an exploded state defined in the assembly document. Generate the isometric view of the assembly on the drawing sheet. Select the view, invoke the shortcut menu, and choose the **Properties** option from it; the **View Properties** tab in the **Drawing View Properties** dialog box will be displayed. Select the **Show in exploded state** check box from the **Configuration information** area and choose the **OK** button. Figure 14-45 shows the drawing view of the exploded state of an assembly with explode lines.

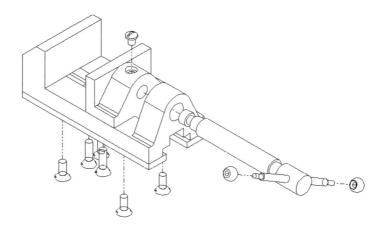

Figure 14-45 *Drawing view of the exploded state of an assembly with explode lines*

Tip. *If the assembly in the assembly document is in the exploded state and you drag and drop the assembly to generate the drawing views, then all views of the assembly will be generated in the exploded state.*

To collapse the exploded state in the drawing view, select the view and invoke the **Drawing View Properties** *dialog box. Clear the* **Show in exploded state** *check box from the* **View Properties** *tab in this dialog box .*

WORKING WITH INTERACTIVE DRAFTING IN SolidWorks

As mentioned earlier, you can also sketch the 2D drawings in the drawing document of SolidWorks. In technical terms, sketching 2D drawings is known as interactive drafting. Before starting the drawing, it is recommended that you insert an empty view. To create an empty view, choose **Insert > Drawing View > Empty** from the SolidWorks menus; an empty view will be attached to the cursor. Select a point at the desired location to place an empty view. Now, select the empty view to activate and use the tools in the **Sketch CommandManager** to sketch the view.

If you move the empty view by selecting and dragging it, the sketched entities will also move. This is because the sketch that you draw is associated to the empty view.

EDITING AND MODIFYING DRAWING VIEWS

In SolidWorks, you can perform various kinds of editing operations and modifications on the drawing views. For example, you can change the orientation of the view or the view scale, or you can also delete the view. All these operations are discussed next.

Changing the View Orientation

You can change the orientation of the views generated using the **Model View** or the **Predefined View** option. To change the orientation, select the view; the **Drawing View PropertyManager** will be displayed in both the cases. Double-click on the view orientation that you want as the current one in the **Orientation** rollout; the orientation of the selected view will be modified. Choose the **OK** button from the **Drawing View PropertyManager**.

All the derived views will also change their orientation, when you change the orientation of the parent view.

Changing the Scale of Drawing Views

In SolidWorks, you can also change the scale of the drawing views. To do so, select the drawing view and then select the **Use custom scale** radio button in the **Scale** rollout. Select the new scale of the drawing view from the drop-down list available below this radio button. You can also change the scale of the derived views. However, the scale of the parent view will not be changed if you change the scale of a derived view.

Deleting Drawing Views

The unwanted views are deleted from the drawing sheet using the **FeatureManager design tree** or directly from the drawing sheet. Select the view to be deleted from the **FeatureManager design tree**. Next, invoke the shortcut menu and choose the **Delete** option from it; the **Confirm Delete** dialog box will be displayed. Choose the **Yes** button from this dialog box. You can also delete a view by selecting it directly from the drawing sheet and pressing the DELETE key; the **Confirm Delete** dialog box will be displayed. Choose the **Yes** button from this dialog box. On deleting a parent view, the projected views will not be deleted. However, if you delete a view that has a section, detail, or an auxiliary view generated, the name of the dependent view will also be displayed in the **Confirm Delete** dialog box. If you choose **Yes**, the dependent views will also be deleted.

Rotating Drawing Views

SolidWorks allows you to rotate a drawing view in the 2D plane. Select the view and choose the **Rotate View** button from the **Heads-up View** toolbar; the **Rotate Drawing View** dialog box will be displayed, as shown in Figure 14-46. You can enter the value or the rotation angle in this dialog box or you can also dynamically rotate the drawing view by dragging the mouse. If you select the **Dependent views update to change in orientation** check box, the views dependent on the rotated view will also change their orientation.

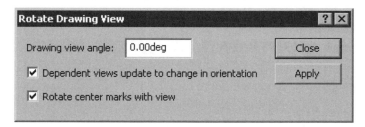

*Figure 14-46 The **Rotate Drawing View** dialog box*

Tip. *You can also copy and paste the drawing view in the drawing sheet. To do so, select the view to copy and press CTRL+C on the keyboard. Now, click anywhere on the drawing sheet to select the sheet and press CTRL+V to paste the drawing view.*

Manipulating the Drawing Views

SolidWorks allows you to manipulate the drawing views dynamically. Select a view and invoke the **3D Drawing View** tool in the **Heads-up View** toolbar; a pop up toolbar will be displayed. Invoke a tool from the toolbar and manipulate the drawing view. After manipulating the view, choose the **OK** button; the drawing will revert to the original view.

MODIFYING THE HATCH PATTERN IN SECTION VIEWS

As discussed earlier, when you generate a section view of an assembly or a component, a hatch pattern is applied to the component or components. This hatch pattern is based on the material assigned to the components in the part document. If you need to modify the default hatch pattern, select it from the section view; the **Area Hatch/Fill PropertyManager** will be displayed, as shown in Figure 14-47. The rollouts in this dialog box are discussed next.

Properties Rollout

The **Properties** rollout is used to define the type of hatch pattern and its properties. Some of the options in this area are not available by default. This is because, by default, the material-dependent hatch pattern is applied to the component. If you want to make the other options also available, clear the **Material crosshatch** check box. The options in this rollout are discussed next.

Preview

The **Preview** area displays the preview of the hatch pattern with the current setting.

Figure 14-47 The Area Hatch/Fill PropertyManager

Hatch

The **Hatch** radio button is selected to apply the standard hatch patterns to the section view. On selecting this button, some options available in the dialog box are invoked to define the properties of the hatch pattern. The options used to define the properties of the hatch pattern are discussed next.

Solid

The **Solid** radio button is used to apply the solid filled hatch pattern to the section view. By default, the black color is applied to the solid filled hatch pattern.

None

Select the **None** radio button, if you do not need to apply any hatch pattern in the section view.

Hatch Pattern

The **Hatch Pattern** drop-down list is used to define the style of the standard hatch pattern that you need to apply to the section view. The preview of the hatch pattern selected from this drop-down list is displayed in the **Preview** area of the **Area Hatch/Fill PropertyManager**.

Hatch Pattern Scale

The **Hatch Pattern Scale** spinner is used to specify the scale factor of the standard hatch pattern selected from the **Pattern** drop-down list. When you change the scale factor using this spinner, the preview displayed in the **Preview** area updates dynamically.

Hatch Pattern Angle

The **Hatch Pattern Angle** spinner is used to define the angle of the selected hatch pattern.

Material crosshatch

The **Material crosshatch** check box is selected to apply the hatch pattern based on the material assigned to the model. Clear this check box to change the type of the hatch pattern.

Apply to

The **Apply to** drop-down list is used to specify whether you need to apply this hatch pattern to the selected component, region, body, or to the entire view. Note that some of these options are available only while modifying the hatch pattern of an assembly section view.

Options Rollout

On selecting the **Apply changes immediately** check box in this rollout, the changes will be applied immediately on the view and the preview will be modified dynamically. If you clear this check box, you need to choose the **Apply** button after making the changes to reflect the changes in the preview.

TUTORIALS

Tutorial 1

In this tutorial, you will generate the front view, top view, right view, aligned section view, detail view, and isometric view of the model created in Tutorial 2 of Chapter 8. Use the Standard A4 Landscape sheet format for generating the views.   **(Expected time: 30 min)**

The following steps are required to complete this tutorial:

a.   Copy the part document of Tutorial 2 of Chapter 8 in the folder of the current chapter.
b.   Open the copied part document and start a new drawing document from within the part document.
c.   Select the standard A4 landscape sheet format and generate the parent view, refer to Figure 14-48.
d.   Generate the projected views using the **Projected View** tool, refer to Figure 14-48.
e.   Generate the aligned section view using the **Aligned Section View** tool, refer to Figures 14-49 and 14-50.
f.   Generate the detail view, refer to Figure 14-51.
g.   Save and close the drawing document.

Copying and Opening the Part Document

1.   Create a folder with the name *c14* in the *SolidWorks* directory and copy *c08tut2.sldprt* from the *My Documents\SolidWorks\c08* folder to this folder.

2.   Start SolidWorks and open the part document of Tutorial 2 of Chapter 8 that you copied in the *c14* folder.

Starting a New Drawing Document

As mentioned earlier, in SolidWorks you can start a new drawing document from the part document. This way, the model in the part document is automatically selected and you can generate its drawing views.

1. Choose **New** > **Make Drawing from Part/Assembly** from the Menu Bar; the **Sheet Format/Size** dialog box is displayed.

 Note

*If you generally use the advanced form of the **New SolidWorks Document** dialog box, the **New SolidWorks Document** dialog box will be displayed every time you choose **Make Drawing from Part/Assembly**. From the **New SolidWorks Document** dialog box, select the drawing template from the **Template** tab and choose **OK**. Remember that if you are not using the advanced form of the **New SolidWorks Document** dialog box, then a new drawing document is started directly and the **Sheet Format/Size** dialog box is displayed.*

2. Select the **A4 - Landscape** sheet from the list box in this dialog box and choose the **OK** button; the new drawing document is started with the standard A4 sheet and the **View Palette** is displayed automatically. The model of Tutorial 2 of Chapter 8 is selected by default for generating the drawing views.

Generating the Parent View and the Projected Views

Before you proceed to generate the drawing views, you need to confirm whether the projection type for the current sheet is set to the third angle.

1. Click anywhere on the sheet to close the **View Palette**. Select **Sheet1** from the **FeatureManager design tree** and then right-click on it. Choose the **Properties** option from the shortcut menu; the **Sheet Properties** dialog box is displayed.

2. Select the **Third angle** radio button from the **Type of projection** area and choose the **OK** button.

3. Now, to open the **task pane**, choose the **View Palette** tab, if the **View Palette** is not displayed by default.

4. Select the **Front** view from the **View Palette** and drag it to the middle left of the drawing sheet just above the title block. Drop the view at this location to place the front view, refer to Figure 14-48.

    The front view is generated and placed at this location. This view is generated at a 1:1 scale. Note that because you selected the option to start the projected views immediately after generating the front view, the **Projected View PropertyManager** is invoked and the preview of the projected view is attached to the cursor. This view is being generated by referencing the front view as the parent view.

5. Move the cursor above the front view and specify a point to place the top view, refer to Figure 14-48. The top view of the model is generated and the preview of the another projected view with the front view as the base view is attached to the cursor.

6. Move the cursor to the right of the front view and place the right view, refer to Figure 14-48.

7. Similarly, move the cursor horizontally toward the right and then move it upward; the preview of the isometric view is displayed. Specify a point to place the isometric view. Now, exit the **Projected View PropertyManager**.

    The current location of the isometric is such that it will interfere with the aligned section view that you need to place next. Therefore, you need to move the isometric view close to the top right corner of the drawing sheet.

8. Move the cursor over the isometric view; the bounding box of the view is displayed in orange.

9. Click to select the view; the border of the view is displayed in different color.

10. Move the cursor on one of the borderlines of the view; the cursor changes to the move cursor.

11. Press and hold the left mouse button and drag the view close to the upper right corner of the drawing sheet. The drawing sheet after generating and moving the drawing view is shown in Figure 14-48.

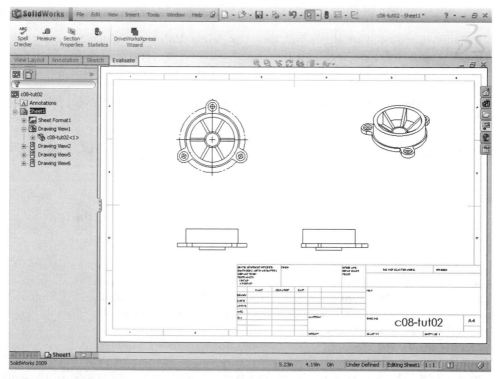

Figure 14-48 *Drawing sheet after generating the front, top, right, and isometric views*

Tip. *You can turn off the origins displayed in the drawing views by using the* ***Heads-up View*** *toolbar.*

The center marks are automatically created in the drawing views of the circular features in a model.

Generating the Aligned Section View

Next, you need to generate the aligned section view. The line segments that are used to generate this view will be drawn before invoking the **Aligned Section View** tool. Remember that the view is projected normal to the line selected last, irrespective of the last line drawn. This means that you can draw any line first. In this tutorial, you will first select the inclined line and then the vertical line.

1. Click on the top view to activate the view.

2. Choose the **Sketch** tab to invoke the **Sketch CommandManager**. Draw the lines using the **Line** tool and apply the relations and dimensions to the sketch, as shown in Figure 14-49.

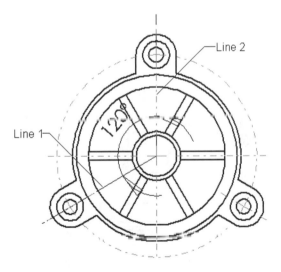

Figure 14-49 *Sketch to be used as the section sketch for the aligned section view*

3. Select the dimension and invoke the shortcut menu. Choose the **Hide** option from the shortcut menu to hide the dimension.

Next, you need to select the lines to generate the aligned section view. Note that the vertical line should be selected last to generate the view normal to this line. However, it will be difficult to select the line because the vertical line coincides with the center marks. You will use the **Select Other** option to select this line.

4. Select the inclined line. Make sure you do not select any segment of the center mark.

5. Next, press and hold the CTRL key and move the cursor to the vertical line. Right-click on the vertical line and choose the **Select Other** option from the shortcut menu; the **Select Other** list box is displayed.

6. Select the **Line** option from the **Select Other** list box. As the CTRL key was pressed, the inclined line will also be still in the current selection set.

7. Now, invoke the **View Layout CommandManager** and choose **Section View > Aligned Section View**; the aligned section view is attached to the cursor.

    The view generated is normal to the vertical line. If the direction of viewing the aligned section view is reversed, you need to flip it after placing the view.

8. Move the cursor to the right of the top view and place the aligned section view. The **Section View PropertyManager** is displayed. If the direction of viewing is not the one, as required, select the **Flip direction** check box. Click anywhere on the sheet to exit the **PropertyManager**. The sheet after generating the aligned section view is shown in Figure 14-50.

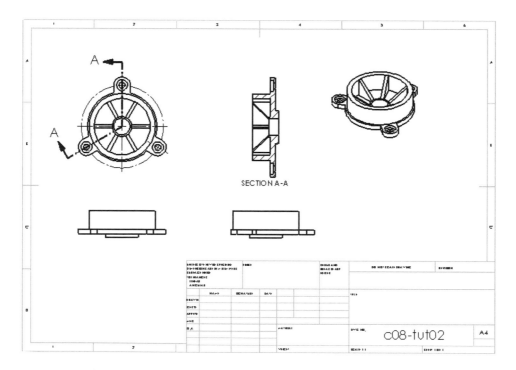

Figure 14-50 *Sheet after generating the aligned section view*

Modifying the Hatch Pattern of the Aligned Section View

The gap between the hatching lines in the aligned section view is large. Therefore, you need to modify the spacing.

1. Select the hatch pattern from one of the sections in the aligned section view; the **Area Hatch/Fill PropertyManager** is displayed.

2. Clear the **Material crosshatch** check box; the **Hatch Pattern**, **Hatch Pattern Scale**, and **Hatch Pattern Angle** options are available. Set the value in the **Hatch Pattern Scale** spinner to **2** and exit the **PropertyManager**.

Generating the Detail View

Next, you need to generate the detail view of the right circular feature of the model. Before doing so, you need to activate the view from which you will drive the detail view.

1. Activate the top view and choose the **Detail View** button from the **View Layout CommandManager**; the **Detail View PropertyManager** is displayed and you are prompted to sketch a circle to continue viewing the creation. Also, the cursor is replaced by the circle cursor.

2. Draw a small circle on the right circular feature of the model in the top view, refer to Figure 14-51. As you draw the circle, the detail view is attached to the cursor.

3. Place the view on the right side of the drawing sheet above the title block, refer to Figure 14-51.

4. Select the **Use custom scale** radio button in the **Scale** rollout. Then, select the **User Defined** option from the drop-down list below the **Use custom scale** radio button.

5. Set the value of the scale factor of the detail view to **3:1** and choose the **OK** button from the **Detail View PropertyManager**.

    You may need to move the drawing view and its label so that the view does not overlap the title block. Figure 14-51 shows the final drawing sheet, after generating the detail view from the top view.

Saving the Drawing

1. Choose the **Save** button from the Menu Bar and save the drawing document with the name and location given below:

    \My Documents\SolidWorks\c14\c14tut1.slddrw

2. Choose **File** > **Close** to close this document. Also, close the part document of Tutorial 2 of Chapter 8.

Tip. *If you suppress the features of a model whose drawing views have been generated, the suppressed features will not be displayed in the drawing views. On unsuppressing the features, they will be displayed again in the drawing views.*

When you hide or suppress the components of an assembly, the hidden or suppressed components are not displayed in the drawing views.

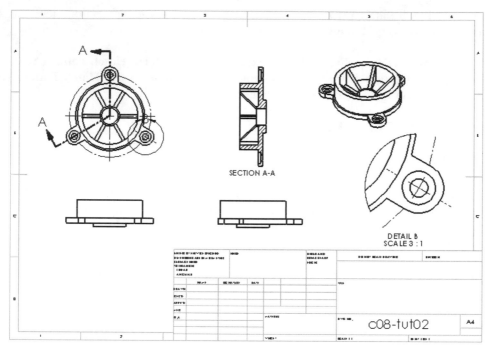

Figure 14-51 The detail view derived from the top view

Tutorial 2

In this tutorial, you will generate the drawing view of the Bench Vice assembly created in Chapter 12. You will generate the top view, sectioned front view, right view, and isometric view of the assembly in the exploded state.   **(Expected time: 45 min)**

The following steps are required to complete this tutorial:

a. Copy the folder of the Bench Vice assembly from Chapter 12 to the *c14* folder.
b. Create the exploded view of the Bench Vice assembly, refer to Figure 14-52.
c. Start a new drawing document from the assembly document using A4 landscape sheet format and generate the top view, refer to Figure 14-53.
d. Generate the section view using the **Section View** tool, refer to Figure 14-54.
e. Generate the right view using the **Projected View** tool, refer to Figure 14-55.
f. Generate the isometric view and change the state of the isometric view to the exploded state, refer to Figure 14-56.
g. Save and close the drawing and assembly documents.

Copying the Folder of the Bench Vice Assembly

First, you need to copy the folder of the Bench Vice assembly to the *c14* folder.

1. Copy the folder of the Bench Vice assembly from the *\My Documents\SolidWorks\c12* folder to the *c14* folder.

Creating the Exploded View of the Assembly

Before proceeding further to generate the drawing views of the assembly, you need to create the exploded state of the assembly in the **Assembly** mode.

1. Open the Bench Vice assembly and create the exploded state and the explode lines, as shown in Figure 14-52.

    It is recommended that whenever you create an exploded state of an assembly, you must revert to the collapsed state. On saving the assembly in the exploded state, whenever you generate the drawing views of the assembly, it will generate views with the exploded state.

2. Right-click on **Bench Vice Configuration(s)** in the **ConfigurationManager** and choose **Collapse** to unexplode the assembly.

3. Save the assembly.

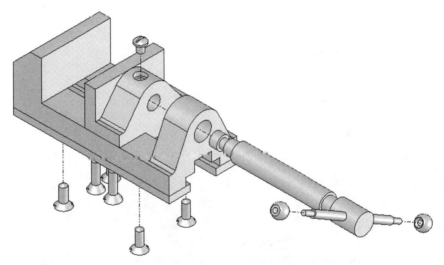

Figure 14-52 Exploded view of the assembly with explode lines

Starting a New Drawing Document From the Assembly Document

As mentioned earlier, you can also start a drawing document from the assembly document.

1. Choose **New > Make Drawing from Part/Assembly** from the Menu Bar; the **Sheet Format/Size** dialog box is displayed.

2. Select the **A4 - Landscape** sheet and choose the **OK** button. Right-click on **Sheet Format1** and choose **Properties** from the shortcut menu. Set the current projection type to third angle using the **Sheet Properties** dialog box.

Generating the Top View

1. Invoke the **Model View** tool and double-click on **Bench Vice** in the **Part/Assembly to Insert** rollout.

2. Select the **Top** button from the **Standard views** area in the **Orientation** rollout of the **Model View PropertyManager**.

3. Select the **Use custom scale** radio button from the **Scale** rollout.

4. Set the value of the scale factor to **1:2** and then select the **Preview** check box from the **Orientation** rollout; the preview of the top view of the assembly is displayed.

5. Make sure that the **Auto-start projected view** check box is cleared in the **Options** rollout.

6. Place the view close to the top left corner of the drawing sheet, refer to Figure 14-53. Click anywhere on the sheet to exit the **PropertyManager**.

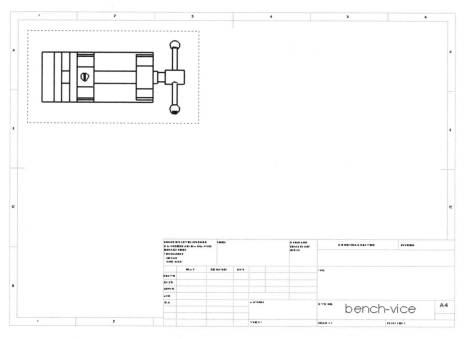

*Figure 14-53 Top view generated using the **Model View** tool*

Creating the Sectioned Front View

Next, you need to generate the sectioned front view that is derived from the top view.

1. Activate the top view and choose the **Section View** button from the **View Layout CommandManager**; the **Section View PropertyManager** is displayed and you are prompted to sketch a line in order to continue viewing the creation. The cursor will be replaced by the line cursor.

2. Draw a horizontal line such that it passes through the center of the Bench Vice assembly.

    On specifying the endpoint of the line, the **Section View** dialog box is displayed. This dialog box is used to exclude the components from the section cut.

3. Click on the + sign located on the left of the **Drawing View1** to display the name of the assembly. Next, expand the assembly.

4. Select Screw Bar, Bar Globes, Jaw Screw, Oval Fillister, Set Screw1, and Set Screw2. Next, click on the **Section View** dialog box in the drawing area to activate it. Select one of the components displayed in the **Exclude components/rib features** selection box and then select the **Don't cut all instances** check box. Similarly, one by one select all components from this selection box individually and then select the **Don't cut all instances** check box.

5. Next, select the **Auto hatching** check box and choose the **OK** button from the **Section View** dialog box; the preview of the section view is displayed in the drawing sheet as you move the cursor up and down.

6. If the direction of viewing of the section view is not as required, flip the direction by selecting the **Flip direction** check box from the **Section Line** rollout.

7. Place the section view below the top view. Click anywhere on the sheet to exit the **PropertyManager**.

8. Modify the hatch scale for the components. Figure 14-54 shows the section view generated using the **Section View** tool, after modifying the hatch scale.

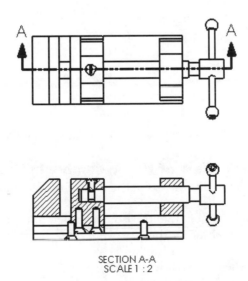

SECTION A-A
SCALE 1 : 2

*Figure 14-54 Section view generated using the **Section View** tool*

Generating the Right Side View

The next view that you need to generate is the right side view derived from the sectioned front view and it will be generated using the **Projected View** tool.

1. Select the sectioned front view and invoke the **Projected View** tool; the **Projected View PropertyManager** is displayed and a projected view is attached to the cursor.

2. Move the cursor to the right of the sectioned front view and place the view on the right of the sectioned front view.

3. Choose **OK** from the **Drawing View PropertyManager**. The sheet, after generating the projected view, is shown in Figure 14-55.

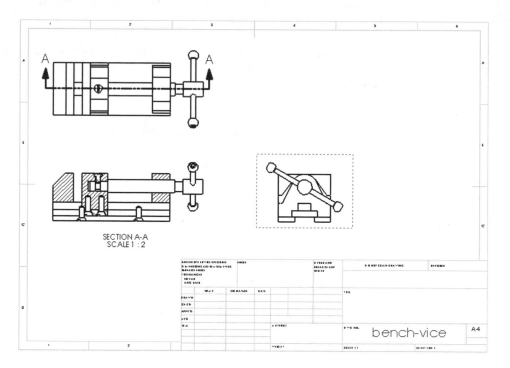

Figure 14-55 Right side view generated using the **Projected View** tool

Creating the Isometric View of the Assembly in the Exploded State

The last view to be generated is the isometric view of the assembly in the exploded state.

1. Use the **Model View** tool to generate the isometric view and place it close to the upper right corner of the drawing sheet.

2. Set the scale factor of the drawing view to **1:2**.

3. Right-click on the view to invoke the shortcut menu. Choose the **Properties** option from the shortcut menu; the **Drawing View Properties** dialog box is displayed.

4. Select the **Show in exploded state** check box in the **View Properties** tab of the **Drawing View Properties** dialog box and choose the **OK** button.

5. Move the views to place all of them in the drawing sheet. Figure 14-56 shows the final drawing sheet after generating all the drawing views.

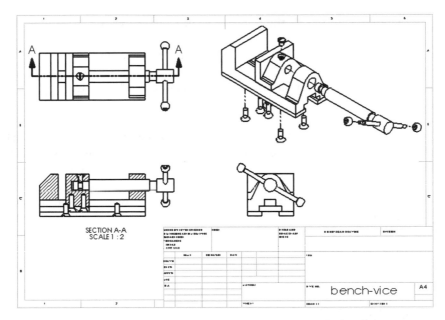

Figure 14-56 Drawing sheet after generating all the views

Saving the Drawing

Next, you need to save the drawing document.

1. Choose the **Save** button from the Menu Bar and save the drawing document with the name and location given below:

    \My Documents\SolidWorks\c14*c14tut2.slddrw*

2. Close the drawing and assembly documents.

SELF-EVALUATION TEST

Answer the following questions and then compare them to those given at the end of this chapter:

1. The **Standard sheet size** radio button is selected by default in the **Sheet Format/Size** dialog box. (T/F)

2. If you want to use the empty sheet without any margin lines or a title block, then select the **Display sheet format** check box in the **Sheet Format/Size** dialog box. (T/F)

3. The **Relative View** tool is used to generate an orthographic view by defining its orientation using reference planes or planar faces of the model. (T/F)

4. An auxiliary view is a drawing view that is generated by projecting the lines normal to a specified edge of an existing view. (T/F)

5. You cannot change the style of the break lines in a broken view. (T/F)

6. In technical terms, creating a 2D drawing in the drawing document is known as _____.

7. To start a new drawing document from the part document, choose the _____ button from the Menu Bar.

8. The _____ check box available in the **Detail View** rollout of the **Detail View PropertyManager** is used to display the complete outline of the closed profile in the detail view.

9. To change the scale of the drawing views, first select the drawing view and then select the _____ radio button from the **Scale** rollout.

10. To rotate a drawing view, select the view and choose the _____ button from the **Heads-up View** toolbar.

REVIEW QUESTIONS

Answer the following questions:

1. Choose the _____ button from the **View Layout CommandManager** to create an alternate position view.

2. The _____ dialog box is used to modify the hatch pattern of a section view.

3. The _____ check box needs to be cleared to modify the scale of the hatch pattern.

4. A _____ view is a section view in which only the sectioned surface is displayed in the section view.

5. The _____ dialog box is displayed to confirm the deletion of the views.

6. Select a view and invoke the _____ tool in the **Heads-up View** toolbar to manipulate the drawing view.

7. The views that are generated from a view already placed in the drawing sheet are known as the

    (a) Child views   (b) Derived views
    (c) Predefined views   (d) Empty views

8. In which shape is the detail view boundary displayed, by default?

    (a) Circle   (b) Ellipse
    (c) Rectangle   (d) None

9. Which of the following edit boxes is used to specify the name of the auxiliary view?

    (a) **Label**   (b) **Arrow**
    (c) **Name**   (d) **Detail view label**

10. Which of the following rollout is used to select the view orientation in the **Named View PropertyManager**?

    (a) **Orientation**   (b) **Define View**
    (c) **Specify View**   (d) **Scale View**

EXERCISE

Exercise 1

In this exercise, you will generate the front view, section right view, isometric view, and the alternate position view on the isometric view of Exercise 1 of Chapter 11. You need to scale the parent view to the scale factor of **1:3**. The views that you need to generate are shown in Figure 14-57. **(Expected time: 30 min)**

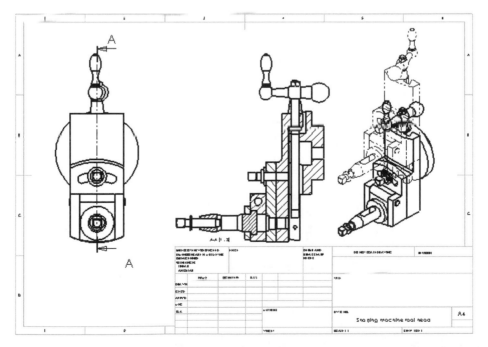

Figure 14-57 Views of Exercise 1

Answers to Self-Evaluation Test

1. T, **2.** T, **3.** T, **4.** T, **5.** F, **6.** Interactive drafting, **7. Make Drawing from Model/Assembly**, **8. Full outline**, **9. Use custom scale**, **10. Rotate View**

Chapter 15

Working with Drawing Views-II

Learning Objectives

After completing this chapter, you will be able to:
- *Add annotations to the drawing views.*
- *Add reference dimensions.*
- *Add notes to the drawing views.*
- *Add surface finish symbols to the drawing views.*
- *Add datum feature symbols to the drawing views.*
- *Add geometric tolerance to the drawing views.*
- *Add datum target symbols to the drawing views.*
- *Add center marks and centerlines to the drawing views.*
- *Add hole callouts to the drawing views.*
- *Add cosmetic threads to the drawing views.*
- *Add multi-jog leader to the drawing views.*
- *Add dowel pin symbol to the drawing views.*
- *Edit annotations.*
- *Add Bill of Material (BOM) to the drawing sheet.*
- *Add balloons to the assembly.*
- *Add new sheets in the drawing document.*
- *Edit the sheet format.*
- *Create a user-defined sheet format.*

ADDING ANNOTATIONS TO THE DRAWING VIEWS

After generating the drawing views, you need to generate the dimensions and add annotations such as notes, surface finish symbols, geometric tolerance, and so on to them. Two types of annotations can be displayed in the drawing views. The first type of annotations are the generative annotations that are added while creating the part in the **Part** mode. For example, the dimensions that you add to the sketch and features of the part are generating annotations. The second type of annotations are added manually to the geometry of drawing views such as reference dimensions, notes, surface finish symbols, and so on. Both these types of annotations are discussed next.

Generating Annotations Using the Model Items Tool

CommandManager:	Annotation > Model Items
SolidWorks menus:	Insert > Model Items
Toolbar:	Annotation > Model Items

 The **Model Items** tool is used to generate the annotations that were added while creating the model in the **Part** mode. To invoke this tool, choose the **Model Items** button from the **Annotation CommandManager**; the **Model Items PropertyManager** will be displayed, as shown in Figure 15-1. The options in this **PropertyManager** are discussed next.

Source/Destination Rollout

The **Source** drop-down list in the **Source/Destination** rollout defines the options from where the annotations are imported. The options in this drop-down list are discussed next.

Entire model

When a feature of a model is selected from the **FeatureManager design tree** in the **Drawing** mode, the **Entire model** option is selected to import the annotations from the entire model. In case of assemblies, the annotations from the entire assembly are imported, even if a single component of the assembly is selected.

Selected component

The **Selected component** option is available only when you generate the drawing views of an assembly. This option is selected to import annotations only from the selected component.

*Figure 15-1 Partial view of the **Model Items PropertyManager***

Selected feature

The **Selected feature** option is selected to import the annotations only from the selected feature or features.

Only Assembly

The **Only Assembly** option is also available only when you generate the drawing views of an assembly. This option is selected to import the annotations that are applied to the assembly in the **Assembly** mode such as the offset distance and so on.

Import items into all views

This check box is selected to import the dimensions to all the drawing views available on the sheet. This check box is selected by default. If this check box is cleared, the **Destination view(s)** selection box will be displayed in this rollout. Use this selection box to select the drawing views in which the dimensions will be placed.

Dimensions Rollout

This rollout is used to select the type of dimensions, pattern annotations, and the hole annotations that you need to generate in the drawing views. You can choose the button of the required annotation type. You can also select all buttons in this rollout. The **Eliminate duplicates** check box is selected to remove duplicate instances of annotations.

Annotations Rollout

The **Annotations** rollout is used to select the annotations that are to be generated in the drawing views. Use the buttons in this rollout to generate the cosmetic threads, datums, datum targets, dimensions, geometric tolerances, notes, surface finish, and weld symbols. You can also select the **Select all** check box to select all options.

Reference Geometry Rollout

The **Reference Geometry** rollout is used to generate the reference geometries that were used for creating the part. You can generate axes, curves, planes, surfaces, and so on through this rollout. Choose a button to specify the type of reference geometry that you need to generate in the drawing views. You can also select the **Select all** check box to select all buttons.

Options Rollout

The options in this rollout are discussed next.

Include items from hidden features

The **Include items from hidden features** check box is selected to display the annotation that belongs to a hidden feature of the model. By default, this check box is cleared. It is recommended to keep this check box cleared as it helps in eliminating the display of the unwanted annotations.

Use dimension placement in sketch

This check box is selected to place the dimension at the exact location where it was placed in the sketch while creating the part.

Layer Rollout

This rollout allows you to select the layers in which the dimensions will be placed.

After setting all the parameters in the **Model Items PropertyManager**, choose the **OK** button to display the annotations.

Tip. *You can toggle the display of annotations when the* ***Model Items*** ***PropertyManager*** *is displayed by right-clicking on the annotation.*

The annotations mostly overlap each other when they are generated. Therefore, you may need to move the annotations after generating them. To move an annotation, move the cursor on the annotation; the annotation will be highlighted in red. Press and hold the left mouse button and drag the cursor to place the annotation at the desired location. Release the left mouse button when the cursor is placed at the desired location.

The dimensions generated, while generating the annotations, are the same as the one used to create the model. These dimensions are linked to the model because of the bidirectional associativity in SolidWorks.

Double-click on the dimension to modify it; the ***Modify*** *dialog box will be displayed. Modify the value of the dimension in this dialog box and rebuild the drawing views using the* ***Rebuild*** *button; the dimension will be changed in the drawing as well as in the original model. If the model is used in an assembly, the changes will also be reflected in the assembly.*

Adding Reference Annotations

In SolidWorks, you can add reference annotations in the drawing views. These include reference dimensions, notes, surface finish symbols, datum feature symbols, geometric tolerance, and so on. The method of adding reference annotations is discussed next.

Adding Reference Dimensions

CommandManager:	Annotation > Smart Dimension
SolidWorks menus:	Tools > Dimensions > Smart
Toolbar:	Annotations > Smart Dimension

 You can use the **Smart Dimension** tool to add reference dimensions to the drawing views in the **Drawing** mode of SolidWorks.

On invoking the **Smart Dimension** tool, the **Dimension PropertyManager** will be displayed, as shown in Figure 15-2. By default, the **Smart dimensioning** button is chosen in the **Dimension Assist Tools** rollout of this **PropertyManager**. So, you can create dimensions in the drawing views as discussed in the earlier chapters.

If you choose the **DimXpert** button in the **Dimension Assist Tools** rollout, the **Dimension PropertyManager** will be modified, as shown in Figure 15-3. Specify the datum by selecting an option in the **Datum** rollout. Next, specify the dimensioning scheme and dimensioning pattern scheme in the corresponding rollouts. Then, select an entity to create dimension. Choose **OK** to exit the **PropertyManager**.

You can also create the dimensions automatically. To do so, choose the **Autodimension** tab in the **Dimension PropertyManager**, specify the parameters, and choose **OK.**

Figure 15-2 The *Dimension PropertyManager*

Figure 15-3 The *Dimension PropertyManager displayed on choosing the DimXpert button*

Adding Chamfer Dimensions

CommandManager:	Annotation > Smart Dimension > Chamfer Dimension
SolidWorks menus:	Tools > Dimensions > Chamfer
Toolbar:	Annotations > Smart Dimension > Chamfer Dimension

The **Chamfer Dimension** tool is used to add the dimension to the chamfers in the drawing view. To add a chamfer dimension, choose **Smart Dimension** > **Chamfer Dimension** from the **Annotation CommandManager**; the cursor will be replaced by the chamfer dimension cursor. Now, select the inclined chamfered edge and then select a horizontal or a vertical edge; the chamfer dimension will be attached to the cursor. Select a point on the sheet to place the dimension. Figure 15-4 shows a chamfer dimension added using the **Chamfer Dimension** tool.

Figure 15-4 *Chamfer dimension added using the* **Chamfer Dimension** *tool*

Adding Notes to the Drawing Views

CommandManager: Annotation > Note
SolidWorks menus: Insert > Annotations > Note
Toolbar: Annotation > Note

 In SolidWorks, you can add notes to the drawing views in the **Drawing** mode. To do so, choose the **Note** button from the **Annotation CommandManager**; the **Note PropertyManager** will be displayed, as shown in Figure 15-5.

On invoking the **Note PropertyManager**, a shape defined using the **Style** drop-down list in the **Border** rollout will be attached to the cursor. If you move the cursor close to an edge in the drawing view, a leader will be displayed with a text box. This is because the **Auto Leader** button is chosen in the **Leader** rollout. You can also place a multi-jog leader line. After selecting an edge, place the endpoint of the leader at the desired location; the **Formatting** toolbar and the **Text** edit box will be displayed in the drawing area. Enter the text in the edit box. Next, choose **OK** from the **Note PropertyManager**. The rollouts in the **Note PropertyManager** are discussed next.

Style Rollout

You can save a note as a favorite using the options in the **Style** rollout. The options available in this rollout are the same as those discussed in Chapter 4.

Text Format Rollout

The **Text Format** rollout is used to set the format of the text such as font, size, justification, and rotation of the text. You can also add symbols and hyperlinks to the text using the options available in this rollout.

Leader Rollout

The options in the **Leader** rollout are used to define the style of arrows and leaders that are displayed in the notes.

Figure 15-5 *Partial view of the* **Note** *PropertyManager*

Leader Style Rollout

The options in this rollout are used to define the style and thickness of the leader. By default, the **Use document display** check box is selected. So, the leader will be displayed with the default style and thickness. On clearing this check box, the **Leader Style** and **Leader Thickness** drop-down lists will be enabled. Using these drop-down lists, you can specify different styles and thickness for the leader.

Border Rollout

The options in the **Border** rollout are used to define the border in which the note text will be displayed. You can assign various types of borders from the **Style** drop-down list.

The **Size** drop-down list available in this rollout is used to define the size of the border in which the text will be placed.

Parameters Rollout

The **Parameters** rollout is used to specify the X and Y coordinate values of the note center.

Adding Surface Finish Symbols to the Drawing Views

CommandManager:	Annotation > Surface Finish
SolidWorks menus:	Insert > Annotations > Surface Finish Symbol
Toolbar:	Annotation > Surface Finish

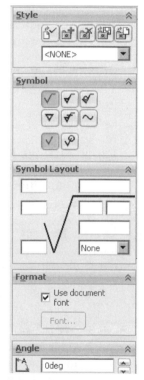

You can add the surface finish symbols to the edges or the faces in the drawing views using the **Surface Finish** tool. To do so, choose the **Surface Finish** button from the **Annotation CommandManager**; the **Surface Finish PropertyManager** will be displayed, as shown in Figure 15-6. When you invoke this tool, a surface finish symbol is attached to the cursor. The rollouts in the **Surface Finish PropertyManager** dialog box are discussed next.

Style Rollout

The options in this rollout are the same as those discussed in Chapter 4. You can use the options in the **Style** rollout to save a surface finish as a favorite.

Symbol Rollout

The **Symbol** rollout is used to define the type of surface finish symbol that you need to add to the drawing views. There are many types of surface finish symbols such as **Basic, Machining Required, Machining Prohibited, JIS Basic, JIS Machining Required, JIS Machining Prohibited**, and so on.

Symbol Layout Rollout

The options in the **Symbol Layout** rollout are used to define the parameters of the surface finish symbol.

Format Rollout

The options in the **Format** rollout are used to define the font size and the orientation of the surface finish symbol.

*Figure 15-6 Partial view of the **Surface Finish** PropertyManager*

Angle Rollout

The options in the **Angle** rollout are used to define the angle of the surface finish symbol. You can enter the angle value in the spinner provided in this rollout or choose the buttons available below the spinner.

The other options in the **Surface Finish PropertyManager** are the same as those discussed while adding notes.

Adding a Datum Feature Symbol to the Drawing Views

CommandManager: Annotation > Datum Feature
SolidWorks menus: Insert > Annotations > Datum Feature Symbol
Toolbar: Annotation > Datum Feature

The **Datum Feature** tool is used to add a datum feature symbol to an entity in the drawing view. The datum feature symbols are used as datum references while adding the geometric tolerances in the drawing view. To add the datum feature symbol, choose the **Datum Feature** button from the **Annotation CommandManager**; the **Datum Feature PropertyManager** will be displayed, as shown in Figure 15-7. Also, a datum feature symbol with the default parameters will be attached to the cursor. The options in the **Datum Feature PropertyManager** are discussed next.

*Figure 15-7 The **Datum Feature PropertyManager***

Style Rollout
The options in this rollout are the same as those discussed in Chapter 4. You can use the options in the **Style** rollout to save a datum feature symbol as a favorite.

Label Settings Rollout
The **Label Settings** rollout is used to define the label to be used in the datum feature symbol. You can use alphabets or numeric characters as labels.

Leader Rollout
The **Use document style** check box is selected in this rollout to use the datum feature style that is defined in the document to display the datum feature symbol.

Square
If you clear the **Use document style** check box, the **Square** button is enabled below it. This button is used to place the text of the datum feature inside a square. By default, the text of the datum feature is placed using this option. By using the buttons available below the **Square** button, you can set the type of datum feature such as filled triangle, filled triangle with shoulder, empty triangle, and empty triangle with shoulder.

Round (GB)
The **Round (GB)** button is also enabled below the **Use document style** check box when you clear it. This button is used to place the text of the datum feature inside a circle. To do so, you first need to clear the **Use document style** check box and then choose the **Round (GB)** button. On choosing this button, additional buttons will be displayed below the **Round (GB)** button. These buttons are used to set the style of the datum feature.

Text Rollout

This rollout is used to enter text or insert symbols along with the datum feature. To do so, left-click in the **Text** edit box to enter the text. To add symbols, choose the **More** button located in the lower part of this rollout; the **Symbol** dialog box will be displayed. Select the required symbol from this dialog box and choose **OK**; the preview of the selected symbol will also be attached with the preview of datum feature.

Leader/Frame Style Rollout

The **Leader/Frame Style** rollout is used to specify the style and thickness of the leader/frame using the **Leader/Frame Style** and **Leader/Frame Thickness** drop-down lists, respectively.

After defining all parameters of the datum feature symbol, specify a point on an existing entity in the drawing sheet. Next, move the cursor to define the length and the placement of the datum feature symbol. As soon as you place one datum feature symbol, another datum feature symbol will be attached to the cursor. Therefore, you can place as many datum feature symbols as you want using the **Datum Feature PropertyManager**. As you place the multiple datum feature symbols, the sequence of the names of the datum feature symbols automatically follows the order based on the labels.

Adding a Geometric Tolerance to the Drawing Views

CommandManager:	Annotation > Geometric Tolerance
SolidWorks menus:	Insert > Annotations > Geometric Tolerance
Toolbar:	Annotations > Geometric Tolerance

In a shop floor drawing, you need to provide various other parameters along with the dimensions and dimensional tolerance. These parameters can be geometric condition, surface profile, material condition, and so on. All these parameters are defined using the **Geometric Tolerance** tool. To add the geometric tolerance to the drawing views, choose the **Geometric Tolerance** button from the **Annotation CommandManager**; the **Properties** dialog box will be displayed, as shown in Figure 15-8. Also, a geometric tolerance will be attached to the cursor.

Both the rows in this dialog box are separate frames. You can add additional frames using the **Frames** spinner provided on the right of the **Tertiary** edit box. The parameters that can be added to these frames are geometric condition symbols, diameter symbol, value of tolerance, material condition, and datum references. The options in the **Properties** dialog box are used to add the geometric tolerance to the drawing views and are discussed next.

Symbol

The **Symbol** drop-down list is used to define the geometric condition symbol. When you choose the down arrow button on the right of this drop-down list, the **Symbols** flyout will be displayed, as shown in Figure 15-9. This flyout is used to define the geometric condition symbols in the geometric tolerance. You can select the standard of the geometric condition symbol from this flyout. As soon as you select a symbol, the flyout will be closed and the selected symbol will be displayed in the **Symbol** edit box. Also, the preview of the geometric tolerance will be displayed in the preview area.

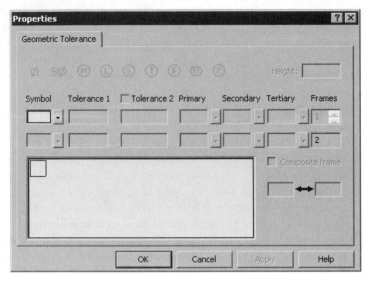

*Figure 15-8 The **Properties** dialog box used to apply the geometric tolerance*

*Figure 15-9 The **Symbols** flyout used to define the geometric condition symbols*

Tolerance 1

The **Tolerance 1** edit box is used to specify the tolerance value with respect to the geometric condition defined using the **Symbols** flyout. You can use the buttons available above the rows of frames to add the symbols such as diameter, spherical diameter, material conditions, and so on.

Tolerance 2

The use of the **Tolerance 2** edit box is the same as that of **Tolerance 1** edit box. This edit box is used to define the second geometric tolerance, if required.

Primary

The **Primary** edit box is used to specify the characters to define the datum reference added to the entities in the drawing view using the **Datum Feature Symbol** tool.

Similarly, you can define the secondary datum reference and the tertiary datum reference.

Frames

The **Frames** spinner is used to increase the number of frames for applying more complex geometric tolerances.

Projected tolerance

The **Projected tolerance** button is the last button available above the frame rows. This button is chosen to define the height of the projected tolerance. When you choose this button, the **Height** edit box will be enabled and you can specify the projected tolerance zone height in this edit box.

Composite frame

The **Composite frame** check box is selected to use a composite frame to add the tolerance. When you select this check box, the tolerance frame is converted into a composite frame and the preview will be modified accordingly.

Between two points

The **Between two points** edit boxes are used to apply a geometric tolerance between two points or entities. To do so, specify the reference in the edit boxes provided in the **Between two points** area.

Figure 15-10 shows a drawing after adding annotations to some of the entities in the drawing view.

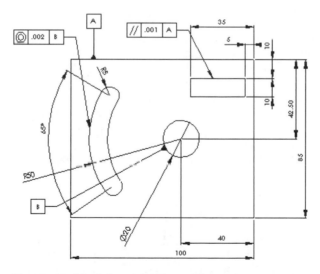

Figure 15-10 *A drawing after adding some annotations*

Adding Datum Target Symbols to the Drawing Views

CommandManager:	Annotation > Datum Target
SolidWorks menus:	Insert > Annotations > Datum Target
Toolbar:	Annotation > Datum Target

The **Datum Target** tool is used to add the datum targets to the entities in the drawing view. To add the datum targets, choose the **Datum Target** button from the **Annotation CommandManager**; the cursor will be replaced by the datum target cursor and the **Datum Target PropertyManager** will be displayed, as shown in Figure 15-11. Select a model face, edge, or a line from the view on which you need to add the datum target and then place the datum target.

The **Datum Target PropertyManager** is used to define the properties of the datum target symbol. Set the parameters of the datum target symbol in the **Settings** rollout of this **PropertyManager**. You can set the target shape as a point, circle, or a rectangle. You can also define the diameter of the target area, if the shapes of the target are selected as a point and a circle. If the shape of the selected target is a rectangle, you need to define its width and height. You can specify the datum references to the datum target symbol by using the **First Reference**, **Second Reference**, and **Third Reference** edit boxes. Figure 15-12 shows the datum target symbols added to the entities in the drawing view.

Figure 15-11 The Datum Target PropertyManager

Adding Center Marks to the Drawing Views

CommandManager:	Annotation > Center Mark
SolidWorks menus:	Insert > Annotations > Center Mark
Toolbar:	Annotations > Center Mark

The **Center Mark** tool is used to add center marks to the circular entities. As discussed earlier, center marks are generated automatically when you generate the dimensions for the model. But if the center marks are not generated while generating the drawing view, or if you have sketched a view, you can use this tool to add the center marks to the drawing views. To add the center marks to the drawing views, choose the **Center Mark**

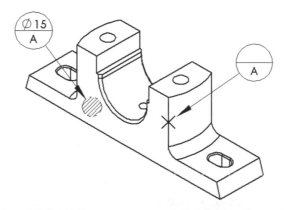

Figure 15-12 Datum target symbols added to the model

button from the **Annotation CommandManager**; the **Center Mark PropertyManager** will be displayed, as shown in Figure 15-13. Also, the cursor will be replaced by the center mark cursor and you will be prompted to select a circular edge or an arc for the center mark insertion.

By default, the **Single Center Mark** button is chosen in the **Options** rollout of the **Center Mark PropertyManager**. Select the circular edge or the arc to add the center mark, as shown in Figure 15-14. On selecting an arc, representing a hole that is part of a linear or a circular pattern, the **Propagate** button will be displayed near the center mark. If you choose this button, the center marks will be added to all the remaining instances of the pattern.

The center marks in rectangular and circular patterns can also be applied using the **Linear Center Mark** and **Circular Center Mark** buttons, respectively. You can add the center marks in the lincar pattern format by using the **Linear Center Mark** button from the **Options** rollout. The center marks will be connected using the centerlines, as shown in Figure 15-15 because the **Connection lines** check box is selected by default.

You can create the center mark in the circular pattern format by using the **Circular Center Mark** button. When you choose this button, the **Circular lines**, **Radial lines**, and **Base center mark** check boxes will be displayed. The **Circular lines** check box is used to create a circular line passing through the centers of the circles arranged in a circular pattern. The **Radial lines** check box is used to display the radial lines from the center of the pattern to

Figure 15-13 The Center Mark PropertyManager

the center of each instance. The **Base center mark** check box is used to display the center mark at the center of the base circle of the pattern. Figure 15-16 shows the center mark created with the **Base center mark** check box cleared. Figure 15-17 shows the center mark created with the **Base center mark** check box selected. Figure 15-18 shows the center mark created with the **Radial lines** check box selected. Observe that in all these figures, the **Circular lines** check box is selected.

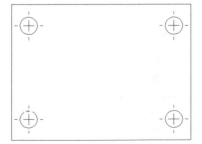

Figure 15-14 Center marks added using the Single Center Mark option

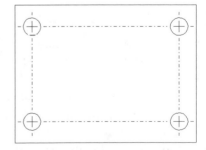

Figure 15-15 Center marks added using the Linear Center Mark option

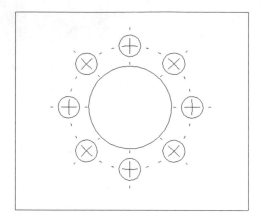

Figure 15-16 *Center marks created with the* **Base center mark** *check box cleared*

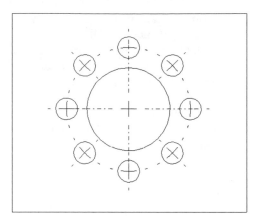

Figure 15-17 *Center marks created with the* **Base center mark** *check box selected*

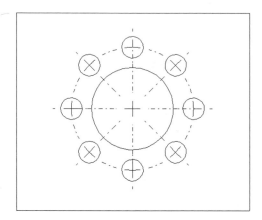

Figure 15-18 *Center marks created with the* **Radial lines** *check box selected*

The **Display Attributes** rollout available in the **Center Mark PropertyManager** is used to define the size of the center mark and the extended lines. The **Angle** rollout is used to rotate the center mark at an angle.

Adding Centerlines to the Drawing Views

CommandManager:	Annotation > Centerline
SolidWorks menus:	Insert > Annotations > Centerline
Toolbar:	Annotations > Centerline

The **Centerline** tool is used to add the centerlines to the views by selecting two edges/sketch segments or a single cylindrical/conical face. To add a centerline, choose the **Centerline** button from the **Annotation CommandManager**; the **Centerline PropertyManager** will be invoked and it will prompt you to select two edges/sketch segments or a single cylindrical/conical face. Select the entity or entities from the view to add the centerline. Figure 15-19 shows the centerlines added to the drawing views by selecting the surface of the cylinder.

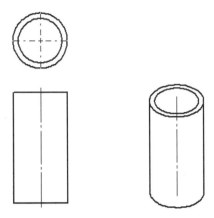

Figure 15-19 *Centerlines added to the front and isometric views using the Centerline tool*

Tip. *To display the hidden lines in a drawing view, select a view, and choose* *Display Style > Hidden Lines Visible from the Heads-up View toolbar.*

You can also set the option for the automatic creation of a centerline while generating the drawing views. To do so, choose Options from the Menu Bar to invoke the System Options - General dialog box and choose the Document Properties tab. Next, select the Centerlines check box from the Auto insert on view creation area and choose OK to close the dialog box.

You can also right-click on a view and choose Annotations > Center Mark/ Centerline to add the centerlines.

Adding a Hole Callout to the Drawing Views

CommandManager:	Annotation > Hole Callout
SolidWorks menus:	Insert > Annotations > Hole Callout
Toolbar:	Annotation > Hole Callout

The **Hole Callout** tool is used to generate the hole callouts for the holes that are created in the **Part** mode using the **Simple Hole** tool, the **Hole Wizard** tool, or the **Extruded Cut** tool. To generate a hole callout, choose the **Hole Callout** button from the **Annotation CommandManager**; the cursor will be replaced by the hole callout cursor. Select the hole from the drawing views; the hole callout will be attached to the cursor. Pick a point on the drawing sheet to place the hole callout; the **Dimension PropertyManager** will be displayed when you place the hole callout. Exit this **PropertyManager**. Figure 15-20 shows a drawing view with the hole callouts generated using the **Hole Callout** tool.

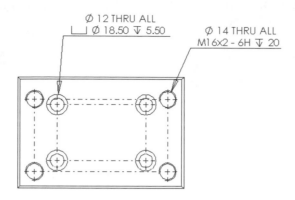

Figure 15-20 *Hole callouts generated using the*
Hole Callout *tool*

Adding Cosmetic Threads to the Drawing Views

CommandManager:	Annotation > Cosmetic Thread *(Customize to add)*
SolidWorks menus:	Insert > Annotations > Cosmetic Thread
Toolbar:	Annotation > Cosmetic Thread *(Customize to add)*

The **Cosmetic Thread** tool is used to add the cosmetic threads that will display the thread conventions in the drawing views. To do so, select the circular edge from the drawing view on which you need to apply the cosmetic thread. Now, choose the **Cosmetic Thread** button from the **Annotation CommandManager**; the **Cosmetic Thread PropertyManager** will be displayed, as shown in Figure 15-21.

The rollouts in the **Cosmetic Thread PropertyManager** are discussed next.

Thread Settings Rollout
The options in the **Thread Settings** rollout are used to define various parameters of the cosmetic thread. On invoking the **Cosmetic Thread** tool, you will be prompted to select the edges for the threads and set the parameters. Select the required circular edges on which you need to add a cosmetic thread; the name of the selected edge will be displayed in the **Circular Edges** selection area. Specify the end condition and set the minor diameter of the thread. It will be displayed in both the current view and in the projected view. Note that the thread will be displayed in the projected view only if the hidden lines are displayed in that view.

Thread Callout Rollout
The edit box in this rollout is used to specify the text to be used in the thread callout for the cosmetic thread.

After setting all the parameters, choose the **OK** button from the **Cosmetic Thread PropertyManager**. When you add a cosmetic thread to a generated drawing view, the thread convention will be displayed in all the drawing views. Figure 15-22 shows the cosmetic thread added to the drawing views.

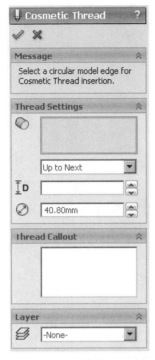

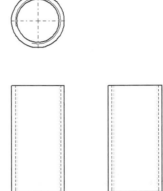

Figure 15-21 The Cosmetic Thread PropertyManager

Figure 15-22 Cosmetic threads added to the drawing views

Note
*The thread conventions added in the drawing views can be deleted only from the part document. You cannot delete the thread conventions from the drawing document. To delete the thread convention in the part document, expand the **Hole** or **Cut** feature in the **FeatureManager design tree**. Now, select the thread convention and delete it.*

Tip. *If you add the cosmetic threads to the drawing views, you can also view them in the part document because of the bidirectional associativity. You can use any display mode to view the cosmetic threads in the model.*

Adding the Multi-jog Leader to the Drawing Views

CommandManager:	Annotation > Multi-jog Leader (*Customize to add*)
SolidWorks menus:	Insert > Annotations > Multi-jog Leader
Toolbar:	Annotation > Multi-jog Leader (*Customize to add*)

You can add a multi-jog leader line to the drawing views by using the **Multi-jog Leader** tool. A multi-jog leader is a leader in which you can add multiple jog lines with arrowheads at both the ends. To add a multi-jog leader line, choose the **Multi-jog Leader** button from the **Annotation CommandManager**; the cursor will be replaced by the multi-jog line cursor. Select a point on the sheet or on an entity from where you need to start the leader. Now, specify the points on the drawing sheet to mark the location of the jogs and then select the second entity where the end of the leader will be placed; a multi-jog leader will be created. You can also double-click anywhere on the sheet to specify the second end of the multi-jog leader. Figure 15-23 shows a multi-jog leader added to the drawing view. Note that in this figure, the text is written separately.

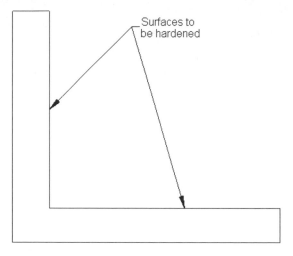

Surfaces to
be hardened

Figure 15-23 Multi-jog leader added to the drawing view

Adding the Dowel Pin Symbols to the Drawing Views

CommandManager:	Annotation > Dowel Pin Symbol (*Customize to add*)
SolidWorks menus:	Insert > Annotations > Dowel Pin Symbol
Toolbar:	Annotation > Dowel Pin Symbol (*Customize to add*)

 The **Dowel Pin Symbol** tool is used to add the dowel pin symbol to the holes in the drawing views. It is also used to confirm the size of the selected hole. To create a dowel pin symbol, select a hole or a circular edge from the drawing view and choose the **Dowel Pin Symbol** button from the **Annotation CommandManager**; the dowel pin symbol will be created and the **Dowel Pin Symbol PropertyManager** will be displayed. You can flip the direction of the dowel pin symbol by using the **Flip symbol** check box in the **Display Attributes** rollout.

EDITING ANNOTATIONS

You can edit the annotations added to the drawing views by selecting them or by double-clicking on them. As a result, their respective **PropertyManagers** or dialog boxes will be displayed, in which you can edit the parameters of the selected annotation.

ADDING THE BILL OF MATERIALS (BOM) TO A DRAWING

CommandManager:	Annotation > Tables > Bill of Materials
SolidWorks menus:	Insert > Tables > Bill of Materials
Toolbar:	Annotation > Tables > Bill of Materials

The Bill of Materials (BOM) is a table that displays the list of the components used in an assembly. This table can also be used to provide information related to the number of components in an assembly, their names, quantity, and any other information required to assemble the components. Remember that the sequence of the parts in the BOM depends on the sequence in which they were inserted in the assembly document. The BOM, placed in the drawing document, is parametric. Therefore, if you add or delete a part from the assembly in the assembly document, the change will be reflected in the corresponding BOM in the drawing document.

To insert a BOM in the drawing file containing the assembly drawing views, select any one view from the drawing document and choose the **Tables > Bill of Materials** button from the **Annotation CommandManager**; the **Bill of Materials PropertyManager** will be displayed, as shown in Figure 15-24. Specify the required parameters. After setting all parameters in the **Bill of Materials PropertyManager**, choose the **OK** button; the BOM will be attached to the cursor. Specify a point on the drawing sheet to place the BOM. Next, select the BOM added to the drawing sheet; the modified **Bill of Materials PropertyManager** will be displayed, as shown in Figure 15-25. Figure 15-26 shows a BOM added to a drawing sheet. The rollouts in the modified **Bill of Materials PropertyManager** are discussed next.

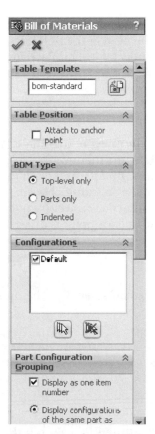

Figure 15-24 *Partial view of the* ***Bill of Materials PropertyManager***

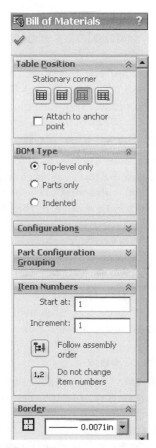

Figure 15-25 *Partial view of the modified* ***Bill of Materials PropertyManager***

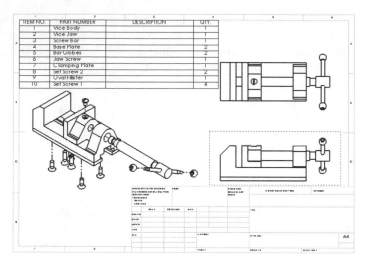

Figure 15-26 *BOM added to a drawing sheet*

Table Template Rollout

The **Table Template** rollout is used to define the template to be used in the BOM. By default, the **bom-standard** template is chosen. If you choose the **Open table template for Bill of Materials** button, the **Select BOM Template** dialog box will be displayed. You can choose any of the default templates available in SolidWorks by using this dialog box.

Table Position Rollout

You can specify the stationary position of the BOM using the buttons in the **Table Position** rollout. If the **Attach to anchor point** check box is selected in this rollout, the table will be automatically attached to the anchor point of the drawing sheet. But, if the **Attach to anchor point** check box is cleared, the table will be attached to the cursor only after choosing the **OK** button from the **Bill of Materials PropertyManager**. Next, you need to specify a point in the drawing sheet to place the table. The procedure to define the anchor point is discussed later in this chapter.

BOM Type Rollout

The **BOM Type** rollout is used to specify the different levels of an assembly. The options in this rollout are discussed next.

Top level only

The **Top level only** radio button is used to list only the parts and the subassemblies in BOM. The parts of the subassemblies are not listed in the BOM.

Parts only

If you select the **Parts only** radio button, the subassemblies will not be listed in the BOM. The components of the subassemblies will be listed as individual components in the BOM.

Indented assemblies

The **Indented assemblies** radio button is selected to list the components along with their subassemblies. The components of the subassemblies are listed as indented below their respective subassemblies, and are not listed with their respective item numbers.

Configurations Rollout

The **Configurations** rollout is used to specify the configuration for creating the BOM. By default, the **Default** configuration is selected.

Part Configuration Grouping Rollout

This rollout is used to set the grouping options for a part having more than one configuration. Selecting the **Display as one item number** check box ensures that if a component has multiple configurations, all of them will be listed in the BOM with the same item number. Selecting the **Display configurations of the same part as separate items** radio button ensures that if a component has multiple configurations, they will be listed as separate items in the BOM. Selecting the **Display all configurations of the same part as one item** radio button ensures that all configurations of a part will be listed as one item in the BOM. Similarly, selecting the **Display configurations with the same name as one item** radio button ensures that if the multiple components have configurations with the same name, they will be listed as a single item in the BOM.

Item Numbers Rollout

You can specify a numeric value from where the sequence of the components will start in a BOM. Enter this value in the **Start at** edit box of this rollout. Additionally, you can specify the increment for the numeric value in the BOM using the **Increment** edit box.

After setting all the parameters in the **Bill of Materials PropertyManager**, choose the **OK** button; a BOM will be attached to the cursor. Specify a point on the drawing sheet to place the BOM.

Setting Anchor Point for the BOM

In SolidWorks, you can also set the anchor point for the BOM. To do so, expand the **Sheet Format1** node in the **FeatureManager design tree**. Next, right-click on the **Bill of Materials Anchor1** option; a shortcut menu will be displayed. Choose the **Set Anchor** option from it; the drawing sheet will be displayed in the edit sheet format. If you move the cursor on any intersection, an orange colored point will be displayed. This point defines the anchor point for the BOM. Specify a position in the drawing sheet where you need to anchor the BOM; the anchor point will be specified and drawing sheet will be displayed in the normal mode.

Note that you can specify the anchor point after placing the BOM in the drawing sheet.

Tip. *In SolidWorks 2009, you can add Bill of Materials both in the Part as well as the Assembly environment. To do so, open the part or assembly files and then choose* **Insert > Tables > Bill of Materials** *from the SolidWorks menus; the Bill of Materials will be added.*

ADDING BALLOONS TO THE DRAWING VIEWS

CommandManager:	Annotation > Balloon
SolidWorks menus:	Insert > Annotations > Balloon
Toolbar:	Annotation > Balloon

After adding the BOM, you need to add the balloons to the components in the drawing views. The balloons can be added manually using the **Balloon** tool. The naming of balloons depends on the sequence of the parts in the BOM. The method of adding balloons to the components in the drawing views is discussed next.

To add the balloons to a drawing view, choose the **Balloon** button from the **Annotation CommandManager**; the **Balloon PropertyManager** will be displayed, as shown in Figure 15-27.

On invoking the **Balloon PropertyManager**, you will be prompted to select one or more locations to place the balloons. Set the properties of the balloon using the options in the **Balloon Settings** rollout. Select the components from the assembly drawing view to add the balloons. If you select the face of a component, the balloon will have a filled circle at the attachment point. However, if you select an edge of the component, the balloon will have a closed filled arrow. After adding the balloons to all components, choose the **OK** button from the **Balloon PropertyManager**. Figure 15-28 shows the drawing sheet in which the balloons have been added to the assembly drawing.

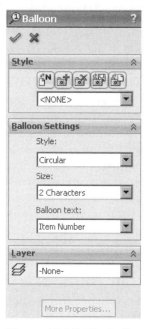

Figure 15-27 The Balloon PropertyManager

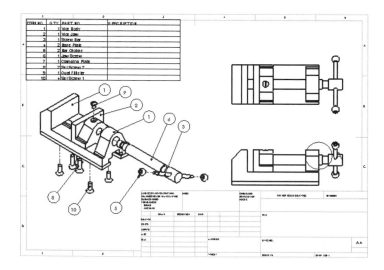

Figure 15-28 Balloons added to the assembly drawing view

Adding Balloons Using the AutoBalloon Tool

CommandManager:	Annotation > AutoBalloon
SolidWorks menus:	Insert > Annotations > Auto Balloon
Toolbar:	Annotation > AutoBalloon

The **AutoBalloon** tool is used to add the balloons automatically. To do so, select the drawing view in which you need to add the balloons and choose the **AutoBalloon** button from the **Annotation CommandManager**; the balloons will be added to the selected drawing view with the default settings and the **Auto Balloon PropertyManager** will be displayed, as shown in Figure 15-29. The rollouts in the **Auto Balloon PropertyManager** are discussed next.

Balloon Layout Rollout

The options in the **Balloon Layout** rollout are used to set the layout of the balloons when they are placed automatically. By default, the **Square** button is chosen in the **Balloon Layout** rollout, therefore the balloons are placed in a square form. You can also arrange the balloons in circular, aligned to top, aligned to bottom, aligned to left, and aligned to right forms by choosing the corresponding buttons in this rollout. The **Ignore multiple instances** check box is selected by default to eliminate the creation of multiple instances of a balloon.

Balloon Settings Rollout

The **Balloon Settings** rollout is used to set the style, size, and type of the text of balloons.

After setting all parameters, choose the **OK** button from the **Auto Balloon PropertyManager**.

Figure 15-29 Partial view of the Auto Balloon PropertyManager

ADDING NEW SHEETS TO THE DRAWING VIEWS

You can also add new sheets to a drawing document. A multisheet drawing document can be used to generate the drawing views of all the components and the drawing views of the assembly in the same document. You can switch between the two sheets easily to refer to the drawings views of the different parts of an assembly within the same document, without opening the separate drawing documents. To add a sheet to the drawing document, choose the **Add Sheet** tab above the status bar; a new sheet will be added to it. Figure 15-30 shows a drawing document with the **Add Sheet** tab chosen, and three new drawing sheets added to it. To add a sheet to the drawing document, you can also select **Sheet1** from the **FeatureManager design tree**; the shortcut menu will be invoked. Now, choose the **Add Sheet** option to add a sheet to the drawing document.

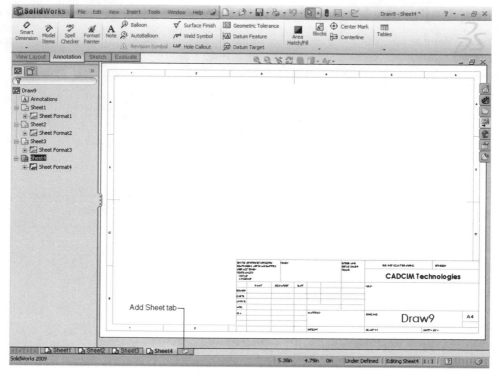

Figure 15-30 *Drawing sheets added to the drawing document*

To activate a drawing sheet, select it by choosing the corresponding tab above the status bar. To change the properties of a sheet, select it, invoke the shortcut menu, and choose the **Properties** option from it.

EDITING THE SHEET FORMAT

You can edit the standard sheet format according to your requirement. To do so, ensure that the required sheet is active. To do so, select it from the **FeatureManager design tree**. Next right-click on the sheet to invoke the shortcut menu and choose the **Edit Sheet Format** option from it. All the entities, annotations, and views will disappear from the drawing sheet. You can edit the sheet format by using the sketching tools in the **Sketch CommandManager**. After editing the sheet format, select the active sheet again and invoke the shortcut menu. Choose the **Edit Sheet** option from the shortcut menu to switch back to the edit sheet environment.

CREATING USER-DEFINED SHEET FORMATS

You can also create a user-defined sheet format in SolidWorks. To do so, when you start a new drawing document, select the **Custom sheet size** radio button from the **Sheet Format/Size** dialog box. On the basis of your design requirements, set the size of the sheet in the **Width** and **Height** edit boxes in this dialog box and choose **OK**; the new customized drawing sheet will be displayed. Select **Sheet1** from the **FeatureManager design tree** and invoke the shortcut menu. Choose the **Edit Sheet Format** option; the edit sheet format environment will be invoked. You can create or modify the sheet format by using the sketching tools in the **Sketch CommandManager**. After creating or modifying the sheet format, switch back to the edit sheet environment. Choose **File > Save Sheet Format** from the SolidWorks menus; the **Save Sheet Format** dialog box will be displayed. Browse to the location where you need to save the sheet format. Specify the name of the sheet format and choose the **Save** button from the **Save Sheet Format** dialog box.

To use the saved sheet format, start a new drawing document; the **Sheet Format/Size** dialog box will be displayed, select the **Standard sheet format** radio button, choose the **Browse** button, and browse to the location where you have saved the sheet format and open it. Figure 15-31 shows a user-defined sheet format.

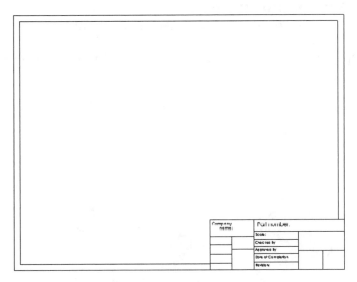

Figure 15-31 *A user-defined sheet format*

TUTORIALS

Tutorial 1

In this tutorial, first you will open the drawing created in Tutorial 2 of Chapter 14 and then generate dimensions and add annotations to it. Next, you will change the display of the front and the right view to make hidden lines visible. Finally, change the display of the isometric and aligned section views to the shaded mode. **(Expected time: 45 min)**

The following steps are required to complete this tutorial:

a. Copy the part and drawing documents from Chapter 14 to the folder of the current chapter.
b. Configure the font settings and generate the dimensions using the **Model Items** tool.
c. Arrange the dimensions and delete the unwanted dimensions, refer to Figures 15-33 and 15-34.

d. Add the datum symbol and geometric tolerance to the drawing views, refer to Figures 15-35 and 15-36.

e. Change the model display state of the drawing views, refer to Figure 15-37.

Copying the Documents in the Folder of the Current Chapter

Before proceeding further, you need to copy the model and the drawing document in the folder of the current chapter.

1. Create a folder with the name *c15* in the *SolidWorks* folder and copy *c08_tut02.sldprt* and *c14_tut01.slddrw* from the *\My Documents\SolidWorks\c14* folder to the *c15* folder.

Opening the Drawing Document

Next, you need to open the drawing document in the SolidWorks window.

1. Invoke the **Open** dialog box and open the *c14_tut01.slddrw* document from the folder of the current chapter.

The drawing document in which you need to add the dimensions is displayed in the drawing area, as shown in Figure 15-32.

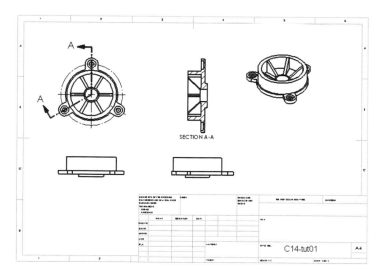

Figure 15-32 *Drawing views generated in Chapter 14*

Applying the Document Settings

Before generating the model dimensions, you need to configure the document settings. These settings will allow the dimensions and other annotations in the current sheet to be viewed properly.

1. Invoke the **Document Properties - Drafting Standard** dialog box and choose the **Annotations > Notes** from the area on the left.

2. Choose the **Font** button from the **Text** area of the dialog box; the **Choose Font** dialog box is invoked.

3. Select the **Points** radio button from the **Height** area and set the value of the font size to **9** from the list box.

4. Choose the **OK** button from the **Choose Font** dialog box. Similarly, set the font size for the **Dimension**, **Detail View**, and **Section View** options to **9**.

5. Choose the **Dimension** option from the area on the left; the related options are displayed on the right.

6. Set the values of height, width, and length of the arrows as **1**, **3**, and **6** using their respective edit boxes in the **Arrows** area.

7. Now, choose **View Labels > Section** from the left of the dialog box; the related options are displayed on the right. Set the values of height, width, and length of the section arrows as **2**, **4**, and **8** using their respective edit boxes in the **Section/View size** area.

8. Choose the **OK** button from the **Document Properties** dialog box.

Generating the Dimensions

Next, you need to generate the dimensions using the **Model Items** tool. As discussed earlier, if you do not select any view on generating the dimensions using the **Model Items** tool, all dimensions will be displayed in all views. Sometimes, the dimensions may overlap each other. Therefore, you will select the view in which you need to generate the dimension and then you will invoke the **Model Items** tool.

1. Select the top view and choose the **Model Items** button from the **Annotation CommandManager**; the **Model Items PropertyManager** is displayed and the name of the selected view is displayed in the **Source/Destination** rollout.

2. Select the **Entire model** option from the **Source** drop-down list and choose the **OK** button from the **Model Items PropertyManager**; the dimensions of the model, which can be displayed in the selected view, are generated.

   Note that the generated dimensions are scattered arbitrarily on the drawing sheet. Therefore, you need to arrange the dimensions by moving them to the required locations.

3. Select the dimensions one by one and drag them to the desired location. You can reverse the direction of arrowheads by clicking on the control point that is displayed on them.

   Any radial dimension attached to the counterbore hole in the top view needs to be deleted because you will add a hole callout to this counterbore hole later.

4. Select the radial dimension and press the DELETE key to delete the dimension. Similarly, delete the diameter dimension value 20. The drawing view after arranging the dimensions and deleting the diameter dimension is shown in Figure 15-33.

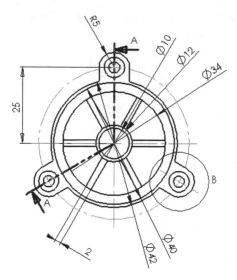

Figure 15-33 Top view after generating and arranging the dimensions

Note that if SolidWorks 2009 is configured for the ANSI system on your system, the dimension arrowheads are displayed as not filled. You need to change the arrowheads to filled.

5. Drag a window such that all the dimensions are enclosed inside it. Release the left mouse button to select all the generated dimensions; the **Dimension PropertyManager** is displayed.

6. Choose the **Leaders** tab and select the **Filled Arrow** option from the **Style** drop-down list in the **Witness/Leader Display** rollout. Choose **OK** to close the **Dimension PropertyManager**; the arrowheads are changed to the filled arrowheads.

7. Select the aligned section view and generate the dimensions using the **Model Items** tool. After placing the dimensions, move them to the appropriate places, refer to Figure 15-34. You may need to change the arrowheads to closed filled, if they are not filled already.

8. Choose the **Hole Callout** button from the **Annotation CommandManager** and select the outer circle of one of the counterbore features in the top view; the hole callout is attached to the cursor. Pick a point on the drawing sheet to place the hole callout.

Adding the Datum Feature Symbol to the Drawing View

After generating the dimensions, you need to add the datum feature symbol to the drawing view. The datum feature symbols are used as the datum reference for adding the geometric tolerance to the drawing views.

1. Select the edge of the outer cylindrical feature from the top view and then choose the

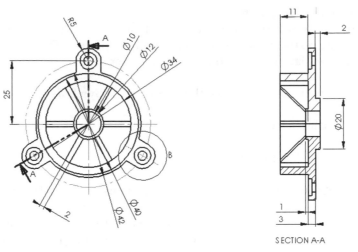

Figure 15-34 *Partial view of the sheet after generating and arranging the dimensions in the aligned section view*

Datum Feature button from the **Annotation CommandManager**; the **Datum Feature PropertyManager** is displayed and a datum callout is attached to the cursor.

2. Place the datum symbol at an appropriate location, refer to Figure 15-35.

3. Choose the **OK** button from the **Datum Feature PropertyManager**.

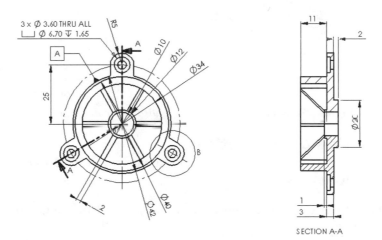

Figure 15-35 *Datum feature symbol and the hole description added to the top view*

Adding the Geometric Tolerance to the Drawing View

After defining the datum feature symbol, you will add the geometric tolerance to the drawing view.

1. Select the circular edge that has a diameter of 12 mm from the top view and choose the **Geometric Tolerance** button from the **Annotation CommandManager**; the **Properties** dialog box is displayed. This dialog box is used to specify the parameters of the geometric tolerance.

2. Select the arrow in drop-down list of the first row; the **Symbols** flyout is displayed.

3. Choose the **Concentricity** option from this flyout.

4. Enter the value **0.002** in the **Tolerance 1** edit box.

5. Enter **A** in the **Primary** edit box to define the primary datum reference.

6. Choose the **OK** button from the **Properties** dialog box; the geometric tolerance is attached to the selected circular edge. You may need to move the geometric tolerance, if it overlaps the dimensions. Figure 15-36 shows the drawing view after adding and rearranging the geometric tolerance.

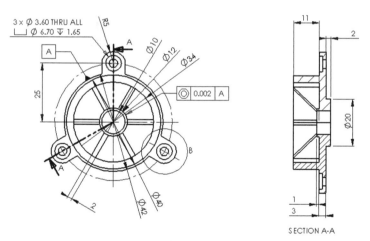

Figure 15-36 Geometric tolerance added to the drawing view

Changing the View Display Options

After adding all the annotations to the drawing views, you need to change the display setting of the drawing views.

1. Press and hold the CTRL key, select the front view and the right-side view from the drawing sheet.

2. Choose the **Hidden Lines Visible** button from the **Heads-up View** toolbar; the hidden lines are displayed in the selected drawing views. You can also choose this button from the **Display Style** rollout in the **Multiple Views PropertyManager** that is displayed when you select the two views.

3. Now, select the isometric view and the aligned section view from the drawing sheet.

4. Choose the **Shaded With Edges** button from the **Heads-up View** toolbar or the **Multiple Views PropertyManager**. Figure 15-37 shows the final drawing sheet after changing the display view settings.

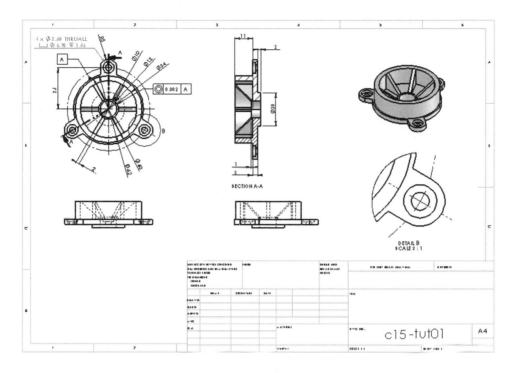

Figure 15-37 Final drawing sheet

5. Save and close the drawing document.

Tutorial 2

In this tutorial, you will generate the BOM of the Bench Vice assembly and then add balloons to the isometric view in the exploded state.   **(Expected time: 45 min)**

The following steps are required to complete this tutorial:

a. Copy the Bench Vice folder, which contains parts, assembly, and the drawing document, to the folder of the current chapter.
b. Delete the views that are not required in the drawing sheet, refer to Figure 15-39.
c. Move the views and arrange them in the drawing sheet, refer to Figure 15-39.
d. Set the anchor on the drawing sheet where the BOM will be attached.
e. Generate the BOM, refer to Figure 15-40.
f. Add balloons to the isometric view, refer to Figure 15-41.

Copying the Bench Vice Assembly Folder to the Current Folder

1. Copy the Bench Vice folder from the *\My Documents\SolidWorks\c14* folder to the folder of the current chapter, if it is not done earlier.

Opening the Drawing Document

After copying the folder, you need to open the drawing document in the SolidWorks window.

1. Open the *c14_tut02.slddrw* document.

   The drawing document, in which you need to generate the BOM and balloons is displayed in Figure 15-38.

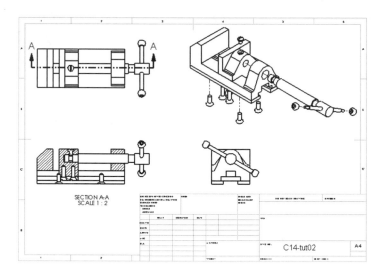

Figure 15-38 *Drawing views generated in Chapter 14*

Deleting the Unwanted View

You need to delete the right view because it is not required in this tutorial.

1. Select the right-side view and press the DELETE key; the **Confirm Delete** dialog box is displayed.

2. Choose the **Yes** button from this dialog box; the view is deleted from the current drawing sheet.

Moving the Isometric View

You need to move the exploded isometric view, because the BOM will be generated and placed at the top right corner of the drawing sheet.

1. Select the isometric view; the border of the view is highlighted.

2. Move the cursor to the border; the cursor is replaced by the move cursor.

3. Drag the cursor to move the drawing view. Place it at the required location, refer to Figure 15-39.

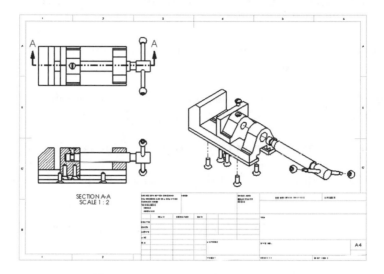

Figure 15-39 *Drawing sheet after deleting and moving the drawing views*

Setting the Anchor for the BOM

Before generating the BOM, you need to set its anchor. The anchor is a point on the drawing sheet to which one of the corners of the BOM coincides. By default, the anchor is defined at the top left corner of the drawing sheet. But in this tutorial, you need to add the BOM on the top right corner of the drawing sheet. Therefore, you need to set the anchor before generating the BOM.

1. Expand **Sheet1** from the **FeatureManager design tree** and then expand **Sheet Format1**.

2. Select the **Bill of Materials Anchor1** option, right-click to invoke the shortcut menu and choose the **Set Anchor** option from it; the drawing views will disappear from the sheet.

3. Specify the anchor point on the inner top right corner of the drawing sheet; a point is placed at the selected location.

   After you specify the anchor point, the drawing views are displayed automatically in the sheet because the sheet editing environment is invoked automatically.

Generating the BOM

Next, you need to generate the BOM. As discussed earlier, the BOM generated in SolidWorks is parametric. If a component is deleted or added in the assembly, the change is reflected automatically in the BOM. But before generating the BOM, you need to set its text parameters.

1. Invoke the **Document Properties - Drafting Standard** dialog box and choose **Annotations > Notes** from the area on the left.

2. Choose the **Font** button from the **Text** area of the dialog box; the **Choose Font** dialog box is invoked. Select the **Points** radio button from the **Height** area and set the value of the font size to **9** from the list box.

3. Choose the **OK** button from the **Choose Font** dialog box. Similarly, change the text height of balloons to **12** points.

4. Select the isometric view and choose **Tables > Bill of Materials** from the **Annotation CommandManager**; the **Bill of Materials PropertyManager** is displayed.

5. Select the **Attach to anchor point** check box in the **Table Position** rollout.

6. Choose the **OK** button from the **Bill of Materials PropertyManager**; the BOM is generated.

   You will notice that the **Description** column is also displayed in the BOM. But this column is not required. So you need to delete it.

7. Move the cursor over the **Description** heading and right-click to display the shortcut menu. Choose **Delete > Column** from the cascading menu; this column is deleted. The drawing sheet, after generating the BOM and deleting the **Description** column is displayed, as shown in Figure 15-40.

   Note
   *If the color of the BOM is gray and is not clearly visible, invoke the **System Options - Colors** dialog box. Select **Annotations, Imported** from the **Color scheme settings** list box and change its color to black.*

Adding Balloons to the Components

After generating the BOM, you need to add balloons to the components. Before proceeding further, make sure that you have changed the font height of balloons to **12** points as discussed in the previous section.

1. Select the isometric view and choose the **AutoBalloon** button from the **Annotation CommandManager**; the balloons are automatically added to all the components in the isometric view and the **Auto Balloon PropertyManager** is also displayed.

   The multiple instances of any component are ignored because the **Ignore multiple instances** check box is selected in the **Balloon Layout** rollout.

2. Select **1 Character** from the **Size** drop-down list in the **Balloon Settings** rollout. Choose **OK** to close this **PropertyManager**.

   The balloons are added to all the components, except the Clamping Plate. This is because the clamping plate is not visible in the isometric view. You will notice that the balloons

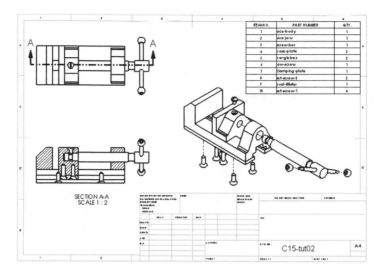

Figure 15-40 Drawing sheet after generating the BOM

are not properly arranged on the sheet and are placed arbitrarily. Therefore, you need to manually drag each balloon and place it properly.

3.   Move the cursor over one of the balloons, and when it is highlighted, drag it to place it at another location, refer to Figure 15-41.

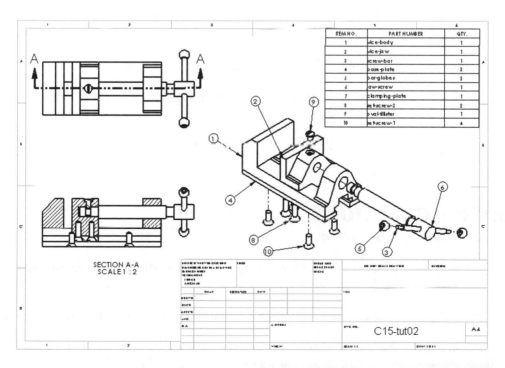

Figure 15-41 Final drawing sheet after adding balloons

4. Similarly, drag and place the remaining balloons at proper locations. The final drawing sheet after adding and rearranging balloons is shown in Figure 15-41.

5. Save the drawing and close the document.

SELF-EVALUATION TEST

Answer the following questions and then compare them to those given at the end of this chapter:

1. You cannot add annotations while creating the part in SolidWorks. (T/F)

2. You can add the surface finish symbols to the drawing views. (T/F)

3. The **Projected tolerance zone** area is used to define the quality of the projected tolerance. (T/F)

4. You can set the target shape as a point, circle, or a rectangle while adding a datum target. (T/F)

5. You can also set the option for the automatic creation of the centerline while generating the drawing views. (T/F)

6. The _____ spinner is used to define the major diameter of the thread.

7. The _____ tool is used to add the balloons to the components of the assembly in the drawing view.

8. You can also create automatic balloons using the _____ tool.

9. The _____ rollout in the **Bill of Materials PropertyManager** is used to specify the template needed to create the BOM.

10. The _____ tool is used to create a hole callout.

REVIEW QUESTIONS

Answer the following questions:

1. The _____ tool is used to add the cosmetic threads to display the thread conventions in the drawing views.

2. The _____ tool is used to add reference dimensions to the drawing views.

3. You can change the model display setting from the hidden lines removed to the hidden lines visible, wireframe, or shaded using the options available in the _____ toolbar.

4. Select the _____ check box in the **Auto insertion on view creation** area to automatically create the centerlines, while generating the views.

5. The _____ tool is used to create the centerlines in the views.

6. Which **PropertyManager** is invoked to add automatic balloons to the selected drawing view?

    (a) **AutoBalloon**   (b) **Balloon**
    (c) **Properties**   (d) **Center Mark**

7. Which **PropertyManager** is displayed when you choose the **Cosmetic Thread** button from the **Annotation CommandManager**?

    (a) **Cosmetic Thread Properties**   (b) **Cosmetic Thread**
    (c) **Cosmetic Thread Convention**   (d) None of the above

8. Which **PropertyManager** is used to add center marks to the drawing views?

    (a) **Add Center Mark**   (b) **Create Center Mark**
    (c) **Center Mark**   (d) **Cosmetic Thread**

9. Which rollout in the **Cosmetic Thread PropertyManager** is used to define the depth of the cosmetic thread?

    (a) **Thread Settings**   (b) **Thread Depth**
    (c) **Cosmetic Thread**   (d) None of the above

10. Which **PropertyManager** is used to add balloons in the drawing views?

    (a) **Add Balloons**   (b) **Balloon Properties**
    (c) **Balloons**   (d) None of these

EXERCISE

Exercise 1

Generate the isometric view of the exploded view of the assembly created in Tutorial 1 of Chapter 13 on the standard A4 sheet format. The scale of the view will be 1:5. After generating the view, generate the BOM and add balloons to the assembly view, as shown in Figure 15-42.

(Expected time: 30 min)

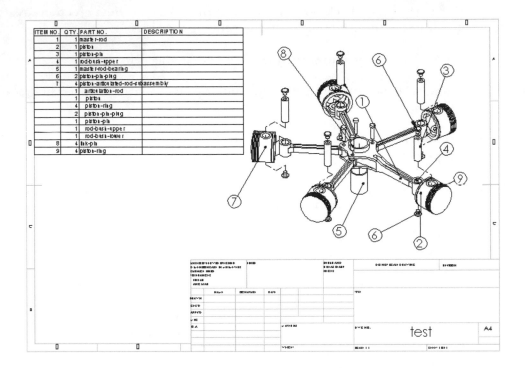

ITEM NO.	QTY.	PART NO.	DESCRIPTION
1	1	master-rod	
2	1	piston	
3	1	piston-pin	
4	1	rod-bush-upper	
5	1	master-rod-bearing	
6	2	piston-pin-plug	
7	4	piston-articulated-rod-sub-assembly	
	1	articulation-rod	
	1	piston	
	4	piston-ring	
	2	piston-pin-plug	
	1	piston-pin	
	1	rod-bush-upper	
	1	rod-bush-lower	
8	6	link-pin	
9	6	piston-ring	

Figure 15-42 *Drawing view for Exercise 1*

Answers to Self-Evaluation Test
1. T, **2.** T, **3.** F, **4.** T, **5.** T, **6. Major Diameter**, **7. Balloon**, **8. AutoBalloon**, **9. Table Template**, **10. Hole Callout**

Chapter 16

Sheet Metal Design

- *Create base flange.*
- *Understand the FeatureManager design tree of a sheet metal component.*
- *Create edge flange.*
- *Create tabs.*
- *Create sketched bends.*
- *Create miter flange.*
- *Create closed corners.*
- *Create hems.*
- *Create jog bend.*
- *Break corners.*
- *Create cuts on the flat faces of the sheet metal components.*
- *Create lofted bends.*
- *Create flat pattern of the sheet metal components.*
- *Create sheet metal components from a flat sheet.*
- *Create sheet metal components from a flat part.*
- *Create a sheet metal component by designing it as a part.*
- *Design a sheet metal part from a shelled solid model.*
- *Create cuts in the sheet metal component across the bends.*
- *Create cylindrical and conical sheet metal components.*
- *Generate the drawing views of the flat pattern of the sheet metal components.*

SHEET METAL DESIGN

In SolidWorks, you can design the sheet metal components using various tools available for manipulating the sheet metal components in the **Part** mode. Generally, the solid models of the sheet metal components are created to generate the flat pattern of the sheet, study the design of the dies and punches, and study the process plan for designing the tools needed for manufacturing the sheet metal components. In a tool room or a machine shop, the most important thing that you need before designing the press tool, bending tool or any other tool for creating a sheet metal component is the flat pattern layout of the component. Figure 16-1 shows the model of a sheet metal component and Figure 16-2 shows its flat pattern layout. A flat pattern layout displays the flattened view of the sheet metal component, refer to Figure 16-2.

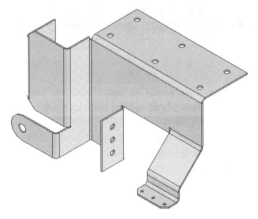

Figure 16-1 *Solid model of a sheet metal component*

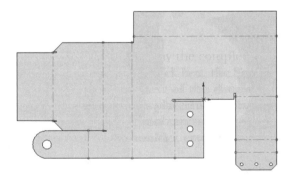

Figure 16-2 *Flat pattern layout of the sheet metal component*

As discussed earlier, the sheet metal components are designed in the **Part** mode of SolidWorks. To create a sheet metal component, start a new SolidWorks document in the **Part** mode and then invoke the **SheetMetal CommandManager**. If this **CommandManager** is not available by default, invoke this **CommandManager** by right clicking on the tab of a **CommandManager** and choose **SheetMetal** from the shortcut menu. All tools that are used to design a sheet metal component are available in this **CommandManager**. You can also invoke these tools from the **Sheet Metal** toolbar. The different methods to create sheet metal components are discussed in this chapter.

DESIGNING THE SHEET METAL COMPONENTS BY CREATING THE BASE FLANGE

The most widely used method of designing the sheet metal component is by first creating the base flange. In this method, first you will create the base flange and then add the sheet metal feature on the base flange to obtain the required sheet metal component. In this method, all the parameters related to the sheet metal such as the bending radius, the bend allowance, and the relief are defined while creating the base flange. Various tools used to create the sheet metal components are discussed next.

Creating the Base Flange

CommandManager:	Sheet Metal > Base Flange/Tab
SolidWorks menus:	Insert > Sheet Metal > Base Flange
Toolbar:	Sheet Metal > Base Flange/Tab

To create a sheet metal component, you first need to create a base feature or a base sheet. This base sheet is known as the base flange. You can create a base flange from a closed sketch or an open sketch. To create a base flange, draw the sketch of the base flange and then choose the **Base Flange/Tab** button from the **Sheet Metal CommandManager**; the **Base Flange PropertyManager** will be displayed. Also, the preview of the base flange will be displayed with the default values. Figure 16-3 shows the **Base Flange PropertyManager** for an open sketch. The rollouts in the **Base Flange PropertyManager** are discussed next.

Note
*The parameters that you define in the **Base Flange PropertyManager** are used as the default parameters throughout the current document. However, you can modify these values using the **PropertyManagers** of other tools.*

Direction 1 Rollout
This rollout is displayed only if the sketch of the base flange is open. The options in the **Direction 1** rollout are used to define the feature termination in the first direction.

Direction 2 Rollout
The options in the **Direction 2** rollout are used to define the feature termination in the second direction. The **Direction 2** rollout is also displayed only if the sketch for the base flange is open.

Figure 16-3 The Base Flange PropertyManager

Sheet Metal Gauges Rollout

This rollout enables you to use the gauge table to create the sheet metal parts. Select the **Use gauge table** check box; the **Select Table** drop-down list will be displayed. Choose any of the default gauge tables from this drop-down list. You can also choose the **Browse** button and select a user-defined gauge table.

Sheet Metal Parameters Rollout

The options in the **Sheet Metal Parameters** rollout are used to define the thickness and the bend radius of the sheet. These options are discussed next.

Thickness

The **Thickness** spinner in the **Sheet Metal Parameters** rollout is used to define the thickness of the sheet.

Reverse direction

The **Reverse direction** check box is used to flip the direction of material addition while specifying the thickness to the base flange.

Bend Radius

The **Bend Radius** spinner is used to specify the bend radius of the base flange. If the sketch of the base flange is closed, the **Bend Radius** spinner will not be available in the **Sheet Metal Parameters** rollout.

Bend Allowance Rollout

The options in the **Bend Allowance Type** drop-down list of this rollout are used to specify the bend allowance for all the bends in the sheet metal component. These options are discussed next.

Bend Table

The **Bend Table** option is selected to specify the bending allowance using the bend tables. When you select this option, the **Bend Table** drop-down list will be displayed below the **Bend Allowance Type** drop-down list. In SolidWorks, various bend tables are provided to calculate the bending radius. The **BASE BEND TABLE** option is selected by default in the **Bend Table** drop-down list. The other bend tables available in this list are **METRIC BASE BEND TABLE**, **KFACTOR BASE BEND TABLE**, and **SAMPLE**. Choose the **Browse** button available below this drop-down list to browse the location of the folder if you have saved a user-defined bending table file that is created in Microsoft Excel.

K-Factor

The **K-Factor** option is used to define the K-Factor. The K-Factor is defined as the ratio of the location of the neutral sheet to the thickness of the sheet. When you select this option, the **K-Factor** spinner will be displayed. Specify the K-Factor value in this spinner.

Bend Allowance

The **Bend Allowance** option is used to define the bend allowance by specifying a numeric value. When you select this option, the **Bend Allowance** spinner will be displayed. You can specify the bend allowance value in this spinner.

Bend Deduction

The **Bend Deduction** option is used to define the bend deduction. When you select this option, the **Bend Deduction** spinner will be displayed. Specify the bend deduction value in this spinner.

Auto Relief Rollout

The **Auto Relief** rollout is used to define the relief in the sheet metal component. The reliefs are provided in the sheet metal components to avoid tearing of the sheet while bending. The options available in this rollout are discussed next. You will learn about the types of reliefs in detail later in this chapter.

Auto Relief Type

The **Auto Relief Type** drop-down list is used to define the type of relief that you need to specify to the base flange. The types of reliefs available in this drop-down list are **Rectangle**, **Tear**, and **Obround**. If you select the **Rectangle** or the **Obround** type of relief, the **Relief Ratio** spinner will be displayed to define the relief ratio.

The base flange can be created using an open sketch with the single sketched entity, as shown in Figure 16-4. Figure 16-5 shows the resulting base flange.

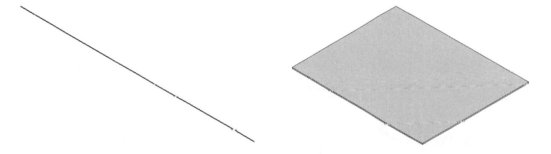

Figure 16-4 *Open sketch with a single entity*   *Figure 16-5* *Resulting base flange*

You can also create the base flange using an open sketch with multiple sketched entities, as shown in Figure 16-6. Figure 16-7 shows the resulting base flange with the bending radius applied automatically to the edges.

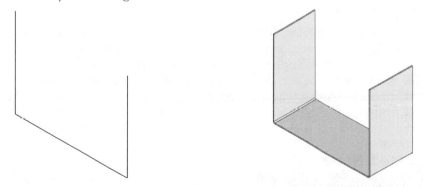

Figure 16-6 *Open sketch with multiple entities*   *Figure 16-7* *Resulting base flange*

Figure 16-8 shows a closed sketch and Figure 16-9 shows the resulting base flange.

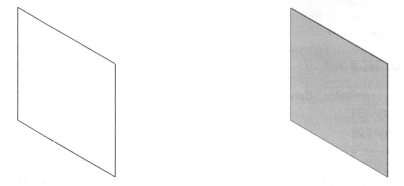

Figure 16-8 Closed sketch   *Figure 16-9* Resulting base flange

Understanding the FeatureManager design tree of a Sheet Metal Component

After creating the base flange, you will notice that some nodes are displayed in the **FeatureManager design tree**, as shown in Figure 16-10. All these nodes are discussed next.

Figure 16-10 Various nodes displayed in the **FeatureManager** *design tree* after creating the base flange

Sheet-Metal1 Node

The **Sheet-Metal1** node contains all the information about the default sheet metal parameters such as bend, bend allowance, and auto relief parameters. The values assigned to these parameters are automatically applied to all the other sheet metal features that you add to the base flange. At any stage of the design, you can edit these parameters. To do so, select **Sheet-Metal1** in the **FeatureManager design tree**; a pop-up toolbar will be displayed. Choose **Edit Feature** from the pop-up toolbar; the **Sheet-Metal1 PropertyManager** will be displayed. You can modify the default sheet metal parameters using this **PropertyManager**.

Base-Flange1 Node

The **Base-Flange1** node is displayed after creating the base flange. You can change the thickness of the sheet by editing this feature. You can also edit the sketch of the base flange using this feature.

Flat-Pattern1 Node

The **Flat-Pattern1** node is also available after creating the base flange. This feature is used to create the flat pattern of the bent sheet metal component. By default, this feature is suppressed. You will learn more about the flat patterns later in this chapter.

Creating the Edge Flange

CommandManager:	Sheet Metal > Edge Flange
SolidWorks menus:	Insert > Sheet Metal > Edge Flange
Toolbar:	Sheet Metal > Edge Flange

Edge flange is a bent sheet metal wall created at an angle at the edge of the existing base flange or an existing flange. To create an edge flange, choose the **Edge Flange** button from the **Sheet Metal CommandManager**; the **Edge-Flange PropertyManager** will be displayed, as shown in Figure 16-11 and you will be prompted to select a linear edge of a planar face to create the edge flange.

Next, you need to select the edge along which the flange will be created, as shown in Figure 16-12. As soon as you select the edge, the preview of the edge flange with the drag handle will be displayed in the drawing area, as shown in Figure 16-13. The length of the resulting flange will change dynamically as you move the cursor.

The rollouts in the **Edge-Flange PropertyManager** are discussed next.

Flange Parameters Rollout

The options in the **Flange Parameters** rollout are used to define the edge reference to be used for creating the edge flange, the bending radius, and the profile of the edge flange. These options are discussed next.

Edge

The **Edge** selection box is used to select the edges to create the edge flange.

Figure 16-11 The Edge-Flange PropertyManager

Edit Flange Profile

The **Edit Flange Profile** button is chosen to edit the profile of the edge flange. By default, the edge flange is created along the entire length of the selected edge. To edit the profile of the edge flange, choose the **Edit Flange**

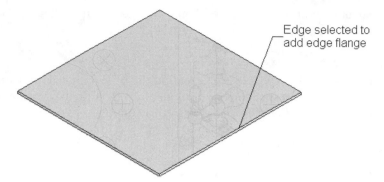

Edge selected to
add edge flange

Figure 16-12 Edge selected to add the edge flange

Figure 16-13 Preview of the edge flange with the drag handle

Profile button; the **Profile Sketch** dialog box will be displayed, which will inform you that the sketch is valid. Also, the sketching environment will be invoked in the background. Edit the sketch of the profile of the edge flange using the sketching tools. You will also notice that while editing the sketch of the edge flange, the **Profile Sketch** dialog box informs you whether the sketch is valid for creating the edge flange or not. If the status of the sketch is shown valid in the **Profile Sketch** dialog box, the preview of the flange will be displayed in the drawing area. After editing the profile, choose the **Finish** button from the **Profile Sketch** dialog box; the flange will be created and the **Edge-Flange PropertyManager** will be automatically closed. Note that if you want to modify the other parameters of the flange, choose the **Back** button from the **Profile Sketch** dialog box. Figure 16-14 shows the edge flange created along the entire length of the selected edge. Figure 16-15 shows the edited sketch of the edge flange and Figure 16-16 shows the resulting edge flange.

Angle Rollout

The **Angle** rollout is used to define the angle of the flange. The default angle of the flange is 90-degree. You can define any other angle of the flange using the **Flange Angle** spinner. The angle of the edge flange can be greater than 0-degree and less than 180-degree. You can also select a face and specify whether the resulting flange will be parallel or normal to it. Figure 16-17 shows an edge flange created at an angle of 45-degree. Figure 16-18 shows an edge flange created at an angle of 135-degree.

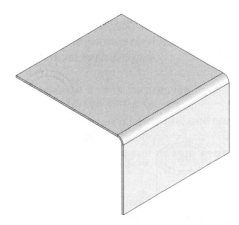

Figure 16-14 Edge flange created along the entire length of the edge

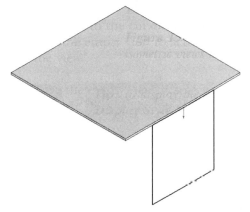

Figure 16-15 Edited sketch of the edge flange

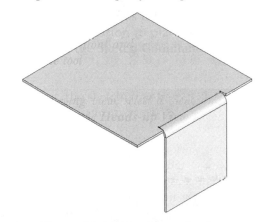

Figure 16-16 Resulting edge flange

Figure 16-17 Edge flange created at an angle of 45-degree

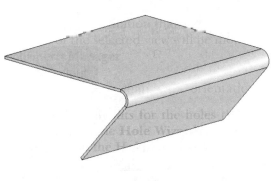

Figure 16-18 Edge flange created at an angle of 135-degree

Flange Length Rollout

The **Flange Length** rollout is used to define the length of the flange. In other words, the options of feature termination are available in this rollout. These options are the same as discussed earlier. The other two options provided in this rollout are discussed next.

Outer Virtual Sharp

The **Outer Virtual Sharp** button is used to define the length of the flange from the outer virtual sharp. The outer virtual sharp is an imaginary vertex created by virtually extending the tangent lines from the outer radius of the bend, as shown in Figure 16-19.

Inner Virtual Sharp

The **Inner Virtual Sharp** button is chosen by default and is used to define the length of the flange from the inner virtual sharp. The inner virtual sharp is an imaginary vertex created by virtually extending the tangent lines from the inner radius of the bend, as shown in Figure 16-19.

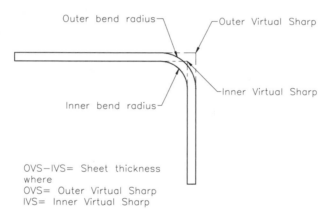

Figure 16-19 *Outer Virtual Sharp and Inner Virtual Sharp*

Flange Position Rollout

The **Flange Position** rollout is used to define the position of the flange on an edge. The options in this rollout are discussed next.

Material Inside

The **Material Inside** button is used to create the edge flange in such a way that the material of the flange after the bend lies inside the maximum limit of sheet. Figure 16-20 shows the edge flange created with the **Material Inside** button chosen.

Material Outside

The **Material Outside** button is chosen by default and it creates the edge flange such that the material of the flange after the bend lies outside the maximum limit of the sheet. Figure 16-21 shows the edge flange created with the **Material Outside** button chosen.

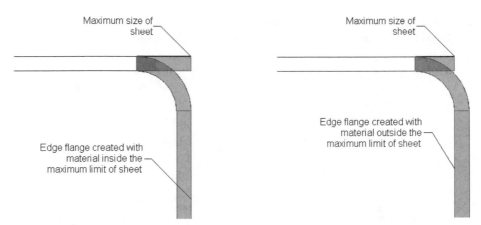

Figure 16-20 *Edge flange created with the* **Material Inside** *button chosen*

Figure 16-21 *Edge flange created with the* **Material Outside** *button chosen*

Bend Outside

The **Bend Outside** button is used to create an edge flange such that the bending of the sheet starts from outside the maximum limit of the sheet, as shown in Figure 16-22.

Bend from Virtual Sharp

The **Bend from Virtual Sharp** button is used to create an edge flange with the bending of the sheet starting from the virtual sharp. The position of the flange depends on whether you select the **Outer Virtual Sharp** button or the **Inner Virtual Sharp** button from the **Flange Length** rollout. Figure 16-23 shows the edge flange created with the **Inner Virtual Sharp** and **Bend from Virtual Sharp** buttons chosen.

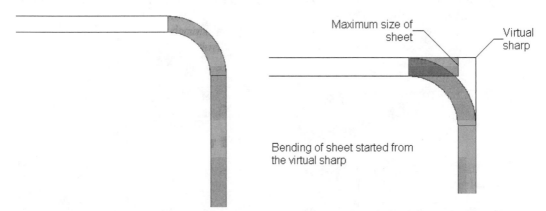

Figure 16-22 *Edge flange created with the* **Bend Outside** *button chosen*

Figure 16-23 *Edge flange created with the* **Bend from Virtual Sharp** *button chosen*

Trim side bends

Select the **Trim side bends** check box to trim extra materials in the bends surrounding the current edge flange. By default, this check box is not selected. Figure 16-24 shows the edge flange created with the **Trim side bends** check box cleared. Figure 16-25 shows the edge flange created with the **Trim side bends** check box selected.

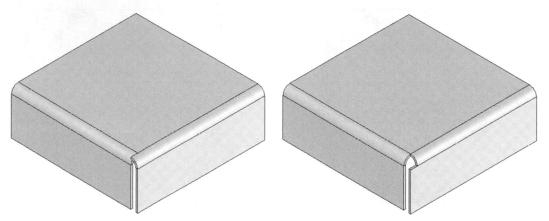

Figure 16-24 *Edge flange created with the*
Trim side bends *check box cleared*

Figure 16-25 *Edge flange created with the*
Trim side bends *check box selected*

Offset

The **Offset** check box is available only when you create an edge flange using the **Material Inside**, **Material Outside**, or **Bend Outside** options. This check box is used to create an edge flange at an offset distance from the selected edge reference. When you select the **Offset** check box, the **Offset End Condition** drop-down list and the **Offset Distance** spinner will be displayed. Specify the offset distance using this spinner. Figure 16-26 shows the edge flange created with the **Offset** check box cleared. Figure 16-27 shows the edge flange created with the **Offset** check box selected and the offset distance specified in the **Offset Distance** spinner.

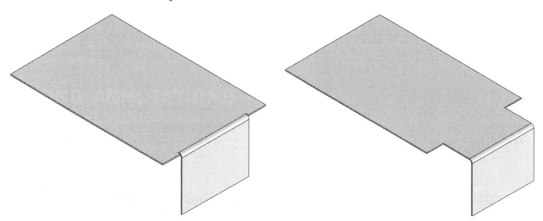

Figure 16-26 *Edge flange created with the*
Offset *check box cleared*

Figure 16-27 *Edge flange created with the*
Offset *check box selected*

Custom Bend Allowance Rollout

The **Custom Bend Allowance** rollout is used to define the bend allowance other than the default bend allowance that you defined while creating the base flange. To apply the custom bend allowance, expand this rollout by selecting the **Custom Bend Allowance** check box. Then, use the options in this rollout to define the bend allowance for the current bend as discussed earlier.

Custom Relief Type Rollout

The **Custom Relief Type** rollout is used to define the type of relief other than the default relief type that you defined while creating the base flange. To apply the custom relief, expand this rollout by selecting the **Custom Relief Type** check box, as shown in Figure 16-28.

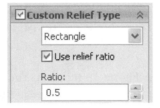

*Figure 16-28 The **Custom Relief Type** rollout*

The types of reliefs that you can define for a sheet metal component are discussed next.

Obround Relief

The **Obround** option is used to provide the obround relief such that the edges of the relief merging with the sheet are rounded. The **Use relief ratio** check box is selected by default. Therefore, you can modify the value of the relief ratio, by setting the value in the **Relief Ratio** spinner. If you clear the **Use relief ratio** check box, the **Relief Width** and the **Relief Depth** spinners will be displayed, as shown in Figure 16-29. You can modify the relief width and relief depth individually using these two spinners.

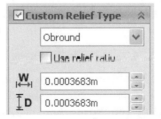

*Figure 16-29 The **Relief Width** and **Relief Depth** spinners displayed in the **Custom Relief Type** rollout*

Figure 16-30 shows the edge flange created by providing the obround relief with the default relief ratio. Figure 16-31 shows the edge flange created by providing obround relief after modifying the relief ratio.

Rectangle Relief

The **Rectangle** option is selected by default. This option specifies the rectangular relief to the sheet metal components. The options available for defining the rectangular relief

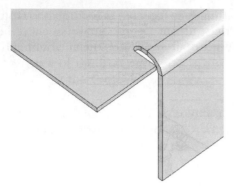

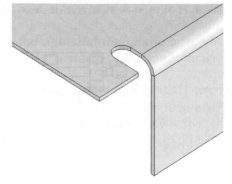

Figure 16-30 *Edge flange created with the default relief ratio*

Figure 16-31 *Edge flange created after modifying the relief ratio*

are the same as discussed above. Figure 16-32 shows the edge flange created by providing the rectangular relief with the default relief ratio. Figure 16-33 shows the edge flange created by providing rectangular relief after modifying the relief ratio.

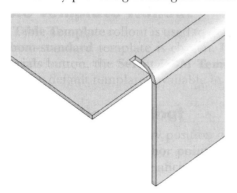

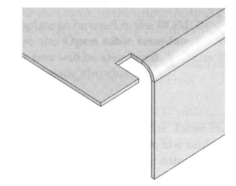

Figure 16-32 *Edge flange created with default relief ratio*

Figure 16-33 *Edge flange created after modifying the relief ratio*

Tear Relief

You can provide the tear relief to the edge flange using the **Tear** option. The tear relief will tear the sheet in order to accommodate the bending of the sheet. When you select the **Tear** option from the **Relief Type** drop-down list, all the other options are replaced by the **Rip** and the **Extend** buttons, as shown in Figure 16-34.

Figure 16-34 *The **Custom Relief Type** rollout with the **Tear** option selected from the **Relief Type** drop-down list*

The **Rip** button is chosen by default. This option rips or tears the sheet to accommodate the bending of the sheet, as shown in Figure 16-35. When the **Extend** button is chosen, the outer faces of the bend will be extended to the outer faces of the sheet on which you create the edge flange, as shown in Figure 16-36.

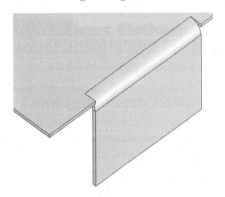

Figure 16-35 Tear relief with the **Rip** button chosen

Figure 16-36 Tear relief with the **Extend** button chosen

Tip. *You can edit the sketch of the edge flange after creating it. To do so, select the edge flange feature from the **FeatureManager design tree** and invoke the pop-up toolbar. Next, choose **Edit Sketch** from it; the sketching environment will be invoked. Now, edit the sketch and exit the sketching environment.*

Creating Tabs

CommandManager:	SheetMetal > Base Flange/Tab
SolidWorks menus:	Insert > Sheet Metal > Tab
Toolbar:	Sheet Metal > Base Flange/Tab

A tab feature is created by adding material to the walls of the sheet metal component. To create a tab, select a face to use as the sketching plane and create the sketch of the tab. Remember that the sketch must be closed. Now, choose the **Base Flange/Tab** button from the **Sheet Metal CommandManager** or choose **Insert > Sheet Metal > Tab** from the SolidWorks menus; a tab will be created and the thickness of the tab will be automatically adjusted according to the thickness of the sheet. Figure 16-37 shows the sketch for creating a tab and Figure 16-38 shows the resulting tab.

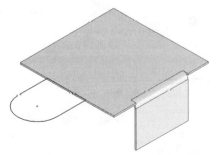

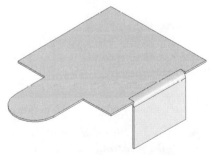

Figure 16-37 Sketch for creating a tab

Figure 16-38 Resulting tab

Note

*If you create a tab feature and select it from the **FeatureManager design tree**, the **Edit Feature** option will not be available in the pop-up toolbar. So, you cannot edit a tab feature. However, you can edit the sketch of the tab feature.*

Creating the Sketched Bend

CommandManager:	SheetMetal > Sketched Bend
SolidWorks menus:	Insert > Sheet Metal > Sketched Bend
Toolbar:	Sheet Metal > Sketched Bend

The **Sketched Bend** tool is used to create a bend by using a sketch as the bending line. To create a sketched bend, select the face of the sheet on which you need to create a bend line and invoke the sketching environment. Draw a line to define the bend line using the **Line** tool. Now, choose the **Sketched Bend** button from the **SheetMetal CommandManager**; the **Sketched Bend PropertyManager** will be displayed, as shown in Figure 16-39. Also, you will be prompted to specify the planar face to be fixed while creating the bend. Select the side of the sheet that will be fixed when you create the bend; a black sphere will be displayed on the selected point and the **Reverse Direction** arrow will also be displayed to reverse the direction of bend creation. You will notice that the **Bend Centerline** button is chosen by default in the **Bend position** area. So, the sheet is bent equally on both the sides of the bend line. The other options in the **Sketched Bend PropertyManager** are the same as those discussed earlier. After setting all the parameters, choose the **OK** button from the **Sketched Bend PropertyManager**. Figure 16-40 shows the sketch to be used as the bending line and the side of the face to be fixed while bending. Figure 16-41 shows the resulting bend.

Figure 16-39 The Sketched Bend PropertyManager

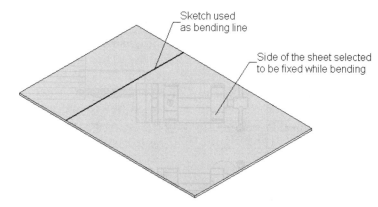

Figure 16-40 The face to be fixed and the bending line

Note

You can also create more than one sketch line for creating multiple bends using a single sketch bend feature. But make sure that the bend sketches do not intersect each other. Figure 16-42 shows the sheet and the two bend lines and Figure 16-43 shows the resulting bends.

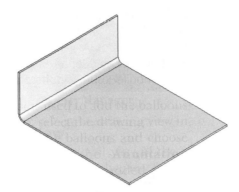

Figure 16-41 *Resulting sketched bend*

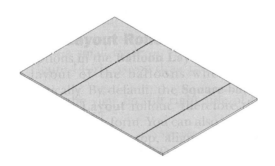

Figure 16-42 *Two bend lines*

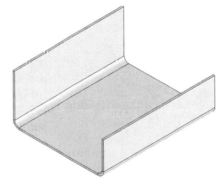

Figure 16-43 *Resulting sketched bend*

Creating the Miter Flange

CommandManager:	Sheet Metal > Miter Flange
SolidWorks menus:	Insert > Sheet Metal > Miter Flange
Toolbar:	Sheet Metal > Miter Flange

 The **Miter Flange** tool is used to create a series of flanges along the edges of the sheet metal component. The profile of the miter flange is defined by the sketch created on a sketching plane normal to the direction of extrusion of flange. To create a miter flange, select the sketching plane and invoke the sketching environment. Create the sketch for the miter flange and then choose the **Miter Flange** button from the **Sheet Metal** toolbar; the **Miter Flange PropertyManager** will be displayed, as shown in Figure 16-44.

The preview of the flange with the default settings will be displayed in the drawing area and you will be prompted to select the linear edge(s) to attach the miter flange. Figure 16-45 shows the sketch for creating the miter flange and Figure 16-46 shows the preview of the miter flange. You can select the other continuous edges, if required, as shown in Figure 16-47. After selecting the edges, choose the **OK** button from the **Miter Flange PropertyManager**; the miter flange is created, as shown in Figure 16-48.

The **Gap distance** area in the **Miter Flange PropertyManager** is discussed next.

Figure 16-44 *The **Miter Flange PropertyManager***

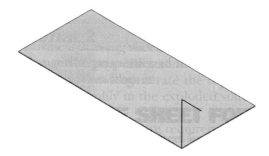

Figure 16-45 *Sketch for creating the miter flange*

Figure 16-46 *Preview of the miter flange*

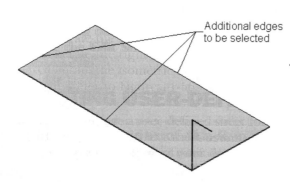

Figure 16-47 *Sketch and the additional edges to be selected*

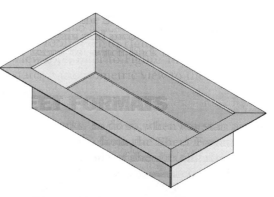

Figure 16-48 *Resulting miter flange*

Gap distance Area

The spinner in this area is used to define the rip distance between the two consecutive flanges. Set the value in the **Rip Gap** spinner to modify the distance value of the rip. While creating a miter flange, if the feature creation is aborted due to default rip distance, the **Rebuild Errors** message box will be displayed and it will prompt you to enter a larger distance value. Figure 16-49 shows the miter flange created using the default distance value and Figure 16-50 shows the miter flange created using the modified rip distance.

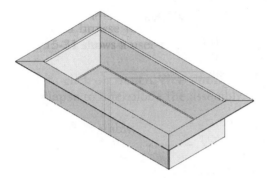

Figure 16-49 *Miter flange with the default rip distance*

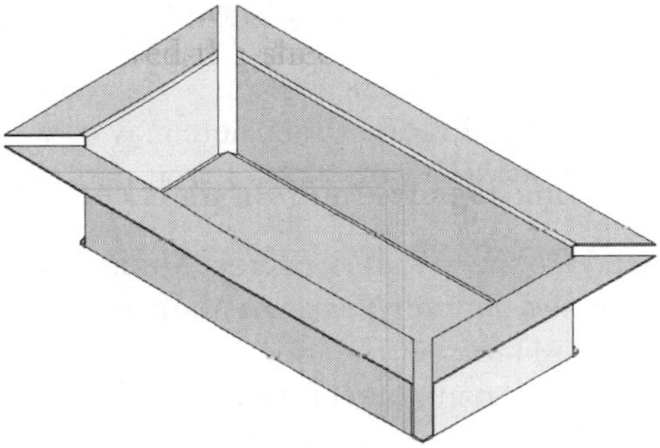

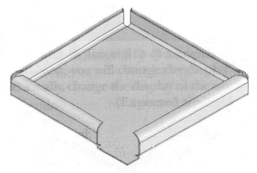

Figure 16-50 *Miter flange with the modified rip distance*

Start/End Offset Rollout

You can specify the start and end offset distances of the miter flange using the options in the **Start/End Offset** rollout. The **Start Offset Distance** spinner is used to specify the offset distance from the start face of the miter flange. The **End Offset Distance** spinner is used to specify the offset distance from the end face of the miter flange. If the start and end offset distances are applied to the miter flange created on the continuous edges of the base flange, the start offset distance is applied to the first edge and the end offset distance is applied to the edge selected at last. Figure 16-51 shows the miter flange created on a single edge with the start and end offsets. Figure 16-52 shows the offsets applied to the miter flange created by selecting all the edges of the base flange.

Figure 16-51 *Offset distances applied to the miter flange created by selecting a single edge*

Figure 16-52 *Offset distances applied to the miter flange created by selecting all the edges*

Tip. *While creating the miter flange, if any of the edge is tangent to the selected edge, then [tab] symbol will be displayed. Click on this symbol; all the edges tangent to the selected edge will be automatically selected.*

Creating Closed Corners

CommandManager:	SheetMetal > Corner > Closed Corner
SolidWorks menus:	Insert > Sheet Metal > Closed Corner
Toolbar:	Sheet Metal > Corner > Closed Corner

In SolidWorks, when you create walls using the **Edge Flange** tool, there may be a gap between the corners due to relief. You can close this gap and create a closed corner. To do so, choose the **Corners > Closed Corner** from the **Sheet Metal** CommandManager; the **Closed Corner PropertyManager** will be displayed, as shown in Figure 16-53, and you will be prompted to select the planar corner face(s) to extend for creating a closed corner. Select the face or the edge that you need to extend, as shown in Figure 16-54; the selected face will be highlighted in green. Note that both the flanges must be normal to each other for creating the closed corners. You cannot close the faces of the flanges if any one of them is not at 90-degree. After selecting the faces, select the type of corner that you need to create by choosing the buttons in the **Corner type** area of the **Faces to Extend** rollout; the preview of the closed corner will be displayed in the drawing area. Choose the **OK** button from the **Closed Corner PropertyManager**. Figures 16-55 through 16-57 show the preview of the closed corners created using the **Butt**, **Overlap**, and **Underlap** options.

Figure 16-53 The Closed Corner PropertyManager

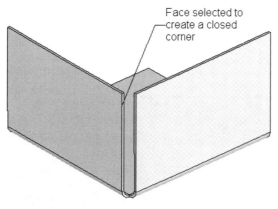

Figure 16-54 Face selected to create a closed corner

Face selected to create a closed corner

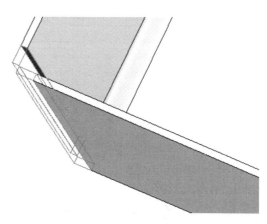

Figure 16-55 Closed corner created with the Butt button chosen

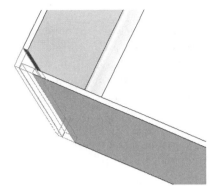

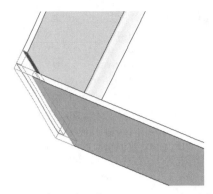

Figure 16-56 *Closed corner created with the* **Overlap** *button chosen*

Figure 16-57 *Closed corner created with the* **Underlap** *button chosen*

Creating Hems

CommandManager:	Sheet Metal > Hem
SolidWorks menus:	Insert > Sheet Metal > Hem
Toolbar:	Sheet Metal > Hem

Hems are generally used to bend a small area of sheet in order to eliminate the sharp edges in a sheet metal component. Hems are also used to join two sheet metal components. To create a hem, choose the **Hem** button from the **Sheet Metal CommandManager**; the **Hem PropertyManager** will be displayed, as shown in Figure 16-58.

You will be prompted to select an edge on a planar face to create a hem feature. Select the edge on a planar face; the preview of the hem with the default settings will be displayed in the drawing area. The rollouts in the **Hem PropertyManager** are discussed next.

Edges Rollout

The options in the **Edges** rollout are used to specify the edges on which will create the hem. As you select the edges, the names of the edges will be listed in the **Edges** selection box and the preview of the hem will be displayed. The **Reverse Direction** button is chosen to reverse the hem direction.

Figure 16-58 *The Hem PropertyManager*

By default, the **Material Inside** button is chosen in the **Edges** rollout. So, the hem is created such that the material of the hem after the bend lies inside the maximum limit of sheet. If you select the **Bend Outside** button, then the hem is created with the bend starting from the maximum limit of the sheet.

Type and Size Rollout

The **Type and Size** rollout is used to define the type and size of the hem that you need to create. The types of hem that you can create using the options in this rollout are discussed next.

Closed Hem

The closed hem is a hem with no gap between the inner face of the hem and the face adjacent to the edge on which the hem is created. To create a closed hem, choose the **Closed** button and set the length of the closed hem using the **Length** spinner. If you select more than one edge to create the hem, the **Miter Gap** rollout will be displayed. You can specify the rip gap in this rollout. Figure 16-59 shows the edge selected to create a closed hem and Figure 16-60 shows the resulting closed hem.

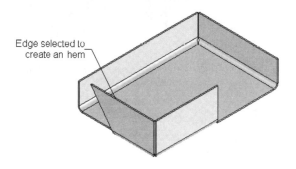

Figure 16-59 Edge selected to create a closed hem

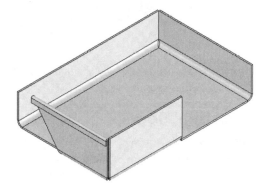

Figure 16-60 Resulting closed hem

Open Hem

The open hem is a hem with a gap between the inner face of the hem and the face adjacent to the edge on which the hem is created. To create the open hem, choose the **Open** button; the **Length** and **Gap Distance** spinners will be displayed. You can specify the value of the length and the gap distance in these spinners. Figure 16-61 shows the edge to be selected to create an open hem and Figure 16-62 shows the resulting open hem.

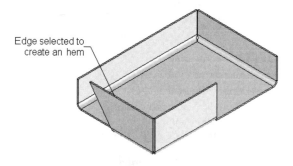

Figure 16-61 Edge selected to create an open hem

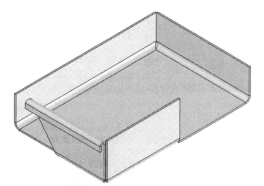

Figure 16-62 Resulting open hem

Tear Drop Hem

By default, the **Tear Drop** button is chosen when you invoke the **Hem PropertyManager**. So the tear drop shaped hem will be created on the selected edge. Set the angle and the radius of the tear drop in the **Angle** and **Radius** spinners, respectively. Figure 16-63 shows the tear drop hem created on a sheet metal component.

Rolled Hem

The **Rolled** button is used to create the rolled shaped hem. When you chosen this button, the **Angle** and **Radius** spinners are displayed to set the respective values.

Figure 16-64 shows the rolled hem created on a sheet metal component.

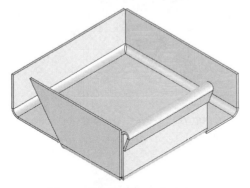

Figure 16-63 Tear drop hem

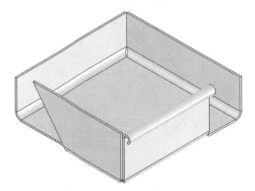

Figure 16-64 Rolled hem

Creating a Jog Bend

CommandManager:	Sheet Metal > Jog
SolidWorks menus:	Insert > Sheet Metal > Jog
Toolbar:	Sheet Metal > Jog

SolidWorks allows you to create a bend that consists of two bends created using a bend line. The bend line is sketched on the face of the sheet metal component from where you need to create the jog bend. Note that the sketch of the bend line must lie inside the face of the sheet metal. After creating the bend line, choose the **Jog** button from the **Sheet Metal CommandManager**; the **Jog PropertyManager** will be displayed, as shown in Figure 16-65 and you will be prompted to select the planar face to be fixed while creating the bend. Select the side of the face to be fixed; the preview of the jog bend with the default values will be displayed in the drawing area. Figures 16-66 and 16-68 show the bend line and the faces to be fixed. Figures 16-67 and 16-69 show the respective jog bends. The rollouts in the **Jog PropertyManager** are discussed next.

Selections Rollout

The options in the **Selections** rollout are used to define the face to be fixed while bending, and also define the radius of the bend. The name of the selected face that needs to be fixed while bending, will be displayed in the **Fixed Face** selection box. By default, the **Use default radius** check box will be selected. If you need to define the bending radius other than the default radius, clear this check box and set the value of the radius in the **Bend Radius** spinner.

Figure 16-65 The **Jog** **PropertyManager**

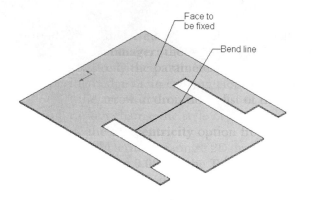

Figure 16-66 *Bend line and face to fix*

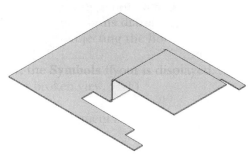

Figure 16-67 *Resulting jog bend*

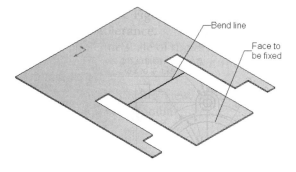

Figure 16-68 *Bend line and face to fix*

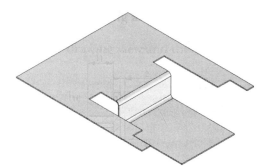

Figure 16-69 *Resulting job bend*

Jog Offset Rollout

The **Jog Offset** rollout is used to define various parameters of the jog. You can define the feature termination option for the jog using this rollout. You can also create a jog with 0 mm blind depth. The options in this rollout are discussed next.

Dimension position Area

The **Dimension position** area of the **Jog Offset** rollout is used to define the position from where the dimension of the jog offset will be calculated. The buttons in this area are used to specify the offset by calculating the inside offset, outside offset, and the overall dimension, refer to Figure 16-70.

Fix projected length

The **Fix projected length** check box is selected by default and is used to maintain the length of the bent sheet equal to the projected length of the original sheet after adding a jog bend. If you clear this check box, then the overall length of the sheet is maintained equal to the original sheet even after adding the jog bend. Figure 16-71 shows the bend line that will be used to create a jog bend. Figure 16-72 shows the preview of the jog bend, created with **Fix projected length** check box selected. Figure 16-73 shows the preview of the jog bend created with the **Fix projected length** check box cleared.

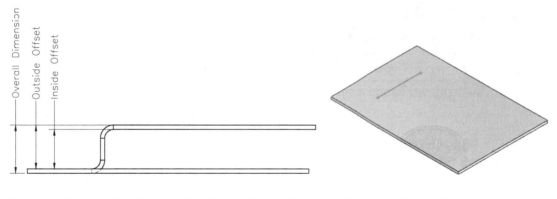

Figure 16-70 *Inside offset, outside offset, and overall dimension*

Figure 16-71 *Bend line to create the jog bend*

Figure 16-72 *Jog bend created with the **Fixed projected length** check box selected*

Figure 16-73 *Jog bend created with the **Fixed projected length** check box cleared*

Jog Position Rollout

The **Jog Position** rollout is used to define the position of bending. The options in this rollout are similar to those discussed earlier.

Jog Angle Rollout

The **Jog Angle** rollout is available to define the angle of the jog bend. The default value of the jog angle is 90-degree. You can set the value of the angle at which you need to create the jog bend in the **Jog Angle** spinner. Figure 16-74 shows the jog bend created at an angle of 135-degree.

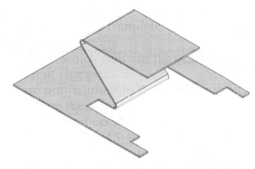

Figure 16-74 *Jog bend created at an angle of 135-degree*

Breaking the Corners

CommandManager	Sheet Metal > Corners > Break-Corner/Corner-Trim
SolidWorks menus:	Insert > Sheet Metal > Break-Corner
Toolbar:	Sheet Metal > Corners > Break-Corner/Corner-Trim

In SolidWorks, you are provided with an option to break the edges of the sheet metal components to create chamfer or fillet. The edges of the sheet metal components are chamfered or filleted using the **Break-Corner/Corner-Trim** tool. To invoke this tool, choose the **Corners > Break-Corner/Corner-Trim** from the **Sheet Metal CommandManager**; the **Break Corner PropertyManager** will be displayed, as shown in Figure 16-75. Also, you will be prompted to select corner edge(s) or flange face(s).

Select the faces or edges that you need to break; the preview of the corner break is displayed in the drawing area with the default settings. As the **Chamfer** button is chosen by default in the **Break Corner Options** rollout, the corner break created by default is a chamfer. You can set the value of the chamfer using the **Distance** spinner. If you need to create a corner break as fillet, choose the **Fillet** button in the **Break Corner Options** rollout; the **Distance** spinner will be replaced by the **Radius** spinner. After setting all the parameters, choose the **OK** button from the **Break Corner PropertyManager**. Figure 16-76 shows the sheet metal component with the chamfers and fillets added using the **Break Corner PropertyManager**.

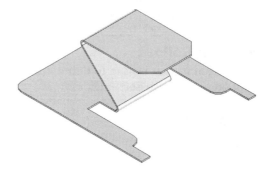

*Figure 16-75 The **Break Corner PropertyManager***

Figure 16-76 Chamfers and fillets added to the sheet metal component

Note
*When you invoke the **Corner** tool after creating a flat pattern of the sheet metal component, some more options will be displayed in the **Break Corner PropertyManager**. These options are discussed later in this chapter.*

Creating Cuts on Planar Faces of the Sheet Metal Components

CommandManager:	Sheet Metal > Extruded Cut
SolidWorks menus:	Insert > Cut > Extrude
Toolbar:	Sheet Metal > Extruded Cut

 In SolidWorks you can create cuts in the sheet metal components. Creating cuts in the sheet metal components is similar to creating cuts in the solid models. To create cuts on the planar faces of the sheet metal components, select a face or a plane as the sketching plane and invoke the sketching environment. Draw the sketch for creating the cut feature and choose the **Extruded Cut** button from the **Sheet Metal CommandManager**; the **Extrude PropertyManager** will be displayed. Set the options for feature termination in the **Extrude PropertyManager**. You will observe that some additional options are displayed in the **Distance 1** rollout of the **Extrude PropertyManager**. These additional options are discussed next.

Link to thickness

The **Link to thickness** check box is used to set the value of the feature termination according to the thickness of the sheet. When you select this check box, the cut feature will be terminated at the blind distance equal to the sheet thickness, irrespective of the feature termination option selected.

Flip side to cut

This check box is used to reverse the side of the sheet metal part to cut.

Normal cut

The **Normal cut** check box is selected by default and is used for the bent sheet metal components. If this check box is selected, the cut feature is created normal to the sheet thickness. If you clear this check box, the cut feature will be created normal to the sketching plane. Figure 16-77 shows the side view of a sheet metal component in which a cut feature is created with the **Normal cut** check box selected and a cut feature created with the **Normal cut** check box cleared.

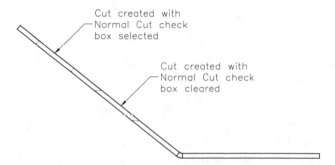

*Figure 16-77 Cut created with the **Normal cut** check box selected and cleared*

Creating Lofted Bends

CommandManager:	Sheet Metal > Lofted-Bend
SolidWorks menus:	Insert > Sheet Metal > Lofted-Bend
Toolbar:	Sheet Metal > Lofted-Bend

 The lofted bends are created by defining a transition of sheet between two open sections placed apart from each other at some offset distance. To create the lofted bends, create the open sections. Remember that the sections should not have vertices. If the sections have vertices, replace them with fillets. Now, choose **Insert > Sheet Metal > Lofted Bends** from the SolidWorks menus; the **Lofted Bends PropertyManager** will be displayed and you are prompted to select two profiles.

Select two profiles to create the lofted bends; the preview of the lofted bend will be displayed in the drawing area. Set the thickness of the sheet using the **Thickness** spinner and choose the **OK** button from the **Lofted Bends PropertyManager**. Figure 16-78 shows the open section that you need to select for creating a lofted bend. Figure 16-79 shows the resulting lofted bend.

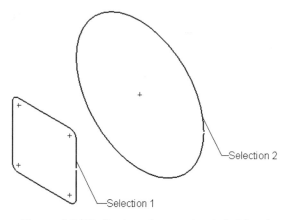

Figure 16-78 Sections for creating lofted bend   *Figure 16-79* Resulting lofted bend

Creating a Flat Pattern View of the Sheet Metal Components

CommandManager:	Sheet Metal > Flatten
SolidWorks menus:	Insert > Sheet Metal > Flatten
Toolbar:	Sheet Metal > Flatten

 The flat pattern view of the sheet metal component is extensively used in the tool room or the machine shop to define the size of the raw sheet, and also the shape of the sheet that you need before bending. It is also used for process planning to start the manufacturing of the tool that will create the sheet metal component. Before creating the flat pattern, you can set the option for the flat pattern. To set the options for the flat pattern, select the **Flat-Pattern1** feature from the **FeatureManager design tree** and invoke the pop-up toolbar. Next, choose the **Edit Feature** option from this toolbar; the **Flat-Pattern PropertyManager** will be invoked, as shown in Figure 16-80. The rollouts in the **Flat-Pattern PropertyManager** are discussed next.

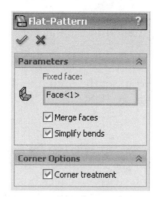

*Figure 16-80 The **Flat-Pattern PropertyManager***

Parameters Rollout

The options in the **Parameters** rollout are used to define various parameters to create the flat pattern of the sheet metal component. The options in this rollout are discussed next.

Fixed face

The **Fixed face** display area is used to specify the face that will be fixed while opening the sheet to create the flat pattern. Select a face; the face will be highlighted in different color and its name is displayed in the **Fixed face** display area. You can select any face from the drawing area that needs to be fixed while creating the flat pattern.

Merge faces

The **Merge faces** check box is used to merge the flat faces and the bending faces while creating the flat pattern. This check box is selected by default. If you clear this check box, the flat faces and bend faces will not be merged. Figure 16-81 shows the flat pattern of a sheet metal component with the **Merge faces** check box selected. Figure 16-82 shows the flat pattern of a sheet metal component with the **Merge faces** check box cleared.

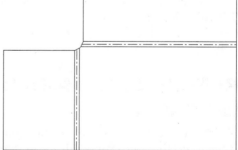

*Figure 16-81 Flat pattern with the **Merge faces** check box selected*

*Figure 16-82 Flat pattern with the **Merge faces** check box cleared*

Simplify bends

The **Simplify bends** check box is selected by default and is used to straighten the curved edges of the sheet metal component in the flat pattern. If you clear this check box, the curved edge will not be straightened in the flat pattern.

Corner Options

The **Corner Options** rollout is used to set the option to dress up the corners of the flattened sheet metal component. The option available in this rollout is discussed next.

Corner Treatment

The **Corner Treatment** check box is selected by default and is used to automatically apply the corner treatment to the flattened sheet. This option removes or adds the material at the corners of the sheet. If you clear this check box, the corner treatment is not applied to the flattened sheet. Figure 16-83 shows the flat pattern of a sheet metal component with the **Corner Treatment** check box selected. Figure 16-84 shows the flat pattern of a sheet metal component with the **Corner Treatment** check box cleared.

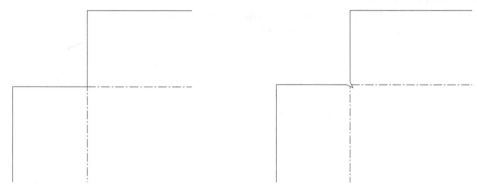

*Figure 16-83   Flat pattern with the **Corner Treatment** check box selected*

*Figure 16-84   Flat pattern with the **Corner Treatment** check box cleared*

After setting all the options, choose the **OK** button from the **Flat-Pattern PropertyManager**. Now, to flatten the sheet metal component, choose the **Flatten** button from the **Sheet Metal** toolbar. You can also select the **Flat-Pattern1** feature from the **FeatureManager design tree** and invoke the pop-up toolbar. Next, choose the **Unsuppress** option from this toolbar to flatten the sheet metal component. The sheet metal component is flattened by selecting the base flange as the face to be fixed.

CREATING SHEET METAL COMPONENTS FROM A FLAT SHEET

In SolidWorks, you can create the sheet metal component by first creating the flat pattern of the sheet and then adding bends to it to get the required shape of the component. Consider an example of the sheet metal component shown in Figure 16-85. The flat pattern of this component is shown in Figure 16-86.

To create this component from a flat sheet, you first need to create the base flange similar to the flat pattern by invoking the **Base Flange/Tab** tool, as shown in Figure 16-87. Next, create

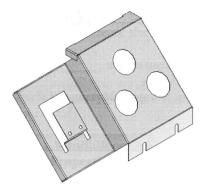

Figure 16-85 *Sheet metal component*

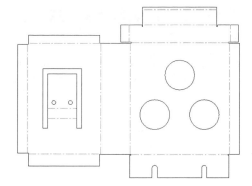

Figure 16-86 *Flat pattern of the sheet metal component*

the bend lines in a single sketch, as shown in Figure 16-88. Now, choose the **Sketched Bend** tool to bend the sheet metal component along the sketch created as the bending lines, as shown in Figure 16-89. You can also add other sheet metal features to complete the component.

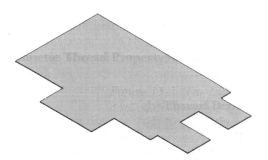

Figure 16-87 *Base flange*

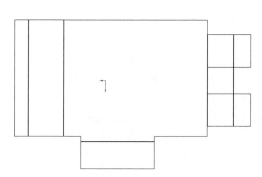

Figure 16-88 *Bend lines*

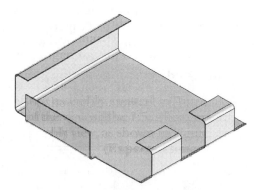

Figure 16-89 *Sheet metal component with bend*

CREATING A SHEET METAL COMPONENT FROM A FLAT PART

In SolidWorks, you can create a sheet metal component by creating the flat state of the sheet as a solid part in the **Part** mode and then converting the solid part into sheet metal. To create a sheet metal component using this method, create a closed sketch that will define the flat state of the sheet. Extrude the sketch using the blind depth equal to the thickness of the flat sheet using the **Extruded Boss/Base** tool. Next, convert the flat part into a sheet metal component in flattened state. The procedure of converting the flat part into a sheet metal component is discussed next.

Converting A Part or Flat Part into Sheet Metal by Adding Bends

CommandManager:	Sheet Metal > Insert Bends
SolidWorks menus:	Insert > Sheet Metal > Insert Bends
Toolbar:	Sheet Metal > Insert Bends

To convert a part into a sheet metal component, you need to add bends in the part. The bends are added to the part using the **Insert Bends** tool. To do so, create the solid part and choose the **Insert Bends** button from the **Sheet Metal CommandManager**; the **Bends PropertyManager** will be displayed and you will be prompted to select the fixed face or edge and set the bend parameters. The partial view of the **Bends PropertyManager** is shown in Figure 16-90.

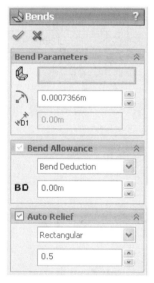

Figure 16-90 Partial view of the Bends PropertyManager

Select the top face of the flat part, as shown in Figure 16-91; the selected face will be highlighted in different color and the name of the face will be displayed in the **Fixed Face or Edge** selection box. Set the parameters of the bend allowance and the relief in the **Bend Allowance** and **Auto Relief** rollouts, respectively. After specifying all these parameters, choose the **OK** button from the **Bends PropertyManager**; the **SolidWorks** message box will be displayed, as shown in Figure 16-92. It will inform you that no bends were found. Choose the **OK** button from the **SolidWorks** message box.

Although no bends are added to the flat part, you will observe that the flat part is converted into a sheet metal part. Then, you can add all features of a sheet metal component to this part. After choosing the **OK** button from the **SolidWorks** message box, you will notice that some new nodes are added to the **FeatureManager design tree**. The usage of these nodes is discussed later in this chapter.

Adding Bends to the Flattened Sheet Metal Component

After converting the solid part into a sheet metal component, you can add bends to the sheet metal component. There are two methods of adding bends to the flattened sheet metal

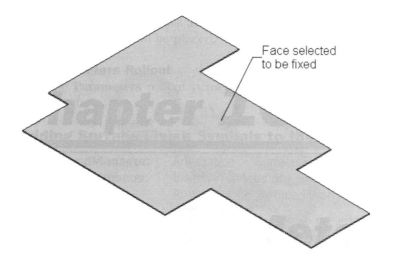

Figure 16-91 *Face selected to be fixed*

Figure 16-92 The SolidWorks message box

components that are extracted from a flat part. The first method of creating sketched bends has already been discussed earlier in this chapter. The second method of creating the sketched bends is discussed next.

Creating Sketched Bends Using the Process Bends Method

The Process Bends method is used to create sketched bends in the sheet metal components extracted from a part. These bends are also called Flat Bends. All the bends created using the bending lines are placed in the **Process-Bends1** node in the **FeatureManager design tree**. To create the bends using this method, expand the **Process-Bends1** node and select the **Flat-Sketch1** node. Next, choose the **Edit Sketch** option from the pop-up toolbar; the sketching environment will be invoked. Create the sketch of the bending lines and exit the sketching environment; the sheet metal component will be bent along the bend lines. If you expand the **Process-Bends1** nodes again, you will observe that all the bend features that you have added using the process bends are displayed. Figure 16-93 shows the sketches that will be used as bend lines to create the bends. Figure 16-94 shows the resulting bent sheet metal component.

Tip. *If you need to edit the radius of the bends individually, expand the Process-Bends1 node in the FeatureManager design tree. Select the bend that you need to modify and invoke the pop-up toolbar. Next, choose the Edit Feature option from this toolbar; the FlatBend PropertyManager will be displayed, which can be used to edit the parameters of the bend.*

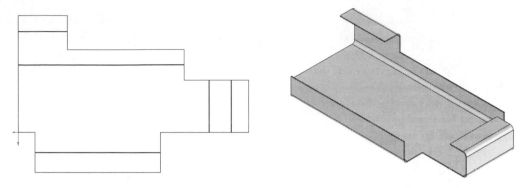

Figure 16-93 *Bend lines*

Figure 16-94 *Resulting bending*

Unbending the Sheet Metal Part Using the No Bends Tool

CommandManager:	SheetMetal > No Bends
Toolbar:	Sheet Metal > No Bends

 The **No Bends** tool is used to straighten the bends in the sheet metal component and roll it back to the stage when it did not have any bends. Choose the **No Bends** button from the **Sheet Metal** toolbar; the **FeatureManager design tree** rollbacks to the stage where no bends were added. It is a toggle tool. You can also rollback the sheet metal component by rolling up the rollback bar above the **Flatten-Bends1** feature from the **FeatureManager design tree**.

After invoking the **No Bends** tool, if you add an extruded feature to the part such that the depth of the extruded feature is equal to the sheet thickness, it will automatically be converted into a flange when you resume the sheet metal part. Consider the model shown in Figure 16-95. This figure shows an extruded feature added to an unbent sheet metal part. Now, if you choose the **No Bends** button from the **Sheet Metal** toolbar, the flange with the default settings for bending and relief will be created, as shown in Figure 16-96. If you want to specify custom bending and relief, expand the **Flatten-Bends1** node in the **FeatureManager design tree** and select **SharpBend1**. Next, invoke the pop-up toolbar and choose the **Edit Feature** option from it. You can define the custom parameters of bend radius, bend allowance, and relief using the **SharpBend PropertyManager**.

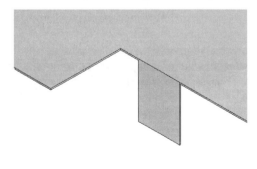

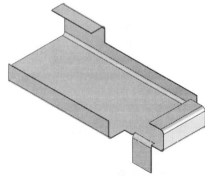

Figure 16-95 *Model with an extruded feature*

Figure 16-96 *Flange with the default settings for bending and relief*

Tip. *Remember that if the original sketch of the sheet metal part had multiple lines at an angle to each other such as the L or U sections, they will not be unbent.*

CREATING A SHEET METAL COMPONENT BY DESIGNING IT AS A PART

SolidWorks provides you with an option to first design the entire part in the part mode and then convert it into a sheet metal component. Consider an example of a sheet metal component shown in Figure 16-97. For creating this component, create the design of the sheet metal component using the part modeling tools, as shown in Figure 16-98.

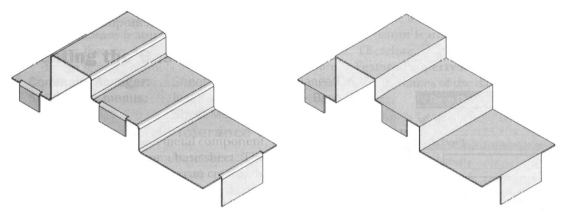

Figure 16-97 *A sheet metal component*   *Figure 16-98* *Component designed as a part*

After designing it as a part, invoke the **Insert Bends** tool from the **Sheet Metal** toolbar; the **Bends PropertyManager** will be displayed. Select the face that will be fixed and specify the sheet metal parameters. Choose the **OK** button from the **Bends PropertyManager**; the part file will be converted into the sheet metal part. If some reliefs are added to the sheet metal component, then the **SolidWorks** message box will be displayed and you will be informed that auto relief cuts were made for one or more bends. Choose the **OK** button from this message window; the sheet metal component will be created. Figure 16-99 shows the flat pattern of the sheet metal component shown in Figure 16-97.

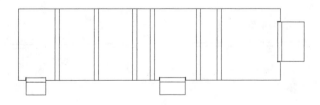

Figure 16-99 *Flat pattern of the sheet metal component*

Understanding the Types of Bends

Now, you need to learn various types of bends that are added to sheet metal components when you create the sheet metal components by converting a part into sheet metal. The types of bends that are added to the sheet metal components during this conversion are discussed next.

Sharp Bends

If you create a part with sharp edges and convert it into a sheet metal component, then the bends added to the sheet metal component are recognized as sharp bends. The sharp bends are placed in the **Flatten-Bends1** feature in the **FeatureManager design tree**. Figure 16-100 shows a part created with sharp edges. Figure 16-101 shows the part converted into sheet metal component.

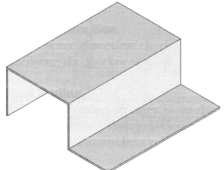

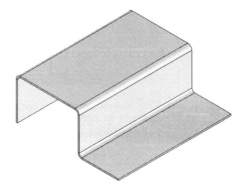

Figure 16-100 *Part created with sharp edges*   *Figure 16-101* *Part converted into sheet metal component*

Round Bends

If you create a part with rounded edges and convert it into a sheet metal component, then the bends added to the sheet metal component are recognized as rounded bends. The rounded bends are placed in the **Flatten-Bends1** feature in the **FeatureManager design tree**. Figure 16-102 shows a part created with rounded edges. Figure 16-103 shows the part converted into sheet metal component.

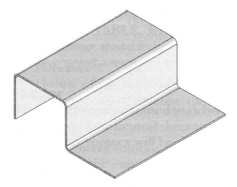

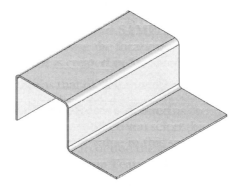

Figure 16-102 *Part with rounded edges*   *Figure 16-103* *Part converted into sheet metal component*

Flat Bends

The flat bends are the bends that are created by bending the flattened sheet. The flat bends are placed in the **Process-Bends1** feature in the **FeatureManager design tree**. The procedure to create these type of bends has been discussed earlier.

CONVERTING A SOLID BODY INTO A SHEET METAL PART

CommandManager:	Sheet Metal > Convert to Sheet Metal
SolidWorks menus:	Insert > Sheet Metal > Convert To Sheet Metal
Toolbar:	Sheet Metal > Convert to Sheet Metal

In SolidWorks 2009, you can convert a solid body into a sheet metal part using the **Convert to Sheet Metal** tool. To convert a solid body into sheet metal using this tool, create a solid body in the **Part** mode and then choose the **Convert to Sheet Metal** button from the **Sheet Metal CommandManager**; the **Convert To Sheet Metal PropertyManager** will be displayed, as shown in Figure 16-104. Next, select the face of the solid body that will be fixed while opening the sheet to create the flat pattern, as shown in Figure 16-105; the selected face will be highlighted in green and its name will be displayed in the **Select a fixed entity** selection box in the **Sheet Metal Parameters** rollout. Set the sheet thickness and the radius of the bend using the **Sheet thickness** and **Default radius for bends** spinners. You can flip the direction of the sheet metal thickness by selecting the **Reverse Thickness** check box in this rollout.

Next, select the edges of the solid body, as shown in Figure 16-106; the name of the selected edges will be displayed in the **Select edges/faces that represent bends** selection box of the **Bend Edges** rollout. Note that the corresponding rib edges of the bend edges are selected automatically and their names will be displayed in the **Automatically found rib edges** selection box. After setting all the required parameters, choose the **OK** button from the **Convert To Sheet Metal PropertyManager**; the solid body will be converted into a sheet metal component. Figure 16-107 shows the solid body to be converted into a sheet metal component and Figure 16-108 shows the flat pattern of the resulting sheet metal component.

*Figure 16-104 Partial view of the **Convert To Sheet Metal PropertyManager***

The other rollouts in this **PropertyManager** are discussed next.

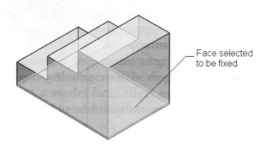

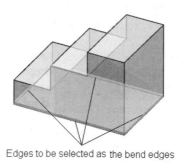

Figure 16-105 *The face selected to be fixed*   **Figure 16-106** *Edges selected*

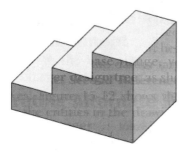

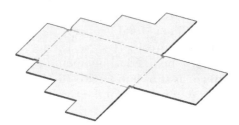

Figure 16-107 *The solid part to be converted into a sheetmetal component*

Figure 16-108 *The flat pattern of the sheetmetal component*

Rip Sketches Rollout

This rollout is used to define the required rips. The **Select a sketch to add a rip** selection box in this rollout is used to select a sketch from the drawing area to define the required rip. To do so, you first need to create a sketch of the rip in the sketching environment. You can specify the gap between the rips using the **Default gap for all rips** spinner in this rollout.

Auto Relief Rollout

The options in the **Auto Relief** rollout of this **PropertyManager** are same as discussed earlier in the **Base Flange PropertyManager**.

DESIGNING A SHEET METAL PART FROM A SOLID SHELLED MODEL

SolidWorks also provides you with an option of designing the sheet metal part as a solid model and then shelling the model. Remember that while shelling the model, you need to remove at least one face. After shelling the model, you need to rip the edges of the thin solid model. The ripping is done in order to cut the sheet so that it can be opened easily while creating the flat pattern. The procedure of ripping the edges of a solid part is discussed next.

Ripping the Edges

CommandManager:	Sheet Metal > Rip
SolidWorks menus:	Insert > Sheet Metal > Rip
Toolbar:	Sheet Metal > Rip

 The **Rip** tool is used to add a gap between the edges of the shelled solid part before converting it into a sheet metal component. To rip the edges, choose the **Rip** button from the **Sheet Metal CommandManager**; the **Rip PropertyManager** will be displayed, as shown in Figure 16-109. Also, you will be prompted to set the rip gap and select the edge(s) to rip. Select the internal edges that you need to rip; the direction arrows are displayed on the selected edge; the name of the selected edge will be displayed in the **Edge to Rip** selection box. The two arrows displayed on the selected edge indicates that the ripping will be done on both the sides of the selected edge. Use the **Change Direction** button to toggle between the two directions. The **Rip Gap** spinner is used to set the value of the rip gap.

Figure 16-109 The Rip PropertyManager

Figure 16-110 shows the edge selected to create the rip in both directions. Figure 16-111 shows the resulting rip.

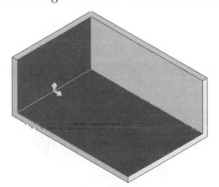

Figure 16-110 Edge selected to create the rip

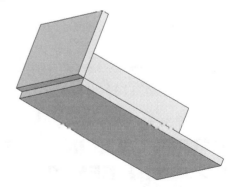

Figure 16-111 Resulting rip

After ripping the edges, choose the **Insert Bends** button to invoke the **Bends PropertyManager**. Select the fixed face, set the sheet metal parameters and choose the **OK** button. Figure 16-112 shows the shelled solid model and Figure 16-113 shows the model after ripping and converting it into a sheet metal component. Figure 16-114 shows the flat pattern of the sheet metal component.

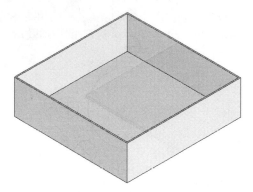

Figure 16-112 *Shelled solid model*

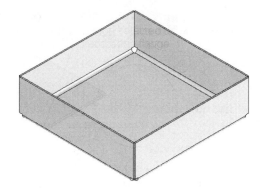

Figure 16-113 *Model after ripping and converting it into a sheet metal component*

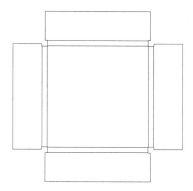

Figure 16-114 *Flat pattern of the sheet metal component*

Tip. *You can also rip the edges using the* **Rip Parameters** *rollout available in the* **Bends PropertyManager**.

CREATING CUTS IN SHEET METAL COMPONENTS ACROSS THE BENDS

In this section, you will learn to create cuts across the bends, as shown in Figure 16-115. The methods of creating cuts across the bends are different for the sheet metal components created from the base flange and the sheet metal component created by converting the solid part. The methods for creating cuts for both types of sheet metal components are discussed next.

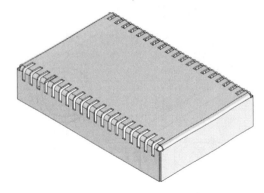

Figure 16-115 *A sheet metal component with cuts across the bends*

Creating Cuts in a Sheet Metal Component Created from a Solid Model

To create a cut in a sheet metal component created by converting a solid model to sheet metal component, you first you need to create the flat pattern of the sheet metal component by invoking the **No Bends** tool. Then, select the face on which you need to create the cut and invoke the sketching environment. Create the sketch and extrude it to create the cut feature. Next, invoke the **No Bends** tool again; the cut will be created across the bends.

Consider an example of a sheet metal component shown in Figure 16-116. Invoke the **No Bends** tool to create the flat pattern of the sheet metal component, as shown in Figure 16-117. Select the top face of the flattened sheet metal component as the sketching plane and invoke the sketching environment. Create the sketch and extrude the cut using the **Link to thickness** option from the **Extrude PropertyManager**. After creating the cut, use the **Linear Pattern** tool to create a linear pattern of the cut feature. The flattened sheet metal component after creating and patterning the cut feature is shown in Figure 16-118. Next, invoke the **No Bends** tool again to display the sheet metal component with cuts across the bends, as shown in Figure 16-119.

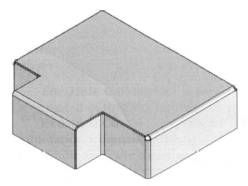

Figure 16-116 *Sheet metal component*

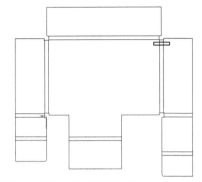

Figure 16-117 *Flat pattern of the sheet metal component*

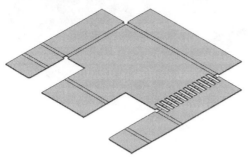

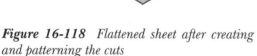

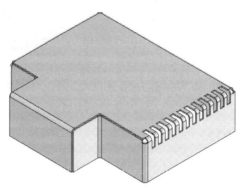

Figure 16-118 *Flattened sheet after creating and patterning the cuts*

Figure 16-119 *Final sheet metal component*

Note

*If you choose the **Flatten** button from the **Sheet Metal** toolbar to create the cuts on a flattened sheet, the cuts will not be displayed in the unflattened sheet metal component.*

Creating Cuts in a Sheet Metal Component Created Using the Base Flange

The sheet metal component designed using the base flange does not include the **Flatten-Bends1** and the **Process-Bends1** features. Therefore, for creating cuts in this type of sheet metal component, you first need to unfold the sheet using the **Unfold** tool and then create the cut feature. After creating the feature, you need to fold the sheet again using the **Fold** tool. Consider the example of the sheet metal component displayed in Figure 16-120. For creating cuts in this sheet metal component, you first need to unfold the sheet. The method of unfolding the sheet is discussed next.

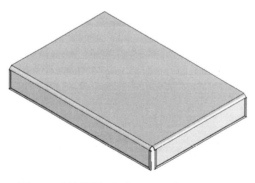

Figure 16-120 *A sheet metal component*

Unfolding the Sheet

CommandManager:	Sheet Metal > Unfold
SolidWorks menus:	Insert > Sheet Metal > Unfold
Toolbar:	Sheet Metal > Unfold

To unfold the sheet, you need to invoke the **Unfold** tool by choosing the **Unfold** button from the **Sheet Metal CommandManager**; the **Unfold PropertyManager** will be displayed, as shown in Figure 16-121. Also, you will be prompted to select a face to be fixed and the bends to be unfolded.

Select the face that you need to fix and the bends that you need to unfold. To unfold all the bends, choose the **Collect All Bends** button in the **Selections** rollout. Choose the **OK** button from the **Unfold PropertyManager**. You will notice that the sheet metal component is unfolded. Figure 16-122 shows the unfolded sheet.

Figure 16-121 The Unfold PropertyManager

After unfolding the sheet, create the required cut feature. The unfolded sheet after creating the cut feature is shown in Figure 16-123. Fold the sheet again after creating the cut feature.

Figure 16-122 The unfolded sheet

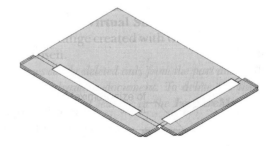

Figure 16-123 The unfolded sheet after creating the cut feature

Folding the Sheet

CommandManager:	SheetMetal > Fold
SolidWorks menus:	Insert > Sheet Metal > Fold
Toolbar:	Sheet Metal > Fold

To fold the unfolded sheet, choose the **Fold** button from the **Sheet Metal CommandManager**; the **Fold PropertyManager** will be displayed, as shown in Figure 16-124. Also, you will be prompted to select a face to be fixed and the bends to be folded.

The face of the sheet that was fixed while unfolding the sheet is selected by default when you invoke the **Fold PropertyManager**. You can also select any other face that you need to fix while folding the sheet. Choose the **Collect All Bends** button to select all bends to be folded and then choose the **OK** button from the **Fold PropertyManager**. Figure 16-125 shows the final sheet metal component after folding it using the **Fold** tool.

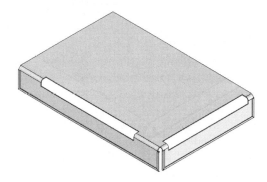

Figure 16-124 The *Fold PropertyManager*   *Figure 16-125* *Sheet metal component after folding*

 Note
If you create edge flanges throughout the length of edges of the base flange, SolidWorks may not fold the component back.

Creating Cylindrical and Conical Sheet Metal Components

SolidWorks also allows you to create cylindrical and conical sheet metal components. For creating a cylindrical or a conical sheet metal component, you need to make sure that there is some gap to unfold the sheet. Create a conical or a cylindrical sheet metal part and invoke the **Bends PropertyManager** to convert the part into the sheet metal component. Now, select a linear edge of the conical or cylindrical part that will be fixed, refer to Figure 16-126. Choose the **OK** button from the **Bends PropertyManager**. Next, choose the **Flatten** button. Figure 16-127 shows the flat pattern of the conical sheet metal component.

Figure 16-126 Edge selected to be fixed

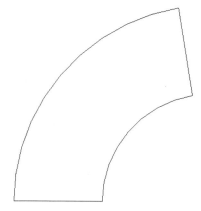

Figure 16-127 Flat pattern of the conical sheet metal component

Note
If you create the cylindrical or conical sheet metal component by lofting, you can directly use the **Flat Pattern** *option to create the flat pattern.*

GENERATING THE DRAWING VIEW OF THE FLAT PATTERN OF THE SHEET METAL COMPONENTS

After creating a sheet metal component, the next step is to generate the drawing view of the flat pattern of the sheet metal component. For generating the drawing view of the flat pattern, select the **Flat Pattern** check box from the **Orientation** rollout in the **Model View PropertyManager** and place the drawing view on the sheet. Figure 16-128 shows a sheet metal component and Figure 16-129 shows its resulting flat pattern view. Figure 16-130 shows the drawing view of the flat pattern of the sheet metal component.

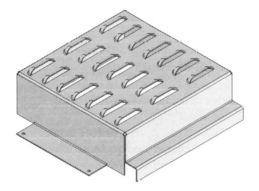

Figure 16-128 Sheet metal component

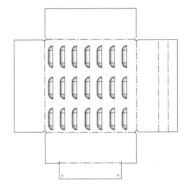

Figure 16-129 Flat pattern

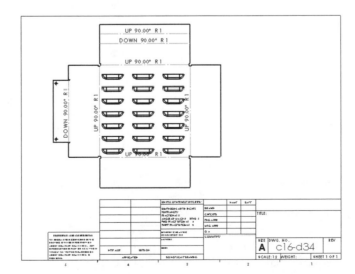

Figure 16-130 Drawing view of the flat pattern

TUTORIALS

Tutorial 1

In this tutorial, you will create the sheet metal component shown in Figure 16-131. The flat pattern of the sheet metal component and its views and dimensions are shown in Figures 16-132 and 16-133, respectively. You will first create the base flange and then the other features. After creating the model, you will create its flat pattern.   **(Expected time: 45 min)**

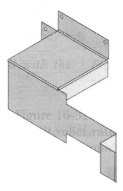

Figure 16-131 *Sheet metal component*

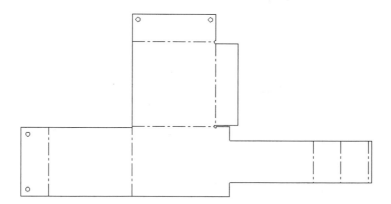

Figure 16-132 *Flat pattern of the sheet metal component*

The following steps are required to complete this tutorial:

a.   Create the base flange of the sheet metal component.
b.   Add the other required flanges to the sheet metal component.
c.   Create the tab feature.
d.   Add a hem to the right most flange.
e.   Create the flat pattern of the sheet metal component.
f.   Save the model.

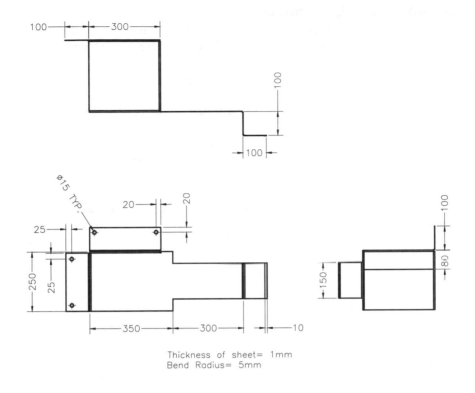

Figure 16-133 *Drawing views and dimensions for Tutorial 1*

Creating the Base Flange

For creating this sheet metal component, you first need to create the base flange. The base flange will be created using a rectangular sketch drawn on the Front Plane.

1. Start a new SolidWorks document in the **Part** mode.

2. Invoke the sketching environment using the Front Plane as the sketching plane.

3. Create a rectangle of 350x250 mm as the sketch of the base flange, refer to Figure 16-134.

4. Choose the **Base Flange/Tab** button from the **Sheet Metal CommandManager**; the **Base Flange PropertyManager** is displayed.

5. Set the value of the following parameters and choose the **OK** button from the **Base Flange PropertyManager**.

   Thickness: **1**   K-Factor: **1**   Auto Relief Type: **Rectangular**   Ratio: **0.5**

   Figure 16-134 shows the base flange created using the sketch created on the Front Plane as the sketching plane.

Creating the First Edge Flange

After creating the base flange, you need to create the first edge flange using the top edge of the base flange as the reference. You will observe that the **Sheet-Metal1** feature is displayed in the **FeatureManager design tree**. Modify the default bend radius using the **Sheet-Metal1** feature before creating the first edge flange.

1. Select the **Sheet-Metal1** node from the **FeatureManager design tree** to invoke the pop-up toolbar. Choose the **Edit Feature** option from the pop-up toolbar.

2. Set the value in the **Bend Radius** spinner to **5** and choose the **OK** button from the **Sheet-Metal1 PropertyManager**.

3. Choose the **Edge Flange** button from the **Sheet Metal CommandManager**; the **Edge-Flange PropertyManager** is displayed. Also, you are prompted to select a linear edge of a planar face to create the edge flange.

4. Select the edge of the base flange, as shown in Figure 16-135.

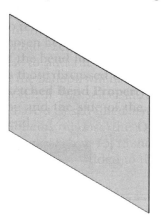

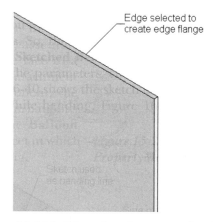

Figure 16-134 *Base flange*   *Figure 16-135* *Edge selected to create edge flange*

5. In the **Flange Length** rollout, set the value in the **Length** spinner to **300**. Choose the **Material Outside** button from the **Flange Position** rollout. Make sure that the flange is being created in the backward direction.

   Next, you need to edit the profile of the edge flange.

6. Choose the **Edit Flange Profile** button from the **Flange Parameters** rollout. If this button is not available, clear the **Use default radius** check box and then select it again; the **Edit Flange Profile** button will be available. As soon as you choose this button, the sketching environment is invoked and the **Profile Sketch** dialog box is displayed.

7. Edit the sketch, refer to Figure 16-136. Choose the **Finish** button from the **Profile Sketch** dialog box. The model after creating the first flange is displayed, as shown in Figure 16-137.

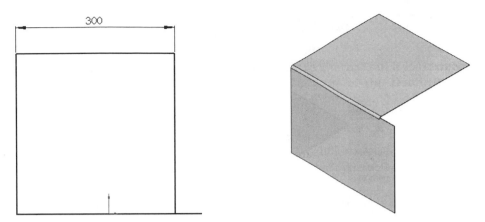

Figure 16-136 *Modified sketch of the edge flange*   *Figure 16-137* *Model after creating edge flange*

Creating the Second Edge Flange

Next, you need to create the second edge flange with the holes.

1. Choose the **Edge Flange** button from the **Sheet Metal CommandManager** to invoke the **Edge-Flange PropertyManager**.

2. Select the edge, as shown in Figure 16-138; the preview of the edge flange is displayed.

3. Set the value in the **Length** spinner to **100** and choose the **OK** button from the **Edge-Flange PropertyManager**.

    The model after creating the second edge flange is shown in Figure 16-139.

4. Similarly, create the edge flanges on the left side of the sheet metal component.

5. Edit the sketch of the edge flanges and draw the sketch for the holes. Refer to Figure 16-133 for dimensions. Edge-flanges with the holes are shown in Figure 16-140.

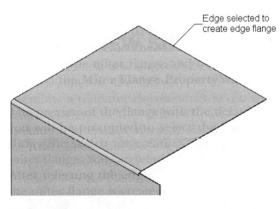

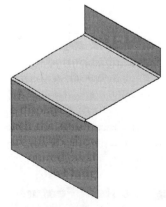

Figure 16-138 *Edge selected to create the edge flange*

Figure 16-139 *Model after creating the second edge flange*

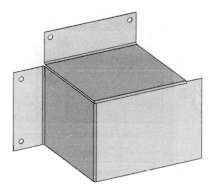

Figure 16-140 Model after creating edge flanges and holes on the left of the model

Creating the Tab and Flange Feature

Next, you need to add a tab feature to the sheet metal component. A tab feature is used to add material to the base flange or any other flange feature.

1. Select the front face of the base flange as the sketching plane and invoke the sketching environment.

2. Draw the sketch of the tab feature, as shown in Figure 16-141.

3. Choose the **Base-Flange/Tab** button from the **Sheet Metal CommandManager** to create the tab feature. The model after creating the tab feature is displayed in Figure 16-142.

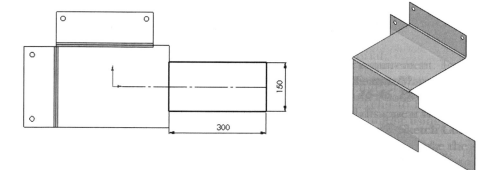

Figure 16-141 Sketch of the tab feature   *Figure 16-142 Model after creating the tab feature*

4. Create three more edge flanges, two of length 100 mm and one of length 80 mm, refer to Figure 16-133. The model after creating all the edge flanges is displayed in Figure 16-143.

Creating the Hem Feature

After creating the other sheet metal features, you need to create the hem on the right most edge flange.

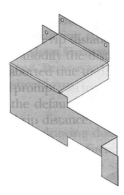

Figure 16-143 *Model after creating all the edge flanges*

1. Choose the **Hem** button from the **Sheet Metal CommandManager**; the **Hem PropertyManager** is displayed.

2. Choose the **Closed** button from the **Type and Size** rollout and set the value in the **Length** spinner to **10**.

3. Select the edge to create the hem, as shown in Figure 16-144; the hem is created, as shown in Figure 16-145.

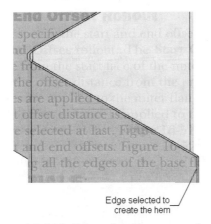

Edge selected to
create the hem

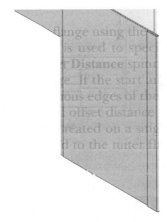

Figure 16-144 *Edge selected to create the hem*

Figure 16-145 *Resulting hem*

Creating the Flat Pattern

After creating the sheet metal component, you need to create its flat pattern.

1. Choose the **Flatten** button from the **SheetMetal CommandManager** to create the flat pattern of the sheet metal component.

2. Orient the flattened model parallel to the screen.

The flattened sheet metal component is displayed in Figure 16-146.

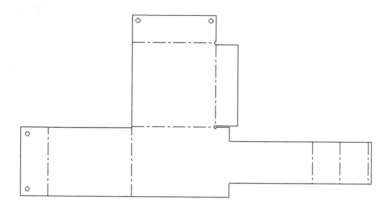

Figure 16-146 *Flattened sheet metal component*

Saving the Model

Next, you need to save the model.

1. Choose the **Save** button from the Menu Bar and save the drawing in the location and the name given below and close the file.

   \My Documents\SolidWorks\c16\c16tut01.sldprt

Tutorial 2

In this tutorial, you will create the sheet metal component shown in Figure 16-147. The flat pattern of the sheet metal component is displayed in Figure 16-148. After creating the model, you need to generate its drawing views, as shown in Figure 16-149. The drawing views and the dimensions for the model are displayed in Figure 16-150.   **(Expected time: 1 hr)**

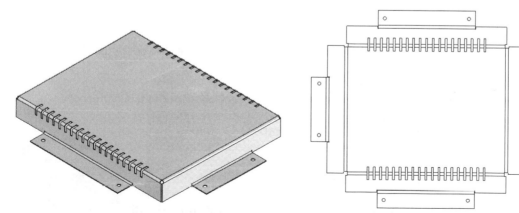

Figure 16-147 *Sheet metal component*   ***Figure 16-148*** *Flattened sheet metal component*

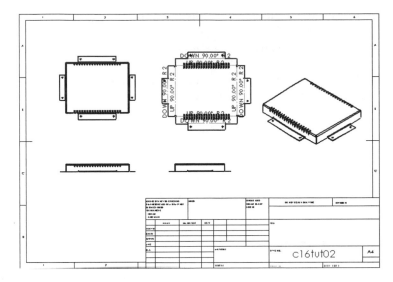

Figure 16-149 *Drawing views of the model*

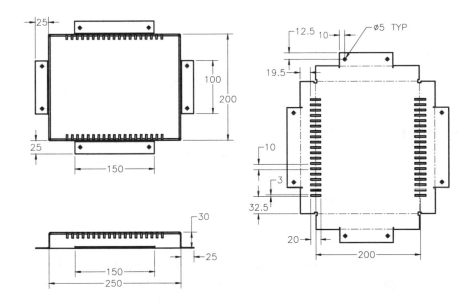

The thickness of sheet is 1mm. Bend radius is 2mm

Figure 16-150 *Views and dimensions for Tutorial 2*

The following steps are required to complete this tutorial:

a. Create the base feature by extruding a sketch created on the Top Plane.
b. Shell the base feature.
c. Convert the shelled solid model into sheet metal component.
d. Rollback the model to the state where no bends were added to the sheet metal component.
e. Add flanges to the sheet metal component.
f. Create the flat pattern of the sheet metal component.
g. Create slots using the cut feature and pattern them on the sides of the flatten sheet metal component.
h. Refold the sheet metal component.
i. Generate the drawing views of the sheet metal component.
j. Save the model.

Creating the Base Feature

You will create this model by converting a shelled part into a sheet metal component. Therefore, you first need to create the base feature of the model by extruding a sketch created on the Top Plane.

1. Start a new SolidWorks document in the **Part** mode.

2. Invoke the sketching environment by selecting the top plane as the sketching plane.

3. Draw the sketch of the base feature that consists of a rectangle of 250x200.

4. Extrude the sketch to a distance of 30 mm; the base feature of the model is displayed, as shown in Figure 16-151.

Shelling the Base Feature

Next, you need to add the shell feature to the model by removing the bottom face of the base feature.

1. Rotate the model so that the bottom face of the model is clearly visible.

2. Invoke the **Shell** tool and select the bottom face of the base feature as the face to remove.

3. Set the value in the **Thickness** spinner to **1** and choose the **OK** button from the **Shell1 PropertyManager**; the shell feature is created, as shown in Figure 16-152.

Converting the Shelled Model into Sheet Metal Component

After creating the base feature and shelling the model, you need to convert it into a sheet metal component using the **Insert Bends** tool.

1. Choose the **Insert Bends** button from the **SheetMetal CommandManager** to invoke the **Bends PropertyManager**.

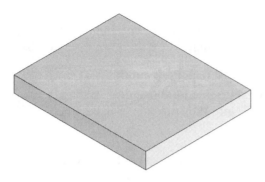

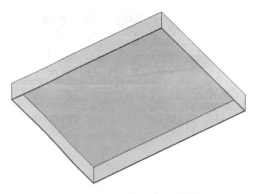

Figure 16-151 *Base feature*   *Figure 16-152* *Model after shelling*

2. Select the top face of the model to fix.

3. Click once in the **Edges to Rip** selection box in the **Rip Parameters** rollout to activate the selection mode.

4. Select all the inner vertical edges of the base feature as the edges to rip.

5. Set the value **2** in the **Bend Radius** spinner and **1** in the **K-Factor** spinner.

6. Choose the **OK** button from the **Bends PropertyManager**; the SolidWorks message box is displayed, which informs you that the auto reliefs are added. Choose the **OK** button from this message box.

The model after converting the solid shelled model into the sheet metal component is shown in Figure 16-153.

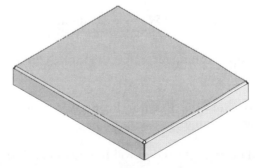

Figure 16-153 *Solid shelled model after converting into sheet metal component*

Tip. *You can also convert a solid model into sheet metal by choosing the **Convert to sheet metal** tool.*

Creating the Edge Flanges

Next, you need to add the edge flanges to the sheet metal component. Before adding the edge flanges, you need to rollback the model to the stage when there were no bends in the sheet metal component.

1. Choose the **No Bends** button from the **Sheet Metal CommandManager** to rollback the model to the stage where it had no bends. Note that the four walls of the model are not unbent.

2. Now, select the bottom face of one of the four walls of the model as the sketching plane and invoke the sketching environment.

3. Draw the sketch of the flanges, as shown in Figure 16-154.

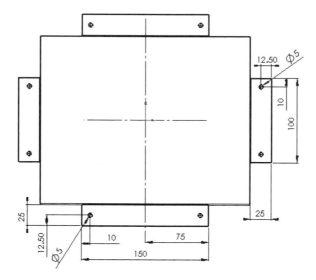

Figure 16-154 Sketch of the flanges

4. Invoke the **Extrude PropertyManager**. Select the **Link to thickness** check box and choose the **Reverse Direction** button.

5. Choose the **OK** button from the **Extrude PropertyManager**. Figure 16-155 shows the model after extruding the flanges.

   After extruding the flanges, you need to roll the model back to the bending stage.

6. Again, choose the **No Bends** button from the **Sheet Metal CommandManager** to roll the model to the bending stage.

   Figure 16-156 shows the model after rolling it to the bending stage.

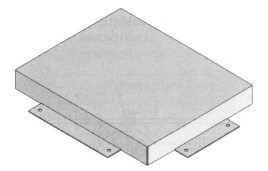

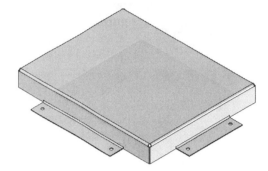

Figure 16-155 *Model after extruding the flanges*

Figure 16-156 *Model rolled to the bending stage*

Creating Cuts across the Bends

The next feature that you need to create is the cut feature across the bends. For creating this feature, you first need to unfold the sheet metal component.

1. Choose the **Unfold** button from the **Sheet Metal CommandManager** and select the top face of the model as the fixed face.

2. Choose the **Collect All Bends** button and then choose **OK** from the **Unfold PropertyManager**. The unfolded view of the model is shown in Figure 16-157.

3. Select the top face of the model and invoke the sketching plane. Next, draw the sketch of the cut feature, as shown in Figure 16-158.

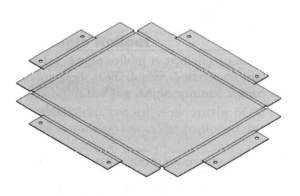

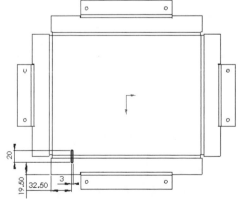

Figure 16-157 *Unfolded view of the model*

Figure 16-158 *Sketch of the cut feature*

4. Invoke the **Extruded Cut** tool and create the cut feature. The model after adding the cut feature is shown in Figure 16-159.

5. Pattern the cut feature. The model after patterning the cut feature is shown in Figure 16-160.

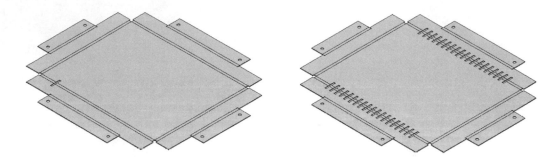

Figure 16-159 *Model after adding the cut feature*

Figure 16-160 *Model after patterning the cut feature*

Refolding the Sheet Metal Part

After creating the sheet metal component, you need to refold the sheet.

1. Choose the **Fold** button from the **SheetMetal CommandManager**; the **Fold PropertyManager** is displayed and the top face is selected by default.

2. Choose the **Collect All Bends** button and then choose **OK**. The sheet metal component after refolding is shown in Figure 16-161.

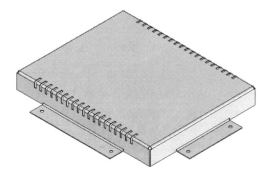

Figure 16-161 *Sheet metal component after refolding*

 Note
You can also create the flat pattern of the sheet metal component as a new configuration. The procedure to add configurations is discussed in the next chapter.

Saving the Model

Next, you need to save the model before generating the drawing views.

1. Choose the **Save** button from the Menu Bar and save the drawing in the location and the name given below:

    \My Documents\SolidWorks\c16\c16tut02.sldprt

Generating the Drawing Views of the Sheet Metal Component

You will generate the drawing views on an A4 size drawing sheet with third angle projection.

1. Choose **New > Make Drawing from Part/Assembly** from the Menu Bar and start the **Drawing** mode with the **A4-Landscape** as the standard sheet size.

2. If the default projection type is in the first angle, change it to the third angle using the **Sheet Properties** dialog box.

3. Generate the three default standard views of the model by dragging it from the **View Palette** task pane. Figure 16-162 shows the drawing sheet after generating the three standard views.

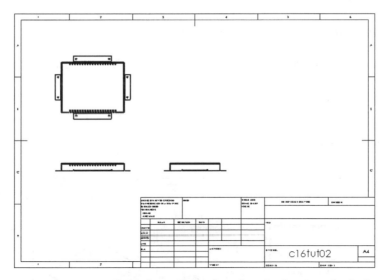

Figure 16-162 *Drawing sheet after generating the three standard views*

After generating the three standard views, you need to generate the drawing view of the flat pattern.

4. Invoke the **Model View** tool and double-click on **c16tut02** in the **Open Documents** area.

5. Select the **Flat pattern** check box in the **Orientation** rollout. Select **Flat Pattern** from the drop-down list available in the **Reference Configuration** rollout and place the flat pattern view.

    Figure 16-163 shows the drawing sheet after generating the drawing view of the flat pattern.

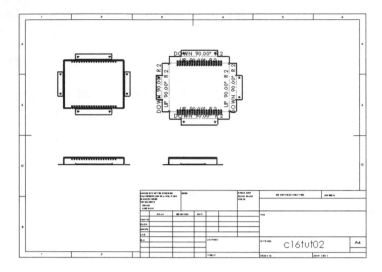

Figure 16-163 *Drawing sheet after generating the flat pattern view*

Next, you need to generate the isometric view.

6. Generate an isometric view and place the view close to the top right corner of the drawing sheet. Change the scale of the isometric view to 1:4.

The drawing sheet after generating all the drawing views is displayed in Figure 16-164.

7. Save the drawing file.

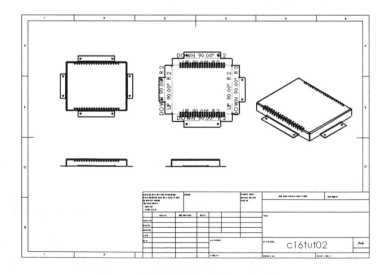

Figure 16-164 *Final drawing sheet*

SELF-EVALUATION TEST

Answer the following questions and then compare them to those given at the end of this chapter:

1. In SolidWorks, the _____ button in the **Sheet Metal** toolbar is used to create the base flange.

2. The _____ option in the **Bend Allowance Type** drop-down list is selected to specify the bending allowance using the bend tables.

3. Select the _____ check box in the **View Orientation** rollout to generate the drawing view of the flat pattern of the sheet metal component.

4. The _____ button in the **Sheet Metal** toolbar is provided to create hems.

5. The _____ rollout is used to define the bend allowance other than the default bend allowance that you have defined while creating the base flange.

6. To create the flat pattern of a sheet metal component, which is created by converting a part, you need to choose the **Flatten** button. (T/F)

7. If you create a part with sharp edges and convert it into a sheet metal component, then the bends added to the sheet metal component are recognized as round bends. (T/F)

8. For creating a closed corner, choose the **Closed Corner** button from the **Features** toolbar. (T/F)

9. The **Rip Gap** spinner in the **Rip Parameters** rollout is used to define the rip distance between two consecutive flanges. (T/F)

10. The **Sketched Bend** tool is used to create a bend using a sketch as the bending line. (T/F)

REVIEW QUESTIONS

Answer the following questions:

1. The _____ option in the **Bend Allowance Type** drop-down list is used to define the K-Factor.

2. The _____ tool is used to create a series of flanges along the edges of the sheet metal component.

3. The _____ check box is used to set the value of the feature termination according to the thickness of the sheet.

4. While creating the miter flange, the distance value of the rip is modified using the _____ spinner.

5. To create lofted bends, choose the _____ button from the **Sheet Metal** toolbar.

6. Which button in the **Sheet Metal** toolbar is used to fold the unfolded sheet?

    (a) **Flattened**   (b) **Fold**
    (c) **Bends**   (d) **Unfold**

7. Which tool is used to rollback the sheet metal component to the stage when it did not have any bends?

    (a) **Flattened**   (b) **No Bends**
    (c) **Unfold**   (d) **Remove Bends**

8. To unfold the sheet, you need to invoke the _____ tool?

    (a) **Unfold**   (b) **Flattened**
    (c) **No Bends**   (d) None of these

9. Which tool is used to draw the bending lines?

    (a) **Centerline**   (b) **Arc**
    (c) **Spline**   (d) **Line**

10. Lofted bends are created between_____.

EXERCISE

Exercise 1

In this exercise, you will create the sheet metal component shown in Figure 16-165. The flat pattern of this model is shown in Figure 16-166. To create this model, first create the base flange. Then, you need to create a miter flange to complete the sheet metal component. The default bend radius is 2 mm, K-Factor is 0.5, and Rectangular Relief ratio is 0.5. Thickness of the sheet is 1 mm. Rip gap for miter flange is 2 mm. Views and dimensions for this model are shown in Figure 16-167.   **(Expected time: 20 min)**

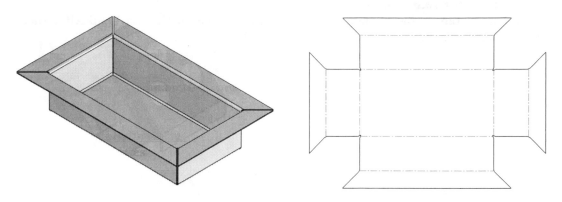

Figure 16-165 *Sheet metal component*

Figure 16-166 *Flat pattern of the sheet metal component*

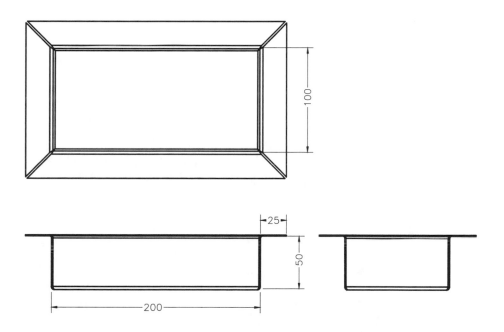

Figure 16-167 *Views and dimensions of the sheet metal component for Exercise 1*

Answers to Self-Evaluation Test
1. Base-Flange/Tab, **2. Bend Table**, **3. Flat Pattern**, **4. Hem**, **5. Custom Bend Allowance**, **6.** T, **7.** F, **8.** F, **9.** T, **10.** T

Chapter 17

Equations, Configurations, and Library Features

Learning Objectives

After completing this chapter, you will be able to:
- *Work with equations.*
- *Work with configurations.*
- *Create configurations using design tables.*
- *Change the suppression state of the components using design table.*
- *Change visibility of the components using design table.*
- *Edit the design tables.*
- *Delete the design tables.*
- *Create library features.*

EQUATIONS AND CONFIGURATIONS

In this chapter, you will learn some of the advanced tools that are used to increase the productivity in the **Part**, **Drawing**, and **Assembly** modes of SolidWorks. These tools are used to create equations in part modeling, configurations, and library feature. The tools and the procedure to create the equations and configurations are discussed next.

Working with Equations

SolidWorks menus:	Tools > Equations
Toolbar:	Tools > Equations

Equations are the mathematical relations between the dimensions. The dimensions can be the dimension of a sketch, a feature, or dimension on the drawing sheet. The dimension names are used as variables for adding the equations in the design. To add the equations in the sketching environment or in the part modeling environment, choose the **Equations** button from the **Tools** toolbar; the **Equations** dialog box will be displayed, as shown in Figure 17-1.

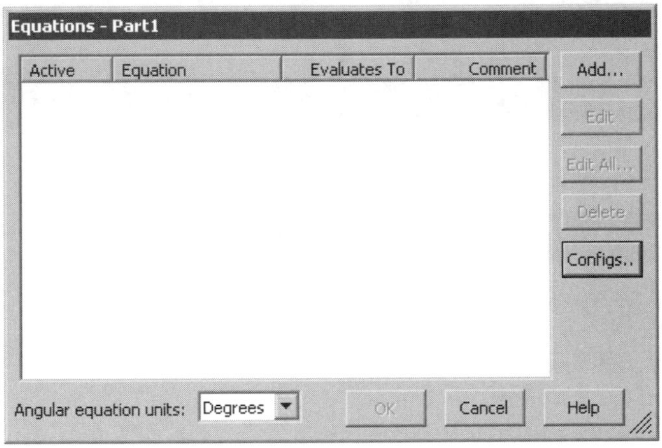

*Figure 17-1 The **Equations** dialog box*

The options in this dialog box are used to add the equations to the design. These options are discussed next.

Adding the Equations

You can add dimensions to a sketch or a feature. To add the equations to a sketch, create a sketch, apply dimension to it, and then choose the **Add** button from the **Equations** dialog box; the **Add Equation** dialog box will be displayed, as shown in Figure 17-2. If you add the equations in the **Part** mode, then you need to double-click the feature or features whose dimensions are to be included in the equation. Select a dimension from the drawing area. This dimension is known as the driven dimension and it has to equate to other dimensions. The other dimension is called as driving dimension. On selecting a driven dimension, its name will be displayed as a variable in the edit box provided in the **Add Equation** dialog box. Next, press the **=** (equal to) key, then select the driving dimension from the drawing area and

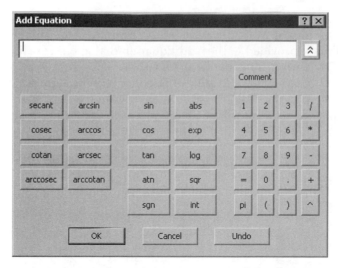

Figure 17-2 The **Add Equation** dialog box

add the mathematical relation. Note that if you select the dimension and invoke the **Add Equation** dialog box, then the name of the dimension along with the = (equal to) symbol will be displayed in the **Add Equation** dialog box.

Consider a case of the sketch of a rectangle in which you need the width of the rectangle to be 0.5 times the length of the rectangle. Also, you need to drive the width of the rectangle with respect to the length of the rectangle. Figure 17-3 shows the sketch of the rectangle with the dimensions added to the sketch.

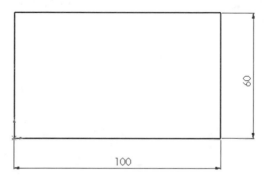

Figure 17-3 Sketch of the rectangle with dimensions

Invoke the **Equations** dialog box and choose the **Add** button from this dialog box to invoke the **Add Equation** dialog box. Select the dimension with the value 60; the name of the dimension will be displayed in the edit box provided in the **Add Equation** dialog box. Choose the **=** (equal to) button in this dialog box. Now, select the dimension with the value 100 from the drawing area. Choose the **Multiplication** button from the **Add Equation** dialog box and enter **0.5** in the edit box provided in the **Add Equation** dialog box, as shown in Figure 17-4. Next, choose the **OK** button from the **Add Equation** dialog box. The value after solving the equation will be displayed in the **Evaluates To** column of the **Equations** dialog box. Now, choose the **OK** button from this dialog box. The sketch will be regenerated and the dimension value of the width of the rectangle will be modified with respect to the relation applied to it. Also, the equation symbol will be added to the width of the rectangle.

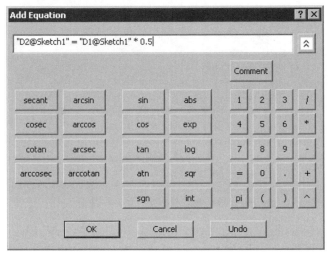

*Figure 17-4 The **Add Equation** dialog box after adding the equation*

When you add the equations in the part or in the sketch, the **Equations** folder is automatically created in the **FeatureManager design tree**, as shown in Figure 17-5. You will learn more about this folder later in this chapter.

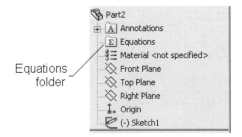

*Figure 17-5 The **Equations** folder created in the*
FeatureManager design tree

Editing the Equations

You can also edit the equations that are added to the design using the **Add Equation** dialog box. If the **Equations** dialog box is already invoked, select the equation to be edited and choose the **Edit** button from the **Equations** dialog box; the **Edit Equation** dialog box will be displayed, in Figure 17-6. Alternatively, you can use the **Equations** tool to invoke the

Equations dialog box, then select an equation, and choose the **Edit** button from this dialog box. You can also invoke the **Edit Equation** dialog box by selecting the **Equations** folder from the **FeatureManager design tree.** Then, right-click and choose the **Edit Equation** option from the shortcut menu.

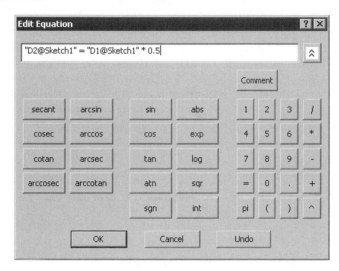

*Figure 17-6 The **Edit Equation** dialog box*

If you choose the **Edit All** button from the **Equations** dialog box, all the equations that are added to the model will be displayed in the **Edit Equations** dialog box, as shown in Figure 17-7. You can edit an equation by clicking on it in the list box. After editing the equations, choose the **OK** button from the **Edit Equations** dialog box. Then, choose the **OK** button from the **Equations** dialog box so that the changes made to the equations are reflected in the design. You may also need to rebuild the model after editing the equations.

*Figure 17-7 The **Edit Equations** dialog box*

Tip. *To invoke the **Equations** dialog box, you can also double-click on a dimension to display the **Modify** dialog box and select the **Add Equation** option from the drop-down list in this dialog box.*

*To edit or delete an equation, double-click on the dimension that has the equations; the **Modify** dialog box will be displayed. Select the **Edit Equation** or the **Delete Equation** option from the drop-down list.*

Suppressing and Unsuppressing the Equations

You can also suppress the equations that are not required at a particular stage. To suppress an equation, invoke the **Equations** dialog box and clear the check box in the **Active** column of the **Equations** dialog box; the status of the equation will be displayed as **Suppressed** in the **Evaluates To** column of this dialog box. Now, choose the **OK** button from the **Equations** dialog box. On suppressing an equation, you can modify the corresponding driven dimension.

To unsuppress the suppressed equation, you need to select the check box in the **Active** column of the **Equations** dialog box; a green check mark will be displayed and the value of the driven dimension will be displayed in the **Evaluates To** column. Now, choose the **OK** button from the **Equations** dialog box. As you unsuppress the equation, the driven dimension will revert to the same value that was applied to it using the equation.

Deleting the Equations

You can delete the unwanted equations by selecting them in the **Equations** dialog box and then choosing the **Delete** button from this dialog box. Alternatively, you can double-click on the dimension value to invoke the **Modify** dialog box and then select the **Delete equation** option to invoke the **Equations** dialog box.

Applying Equations to the Configurations

You can apply equations only to some of the specified configurations using the **Equations** dialog box. To apply equations to the configurations, choose the **Configs** button from the **Equations** dialog box; a dialog box will be displayed with the name of the current document. This dialog box displays the list of all configurations. Select the configurations using this dialog box and apply equations. You will learn about configurations later in the next topic.

Working with Configurations

In SolidWorks, you can create multiple instances of a part or assembly with ease. For example, if you need to create a bolt and nut of different dimensions, you need not create the parts of different dimensions in part document, instead you can create multiple configurations. There are two methods of creating configurations: manually and by using the design table. The method of creating configurations manually is discussed next and the second method will be discussed later in this chapter.

Creating Configurations Manually

You can create the configurations manually and specify the properties of these configurations. Then, you can modify the model or the assembly to create the variations in the new configuration. Consider the case of a machine bed shown in Figure 17-8. You need to create two types of designs of the same machine bed. In the first design, you need to have a circular pocket on the top face of the machine bed. In the second design, the circular pocket is removed from the top face of the machine bed.

To create the configurations manually, you need to invoke the **ConfigurationManager**. To do so, choose the **ConfigurationManager** button next to the **PropertyManager** button below the **CommandManager**. You will observe that the model of the machine bed shown in

Figure 17-8 is saved as the **Default** configuration and is active. The node of the active configuration is shown in yellow color.

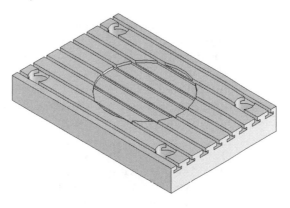

Figure 17-8 *Model of a machine bed*

To create a new configuration, select the name of the part in the **ConfigurationManager** and right-click to invoke the shortcut menu. Choose the **Add Configuration** option from the shortcut menu as shown in Figure 17-9. On selecting this option from the shortcut menu, the **Add Configuration PropertyManager** will be displayed, as shown in Figure 17-10. In the **Configuration Properties** rollout, you can specify the name of the configuration in the **Configuration name** edit box. The description of the configuration can be specified in the **Description** edit box. You can use the **Comment** edit box to specify the comment about the configuration.

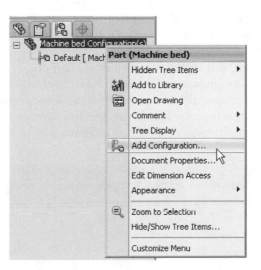

Figure 17-9 *Cursor choosing the **Add Configuration** option from the shortcut menu*

Figure 17-10 *The **Add Configuration** PropertyManager*

The drop-down list in the **Bill of Materials Options** rollout is used to specify the name of the part that has to be displayed in BOM when the drawing views are generated with the selected configuration.

On expanding the **Advanced Options** rollout, you will observe that the **Suppress new features and mates** check box is selected, by default. Therefore, the new features and mates added in some other configuration of the same part will be automatically suppressed in this configuration. Select the **Use configuration specific color** check box to specify a color for the newly created configuration. On selecting this check box, the **Color** button will be enabled. Invoke the **Color** dialog box by choosing this button and specify the color for the configuration.

After adding all the information in the **Add Configuration PropertyManager**, choose the **OK** button; the new configuration is created and it is activated automatically. So, the node of the new configuration will be displayed in yellow color in the **ConfigurationManager**. Figure 17-11 shows the name of the new configuration displayed in the **ConfigurationManager**.

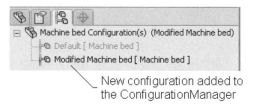

Figure 17-11 *New configuration displayed in the* **ConfigurationManager**

After creating the configuration, edit the features of the model that needed to be displayed in the newly created configuration. The design requirement for the machine bed is that the circular recess needs to be removed in the second configuration of the machine bed. Therefore, you need to suppress the cut feature that is used to create the circular recess in the machine bed. To do so, invoke the **FeatureManager design tree** and suppress the cut feature. Now, if you want to switch back to the **Default** configuration, select the **Default** configuration from the **ConfigurationManager** and invoke the shortcut menu. Choose the **Show Configuration** option; the **Default** configuration will be displayed and you will observe that the circular recess is not suppressed in this configuration. On the other hand, when you invoke the newly created configuration, you will observe that the circular recess is not displayed in the machine bed. Figure 17-12 shows the machine bed with the **Default** configuration and Figure 17-13 shows the machine bed with the modified design configuration.

Tip. *If you want to open a particular configuration of a part or an assembly document that has multiple configurations, invoke the* **Open** *dialog box, select the configuration from the drop-down list in the* **Configuration** *area of this dialog box, and choose the* **Open** *button.*

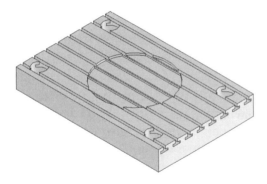

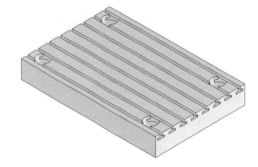

Figure 17-12 *Machine bed with the **Default** configuration*

Figure 17-13 *Machine bed with the modified design configuration*

Tip. *You can also drag and drop the specific configuration from the **ConfigurationManager** to an assembly or a drawing document. When you place a component with multiple configurations in an assembly document, the name of the current configuration will be displayed along with the name of the part in the **FeatureManager design tree**.*

*To change the configuration of the components placed in an assembly document, select a component and invoke the shortcut menu. Choose the **Component Properties** option from the shortcut menu; the **Component Properties** dialog box will be displayed. Select the required configuration from the **Referenced configuration** area and choose the **OK** button.*

*You can also change the configurations of a part in each drawing view independently. To do so, select the drawing view and choose the **Properties** option from the shortcut menu; the **Drawing View Properties** dialog box will be displayed. Now, you can change the configuration by selecting different options from the **Use named configuration** drop-down list.*

Editing the Features of a Part with Multiple Configurations

When you edit the features of a part with multiple configurations, the **Configurations** rollout will be displayed in the **PropertyManager** of the feature to be edited, as shown in Figure 17-14. You can specify the configuration that you need to modify using the options in this rollout. These options are discussed next.

This configuration

If you select the **This configuration** radio button, the modification made in the feature is applied only to the current configuration. The same feature will not be modified in the remaining configurations.

Figure 17-14 *The **Configurations** rollout*

All configurations

The **All configurations** radio button is selected by default. So, the modification made in a feature will be applied to all the configurations of the current part document.

Specify configurations

Select the **Specify configurations** radio button to apply the modification only to the selected configurations. When you select this radio button, the configurations in the part document are listed in the list box. The current configuration is selected by default. Select the configuration in which you want to apply the modification. The **All** button is used to select all configurations displayed in the list box.

Creating Configurations Using Design Tables

SolidWorks menus:	Insert > Design Table
Toolbar:	Tools > Design Table

 Sometimes you may need to create a part that is used repeatedly in your design work. Each instance of that part may have same geometry, but different dimensions. You can create the part having different configurations by modifying the dimensions manually. But it is recommended to create these types of configurations using the **Design Table** tool. To do so, choose the **Design Table** button from the **Tools** toolbar or choose **Insert > Design Table** from the SolidWorks menus; the **Design Table PropertyManager** will be displayed, as shown in Figure 17-15.

The rollouts in the **Design Table PropertyManager** are discussed next.

Source Rollout

The **Source** rollout is used to specify the type and the source for inserting the design table in the part or assembly document. The options in this rollout are discussed next.

Blank

The **Blank** radio button is used to insert a blank design table. You need to manually enter the parameters in a blank design table.

Auto-create

The **Auto-create** radio button is selected by default when you invoke the **Design Table PropertyManager**. This radio button allows you to insert a new design table in the part or the assembly document. It will also load all the parameters and their associated values in the design table.

Figure 17-15 The **Design Table PropertyManager**

From file

Select the **From file** radio button if you need to insert an existing design table. The design tables are created as Microsoft Excel files. To retrieve a saved design table, select this radio button and choose the **Browse** button provided in this rollout; the **Open** dialog box will be displayed. Browse and open the file that you need to insert as design table; the name and path of the selected file will be displayed in the display box provided below the radio button. The **Link to file** check box is available only when you select the **From file** radio button. If you select this check box, any change made in the Microsoft Excel file will be reflected in the part model or the assembly, and vice versa.

Edit Control Rollout

The **Edit Control** rollout is used to specify the settings of bidirectional control on the design table. The options available in this rollout are discussed next.

Allow model edits to update the design table

The **Allow model edits to update the design table** radio button is selected by default and is used to add a bidirectional relation between the model and the design table. If you select this radio button, the changes made in the model will be updated in the design table automatically.

Block model edits that would update the design table

The **Block model edits that would update the design table** radio button is selected to block the editing of the parameters of the model that tend to update the design table.

Options Rollout

The options in the **Options** rollout are used to add rows or columns to the design table and warn you before updating the design table. The options in this rollout are discussed next.

New parameters

The **New parameters** check box is selected by default and is used to automatically add new rows or columns in the design table when new parameters are added in the drawing view.

New configurations

The **New configurations** check box is selected by default and is used to automatically add new columns and rows in the design table when a new configuration is added to the model.

Warn when updating design table

The **Warn when updating design table** check box is selected by default and gives a warning message every time the design table updates.

Consider a case in which you need to create a washer of 100 mm outer diameter, 50 mm inner diameter, and 10 mm thickness, as shown in Figure 17-16. Also, you need to create five more washers with different dimensions. As the geometry of the washers is the same and only the dimensions are different, it is recommended to create a single part document of the washer and then create different configurations of the washer using the design table.

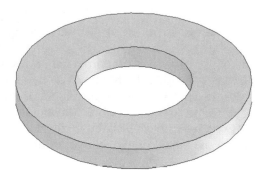

Figure 17-16 *Washer created using the given dimensions*

After creating the part model, invoke the **Design Table PropertyManager**. Select the **Auto-create** radio button and choose the **OK** button from the **Design Table PropertyManager**; the design table will be created using the default settings. The tools in the toolbars of SolidWorks window will be replaced by the Microsoft Excel tools. Also, the **Creating design table** dialog box will be displayed, overlapped by the **Dimensions** dialog box. Figure 17-17 shows the SolidWorks window after you choose the **OK** button from the **Design Table PropertyManager** to create the design table.

Now, press and hold the CTRL key and select all the dimensions displayed in the **Dimensions** dialog box. Choose the **OK** button; the name of the selected dimensions with the dimensional values of the **Default** configuration will be displayed in the Microsoft Excel sheet in the drawing area, as shown in Figure 17-18. Now, you need to specify the name of the second instance to be created for the model and enter the dimensions for that instance in the excel sheet. Similarly, specify the names and dimensions for other instances, as shown in Figure 17-19.

After specifying the configurations and dimensions in the Microsoft Excel sheet, click anywhere in the drawing area; the **SolidWorks** message box will be displayed with the names of the configurations generated by design table. Choose the **OK** button from this information box.

Now, you can observe that different configurations are created in the **ConfigurationManager** and the **Default** configuration is activated as shown in Figure 17-20. The Microsoft Excel icon displayed before the **Design Table** node in the **ConfigurationManager** confirms that the configuration is generated using the design table. If you need to view any other configuration, select the configuration and invoke the shortcut menu. Choose the **Show Configuration** option from the shortcut menu. Alternatively, you can double-click on the configuration in the **ConfigurationManager**.

Note
You can create only one design table in a part or an assembly document.

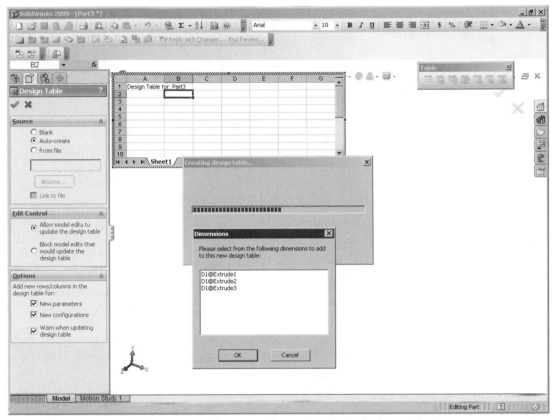

Figure 17-17 *SolidWorks window while creating the design table*

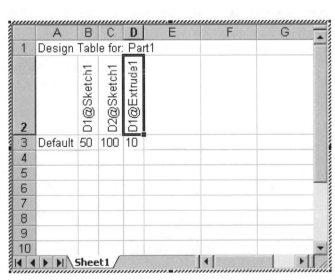

Figure 17-18 *Microsoft Excel sheet after selecting the dimensions from the **Dimensions** dialog box*

	A	B	C	D	E	F	G
1	Design Table for: Part1						
2		D1@Sketch1	D2@Sketch1	D1@Extrude1			
3	Default	50	100	10			
4	2nd	50	70	10			
5	3rd	50	85	7.5			
6	4th	25	100	5			
7	5th	25	75	5			
8							
9							
10							

Sheet1

Figure 17-19 *Microsoft Excel sheet after specifying the name of the new instances and adding dimensions to those instances*

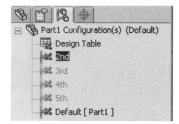

Figure 17-20 *The ConfigurationManager with the configurations*

Tip. *If you have invoked the configuration once and saved it, you can preview the it before using the* **Show Configuration** *option from the shortcut menu. To display the preview of the configuration, select the configuration from the* **ConfigurationManager** *and choose the* **Show Preview** *option from the shortcut menu; the preview of the selected configuration will be displayed in the* **PropertyManager**. *After displaying the preview of all the documents, click anywhere in the drawing area to close the preview window.*

Changing the Suppression State Using the Design Table

You can change the suppression state of the features of a component using the design table. This method is of great use in the design departments because you can generate different configurations of a part, showing the feature to be created after each stage of the manufacturing process. Assume you are provided with the finished billet stock and you need to manufacture the plate shown in Figure 17-21.

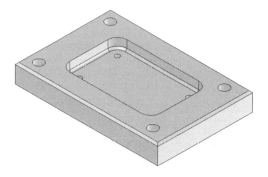

Figure 17-21 *Finished plate after manufacturing*

To manufacture the plate from the billet, you first need to perform the pocket milling operation to remove the material from inside the plate. Then, you need to drill the holes inside the pocket as well as on the top face of the plate. After performing all the operations, you need to chamfer the top edges of the plate.

To represent all these processes in a CAD part in SolidWorks, you need to create different configurations displaying each stage of the manufacturing process using the design table. You can also create these configurations manually, but that will be a time-consuming process.

Before creating these types of configurations, you need to change the names of the feature in the **FeatureManager design tree**. To change the name of a feature, select a feature and again left-click on it; name of the feature will be displayed in a text edit box. Enter a new name for the feature. Remember that it is not mandatory to change the names of the features. It is done to avoid confusion. Save the model and then invoke the **Design Table PropertyManager**, select the **Auto-create** radio button, and choose the **OK** button; the **Dimensions** dialog box will be displayed. Without selecting any dimension from the **Dimensions** dialog box, choose the **OK** button. You will notice that only the name of the design table is displayed in the design table. Next, double-click on all the features displayed in the **FeatureManager design tree**. You will notice that the names of the features will be displayed in the top row and their respective suppression states will be displayed under the names of the features in the Microsoft Excel, refer to Figure 17-22.

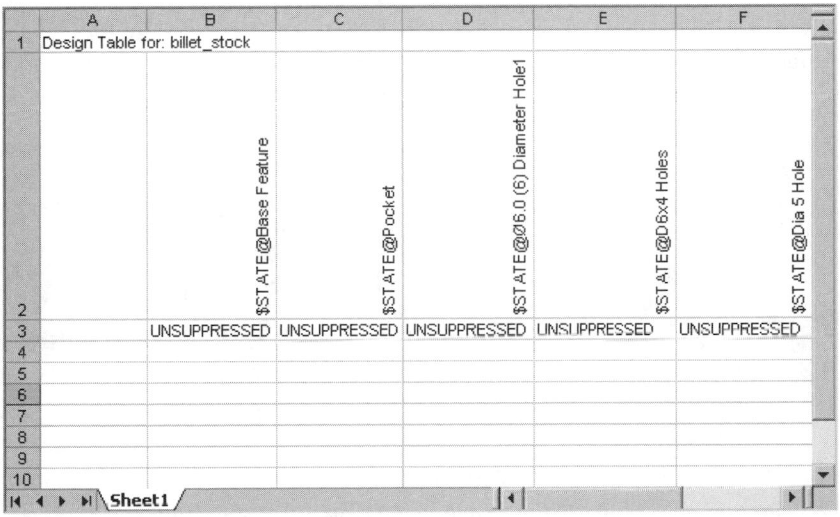

Figure 17-22 The Microsoft Excel sheet after adding features to the design table

Note that the suppression state of all the features is displayed as unsuppressed. Enter the name of the configuration in the **A3** cell as **Finished Plate**. Enter the name of the second configuration in the **A4** cell as **Billet Stock**. Now, specify the suppression state as suppressed in all the features in the design table, except the base feature. Instead of specifying the complete spelling of suppress and unsuppress, you can enter **S** for suppressed state and **U** for unsuppressed state. Next, enter the name of the third configuration in the **A5** cell as **Pocket Milling** and suppress all the features except the base feature, pocket, and fillet features. Similarly, create other configurations. Figure 17-23 shows the design table after specifying all the configurations and their respective suppression states.

	A	B	C	D	E	F	G	H	I	J	K
1	Design Table for: billet_stock										
2		$STATE@Base Feature	$STATE@Pocket	$STATE@Ø6.0 (6) Diameter Hole1	$STATE@D6x4 Holes	$STATE@Dia 5 Hole	$STATE@Dia 5x4	$STATE@Fillet1	$STATE@Chamfer2		
3	Finished Table	U	U	U	U	U	U	U	U		
4	Billet Stock	U	S	S	S	S	S	S	S		
5	Pocket Milling	U	U	S	S	S	S	U	S		
6	Dia 5 Holes	U	U	S	S	U	U	U	S		
7	Dia 6 Holes	U	U	U	U	U	U	U	S		
8	Chamfer	U	U	U	U	U	U	U	U		
9											
10											

Figure 17-23 *Design table after specifying all the configurations and their respective suppression states*

Click anywhere in the drawing area and choose **OK** from the message box to return to the part modeling environment. Figures 17-24 through 17-28 show the different configurations of the plate created by changing the suppression state of the feature using the design table.

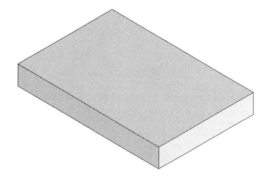

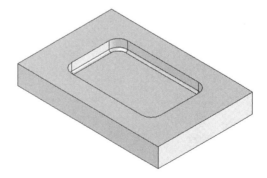

Figure 17-24 *Plate shown in the* **Billet Stock** *configuration*

Figure 17-25 *Plate shown in the* **Pocket Milling** *configuration*

Tip. *While modifying the dimensions of the features or sketches, specify the configuration that needs to be modified in the **PropertyManager** displayed while editing.*

*While modifying the relations of the sketches using the **Display/Delete Relations** tool, specify the configuration that needs to be modified in the **PropertyManager** displayed.*

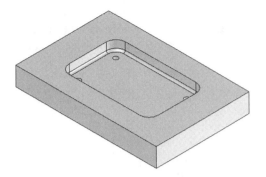

Figure 17-26 *Plate shown in* **Dia 5 Holes** *configuration*

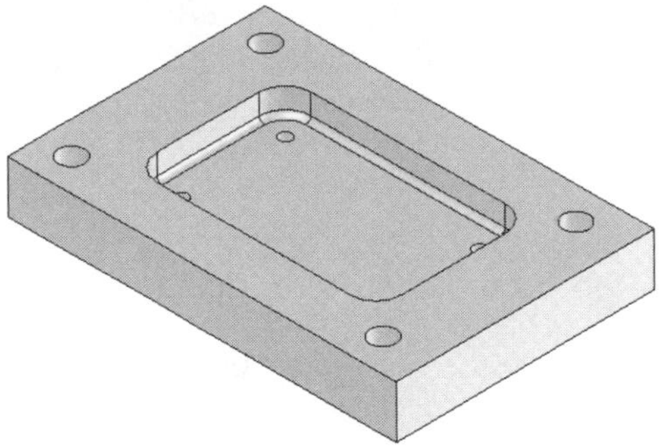

Figure 17-27 *Plate shown in* **Dia 6 Holes** *configuration*

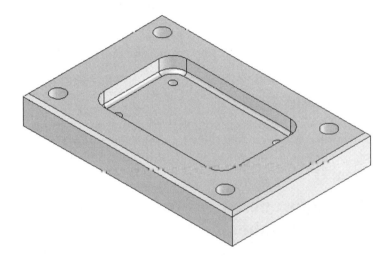

Figure 17-28 *Plate shown in the* **Chamfer** *configuration*

Editing the Design Table

You can also edit the design table created in the part or the assembly document. To edit the design table, right-click on the design table icon from the **ConfigurationManager** to invoke the shortcut menu. Choose the **Edit Table** option from the shortcut menu; the **Add Rows and Columns** dialog box will be displayed. If some configurations or parameters are added to the model after creating the design table, those configurations and parameters will be listed in the **Configurations** and **Parameters** areas of the **Add Rows and Columns** dialog box. You can select the parameters or the configurations displayed in this dialog box to be included in the design table and choose the **OK** button from this dialog box; the part modeling environment will be replaced by the Microsoft Excel application environment and the Microsoft Excel sheet will be displayed in the drawing area. Edit the sheet and then click anywhere in the drawing area to return to the part modeling environment of SolidWorks.

Tip. *You can also edit the design table in a separate Microsoft Excel window. To do so, right-click on the design table icon from the **ConfigurationManager** to invoke the shortcut menu. Choose the **Edit Table in New Window** option from the shortcut menu; a separate Microsoft Excel window will be invoked. After editing the design table, choose **File** > **Update** from the SolidWorks menus.*

*You can also save the design table created in the part or the assembly document. To do so, right-click on the design table icon from the **ConfigurationManager** and invoke the shortcut menu. Choose the **Save Table** option from the shortcut menu, the Microsoft Excel sheet will be displayed. If you have updated the model after creating the design table, the **Add Rows and Columns** dialog box will be displayed. Choose the **OK** button from this dialog box; the **Save Design Table** dialog box will be displayed. Use this dialog box to save the design table.*

You can also edit the properties of the design table by invoking the **Design Table PropertyManager**. To do so, select the design table icon from the **ConfigurationManager** and invoke the shortcut menu. Choose the **Edit Feature** option from the shortcut menu; the **Design Table PropertyManager** will be displayed and now you can edit the properties of the design table.

Deleting the Design Table

You can also delete the design table if it is not required in the part or assembly document. To do so, select the icon of the design table from the **ConfigurationManager** and press the DELETE key. Note that even if you delete the design table, the configurations created by using it, will not be deleted.

Changing the Suppression State of a Component without Invoking the Design Table

In the previous section, you learned to change the suppression state of various features of a component using the design table. However, you can also change the suppression state of a feature without invoking the design table.

To change the suppression state of the features, select all the features from the **FeatureManager design tree** and invoke the shortcut menu. Choose the **Configure Feature** option from the shortcut menu; the **Modify Configurations** window will be displayed with the names of selected features along the columns, as shown in Figure 17-29.

Modify Configurations								
	Base Feature	**Pocket**	**Ø6.0 (6) Diameter Hole1**	**D6x4 Holes**	**Dia 5 Hole**	**Dia 5x4**	**Fillet1**	**Chamfer2**
	Suppress	Suppress	Suppress	Suppress	Suppress	Suppress	Suppress	Suppress
Finished Table	☐	☐	☐	☐	☐	☐	☐	☐
< Creates a new configuration. >								

*Figure 17-29 The **Modify Configurations** window*

Left-click once in the **<Creates a new configuration.>** cell, enter a name for the new feature and click once in any of the cell; a new row will be created for the new configuration with check boxes in it. Similarly, create other configurations. To suppress a particular feature in a configuration, select the check box of their corresponding feature, as shown in Figure 17-30. Choose the **OK** button; the configurations will be created and displayed in the **ConfigurationManager**.

Modify Configurations	Base Feature	Pocket	Ø6.0 (6) Diameter Hole1	D6x4 Holes	Dia 5 Hole	Dia 5x4	Fillet1	Chamfer2
	Suppress	Suppress	Suppress	Suppress	Suppress	Suppress	Suppress	Suppress
Billet Stock	☐	☑	☑	☑	☑	☑	☑	☑
Pocket	☐	☐	☑	☑	☑	☑	☐	☑
D5 Holes	☐	☐	☑	☑	☐	☐	☐	☑
D6 Holes	☐	☐	☐	☐	☐	☐	☐	☑
Finished Table	☐	☐	☐	☐	☐	☐	☐	☐
< Creates a new configuration. >								

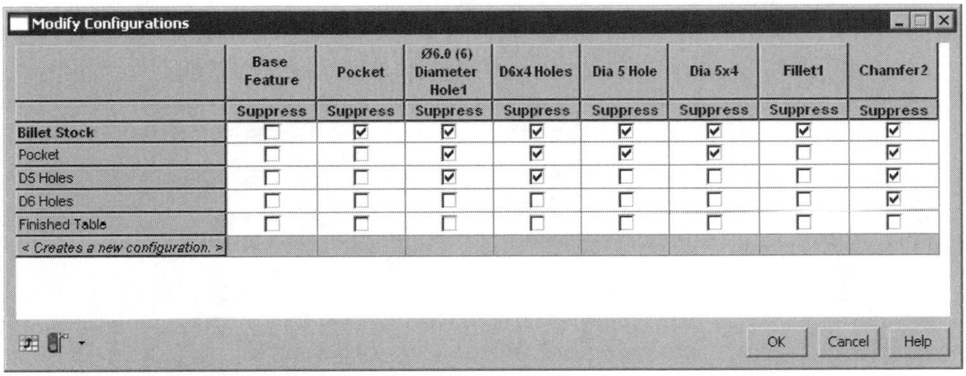

Figure 17-30 *The* **Modify Configurations** *window after specifying the features to be suppressed in various configurations*

To change the name of a configuration or to delete a configuration, select the configuration and right-click to invoke the shortcut menu. Choose the corresponding option from the shortcut menu to change the name or to delete the configuration.

To edit a configuration, select the features or a feature and invoke the **Modify Configurations** window. Select or clear the check boxes to modify the configuration and choose **OK**.

Changing the Visibility of the Components in Different Configurations of an Assembly

In the **Assembly** mode, you can also change the visibility of the components in the different configurations. To do so, invoke the **ConfigurationManager** and right-click in the **ConfigurationManager**. Choose the **Add Display State** option from the shortcut menu; the **Display States ShowFeatureManager** will be displayed with a new display state. Similarly, add as many display states as required. If this **ShowFeatureManager** is not displayed by default, you need to drag the two lines displayed above the **ConfigurationManager** to display the **Display States ShowFeatureManager**, as shown in Figure 17-31.

To change the color, texture, and the display state, invoke the **FeatureManager** and click on the arrow symbol to display the display pane, as shown in Figure 17-32. Now, change the color, display state, or texture of a feature in the assembly.

To view the different display states, you can double-click on the corresponding display state in the **Display States ShowFeatureManager**. Alternatively, invoke the **Display States** toolbar and select the corresponding display state from the drop-down list.

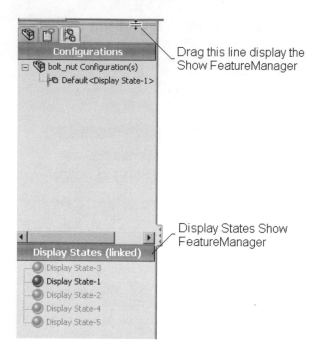

Drag this line display the
Show FeatureManager

Display States Show
FeatureManager

Figure 17-31 The *Display States*
ShowFeatureManager

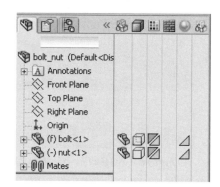

Figure 17-32 The *FeatureManager*
with the display pane

LIBRARY FEATURES

In most of the designs, some features are used frequently. Therefore, you can create and save such features as library features. Later on, you can drag and place the saved library features in the part, whenever required. This reduces the time to create the same part or feature repeatedly. In this section, you will learn how to create the library feature, place them in a part, edit them, and dissolve the library feature.

Creating a Library Feature

A library feature is created by saving an existing feature with different file extension. To save a feature as a library feature, you first need to create a base feature and then create the feature or features to be added as the library feature. After creating the features, you need to select the features to be added as the library feature and then save them with *.sldlfp* file extension.

Consider a case in which you need to save an extruded feature and fillet feature as the library feature. You need to create a base feature and then create an extruded feature and add fillets to this extruded feature. After creating the model, select the name of the model from the **FeatureManager design tree** and invoke the shortcut menu. Choose the **Add to Library** option from it; the **Add to Library PropertyManager** will be displayed, as shown in Figure 17-33. You will notice that the name of the model is displayed by default in the selection box in the **Items to Add** rollout. Clear the current selection, press and hold the CTRL key, and select the features to be added as the library feature from the **FeatureManager design tree**. The extruded feature and the fillet feature of the model, as shown in Figure 17-34, are selected as the library features.

Specify the name for the library features in the **File name** edit box of the **Save To** rollout. Then, select the location to save the library feature by expanding the nodes in the **Design Library folder** list box.

Select the **Lib Feat Part (*.sldlfp)** option from the **File type** drop-down list in the **Options** rollout, if it is not selected by default. If you want to give a brief description about the feature, specify it in the **Description** edit box in the **Options** rollout.

Choose **OK** after setting all parameters; the features are saved as the library feature. The features that are selected to be saved as library features will have an **L** symbol displayed on their icons, and the library symbol will be displayed with the name of the part document in the **FeatureManager design tree**, as shown in Figure 17-35. Invoke the **Design Library** task pane and browse to the location where you have saved the library feature to view it.

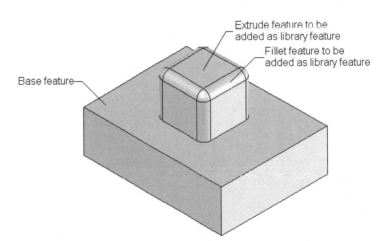

Figure 17-34 *The features to be added as library feature*

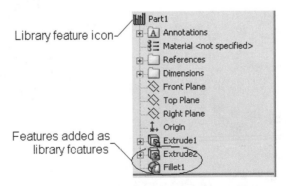

Figure 17-33 *The **Add to Library** PropertyManager*

Figure 17-35 *Library icon and the **L** symbols displayed on the feature icons*

Note

If the library feature is located with respect to an entity in a feature in which it has been created, then you need to specify the reference while placing the library feature.

Placing the Library Feature in a Part

After creating and saving the library features, you can place them in a part document. To place a library feature, invoke the **Design Library** task pane by choosing the **Design Library** tab and browse to the location where you have saved the library feature. Then, drag the feature and drop it on a face of the model; the **PropertyManager** of the corresponding library feature will be displayed, as shown in Figure 17-36. If you need to change the placement plane for the library feature, clear the existing placement plane displayed in the **Placement Plane** rollout of the **Library Feature PropertyManager** and select a new placement plane. If the selected library feature has more than one configurations, it will be displayed in the **Configuration** rollout.

On selecting a library feature created with references, the preview of the feature will be displayed in a window. Also, you will be prompted to specify the references. If you click in the preview window, the **Heads-up View** toolbar will be displayed and you can view the feature using the tools in this toolbar. Specify the references in the drawing area; the preview window

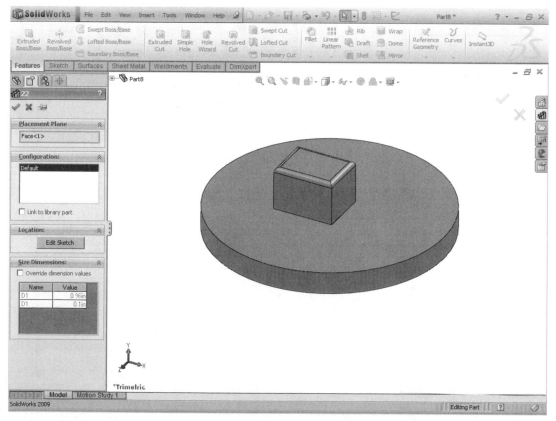

*Figure 17-36 Part document with the **Library Feature PropertyManager***

will disappear and the location of the feature with respect to the selected references will be displayed in the **Locating Dimensions** area of the **Library Feature PropertyManager**.

If the selected library feature does not have any references, the **Location** rollout will be displayed. Choose the **Edit Sketch** button from this rollout and specify the location of the feature.

If you want to modify the existing dimensions of the library feature, select the **Override dimension values** check box in the **Size Dimensions** rollout and modify the values. The modified feature will be displayed with the name **Custom configuration** in the **Configuration** rollout.

If you select the **Link to library part** check box in the **Configuration** rollout, the references of the library feature will be saved in the part. So, if you modify the library feature, the modification will be reflected in the model.

Figure 17-37 shows the library feature placed on the top face of the model.

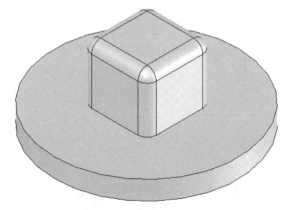

Figure 17-37 Library feature placed on the top face of the model

 Tip. *If you include the base feature in a library feature, you can place the library feature only in an empty SolidWorks part document. Instead, if you place it in a part document that already has a base feature, the **SolidWorks** warning box will be displayed. It will inform you that a library feature with a base feature can be inserted only into an empty part document.*

Editing the Library Features

You can edit or change the features included in the library feature part document. To remove a library feature from the library, select that library feature from the **Design Library** task pane. Now, invoke the shortcut menu and choose the **Delete** option from it. If you need to edit the library feature, select the feature from the **Design Library** task pane and invoke the shortcut menu. Then, choose the **Open** option from the shortcut menu; the part document of the library feature will be opened. Edit the feature and save it. If you have selected the **Link to library part** check box in the **Configuration** rollout while placing the library feature, then the modification made in the library feature will be reflected in the document in which the library feature is placed.

Dissolving the Library Features

If you place a library feature, the library icon will be displayed before the name of the feature. So, if you try to edit the library feature, the **Library Feature PropertyManager** will be displayed. To convert the library feature into the individual part feature, you need to dissolve the library feature. To do so, select the library feature from the **Feature Manager design tree** and invoke the shortcut menu. Choose the **Dissolve Library Feature** option from the shortcut menu; the library feature will be dissolved into individual features.

TUTORIALS

Tutorial 1

In this tutorial, you will open the Tutorial 3 of Chapter 2. The dimensions of the sketch are shown in Figure 17-38. Extrude the sketch up to a depth of 50 mm. Then you will add equations to the dimensions of the sketch. The dimension 150 will be the driving dimension. While adding the equations, you can change the vertical dimensions 20 and 40 to 25 and 50 for the convenience of calculation. **(Expected time: 30 min)**

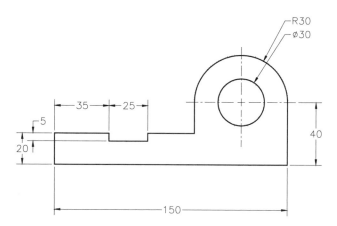

Figure 17-38 *Sketch for Tutorial 1*

The following steps are required to complete this tutorial:

a.   Start a new part document and open the Tutorial 3 of Chapter 2.
b.   Extrude the sketch to a depth of 50 mm.
c.   Edit the dimensions and add equations using the **Equations** tool.
d.   Save the model.

Starting a New SolidWorks Document and Creating the Extrude Feature

1. Start a new SolidWorks document and open the Tutorial 3 of Chapter 2.

2. Add relations and dimensions to fully define the sketch. Refer to Figure 17-38.

3. Extrude the sketch to a depth of 50 mm.

4. Choose the **Save As** button and save the model with the name c17_tut01.

Adding Equations to the Dimensions in the Sketch

For this model, you will keep the horizontal dimension 150 as the driving dimension and other dimensions as the driven dimensions. Also, the you will change the vertical dimensions to 25 and 50 mm for the ease of calculation.

1. Invoke the sketching environment to edit the sketch of the base feature, double-click on the vertical dimensions in succession and change the dimension value 20 to **25** and 40 to **50**.

2. Choose the **Equations** button from the **Tools** toolbar; the **Equations** dialog box is displayed.

3. Choose the **Add** button; the **Add Equation** dialog box is displayed.

4. Select the radius value 30; its name is displayed in the **Add Equation** dialog box.

5. Choose the = (equal to) button from the **Add Equation** dialog box and then select the horizontal dimension value 150.

6. Choose the / (forward slash) button and then by the value **5** button; the equation in the edit box in the **Add Equation** dialog box will be **"D5@Sketch1" = "D1@Sketch1" / 5**. Where, **D5@Sketch1** − 30 and **D1@Sketch1** − 150. The names of the dimensions can be different as they are based on the sequence in which they are added to the sketch.

7. Choose the **Comment** button and enter **Radius** in the edit box next to the equation added.

8. Choose the **OK** button; the equations will be displayed in the **Equations** dialog box with a green colored check mark and the value 30 mm are displayed in the **Evaluates To** column with the comment **Radius**.

9. Select the radius value 30 and choose the **Add** button; the **Add Equation** dialog box will be displayed with the name of the selected dimension.

10. Select the horizontal dimension value 150.

11. Choose the / (forward slash) button and then the **5** button; the equation in the edit box of

the **Add Equation** dialog box will be **"D4@Sketch1" = "D1@Sketch1" / 5**. Where, **D4@Sketch1** = 30 and **D1@Sketch1** = 150.

12. Choose the **Comment** button and enter **Diameter** in the edit box next to the equation added.

13. Choose the **OK** button; the equations will be displayed in the **Equations** dialog box with the green colored check mark. Also, the value 30 mm is displayed in the **Evaluates To** column with the comment **Diameter**.

14. Similarly, add equations to all dimensions as given below:

Dimension to be selected	Equation to be added	Comment
Vertical dimension 25	150/6	Height
50	150/3	Hole location
35	150/30*7	Slot location
Horizontal dimension 25	150/6	Slot
5	150/30	Slot depth

15. Resize the **Equations** dialog box, if required. The **Equations** dialog box after adding all equations is shown in Figure 17-39.

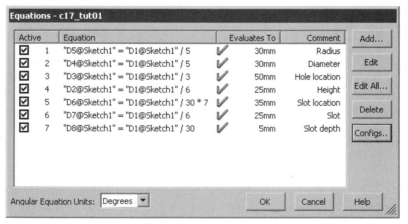

*Figure 17-39 The **Equations** dialog box after adding all equations*

16. Choose the **OK** button from the **Equations** dialog box; the dimensions are displayed in the sketch with the equation symbol. Also, the **Equations** folder is added to the **FeatureManager design tree**.

Adding Equation to the Extrude Feature

Next, you need to add equations to the extrude feature such that it is controlled by the horizontal dimension value of 150.

1. Choose the **Equations** button from the **Tools** toolbar; the **Equations** dialog box is displayed.

2. Double-click on the model; the dimensions of the sketch and feature are displayed.

3. The dimensional value 50 displayed in blue is the dimension of the extrude feature. Select this dimension and choose the **Add** button in the **Equations** dialog box.

4. Select the horizontal dimension value 150 in the drawing area. Then, choose the / (forward slash) and the value **3** in succession in the **Equations** dialog box.

5. Choose the **Comment** button and enter the comment **Extrude**.

6. Choose the **OK** button from the **Add Equation** dialog box and then from the **Equations** dialog box.

Changing the Dimensions of the Model

1. Double-click on the model; all dimensions of the model are displayed.

2. Double-click on the dimensional value 150 and enter **300** in the text box.

3. Rebuild the model; all dimensions of the model are modified.

Note

For the purpose of tutorial, all dimensions have been equated to round figure. However, you can add any mathematical relation to a feature/dimension such that it does not override the design intent of the model.

4. Save the model.

Tutorial 2

Create the Socket Head Screw shown in Figure 17-40. Assume the base diameter of the screw, d, as 30 mm. Create the model using the relations given in Figure 17-41. Then, create different configurations by changing the base diameter to 20 mm, 50 mm, 40 mm, and 5 mm and other related parameters with respect to the relations given in Figure 17-41.

(**Expected time: 30 min**)

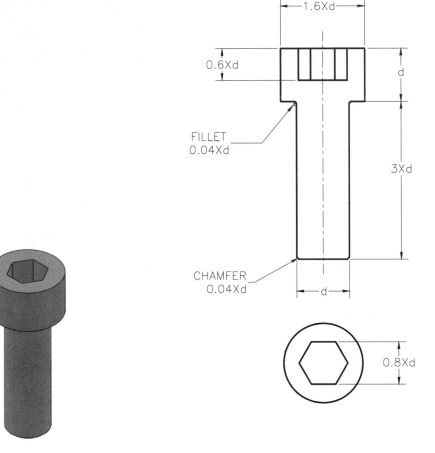

Figure 17-40 *Socket Head Screw*   **Figure 17-41** *The parameters of the Socket Head Screw*

The following steps are required to complete this tutorial:

a. Create the socket head screw using the **Revolved Boss/Base** and the **Extruded Cut** tools.
b. Create different configurations using the design table.
c. Save the model.

Creating the Socket Head Screw

1. Start a new SolidWorks document, draw the sketch of the base feature and dimension it. Note that the base diameter is 30 mm and other entities are dimensioned with respect to the relations shown in Figure 17-41.

2. Create the base feature using the **Revolved Boss/Base** tool.

3. Create the hexagonal cut on the base feature using the **Extruded Cut** tool.

4. Add fillets and chamfers.

5. Save the model as c17_tut02 in the folder created for Chapter 17.

Creating Configurations Using the Design Table

As you need to create Socket Head Screw of same geometry and different dimensions, it needs to be created using the **Design Table**.

1. Choose **Insert > Design Table** from the SolidWorks menus; the **Design Table PropertyManager** is displayed.

2. Select the **Auto-create** radio button from the **Source** rollout. Make sure that the **Allow model edits to update the design table** radio button and all other check boxes in the **Design Table PropertyManager** are selected.

3. Choose the **OK** button from the **Design Table PropertyManager**; the **Dimensions** dialog box is displayed.

4. Select the names of all dimensions from the list box in the **Dimensions** dialog box, except the **D1@Revolve1**, **D1@Fillet1**, **D1@Chamfer1**, **D2@Chamfer1**. These names correspond to revolve, fillet and chamfer features.

5. Choose **OK** from the **Dimensions** dialog box; the design table with the default dimensions will be displayed, as shown in Figure 17-42.

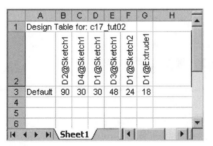

Figure 17-42 The design table with the default dimensions

6. Enter the names of the new instances as **20x60**, **50x150**, **40x120**, and **5x15** in the **A4**, **A5**, **A6**, and **A7** cells, respectively.

Note
*If you click in the drawing area by mistake, the design table will disappear. To display it again, invoke the **ConfigurationManager**, right-click on the **Design Table** node, and choose the **Edit Table** option from the shortcut menu.*

7. Enter the dimensions for the new instances with respect to the equations shown in Figure 17-41. The excel sheet after adding the dimensions is shown in Figure 17-43.

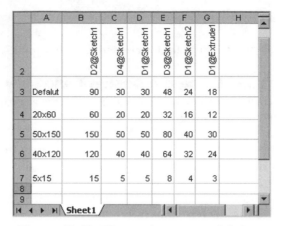

Figure 17-43 *The new instances and their dimensions*

8. In the **A3** cell, change the **Default** name to **30x90**.

9. Click anywhere in the drawing area; the **SolidWorks** message box is displayed with the names of the configurations created.

10. Choose **OK** in the message box; the **ConfigurationManager** is displayed with the configurations created. Double-click on a configuration to make it active.

11. Save the model.

SELF-EVALUATION TEST

Answer the following questions and then compare them to those given at the end of this chapter:

1. You can add the mathematical relations between the model dimensions, sketch dimensions, and dimensions on the drawing sheet using the **Equations** tool. (T/F)

2. You can edit the equations that are added to the design using the **Add Equation** dialog box. (T/F)

3. You can suppress the equations that are not required at a particular stage. (T/F)

4. The configurations help you to create the multiple instances of a part or an assembly within a single SolidWorks document. (T/F)

5. You can change the suppression state of the features of a component using the design table. (T/F)

6. To dissolve a library feature, choose the _____ option from the shortcut menu.

7. Which **PropertyManager** is used to create a design table?

    (a) **Design Table**   (b) **Create Design Table**
    (c) **Physical Dynamics**   (d) None of these

8. The _____ radio button is selected by default when you invoke the **Design Table PropertyManager**.

9. You cannot suppress the feature of the configuration without using the design table. (T/F)

10. The features to be added as library feature arc saved with the _____ file extension.

REVIEW QUESTIONS

Answer the following questions:

1. If you try to edit the library feature, the **Library Feature PropertyManager** will be displayed. (T/F)

2. If you include the base feature in the library feature, you can place the library feature only into an empty SolidWorks part document. (T/F)

3. Which of the following should be invoked to change the color, texture, and the display state of the configuration?

    (a) Display Pane in the **FeatureManager**
    (b) Display Pane in the **PropertyManager**
    (c) Display Pane in the **ConfigurationManager**
    (d) None

4. You can preview the configuration in the **ConfigurationManager** even if it has not been opened and saved once. (T/F)

5. You can create only one design table in a part or an assembly document. (T/F)

6. You need to suppress an equation to modify the corresponding driven dimension.

7. You can invoke the **Add Equation** dialog box by right-clicking on the **Equations** node in the **FeatureManager design tree**. (T/F)

8. If the library feature is located with respect to an entity in the feature in which it has been created, then you need to specify the reference while placing the library feature. (T/F)

9. You can also change the visibility of the components in the different configurations. (T/F)

10. You can drag and drop a specific configuration from the **ConfigurationManager** to an assembly or a drawing document. (T/F)

EXERCISES

Exercise 1

Create the model shown in Figure 17-44. The dimensions of the model are shown in Figure 17-45. Extrude the sketch up to a depth of 20 mm. Then, you will add equations to the dimensions of the sketch and the feature. The dimension 80, will be the driving dimension. While adding the equations, you can change the dimensions 30 and 15 to 40 and 20 for the convenience of calculation.   (**Expected time: 30 min**)

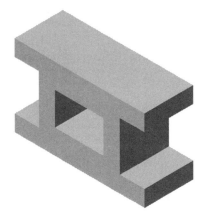

Figure 17-44 Solid model for Exercise 1

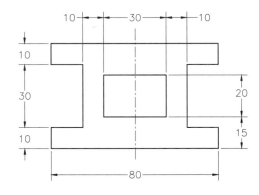

Figure 17-45 Dimensions of the model for Exercise 1

Exercise 2

Create the Cheese Head Screw shown in Figure 17-46. Assume the base diameter of the screw, d as 25 mm. Create the model using the relations given in Figure 17-47. Then, create different configurations by changing the base diameter to 20 mm, 15 mm, 12 mm, and 6 mm. Create the other related parameters with respect to the relations given in Figure 17-47.   (**Expected time: 30 min**)

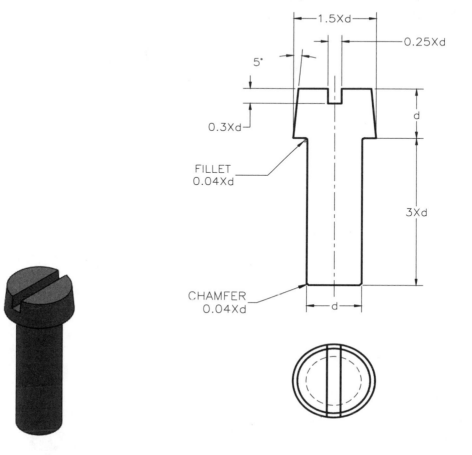

Figure 17-46 *The Cheese Head Screw*

Figure 17-47 *Parameters of the Cheese Head Screw*

Answers to Self-Evaluation Test
1. T, **2.** T, **3.** T, **4.** T, **5.** T, **6. Dissolve Library Feature**, **7. Design Table**, **8. Auto-create**, **9. F**, **10.** *.sldlfp*

Chapter 18

Working with Blocks

Learning Objectives

After completing this chapter, you will be able to:

- *Use tools in the Blocks toolbar.*
- *Save sketch as a block in the Design Library.*
- *Create mechanisms using blocks.*
- *Create parts from blocks.*

INTRODUCTION TO BLOCKS

A block is a set of entities grouped together as a single entity. The blocks are used to create complex mechanisms as sketches and check their functioning before developing them into complex 3D model. You can create a block from a single or combination of multiple sketch entities. To create a block, you first need to draw an object and then convert it into a block using the tools from the **Blocks** toolbar. This toolbar is also used to perform other operations such as edit, save, explode, rebuild, and so on. You can convert a block into part in the Layout environment. In this chapter, you will learn how to create a part and an assembly from blocks.

Blocks Toolbar

The **Blocks** toolbar, as shown in Figure 18-1, is used to control the sketched entities of the blocks. You can perform different operations related to blocks such as create, edit, insert, save, and so on by using the **Blocks** toolbar. The tools in this toolbar are discussed next.

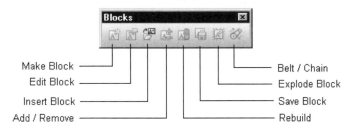

*Figure 18-1 The **Blocks** toolbar*

Make Block

The **Make Block** tool is used to convert the sketch entities into a block. Using this tool, you can make each entity of the sketch as a separate block that can be moved with respect to one another. In such a case, there will be a motion between sketched entities. This tool will be available only when you invoke the sketching environment. To create a block, select any entity from the sketch that has multiple entities. Next, choose the **Make Block** button from the **Blocks** toolbar or choose **Tools > Blocks > Make** from the SolidWorks menus; the **Make Block PropertyManager** will be displayed, as shown in Figure 18-2 and the name of the selected entity will be displayed in the selection area of the **Block Entities** rollout. Finally, choose the **OK** button; the sketched entity will be converted into a block. Similarly, convert other entities of the sketch into blocks. The **Insertion Point** rollout of the **Make Block PropertyManager** is used to insert a point at the required position. To do so, click on

*Figure 18-2 The **Make Block** PropertyManager*

the down arrow on the right of this rollout; a manipulator will be displayed in the drawing area. Drag the manipulator and place it at the location where the insertion point is to be insertcd. Using this insertion point, you can drag the block, in the desired direction. You can also add relations between the insertion point and the sketched entity.

Note

It is recommended to create each entity of the sketch as a separate block, else there will be no motion between the sketch entities.

Save Block

The **Save Block** tool is used to save the current sketch as a block file. Using this tool, you can save the sketch of multiple entities as a single block. In this case, the motion between the sketched entities will be frozen. To save a sketch, create a sketch of multiple entities and then save it directly by choosing the **Save Block** button from the **Blocks** toolbar. Alternatively, choose **Tools > Blocks > Save** from the SolidWorks menus; the block will be saved as *.Sldblk* file. *.Sldblk* is the default extension of blocks.

Insert Block

The **Insert Block** tool is used to insert the blocks created by you into the active sketch. To insert a block, choose the **Insert Block** button from the **Blocks** toolbar; the **Edit Sketch PropertyManager** will be displayed, as shown in Figure 18-3 and you will be prompted to select a sketching plane. Select the sketching plane from the drawing area or from the **FeatureManager design tree**; the **Insert Block PropertyManager** will be displayed, as shown in Figure 18-4. Note that if you are in the sketching environment, then the **Insert Block PropertyManager** will be displayed directly. The options available in this **PropertyManager** are discussed next.

Figure 18-3 The Edit Sketch PropertyManager

Figure 18-4 The Insert Block PropertyManager

Blocks to Insert

The existing blocks of the active sketch are listed under the **Open Blocks** area of the **Blocks to Insert** rollout. You can insert multiple copies of the existing blocks into the active sketch. To do so, select a block from the **Open Blocks** selection area in the **Blocks to Insert** rollout; the selected block will be attached to the cursor. Next, click the left mouse button in the drawing area to insert it into the current sketch. Note that the block will still be attached to the cursor, which implies that you can insert multiple copies of that block by clicking the left mouse button repeatedly in the drawing area. You can also browse to the blocks by choosing the **Browse** button from the **Blocks to Insert** rollout. Choose the **OK** button from the **Insert Block PropertyManager** to exit from it.

Parameters

In this rollout, the **Block Scale** and **Block Rotation** spinners are available. By default, 1 is displayed as the scale value in the **Block Scale** spinner. It indicates that the current scale factor of the entity is 1. You can change the scale value of the block by using this spinner or by entering the scale value using the keyboard. The **Block Rotation** spinner is used to rotate the block by an angle or adjust the orientation of the block. The default angle value in the **Block Rotation** spinner is 0. You can change the default rotational angle value by using the spinner.

Edit Block

 The **Edit Block** tool is used to add, remove, or modify the block entities, as well as change the existing relations and dimensions of the block entities. This tool is enabled in the **Blocks** toolbar only when you select a block in the drawing area. To edit a block, first ensure that the sketching environment is activated. Then, click on the **+**sign available on the left of the **Sketch** in the **FeatureManager design tree** to expand the node and display the blocks, if they are not already displayed. Next, select the required block from the design tree and right click; a shortcut menu will be displayed. Choose the **Edit Block** option from the shortcut menu. Alternatively, you can choose the **Edit Block** button from the **Blocks** toolbar. Now, you can edit the selected block as per the requirement. Once the changes are done, click on the block confirmation corner available on the top right corner of the drawing area to exit from it.

Add/Remove

The **Add/Remove** tool is used to add or remove the sketch entities from a block. To add the sketch entities to a block using the **Add/Remove** tool, select the required block from the drawing area or from the **FeatureManager design tree** and right-click; a shortcut menu will be displayed. Next, choose the **Edit Block** option from the shortcut menu; the **Add/Remove** button will be enabled in the **Blocks** toolbar. Choose the **Add/Remove** button from the **Blocks** toolbar to add or remove the sketch entities from a block; the **Add/Remove Entities PropertyManager** will be displayed, as shown in Figure 18-5. The names of the entities of the selected block will be displayed in the selection area of the **Block Entities** rollout. Select the required sketch

*Figure 18-5 The Add/Remove
Entities PropertyManager*

entities from the drawing area to add it into the block. Note that the selected sketch entities will also be added to the selection area of the **Block Entities** rollout. Choose the **OK** button from the **Add/Remove Entities PropertyManager**; the selected sketch entities will be add to the block. To remove an entity from the selected block, invoke the **Add/Remove Entities PropertyManager** and then select the entity from the selection area of the **Block Entities** rollout. Next, press the DELETE key.

Rebuild

 The **Rebuild** tool enables you to refresh or update the parent sketches after editing the block. If you have edited the position of a block using the **Edit Block** tool, you will notice that the block no longer maintains relations with the other entities. To reestablish the relations, you need to choose the **Rebuild** button from the **Blocks** toolbar. Alternatively, choose **Tools > Blocks > Rebuild** from the SolidWorks menus to reestablish or update the sketch entities.

Explode Block

 The **Explode Block** tool is used to explode the selected block and dissolve into the sketch entity. To explode the block, select the block from the **FeatureManager design tree**; the **Explode Block** button will be enabled in the **Blocks** toolbar. Choose the **Explode Block** button from the **Blocks** toolbar or choose **Tools > Blocks > Explode** from the SolidWorks menus; the selected block will dissolve into the sketch. After dissolving a block into the sketch, you can again turn it into a block using the **Make Block** button, but a new name will be assigned to it.

Belt/Chain

 The **Belt/Chain** tool is used to insert a belt between pulleys. This tool helps you to create the mechanisms such as multiple gear sets, cable and belt pulleys, chain sprocket system, and so on. The belt automatically creates the link motion of the pulleys based on their diameters. To add a belt/chain between pulleys, create sketches of two pulleys in the drawing area and then convert them into separate blocks. The sketch of pulley is a circle or an arc only. Choose the **Belt/Chain** button from the **Blocks** toolbar or choose **Tools > Sketch Entities > Belt / Chain** from the SolidWorks menus; the **Belt / Chain PropertyManager** will be displayed, as shown in Figure 18-6 and you will be prompted to select the circle or arc to define the belt members around which the belt will pass. The options in this **PropertyManager** are discussed next.

Belt Members

The **Belt Members** rollout is used to display the name of the blocks that are selected to define the belt members. Select the circular blocks from the drawing area to define the belt members. The selected blocks will be displayed in the **Pulley Components** selection area of this rollout

Figure 18-6 The Belt / Chain PropertyManager

and the preview of belt/chain mechanism will be displayed in the drawing area. You can also remove a selected block from the **Pulley Components** selection area. To do so, select the block from the **Pulley Components** selection area and invoke the shortcut menu. Next, choose the **Delete** option from the shortcut menu; the selected block will be removed from the selection area. If you choose the **Clear Selection** option from the shortcut menu, then all blocks will be removed from the selection area of the **Belt Members** rollout. Figure 18-7 shows the preview of the belt/chain mechanism after selecting the belt members.

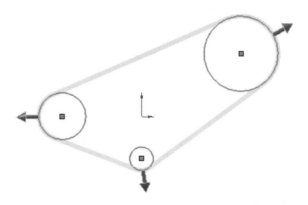

Figure 18-7 Preview of the belt/chain mechanism

The **Move Up** and **Move Down** buttons available on the left of the **Belt Members** rollout are used to change the order of the belt members. To move a particular block up in the selection area, select it and then choose the **Move Up** button. Similarly, the **Move Down** button is used to move the selected belt member down in the order. Using these buttons, you can arrange the sequence of the belt members in the selection area of the **Belt Members** rollout. You can also flip the side of the selected belt member, on which the belt is placed, by choosing the **Flip belt side** button available in this rollout. Alternatively, you can flip the side of the belt member by clicking on the arrow of the belt member from the drawing area. Figure 18-8 shows the belt member whose side has to be flipped and the Figure 18-9 shows the belt member after flipping the side.

Properties

By default, the **Driving** check box is clear in this rollout and therefore, the driving length of the belt is calculated automatically. Select the **Driving** check box to define the length of the belt as per your requirement; the length spinner will be available. You can specify the driving length of the belt using this spinner. To specify the thickness of the belt, select the **Use belt thickness** check box; the **Belt thickness** spinner will be displayed. You can specify the value of the thickness of the belt in this spinner. The **Engage belt** check box is used to engage or disengage the belt mechanism. By default, this check box is selected and engages the belt mechanism. To disengage the belt mechanism, clear this check box. Figure 18-10 shows the mechanism without specifying any belt thickness and Figure 18-11 shows the same mechanism after specifying some belt thickness.

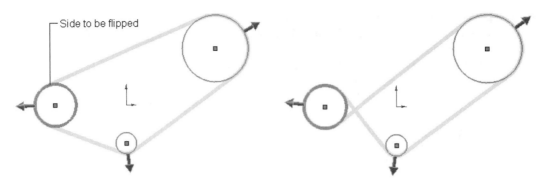

Figure 18-8 *The block entity before flipping the side*

Figure 18-9 *The block entity after flipping the side*

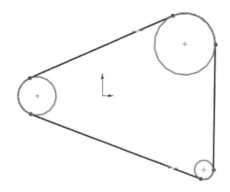

Figure 18-10 *Mechanism without specifying the belt thickness*

Figure 18-11 *Mechanism after specifying the belt thickness*

Tip. *If you draw an axis in the pulley, you can easily visualize the rotation when it is rotated.*

SAVING A SKETCH AS A BLOCK IN THE DESIGN LIBRARY

In the earlier versions of SolidWorks, first you need to make blocks from the sketches using the tools in the **Blocks** toolbar and then save them in the **Design Library**. In SolidWorks 2009, you can directly save a sketch as a block in the **Design Library**.

To save a sketch as a block in the **Design Library**, select the sketch from the **FeatureManager design tree** and then choose the **Design Library** tab from the task pane; the **Design Library** task pane is invoked. Next, choose the **Add to Library** button from the **Design Library** task pane; the **Add to Library PropertyManager** will be displayed, as shown in Figure 18-12 and the name of the selected sketch will be displayed in the **Items to Add** rollout of the **PropertyManager**. Enter the file name in the **File name** edit box in the **Save To** rollout of the **PropertyManager**. Next, select the folder in which you want to save this file from the **Design Library folder** area. You can also create a new folder in the **Design Library folder** area by choosing the **Create New Folder** button from the **Design Library** task pane. The **Option** rollout in the **Add to Library PropertyManager** is used to view the file type or extension of the file. Specify the file type **SolidWorks (.Sldblk)** from the **File Type** drop-down list, if it is not already selected. The **Enter Description** edit box in this rollout is used to enter the description of the block; this description will be displayed as a tooltip. After setting all the required parameters in the rollout, choose the **OK** button from the **Add to Library PropertyManager** to exit.

CREATING MECHANISMS USING BLOCKS

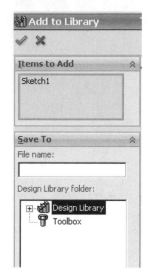

Figure 18-12 The Add to Library PropertyManager

In SolidWorks, you can create simple mechanisms by adding a suitable relation between the blocks. For example, the **Traction** relation is used to create mechanisms such as gear trains, rack and pinion, and so on. Similarly, you can create the cam and follower mechanism using the **Make Path** relation. The procedures to create these mechanisms are discussed next.

Creating the Rack and Pinion Mechanism

In SolidWorks, you can create a rack and pinion mechanism using the **Traction** relation. To do so, create two sketches, as shown in Figure 18-13 and convert them into two separate

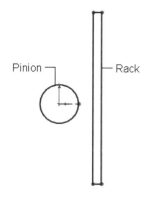

Figure 18-13 Sketches to the blocks

blocks. Next, select the circular block and then the vertical line of the other block by pressing the CTRL key; the **Properties PropertyManager** will be displayed, as shown in Figure 18-14.

*Figure 18-14 The **Properties PropertyManager***

Note that the **Traction** button is available in the **Add Relations** rollout of the **Properties PropertyManager**. Choose the **Traction** button from the **Add Relations** rollout and then click anywhere in the drawing area to exit from this **PropertyManager**. Similarly, apply other suitable constraints as well. Figure 18-15 shows the blocks before applying the **Traction** relation and Figure 18-16 shows the resultant blocks after applying the **Traction** relation. To check the linkage between these blocks, click on the vertical line of the block and drag it up or down in the drawing area. You will notice that the linear translation of one part results in a circular motion of the other part and vice-versa.

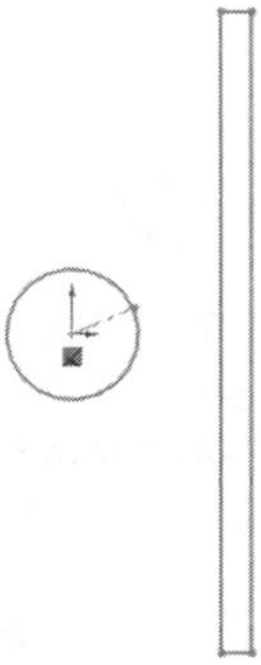

*Figure 18-15 The blocks before applying the **Traction** relation*

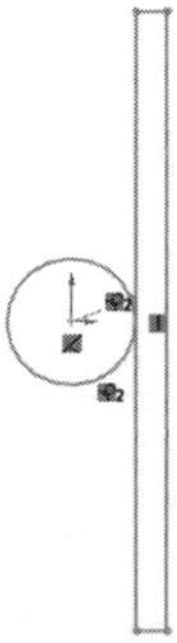

*Figure 18-16 The resultant blocks after applying the **Traction** relation*

Creating the Cam and Follower Mechanism

A cam is a rotating machine element which gives reciprocating or oscillating motion to another element known as follower. In SolidWorks, you can create a cam and follower mechanism between two blocks using the **Make Path** tool. To create a cam and follower mechanism, first you need to convert a cam profile into a single path using the **Make Path** tool and then apply tangent relation between the cam and follower profiles. Note that, the sketched entities of the cam profile to be converted as path should be coinciding with each other and forming a single chain. The procedure to create a cam and follower mechanism is given below.

Create two sketches representing the sketch of the cam and the follower, as shown in Figure 18-17, and then convert them into separate blocks. Now, you need to convert the cam profile into a single path by using the **Make Path** tool. To do so, select the lower arc of the cam, as shown in Figure 18-18 and then choose **Tools > Sketch Tools > Make Path** from the SolidWorks menus; the **Path Properties PropertyManager** will be displayed, as shown in Figure 18-19. In this **PropertyManager**, the selection area of the **Existing Relations** rollout displays the relations between the sketch entities that make up the path and the sketch entities with which the path interacts. Choose the **Edit Path** button from the **Definition** rollout of this **PropertyManager**; the **Path PropertyManager** will be displayed, as shown in Figure 18-20 and you will be prompted to select the entities that are coincident end to end and form a single chain. Note that the selected arc of the cam will be displayed in the **Selected Entities** rollout of the **Path PropertyManager**. Now, select the remaining sketched entities of the cam that have a tangent relation with each other from the drawing area to make a path. Choose the **OK** button to exit from the **PropertyManager**. Next, apply the relations, as shown in Figure 18-21. Figure 18-22 shows the cam and follower mechanism after applying the relations. To check the motion between the cam and follower, click on the cam and drag it clockwise in the drawing area.

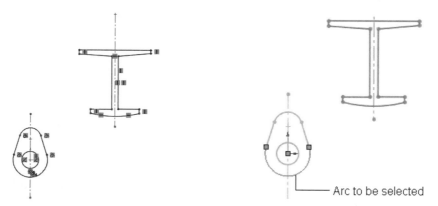

Figure 18-17 *Sketches of cam and follower*   *Figure 18-18* *The arc of the cam to be selected*

*Figure 18-19 The **Path Properties** PropertyManager*

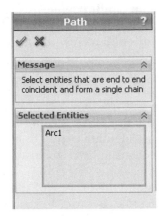

*Figure 18-20 The **Path** PropertyManager*

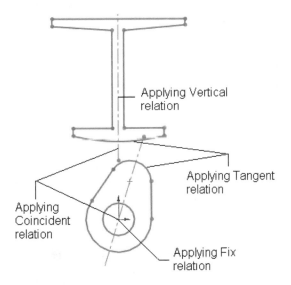

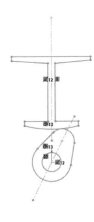

Figure 18-21 Entities to be selected for adding relations

Figure 18-22 Cam and follower after applying the relation

APPLYING MOTION TO BLOCKS

In SolidWorks, you can animate the mechanism created using blocks by applying motion to it. To do so, you need to create all entities of the mechanism individually and then save them as separate blocks. Next, start a new SolidWorks Assembly document by choosing the **Assembly** button from the **New SolidWorks Documents** dialog box; a new Assembly session will be started and the **Begin Assembly PropertyManager** will be invoked. Choose the **Create Layout** button from the **Begin Assembly PropertyManager**; the layout environment will be invoked. Insert all blocks one-by-one in the drawing area by choosing the **Insert Blocks** button from the **Blocks** toolbar and apply the required relations between the blocks of the mechanism. After applying the required relation, choose the **Layout** button from the

Layout CommandManager to exit from it. To add the motor, choose the **Motion Study** tab available at the lower left corner of the drawing area; the **MotionManager** will be displayed. In this **MotionManager**, the **Animation** option is selected by default in the **Type of Study** drop-down list. Choose the **Motor** button from the **MotionManager** toolbar; the **Motor PropertyManager** will be displayed. Select the required motor from the **Motor Type** rollout and specify the direction of the motor in the **Motor direction** selection box of the **Component/Direction** rollout. After specifying all the required parameters, choose the **OK** button from the **Motor PropertyManager** to exit. To calculate the animation motion study, choose the **Calculate** button from the **MotionManager** toolbar. Now, you can view the motion of the mechanism by choosing the **Play** button from the **MotionManager** toolbar.

To understand the process of applying motion to blocks, we will take the example of pulleys. In this example, in order to create a driver-driven mechanism between three pulleys having diameters 10, 20, and 30, and to animate it, you need to draw three circles of diameters 10, 20, and 30 respectively in separate sketching environments and save them as a block files. Next, open the layout environment by choosing the **Create Layout** button from the **Begin Assembly PropertyManager**. Now, insert the circles, which are saved as a block, one-by-one into the drawing area by choosing the **Insert Block** button from the **Blocks** toolbar, as shown in Figure 18-23. Next, select the bigger and medium sized circles from the drawing area by pressing the CTRL key; the **Properties PropertyManager** will be displayed. Choose the **Traction** button from the **Add Relations** rollout of the **PropertyManager** to apply the **Traction** relation. Similarly, select the bigger and smaller circles from the drawing area and apply the **Traction** relation on them. Figure 18-24 shows the circles after applying the **Traction** relation on them. Finally, choose the **Layout** button from the **Layout CommandManager** to exit.

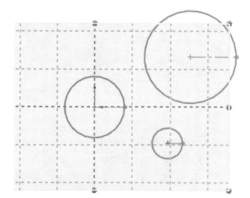

Figure 18-23 Circles before applying the **Traction** relation

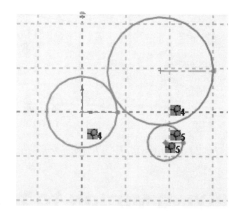

Figure 18-24 Circles after applying the **Traction** relation

Now, to animate these circles, choose the **Motion Study** tab, the **MotionManager** will be displayed. In the **MotionManager**, the **Animation** option is selected by default in the **Type of Study** drop-down list. Choose the **Motor** button from the **MotionManager** toolbar; the **Motor PropertyManager** will displayed. By default, the **Rotary Motor** button is chosen in the **Motor Type** rollout of the **PropertyManager**. Now, you need to select the direction of the motor. To do so, select any one of the circle as a direction of the motor and then choose the **OK** button from the **PropertyManager** to exit. To calculate the motion study, choose the **Calculate** button from the **MotionManager** toolbar. Next, choose the **Play** button to run the motion between the three circles after applying the **Traction** relation.

Note
You can also create the sketches of the mechanism and convert them into separate blocks in the layout environment itself.

CREATING PARTS FROM BLOCKS

As discussed earlier, you can create parts from the blocks. To make a part from the bock, choose the **Make Part from Block** button from the **Layout CommandManager**; the **Make Part from Block PropertyManager** will be displayed, as shown in Figure 18-25. The option in this **PropertyManager** are discussed next.

*Figure 18-25 The **Make Part** from Block PropertyManager*

Selected Blocks

This rollout lists the blocks that will be selected for creating parts from the drawing area. Select the block from the drawing area; the selected block will be displayed in the **Selected Blocks** rollout. You can select more than one block from the drawing area.

Block to Part Constraint

In this rollout, there are two buttons namely, **Project** and **On Block**. These buttons are used to make parts from the blocks. By default, the **On Block** button is chosen in this rollout. On choosing the **Project** button from the **Block to Part Constraint** rollout, you can create a part from the block, this part will be projected on the plane of the block in the layout environment. You can drag this part in the drawing area, normal to the plane of the block and it is not constrained to be co-planar with the plane of the block in the layout environment, but the part that is created by choosing the **On Block** button is constrained to be co-planar with the plane of the block in the layout environment.

Select the block from the drawing area of the layout environment; the selected block will be displayed in the selection area of the **Selected Blocks** rollout. Choose the **OK** button from the **PropertyManager** to conform the selection. The selected block will be displayed as a part in the **FeatureManager design tree**. The part name is the same as the block name. Note that the name of the part in the design tree will be covered by a square bracket, indicating that it is a virtual component. The virtual components are saved internally in the assembly file in which they are created. You can save these components into external files later on. Next, select the part name or virtual component from the design tree; the pop-up toolbar will be displayed. Choose the **Open Part** button from the pop-up toolbar; the selected part will be opened in the **Part** environment. Now, you can convert it into a solid feature using the tools available in the **Feature CommandManager**. Next, open the layout environment again by choosing **Window > name of the layout assembly** from the SolidWorks menus; the **SolidWorks 2009** message window will be displayed. Choose the **Yes** button to rebuild the change.

TUTORIALS

Tutorial 1

In this tutorial, you will create a reciprocating mechanism using blocks, as shown in Figure 18-26. You will also convert the blocks of the reciprocating mechanism into parts. The final assembly of the mechanism after converting the blocks into parts is shown in Figure 18-27. Figure 18-28 to 18-31 show different views of the parts of the mechanism with required dimensions. Assume the missing dimensions.

(Expected time: 45 min)

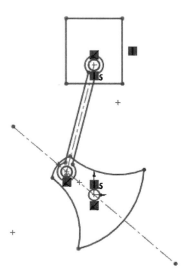

Figure 18-26 *The reciprocating mechanism created by assembling the blocks*

Figure 18-27 *The reciprocating mechanism after converting the blocks into parts*

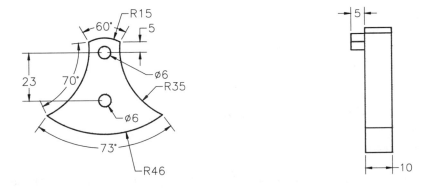

Figure 18-28 *Front view of the crank*

Figure 18-29 *The right view of the crank*

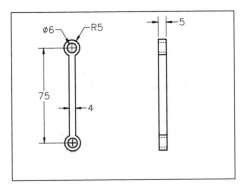

Figure 18-30 *The front view of the piston-rod*

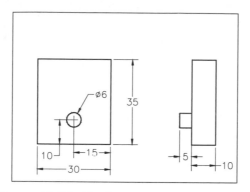

Figure 18-31 *The front view of the piston tank*

The following steps are required to complete this tutorial:

a. Create sketches of the mechanism using the **Sketch** tools.
b. Save the sketches as different block files.
c. Insert the blocks into the Layout environment, refer to Figure 18-32.
d. Apply relations between the blocks, refer to Figure 18-33 and 18-34.
e. Convert the blocks into parts, refer to Figure 18-37 and 18-38.
f. Save and close the document.

Creating the First Sketch of the Mechanism

1. Start a new SolidWorks part document using the **New SolidWorks Document** dialog box and invoke the sketching environment.

2. Draw the front view of the crank, refer to Figure 18-28, using the tools available in the **Sketch CommandManager**.

Saving a Sketch as a Block File

You need to save the sketch of the crank as a block.

1. Choose the **Save Sketch as Block** button from the **Blocks** toolbar; the **Save As** dialog box is displayed. Enter the name of the sketch as **Crank** in the **File name** edit box. Browse to the required location and then choose the **Save** button to exit from it. Alternatively, choose **Tools > Blocks > Save** from the SolidWorks menus to save the sketch as a block file.

2. Close the current sketching environment by choosing **File > Close** from the SolidWorks menus; the SolidWorks message window is displayed. Choose the **Yes** button.

Creating Other Sketches of the Mechanism and Saving them as Block Files

Create other sketches of the mechanism in different sketching environments and save them as a separate block file.

1. Start a new SolidWorks part document using the **New SolidWorks Document** dialog box and then switch to the sketching environment.

2. Draw the sketch of the piston rod, refer to Figure 18-30.

3. Save this sketch as a block file by choosing the **Save Sketch as Block** button from the **Blocks** toolbar. Enter **Piston_rod** in the **File name** edit box of the **Save As** dialog box and then exit from it.

4. Draw the sketch of the piston tank, refer to Figure 18-31, and then save the sketch as a separate block file, named **Piston_tank**.

Inserting the Blocks into the Layout Environment

You need to insert the blocks in the layout environment and then apply the required relation between them.

1. Start a new SolidWorks Assembly environment using the **New SolidWorks Document** dialog box and then choose the **Create Layout** button from the **Begin Assembly PropertyManager**; the layout environment is invoked.

2. Choose the **Insert Block** button from the **Layout CommandManager**; the **Insert Block PropertyManager** is displayed.

3. Choose the **Browse** button from the **Blocks to Insert** rollout of the **Insert Block PropertyManager**; the **Open** dialog box is displayed.

4. Select **Crank** from the **Open** dialog box and then choose the **Open** button; the selected block is attached to the cursor.

5. Click anywhere in the drawing area to place the block and then right-click to display the shortcut menu. Choose **OK** from the shortcut menu.

6. Similarly, insert the **Piston_rod** and **Piston_tank** in this layout environment. To change the current view orientation normal to the screen, choose the **View Orientation** button from the **Heads-Up View** toolbar; a flyout is displayed. Choose the **Normal To** button from the flyout. Figure 18-32 shows all the blocks inserted into the layout environment.

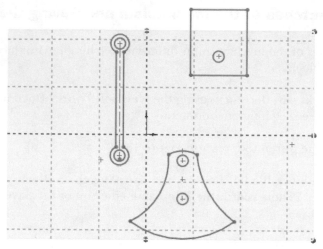

Figure 18-32 Blocks after inserting into the layout environment

Applying Relations to the Blocks

You need to apply relations to the blocks to assemble them and to view the motion of the mechanism.

1. Press and hold the CTRL key, and then select the center of the lower circle of the **Crank** and the origin, as shown in Figure 18-33; the **Properties PropertyManager** is displayed.

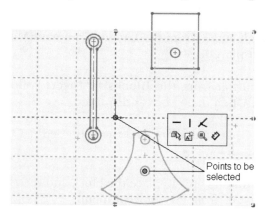

Figure 18-33 Points to be selected to apply the **Coincident** *relation*

2. Choose the **Coincident** button from the **Add Relations** rollout of the **Properties PropertyManager**; the coincident relation is applied between the selected points. Click anywhere in the drawing area.

3. Next, apply the relations, as shown in Figure 18-34. Figure 18-35 shows the blocks after applying the required relations. Now, the blocks act as a reciprocating mechanism.

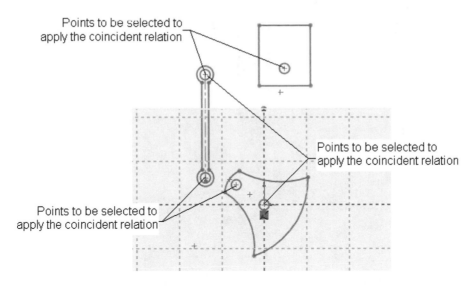

Points to be selected to
apply the coincident relation

Points to be selected to
apply the coincident relation

Points to be selected to
apply the coincident relation

Figure 18-34 Points selected to apply the relations

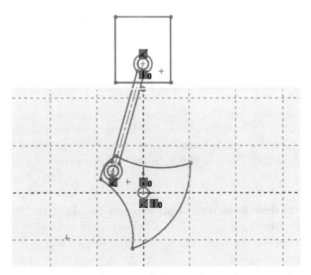

*Figure 18-35 The blocks after applying the required
relations*

4. To view the motion of the mechanism, press and hold the left mouse button on the point, as shown in Figure 18-36, and rotate the cursor in the clockwise direction.

Converting Blocks into Parts

Now, you need to convert the blocks into parts to create a 3D mechanism.

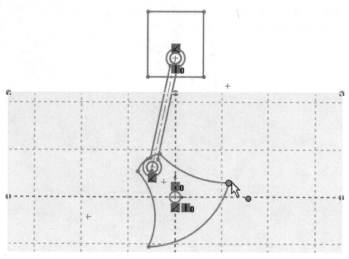

Figure 18-36 *Point selected to view the motion of the mechanism*

1. Choose the **Make Part from Block** button from the **Layout CommandManager**; the **Make Part From Block PropertyManager** is displayed.

2. Select all blocks from the drawing area; the names of the selected blocks are displayed in the **Selected Blocks** rollout of the **PropertyManager**. Choose the **OK** button; all blocks are displayed as parts in the **FeatureManager design tree** with the part symbol on their left.

3. Select the **Crank** block from the **FeatureManager design tree**; the pop-up toolbar is displayed. Choose the **Edit Part** button from the pop-up toolbar, the sketching environment is invoked. Choose the **Feature** tab from the **CommandManager** to invoke the Part environment.

4. Choose the **Extruded Boss/Base** button from the **Feature CommandManager**; the **Extrude PropertyManager** is displayed and you are prompted to select the sketching plane or the existing sketch. Select the sketch from the drawing area; its preview is displayed in the drawing area.

5. In the **Direction 1** rollout of the **PropertyManager**, the **Blind** option is selected by default the **End Condition** drop-down list. Enter **10** mm in the **Depth** spinner of the **Direction 1** rollout and choose the **Reverse Direction** button to flip the direction of the extrude. Choose the **OK** button to exit from it.

    Next, you need to extrude the upper hole of the **Crank**, refer to Figure 18-29.

6. Select the **Sketch** of the extrude feature from the **FeatureManager design tree** and then choose the **Extruded Boss/Base** button from the **Feature CommandManager**; the **Extrude PropertyManager** is displayed.

7. Click on the arrows available on the right of the **Selected Contours** rollout in this **PropertyManager** to expand it. Move the cursor toward the upper hole of the **Crank** and select the upper hole of the **Crank** when it appears in a different color, as shown in figure 18-37.

Figure 18-37 Hole of the crank to be selected

8. Enter **5** mm in the **Depth** spinner. Invoke the **Direction 2** rollout and enter the value **10** mm in the **Depth** spinner of the **PropertyManager**. Choose the **OK** button to exit from it; the crank feature is displayed in the drawing area.

9. Click on the conformation corner in the upper right of the drawing area. Note that the rebuild icon is available on the left of the **Crank** in the design tree. Choose the **Rebuild** button from the Menu Bar to rebuild the part.

10. Select the **Piston_rod** block from the **FeatureManager design tree**; the pop-up toolbar is displayed.

11. Choose the **Edit Part** button from the pop-up toolbar and invoke the **Part** environment by choosing the **Feature** tab, if it is not already invoked.

12. Invoke the **Extrude PropertyManager**, select the sketch of the **Piston_rod** from the drawing area and enter **5** mm in the **Depth** spinner of the **PropertyManager**. Choose the **OK** button to exit from it.

13. Next, click on the conformation corner in the upper right of the drawing area and then choose the **Rebuild** button from the Menu Bar.

14. Similarly, select the **Piston_tank** from the **FeatureManager design tree** and invoke the **Part** environment.

15. Invoke the **Extrude PropertyManager** and select the sketch from the drawing area; its preview is displayed.

16. Enter **10** mm in the **Depth** spinner of the **PropertyManager**.

17. Choose the **Reverse Direction** button from the **Direction 1** rollout of the **PropertyManager** and choose **OK**.

    Next, you need to extrude the hole of the **Piston_tank**, refer to Figure 18-32.

18. Select the **Sketch** of the **Piston_tank** from the **FeatureManager design tree** and then invoke the **Extrude PropertyManager**.

19. Expand the **Selected Contours** rollout of the **PropertyManager** and move the cursor towards the hole of the **Piston_tank**. Next, select it by using the left mouse button when it is displayed in a different color.

20. Enter **5** mm in the **Depth** spinner of the **Direction 1** rollout. Next, invoke the **Direction 2** rollout and enter 10 mm in the **Depth** spinner of this rollout and exit by clicking on the conformation corner.

21. Choose the **Rebuild** button from the Menu Bar to rebuild the part. Next, choose the **Hide/Show items** button from the **Heads-Up View** toolbar; the flyout is displayed. Choose the **View Sketches** button to hide the sketches and vice-versa. Figure 18-38 shows the resultant mechanism after hiding the sketches of the parts.

Figure 18-38 *Reciprocating mechanism after hiding the sketches*

Saving the Model

1. Choose the **Save** button from the Menu Bar and save the mechanism with the name and location given below:

   \My Documents\SolidWorks\c18\c18tut1.sldasm

2. Close the document by choosing **File > Close** from the SolidWorks menus.

Tutorial 2

In this tutorial, you will convert 2D blocks into parts in the layout environment and then assemble them to create a mechanism, as shown in Figure 18-39. Also, you will animate the mechanism by applying the rotary motor. Figures 18-40 to 18-43 show different views of the parts of the mechanism with required dimensions. **(Expected time: 45 min)**

Figure 18-39 *The mechanism created by assembling the parts*

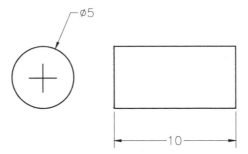

Figure 18-40 *The front and side views of the Shaft*

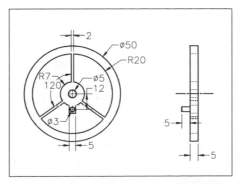

Figure 18-41 *The front view of the Wheel*

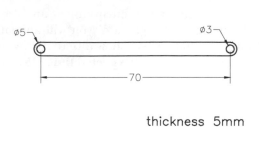

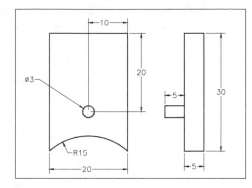

Figure 18-42 *The front view of the Connecting rod*

Figure 18-43 *The front and side views of the Slider*

The following steps are required to complete this tutorial:

a. Create the sketches of the mechanism using the sketch tools and save them as different block files.
b. Insert blocks into the layout environment, as shown in Figure 18-44.
c. Convert the blocks into parts, as shown in Figure 18-46.
d. Assemble the parts, as shown in Figure 18-48.
e. Animate the mechanism by applying the rotary motor.
f. Save the mechanism and then close the document.

Creating the Sketches of the Mechanism and Save them as Block Files

1. Start a new SolidWorks part document using the **New SolidWorks Document** dialog box and invoke the sketching environment.

2. Draw the sketch of the Shaft using the tools available in the **Sketch CommandManager**. For dimensions of the shaft, refer to Figure 18-40. Save the sketch of the Shaft in the *c18* folder as a block file using the **Save Sketch as Block** button from the **Blocks** toolbar.

3. Similarly, create the sketches of the Wheel, Connecting rod, and Slider in a separate sketching environment. For dimension of the sketches, refer to Figure 18-41 to 18-43. Save all sketches as separate block files in the *c18* folder.

Inserting All Blocks in the Layout Environment

After you have saved all sketches as a separate block files, you need to place these blocks one by one in the layout environment to convert them into parts.

1. Start a new Assembly document by choosing the **Assembly** button from the **New SolidWorks Document** dialog box. Choose the **Create Layout** button from the **Begin Assembly PropertyManager**; the layout environment is invoked.

2. Choose the **View Orientation** button from the **Heads-Up View** toolbar; the flyout is displayed. Choose the **Normal To** button from the flyout for changing orientation of the plane normal to the screen.

3. Choose the **Insert Block** button from the **Layout CommandManager** and insert a Shaft, Wheel, Connecting rod, and Slider in the layout environment, as shown in Figure 18-44.

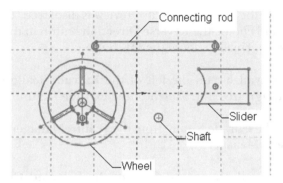

Figure 18-44 The blocks inserted into the layout environment

Converting Blocks into Parts

Now, you need to convert all the blocks into parts to create a 3D mechanism.

1. Choose the **Make Part from Block** button from the **Layout CommandManager**; the **Make Part From Block PropertyManager** is displayed.

2. Select all blocks from the drawing area or from the **FeatureManager design tree**. Note that the names of the selected blocks are displayed in the **Selected Blocks** selection area. Choose the **OK** button from the **PropertyManager** to exit; all blocks are displayed with the part symbol on the left in the **FeatureManager design tree**.

3. Choose the **Rebuild** button from the Menu Bar to update the change.

4. Select **Shaft** from the **FeatureManager design tree**, the pop-up toolbar is displayed. Choose the **Edit Part** button from this toolbar, the sketching environment is invoked.

5. Choose the **Features** tab from the **CommandManager**.

6. Choose the **Extruded Boss/Base** button from the **Feature CommandManager**; the **Extrude PropertyManager** is displayed and you are prompted to select the sketch.

7. Select the Shaft from the drawing area, its preview is displayed.

8. Enter **5 mm** in the **Depth** spinner of the **Direction 1** rollout, choose the **Reverse Direction** button and then choose the **OK** button.

9. Click on the conformation corner available in the upper right corner of the screen.

10. Similarly, select the Wheel from the **FeatureManager design tree** and invoke the **Part** environment.

11. Invoke the **Extrude PropertyManager** by choosing the **Extruded Boss/Base** button from the **Feature CommandManager**.

12. Select the Wheel from the drawing area; its preview is displayed. Enter the value **5 mm** in the **Depth** spinner and choose the **Reverse Direction** button in the **Direction 1** rollout of the **PropertyManager**. Finally, choose the **OK** button.

13. Click on the +sign available on the left of the **Extrude** feature of the Wheel in the **FeatureManager design tree**; the **Sketch** of the extrude feature is displayed.

14. Select the **Sketch** of the extrude feature from the **FeatureManager design tree** and invoke the **Extrude PropertyManager**.

15. Click on the arrow available on the right of the **Selected Contours** rollout in the **PropertyManager** to expand it. Zoom the wheel feature and select the area of the Wheel to be extruded, as shown in Figure 18-45.

Figure 18-45 *The area selected to be extruded*

16. Enter **5 mm** in the **Depth** spinner of the **Direction 1** rollout and extrude it using the **Mid Plane** option. Click on the conformation corner to exit from it.

17. Select the Connecting rod from the **FeatureManager design tree**; the pop-up toolbar is displayed. Invoke the Part environment.

18. Invoke the **Extrude PropertyManager** and select the sketch of the Connection rod from the design tree. Enter **5 mm** in the **Depth** spinner of the **Direction 1** rollout and then choose the **OK** button to exit from the **PropertyManager**. Next, click on the conformation corner.

19. Select the Slider from the **FeatureManager design tree** and invoke the **Part** environment by choosing the **Edit Part** button from the pop-up toolbar.

20. Invoke the **Extrude PropertyManager** and select the sketch of the slider from the drawing area; its preview is displayed.

21. Enter **5 mm** in the **Depth** spinner and choose the **Reverse Direction** button in the **PropertyManager**. Next, choose the **OK** button to exit.

22. Click on the +sign available on the left of the **Extrude** feature of the slider in the design tree; the **Sketch** of the extrude feature is displayed.

23. Select the **Sketch** of the extrude feature from the design tree and invoke the **Extrude PropertyManager**. Next, expand the **Selected Contours** rollout and select the area enclosed by the hole of diameter 3 mm in the Slider; its preview is displayed.

24. Enter **5 mm** in the **Depth** spinner of the **Direction 1** rollout and extrude it using the **Mid Plane** option. Finally, choose the **OK** button to exit from the **PropertyManager**.

25. Click on the conformation corner to exit from the **Part** environment. Figure 18-46 shows the blocks after converting into parts.

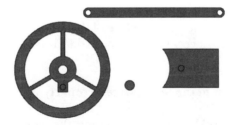

Figure 18-46 The blocks after being converted into parts

Assembling the Parts

Once all parts are created, you need to assemble them in the **Assembly** environment using the mate relations.

1. Choose the **Assembly** tab from the **CommandManager**, the assembly environment is invoked.

   First, you need to assemble the Wheel with the Shaft. Therefore, you need to fix the Shaft.

2. Select the Shaft from the drawing area and right-click to display the shortcut menu. Select the **Fix** option from the shortcut menu; the Shaft is fixed and you cannot move or rotate it.

3. Invoke the **Move Component PropertyManager** and choose the **SmartMates** button from the **Move** rollout. Next, double-click on the inner-most circular face of the Wheel; the Wheel appears transparent.

4. Next, double-click on the shaft; the **Mate** pop-up toolbar is invoked. The **Concentric** button is highlighted in this toolbar. Choose the **Add/Finish Mate** button from the **Mate** pop-up toolbar.

5. Right-click in the drawing area and choose the **Clear Selection** option to clear the current selection.

6. Double-click on the left-most inner circular face of the Connecting rod; the Connecting rod appears transparent.

7. Double-click on the outer cylindrical handle face of the Wheel; the concentric mate is applied between the two selected faces. Choose the **Add/Finish Mate** button from the **Mate** pop-up toolbar.

8. Right-click in the drawing area and choose the **Clear Selection** option to clear the current selection.

9. Rotate the assembly and double-click on the right most inner circular face of the Connecting rod; the Connecting rod appears transparent.

10. Next, select the outer cylindrical handle face of the Slider; the concentric mate is applied between the two selected faces. Choose the **Add/Finish Mate** button from the **Mate** pop-up toolbar.

11. Choose the **OK** button from the **SmartMates PropertyManager**.

12. Invoke the **Mate PropertyManager** by choosing the **Mate** button from the **Assembly CommandManager**. Then, select the horizontal planes of the Slider and Shaft from the drawing area, as shown in Figure 18-47. The selected planes are displayed in the **Entities to Mate** selection area of the **Mate Selections** rollout. Next, exit from the **PropertyManager**. Figure 18-48 shows the final assembly of the mechanism.

Figure 18-47 *The planes to be selected*   *Figure 18-48* *The final mechanism*

Applying Motion to the Mechanism

Next, you need to apply motion to the mechanism to check its working.

1. Choose the **Motion Study** tab available at the lower left corner of the drawing area; the **MotionManager** is displayed.

2. Choose the **Motor** button from the **MotionManager** toolbar; the **Motor PropertyManager** is displayed.

3. The **Rotary Motor** is selected by default in this **PropertyManager**. Select the front face of the Wheel as the direction of rotation. The selected face is displayed in the **Motor direction** area of the **Component / Direction** rollout of the **PropertyManager**. You can flip the direction of the rotation of the motor, if required, by choosing the **Reverse Direction** button from the **Component / Direction** rollout.

4. Choose the **OK** button from the **Motor PropertyManager** to exit.

5. Choose the **Calculate** button from the **MotorManager** toolbar to calculate the motion study of the mechanism.

6. Choose the **Play** button from the **MotorManager** toolbar to view the motion of the mechanism and then choose the **Stop** button to stop the motion of the mechanism.

Saving the Model

1. Choose the **Save** button from the Menu Bar and save the mechanism with the name and location given below:

    \My Documents\SolidWorks\c18\c18tut2.sldasm

2. Close the document by choosing **File > Close** from the SolidWorks menus.

SELF-EVALUATION TEST

Answer the following questions and then compare them to those given at the end of this chapter:

1. In SolidWorks, the _____ button in the **Blocks** toolbar is used to make each entity of the sketch as a separate block.

2. The _____ check box in the **Belt/Chain PropertyManager** is selected to specify the thickness of the belt.

3. Choose the _____ button in the **Definition** rollout of the **Path Properties PropertyManager** to invoke the **Path PropertyManager**.

4. The _____ button in the **Blocks** toolbar is provided to edit a block.

5. The _____ button in the **Belt Members** rollout of the **Belt/Chain PropertyManager** is used to flip the side of the selected belt member.

6. The **Traction** relation is used to create a driver-driven mechanism. (T/F)

7. In SolidWorks 2009, you can save a sketch directly as a block in the **Design Library**. (T/F)

8. In SolidWorks, you cannot animate the mechanism created out of blocks by applying motor to it. (T/F)

9. You cannot change the order of the belt members that are selected in the selection area of the **Belt Members** rollout. (T/F)

10. The **Insert Block** tool is used to insert the blocks into an active sketch. (T/F)

REVIEW QUESTIONS

Answer the following questions:

1. The _____ tool helps you to create a path of sketch entities that are coincident end to end and form a single chain.

2. The _____ button in the **Make Part From Block PropertyManager** is used to create a part that is constrained to be co-planar with the plane of the block in the layout environment.

3. The _____ button is used to invoke the **Make Part From Block PropertyManager**.

4. While inserting a block into the active sketch, you can change its scale value using the _____ spinner.

5. To refresh or update the sketches, choose the _____ button from the **Blocks** toolbar.

6. Which button in the **Blocks** toolbar is used to add or remove the sketch entities?

    (a) **Edit Block**   (b) **Make Block**
    (c) **Add/Remove**   (d) **Explode Block**

7. Which of the following tools is used to make each entity of the sketch as a separate block?

    (a) **Save Blocks**   (b) **Make Block**
    (c) **Edit Block**   (d) **Add/Remove**

8. To create a part from the block, you need to invoke the _____ **PropertyManager**?

    (a) **Path Properties**   (b) **Make Block**
    (c) **Make Part From Block**   (d) None of these

9. Which of the following tools is used to dissolve a block into an sketched entity?

   (a) **Belt/Chain**   (b) **Rebuild**
   (c) **Add/Remove**   (d) **Explode Block**

10. The **Belt/Chain** tool is used to insert a belt between_____.

EXERCISES

Exercise 1

Create a mechanism using the blocks, as shown in Figure 18-49, and then convert the blocks of the mechanism into parts. Figure 18-50 shows the mechanism after converting the blocks into parts. Figures 18-51 through 18-54 show different views of the parts of the mechanism with required dimensions.   **(Expected time: 45 min)**

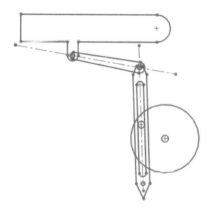

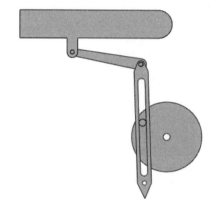

Figure 18-49 *The mechanism created by assembling the blocks*

Figure 18-50 *The mechanism after converting the blocks into parts*

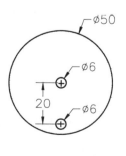

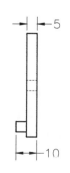

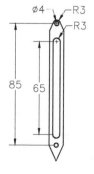

Figure 18-51 *The front and side views of Wheel*

Figure 18-52 *The front and side views of the Connecting rod1*

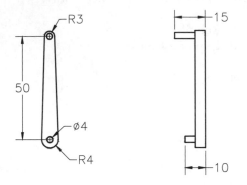

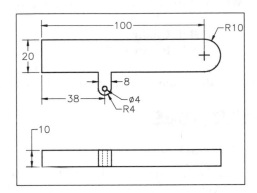

Figure 18-53 *The front and side views of the Connecting rod2*

Figure 18-54 *The front and top views of the Ram*

Chapter 19

Surface Modeling

Learning Objectives

After completing this chapter, you will be able to:

- Create an Extruded surface.
- Create a Revolved surface.
- Create a Swept surface.
- Create a Lofted surface.
- Create a Planar surface.
- Create a Boundary surface.
- Create a Fill surface.
- Create a Radiated surface.
- Offset surfaces.
- Trim surfaces.
- Untrim surfaces.
- Extend surfaces.
- Knit surfaces.
- Fillet surfaces.
- Create a Mid-surface.
- Delete Holes.
- Replace faces.
- Delete faces.
- Move and copy surfaces.
- Thicken the surface body.
- Create a thicken the surface cut.
- Create a surface cut.

SURFACE MODELING

Surface modeling is a technique of creating planar or non planar geometry of zero thickness. This zero thickness geometry is known as surface. Surfaces are generally used to create models of complex shapes. You can easily convert surface models into solid models. You can also extract a surface from a solid model using the surface modeling tools. This chapter deals with the surface modeling tools in SolidWorks. Using these tools, you can create complex shapes as surfaces and then convert them into solid models, if required.

Most of the real world components are created using solid modeling. But sometimes, you may need to create some complex features that can only be created by surface manipulation. Surface manipulation is done by using surface modeling tools. After creating the required complex surface, you can convert it into a solid model. The reasons to convert a surface model into a solid model are that a surface is a zero thickness geometry, and it has no mass and mass properties. But, while designing real world models, you may need mass and mass properties. The other reason is that you can generate a section view only if the model is a solid.

In SolidWorks, surface modeling is done in the **Part** mode and the tools used for surface modeling are available in the **Surfaces CommandManager**. The **Surfaces CommandManager** is not available, by default. Therefore, you need to right-click on any **CommandManager** tabs to invoke a shortcut menu and then choose the **Surfaces** option from it. The surface modeling tools can also be invoked by choosing **Insert > Surface** from the SolidWorks menus. You will notice that some of the tools available in the **Surfaces CommandManager**, such as extrude, revolve, sweep, and loft are similar to those discussed in the solid modeling.

The above mentioned tools and the other advanced surface modeling tools are discussed next.

Creating an Extruded Surface

CommandManager:	Surfaces > Extruded Surface
SolidWorks menus:	Insert > Surface > Extrude
Toolbar:	Surfaces > Extruded Surface

 In SolidWorks, the **Extruded Surface** tool is used to extrude a closed or an open sketch for creating an extruded surface. To create an extruded surface, create a sketch in the sketching environment and then, choose the **Extruded Surface** button from the **Surfaces CommandManager**; the **Surface-Extrude PropertyManager** will be displayed, as shown in Figure 19-1. The preview of the extruded surface with the default values will also be displayed in the drawing area. To define feature termination, select the required option from the **End Condition** drop-down list in the **PropertyManager**. The feature termination options are available in the **Direction 1** and **Direction 2** rollouts. The other options in this **PropertyManager** are the same as those discussed in part modeling. You can also define the extrusion depth dynamically by dragging the handle provided in the drawing area.

Figure 19-2 shows a closed sketch and Figure 19-3 shows the surface created by extruding the closed sketch. Figure 19-4 shows an open sketch and Figure 19-5 shows the surface created by extruding that open sketch.

Figure 19-1 *The **Surface-Extrude PropertyManager***

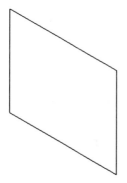

Figure 19-2 *A closed sketch*

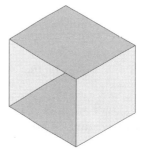

Figure 19-3 *Surface created by extruding the closed sketch*

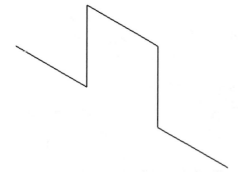

Figure 19-4 *An open sketch*

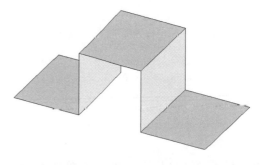

Figure 19-5 *Surface created by extruding the open sketch*

Creating a Revolved Surface

CommandManager:	Surfaces > Revolved Surface
SolidWorks menus:	Insert > Surface > Revolve
Toolbar:	Surfaces > Revolved Surface

You can also create a surface by revolving a closed or an open sketch along a centerline. Revolving a sketch along a centerline to create a revolved surface is similar to revolving a sketch along a centerline to create a solid feature. To create a revolved surface, first create a sketch and a centerline in the sketching environment. Next, choose the **Revolved Surface** button from the **Surfaces CommandManager**; the **Surface-Revolve PropertyManager** will be displayed, as shown in Figure 19-6. The preview of the revolved surface with the drag handle will be displayed in the drawing area. The feature termination options and other options in this **PropertyManager** are similar to those discussed while revolving a solid feature.

Figure 19-6 *The **Surface-Revolve PropertyManager***

Figure 19-7 shows an open sketch for creating a revolved surface. Figure 19-8 shows the resulting revolved surface created by revolving a sketch through an angle of 270-degree.

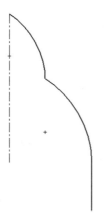

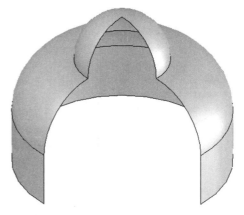

Figure 19-7 *Sketch for creating a revolved surface*

Figure 19-8 *Surface created by revolving a sketch through an angle of 270-degree*

Creating a Swept Surface

CommandManager:	Surfaces > Swept Surface
SolidWorks menus:	Insert > Surface > Sweep
Toolbar:	Surfaces > Swept Surface

You can also create a swept surface by sweeping a closed or an open profile along a closed or an open path. To create a swept feature, first draw a closed or an open sketch as a sweep profile and another sketch as a sweep path in the sketching environment. Next, choose the **Swept Surface** button from the **Surfaces CommandManager**; the **Surface-Sweep PropertyManager** will be displayed, as shown in Figure 19-9. Also, you will be prompted to select a sweep profile. Select a closed sketch or an open sketch as the profile of the sweep feature. Next, you will be prompted to select the sweep path. Select a closed or an open sketch as the sweep path. The preview of the sweep feature will be displayed in the drawing area.

*Figure 19-9 The **Surface-Sweep PropertyManager***

You can also select guide curves while creating the sweep surface. All the other options used to create a sweep surface are similar to those discussed while creating the solid sweep feature. Figure 19-10 shows an open profile and an open path and Figure 19-11 shows the resultant sweep surface. Figure 19-12 shows a closed profile and an open path and Figure 19-13 shows the resultant sweep surface. Figure 19-14 shows an open profile and a closed path and Figure 19-15 shows the resultant sweep surface.

Figure 19-16 shows a closed profile and a closed path and Figure 19-17 shows the resultant sweep surface.

Figure 19-18 shows a profile, path, and guide curves and Figure 19-19 shows the resultant sweep surface.

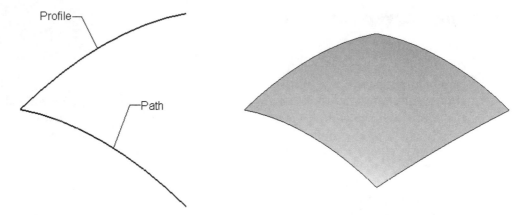

Figure 19-10 *A open profile and open path*

Figure 19-11 *Resultant sweep surface*

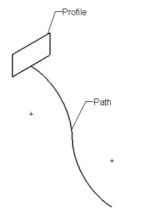

Figure 19-12 *A closed profile and an open path*

Figure 19-13 *Resultant sweep surface*

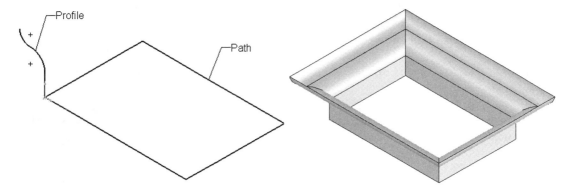

Figure 19-14 *An open profile and a closed path*

Figure 19-15 *Resultant sweep surface*

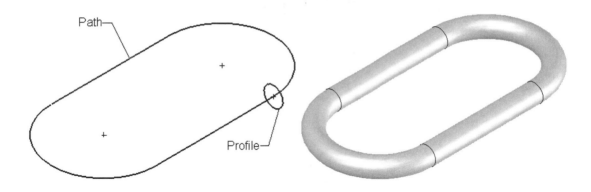

Figure 19-16 *A closed profile and closed path*   **Figure 19-17** *Resultant sweep surface*

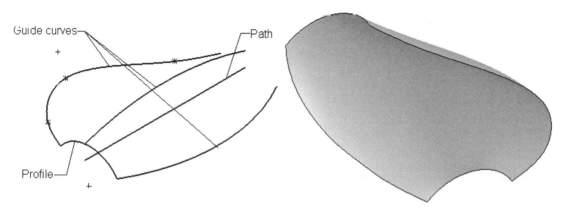

Figure 19-18 *Profile, path, and guide curves*   **Figure 19-19** *Resultant sweep feature*

Creating a Lofted Surface

CommandManager:	Surfaces > Lofted Surface
SolidWorks menus:	Insert > Surface > Loft
Toolbar:	Surfaces > Lofted Surface

In SolidWorks, you can also create a surface by lofting two or more sections. To create a lofted surface, choose the **Lofted Surface** button from the **Surfaces CommandManager**; the **Surface-Loft PropertyManager** will be displayed, as shown in Figure 19-20 and you will be prompted to select at least two profiles. Select the profiles to be lofted. All the options for creating a lofted surface are similar to those discussed while creating a solid lofted feature.

Note that if you want to create a loft surface with open section, all the sections to be lofted must be opened. Similarly, if you want to create a closed lofted surface, all the sections must be closed. The combination of closed and opened sections in a lofted surface is not possible. Figure 19-21 shows two open sections to be lofted and Figure 19-22 shows the resultant lofted surface.

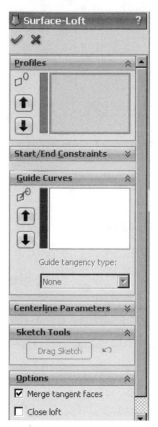

Figure 19-20 The Surface-Loft PropertyManager

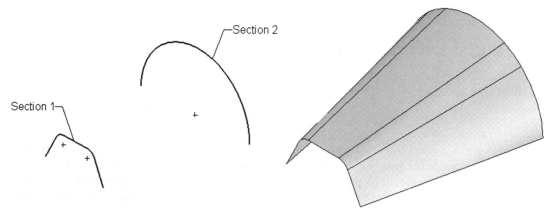

Figure 19-21 Open sections   *Figure 19-22 Resultant lofted surface*

Figure 19-23 shows two closed sections to be lofted and Figure 19-24 shows the resultant lofted surface. Figure 19-25 shows two sections and a centerline and Figure 19-26 shows the resultant lofted surface.

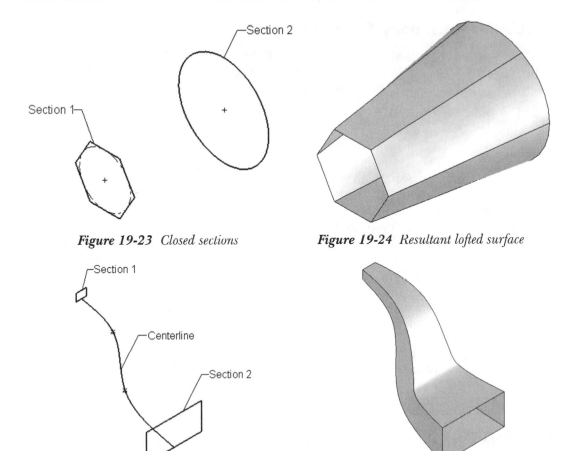

Figure 19-23 *Closed sections*

Figure 19-24 *Resultant lofted surface*

Figure 19-25 *Sections and centerline*

Figure 19-26 *Resultant lofted surface*

Figure 19-27 shows two sections and guide curves and Figure 19-28 shows the resultant lofted surface.

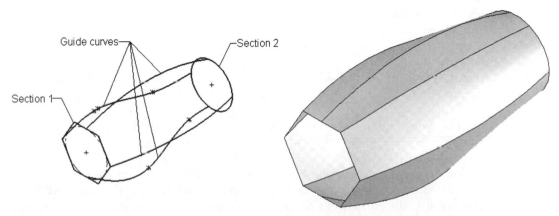

Figure 19-27 *Sections and guide curves*

Figure 19-28 *Resultant lofted surface*

Creating a Boundary Surface

CommandManager:	Surfaces > Boundary Surface
SolidWorks menus:	Insert > Surface > Boundary Surface
Toolbar:	Surfaces > Boundary Surface

 The **Boundary Surface** tool is used to create complex shaped models with high accuracy as well as high surfaces quality with curvature continuity. To create a boundary surface, choose the **Boundary Surface** button from the **Surfaces CommandManager**; the **Boundary-Surface PropertyManager** will be displayed, as shown in Figure 19-29 and you will be prompted to select the profile for the boundary surface. Select the curves from the drawing area; the selected curves will be displayed in the **Direction 1** rollout of the **PropertyManager** and the preview will be displayed in the drawing area. To select the curves for the **Direction 2** rollout, click on the **Curve** selection area of the **Direction 2** rollout and then select the curves from the drawing area; the selected curves will be displayed in the **Curve** selection area of the **Direction 2** rollout. The other options in this **PropertyManager** are discussed next.

Direction 1 Rollout

The **Direction 1** rollout is used to control the tangency and curvature continuity of curves in direction 1. The boundary surface is created based on the order of curves selected from the drawing area. You can change the order of curves in the **Curve** selection box by choosing the **Move Up** and **Move Down** buttons. The options that affect curves in the direction 1 are discussed next.

Figure 19-29 *The Boundary-Surface PropertyManager*

Tangent Type

The **Tangent Type** drop-down list is used to display options that control the tangency of the curvature. The options in this drop-down list are discussed next.

None. The **None** option is used to apply zero curvature or no tangency constraint to curves.

Direction Vector. The **Direction Vector** option is used to apply tangency constraint to curves. When you select the **Direction Vector** option from the **Tangent Type** drop-down list, the **Alignment** drop-down list and the **Direction Vector** area will be enabled below this drop-down list. Select the required alignment option from the **Alignment** drop-down list and then select the direction based on the selected curves. You can also specify the draft angle and tangent length for curves in the **Draft angle** and **Tangent Length** spinners, respectively.

Default. The **Default** option will be available in the **Tangent Type** drop-down list, only when atleast three curves are selected in one direction.

Normal To Profile. The **Normal To Profile** option is used to apply the tangency constraint normal to the selected curves. You can also set the draft angle and tangent length for curves using this option.

Direction 2 Rollout

The options in the **Direction 2** rollout are the same as those discussed in the **Direction 1** rollout.

Curve Influence

The **Curve Influence** drop-down list will be displayed in the **Direction 1** and **Direction 2** rollouts, only when you select a curve for the second direction. The options available in this drop-down list are discussed next.

Global. The **Global** option is selected by default in this drop-down list. This option is used to extend the curve influence upto the entire boundary feature.

To Next Curve. The **To Next Curve** option is used to extend the curve influence upto the next curve only.

To Next Sharp. The **To Next Sharp** option is used to extend the curve influence upto the next sharp only. Sharp is a hard corner of the sketch entity. This option is applicable between two sketch entities that do not have a tangency and curvature relation with each other.

To Next Edge. The **To Next Edge** option is used to extend the curve influence upto the next edge only.

Linear. The **Linear** option is used to extend the curve influence linearly upto the entire boundary feature.

Note
*While selecting curves from the drawing area, select a point on the curve such that it follows the required path of the boundary feature. The selected points on curves act as connectors of the boundary feature. You can also flip the boundary feature connectors. To do so, right-click in the drawing area; a shortcut menu will be displayed. Choose the **Flip Connectors** option from the shortcut menu to flip the direction of connectors.*

Options and Preview Rollout

You can merge the tangent faces of a boundary feature by selecting the **Merge tangent faces** check box available in this rollout. To unmerge the tangent faces of the boundary feature, you need to clear this check box. You can trim surfaces to make a closed boundary feature by selecting the **Trim by direction 1** and **Trim by direction 2** check boxes. These check boxes are cleared by default in this rollout. To view the preview of the boundary feature, select the **Show preview** check box available in this rollout. This check box is selected by default in this rollout.

Display Rollout

The **Display** rollout is used to display the mesh preview, zebra stripes, and curvature combs of the boundary feature. The **Mesh preview** and **Curvature combs** check boxes are selected by default in the **Display** rollout of the **Boundary-Surface PropertyManager**. The **Mesh preview** check box allows you to toggle the mesh preview of the boundary surface. You can increase or decrease the number of lines of the mesh by using the **Mesh density** spinner available below the **Mesh preview** check box in this rollout. By selecting the **Zebra stripes** check box, you can visually determine the type of boundary existing between surfaces such as contact, tangency, and curvature continuous. Using the **Zebra stripes** check box, you can also identify wrinkles or defects in surfaces. On selecting the **Curvature combs** check box, you can visualize the continuity of the curve and also get a better idea of the quality of the surfaces that will be generated. It also helps you magnify discontinuities in a curve. The **Direction 1** and **Direction 2** check boxes, available below the **Curvature combs** check box in this rollout, are used to toggle the display of curvature combs along the direction 1 and direction 2. You can also adjust the scale and density of curvature combs by using the **Curvature Combs Scale** and **Curvature Combs Density** spinners, respectively.

Figure 19-30 shows three curves for creating a boundary surface in direction 1 and Figure 19-31 shows the resultant boundary surface. Figure 19-32 shows six curves for creating a boundary surface in direction 1 and direction 2 and Figure 19-33 shows the resultant boundary surface.

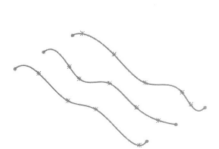

Figure 19-30 *Three curves for a creating boundary surface in direction 1*

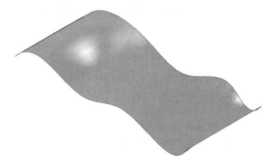

Figure 19-31 *Resultant boundary surface*

Figure 19-34 shows the direction 2 curves extended beyond the direction 1 curves and Figure 19-35 shows the resultant preview of the boundary surface without trimming the direction 2 curves and Figure 19-36 shows the resultant preview of the boundary surface after trimming the direction 2 curves by direction 1 curves.

Figure 19-37 shows two sketches for creating a boundary surface in direction 1 and Figure 19-38 shows the resultant boundary surface with merge tangent faces and Figure 19-39 shows the resultant boundary surface without merge tangent faces.

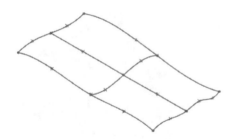

Figure 19-32 *Curves for creating a boundary surface in direction 1 and direction 2*

Figure 19-33 *The resultant boundary surface*

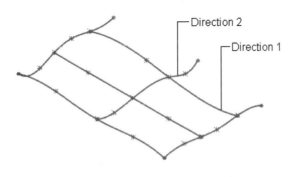

Figure 19-34 *The direction 2 curves extended beyond the direction 1 curves*

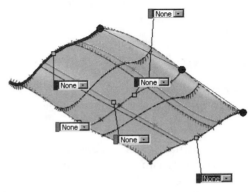

Figure 19-35 *The preview of the boundary surface without trimming the direction 2 curves*

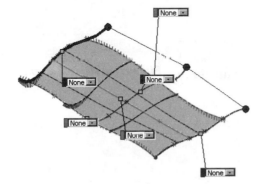

Figure 19-36 *The preview of the boundary surface after trimming the direction 2 curves by direction 1 curves*

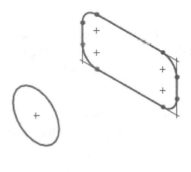

Figure 19-37 *The sketches for creating boundary surface*

Figure 19-38 *The boundary surface with merge tangent faces*

Figure 19-39 *The boundary surface without merge tangent faces*

Creating a Planar Surface

CommandManager:	Surfaces > Planar Surface
SolidWorks menus:	Insert > Surface > Planar
Toolbar:	Surfaces > Planar Surface

 A planar surface is generally used to fill gaps between surfaces using a planar patch. To create a planar surface, choose the **Planar Surface** button from the **Surfaces CommandManager** or choose **Insert > Surface > Planar** from the SolidWorks menus; the **Planar Surface PropertyManager** will be displayed, as shown in Figure 19-40 and you will be prompted to select the bounding entities such as a sketch, an edge, or a curve.

Select the bounding entities; the name of the bounding entities will be displayed in the **Bounding Entities** rollout. Next, choose the **OK** button from the **Planar Surface PropertyManager**; a planar surface will be created using the selected entities.

Figure 19-40 *The Planar Surface PropertyManager*

Figure 19-41 shows the bounding entities to be selected for creating a planar surface and Figure 19-42 shows the resultant planar surface.

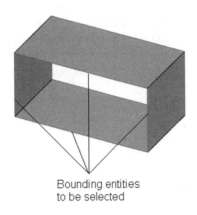

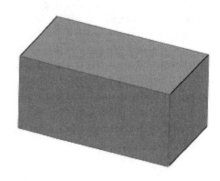

Bounding entities
to be selected

Figure 19-41 *Bounding entities to be selected*   *Figure 19-42* *The resultant planar surface*

Creating a Fill Surface

CommandManager:	Surfaces > Filled Surface
SolidWorks menus:	Insert > Surface > Fill
Toolbar:	Surfaces > Filled Surface

The **Filled Surface** tool is used to create a surface patch along N number of sides. The sides to be selected for creating a fill surface can be edges of the existing model, 2D or 3D sketch entities, or 2D or 3D curves. The difference between planar surface and fill surface is that you cannot create a planar surface using 3D curves or edges. For example, the 3D edge created in Figure 19-43 cannot be used to create a planar surface. But you can fill this gap by selecting the 3D edge and creating a fill surface.

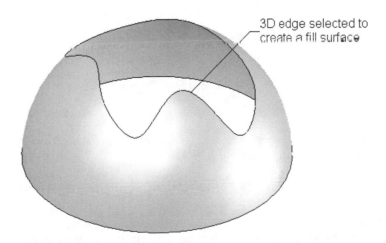

3D edge selected to
create a fill surface

Figure 19-43 *Entities selected for creating a fill surface*

To create a fill surface, choose the **Filled Surface** button from the **Surfaces CommandManager**; the **Fill Surface PropertyManager** will be displayed, as shown in Figure 19-44 and you will be prompted to select bounding entities and set the required options. Select the entities that will define the boundary; the selected entities will be displayed in blue, and callouts will be attached to them. On selecting the last entity that will close the current selection chain, the preview of the fill surface along with the mesh will be displayed in the drawing area. Now, choose the **OK** button from the **Fill Surface PropertyManager**. Figure 19-45 shows the preview of the fill surface along with the mesh and Figure 19-46 shows the resultant fill surface.

Figure 19-44 The Fill Surface PropertyManager

Note
The surface model used in the above example is created by trimming a surface. You will learn about the trimmed surfaces later in this chapter.

The other options in the **Fill Surface PropertyManager** are discussed next.

Edge settings

The options in the **Edge settings** area are used to define various parameters to specify references with respect to the selected edges, type of curvature, and so on. These options are discussed next.

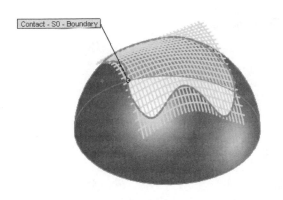

Figure 19-45 *Preview of the fill surface along with the mesh*

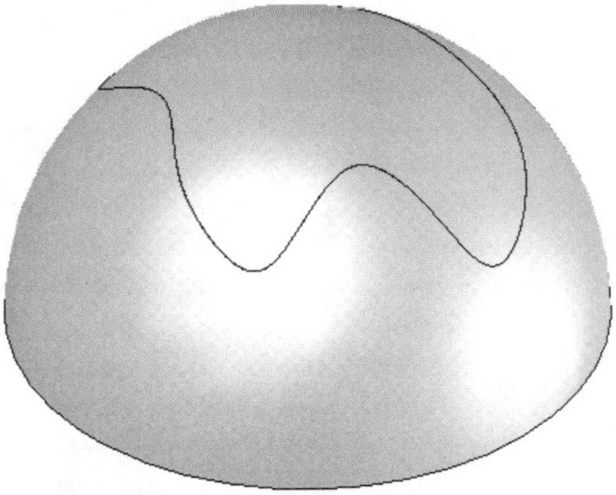

Figure 19-46 *Resultant fill surface*

Alternate Face

The **Alternate Face** button in the **Edge settings** area is used to specify the face reference to be included while creating a fill surface for controlling the curvature of the fill surface. This option is only used when you are creating a fill surface on a solid body.

Curvature Control

The **Curvature Control** drop-down list is used to define the type of curvature that you need to apply on the fill surface. There are different types of curvatures in this drop-down list that are discussed next.

Contact

The **Contact** option is selected by default and is used to create a patch using the fill surface option within the selected patch boundary.

Tangent

The **Tangent** option is selected to create a patch such that the resulting patch maintains tangency with the selected edges. On selecting this option for creating a patch, the **Reverse Surface** button is also displayed, if there is a possibility of creating a patch in the other direction. Choose this button to reverse the direction of the surface created.

Curvature

The **Curvature** option is selected to create a patch such that the resulting patch maintains curvature continuity with the selected edge.

Figure 19-47 shows the circular edge selected as the patch boundary. Figure 19-48 shows the fill surface created with the **Contact** option selected in the **Curvature Control** drop-down list. Figure 19-49 shows the fill surface created with the **Tangent** option selected in the **Curvature Control** drop-down list.

Edge selected as
patch boundary

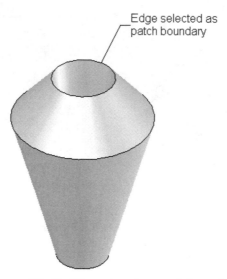

Figure 19-47 *Edge selected as patch boundary*

Figure 19-48 *Fill surface created using the*
Contact *option*

Figure 19-49 *Fill surface created using the*
Tangent *option*

Apply to all edges

This option is used to apply curvature settings to all edges. If this check box is not selected, the current curvature setting will only be applied to the edge of the boundary that is selected in the **Patch boundary** display area.

Optimize surface

The **Optimize surface** option is used to create a simplest patch of the surface along the selected patch boundary. The **Optimize surface** check box is selected by default. Therefore, if you create a surface patch, the time taken to create the surface will be less and the model will be rebuild faster. When you clear this check box, the **Resolution Control** rollout will be displayed, as shown in Figure 19-50. The slider available in this rollout is used to specify the resolution of the fill surface. Higher the resolution, better will be the quality of the surface and more time will it take to rebuild the model. In case of lower resolution, the quality of the surface will not be good. However, in such a case, the rebuilding of the model will take lesser time.

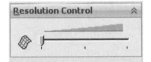

Figure 19-50 The Resolution Control rollout

Show Preview

The **Show Preview** check box is selected by default and is used to display the preview of the fill surface that is created using the selected patch boundary.

Preview Mesh

The **Preview Mesh** check box is selected by default and is used to display the mesh surface in the preview of the fill surface. This option is only available, if the **Show Preview** check box is selected earlier.

Constraint Curves

The **Constraint Curves** rollout is used to define constraint curves while creating a fill surface. To create a fill surface using constraint curves, invoke the **Fill Surface PropertyManager** and then select the patch boundary. Now, click once in the **Constraint Curves** area of the **Constraint Curves** rollout to the invoke selection mode and then select constraint curves. Note that, the constraint curves to be selected can be a sketched entity, an edge, or a curve. The selected constraint curve will be displayed in a different color and a callout will be attached to it. Also, the name of the selected entity will be displayed in the **Constraint Curve** selection area. The preview of the fill surface gets modified when you select the constraint curves. After specifying all constraint curves, choose the **OK** button from the **Fill Surface PropertyManager**. Figure 19-51 shows the sketch selected for patching the boundary and constraint curves. Figure 19-52 shows the resultant fill surface.

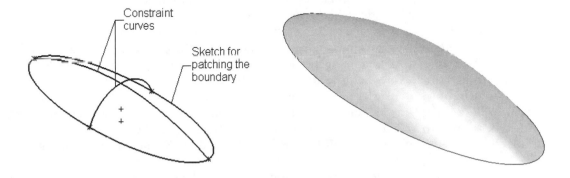

Figure 19-51 Sketch and constraint curves to be selected

Figure 19-52 Resultant fill surface

Creating a Radiated Surface

CommandManager:	Surfaces > Radiate Surface
SolidWorks menus:	Insert > Surface > Radiate
Toolbar:	Surfaces > Radiate Surface

In SolidWorks, you can also create a surface by radiating a surface along an edge or a split line. The radiated surface is always created parallel to the plane or the face selected as the radiate direction reference. This type of surface is generally used in mold design as the parting surface for extracting the core and cavity. To create a radiated surface, choose the **Radiate Surface** button from the **Surfaces CommandManager**; the **Radiate Surface PropertyManager** will be displayed, as shown in Figure 19-53.

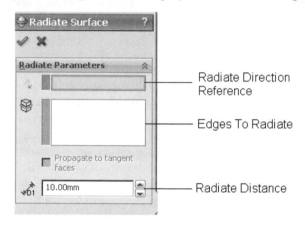

Figure 19-53 The Radiate Surface PropertyManager

You will observe that the **Radiate Direction Reference** selection area is activated, by default in this **PropertyManager**. Therefore, first you need to select a plane or a planar face parallel to which the surface will be radiated. The selected reference will be highlighted in a different color and an arrow symbol normal to the selected face will be displayed. On selecting a face, the **Edges To Radiate** selection area will be activated. Now, select the edges along which the surface will be radiated; the name of the selected edges will be displayed in the **Edges To Radiate** selection area. Note that, the arrows will be displayed in the drawing area, showing the direction in which the surface will be radiated. Now, set the value of the distance of the surface to be radiated in the **Radiate Distance** spinner. The **Propagate to tangent faces** check box is used to radiate surfaces along all edges tangent to the selected edge. After setting all parameters, choose the **OK** button from the **Radiate Surface PropertyManager**.

Figure 19-54 shows the radiate direction reference and the edges to be selected. Figure 19-55 shows the resultant radiated surface with the **Propagate to tangent faces** check box selected.

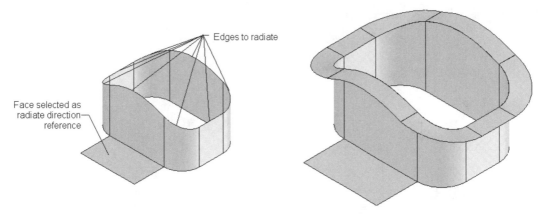

Figure 19-54 *Reference and edges to be selected*

Figure 19-55 *Resultant radiated surface with the Propagate to tangent faces check box selected*

Offsetting Surfaces

CommandManager:	Surfaces > Offset Surface
SolidWorks menus:	Insert > Surface > Offset
Toolbar:	Surfaces > Offset Surface

The **Offset Surface** tool is used to offset the selected surface or surfaces to a given distance. T offset a surface, choose the **Offset Surface** button from the **Surfaces CommandManager**; the **Offset Surface PropertyManager** will be displayed, as shown in Figure 19-56 and you will be prompted to select a face or a surface to offset.

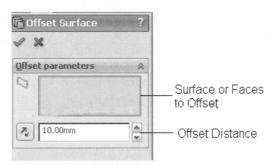

Figure 19-56 *The Offset Surface PropertyManager*

Now, select the face or the surface that you need to offset. The selected face or the surface will be highlighted in a different color and its name will be displayed in the **Surface or Faces to Offset** display area. Also, the preview of the offset surface with the default value will be displayed in the drawing area. Set the value of the offset distance using the **Offset Distance** spinner. You can flip the direction of the surface creation using the **Flip Offset Direction** button available on the left of the **Offset Direction** spinner. After setting all parameters, choose the **OK** button from the **Offset Surface PropertyManager**. Figure 19-57 shows the surface selected to offset and Figure 19-58 shows the resultant offset surface.

Surface selected
to offset

Figure 19-57 Surface selected to offset

Figure 19-58 Resultant offset surface

 Tip. *If you want to extract a surface from a solid or a surface body, invoke the* **Offset Surface PropertyManager** *and select the surfaces to be extracted. Next, set the value of the* **Offset Distance** *spinner to* **0** *and choose the* **OK** *button from the* **Offset Surface PropertyManager**.

Trimming Surfaces

CommandManager:	Surfaces > Trim Surface
SolidWorks menus:	Insert > Surface > Trim
Toolbar:	Surfaces > Trim Surface

 The **Trim Surface** tool is used to trim surfaces using an entity as trim tool. A trim tool can be a surface, a sketched entity, or an edge. To trim a surface, choose the **Trim Surface** button from the **Surfaces CommandManager**; the **Trim Surface PropertyManager** will be displayed, as shown in Figure 19-59 and you will be prompted to select pieces to keep or remove.

There are two methods of trimming a surface namely, Standard and Mutal trim. In the first method, the **Standard** radio button is selected by default in the **Trim Type** rollout of the **PropertyManager**. Select the trimming surface using the cursor; this surface will now act as a trim tool. You can select a surface, a sketch, or an edge as a trimming surface. On doing so, the selected entity will be highlighted in a different color and the name of the trimming surface will be displayed in the **Trim tool** display area. Also, the selection mode in the **Pieces to keep** display area will be activated and you will be prompted to select pieces to keep. Also, the cursor will be replaced by the surface body cursor. Move the cursor on the surface being trimmed; the pieces

Figure 19-59 The Trim Surface PropertyManager

of the surface on which you place the cursor will be displayed in a different color. Select the piece or pieces of the surface to keep. The selected pieces will be displayed in a different color and their names will be displayed in the **Pieces to keep** display area. Next, choose the **OK** button from the **Trim Surface PropertyManager**.

Figure 19-60 shows the trimming surface and the piece to keep after trimming. Figure 19-61 shows the resultant trimmed surface. Figure 19-62 shows the sketch selected as a trimming surface and Figure 19-63 shows the resultant trimmed surface.

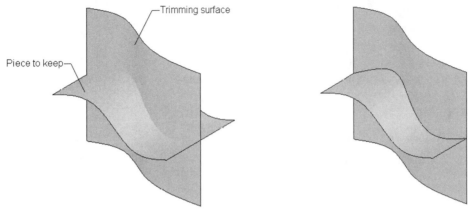

Figure 19-60 *Trimming surface and piece to keep after trimming the surface*

Figure 19-61 *Resultant trimmed surface*

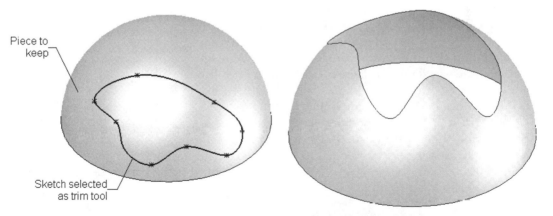

Figure 19-62 *Sketch selected as trimming surface*

Figure 19-63 *Resultant trimmed surface*

The other method of trimming a surface is known as the Mutual trim method. In this method, you need to select two surfaces as the trimming surfaces. To trim these surfaces, invoke the **Trim Surface PropertyManager** and then choose the **Mutual** radio button from the **Trim Type** rollout; you will be prompted to select the surfaces to trim, followed by the pieces to keep. First select the trimming surfaces and then select the pieces to keep, refer to Figure 19-64. After setting all parameters, choose the **OK** button from the **Trim Surface PropertyManager**. Figure 19-65 shows the resultant trimmed surface.

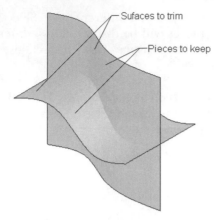

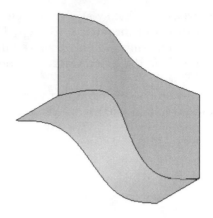

Figure 19-64 *Surfaces to trim and the pieces to keep*

Figure 19-65 *Resultant trimmed surface*

Untrimming Surfaces

CommandManager:	Surfaces > Untrim Surface
SolidWorks menus:	Insert > Surface > Untrim
Toolbar:	Surfaces > Untrim Surface

The **Untrim Surface** tool is used to create a surface patch by extending the existing surfaces. Using this tool, you can fill the trimmed portion of a surface with a surface patch. To untrim a surface, choose **Insert > Surface > Untrim** from the SolidWorks menus. Alternatively, choose the **Untrim Surface** button from the **Surfaces CommandManager**; the **Untrim Surface PropertyManager** will be invoked, as shown in Figure 19-66 and you will be prompted to select the surface bodies or edges of a surface. Select the surface bodies to be untrimmed.

Figure 19-66 *The Untrim Surface PropertyManager*

In SolidWorks, there are two methods of untrimming the surfaces. In the first method, you need to select the face that you want to untrim and in the second method, you need to select the edges of the trimmed portion of the surface. Both these methods are discussed next.

Untrimming Surfaces by Selecting the Faces

In this method, you will untrim the surface by selecting the face or faces of the surface to untrim. To do so, invoke the **Untrim Surface PropertyManager** and then select the face of the surface from the drawing area that needs to be untrimmed; the preview of the untrimmed surface with the default settings will be displayed in the drawing area. As soon as you select the face or faces of the surface to untrim, the **Options** rollout will be displayed with different options, as shown in Figure 19-67. These options are discussed next.

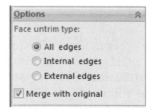

Figure 19-67 *The Options rollout*

Face untrim type

The **Face untrim type** area is used to specify the type of edges along which you want to untrim the surface. The options in this area are discussed next.

All edges

The **All edges** radio button is selected by default. As a result, all internal and external edges of the selected surface are extended to be untrimmed. Figure 19-68 shows the surface to be selected and Figure 19-69 shows the resultant untrimmed surface with the **All edges** radio button selected.

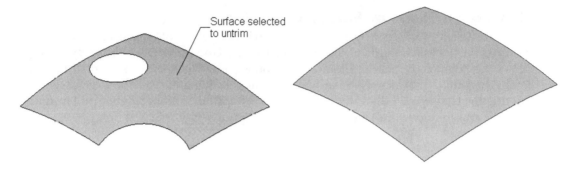

Figure 19-68 Surface selected to untrim   *Figure 19-69 Resultant untrimmed surface with the **All edges** radio button selected*

Internal edges

The **Internal edges** radio button is used if you need to patch only the internal edges of the selected surface using the **Untrim Surface** tool. Figure 19-68 shows the surface selected to untrim and Figure 19-70 shows the untrimmed surface created with the **Internal edges** radio button selected.

External edges

The **External edges** radio button is used if you need to patch only the external edges of the selected surface using the **Untrim Surface** tool. Figure 19-68 shows the surface selected to untrim and Figure 19-71 shows the untrimmed surface created with the **External edges** radio button selected.

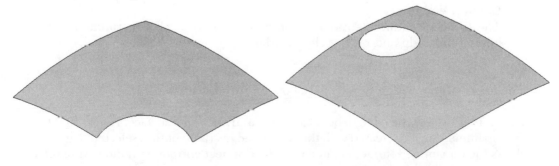

*Figure 19-70 Resultant untrimmed surface with the **Internal edges** radio button selected*   *Figure 19-71 Resultant untrimmed surface with the **External edges** radio button selected*

Merge with original

The **Merge with original** check box is used to merge the untrimmed surface created with the original surface. This check box is selected by default in the **Options** rollout. If you clear this check box, the resultant untrimmed surface will be a separate surface body.

You can also specify the percentage of distance upto which you need to extend the surface depending on the type of edges selected from the **Face untrim type** area of the **Options** rollout. The **Distance** spinner is used to define the percentage of distance for extending the surface. The preview of the surface extension is displayed in the drawing area.

Untrimming Surfaces by Selecting the Edges

You can also patch a trimmed surface using the **Untrim Surface** tool by selecting the edges of the trimmed portion of the surface. To do so, invoke the **Untrim Surface PropertyManager** and select the edge of the surface along which you want to patch the trimmed surface; the preview of the patched surface will be displayed in the drawing area. As soon as you select the edge of the surface to patch the trimmed surface, the **Options** rollout will be displayed with different options, as shown in Figure 19-72. These options are discussed next.

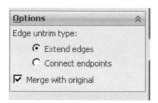

*Figure 19-72 The **Options** rollout with different options*

Edge untrim type

The **Edge untrim type** area is used to specify the options for patching the trimmed surface by using the selected edges. The options in this area are discussed next.

Extend edges

The **Extend edges** radio button is selected by default and is used to extend the edge to create a corner for untrimming the trimmed surface.

Connect endpoints

The **Connect endpoints** radio button is selected to patch the trimmed surface by joining the endpoints of the selected edge.

Merge with original

The use of **Merge with original** check box is same as discussed earlier.

Figure 19-73 shows the edge to be selected for untrimming a surface. Figure 19-74 shows an untrimmed surface created with the **Extend edges** radio button selected. Figure 19-75 shows the untrimmed surface created with the **Connect endpoints** radio button selected.

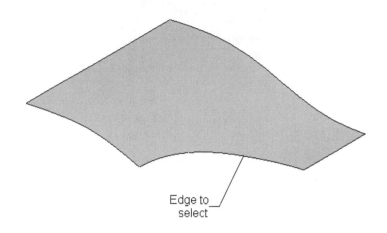

Edge to
select

Figure 19-73 Edge selected for untrimming the surface

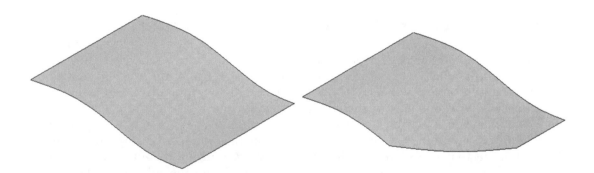

*Figure 19-74 Untrimmed surface created
with the **Extend edges** radio button selected*

*Figure 19-75 Untrimmed surface created with
the **Connect endpoints** radio button selected*

Extending Surfaces

CommandManager:	Surfaces > Extend Surface
SolidWorks menus:	Insert > Surface > Extend
Toolbar:	Surfaces > Extend Surface

The **Extend Surface** tool is used to extend the surface along a selected edge or selected face. To extend the surface, choose the **Extend Surface** button from the **Surfaces CommandManager**; the **Extend Surface PropertyManager** will be displayed, as shown in Figure 19-76 and you will be prompted to select a face or edge(s) and set the properties to extend. There are two methods of extending a surface and these are discussed next.

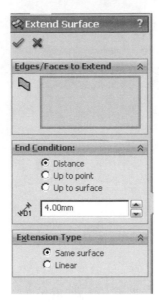

Figure 19-76 The *Extend Surface PropertyManager*

Extending the Surface Using the Same surface Option

You can extend a surface with the **Same surface** radio button selected in the **Extension Type** rollout of the **Extend Surface PropertyManager**. Using this radio button, you can extend a surface by maintaining its curvature. To extend the surface using this method, invoke the **Extend Surface PropertyManager**. The **Same surface** radio button is selected by default in the **Extension Type** rollout. Now, you need to select the edge or face that you need to extend. Note that when you select the face to extend the surface, the surface extends equally in all directions. You can extend a surface dynamically using the drag handle or set the extending distance in the **Distance** spinner available in the **End Condition** rollout. You can also use other feature termination options available in the **End Condition** rollout. By default, the **Distance** radio button is selected in the **End Condition** rollout. If you want to extend the surface up to a particular point or vertex, select the **Up to point** radio button from the **End Condition** rollout and then select the required point or vertex from the drawing area. If you want to extend the surface up to a particular surface, select the **Up to surface** radio button and then select the required surface from the drawing area. After setting all parameters, choose the **OK** button from the **Extend Surface PropertyManager**.

Figure 19-77 shows the edge selected to extend the surface. Figure 19-78 shows the preview of the surface being extended by selecting the edge with the **Same surface** radio button selected. Figure 19-79 shows the face selected to extend the surface. Figure 19-80 shows the preview of the surface being extended by selecting the face with the **Same Surface** radio button selected.

Note
If any edge of the selected surface is merged with another surface, the surface will not be extended along that edge.

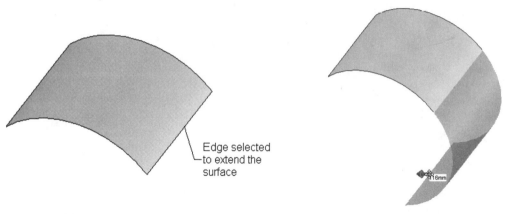

Figure 19-77 *Edge selected to extend the surface*   Figure 19-78 *Preview of the extended surface*

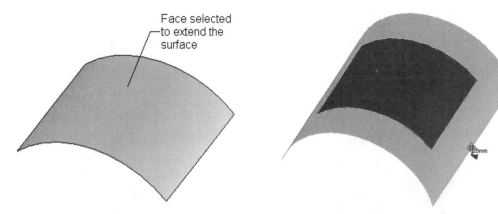

Figure 19-79 *Face selected to extend the surface*   Figure 19-80 *Preview of the extended surface with the Same surface radio button selected*

Extending the Surface Using the Linear Option

You can extend a surface in the linear direction upto an existing surface by maintaining tangency. To do so, invoke the **Extend Surface PropertyManager** and then select the **Linear** radio button from the **Extension Type** rollout. Next, select the face or the edge along which you need to extend the surface and then specify the feature termination using the **End Condition** rollout. After setting all parameters, choose the **OK** button.

Figure 19-81 shows the edge selected to extend the surface and Figure 19-82 shows the preview of the surface being extended with the **Linear** radio button selected. Figure 19-83 shows the face selected to extend the surface and Figure 19-84 shows the preview of the surface being extended with the **Linear** radio button selected.

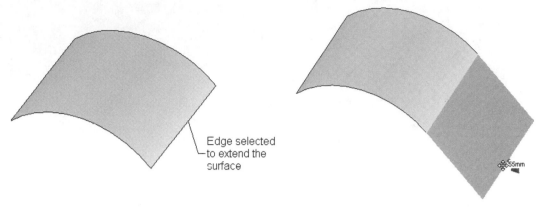

Figure 19-81 *Edge selected to extend the surface*

Figure 19-82 *Preview of the extended surface with the **Linear** radio button selected*

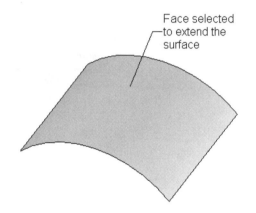

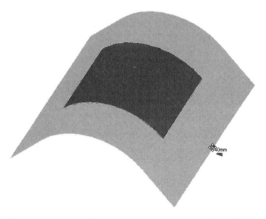

Figure 19-83 *Face selected to extend the surface*

Figure 19-84 *Preview of the extended surface with the **Linear** radio button selected*

Knitting Surfaces

CommandManager:	Surfaces > Knit Surface
SolidWorks menus:	Insert > Surface > Knit
Toolbar:	Surfaces > Knit Surface

 Using the **Knit Surface** tool, you can knit multiple surfaces together to create a single surface. You can also knit a surface with the faces of a solid body. The surfaces that you want to knit together must have contact with each other. You cannot knit disjoint surfaces or faces. The **Knit Surface** tool is widely used for extracting core and cavity while designing a mold. To knit surfaces, choose the **Knit Surface** button from the **Surfaces CommandManager**; the **Knit Surface PropertyManager** will be displayed, as shown in Figure 19-85.

Figure 19-85 *The **Knit Surface** PropertyManager*

Also, you will be prompted to select the surfaces to knit. Select the surfaces; the names of surfaces will be displayed in the **Surfaces and Faces to Knit** selection area of the **Selections** rollout. After selecting all surfaces and faces, choose the **OK** button from the **Knit Surface PropertyManager**; a knitted surface will be created.

Filleting Surfaces

CommandManager:	Surfaces > Fillet
SolidWorks menus:	Insert > Fillet/Round
Toolbar:	Surfaces > Fillet

 The procedure of filleting the surfaces is the same as discussed earlier while filleting the solid models. But there are some exceptions. These exceptions are discussed next.

1. You cannot create a variable radius fillet at the edges.

2. While applying the face fillet to a surface, you need to define the direction in which the fillet needs to be added.

3. You cannot use the **Keep features** option while filleting a surface.

4. You cannot select a surface using the **FeatureManager design tree** while filleting all edges in a surface.

 Note
You can only fillet the edge of the surface that is created at the intersection of two surfaces. Make sure that if the edge is created using two surfaces, then you need to knit them before filleting.

Creating a Mid-Surface

CommandManager:	Surfaces > Mid-Surface	(Customize to add)
SolidWorks menus:	Insert > Surface > Mid-Surface	
Toolbar:	Surfaces > Mid-Surface	(Customize to add)

The **Mid-Surface** tool is used to create a surface between two parallel faces of a solid model. You can define the placement of surface in terms of percentage value with respect to the face selected first. Note that, the faces to be selected to create a mid-surface should be two parallel faces or two concentric curved faces. To create a mid surface, choose the **Mid-Surface** button from the **Surfaces CommandManager**; the **MidSurface1 PropertyManager** will be displayed, as shown in Figure 19-86.

Also, you will be prompted to either select the face pairs manually or use the **Find Face Pairs** button to automatically recognize the face pairs. Next, select the faces between which you need to create the mid-surface. On doing so, both the selected faces will be highlighted in different colors. Also, the names of the selected faces will be displayed in the **Face pairs** display area. By default, the mid-surface is placed in the middle of the selected faces. You can

Figure 19-86 *The* **MidSurface1 PropertyManager**

also define the percentage distance for the placement of the mid-surface using the **Position** spinner that is available in the **Selections** rollout of the **PropertyManager**. The position of the mid-surface is defined from the first selected surface. After setting all parameters, choose the **OK** button from the **MidSurface1 PropertyManager**.

Figure 19-87 shows the offset faces to be selected and Figure 19-88 shows the mid-surface created in the middle of the selected faces.

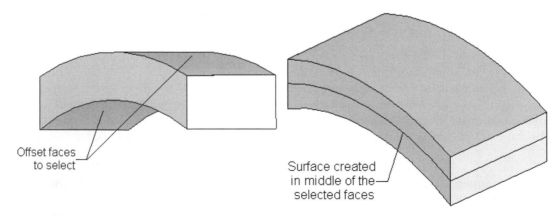

Figure 19-87 *Offset faces selected*   *Figure 19-88* *Resultant mid-surface*

The **Find Face Pairs** button is used to find the faces that are adjacent to the selected face. The options in the **Recognition threshold** area are used to filter faces depending on the wall thickness of the face searched using the **Find Face Pairs** option. Using the **Threshold Operator** drop-down list in the **Recognition threshold** area, you can set the mathematical operators such as >, <, =, and so on. Using the **Threshold Thickness** spinner, you can specify the threshold thickness.

Deleting Holes from Surfaces

To delete holes from a surface or any closed contours that cut surface, select any one edge of the contour from the drawing area and invoke the shortcut menu. Choose the **Delete** option from the shortcut menu; the **Choose Option** dialog box will be displayed, as shown in Figure 19-89.

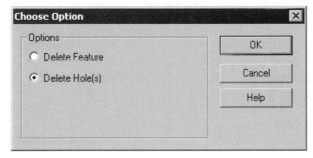

Figure 19-89 The **Choose Option** *dialog box*

The **Delete Hole(s)** radio button is selected by default. As a result, the empty area of the selected contour will be patched and the tangency and curvature with the surrounding surfaces will be maintained. If you delete a hole with the **Delete Hole(s)** radio button selected, you will notice that the **DeleteHole** node is added in the **FeatureManager design tree**. But, if you select the **Delete Feature** radio button, the feature associated with the contour will be deleted. Select the required option from the **Choose Option** dialog box and then choose the **OK** button from this dialog box, the **Confirm Delete** dialog box will be displayed and you will be informed about the name of the feature to be deleted and also the names of the dependent items to be deleted.

Figure 19-90 shows the edge of the closed contour to be selected. Figure 19-91 shows the hole deleted using the delete feature option.

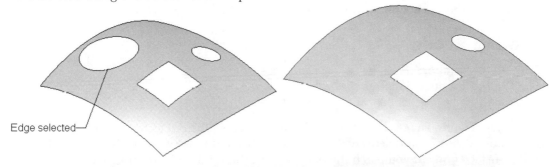

Edge selected

Figure 19-90 Edge to be selected   *Figure 19-91* Resultant surface

Replacing Faces

CommandManager: Surfaces > Replace Face
SolidWorks menus: Insert > Face > Replace
Toolbar: Surfaces > Replace Face

In SolidWorks, you can replace the selected faces of a solid body with one or more surfaces. When you replace the selected faces with another surface or surfaces, the resultant solid body retains the shape of the replaced surface by adding or subtracting material from the solid body. To replace a surface, choose the **Replace Face** button from the **Surfaces CommandManager**; the **Replace Face1 PropertyManager** will be displayed, as shown in Figure 19-92.

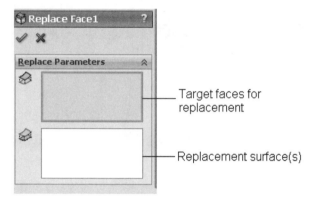

*Figure 19-92 The **Replace Face1 PropertyManager***

Select the face to be replaced; the name of the selected face will be displayed in the **Target faces for replacement** selection area. Next, click once in the **Replacement surface(s)** display selection area to invoke the selection environment of this area. Now, select the replacement surface; the name of the replacement surface will be displayed in the **Replacement surface(s)** selection area. Choose the **OK** button from the **Replace Face1 PropertyManager**; the selected face of the solid body will be replaced.

Figure 19-93 shows the target face to be replaced and the replacement surface. Figure 19-94 shows the resultant replaced face. Figure 19-95 shows the solid body after hiding the surface body. To hide the surface body, select the surface body and then invoke the shortcut menu. Then, choose the **Hide** option from the shortcut menu.

Deleting Faces

CommandManager: Surfaces > Delete Face
SolidWorks menus: Insert > Face > Delete
Toolbar: Surfaces > Delete Face

The **Delete Face** tool is used to delete the faces of the selected surface or the solid body. When you delete the face of a solid body, the deleted face is converted into a surface body. If you patch the deleted face, the solid body will not be converted into a surface body. To delete a face, choose the **Delete Face** button from the **Surfaces**

CommandManager; the **Delete Face PropertyManager** will be displayed, as shown in Figure 19-96.

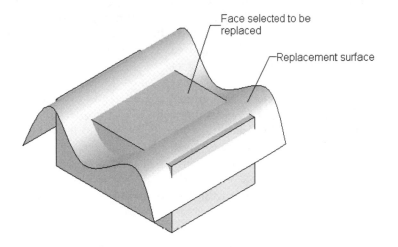

Figure 19-93 *The target face and the replacement surface*

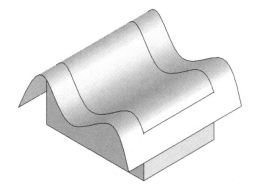

Figure 19-94 *Resultant replaced face*

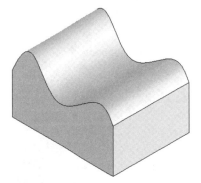

Figure 19-95 *Model after hiding the surface*

Figure 19-96 *The **Delete Face PropertyManager***

The **Delete** radio button is selected in the **Options** rollout of the **Delete Face PropertyManager** to deletes the faces of solid body without patching and trimming it. In this case, the solid body is converted into the surface body. The **Delete and Patch** radio button is used to delete the faces of a solid or surface body by patching and trimming it. If you select the choose **Delete and Patch** radio button, the **Show preview** check box will be invoked and the preview of the model will be displayed in the drawing area. The **Delete and Fill** radio button is used to delete multiple faces and generate a single face.

Select the face or faces to be deleted; the name of the selected face will be displayed in the **Faces to delete** selection area of the **Selections** rollout. Next, select the **Delete and Patch** radio button, if it is not selected by default; the preview of the model will be displayed in the drawing area. If the preview of the patch is not displayed, it confirms that the selected face cannot be deleted and patched. In this case, you need to select the **Delete** radio button from the **Options** rollout so that the face is only deleted, but not patched. After setting all parameters, choose the **OK** button from the **Delete Face PropertyManager**; the resulting model will be displayed.

Figure 19-97 shows the face selected to be deleted. Figure 19-98 shows the face deleted with the **Delete and Patch** radio button selected. Figure 19-99 shows the face deleted with the **Delete** radio button selected. Figure 19-100 shows multiple faces selected to generate a single face. Figure 19-101 shows a single face generated using the **Delete and Fill** radio button.

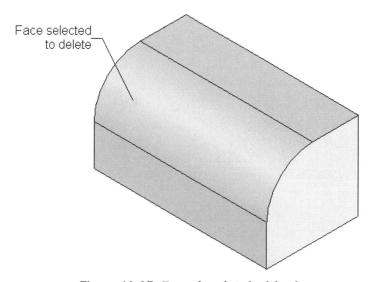

Face selected to delete

Figure 19-97 *Face selected to be deleted*

Note
*You can also delete surface bodies using the **Delete Body PropertyManager**. The procedure of deleting surface bodies is the same as discussed in the solid bodies.*

Tip. *You can also delete a face by selecting it and then invoking the shortcut menu. Choose the **Delete Face** option from the shortcut menu; the **Delete Face PropertyManager** will be displayed.*

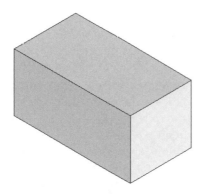

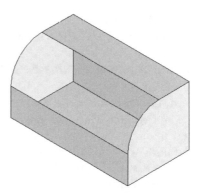

Figure 19-98 *Face deleted with the **Delete and Patch** radio button selected*

Figure 19-99 *Face deleted with the **Delete** radio button selected*

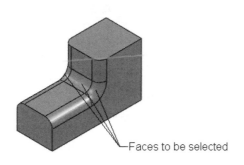

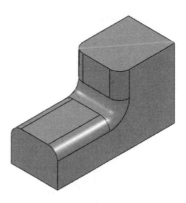

Figure 19-100 *Faces to be selected to generated a single face*

Figure 19-101 *Face deleted with the **Delete and Fill** radio button selected*

Moving and Coping Surfaces

You can move and copy the surfaces using the **Move/Copy Bodies** tool. The methods of moving and coping the surface bodies using the **Move/Copy Bodies** tool is the same as discussed in moving and coping the solid bodies.

Mirroring Surface Bodies

You can mirror the surface bodies using the **Mirror** tool. The procedure of mirroring surface bodies is the same as that discussed in the solid bodies.

Adding Thickness to Surface Bodies

CommandManager:	Surfaces > Thicken
SolidWorks menus:	Insert > Boss/Base > Thicken

In SolidWorks, you can also add thickness to the surface bodies. There are two methods of adding thickness to surface bodies. In the first method, you need to add wall thickness to the surface body. In the second method, you need to solidify the closed, stitched surface body to create a solid body. These two methods are discussed next.

Adding Thickness to the Surface Body

To add thickness to a surface body, choose the **Thicken** button from the **Surface CommandManager** or choose **Insert > Boss/Base > Thicken** from the SolidWorks menus; the **Thicken PropertyManager** will be displayed, as shown in Figure 19-102. Also, you will be prompted to select the surface to thicken. Select the required surface; the preview of the thickened body with default values will be displayed in the drawing area. Using the buttons in the **Thickness** area of this **PropertyManager**, you can specify the side on which you want to thicken the surface. You can also specify the wall thickness by using the **Thickness** spinner in the **Thicken Parameters** rollout. After setting all parameters, choose the **OK** button from the **Thicken PropertyManager**; the thickness will be added to the surface body.

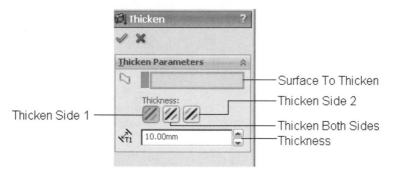

*Figure 19-102　The **Thicken PropertyManager***

Figure 19-103 shows the surface body to thicken and Figure 19-104 shows the model after adding thickness to the surface body.

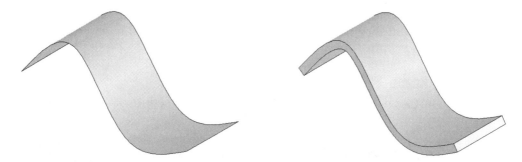

Figure 19-103　Surface to thicken　　　　　　*Figure 19-104　Model after thickening the surface*

Solidifying a Closed Surface Body

To solidify a closed surface body, the surface body needs to be free from any type of gap and all surfaces should be stitched together using the **Knit** tool. To solidify the surface body, invoke the **Thicken PropertyManager** and then select a closed surface body; the **Create solid from enclosed volume** check box will be enabled. Select this check box; the options available in the **Thickness** area and the **Thickness** spinner will be inactivated. Next, choose the **OK** button from the **Thicken PropertyManager**; a solid volume will be created from the closed surface.

 Tip. *If the surface model to be thickened consists of multiple joined surface bodies, you first need to knit the surfaces together and then add thickness to them.*

Creating a Thicken Surface Cut

CommandManager:	Surface > Thickened Cut
SolidWorks menus:	Insert > Cut > Thicken

In SolidWorks, you can cut a solid body by thickening a surface. To do so, create a solid body and a surface intersecting each other and then choose the **Thickened Cut** button from the **Surface CommandManager**; the **Cut-Thicken PropertyManager** will be displayed, as shown in Figure 19-105.

*Figure 19-105 The **Cut-Thicken PropertyManager***

Also, you will be prompted to select the surface to thicken. Select the surface that you want to use as the cutting tool and then specify parameters for defining the side, in which you want to add thickness and thickness of cut. On doing so, the preview will be displayed in the drawing area. Now, choose the **OK** button from the **Cut-Thicken PropertyManager**. If the thicken cut results in the creation of multiple bodies, the **Bodies to Keep** dialog box will be displayed. Using this dialog box, you can define the bodies that you need to keep.

Figure 19-106 shows the surface selected for creating the thicken cut. Figure 19-107 shows the resultant thicken cut.

Creating a Surface Cut

CommandManager:	Surfaces > Cut With Surface
SolidWorks menus:	Insert > Cut > With Surface

In SolidWorks, you can also cut a solid body using a surface. To create this type of surface cut,

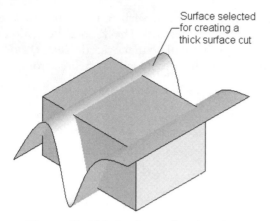

Figure 19-106 *Surface to be selected*

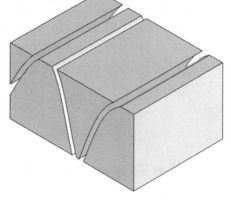

Figure 19-107 *Resultant thicken surface cut*

choose the **Cut With Surface** button from the **Surface CommandManager**; the **SurfaceCut PropertyManager** will be displayed, as shown in Figure 19-108.

Figure 19-108 *The SurfaceCut PropertyManager*

Also, you will be prompted to select the cutting surface. Select the cutting surface; the name of the selected surface will be displayed in the **Selected surface for cut** selection area in the **Surface Cut Parameters** rollout. Also, an arrow will be displayed in the drawing area indicating the direction of removal of the material. Using the **Flip Cut** button, available in the left of the **Selected surface for cut** selection area, you can flip the direction of material removal. Now, choose the **OK** button from the **SurfaceCut PropertyManager**; the surface cut will be created. Figure 19-109 shows the surface selected to create a surface cut. Figure 19-110 shows the resultant surface cut after hiding the surface body.

Tip. *If the surface cut results in the creation of multiple bodies, the **Bodies to Keep** dialog box will be displayed after exiting the **SurfaceCut PropertyManager**.*

*If you create a thicken surface cut or a surface cut on multiple solid bodies, the **Feature Scope** rollout will be displayed with different options and you can specify the bodies on which you need to add this feature.*

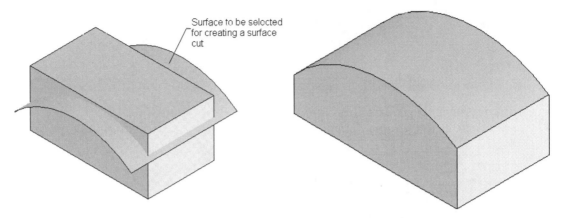

Figure 19-109 *Surface selected to create a surface cut*

Figure 19-110 *Resultant surface cut after hiding the surface body*

TUTORIALS

Tutorial 1

In this tutorial, you will create the model shown in Figure 19-111. Create the model using the surface modeling tools available in SolidWorks and then add wall thickness to the surface model. The views and dimensions of the model are shown in Figure 19-112.

(Expected time: 1hr)

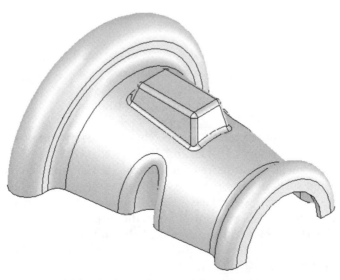

Figure 19-111 *Model for Tutorial 1*

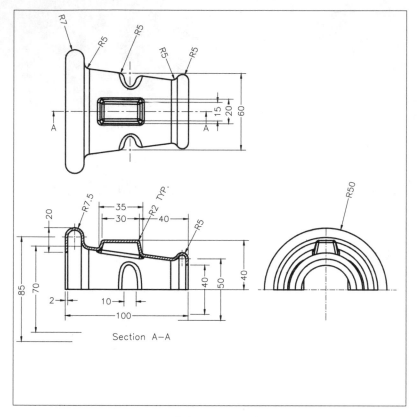

Figure 19-112 *Views and dimensions of the model for Tutorial 1*

The following steps are required to complete this tutorial:

a. Create the base surface of the model by revolving the sketch using the **Mid Plane** option to 180-degree, refer to Figures 19-113 and 19-114.
b. Create the second surface feature, refer to Figures 19-115 and 19-116.
c. Trim the extruded surface using the trim tool, refer to Figures 19-117 and 19-118.
d. Add fillet to the trimmed base surface, refer to Figures 19-119 and 19-120.
e. Create a plane at an offset distance of 40 from the **Top** plane.
f. Create a lofted surface, refer to Figures 19-121 through 19-125.
g. Create a planar surface on the top of the lofted feature and trim the base feature using the lofted feature, Figures 19-126 and 19-127.
h. Trim and knit all the surfaces together, refer to Figure 19-128.
i. Add fillets to the surface model, refer to Figure 19-129.
j. Add thickness to the knitted surface, Figure 19-130.

Creating the Base Surface

To create this model, first you need to create the base surface. The base surface will be created by revolving a sketch created on the **Front** plane.

1. Start SolidWorks part document using the **New SolidWorks Document** dialog box.

2. Invoke the sketcher environment using the **Front** plane as the sketching plane and create the sketch of the base surface, as shown in Figure 19-113.

3. Choose the **Revolve Surface** button from the **Surfaces CommandManager**; the **Surface-Revolve PropertyManager** is displayed.

4. Select the **Mid-Plane** option from the **Revolve Type** drop-down list and set the value of the **Angle** spinner to **180**.

5. Choose the **OK** button from the **Surface-Revolve PropertyManager**. Figure 19-114 shows the resulting revolved base feature.

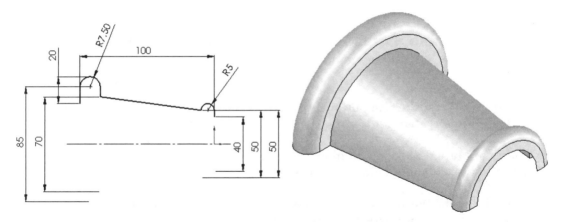

Figure 19-113 Sketch of the base surface   *Figure 19-114 Revolved base surface*

Creating the Second Surface Feature

The second surface feature will be an extruded surface. This surface will be created by extruding a sketch created on the **Top** plane.

1. Invoke the sketching environment and then select the **Top** plane as the sketching plane.

2. Create the sketch of the second surface feature, as shown in Figure 19-115. Note that you may have to apply the **Horizontal** or **Vertical** relation between the points of the ellipse.

3. Next, choose the **Extruded Surface** button from the **Surfaces CommandManager**; the **Surface-Extrude PropertyManager** is displayed.

4. Set the value of the **Depth** spinner to **40** and choose the **OK** button from the **Surface-Extrude PropertyManager**.

    The surface created after extruding the sketch is shown in Figure 19-116.

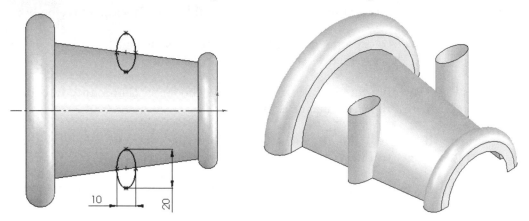

Figure 19-115 *Sketch of the second surface feature*   **Figure 19-116** *Extruded surface*

Trimming the Base Surface Using the Extruded Surface

Next, you need to trim the unwanted portions of the surface by using the extruded surface.

1. Choose the **Trim Surface** button from the **Surfaces CommandManager**; the **Trim Surface PropertyManager** is invoked.

2. Select the **Mutual** radio button from the **Trim Type** rollout and then select the surfaces to be used as trimming surfaces, as shown in Figure 19-117.

3. Now, click in the **Pieces to Keep** selection area to invoke the selection mode. Next, select the pieces to keep, as shown in Figure 19-117.

4. Choose the **OK** button from the **Trim Surface PropertyManager**. The model after trimming the base surface is displayed in Figure 19-118.

Filleting the Edges of the Trimmed Surface

Next, you need to fillet the edges created at the intersection of the base surface.

1. Choose the **Fillet** button from the **Surface CommandManager**; the **Fillet PropertyManager** is displayed.

2. Select the edges to fillet, as shown in Figure 19-119.

3. Set the value of the **Radius** spinner to **5** and then choose the **OK** button from the **Fillet PropertyManager**. Figure 19-120 shows the model after adding fillet.

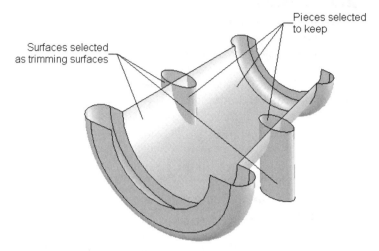

Figure 19-117 *Surfaces selected for trimming*

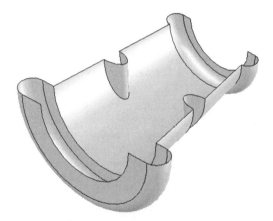

Figure 19-118 *Model after trimming the base surface*

Figure 19-119 *Edges selected to fillet*   **Figure 19-120** *Resultant fillet feature*

Creating a Lofted Surface

Next, you need to create a lofted surface. The lofted surface will be created between two curves. The first curve is to be created on the **Top** plane and projected on the surface. The next curve is to be created on an offset plane.

1. Create a plane at an offset distance of 40 mm from the **Top** plane and then invoke the sketching environment using the newly created plane as the sketching plane.

3. Create the sketch, as shown in Figure 19-121, and exit the sketching environment.

    Next, you need to project this sketch on the base surface.

3. Choose **Curves > Project Curve** from the **Surfaces CommandManager**; the **Projected Curve PropertyManager** is invoked.

4. Select the **Sketch on faces** radio button from the **Projection Type** area.

5. Next, select the sketch and then click once in the **Projection Faces** selection area to activate the selection mode.

6. Select the base surface from middle and select the **Reverse Projection** check box. Choose the **OK** button from the **Projected Curve PropertyManager**.

    Next, you need to create second curve for creating the loft surface.

7. Invoke the sketching environment with the newly created plane as the sketching plane and then create the sketch, as shown in Figure 19-122, and exit the sketching environment.

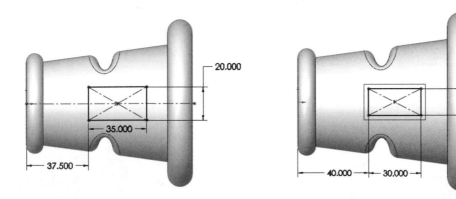

Figure 19-121 *Sketch to create the projected curve*

Figure 19-122 *First sketch for the loft surface*

Figure 19-123 shows the model after creating the sketch and the projected curve.

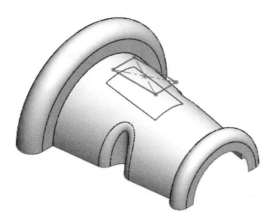

Figure 19-123 *Model after creating the sketch and the projected curve*

8. Choose the **Lofted Surface** button from the **Surfaces CommandManager**; the **Surface-Loft PropertyManager** is displayed.

9. Select the loft section, as shown in Figure 19-124, and choose the **OK** button from the **Surface-Loft PropertyManager**. Figure 19-125 shows the model after creating the lofted surface.

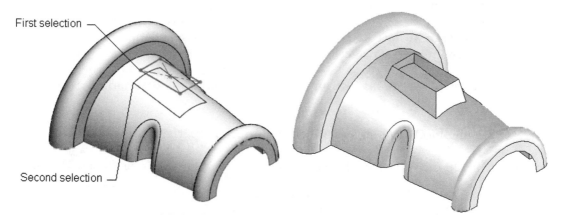

Figure 19-124 *Section selected for the lofted surface*

Figure 19-125 *Resultant lofted surface created*

Creating the Planar Surface

Next, you need to create the planar surface using the top edges of the lofted surface.

1. Choose the **Planar Surface** button from the **Surfaces CommandManager**; the **Planar Surface PropertyManager** is displayed.

2. Select the edges, as shown in Figure 19-126, to create the planar surface; the name of the selected edges is displayed in the **Bounding Entities** selection area of the **Planar Surface PropertyManager**.

3. Choose the **OK** button from the **Planar Surface PropertyManager**; the planar surface is created. Figure 19-127 shows the resultant planar surface.

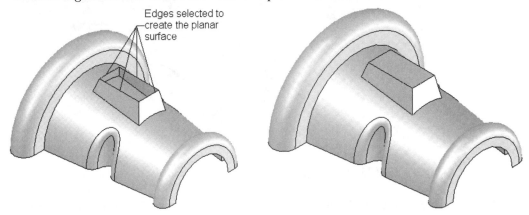

Edges selected to
create the planar
surface

Figure 19-126 Edges selected to create the planar surface   *Figure 19-127 Resultant planar surface*

Trimming the Base Surface Using the Lofted Surface

Next, you need to trim the base surface using the lofted surface.

1. Choose the **Trim Surface** button from the **Surfaces CommandManager** to invoke the **Trim Surface PropertyManager**.

2. Select the lofted surface as the trim tool and then select the base surface as pieces to keep.

3. Next, choose the **OK** button from the **Trim Surface PropertyManager**.

Figure 19-128 shows the model after trimming the base surface using the lofted surface.

Figure 19-128 Model after trimming the base surface using the lofted surface

Knitting all Surfaces

Next, you need to knit the base surface, lofted surface, and planar surface using the **Knit Surface** tool to create fillets on the edges. Note that, if you want to add wall thickness to the surface model created using multiple surfaces, you need to knit all surfaces first.

1. Choose the **Knit Surface** button from the **Surfaces CommandManager** to invoke the **Knit Surface PropertyManager**.

2. Select the base surface, lofted surface, and planar surface from the drawing area; the names of the selected surfaces are displayed in the **Surfaces and Faces to Knit** selection area.

3. Next, choose the **OK** button from the **Surface Knit PropertyManager**; the selected surfaces are knitted.

    Next, you need to add the required fillets to the model. The final surface model after adding fillets is shown in Figure 19-129. For dimensions of fillers, refer to Figure 19-112.

Figure 19-129 *Final surface model*

Adding Thickness to the Surface Model

Next, you need to add thickness to the surface model.

1. Choose the **Thicken** button from the **Surfaces CommandManager** to invoke the **Thicken PropertyManager**.

2. Select the surface model and then set the value of the **Thickness** spinner to **2**.

3. Choose the **OK** button from the **Thicken PropertyManager**.

Figure 19-130 shows the final model after thickening the surface. The order of feature creation can be seen from the **FeatureManager design tree** shown in Figure 19-131.

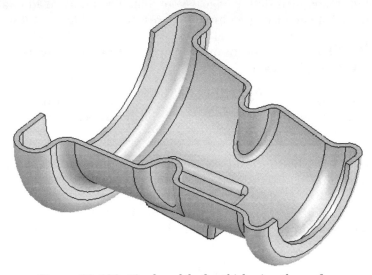

Figure 19-130 Final model after thickening the surface

*Figure 19-131 The **FeatureManager** design tree*

Saving the Model

1. Choose the **Save** button from the Menu Bar and save the drawing with the name given below and close the file.

\My Documents\SolidWorks\c19\c19-tut01.SLDPRT.

Tutorial 2

In this tutorial, you will create the cover of a hair dryer, as shown in Figure 19-132. You will first create the model using surfaces and then thicken it. The views and dimensions of the model are displayed in Figure 19-133. **(Expected time: 1.5 hr)**

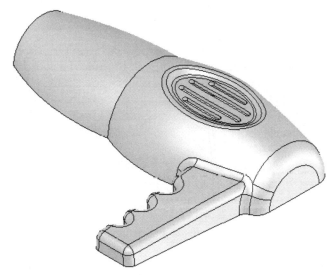

Figure 19-132 Cover of hair dryer

The following steps are required to complete this tutorial:

a. First, create the base surface. The base surface is created by lofting the open sections along the guide curves, refer to Figures 19-134 and 19-135.
b. Create a planar surface to close the right face of the base surface, refer to Figures 19-136 and 19-137.
c. Next, create the basic structure of the handle of the hair dryer cover by creating a lofted surface between two open sections, refer to Figures 19-138 through 19-139.
d. Trim the unwanted portion of the lofted surface that is used to create handle, refer to Figures 19-140 and 19-141.
e. Create a planar surface to close the front face of the handle, refer to Figure 19-143.
f. Extrude the elliptical sketches to create the grips of the handle and then trim the unwanted surfaces, refer to Figures 19-144 through 19-147.
g. Create a dip on the top surface of the hair dryer, refer to Figures 19-148 thought 19-153.
h. Trim the surface to create air vents, refer to Figure 19-154.
i. Knit all the surfaces together and add the required fillets to the model, refer to Figure 19-155.
j. Thicken the surface, refer to Figure 19-156.

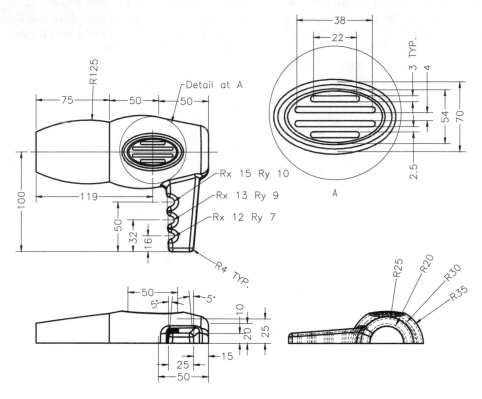

Figure 19-133 *Views and dimensions for the model of Tutorial 2*

Creating the Base Surface

To create hair dryer, you first need to create the base surface of the model. The base surface will be created by lofting the semicircular sections along the guide curves. The sections will be created on different planes. So, you first need to create three planes at an offset distance from the **Right** plane .

1. Start SolidWorks part document using the **New SolidWorks Document** dialog box.

2. Create three planes at an offset distance from the **Right** plane, refer to Figure 19-134. For the offset distance of planes, refer to Figure 19-133.

3. Next, you need to create the sections and guide curves to create a lofted surface, as shown in Figure 19-134. For dimensions, refer to Figure 19-133.

4. Using the **Lofted Surface** tool, create the lofted surface, as shown in Figure 19-135.

5. Create a planar surface to close the right face of the base surface.

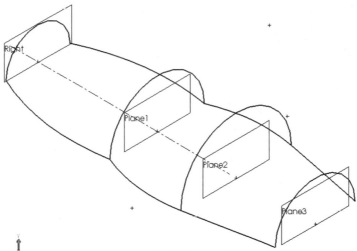

Figure 19-134 Sections and guide curves to create a lofted surface

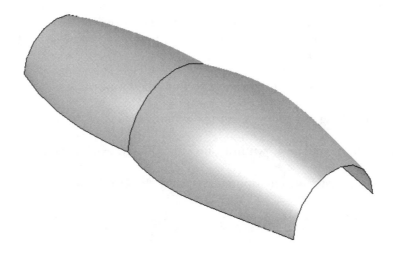

Figure 19-135 Resultant lofted surface

6. Invoke the sketching environment by selecting **Plane3** as the sketching plane.

7. Create a closed sketch to create the planar surface, as shown in Figure 19-136.

8. Invoke the **Planar Surface PropertyManager** and then, select the closed sketch from the drawing area. Next, choose the **OK** button from the **Planar Surface PropertyManager**; the planar surface is created, as shown in Figure 19-137.

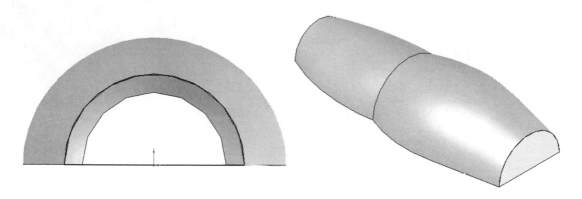

Figure 19-136 *Sketch for creating the planar surface*   ***Figure 19-137*** *Resultant planar surface*

Creating the Base Surface for the Handle

Next, you need to create the base surface for the handle. The base surface for the handle will be created by lofting two open sections. The first section for the lofted surface will be created on a plane at an offset distance from the **Front** plane and the second section will be created on the **Front** plane. Therefore, you first need to create a plane at an offset distance from the **Front** plane.

1. Create a plane at an offset distance of 100 from the **Front** plane.

2. Invoke the sketching environment using the newly created plane as the sketching plane.

3. Create an open sketch, as shown in Figure 19-138, and exit the sketching environment.

4. Now, invoke the sketching environment by using the **Front** plane as the sketching plane.

5. Next, create an open sketch, as shown in Figure 19-139, and exit the sketching environment.

6. Using the **Lofted Surface** tool, create the lofted surface, as shown in Figure 19-140.

Trimming the Unwanted Lofted Surface of the Handle

If you rotate the model after creating the lofted surface for the handle, you will observe that a portion of the lofted surface needs to be trimmed. The method of trimming the unwanted portion of the lofted surface is discussed next.

1. Invoke the **Trim Surface PropertyManager** and then select the **Mutual** radio button from the **Trim Type** rollout.

2. Select the trimming surfaces and the pieces to keep, as shown in Figure 19-141. Next, choose the **OK** button from the **Trim Surface PropertyManager**. Figure 19-142 shows the resultant trimmed surface.

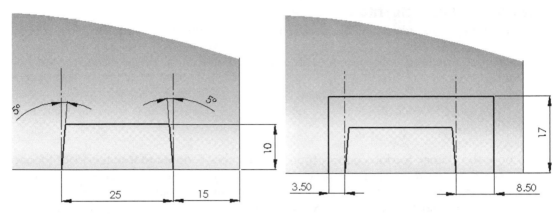

Figure 19-138 *Sketch of the first section for creating the lofted surface of the handle*

Figure 19-139 *Sketch of the second section for creating the lofted surface of the handle*

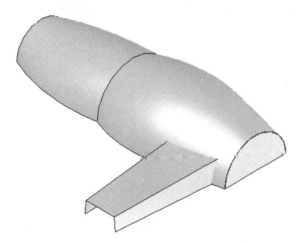

Figure 19-140 *Resultant lofted surface*

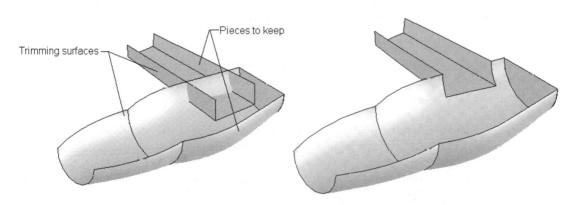

Figure 19-141 *Trimming surfaces and pieces to keep*

Figure 19-142 *Resultant trimmed surface*

Creating a Planar Surface

Next, you need to create a planar surface to close the front face of the handle.

1. Invoke the sketching environment with a plane created at an offset distance from the **Front** plane.

2. Create a closed sketch to create the planar surface and then exit from the sketching environment.

3. Choose the **Planar Surface** button from the **Surfaces CommandManager**; the **Planar Surface PropertyManager** is displayed. Next, select the close sketch from the drawing area; the name of the selected sketch is displayed in the **Bounding Entities** selection area of the **Planar Surface PropertyManager** and the preview of the planar surface is displayed in the drawing area. Next, choose the **OK** button from the **PropertyManager**.

    Model after creating the planar surface is shown in Figure 19-143.

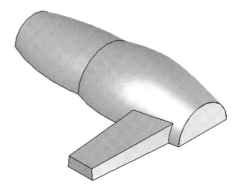

Figure 19-143 Model after creating the planar surface

Creating Grips on the Handle

Next, you need to create grips on the handle to hold the hair dryer. The grip will be created by extruding the elliptical surface and then trimming the unwanted portion of the surfaces.

1. Invoke the sketching environment using the **Top** plane as the sketching plane.

2. Create the sketch for extruding the surface to create grips, as shown in Figure 19-144.

3. Invoke the **Surface-Extrude PropertyManager** and extrude the sketch to the depth of 25 mm. The extruded surface is displayed, as shown in Figure 19-145.

    Next, you need to trim portions of the extruded surface and the handle to achieve the desired shape of grips.

4. Invoke the **Trim Surface PropertyManager** and then select the **Mutual** radio button from the **Trim Type** rollout.

5. Select the trimming surfaces and the pieces to keep, as shown in Figure 19-146.

6. Next, choose the **OK** button from the **Trim Surface PropertyManager**; the surface is trimmed. Figure 19-147 shows the resultant trimmed surface.

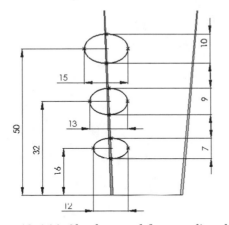

Figure 19-144 *Sketch created for extruding the surface*

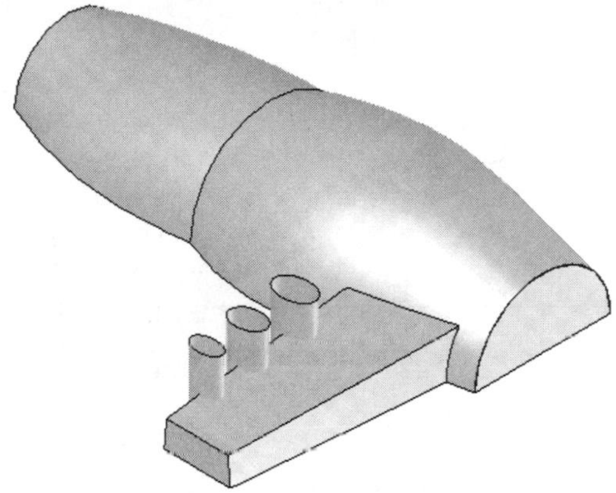

Figure 19-145 *Resultant extruded surface*

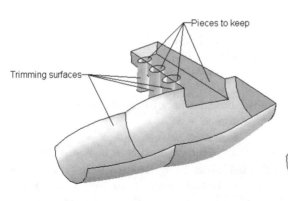

Figure 19-146 *Trimming surfaces and pieces to keep*

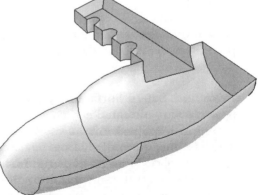

Figure 19-147 *Resultant trimmed surface*

Creating the Dip on the Upper Surface of the Base Surface

Next, you need to create the dip on the base surface. To do so, you need use various tools for offsetting the planes, creating lofted surface, trimming, and for creating planar surface.

1. Create a plane at an offset distance of 35 from the **Top** plane.

2. Invoke the sketching environment using the newly created plane as the sketching plane.

3. Create the sketch, as shown in Figure 19-148, and exit the sketching environment.

4. Next, choose **Curves > Project Curve** from the **Surfaces CommandManager** and project the newly created sketch on the base surface. The model, after projecting the sketch, is displayed, as shown in Figure 19-149.

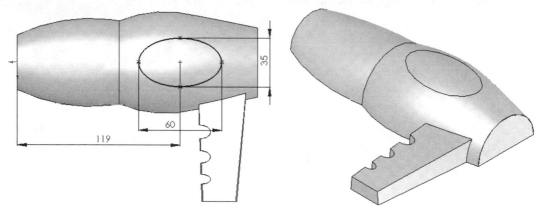

Figure 19-148 Sketch to be created   *Figure 19-149* Resultant projected curve

5. Create a plane at an offset distance of 6 from the newly created plane in the downward direction.

6. Now, invoke the sketching environment using the newly created plane as the sketching plane and create the sketch, as shown in Figure 19-150. Next, exit the sketching environment.

7. Invoke the **Lofted Surface** tool and create the lofted surface using the sketch and the projected curve created earlier.

8. The lofted surface, after hiding the base surface, is displayed, as shown in Figure 19-151. To hide surface bodies, expand the **Surface Bodies** folder in the **FeatureManager design tree**. Next, select the surface and right-click to invoke the shortcut menu. Choose **Hide** from the shortcut menu; the selected surface is hidden.

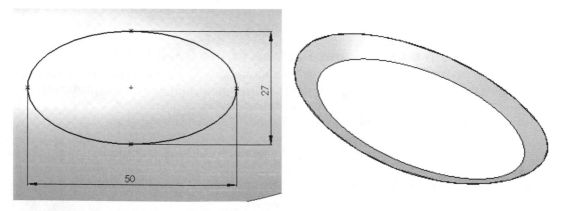

Figure 19-150 Sketch to be created   *Figure 19-151* Lofted surface

9. Invoke the **Trim Surface** tool and trim the base surface using the newly created lofted surface. The model, after trimming the surface, is displayed in Figure 19-152. Next, using the **Planar Surface** tool, create the planar surface, as shown in Figure 19-153.

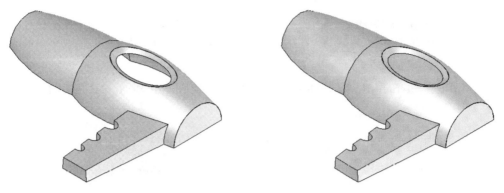

Figure 19-152 *Model after trimming the surface*   *Figure 19-153* *Planar surface*

Creating Air Vents

Next, you need to create air vents on the newly created planar surface. Air vents are created by drawing the sketch on the planar surface and then using the trimming tool to trim the surface.

1. Select the newly created planar surface as the sketching plane and then invoke the sketching environment.

2. Create the sketch of air vents, refer to Figure 19-133.

3. Invoke the **Trim Surface** tool by choosing the **Trim Surface** button from the **Surfaces CommandManager**. Then, select a sketch as the trimming tool to trim the planar surface for creating air vents.

The surface model, after creating air vents, is displayed in Figure 19-154.

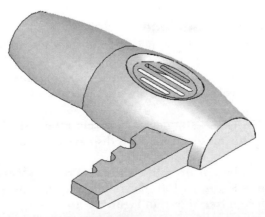

Figure 19-154 *Surface model after trimming the planar surface*

Knitting All Surfaces

After creating all surfaces, you need to knit all surfaces together to add fillets to surfaces and thicken the model.

1. Choose the **Knit Surface** button from the **Surfaces CommandManager**; the **Knit Surface PropertyManager** is invoked and you are prompted to select the surfaces to knit.

2. Expand the **Surface Bodies** folder in the **FeatureManager design tree** and then select all surface bodies from it.

3. Next, choose the **OK** button from the **Knit Surface PropertyManager**.

4. Add all required fillets to the surface model. The model, after adding fillets, is displayed in Figure 19-155.

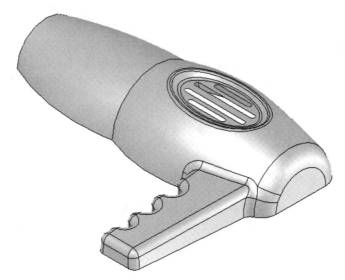

Figure 19-155 *Surface model after adding fillets*

Adding Thickness to the Surface Model

After creating the entire model, you need to add thickness to the surface model.

1. Choose the **Thicken** button from the **Surfaces CommandManager**; the **Thicken PropertyManager** is invoked and you are prompted to select the surface to thicken.

2. Set the value of the **Thickness** spinner to 2 and select the surface model from the drawing area; the preview of the thickened model is displayed in the drawing area.

3. Next, choose the **OK** button from the **Thicken PropertyManager**; the final model is displayed, as shown in Figure 19-156. The order of feature creation can be seen from the **FeatureManager design tree** shown in Figure 19-157.

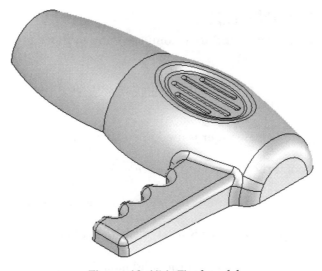

Figure 19-156 *Final model*

Figure 19-157 *The FeatureManager design tree*

Saving the Model

1. Choose the **Save** button from the Menu Bar and save the drawing with the name given below and close the file.

    \My Documents\SolidWorks\c19\c19-tut02.SLDPRT.

SELF-EVALUATION TEST

Answer the following questions and then compare them to those given at the end of this chapter:

1. In SolidWorks, the _____ tool is provided to extrude a closed or an open sketch to create an extruded surface.

2. The _____ **PropertyManager** is used to create a revolved surface.

3. The _____ tool is used to create a surface patch by extending the existing surfaces.

4. The _____ tool is used to offset the selected surface or surfaces to a given distance.

5. The _____ **PropertyManager** is used to create a lofted surface.

6. You cannot patch the deleted faces of the solid model using the **Delete Face** tool. (T/F)

7. Using the **Kint Surface** tool, you can knit multiple surfaces together to create a single surface. (T/F)

8. You cannot create a filled surface by selecting a 3D sketch as patch boundary. (T/F)

9. The **Curvature Control** drop-down list is used to define the type of curvature that you need to apply while creating the fill surface. (T/F)

10. The **SurfaceCut PropertyManager** is used to create a surface cut. (T/F)

REVIEW QUESTIONS

Answer the following questions:

1. The _____ **PropertyManager** is used to add thickness to a surface body.

2. To extend the surface in the linear direction to an existing surface, invoke the **Extend Surface PropertyManager** and select the _____ radio button from the **Extension Type** rollout.

3. The _____ check box is used to solidify a closed surface model.

4. The _____ tool is used to delete the faces of a surface or a solid body.

5. The **Mid-Surface** tool is used to create a surface between the selected faces.

6. Which of the following **PropertyManager** is used to created a fillet surface?

    (a) **Fill Surface**   (b) **Surface Fill**
    (c) **Fillet**   (d) None of these

7. Which of the following buttons in the **Surfaces CommandManager** is used to invoke the **Replace Face1 PropertyManager**?

    (a) **Face Replace**   (b) **Replace Face**
    (c) **Offset Surface**   (d) **Fillet Surface**

8. The **Mid-Surface** tool is used to create a surface between two parallel faces of the solid model. (T/F)

9. Which rollout is used to define constraint curves while creating the fill surface?

    (a) **Define Constraint Curves**   (b) **Constraint Curves**
    (c) **Patch Boundaries**   (d) None of these

10. Which of the following **PropertyManager** is used to created surface by radiating along an edge, edges, or a split line?

    (a) **Surface Fill**   (b) **Surface-Sweep**
    (c) **Radiate Surface**   (d) **Thicken**

EXERCISES

Exercise 1

In this exercise, you will create the model, shown in Figure 19-158, by using surfaces. After creating and knitting all surfaces, you will add required thickness to the model. The views and dimensions of the model are shown in Figure 19-159.   **(Expected time: 1hr)**

Hint:

In this model, you need to knit the surfaces first and then fillet its edges.

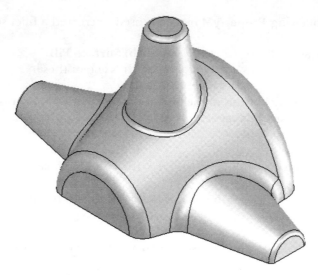

Figure 19-158 *Model for Exercise 1*

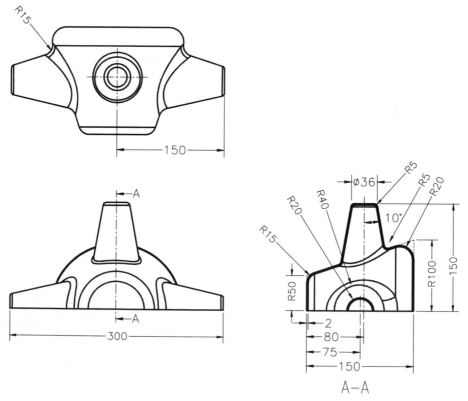

Figure 19-159 *Views and dimensions for Exercise 1*

Exercise 2

In this exercise, you will create the model of the binoculars, shown in Figure 19-160, by using surfaces. First, you need to create a closed surface model and knit all surfaces together and then solidify it. The views and dimensions of the model are shown in Figure 19-161.

(Expected time: 1hr)

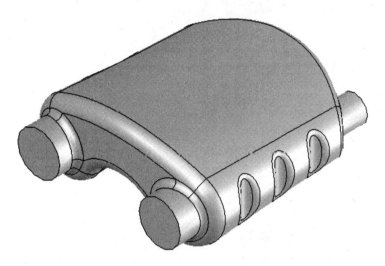

Figure 19-160 Model for Exercise 2

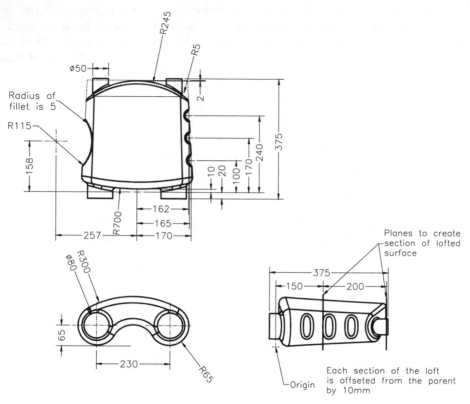

Figure 19-161 *Views and dimensions of Exercise 2*

Index

E

Z

Other Publications by CADCIM Technologies

The following is the list of some of the publications by CADCIM Technologies. Please visit www.cadcim.com for the complete listing.

Autodesk AliasStudio Textbook
- Autodesk AliasStudio 2009 for Designers

Computer Animation Textbooks
- 3ds Max Design 2009: A Tutorial Approach
- 3ds Max 2008: A Comprehensive Guide
- Autodesk Maya 2009: A Comprehensive Guide

Computer Programming Textbooks
- Learning Java Programming
- Learning Visual Basic.NET 2008
- Learning C++ Programming Concepts
- Learning VB.NET Programming Concepts

Autodesk Inventor Textbooks
- Autodesk Inventor 2009 for Designers
- Autodesk Inventor 2008 for Designers

Solid Edge Textbooks
- Solid Edge ST for Designers
- Solid Edge V20 for Designers

NX Textbooks
- NX 6 for Designers
- NX 5 for Designers

SolidWorks Textbooks
- SolidWorks 2008 for Designers
- SolidWorks 2007 for Designers

CATIA Textbooks
- CATIA V5R18 for Designers
- CATIA V5R17 for Designers

EdgeCAM Textbooks
- EdgeCAM 11.0 for Manufacturers
- EdgeCAM 10.0 for Manufacturers

Pro/ENGINEER Textbooks
- Pro/ENGINEER Wildfire 4.0 for Designers
- Pro/ENGINEER Wildfire 3.0 for Designers

Autodesk Revit Textbooks
- Autodesk Revit Architecture 2009 for Architects & Designers
- Autodesk Revit Architecture 2008 for Architects & Designers

AutoCAD LT Textbooks
- AutoCAD LT 2009 for Designers
- AutoCAD LT 2008 for Designers

Textbooks Authored by CADCIM Technologies and Published by Other Publishers
- AutoCAD 2009: A Problem-Solving Approach
  Autodesk Press
- Customizing AutoCAD 2009
  Autodesk Press

Coming Soon: New Textbooks from CADCIM Technologies
- ANSYS for Design Analysts
- AutoCAD Civil 3D 2009 for Engineers
- Mastercam for Manufacturers
- AutoCAD Electrical 2009 for Electrical Control Designers
- Learning AJAX
- Learning Oracle 11g
- Learning Excel 2007
- Learning Dreamweaver CS3

Online Training Program Offered by CADCIM Technologies

CADCIM Technologies provides effective and affordable virtual online training on various software packages including computer programming languages, Computer Aided Design and Manufacturing (CAD/CAM), animation, architecture, and GIS. The training will be delivered 'live' via Internet at any time, any place, and at any pace to individuals, students of colleges, universities, and CAD/CAM training centers. For more information, please visit the following link: **http://www.cadcim.com**